MW00522694

BUSINESS
COMMUNICATION

BUSINESS COMMUNICATION

CHESTER WOLFORD

The Pennsylvania State University, Erie

GRETCHEN VANNEMAN

The Pennsylvania State University, Erie

The Dryden Press
A Harcourt Brace Jovanovich College Publisher
Fort Worth   Philadelphia   San Diego   New York   Orlando   Austin   San Antonio
Toronto   Montreal   London   Sydney   Tokyo

Acquisitions Editor:	Scott Isenberg
Manuscript Editor:	Sarah Helyer Smith
Production Editor:	Michael Ferreira
Designer:	Linda Miller
Art Editor:	Elizabeth Banks
Production Managers:	Mary Kay Yearin and Lesley Lenox

ISBN: 0-15-505492-9

Library of Congress Catalog Number: 91-73616

Printed in the United States of America

PREFACE

Business Communication teaches business students how to write and speak well. Whether students are studying accounting, communications, economics, engineering, finance, health, information science, management, marketing, personnel, or science, the medium by which they discuss and convey these disciplines is the same: words. Managers and technicians alike write reports, letters, and memos.

Specialization resulting from the explosion of knowledge and technology has begun increasingly to complicate language at the very time that business demands simple, clear, and accurate writing. Consequently, this book stresses that students not only must keep abreast of new technology in communications, but also continue to learn the time-honored requirements for prose that is simple, straightforward, concise, and precise.

As the United States vies in competitive international markets, and as the population of the United States itself becomes more diverse, American businesses must become multilingual and be able to understand and to communicate effectively with people of different cultures. *Business Communication* thus addresses international communication throughout the text, particularly in Chapters 7 and 15.

FEATURES OF THE TEXT

Although we have used parts of this book in the classroom for five years, *Business Communication* probably contains more information than can be covered in one term. According to scheduling constraints and individual needs, instructors can select parts of the text while omitting others.

Each chapter contains many features that help students learn the material thoroughly:

QUOTATIONS. Quotations appear in every part and chapter opener, as well as occasionally in the margins of the chapters themselves. While not necessarily words to live by, these quotations provide food for thought about work and how to do it better.

CHECKLISTS. Each chapter begins with a checklist of its most important features, allowing students to concentrate on, learn, and remember the key ideas as they read and study.

EXAMPLES. To provide the feel of everyday business communication, this text contains frequent examples of procedures and formats, including entire formal business reports. Many of the examples are adapted from undergraduate business majors and MBA candidates whom we have been privileged to teach for more than fifteen years.

MARGIN EXERCISES.   This text contains more than 150 exercises in the margins of the chapters. Their purpose is twofold: they immediately reinforce the information in the text, and they provide a vehicle for further contemplation of the subject. Most of them are intended for class discussion. The more students consider the questions posed in the margin exercises, the stronger their ability to think well will become.

SUMMARIES.   Concluding each chapter, a summary reiterates the chapter's key points.

EXERCISES.   In addition to the margin exercises, *Business Communication* contains three kinds of exercises at the conclusion of each chapter: end-of-chapter exercises, case studies, and challenge exercises. End-of-chapter exercises reinforce the practical details discussed and illustrated in the text. Case studies pose typical business problems and ask the students to solve them. Challenge exercises test students' knowledge of the text and stimulate their abilities to write and think creatively.

FULL-COLOR INSERTS.   Three full-color inserts provide vivid photographs of the most rapidly developing areas of business communication: the high-tech office, international communication, and desk-top publishing. The eight-page insert on desk-top publishing illustrates the development and production of a business report, demonstrating the textual and graphic capabilities of desk-top systems.

TECHNICAL REPORTS APPENDIX.   Because business is becoming increasingly technical, business people need to know well the rudiments of technical writing. Consequently, Appendix I introduces business communication students to the fundamental aspects of technical writing — that is, formal definitions; expanded, or amplified, definitions; and the prototypical business report — and provides both a sample description of a mechanism manual and a sample operation manual.

EDITING APPENDIX.   Good writing derives from revising and editing. Building on the discussion of revising and editing in Chapter 2, Appendix II details common problems in grammar, punctuation, and mechanics and demonstrates the copy-editing procedures to correct them.

GLOSSARY.   The glossary is the most unusual feature of *Business Communication*. It incorporates hundreds of words and phrases that are commonly used and misused in business writing and speech. A series of quizzes enables instructors to test students' knowledge of the glossary. These quizzes help students develop as precise a sense of word use to solve business problems as they need for numbers and formulas to solve mathematical problems.

ACKNOWLEDGMENTS

For their guidance and support, we thank Carl J. Schlemmer, former Vice President and General Manager of GE Transportation Systems, GE Company; Thomas B. Hagen, Chairman and Chief Executive Officer, Erie Insurance Group; Chester F. Kempinski, President, McCoy Electronics; Joseph Podolosky, former Manager, Learning and Communications Center, Communications, Public Affairs, GE Company; and Robert G. Vanneman, of The Union Bank of Switzerland.

For their helpful comments and suggestions, we thank Jim Gosline, University of Southern California; Maureen Hoag, Wichita State University; Judith Lancioni, Glassboro State University; Carol Lang, Angelo State University; Sue Luckey, Moorehead State University; Paul Martin, Aims Community College; and Robert Motley, Western Illinois University.

Special thanks go to our children, Reeve and Rebecca, whose wit, charm, patience, and encouragement were the catalysts for this project.

Business Communication was written to help teachers help students become better writers and speakers, but we also know that instruction, like writing itself, is infinitely perfectible. Consequently, we encourage instructors and students to send us suggestions for improving this book.

CHESTER L. WOLFORD	**GRETCHEN VANNEMAN**
School of Business	Division of Humanities and Social Science
The Pennsylvania State University	The Pennsylvania State University
Erie, Pennsylvania 16511	Erie, Pennsylvania 16511

BRIEF CONTENTS

CONTENTS

IV REPORTS

BUSINESS COMMUNICATION

THE DUTY OF A WRITER—

THE REVOLUTIONARY

DUTY, IF YOU LIKE—IS

THAT OF WRITING WELL.

GABRIEL GARCÍA

MÁRQUEZ

(1928–)

THE BUSINESS WRITER'S CONTRACT

1 **COMMUNICATIONS IN BUSINESS**

2 **THE WRITING PROCESS IN BUSINESS**

2

Learning Objectives:

☐ Communicate clearly, accurately, briefly, and with courtesy.

☐ Know the personal and professional benefits of good business communications.

☐ Understand the four basic kinds of business communication:
   simple to complex,
   formal to informal,
   up/down/across,
   verbal/nonverbal.

☐ Know the *Business Writer's Contract*.

☐ Know the particulars of a good business-writing style.

☐ Use a fog index to simplify business communications.

☐ Convey information.

PROPER WORDS IN PROPER

PLACES MAKE THE TRUE

DEFINITION OF STYLE.

COMMUNICATIONS

JONATHAN SWIFT

(1667–1745)

IN

BUSINESS

TO A SNAIL: IF "COM-

PRESSION IS THE FIRST

GRACE OF STYLE," YOU

HAVE IT.

MARIANNE MOORE

(1887–1972)

STYLE IN COMMUNICATIONS

Style is the natural product of writing clearly, concisely, honestly, and accurately.

THE IMPORTANCE OF COMMUNICATION

EXERCISE A: IMPORTANCE OF COMMUNICATION

Discuss in class these questions.

1. Can anyone think without using symbols?
2. What do we mean by *symbols*?
3. If clear thinking is the primary product of language, is communication a mere by-product?
4. How many kinds of symbols are available for thinking? Name some.

Communication is often called a prerequisite to civilization, for without it no group can work effectively. When we think of communication, we usually think of language. It could be the language of mathematics, of music, of painting, but usually it is the language of words. If communication is a product of language, and it almost certainly is, then civilization also must be a product of language.

Language has another product, usually overlooked, that is extremely important to civilization and to business: clear thinking. Language is so important to clear thinking that we cannot think without it. Some may say that they can think in pictures, but pictures are symbols, just as words are symbols. Perhaps it would be better to say that we cannot think without symbols, and that words are perhaps the most useful of all symbols.

Words, then, express thought. And using words well, whether to communicate with others or to think clearly ourselves, is essential to business. Good, clear thinking and civilization: both are required by business; both are made possible by language.

PRACTICAL BENEFITS TO YOU

good job ⟶ promotions ⟶ leading others

HELPING YOU GET A GOOD JOB. Clear, sound, and thoughtful communication is perhaps the most important ability required to get a good job. Of course, good grades are paramount, but unless you can present yourself well to prospective employers, others with grades no better than yours may get the jobs.

Résumés and cover letters must be well written, for they *are* you in the sense that the reader probably has never seen you, knows nothing about you, and forms an opinion derived *solely* from words on paper. The clearer and more thoughtful the words are, then, the more favorably impressed the prospective employer will be.

Your appearance, which is also a form of communication, and your ability to speak well are vital in interviews. More people are qualified for any job than are able to convey their qualifications to employers.

HELPING YOU GET PROMOTED. Because writing is permanent, almost anything you write while working becomes part of the record of your successes and failures. The ability to convey information accurately and to persuade honestly will improve your chances for promotion. In fact, many bosses know some of their subordinates *only* by their writing. In this instance, good writing is the *only* way you may be promoted.

Good communication, of course, is essential for doing a good job. The better you communicate with others, the more likely that you will be successful. The more successful you are in your work, the more likely that you will be promoted.

HELPING OTHERS.   By communicating well, you help others do their jobs better. When they do their jobs well, they look good, which in turn makes you look good. Specifically, good communication is essential for good leadership. Finally, after a certain point, the ability to lead people determines how far you will rise in an organization.

PRACTICAL BENEFITS TO BUSINESS

organization ⟶ production ⟶ sales ⟶ growth

ORGANIZATION.   It is conceivable that a self-employed person could keep all the requirements for a business inside the head, with no need to write down or talk about what needs to be done today, tomorrow, and what was done yesterday. When a business employs more than one person, however, communication in writing and speech becomes essential. Businesses must be organized; they must record and plan, usually in great detail. What was done? What is being done? What should be done? Who did it? Who is doing it? Who should do it? Recording and planning cannot occur without writing or speaking or both.

Businesses change constantly, growing here and shrinking there. To keep changes orderly and controlled, communication is essential. For example, a company will waste money if one department performs work that contradicts another department's functions.

PRODUCTION.   No product appears out of thin air. Yet most products sold today did not exist a century ago. They exist because people conceived ideas, developed them, and produced things from them. To get those ideas out of the brain and into reality, the inventors had to organize their thoughts and convey them to others through speech and writing. Given the complexities of modern business, moving a product from idea to reality requires much highly organized communication.

SALES.   Although developing products requires much communication, the best of products would remain on the shelves, unsold, if communication ended with product development. In short, products do not sell themselves. Communication is the lifeblood of sales, just as sales is the lifeblood of business. Businesses whose employees speak and write well tend to sell more products than those whose employees speak and write poorly.

GROWTH.   Change may be inevitable, but growth is not. Companies grow when they are alert to technological advances, and when

One does not manage *people. One* leads *people.*

Admiral Grace Hopper
(1906–)

....
EXERCISE B:
COMMUNICATION AND
PRODUCTION

Discuss in class the number (and kinds) of people who might be involved in taking the idea of an electric car from conception to a buyer's garage.

they quickly and skillfully convey these advances to employees. Competition increases daily, so companies must improve daily. The how and what of improvement occur largely through communication. Quality control, efficiency, marketing, personnel, and even billing must improve constantly or the company loses in a brutally competitive marketplace. Without good communication, companies have little hope of competing.

People do not stop learning on graduation day or after a big sale. Learning continues throughout a career. And learning is most efficiently achieved through reading and writing.

Good communication, then, is integral to the growth and success of both individuals and organizations.

THE KINDS OF COMMUNICATION

To communicate, people must consider the purpose of the messages they wish to convey, the audience (whether readers or listeners) they are addressing, and the manner in which they give the messages. Their messages may be simple or complex, or they may be formal or informal. Their audience may be above, below, or equal to them in their organization's hierarchy. And their messages may be verbal or nonverbal.

SIMPLE AND COMPLEX

Simple and *complex* are terms relative both to the subject and to the reader. What seems simple to the writer may seem complex to the audience, the reader. For example, one person's jargon (specialized, technical language) is another person's bread and butter. Literature professors frequently use the word "genre." Computer scientists use "bits," "bytes," and "nanoseconds." Economists use "marginal revenue" and "servicing the national debt." When talking with others who have studied what they have studied, these people would not think of their terms as jargon. But the jargon includes many words that are unknown to a general audience. A literature professor might need to explain "genre" to a computer scientist, the computer scientist may have to explain "nanosecond" to an economist, and an economist may need to explain "marginal revenue" to a literature professor. Thus, writers and speakers must always use terms that their intended audience will understand.

FORMAL AND INFORMAL

Communication is formal, informal, or somewhere between. Usually, the better we know someone, the less formal our communication is. In writing, two methods immediately identify whether a letter or memo is formal or informal: layout and language. A letter that does not contain a letterhead, formal address and title, and the like is informal. Using contractions (such as "I'm" for "I am") is informal. These, of course, are simple methods of conveying formality or informality. The words themselves, the kinds of information, and the tone of the communications also identify and reflect the level of formality.

Formality in communications depends not only on how well the writer knows the reader, but also on one or more of the following conditions.

The *nationality* of the reader often determines the most suitable level of formality. Americans are often admired for their informality, for it may aid international business communications by saving much time and money. Conversely, informality can destroy communication with those from other cultures who expect a greater degree of formality in business dealings.

The *situation* often dictates the level of formality. Some things said on the golf course should not be said in the office.

The *status* of the reader, particularly within a hierarchical organization, often dictates how formally that person should be addressed and under what circumstances.

UP, DOWN, AND ACROSS AN ORGANIZATION

People are naturally hierarchical. And because organizations reflect many natural inclinations of people, organizations tend to be hierarchical. There are many ways to display one's status. For instance,

··············

**EXERCISE C: DISCERNING
LEVELS OF FORMALITY**

Often the relative formality of a conversation or letter depends on qualities different from simply nationality, situation, or status in an organization. One example might be the differing classes or, in some societies, castes of the people involved. Imagine a conversation between, say, members of the Brahmin and "Untouchable" classes of India (most members now do speak to each other) or between an Oxford-educated, old-family, Fleet Street banker, and an East London Cockney who sweeps streets.

Are you able to think of any situations similar to these that might occur even in the relatively classless society in the United States? What are they? How might such a conversation proceed with regard to formality?

EXERCISE D: LOADED WORDS

All corporations are hierarchical to one degree or another. Discuss in class the connotations of *up*, *down*, and *across* as they relate to communications in a corporation.

EXERCISE E: UP

What are some of the possible pitfalls to clear, honest communications up?

EXERCISE F: DOWN

What are some of the possible pitfalls to clear, honest communications down?

EXERCISE G: ACROSS

What are some of the possible pitfalls to clear, honest communications across?

one government official received a big promotion, which entitled her to a rug of a certain thickness and size. Unfortunately, the size of office that she was entitled to was unavailable for several months. Most people would wait to have the rug delivered after they were in the bigger office. But organizational status is not always logical. The woman insisted that the rug be delivered and that it stand in the corner, still rolled, so that any who entered could see that she, indeed, had been promoted.

Three business terms describe the kinds of communications within a hierarchy: *up, down,* and *across.* Communications *up* are sent to those who occupy positions superior to the writer's within the company. These kinds of communications require more formality and respect than do communications to the other levels. Formal communication requires much thought because the writer's success depends on impressing these people. Upward communications sometimes are responses to downward communications.

At their best, communications up keep superiors informed about two things: necessary details, and the thoughts of subordinates. Both provide superiors with information from which they can make good decisions. Much depends on the quality of communications up.

At their worst, communications up are simply methods by which subordinates tell superiors only those things that superiors want to hear. Such failure in communications most often leads to mistrust, misinformation, and even mismanagement.

Communications *down* are sent to those who occupy positions in the company subordinate to the writer's. These are tricky. Some superiors get better results from informal communications than from formal communications, but other superiors lose their subordinates' respect when communications become too informal. Communications down require as much thought as communications up. Most corporate employees know that a communication from a superior must be answered. But that does not mean the employees have to like it. Many managers get most from their communications down by *asking* rather than *ordering* that something be done. Everyone knows that a question such as "Do you think you could have this inventory list by tomorrow morning?" actually means "Have this inventory list by tomorrow morning." The relative effects on subordinates of these two sentences are very different, however. The first, although one knows what it means, remains a request. The second is an order, and few people like to be told what to do.

Most people think that communications up require the most courtesy. But although being polite is always important, perhaps the most polite communications should be those directed down.

Communications *across* are sent to those who occupy positions similar in corporate rank to the writer's. These tend to be formal or informal largely to the degree that the writer and reader know each other. One important factor in communications across is that, unlike communications up and down, the reader is not always required to respond or to do what the missive requests. Persuasion, which is always part of communication, thus becomes very important in communications across. Details regarding *kinds* of communications up, down, and across appear in Chapter 3.

VERBAL AND NONVERBAL

Any communication using words is verbal, and any communication that does not use words is nonverbal. Facial or hand gestures, style of dress, and body position are the most common nonverbal messages that make up body language. Nonverbal communication expresses ideas and emotions that either reinforce or contradict the detailed information that verbal communication provides. Nonverbal communication is very subtle; we seldom can take a single clue and generalize an entire attitude from it. Still, that very subtlety demands that speakers and audiences attend to nonverbal communications carefully. In short, never underestimate the importance of body language, but never overestimate it, either. Although conveying much about feelings, nonverbal communication is not, and cannot be, a substitute for verbal communication. See Chapter 15 for a detailed discussion of nonverbal communication.

STYLE IN BUSINESS WRITING

In matters of grave importance, style, not sincerity, is the vital thing.

Oscar Wilde
(1854–1900)

Some things are infinitely perfectible: learning to listen, learning to think, learning to do a job well. Writing is one of those things. Trying to write better simply never ends. As people age, many things get worse: a few steps on the softball field and on the running track are lost; recovering from five 18-hour days in a row takes longer than a weekend; enthusiasm wanes more quickly. Writing, on the other hand, should get better and better, for good writing does not depend on strong legs, or even corporate enthusiasm. It depends on the years of practice behind it and the seriousness with which it is practiced. There are few imperfect things in this imperfect world that pay better dividends than good writing.

Good writing displays an organized mind, a sensitivity to other people, and an ability to convey information clearly. Its dividends are both immediate and cumulative. What is learned today pays today; it also pays tomorrow and the next day, and it continues to pay every time something is written. Learn enough and practice enough, and writing improves.

PLAIN STYLE

An honest tale speeds best being plainly told.

William Shakespeare
(1564–1616)

Good business writing uses a plain style, one that is simple and straightforward. Because the purpose is to convey information, long words and windy phrases, used gratuitously, have no place in business writing. Because these do nothing but complicate the writing and confuse the reader, they create an ineffective style.

A good, effective style is clear, efficient, and accurate. Achieving this plain style, however, is not the work of a day or even of a year. It is the product of a careful, thoughtful, analytical writer. Like a pit-bull terrier, a good plain style must be fed, exercised, and *always kept on a short leash.*

THE BUSINESS WRITER'S CONTRACT

THE BUSINESS WRITER'S CONTRACT

I promise to write clearly, concisely, accurately, courteously, and grammatically to make reading and understanding easy.

In business, as elsewhere, the writer has an implied contract with the reader: the writer promises to present information in a certain way, and the reader promises to consider, weigh, and decide, but not to judge or criticize immediately unless the writer's half of the contract is violated. The writer has violated the contract if anything controlled by the writer gets in the way of the reader's attempt to understand.

WRITING CLEARLY

FIVE WAYS TO CREATE CLARITY

1. *Be brief.*
2. *Be accurate.*
3. *Be courteous.*
4. *Convey information, not rot.*
5. *Know the subject.*

Among the many qualities of clear writing are those listed in the business writer's contract. Brevity, accuracy, courtesy, conveying information, and knowing the subject are each vital elements of *clear writing.* There are many ways to say something, most of which are unclear. Here is an example:

> Determining learner cognitive enhancement requires evaluational determinative techniques.

This sentence manages to violate all requirements for a plain style in only eight words. After much thinking, and a few guesses, we may determine that the sentence means the following:

> Testing requires tests.

The person who wrote the first example evidently thought that using big words was more important or more impressive than communicating effectively. In addition, the writer gave more emphasis to how the words sounded than to what they said. "Testing requires tests" gives the readers no new information.

Readers themselves are often intimidated by big words strung together. Just because they do not understand what is written, readers should never assume that the writer is more intelligent than they. Intelligent, hard-working, thoughtful writers make sure the reader can understand.

The first example, then, violates all five requirements for a plain style.

Brevity. When seven words may be rewritten as three words, those seven words are not "brief."

Accuracy. Because the sentence is nearly indecipherable, it is nearly impossible to determine its accuracy.

Courtesy. Any sentence requiring translation by the reader insults the reader.

EXERCISE H: WRITING CLEARLY

Rewrite the following note to Smedley Fahrquart from the director of research: "Smedley: Because of irreconcilable differences in interpersonal relationships with Emily Gooch, an engineer employed by us on a consulting basis for the purpose of resolving a number of production-related problems, it is the purpose of this memo to direct you, as Assistant Director of Research, to terminate said employment of said consultant."

EXERCISE I: DELETING WORDINESS

Rewrite the following sentences to delete wordiness.

1. Smedley is learning the skills of the work of doing the audits.
2. The artificial heart, which is made of plastic, remains in the experimental stages.
3. What the auditor seemed to be saying in so many words was that our accounting system was too often lacking in the exactitude required by the Internal Revenue Service.
4. After beating around the bush for a long time, she made the decision not to renew the contract of the time-management consultant.
5. No American company will be able in the future to escape the consequences of the global competition that will increasingly be forced on American business in the future.

EXERCISE J: IDENTIFYING AND REMOVING REDUNDANCIES

Identify the redundancies in the following sentences and remove them.

1. Smedley then referred back to the memorandum of 3 October 1989.
2. Samantha told them that the building was broad in width and tall in height.
3. It is an accurate fact that American manufacturing needs much more capital investment.
4. The shape of Smedley's new office is rectangular.
5. The color of Samantha's new office rug is beige.

Information, not rot. Nothing is so clear about this example as its lack of clarity and information.

Knowing the subject. A person who does not understand a subject cannot write clearly about it.

WRITING CONCISELY

Brevity is not only the soul of wit, as Shakespeare said, the mark of a good education, and the heart of a good style, but it is also a goal of business communication. Brevity saves readers time and energy. Saving time and energy saves money. Saving money makes money. Making money makes companies happy.

It is one thing to say "Write concisely"; it is another thing to do it. For instance, what are the means for doing so? Exactly how does a writer achieve brevity without removing necessary information? There are many ways to delete words and phrases without destroying meaning, and among the most common are these five:

1. Eliminate redundancies.
2. Eliminate unnecessary prepositional phrases.
3. Eliminate unnecessary nominalizations.
4. Eliminate unnecessary passive constructions.
5. Eliminate the obvious.

ELIMINATE REDUNDANCIES.   A redundancy is any expression that uses more words than necessary, often saying the same thing in two or more ways. Wordiness contributes nothing to the life of a sentence and can often be corrected simply by deleting all unnecessary words and phrases. For example, "We have a working relationship that is good" can be shortened easily to "We work well together." Similarly, "dashing quickly" is redundant because quickly is the only way we can dash. Identify the redundancy in the following sentence:

> Students should not make advance plans to leave campus until they know the date of their last examination.

"Advance plans" is always redundant because we cannot plan for the past or the present; we can plan only for the future.

ELIMINATE UNNECESSARY PREPOSITIONAL PHRASES.   Prepositional phrases can be deleted when they begin to sound wordy and confusing. Sometimes changing prepositional phrases to possessives works best. Instead of "the books of the women," for instance, we might try "the women's books." However, when two prepositional phrases are strung together, such as "the books of the women in the group," be careful how you revise them. Because reducing both prepositional phrases to possessives may sound awkward ("the group's women's books"), use your ear to determine the best way to avoid wordiness. Perhaps reducing only one of the phrases sounds best: "the books of the group's women."

EXERCISE K: CHANGING PREPOSITIONAL PHRASES TO POSSESSIVES

Note that some of these may be better left alone; possessives should be sounded against the ear before written on the page. Change the following prepositional phrases to possessives, if appropriate.

1. The metal handles of the binder clip
2. The page of the chapter of the book
3. The turn of the century
4. The nineteenth track of the second sector of the disk
5. The first entry of the debit sheet of the Fahrquart Company

EXERCISE L: DELETING NOMINALIZATIONS AND PREPOSITIONAL PHRASES

Rewrite the following sentences to make them less abstract and less wordy by eliminating nominalizations.

1. Samantha took the action quickly to reduce our losses.
2. Smedley's communication with Samantha is effective.
3. Samantha was knowledgeable of the corporate strategy regarding the reorganization of the Finance Department.
4. Smedley's smirks were a detraction from the seriousness of the conversation.
5. Reportation of the Product Development Lab's discoveries is the job of the Director of Research.

ELIMINATE UNNECESSARY NOMINALIZATIONS. *Nominalizations* are nouns that have been created from verbs and adjectives, and they are the most common examples of gobbledygook. The active verb *produce*, for example, becomes the abstract noun *production*, and the precise adjective *red* becomes the abstract noun *redness*. Here is a sentence obscured by a nominalization:

> Samantha did all of the work in the creation of the company's quality control program.

The use of the nominalization *creation* forces the writer to double the number of words in the sentence. Compare the edited version of the example:

> Samantha created the company's quality control program.

The edited version converts the abstract noun to an active verb and makes the meaning of the sentence clear and precise.

Nominalizations are not bad by definition; they are bad only when used in place of clearer, more economical writing. For example, if a writer wanted to address specifically the redness of Mars, not about Mars itself, the nominalization *redness* would be appropriate to use. Because nouns are more powerful than adjectives, emphasizing the red quality of Mars is done best by making the adjective *red* a noun: *redness*.

The following lists show how to convert abstract nominalizations (nouns) into active verbs or into verbals (noun or adjective forms that serve the function of verbs):

Nominalization	Verb
action	act
communication	communicate
creation	create
detraction	detract
execution	execute
implementation	implement
nomination	nominate
purgation	purge
reportation	report
service	serve

Nominalization with a Prepositional Phrase	Verbal with a Noun
The processing of inventory	Processing inventory
The standardization of widgitcogs	Standardizing widgitcogs
The use of [any noun]	Using [any noun]
The hiring of engineers	Hiring engineers

EXERCISE M: REMOVING
NOMINALIZATIONS

Change the following nominalizations into precise verbs.

1. to make a drawing
2. to perform the adjustment
3. to give a speech
4. to try an attempt
5. to reach an agreement
6. to do some work
7. to lay the blame
8. to hold a meeting
9. to take a nap
10. to do lunch

EXERCISE N: CONVERTING
PASSIVE VOICE TO ACTIVE
VOICE

Change the following passive-
voice sentences to active-voice
sentences.

1. Recommendations for reducing inventory were made by
the chief financial officer.

2. The final examination was
written by the instructor to
test only the material covered
during the last half of the
course.

3. All the expenses for the corporate retreat were paid in
advance by the Office of Corporate Training.

EXERCISE O: CHANGING
THE ACTIVE TO THE PASSIVE
VOICE

Change the following sentence
from active to passive voice to
emphasize the object of action
rather than the person performing the action:
Smedley ruined a company car.

ELIMINATE UNNECESSARY PASSIVE VOICE.

The active voice is normally best for all prose, especially business writing, because it is economical, direct, and forceful. It makes clear who the actor is (the subject), what the actor does (the action), and to whom or to what the action is done (the object):

IBM [*actor*] promoted [*action*] Jim [*object*].

In contrast, the passive voice is often wordy and obscure. It tells first to whom or what something is done (the object of action), then what is done (the action), and finally who is doing it (the actor):

Jim [*object of action*] was promoted [*action*] by IBM [*actor*].

The passive version of the sentence is two-thirds longer than the active version.

One reason that the passive voice uses more words than the active voice is that the passive voice often requires state-of-being (or linking) verbs: forms of the verbs *be* and *have*. Compare the short active sentence "Smedley sold a million widgitcogs last year" with the longer passive sentence "A million widgitcogs *were* sold by Smedley last year."

The active voice is also the most memorable. The inscription on the Statue of Liberty does not say: "Your tired, your poor, your huddled masses are to be sent to me," as the passive voice would have it. Rather, the inscription is active, even imperative: "Send me your tired, your poor," etc. Lincoln did not say, "Fourscore and seven years ago, a new nation was brought forth by our fathers." Rather, he used the active voice: "our fathers brought forth."

FOUR USES FOR THE PASSIVE VOICE.

In general, use the active voice unless you have good reason to use the passive voice, such as the following:

1. *To emphasize an action rather than the person performing it.* Laboratory reports are written in the passive voice because experiments are more important than experimenters and because rigor of method should make experiments repeatable. That is, the same experiment performed by different people at different times should yield the same result.

   The material was heated to 206 C for 17 minutes.

   Write reports other than laboratory reports in the active voice.

2. *To express what is done when the "who" is unknown.*

   One million dollars has been embezzled from the employees' pension fund.

3. *To omit deliberately the "who done it."*

   Ten percent of the labor force will be laid off in February.

   Writing "Management will lay off ten percent of the labor force in February" creates bad guys. The passive voice in this example also emphasizes the action and the recipient.

EXERCISE P: USING THE PASSIVE VOICE TO EMPHASIZE THE UNKNOWN

Change the following sentence from active to passive voice to emphasize what was done because who did it is unknown: Someone ruined a company car by crashing through a fence and into the president's swimming pool.

EXERCISE Q: USING THE PASSIVE VOICE TO DELETE THE "WHO DONE IT"

Change the following sentence from active to passive voice to delete the "who done it": Smedley crashed a company car through a fence and into a swimming pool after destroying the president's prized rose bushes.

EXERCISE R: DELETING THE OBVIOUS

Rewrite the following sentences, deleting the obvious: After seven hours in the meeting, Smedley heard his stomach growl. He was hungry.

4. *To allow managers to do their jobs.* Good managers use the passive voice when they wish to be diplomatic. Because the passive voice emphasizes the action rather than the actor, it allows managers to deflect blame or to avoid pointing fingers. Compare the specific "Management mishandled the reorganization" in active voice with the general "The reorganization was mishandled" in passive voice.

ELIMINATE THE OBVIOUS.   Do not write what people already know: it wastes their time. Such words and phrases as "obviously," "needless to say," and the like are almost always unnecessary. If something is so well known that it is needless to say it, then why say it? Neither should writers say such obvious things as "On clear days, the sky is blue."

TWO WARNINGS ABOUT BREVITY.   Brevity is an admirable goal of business and technical writing. Once learned, it can become a passion. As with all passions, however, writing concisely may become destructive if carried too far. Heed the following two warnings.

1. Do not write as babies talk or as machines write. That is, do not omit the articles (the *the*'s, *a*'s, and *an*'s) and other words of normal discourse. Also make sure to vary the length and structure of sentences.

2. Do not delete information unintentionally while writing for brevity. The demand for brevity works to reduce the number of words while the demand for providing information works to increase the number of words. Reduce the number of words only as far as essential information is not deleted.

THE FOG INDEX

Writers who use long sentences and long words are more concerned with conveying their own brilliance and education than with conveying the information they are supposed to convey. Long words and long sentences are used also by those who lack the sensitivity and security to make the reader's job easy. The Gunning Fog Index[1] provides a good method of determining how badly something is written. It does not cure bad writing, but it may help cure two major causes of bad business writing: long sentences and long words.

Fog, says Gunning, is that which comes between the reader and the information on the page. His index quantifies the fogginess of prose; that is, it rates the difficulty of seeing through the fog of words to the information. The higher the number of the fog index, the foggier the prose. The number also corresponds to the grade level of the reader. A fog index of six means that a reader needs to have completed sixth grade (six years' study of the language) to understand the prose. It has little to do with the difficulty of the ideas embodied in a piece of writing, but it has much to do with the language itself. Reducing the

---

[1]Robert Gunning. *The Technique of Clear Writing*, rev. ed. (New York: McGraw-Hill, 1968), 38.

fog index may help simplify and clarify a memo, letter, report, or even a speech. Here is how it works.

The Gunning Fog Index

(Average Sentence Length + % "hard" words) × 0.4 = fog index

1. Count the number of words in a passage at least 100 words long (200 is better). In a long report, count the words in two such passages, always ending at the end of a sentence.

2. Divide the number of words by the number of sentences. This provides the average sentence length (ASL). (Independent clauses count as sentences in most fog indexes, but here we shall count only full sentences.)

3. Count the number of "hard" words—that is, those having more than two syllables. Numerals, no matter how long, are one syllable (*April 1, 1987*, contains three words).

4. Count "-ing" words of more than two syllables. Do not, however, count:

a. letters and numbers used in outlines,
b. proper names,
c. words that combine short words like *treetrimmer* and *bookbinder*,
d. words that become three syllables when *-es* or *-ed* is added: "witnesses" and "invited"; that is, do not count two-syllable words that become three syllables when they become plural or past tense.

Divide the number of "hard" words by the number of words in the passage to get the percent of hard words (PHW). Remember to move the decimal point two places to the right to produce the percentage.

4. Add ASL to PHW.

5. Multiply the sum by 0.4. The result is the fog index.

By applying his fog index to a passage written by Albert Einstein, Gunning shows that complex ideas may be conveyed in simple, clear language.

> If we ponder over the question as to how the universe, considered as a whole, is to be regarded, the first answer that suggests itself to us is surely this: As regards space (and time), the universe is infinite. There are stars everywhere, so that the density of matter, although very variable in detail, is nevertheless on the average everywhere the same. In other words, however far we might travel through space, we should find everywhere an attenuated swarm of fixed stars of approximately the same kind of density.

These are the hard or lengthy words from Einstein's passage.

universe	variable
considered	average
universe	attenuated
infinite	approximately
density	density

And here is the computation of the passage.

Sum of words: 89
Sum of sentences: 4

ASL:	$89 \div 4 = 22.3$
Sum of "hard" words:	10
PHW	$10 \div 89 = 11.2\%$
ASL + PHW	$22.3 + 11.2 = 33.5$
Multiply:	$33.5 \times 0.4 = 13.4$
Fog index:	13.4

The following is another example, this time from a tax law for New York State:

> Except as otherwise provided in this section, all of the provisions of this article applicable to the tax imposed by section five hundred three of this article shall apply with respect to the supplemental tax imposed by this section to the same extent as if it were imposed by such section five hundred three, insofar as such provisions can be made applicable to the supplemental tax imposed by this section, with such modification as may be necessary to adapt such provisions to the supplemental tax imposed by this section.

Notice that Einstein is talking about the makeup of the universe, whereas the second example is discussing only taxes. Does it not seem strange that the first passage has a fog index of only thirteen, while the second passage has a fog index higher than forty (far off Gunning's scale)?

Gunning also provides the following chart to clarify the meaning of a fog index.

Fog Index by Grade	**By Magazine**
17 College graduate	(no popular magazine this foggy)
16 College senior	"
15 College junior	"
14 College sophomore	"
13 College freshman	*Playboy*
Danger Line —————————	
12 High school senior	*Harper's*
11 High school junior	*Time, Newsweek*
Easy-reading Line —————————	
10 High school sophomore	*Reader's Digest*
9 High school freshman	*Saturday Evening Post*
8 Eighth grade	*Ladies' Home Journal*
7 Seventh grade	*True Confessions*
6 Sixth grade	comic books

Although this guide is helpful, remember that since Gunning published his book, more than thirty years ago, Americans have taken to reading less. In addition, television and other forms of relatively mind-

EXERCISE S: COMPUTING A FOG INDEX

Compute the fog index of the following passage:
There are several kinds of stories, but only one difficult kind—the humorous. I will talk mainly about that one. The humorous story is American. The comic story is English. The witty story is French. The humorous story depends for its effect upon the manner of the telling. The comic story and the witty story depend upon the matter.[2]

EXERCISE T: REWRITING FOR ACCURACY

Rewrite the following sentence for accuracy. If you are unsure about the exact meaning of certain words, look them up in a dictionary:
Smedley is anxious to discover the parameters of the dialogue between several persons that he read in the quote from the newspaper.

Men's evil manners, we write
* in brass;*
Their virtues
We write in water.

William Shakespeare
(1564–1616)

less diversion have occupied more and more of people's time. One result is that, on average, people, even college graduates, cannot read as well as they used to. Many college textbooks are written with a fog index of nine, although first-year college students presumably begin with a capacity for reading at a level of twelve or thirteen. Moreover, people are more comfortable reading "down" than at a level they are capable of. According to the abilities of your audience, then, you may want to lower the "danger" and "easy-reading" lines by at least one level.

To remain interesting, prose must include sentences of varying lengths. The average length of sentences for business reports, however, should be between 15 and 25 words. Sentences in letters should be two or three words shorter on average. Informal memoranda should have very short sentences. Moreover, Wolford's Law states that there is an inverse relationship between the difficulty of the information to be conveyed and the length of sentences conveying that information: the more complex the information, the simpler the sentences conveying that information should be. Important, complex information should be written in short sentences. Longer sentences are valuable for conveying the reader from one important idea to the next. Sometimes, they are simply necessary.

Short sentences and words do not automatically produce a good style. Consequently, the fog index is helpful for diagnosing problems in diction and sentence length, but it only *diagnoses*. It does not correct the many other problems of bad writing.

WRITING ACCURATELY

Using precise words leads to precise understanding. Many words used in business are vague and some are used inaccurately. For instance, *anxious* does not mean "eager," yet *anxious* is often misused that way. See the glossary for discussions of such misused words as *dialogue, enormity, gratified, input, lifestyle, level, parameter, quote, service, unique,* and *value.*

WRITING COURTEOUSLY

Rhetoric is little more than applied manners. Offending readers, unintentionally or intentionally, conveys one of two things. First, if readers believe the offense is intentional, the result is hurt feelings or anger. Second, if readers believe the offense is unintentional, they may believe the writer is either careless or ignorant. Whatever readers believe, the result is the same: the writer loses.

First, address the reader respectfully. If the form of the writing calls for the reader to be addressed formally by title, such as in a letter, use "Mr." or "Ms." (unless you know the woman prefers to be addressed as Miss or Mrs.). Avoid stereotyping people or references to

---

[2]Adapted from Mark Twain, "How to Tell a Story."

their behavior. While cleanliness is possible without courtesy, courtesy is difficult without clean unwrinkled paper, clean type, new ribbons, and even margins. Carelessness betrays a sense that the writer cares little for the sensibilities of the reader.

Edit carefully and sensitively to avoid unintentional discourtesies. Do not write, for example, "We are sorry that you have received your bank statements in unsealed envelopes and are especially sorry that this should happen to one of our oldest depositors." Although the offense may be unintentional, it remains an offense. Write instead "We are sorry that your bank statements are arriving in unsealed envelopes and are sorry especially that a depositor whom we have been privileged to serve for many years should be inconvenienced."

Yet do not become so preoccupied with avoiding offense that the language becomes so bland that it imitates a home on the range: where seldom is heard a discouraging word. Where the skies are not cloudy all day, there is sure to be a drought of clear expression.

Please is an important word. "Send me the Fahrquart report right away" is made palatable by adding *please*: "Please send me the Fahrquart report right away." *Thank you* is also important.

Although a writer should never offend gratuitously or unintentionally, avoiding argument at all costs is a mistake for society in general and for business in particular. The notion seems to be widespread in this country that disagreeing vigorously with a person's ideas is the same as attacking that person. This is not so, nor should it be. Only through debate, sometimes heated, can meaningful change occur. For example, more than two thousand years ago Aristotle was asked why he constantly attacked Plato's philosophy, given that Plato and Aristotle were close friends. Aristotle responded by saying, "Plato is dear, but the truth is dearer." Recently, Jack Welch, president and CEO of General Electric, instituted a new method of communications in which argument, sometimes heated, was to be the norm and not the exception. Welch reasoned that telling the boss what the boss wanted to hear created the enormous and enormously expensive bureaucracy of management. Initially, his employees were offended by this method of communication. The problem began to be solved, however, when Welch prefaced every exchange by saying that he was not disagreeing *personally*, he was disagreeing with regard to *ideas*. Managers who invite what Wilcome Washburn calls "vexatious oral exchange," which means that subordinates should not be fearful of arguing with the boss, will discover a more exciting and productive staff.

CONVEYING INFORMATION, NOT ROT

Too often, writers try so hard to convey how educated they are by using big words and long sentences that they fail to convey anything else. Few readers are impressed. The true mark of the educated is the ability to say what one has to say clearly, briefly, brightly, grammatically, and accurately. All else is rot—that is, worthless. Do not write, for example, "Mr. Fahrquart, your request for the purchase of 14 JSEF 280K multi-linkage mainframe computers is seen by this office as

---

....

EXERCISE U: REWRITING FOR COURTESY

Rewrite the following memorandum to Samantha Fahrquart from her subordinate:
Miss Fahrquart: Got your suggestions two weeks after I asked for them. Don't like the first one, but the rest are ok, I guess. Send me some more by tomorrow. The deadline you set is three days away, so hurry up.

EXERCISE V: REWRITING TO ELIMINATE ROT

Rewrite the following sentence to eliminate the rot:
Dear Mr. Fahrquart: It is an unfortunate circumstance that I am led to have to report to you that there has been a discontinuation of the offering of our erstwhile product called "Hirsute Hair Restorer."

EXERCISE W: RECOGNIZING THE IRRESPONSIBLE

Discuss in class the reason that the following sentences are irresponsible:
Europeans driving in America and Americans driving in Europe cause many accidents. Either Americans should drive on the left side of the road as they do in Europe, or Europeans should drive on the right side as they do in America.

not part of the optimal efficiency usage toward which we are striving for the use of corporate monies." Write instead "Smedley, those computers you want us to buy are too expensive."

Rot, which some call "Gobbledygook," or, in business, "commercialese," is the use of many words to say nothing. It derives partly from people's overuse of nominalization, partly from trying to sound intelligent by using bits and pieces of jargon, and partly from insensitivity. The sole purpose of an education, said an Oxford don in 1914, is to teach people to know when someone is talking rot. Rot is a disease of language and thought, the symptoms of which include a pouring forth of verbal nonsense. So little sense is spoken or written these days that it has become difficult to train ourselves by listening or reading. Good books help. Paying attention to what people are saying exactly also helps. Paying attention to what we are saying exactly helps most.

WRITING RESPONSIBLY

Responsible writers know their subjects well. When ignorant of a subject, most writers know they must learn about it before beginning to write. The problem usually derives from writers who know a little about a subject, but not enough. Limited knowledge is dangerous. In business, limited knowledge is deadly. For instance, when General Motors began marketing one of its little cars, the Nova, in Hispanic countries, no one seemed to realize that, in Spanish, *no va* can mean "it does not go." No car company wants to suggest to people that one of its cars does not go. By the time they discovered the error, GM had already spent millions on advertising. This was an expensive error derived from ignorance—in this instance, ignorance of another culture. Similarly, a writer should never state "Assembly-line workers are taking too many coffee breaks" unless the writer has read the latest labor contract.

SUMMARY

1. Learning to communicate is important for two reasons: it teaches us to think and it promotes understanding among people.

2. Good communication provides personal opportunities and practical benefits to business.

3. Communication must also be examined for its relative *simplicity* and *complexity*. The requirements of the subject and the audience determine just how simple or complex a communication must be.

4. Communication can be perceived as running from extreme *formality* to extreme *informality*. The degree of formality is determined by the material, the situation, the audience, and the purpose.

5. Communication can be perceived from the direction in which it is to be sent: *up* to one's corporate superiors; *down* to one's corporate subordinates; *across* to one's colleagues.

6. Communications may also be *verbal* (that is, by words, oral or written) or *non-verbal* (that is, by such methods as body language).

7. Learning to write well requires learning new things about writing and remaining alert in order to maintain those qualities already learned.

8. The *business writer's contract* must be kept in mind always: "I promise to write clearly, concisely, accurately, courteously, and grammatically to make reading and understanding easy."

9. Good style is the result of achieving those qualities discussed in the *business writer's contract*.

10. Brevity may be achieved by avoiding the following: redundancies; unnecessary prepositional phrases and nominalizations; unnecessary use of the passive voice; and the obvious.

11. Brevity should not be achieved at the expense of necessary information, nor does brevity demand that we write as a baby or as a computer talks.

12. The *fog index* is a good diagnostic tool for determining whether sentences and words are too long. Because it is simplistic, the fog index does not by itself determine the quality of the writing.

13. Accuracy requires that a writer know both the subject and the precise meaning of the words used for conveying the subject. Vague words confuse readers.

14. While few people are intentionally discourteous, we must be careful to write in such a way as to avoid even unintentional offense. *Please* and *thank you* remain important words for courteous writing.

15. Writing *rot* is common. Good writers dig out rot before they complete the memo or letter. Writers should never write about something they know nothing about: hence the value of research.

EXERCISES

1. *Communication and humanity*. Make a mental list of human activities that do not require verbal communication. Do you agree that all exclusively human activities—as opposed to the activities of other living things—involve verbal communications? Do you think that verbal communications makes humans human? Which activity—oral or written—is most exclusively human?

2. *Formal and informal communications*. In order to see clearly the difference between formal and informal communications, write a letter to your best friend without using any contractions. Now, write a letter to the dean of your college in which you use every contraction possible. Compare the two.

3. *Directions of business communication*:

   What does communication *up* mean?

   What does communication *down* mean?

   What does communication *across* mean?

4. *Differences in "directions" of business communication*. List and discuss several differences between communications *up*, *down*, and *across*.

5. *Simple and complex as relative terms*. List five words or phrases commonly used by economists, accountants, marketing people, or people in your field. Define those terms. Now make a list of alternatives—that is, write simple words or phrases that would explain in simple language the same notions expressed by the first list.

6. *Verbal and non-verbal*. Using the first list from exercise 5 (or a list prepared by the instructor or the class), play a game of charades.

7. *Body language: Movement and gesture.* Although we seldom see more than the top third of television newscasters' bodies, they nevertheless display much body language. Moreover, each newscaster has been schooled in body language. By switching channels, try to discover the differences in body language expressed by each. List those differences. Discuss the relative effectiveness on viewer interest of those different movements.

8. *Brevity (out-of-class).* Rewrite the following sentences, trying to cut the number of words by at least one-third.

   a. As I am sure you already have been informed and therefore know very well, Smedley is back to work.

   b. The prioritization of our present and future orders will be done by way of a new and vastly improved computerization technique.

   c. When you next have occasion to get in contact with payroll, you may ask that your W-2 form be changed.

   d. Please be advised that we have enclosed in this package the books you ordered from us.

   e. Model 874 Widgitcogs are being discontinued from manufacturing due to the fact that they no longer serve any particular purpose and are not selling well.

   f. He described in a very real sense my personal preference.

   g. The modern student in the world of today must study hard.

   h. We share very much of the common and everyday values of our former backgrounds of upbringing.

   i. She decided that she was in a no-win type of situation, and as a consequence, she would sit back and sort of do nothing.

   j. Unnecessary words that are not needed in a sentence or a paragraph should be taken out and removed from the sentence or paragraph.

CASE STUDY 1: PROFESSOR "OUTLAW" FAHRQUART

For years, Professor Fahrquart has been parking illegally on weekends in front of his office building. Having ignored parking tickets for all those years, and having had the campus police finally give up, the professor has not received a ticket for four years. A new chief of campus security, Preston Yukon, was appointed last month. He wants everyone who parks illegally to be ticketed, and he has been given authority to see that they are paid. The new policy goes into effect on the first day of next month.

You are a student patrol officer. Chief Yukon has given all officers a list of people who have been parking illegally. Moreover, all officers are required to write to the people on their lists, informing them of the new policy.

Write a letter to Professor Fahrquart, telling him of the new policy. Remember that, as a *student* patrol officer, your letter should be considered a letter up.

CASE STUDY 2: FORM LETTERS

Add to the information provided in case study 1 the following information: Chief Yukon has given the list of all people parking illegally to the president of the university. You are the president.

Write a form letter to all violators informing them of the new policy.

CASE STUDY 3: USING THE PASSIVE VOICE

You are the manager of environmental engineering for Fahrquart Industries, Inc. One day, you receive a call from Smedley Fahrquart, CEO of the company. In essence, he says, "I've just written a letter in response to some maverick reporter who suggests that our landfill over in Swampville threatens to bury us all—the whole town included—in toxic waste. It's not pretty. And most of it is a lie. Would you look this over and make sure that I have my facts straight? And while you're at it, would you mind checking to make sure that I don't go overboard in some places. I was pretty hot when I wrote it, and I may have said some things that really ought to be reworded."

You read the letter and decide that Mr. Fahrquart does, indeed, have all his facts straight; you are impressed. On the other hand, the letter is often injudicious, to say the least. In particular, Fahrquart lays direct blame for a number of things on particular people and on particular companies, most of which, if printed, would put the company in hot water, if not in a courtroom, for years. You decide that the best method is to retain the accusations Fahrquart includes but to remove the names of people and companies he accuses. The best method, you decide, is to write the letter in the passive voice, thereby avoiding naming names.

Rewrite the letter that begins at the top of the next page.

Dear Ms. Pulitzer:

You and your paper ought to be ashamed to publish misinformation about a company such as Fahrquart Industries, a company that has been the largest employer in this town for more than 70 years.

You say that the Swampville Landfill, which we now own, is "laced with PCPs put there by Fahrquart Industries." While it is true that there are some PCPs in the landfill, it is not true that we put them there. Probably, they were put there by the old Transformer Electric Company, which owned the landfill before we bought it six years ago. Transformers, as most people know, contain PCPs. Nothing Fahrquart makes contains PCPs. How could we have done it?

You say, "Fahrquart is making no effort to clean up its potentially disastrous mess." Come now, Ms. Pulitzer, had you checked with Ms. Pureair, in the state Environmental Protection Agency office, you would have discovered that we have been working with the state for five years now to try to find a way to reduce the PCP level in the landfill.

Moreover, you would have discovered that Ms. Pureair and her crew checked the level five years ago—at our cost—and found that the PCP level does not exceed state standards for toxicity. Why don't you get off my back?

Smedley Fahrquart, CEO
Fahrquart Industries, Inc.

Rewrite the letter, using the passive voice where appropriate. Be sure that you can justify each instance of the passive voice.

CHALLENGE EXERCISE 1: FINDING ROT

Find a passage from a trade journal, textbook, or memo from work that shows evidence of rot. Write why it is rot.

CHALLENGE EXERCISE 2: BREVITY

Choose a small topic and write 100–150 words about it. Use words of *no more than one syllable.*
Here is an example:

Fishing

The chance for me to fish comes at best once a week; at worst, it comes twice a month. But I could fish once a day and not tire of it. I love the tugs and jerks as the fish swims back and forth and jumps in its quest to throw the hook from its mouth. I do not place great worth on the size of the fish. I have caught them all: big fish, small fish, fat, thin, long and short. I have caught some things that were not fish at all.

I like to fish for more than the mere tug from the end of the line. It soothes the mind, rests the body, and frees the soul. One can feel at peace with the world as one floats in a boat on a still lake and breathes the crisp clean air. Most days I watch dawn break and see the bright red sun climb in the sky to burn off the mist.

But for a real lift, I like to take a child with me when I get a chance to fish. I can see the great joy and the gleam in the child's eyes when the first fish tugs on the small one's pole.

CHALLENGE EXERCISE 3: CONVEYING INFORMATION, NOT ROT

Rewrite the following letters to convey information, not rot.

a. Dear Daughter,
Given the optimal meteorological conditions of today, it is imperative that, immediately upon returning from the furtherance of your educational opportunities, you should consider the efficacy of engaging the machine for equalizing the length of the green monocots profusely growing in the area surrounding our dwelling place.

Mom

b. Dear Mom,
While the meteorological conditions remain optimal and, one can only assume, the machine for monocot-equalizing is similarly in optimal condition, the job task you assigned to me could not be effected because we are in a state of lacking the petroleum-based power source with which the machine is brought into a condition of readiness.

Daughter

c. Dear Son,
Whensoever you return from enhancing your equestrian abilities, it is considered important and crucial by your parent that the sanitation device for eating utensils be opened, the contents removed from their places in the machine, sorted according to type and use, and efficiently replaced in the storage area for such utensils.

Dad

d. Dear Dad,

Thank you for bringing to my considered attention the need for removing the sanitized eating utensils from the machine effecting such a result.

Upon examination of said machine, however, it was discovered that the utensils had not yet been sanitized, and, as a result, removing them to their usual pre-use residence would have resulted in a less than effective activity. I have saved you much time and effort by not effecting such a removal. Rather, I have gathered my equipment for playing the following game — baseball — and engaged in the activity appropriate to that game, having been asked to do so by my peer group.

Son

WRITING AS PROCESS

DEFINING PURPOSE, GOALS, AND SCOPE

Purpose
Defining the Purpose
Goals
Scope

ANALYZING THE READER

Knowledgeable Readers
Unknowledgeable Readers
Primary and Secondary Readers

SCHEDULING TIME

GATHERING IDEAS AND DATA

ORGANIZING IDEAS AND DATA

Managing Data

DRAFTING AND REVISING

PERSUADING THE READER

Classical Rhetoric and Methods of
Persuasion
Writing Persuasively
The Four Appeals of Persuasion
Logical Fallacies

EARNING THE RIGHT TO BE READ

Condescending Language
Dull Language
Tone

EDITING AND PROOFREADING

SUMMARY

EXERCISES

Learning Objectives:

☐ See writing as a process.

☐ Grasp these three activities of the
writing process:
Preparing to write,
Writing,
Revising and editing.

☐ Discover the advantages of business writing over other types of
writing.

☐ Use nine steps to writing
effectively:
Defining purpose, goals, and
scope,
Analyzing the reader,
Scheduling time,
Gathering ideas and data,
Organizing ideas and data,
Drafting and revising,
Persuading the reader,
Earning the right to be read,
Editing and proofreading.

2

THE WRITING PROCESS IN BUSINESS

WRITING AS PROCESS

Good cooks prepare meals by gathering fresh ingredients, cooking them properly, and arranging them to suit the tastes of dinner guests. Diligent students take examinations by preparing for them, concentrating hard on them, and going over them carefully before submitting them to an instructor. Similarly, writers produce a good piece of communication by *preparing* for it, *writing* it, and *revising and polishing* it before presenting it to a reader.

In short, writing, like other complex activities, is a *process*.

THE THREE STEPS OF THE WRITING PROCESS

1. *Preparing to write*
2. *Writing*
3. *Revising and polishing*

1. *Preparing to write.* Long assumed and often ignored, preparing to write now goes by many names, but this chapter will emphasize and analyze the *process*, including the sequence of activities that writers must perform one way or another, before the writing begins.

   In preparing to write, business writers enjoy at least four advantages over writers of other kinds of work:

   a. Often the purpose and goals are easier to define;

   b. Although not completely homogeneous, the readership is easier to analyze;

   c. The resources for research are more readily available;

   d. The writing is easier to arrange because formats are usually already established.

2. *Writing.* Writing is fundamentally an individual activity. That is, when all is said and done, there is one brain, one pen or typewriter or word processor, and the interaction between the two. This is inescapable. Fortunately, because of conventional (sometimes even rigid) methods for preparation, the availability of other people interested in helping, and clear goals for editing, business writing often is easier than, say, creative writing.

3. *Revising and polishing.* The revising and polishing process of business writing—which comprises rewriting, rearranging, editing, and proofreading—has clear aims: clarity, accuracy, courtesy, and good grammar. Detailed examination of this part of the writing process may be found in Appendix I. Here it is important only to say that most of the quality of any writing comes from the revising and polishing, just as the quality of any work comes mostly from careful attention to detail.

   The degree to which writers need to follow each formal step is determined by the *kind* of business writing that they are undertaking. For example, in formal reports writers should follow each detail carefully; in memos simply dashed off to colleagues, however, writers can skip or modify parts of the formal process and do much of the thinking and planning inside their heads.

   Those who fear writing usually spend much time gathering material, piling it on a desk, and shuffling and rearranging it until the panic of a deadline gets the better of them. Then the mad rush of

EXERCISE A: WRITING

Discuss briefly in class the following question: Why is it that writers of business letters probably (not always) may find others to help more readily than, say, poets do?

writing begins. The result of this haphazard process is that they omit much important material, misrepresent much, and badly place much. Finally, when they submit the report, the pleasure of enormous relief is reduced by the nagging feeling that the work is not so good as it might have been.

Writers can make writing far easier by doing much of the work before beginning to write.

DEFINING PURPOSE, GOALS, AND SCOPE

PURPOSE

While everything in business must be written well, the degree of study and preparation required depends on the amount and complexity of the information to be imparted. Preparation begins with understanding the object of and the audience for the writing. The three common purposes of business communications are to *inform*, to *persuade*, and to *express*.

INFORM.   The simplest informational communication does little but tell someone something. How the information was found and what was considered previously are seldom related. Writers create this kind of communication for those who want only the facts. Complex informational reports, on the other hand, provide all the facts, including background, methods, and predictions.

PERSUADE.   Persuading the reader of a given point is the goal of all rhetoric and as such includes all principles of good writing. In business writing, the readers who frequently need to be persuaded are bosses. Thus, the writer should know what bosses like and do not like in communications. These likes and dislikes are given here.[1]

WHAT BOSSES LIKE TO READ	WHAT BOSSES DO NOT LIKE TO READ
■ The main idea first	■ Criticism
■ *All* the *pertinent* facts	■ Personal complaints
■ Plain English	■ Alibis and buck-passing
■ Anything making their job easier	■ Unasked-for opinions
	■ Insufficient information
	■ "Slanted" or "hyped" information

----

[1]See Roger P. Wilcox, *Communication at Work: Writing and Speaking* (Boston: Houghton Mifflin, 1977). Pages 49–51 report a study of what bosses like and dislike about reading reports.

In business, persuading readers derives from showing them how much money could be made, is being lost, or will be lost, and how quickly. Even non-profit companies are concerned about money, but their primary goals are usually better and more efficient service. Consequently, arguments concentrate on improving service and efficiency.

Express.   Most communication in business attempts to express opinions and convey directives. That is, subordinates provide opinions about business matters to their bosses, and bosses convey directives to their subordinates. To be persuasive, however, writers should remember that the key to such communication is *reasoned opinion*.

No matter that bosses want to hear their subordinates' opinions or that subordinates must obey their bosses' orders: everyone wants to know *why*. Bosses are more likely to accept the opinions and advice of their subordinates when those opinions are accompanied by good, logical reasons. Subordinates tend to do a better job and more willingly when their bosses accompany their orders with good, logical reasons for them.

Defining the Purpose

To help define the purpose of any communication, writers should state the purpose in one sentence. Consolidating the purpose into a single statement requires much thought and much rewriting. Once it is written clearly, economically, and accurately, two people benefit: the writer, who knows from this point on exactly what needs to be done; and the reader, who will know exactly what the purpose of the communication is.

Sometimes statements of purpose contain a specific solution as, for example, in proposals: "This report suggests that Widgitcog, Inc., buy two Model 123Z reconditioned cranes from Digit Corp." More often, as in most other kinds of reports, the solution is more general or, as in this example, not implied: "This report determines whether Widgitcog, Inc., should buy two Model 123Z reconditioned cranes from Digit Corp." In any case, writers should not worry when the solution to the communication occurs in the purpose. Business writing is not like mystery fiction: readers do not want to be held in suspense.

Goals

Once the purpose is clearly defined, the writer should then list the goals of the communication. If the purpose statement already encompasses the goals, then the writer may proceed to the job of determining the scope. Often, however, goals differ from the general purpose; they are specific means by which the purpose is achieved. Furthermore, goals may change as the writer learns more about the subject. A list of goals keeps things on track: the writer always knows what the goals are and whether certain information is useful, thus saving much time.

Exercise B: Determining Purpose

Here are two topics for business reports. Each is a quotation from an executive who is assigning you to write the report. Practice creating one-sentence statements of purpose for the report that might come out of that assignment.

1. "We've got to figure out how to reduce the percentage of bad widgitcogs that we're sending out to our customers. I mean, it's really bad in some cases. I've just been listening to a customer complaining that fully 10 percent of our last shipment was bad."

2. "You know, we spend $150,000 a year on that executive dining room upstairs, and just when we've asked our hourly employees to consider a pay reduction because our sales are so low. It's just not right."

······· ·······
EXERCISE C: DISTINGUISHING
BETWEEN *PURPOSE* AND
GOALS

1. Determine the goals that might help achieve the purpose of this report, as given here: "This report suggests that productivity can be increased 7 percent by reducing by 30 minutes the amount of time required to move finished widgitcogs from the assembly line to the packing and shipping rooms."

2. Create a purpose statement from the following list of related goals:
   a. Eliminate 5 engineering positions.
   b. Move the 3 p.m.–11 p.m. janitorial shift to 11 p.m.–7 a.m.
   c. Collapse the present 12 plant divisions into 8.

*A [reader] so various that he seemed
  to be
Not one, but all mankind's epitome.
Stiff in opinions, always in the
  wrong;
Was everything by starts and nothing long:
But in the course of one revolving
  moon,
Was chemist, fiddler, statesman,
  and buffoon.*

John Dryden
(1631–1700)

When goals change as a result of discovering new information, the purpose may change also. Again, this helps the writer keep in mind the purpose.

SCOPE

Deciding on the limits of the scope narrows and focuses the communication for the reader. Imagine the world as a culture placed under a microscope and the subject of a report to be a tiny, single-celled organism in that culture. As a biologist tries to clarify and identify that cell by magnifying and isolating it so the writer magnifies and isolates the subject of the report by defining what is and is not to be considered. The writer narrows the topic by focusing on certain criteria (money, time, capability) required for achieving the purpose of the communication. A clear scope saves the writer much time in gathering, organizing, and writing the communication.

ANALYZING THE READER

Once the purpose, goal, and scope of a communication have been determined, the writer then should consider who will be reading it and what the reader already knows about the topic. Most readers may be classified as either knowledgeable or unknowledgeable and primary or secondary.

KNOWLEDGEABLE READERS

These are people who know much about the subject under discussion. Addressing the knowledgeable reader usually means that the writer does not need to simplify specialized vocabulary, to explain certain acronyms and initialisms, or to alter certain specialized phrases. *If and only if*, for example, means one thing to a mathematician, another thing to a philosopher, and a third to a rhetorician. If the subject is mathematics and the reader is a mathematician, or even an engineer, the writer can use *if and only if* without explanation. Even if the reader is knowledgeable about the subject, however, the writer still must be clear, precise, brief, and accurate.

The writer must know whether or not only knowledgeable readers will read the technical letter, memo, or report. A writer should know, for example, if a report written for the boss, an engineer, will be sent to the next level boss, who does not have an engineering degree. If the communication may be read by people lacking technical knowledge of the subject, then it must be written another way.

UNKNOWLEDGEABLE READERS

Readers are unknowledgeable in varying degrees. This does not mean that they are not intelligent, generally knowledgeable people, or that they do not know much about the subject. It does mean that they may not know much about the specific subject of the memo, letter, or report under consideration. It probably means that they do not know the specialized vocabulary, the background, or even many of the ideas contained in the writing. The writer's job is to know who knows what and so to write in a way that all possible readers will understand.

A good example of the problems and solutions of trying to understand the reader comes from F. F. Colton's article, "Some of My Best Friends Are Scientist":

> A New York plumber of foreign extraction with a limited command of English wrote the National Bureau of Standards and said that hydrochloric acid quickly opened drainage pipes when they got plugged. A bureau scientist replied: "The efficacy of hydrochloric acid is indisputable, but the corrosive residue is incompatible with metallic permanence."
>
> The plumber wrote back thanking the Bureau for telling him the method was all right. The scientist was a little disturbed and showed the correspondence to his boss, another scientist. The latter wrote the plumber: "We cannot assume responsibility for the production of toxic and noxious residue with hydrochloric acid and suggest that you use an alternative procedure."
>
> The plumber wrote back that he agreed with the Bureau—hydrochloric acid works fine. A top scientist—the boss of the first two—broke the impasse by tearing himself loose from technical terminology and writing this letter: "Don't use hydrochloric acid. It eats hell out of the pipes."[2]

PRIMARY AND SECONDARY READERS

Reports generally are written for a variety of readers. Few readers need to know everything in a report. Accountants need to know the costs; personnel managers need to know what and how many people need to be hired, fired, or moved; executives need to know the general aims and implications; and public relations managers need to know the effects on the public. Consequently, different parts of reports are written for different readers.

Shorter forms of communications, such as letters and memos, usually are written only for a few specific readers. They depend for their effect on the writer's knowledge of the reader. Naturally, the writer addresses bosses and subordinates differently.

PRIMARY READERS.   There are two categories of primary readers: the announced reader and the important reader. Often these are the same person or group. A boss who assigns a letter or report, and who is the person who will pass judgment on that letter or report, is both the announced and the most important (perhaps only) reader. On the other hand, a CEO (chief executive officer) may assign a letter or report

---

[2]F. F. Colton, "Some of My Best Friends Are Scientist," *Scientific Monthly*, September 1949.

to be written that will be read also by all members of the board. The CEO, then, becomes the announced reader (and also an important reader), while the board members are important readers.

Primary readers are so important to any communication that it is best to analyze them carefully. This may be done efficiently by using a reader profile.

READER PROFILE. The following form provides the important categories that the writer must be concerned about regarding the reader. All categories are not important all the time, but all are important some of the time, and some all of the time.

READER PROFILE: _____ (name) _____

The reader's relation to the writer

_____ Boss	_____ Subordinate	_____ Colleague
_____ Competitor	_____ Customer/Client	_____ ?
_____ Likes	_____ Dislikes	_____ Neutral
_____ Changeable	_____ Competitive	_____ ?

The reader's relation to the message

Knowledge of subject:	_____ Good	_____ Fair	_____ Poor	_____ ?
Knowledge of message:	_____ Expects it	_____ Does not expect it		
Biases about message:	_____ Positive	_____ Negative	_____ Neutral	_____ ?
Biases about subject:	_____ Positive	_____ Negative	_____ Neutral	_____ ?
Interest in subject:	_____ Strong	_____ Mild	_____ Neutral	_____ ?

The reader

Likes	Dislikes
1. _____	1. _____
2. _____	2. _____
3. _____	3. _____
4. _____	4. _____
5. _____	5. _____

SECONDARY READERS. Although secondary readers, as the name implies, are not primary, they remain very important. Consequently, writers must keep them in mind throughout the planning and writing of communications. One way to distinguish between primary and secondary readers is to contrast the importance to various readers of two parts of a formal report: the personnel section and the cost section. The primary readers for the personnel section would be the human resource managers responsible for hiring, training, and firing personnel. But, because personnel cost money, people in the accounting or finance department will pay attention to this section also, although they may be termed secondary readers. Conversely, the cost section's primary readers would be people in finance and accounting, while human resources, as secondary readers, pay attention to the costs attendant upon hiring, training, or firing personnel.

A word of caution: the terms *primary* and *secondary* do not always refer to the relative importance of a reader. Board members of a corporation may not be the primary readers of a report to a CEO, but they are sufficiently important to require the writer to pay careful attention to them. In short, the terms refer not only to their holders' importance, but also to their relative interest in the communication.

SCHEDULING TIME

Part of the planning process includes scheduling time. Deadlines — the hour or day that a memo or report is due — make scheduling time a necessity. Memos may be written relatively quickly, but long, complex reports may take days or even weeks to write. The more complex the communication, the more important it is to divide the process of writing that communication into segments and to place each segment into a block of time that realistically may allow that task to be accomplished.

Although the detailed and practical discussion of scheduling specific segments and blocks of time for long reports may be found in Chapter 8, it is useful to know here the several steps of the process that remain the same for all writing projects, regardless of their size and complexity. For simple memos and brief letters, most writers may be able to perform the following steps in their heads; for longer and more complex assignments, such as formal reports, each step should be performed on paper and with much thought and revision.

STEP 1. Writers must allow time to conceptualize the project — to define purpose, goals, scope, and readers. It is as important to spend much time on this step as it is to be willing to revise it later as the information and organization demand. That is, the writer's ideas about a project may be firm at the beginning, but many times facts, data, and ideas discovered later will tell a different story. When this happens, the writer may be forced to modify the original concept.

STEP 2. Writers must decide what kind of information they need and schedule time for gathering it. Having been diligent in performing step 1, the writer will have a good idea about the kind of information required. How much time will be required for gathering that information will depend on the kind of information, the sources of that infor-

• • • • • • • • • • • • • •

EXERCISE D: PRIMARY AND SECONDARY READERS

Identify as primary or secondary the following people in the following types of communications. Remember that in some ways some people may be both primary and secondary readers.

1. Letter to supplier for boss's signature: boss, supplier, loading dock supervisor.

2. Memo to your subordinate regarding your boss's concern that all letters be printed on company letterhead: boss, subordinate.

mation, and the ease of collecting it. Books in a library may be found and checked out quickly, but gathering material through interlibrary loan or some other long-distance method may take a much longer time.

STEP 3.   Writers must organize the information; that is, they must decide what format to use and where best in the format to place the information. Usually, a good grasp of steps 1 and 2, and a knowledge of the common business formats for various memos, letters, and reports, such as those presented in this book, will lead the writer to select a good fit between information and organization. Precisely where a given piece of information should go in the communication, however, is slightly more difficult to determine quickly. This is the job of step 4.

STEP 4.   Writers must rework as many drafts as are required to produce clarity, accuracy, brevity, and completeness. This step includes revising, editing, and finally proofreading. Very often, in the process of rewriting, writers will discover a flaw in the organization, which then naturally requires a return to step 3, organizing the information. It is nearly impossible to overestimate the importance of step 4. The quality of any communication derives from rewriting, and much more time is required for it than many people allow. (See Chapter 8.)

GATHERING IDEAS AND DATA

Having determined the purpose, goals, scope, readers, and schedule, the writer is ready to gather information to support the writing project. The degree of research required is always determined by the necessity of having complete and accurate information for the purpose. Occasionally, a brief memo or letter may require much research, but usually the writer either has all the necessary information at hand or may consult a few ready sources. Reports normally require much more information gathering than do other kinds of business communication. Often the writer must mount an organized, extensive search for the information.

Although a detailed and extensive discussion of the research process for reports occurs in Chapter 8, it is useful to mention here three fundamental classifications of the information needed for business communications: *data, information,* and *ideas.*

Data are numbers or facts. *Information* is *meaningful* data; that is, information is numbers or facts, or both, put together in such a way as to create meaning. To understand the difference, try working in class exercise 5 found in the margin.

It is clear that the difference between data and information is great. Data is not information, but information cannot be gathered without data. Now, what about ideas? An *idea* is a thought or opinion. In business writing, ideas should be derived from data and information, for only in that way may the ideas be defended as valuable. Thus, the phrase used to describe good ideas is "informed opinion" or

EXERCISE E: MAKING INFORMATION FROM DATA

Write your name on a slip of paper. Write your address on a different slip of paper. Write your telephone number on a third slip of paper. Place these pieces of paper in a hat with similar slips from your classmates.

1. When pieces of paper are pulled at random from the hat, the result is
   Data? Information? Why?

2. When three pieces match—your name, your address, your telephone number—the result is
   Data? Information? Why?

"informed thought." When writing memos, letters, and reports, business writers should always keep this end in mind: Are the ideas represented here *informed*? That is, is the information derived from solid data, and are the ideas derived from good information?

ORGANIZING DATA AND IDEAS

After writers have collected all the information they need to support their arguments, they must decide how to organize it. Once again, keeping in mind the purpose, goals, and scope of the communication — whether memo, letter, or report — will help determine how the information should be arranged. If the communication, for example, is a report, is it a feasibility study, a progress report, or a proposal? Each type of report, as described in Chapters 9 and 10, has a specific emphasis and, consequently, a specific format. Thus, ideas sometimes should be arranged either chronologically, as in progress reports, or spatially, as in a feasibility study on rearranging the production line for manufacturing widgitcogs. Possibly, one idea may cause a second idea, in which case, a cause-and-effect arrangement is best. In any case, writers must know their ideas well so they can arrange them in the best manner and in the best format.

Occasionally, the data, information, and ideas do not easily fit a standard format. When this happens, writers must be sufficiently flexible to create a format that *does* accommodate everything. To do this well, of course, requires that writers know the several types of formats commonly used in reports. Then the job becomes easier because selected parts of established formats may create a perfect arrangement for the new format. For instance, if a feasibility study attempts to select one of four different cranes as most feasible for a certain demolition project, then the writer not only may say that the job *is* feasible, but also may recommend that the job be done with one particular crane. The result is a format that combines the standard arrangements for both feasibility studies and proposals. Details for this kind of report may be found in Chapter 9.

MANAGING DATA

Managing data means discovering the *meaning* of those data, as well as discovering the best way to present them to readers so the information has meaning. Moreover, just as managing people sometimes means firing those whose work is not good or moving them to jobs that they *can* do well, so managing data means discarding those that are useless or irrelevant and using relevant data productively.

Writers generally determine the meaning of data in one or more of three ways: trends, correlations, and conclusions. Before discussing these, however, it is important to be clear on the meanings of four mathematical terms: average, arithmetic mean, median, and mode. These are important because many trends, correlations, and conclusions are derived from them. *Average* is a general term meaning "somewhere in the middle" and is not to be used when precision is required. *Arithmetic mean* is the sum of a group of numbers divided by the number of elements in that group. Use *mean* when precision is required and when the reader knows its meaning. *Median* is that point in an ordered list of numbers at which half are above and half are below. If the list contains an even number of numbers, the median becomes that point halfway between the two middle numbers. *Mode* is simply the number that occurs most often.

Set of numbers:	1, 9, 9, 12, 20, 24, 30 (= 105)
Arithmetic mean:	15 (105 divided by 7)
Median:	12 (the middle number of the list of 7)
Mode:	9

Although *average* is often sufficient, *median* and *mode* are more precise. In August of 1988, for example, the average selling price of a house in the U.S. was $114,000, but the median selling price was $143,000.

TRENDS.   Trends are patterns that emerge over time. The longer the time span, the more valid the trend. One trend that people on Wall Street watch is that aspect of fashion in clothing that dictates the length of skirts and dresses. Hemlines tend to rise and fall over fairly long periods of time. For example, the miniskirt appeared in the 1960s. Over the years, though, hemlines grew longer, so that by the late 1970s, hemlines had fallen nearly to the ankle. Because the change occurred over more than ten years, one could say that by the early 1970s, the *trend* was toward longer skirts and dresses.

The reason people on Wall Street watch this trend very carefully is that there seems to be *correlation* between the hemlines and the stock market: as hemlines rise, so does the Dow-Jones Industrial Average.

CORRELATIONS.   Correlations are statistically significant relationships between two elements. That is, when A and B have some affect on each other, a *relationship* exists between them. When that relationship can be shown statistically, then it is called a *correlation*. Before the stock market crash of 1929, hemlines were shorter than they had ever been in the United States. At the same time, the stock market had never been higher. As hemlines grew longer, the country fell into the terrible economic depression of the 1930s. As the hemlines rose and fell slightly in advance of the rise and fall of the stock market, people began to think that a correlation existed between hemlines and the Dow-Jones Industrial Average on the stock market. In the 1960s, hemlines again became very short, and again the stock market rose. When hemlines fell in the 1970s, so too did the stock market. This gave rise to the so-called hemline theory, which says that the country does well economically when hemlines are high and badly when hemlines are low. The question remains, however, whether only two or three occurrences of this phenomenon are sufficient to make the correlation valid.

Consequently, human judgment is still required, for mathematics alone does not say that the correlation is meaningful.

CONCLUSIONS. Medicine constantly studies correlations. Medical researchers try to prove, for example, a correlation exists between exercise and longevity, between the amount of vitamin C individuals ingest and the number of colds they contract, and so on. For years, they have reported that cholesterol is related to heart disease, and that reducing cholesterol level increases longevity. Proving this seemingly simple correlation cost the American people $148 million. And even then it was not proven.[3]

The point is that drawing conclusions from correlations is not always easy. Yet they must be drawn. People in business are paid to make decisions, and those decisions derive from conclusions drawn from solid evidence. The academic discipline of logic has much to tell us about bad reasoning—in this case drawing unwarranted conclusions from the evidence. Writers who are aware of logical fallacies and are honest with themselves will be less likely to make decisions that the evidence does not support. (See the list of fallacies, pages 39–41.)

DRAFTING AND REVISING

Drafting and revising are two of the most important stages in the process of writing. *Drafting* involves two steps: describing and discussing each of the ideas organized during the previous stage, and then creating logical links between them. This part of the writing process may be easier than most writers think *if* they forget for the moment about the entire communication and concentrate on the task at hand. Trying to write a long communication all at once usually does not work. Writing out each set of ideas separately allows the writer to produce coherent thoughts about each.

Once writers have drafted the various sets of ideas, they may then begin to put them together. This *revising* process is rather like putting together a puzzle. As in a puzzle, the relationships of the various parts must be *seen*. Similarly, putting together sets of ideas requires that writers *see* the connections between ideas. In the revision stage, writers should remember that writing is a *process* and that the communication may go through several revisions, or drafts, before it is logical and cohesive.

Revising makes the connections more effective by adjusting their arrangement to create logical transitions and so to make the argument as persuasive as possible. At the end of the revising process, most of the thoughts that will end up in the final, polished communication are already on the page. The communication may not yet be especially pretty, but the structure is sound.

---

[3]Thomas J. Moore, "The Cholesterol Myth," *The Atlantic*, September 1989.

PERSUADING THE READER

As *part of* the revising process, the writer must shift perspective. Until now, the focus has been on the information and on the organization of the information. The writer must review the information with a reader's eye. What will the reader understand? Not understand? What words need to be explained? What processes? What are the reader's prejudices? How may they be avoided? In what order should the information be presented so that the reader may best understand? These questions and many others are essential to writing a good letter, memo, or report, because what may seem to be the clearest, most precise, most accurate report to the writer is worthless if it is not clear, precise, and accurate to the reader.

CLASSICAL RHETORIC AND METHODS OF PERSUASION

One problem with writing is the reader. On the one hand, readers have an amazing ability to interpret squiggles on a page, turning them into very sophisticated ideas. On the other hand, they have quirks: irrational likes and dislikes. They are insecure and quick to take offense. They are wise one moment and foolish the next, intelligent and then dense by turns. There is nothing for it except to try to understand the reader and to avoid pitfalls.

There is also the problem of different readers. What is clear, accurate, and brief to some may be fuzzy, inaccurate, and wordy to others. When readers are offended, then clarity, accuracy, and brevity are useless: readers will remain offended, and they will not accept the information.

Given this hopeless tangle of prejudice and openness, knowledge and ignorance, thick heads and thin skins, it is a wonder that people try to communicate at all. But they do. And sometimes it works. It works in business writing when writers understand that the burden lies with them to overcome the vagaries not only of language, but also of human beings. It works, moreover, because persuasion has been studied for several thousand years, and people have learned a few things about it.

The great Athenian politician and orator, Pericles (495?–429 B.C.), said that one who can think but cannot express ideas clearly is on a level with those who cannot think. Pericles was right. People think in symbols. Mathematicians may think well in numbers, chemists in chemical or molecular symbols, composers in musical notes, painters in colors, sculptors in shapes and textures, but by far the most useful symbols for the greatest number of people are words. Before anything can be accomplished in business, there must be words, and before anything can be accomplished well in business, there must be clear words properly arranged.

For Aristotle (384–322 B.C.) and other classical philosophers, rhetoric was the art of persuasion, of saying things to produce a desired result. For managers to manage well, for engineers to engineer well, they must be able to persuade. The most useful medium of persuasion for managers and engineers is words.

WRITING PERSUASIVELY

The object of oratory alone is not truth but persuasion.

Thomas Babington,
Lord Macaulay
(1800–1859)

Most writing, even the most simple forms, involves persuasion. Proposals for changing the grills on next year's automobiles are competitive; the most persuasive are most likely to succeed. Even directives are nominally persuasive: "Joe, bring the Fahrquart Report to my office, pronto" is a simple directive, but in the long run Joe must be persuaded that it is in his interest to do so.

THE FOUR APPEALS OF PERSUASION

Writers persuade their readers by appealing to four human qualities: self-interest, reason, emotion, and ethics.

SELF-INTEREST.   The most effective persuasion appeals to the self-interest of the reader. The writer should always try to discover something appealing to the reader's interest. Although "Joe, bring the Fahrquart Report to my office, pronto" will doubtless bring Joe running, if the writer is Joe's boss, adding the following would bring Joe more quickly and more willingly: "The General Manager is here with me, and we would like your opinion of the report's strong and weak points."

EXERCISE F: DISCOVERING SELF-INTEREST

Discuss in class which of these sentences appeals most to the self-interest of the reader. Why?

1. Smedley, bring the production figures to my office first thing tomorrow morning.
2. Smedley, bring the production figures to my office first thing tomorrow morning. The president will be here and he wants to see them.

REASON.   Reason in business writing is the expression of systematic, coherent, and logical thought and judgment. Sound reasoning tends to be believed because it cannot be refuted. In short, rational appeals work because they make sense. Appeals to reason should be the most common in business: "If you do what I ask, we will make money" or save time, or avoid losing money, time, or one's job. "If we continue to clear-cut our hardwood, the deer population will increase greatly. Browsing deer will keep the trees from growing higher than six feet, making it impossible, short of removing the deer, to renew the resource." An emotional appeal may aid a rational one, as it does if this reason is added to the previous sentence: "The wildlife service will charge $275,000 to survey the population, $45 for each deer killed, and $200 for each deer relocated. Whether they will kill or relocate the deer is unclear."

EXERCISE G: RATIONAL APPEALS

Discuss in class which of the following sentences most appeals to reason. Why?

1. Smedley: Stop producing X347 widgitcogs.
2. Smedley: Our market research analysts told me an hour ago that the market for X347 widgitcogs will drop 87% in the next three months. We now have six months' supply in stock. Because the analysts rarely are wrong, we must stop making X347 widgitcogs.

EMOTION.   Emotional appeals usually are weak and should be avoided in business: "If we continue to clear-cut our hardwood, the deer population will first grow greatly, and then we will have to slaughter many thousands of them to keep them from stunting the growth of the new trees."

One of the most common emotional appeals today is that of sincerity. Writers and speakers seem to be persuaded that if they simply convey sincerity—the sense of strongly held belief—they should be

EXERCISE H: DISCUSSION: DISCOVERING APPEALS TO EMOTION

Discuss in class which of the following sentences most appeals to the emotions. Why?

1. The Statue of Liberty cost $78 million to restore.

2. The Statue of Liberty, symbol of freedom and justice to millions, her torch a beacon of hope to the starved and beaten masses of the world, cost $78 million to restore: less than the price of one roll of breath-mints for every American.

EXERCISE I: DISCUSSION: DISCOVERING ETHICAL APPEALS

Discuss in class which of the following sentences appeals most to ethics. Why?

1. By selling now, we can make several hundred thousand dollars each.

2. By selling now, we shall put 798 people out of work.

(3. Is it possible that *both* statements raise ethical questions? What might they be?)

believed. That is, in the mere presence of sincerity, people will be persuaded. Perhaps, but *should* they be persuaded? No one doubts that Ford was very *sincere* when it brought out the Edsel automobile, but reason, had Ford listened to it, may have predicted the utter disaster the Edsel produced: huge expenses, few sales, great losses. While emotion is a great persuasive device, it should never be used unless accompanied by reason.

ETHICS. Ethics derives from two beliefs: individuals are important and society is important. Ethics tries to make life just for individuals and for society.

Ethical appeals require that readers have ethics and that the writer know what they are. Such appeals also require that readers have no cause to suspect any hidden motives of the writer. "We cannot continue to clear-cut our hardwood, knowing that eventually many thousands of deer either will starve to death or will have to be killed" may produce certain questions. In fact, these questions should occur, for each of us *should* be skeptical. Consequently, the writer *should* anticipate questions and answer them.

Regarding the question of clear-cutting, some of the ethical questions are these: should the individual owner of property be allowed to dispose of it in a way seen fit by that owner? Should society, which according to state law "owns" the deer on anyone's property, be allowed to prevent the owner from acting in such a way as to harm the property of society? These are not easy questions to answer.

Another example might be that of taxes and war. Individuals in the United States legally may oppose war waged by the society. Individuals in the United States may not legally avoid paying taxes to the society. Suppose a person desires to oppose a war by refusing to pay the taxes that fund that war, saying, in effect, "I refuse to allow my earnings to support a war that I do not support." This is an ethical problem. When Henry David Thoreau refused to pay his taxes in 1848 because he opposed the Mexican War, he was thrown in jail. Again, suppose a person refuses to pay taxes to support, say, saving the whales? Should that person be incarcerated?

Notice that while ethical problems may have moral dimensions, they are *not* moral questions. The moral questions of killing deer, opposing war, and saving whales are not quite the same things as the ethical problems of opposing those actions by withholding money owed in taxes to that society.

In business, ethical problems occur daily. Fortunately, most businesses behave responsibly, as do most people in business. Although immoral and unethical business leaders grab most of the headlines, writers should remember that the most important personal quality required for good leadership in business or elsewhere is integrity.

LOGICAL FALLACIES

Arguments in business should be *valid* (correctly derived from the rules of logic) as well as *true* (factual). Opinions themselves are neither valid nor true; they are simply sound or not, depending on whether they have been derived validly from fact. If an argument relies on an invalid or false statement, it is *fallacious*. Some common types of fallacies to avoid and examples of each follow:

1. *Ad hominem* (attacking the person rather than the argument).

   > Jesus Christ has little to tell people about morality since he habitually associated with thieves and prostitutes.

   This charge was actually levied against Jesus. Similar charges brought down many prominent men such as Benjamin Disraeli, a prime minister of England under Queen Victoria, and more recently such American politicians as John Tower of Texas and Gary Hart of Colorado.

   > Vice-president for sales, Smedley Fahrquart cannot argue that the company should stop paying for alcoholic beverages consumed by sales people during lunch because he himself is well known to have several drinks every year at the company's Christmas party.

   People who live in glass houses should not throw stones.

2. *Two wrongs make a right*.

   > A university fails to punish a student caught cheating because, as one administrator says, "everybody does it."

   Whether one or many people cheat does not change the fact that cheating is wrong and should be punished.

   > A company hires people of Religion A, and will not hire people of Religion B. Twenty years later, the unfairness of this policy is realized. Then, people of Religion B are hired and people of Religion A are not.

   One wrong practice is not corrected by another wrong practice; that is, the end does not justify the means to gaining that end.

3. *Straw man* (the "weaker" person, easily defeated; that is, attacking the weakest of your opponent's arguments).

   > A student complains, "Granted I know little about physics, but Professor Fahrquart, who teaches the course, ought to be fired because she shows up only half the time." "Straw man" response: "You want a knowledgeable physics professor fired, but you admit to knowing nothing about physics. That makes no sense!"

   What has knowing or not knowing physics have to do with Professor Fahrquart's attendance record?

   > A professor complains, "This student has come only to five of 18 classes, has failed every examination, never wears shoes to class, and yet still wants me to write a good letter of recommendation for a job." Straw man response: "Humph. Just because students do not wear shoes to college classes does not mean that they will not wear shoes on the job. This student might be an excellent employee."

   Shoelessness is not a good reason for not writing a letter of recommendation; the other reasons are stronger.

4. *Begging the question* (an unwarranted assumption is included in the statement).

> Why would you want to work for such a big and therefore unfeeling company as IBM?

This argument assumes that *big* equals "unfeeling."

> When did you stop beating your children, Mr. Fahrquart?

This argument assumes that Fahrquart used to beat his children.

Many other logical fallacies exist, but there is insufficient space here to consider them all. Remember that writers and speakers must be alert not to let their own emotional or self-promotional desires cloud the truth. Ultimately, people earn the right to be read and listened to by trying to see the truth clearly and acting appropriately on it.

EARNING THE RIGHT TO BE READ

Earning the right to be read requires writers to use language that their readers will understand. Such language cannot condescend, be dull or sloppy, or waste the readers' time and energy by using ten words when five would do.

CONDESCENDING LANGUAGE

Condescending language derives from words that convey a sense of the writer's "superiority" over the reader. The writer indeed may know more than the reader; most people, after all, read for information, and they naturally assume that the writer knows more than they know. There are few excuses, however, for beating the reader over the head with this fact. The reader should be addressed with respect for having sought the writer's knowledge of the subject.

DULL LANGUAGE

Dull language derives from many things: wordiness, unnecessary and irrelevant information, vague words, and statements of the obvious. A good style cannot be dull; a good style is efficient, clear, informative, and engaging.

TONE

Tone is also important. No executive should accept an invitation to a high school reunion by writing "As chief executive officer of Blimp Enterprises, it gives me great pleasure to accept with thanks your kind invitation to join you and my fellow classmates at the Dinkytown Fire Hall at 8:00 p.m. on 12 July 1993." Rather, to convey the appropriate

EXERCISE J: DISCOVERING THE CONDESCENDING AND DULL

Discuss in class the following questions.

1. Why is the following condescending?
   Are you quite sure, Mr. Fahrquart, that you understand the utter clarity of the nature of my remarks? I have tried my utmost best to explain them in a way that could be understood by any child of five.

2. Why is the following dull?
   At each transition, each member in a given state must either stay in that given state or change to another given state. In terms of probabilities, this must mean that the state of the sum of the entries in any of the probabilities of each possible type of transition or change within the population of each type of any column is finite.

Tone is so broad that it is difficult to classify. A given tone may be condescending, flat, happy, sad, imperious, democratic, angry, lugubrious, nostalgic, and on and on.

1. Write a paragraph in which high school is described nostalgically.

2. Write a paragraph in which high school is described condescendingly.

3. Rewrite the following paragraph so that it is efficient, clear, accurate, and human: Dear Mr. Fahrquart: Pursuant to your request of the 19th of July, I have rewritten the attached report so that it may be perceived and understood by the average layman in the street for whom it was intended.

4. Rewrite the following paragraph so it is efficient, clear, accurate, and human: Mr. Fahrquart: Here is the report. You requested it on 19 July. I rewrote it. All can understand it.

tone, the response should be something like this: "Great! I'll be there!" Too often a business-like tone is misperceived as a dull, emotionless one; an efficient tone is often seen as one that reads as if it came from a computer's circuits. A good tone for business varies with the demands of the information and the reader. Most often, however, routine business writing should carry a tone of efficiency, clarity, and accuracy without losing its human qualities. That is, the tone should convey a sense of one human being speaking to another.

EDITING AND PROOFREADING

Editing and proofreading are the final steps to the writing process. Once the argument is persuasive and organized soundly, the writer edits the communication for logical order, proper evidence, and smooth transitions. The best editing is done by writers who can pretend to be the reader while examining the communication. While this ability takes a long time to develop fully, business writers may begin to develop it by allowing time to go by, often several days, if possible, before looking at the communication as if they were readers rather than writers. Time allows the writers to look at their writing freshly, to see it as if it were written by someone else. Consequently, rigorous criticism of the communication may come from the person who wrote it.

Specifically, *editing* has four stages. First, check to see that the ideas follow logically from the first idea to the last. One way to do this is to make sure that each paragraph encompasses a fully developed idea. Second, check to see that each idea is made valid by the logic, the evidence, and the facts. Third, check for smooth transitions between statements. Make sure that such transitional words and phrases as "moreover," "in addition," "also," and "too" are used to move the reader from one example or piece of evidence to another that supports the same idea. Make sure that words such as "but," "however," "although," and "conversely" are used to bridge from one idea to a contrary idea or contradictory fact. Fourth, check that each sentence is grammatical and punctuated properly and that each word is spelled correctly.

Punctuation is best checked by looking at the words and phrases that occasion the punctuation. Do they require punctuation? Do they require *this* punctuation? It is also a good idea to review rules for punctuation before completing the process of editing. Appendix I includes many rules for punctuation.

Checking for spelling has been made much easier by computer programs that do the job for the writer. At least, that is what the instructions say. While spell-checkers do a fine job of correcting many spelling errors, they do not correct a word misspelled in such a way that it spells another word. For example, a spell-checker examining this sentence, "She lead the fight for parental leave in her compnay," would easily correct the misspelling of "compnay," but it would miss the misspelling of "lead" because "lead" is a word. Yet the proper word for the sentence would be either "leads" or "led." Similarly, spell-checkers will not correct such errors as "at" for "it," "in" for "on," and "end" for "and." Consequently, writers must proofread not so much to correct misspellings any more, but rather to make sure that they have used the proper word.

Writers who lack spell-checkers may proofread for spelling by reading *backward*. Because English is read left-to-right, fluent readers tend to skip words and see entire phrases as single entities, thus overlooking some individual words. Reading from right-to-left forces the writers' eyes to stop on each word.

Finally, once these changes have been made, a new copy should be printed out or typed, and then *proofread*. Writers should give the communication one last read-through to catch any typographical errors as well as any errors in formatting or spacing.

SUMMARY

Business communication has three purposes: to inform, to persuade, and to express. Writing is a process. The business writing process has three big steps: *preparing to write, writing,* and *revising and polishing.* Within the three big steps, the writing process includes nine important steps:

1. Defining purpose, goals, and scope: Carefully defined purposes, goals, and scopes make the job of writing much easier.

2. Analyzing the reader: It is easier to persuade people if the writer can classify the likely readers of a persuasive document. The chief method of classification is that of dividing readers into knowledgeable and unknowledgeable.

3. Scheduling time: Blocking a writing job into segments of time allows the job to be done better and faster.

4. Gathering ideas and data: Old-fashioned hard work and modern electronic methods combine to make research more complete.

5. Organizing ideas and data: Organizing ideas and data before beginning to write reduces the panic of beginning to write.

6. Drafting and revising: Good drafting and revising shape a communication and make it logical.

7. Persuading the reader: Readers (and listeners) have been the primary object of communications for millennia. Classical Greek writing suggests that there are four ways of persuading people through rhetoric: self-interest, reason, emotion, and ethics.

8. Earning the right to be read: To persuade people, the writer or speaker must use language that is not condescending, dull, sloppy, or wordy.

9. Editing and proofreading: Editing and proofreading, like washing and polishing a car, make a good product into a great finished product.

EXERCISES

1. *Defining purpose and goals.* Remembering that goals are usually means to the end of accomplishing a purpose, which of the following in each group are purposes and which are goals?

   a. Catching up on all classwork by Friday at 3:00 p.m.
      Going home for the weekend
      Seeing old friends

   b. Getting an *A* in Economics
      Memorizing the definition of marginal profits
      Learning to construct a demand curve

   c. Working an extra shift at the fast food restaurant
      Selling a stereo system
      Buying a new tennis racquet

   d. Denying yourself a second helping of dessert at dinner
      Losing 10 pounds
      Running five instead of three miles every day

2. *Determining scope.* Which subtopic in each group might *not* belong in the scope of the topic? Your professor may choose those most appropriate for your class.

   a. Topic: computers
      Subtopics: keyboard, disk drive, spell-checker program, monitor

   b. Topic: business software
      Subtopics: Fortran, Cobol, Xtree, Pascal

   c. Topic: exclusively Hispanic festivals
      Subtopics: Cinco de Mayo, Hispanidad, Fiesta del Pueblo

3. *Analyzing the reader.* Discuss in class the attributes of the typical viewer of a Stephen King movie. List those attributes on the chalkboard. [You may discover just how difficult it is to analyze a mass audience.]

4. *Persuasion.* Identify the kinds of persuasive appeals made in the following slogans (more than one kind may be involved).

   Kalox has more!

   Mepsi, the Now Generation

   The cool way to go

   No artificial ingredients

   All natural ingredients

5. *Persuasion.* Write a paragraph or two, using vivid and persuasive language, on *one* of the following topics: world hunger, overpopulation. Before writing, however, be sure to decide on a reader whom you will try to persuade.

6. *Dullness.* Rewrite the following passage so it is livelier. Remember that dullness is overcome by obeying the rules for a good style.

> TV set makers are separating the traditional TV receiver model into component parts which can be bought separately and used individually or in groups, as the case may be. The addition of a component stereo system, with the inclusion of a separate tuner, amplifier, turntable, speakers, and tape deck, along with a separate TV monitor and a control device, will allow for the possibility of improving the sound produced by the TV and of allowing users to watch a program, use a computer, watch a video cassette, play games, or many other things. The cost, however, may be prohibitive to those in the middle-income socioeconomic levels of the society.

7. *Tone.* Identify and discuss the predominant tone of the following passages.

  a. Samantha: Send me the specifications on the 3X4000 Rack Washer by Thursday morning, and I'll spring for lunch on Friday.

  b. Ms. Fahrquart: Please send me the specifications on the 3X4000 Rack Washer by 9:00 a.m. on Friday, 13 September.

  c. Ms. Fahrquart: Get the specifications for the 3X4000 Rack Washer on my desk by 9 sharp this Friday (9/13/92).

8. *Words people like and dislike.* Rewrite the following passage replacing words that people dislike with words they like.

> Dear Mr. Fahrquart:
> The widgitcogs my company bought from you are terrible. Many have broken, and your company is probably to blame. No, we were not careless, but I fear that our operations are jeopardized by the waste produced by the negligence and grievous misfortune that does little but discredit your company. We will accept no alibis. Send us 321 better widgitcogs.

9. *Purpose.* Write a one-sentence, general purpose statement for a large project you must complete this semester or quarter.

10. *Logical fallacies.* Here are several statements. Determine whether they exhibit fallacies and identify the fallacy each example contains: ad hominem, two wrongs make a right, straw man, or begging the question.

  a. The proposed legislation will cut off water from farmers now using it and return it to the land currently deprived of water. The farmers, after all, have had the advantage of that water through unfair legislation for 95 years.

  b. Because all professors are forgetful, we had better send an extra graduation invitation to all professors a week after sending the first invitations to students, staff, and faculty.

  c. Proposing to cut the budget for the company's charitable contributions while increasing the budget for corporate retreats to golfing resorts is wrong.

  d. Professor Fahrquart cannot teach a course well on the history of Methodism; he is, as you may know, an Episcopalian.

11. *Trends.* Make a list of three trends. Be prepared to discuss them in class.

12. *Correlations.* Make a list of three correlations. Be prepared to discuss them in class.

13. *Reader profile.* Establish a reader profile of a boss, a parent, or a professor using the model on page 31. Write a memo asking for a raise from the boss, a bigger allowance from a parent, or a better grade from a professor.

CASE STUDY 1: ANALYZING THE PROFESSOR AS READER

Using the form on page 31, create a reader profile of your professor for this course. Naturally, if this is early in the semester, you do not yet have sufficient information with which to write a fully informed profile, but it is often just as important to discover what one does *not* know as it is to discover what one does know.

Your professor will tell you whether your profile will be read and graded or placed on a transparency *without* your name and placed on an overhead projector for class discussion. How honest you are in your profile depends on whether your name will appear on it and whether the professor is willing to have some fun at his or her expense.

CASE STUDY 2: ANALYZING READERS

What in the following memo should be changed (emphasized, de-emphasized, deleted, or inserted) to make it more likely that Fahrquart will look favorably on the memo and the writer? The reader profile of Fahrquart follows the memo.

MEMORANDUM

To: Smedley Fahrquart, Vice-President for Investments
From: Percy B. Shelley, Staff
Date: 22 September 1993
Re: Profit Projections for 1994

The report you asked for on 1 September regarding actuarial tables for setting our profit projections for 1994 will be along in a day or two. I'm still waiting for several sets of figures on the ACLU readjustments for 1994. Still, people are living longer. This is nevertheless offset somewhat by increases in personal injury lawsuits. The old Life/Injury Adjustment Formula may have to be scrapped for that new method from the economists, the Weller/Kurre Forecasting Method for Insurance Rate Adjusters, but I can't tell yet.

Here is a profile of Smedley Fahrquart.

READER PROFILE: ___Smedley Fahrquart_____

Reader's relation to the writer.

__X__ Boss	_____ Subordinate	_____ Colleague
_____ Competitor	_____ Customer/Client	_____ ?
_____ Likes	_____ Dislikes	__X__ Neutral
_____ Changeable	_____ Competitive	_____ ?

Reader's relation to the message.

Knowledge of subject:	_____ Good	_____ Fair	__X__ Poor
Knowledge of message:	__X__ Expects it	_____ Does not expect it	
Biases about message:	_____ Positive	_____ Negative	_____ Neutral
Biases about subject:	_____ Positive	_____ Negative	__X__ Neutral
Interest in subject:	__X__ Strong	_____ Mild	_____ Neutral

The reader.

Likes	**Dislikes**
1. _____details_____	1. _____hates economists_____
2. _____	2. _____
3. _____	3. _____
4. _____	4. _____

CHALLENGE EXERCISE 1: DETERMINING SCOPE

Determining the scope of any communication involves deciding not only what to write about, but also what *not* to write about. To that end, choose a current political issue, define one aspect of that issue, list the specific points that need to be discussed, and then list the specific points that, while related, need not be discussed.

CHALLENGE EXERCISE 2: SCHEDULING TIME

Exactly 72 hours from right now, you have a 10-page report due for a final project in Sociology 101. The title is "Social Assimilation among Left-Handed Lithuanians from 1960 to 1990." Draw up a schedule for completing the report. Be sure to include everything else that has to be done during those 72 hours: eating, sleeping, attending other classes, and doing other classwork.

ARE ALL THY CONQUESTS,

GLORIES, TRIUMPHS, SPOILS,

SHRUNK TO THIS LITTLE

MEASURE?

MEMORANDA

WILLIAM SHAKESPEARE

(1564–1616)

**5
0**

Learning Objectives:

☐ Write properly formatted memos.

☐ Write better memos by understanding their purposes: to provide
a record, to improve efficiency, to
direct, and to inform.

☐ Write better memos to superiors
(memos up), to subordinates
(memos down), and to colleagues
(memos across).

☐ Avoid using memos improperly by
understanding their abuses: covering your flanks, writing instead of
talking, writing rot rather than information, writing on the ladder,
and writing by committee.

▲
CHECKLIST

"THE HORROR OF THAT MOMENT," THE KING WENT ON, "I SHALL NEVER, NEVER FORGET!"

"YOU WILL, THOUGH," THE QUEEN SAID, "IF YOU DON'T MAKE A MEMO-RANDUM OF IT."

LEWIS CARROLL

(1832–1898)

WRITING GOOD MEMORANDA: CONTENT AND STYLE

Introduction

A memorandum is a brief, written form of communication. Less formal than reports and often shorter than letters, memos are the most common form of business writing. Although they can be used to convey information to people outside an organization, they are used almost exclusively as internal documents to share information in an organization.

Memoranda is the plural form of *memorandum*, which in Latin means ''be remembered,'' and memoranda are indeed the memories of business. While formal prose normally uses *memoranda* or the Anglicized form *memorandums*, informal prose frequently shortens the forms to *memo* and *memos*. Regarding old and new forms, and which ones writers should use, Alexander Pope (1688–1744) provides the best advice to people in business:

> Be not the first by whom the new are tried,
> Nor yet the last to lay the old aside.

This book will use the formal *memoranda* in titles and the informal *memo* and *memos* in the text.

Although less formal than letters, memos require standards of writing at least as high as those for letters. From the writer's perspective, memos are often more important than letters because memos are read by people who exercise power over the writer's career. In fact, many companies think that the ability to write clear, brief, accurate memos is so important that they sometimes include this ability as a primary qualification for certain managerial jobs.

Exercise A: Why Clear Memos?

Discuss in class the following question: Why might a company be more concerned with having clarity in memos than in any other form of communication?

Basic Format

Designed to be simple, memos have a specific format that consists of five parts. The first four parts are essentially a list that states clearly the reader, the writer, the date, and the subject of the memo. The fifth part is the text or body of the memo. Following are a list that describes each part and sample memos that demonstrate the format:

1. To *should contain a name and a title or, if no title, at least the department where the addressee works.* If the memo is going to several people, their names should appear here.

2. From *should list names and titles as specific as those in the* To *line.* Authors usually initial their typed names here.

3. Date *should state the month, day, and year.* If numerals instead of letters are used for the month—that is, ''10'' instead of ''October''—make sure the record will be clear, that the reader who later finds the memo in the file understands that the ''10'' refers to the month and not the day. Europeans, the American military, and some com-

EXERCISE B: FORMAL
EUROPEAN METHOD OF
DATING

Discuss in class the following
question: Why might Gua-
dalupe Romero, a systems analyst for Seat, an automobile
manufacturer in San Sebastián,
Spain, date a memo to an
American employee like this:
2.viii.92?

EXERCISE C: WHERE TO
PLACE *RE*?

Discuss in class the following
question: Some companies place
''Re'' (or ''Subject'') above the
date, making ''Date'' last. What
are the advantages and disadvantages of this arrangement?

panies write dates differently from American civilians. Americans
writing ''1/10/92'' mean ''January 10, 1992.'' In contrast, Europeans
progress from the smallest unit of time to the largest (day, month,
year), writing ''1/10/92'' to mean ''1 October 1992.'' Unless a company or a field of business specifies the format for numerical dates
on memos, the safest policy is to spell out the month so that no
readers will be confused. Europeans sometimes solve the problem
in formal writing by using small Roman numerals for the month,
writing ''1.x.92'' for ''1 October 1992.''

4. Re *should state the subject concisely.* Short for ''regarding,'' *Re* is important both for the writer and for the reader. It forces the writer to
summarize and focus the content of the memo, and it succinctly
informs the reader of the content of the memo. Company preferences may be to type the *Re* information in all capital letters, to
emphasize the memo's subject.

   Begin the *To, From, Date,* and *Re* labels on the left margin, type a
colon after each one, and double-space the lines. The style preference of the company will determine whether these labels should be
all capital letters or capital and lowercase. Companies also will indicate their preference about spacing after the colons on each line:
some prefer to have the information begin two spaces after the colons; others prefer to align the first words. The examples in this
book demonstrate both styles.

5. *The* text *of the memo should be brief, organized, and to the point.* Begin
the text three or four lines below the *Re,* depending on the size
of the paper and, again, on the style preferred by the company.
Each paragraph should begin at the left margin. Single-space the
lines of the paragraphs, and double-space between the paragraphs.
Left and right margins should be equal.

*A typewritten memo on a
company's printed memo stationery, ragged arrangement*

MEMORANDUM

TO: Smedley Fahrquart, Vice-President, Accounting

FROM: Samantha Evans, Vice-President, Personnel

DATE: 1 October 1992

RE: Need the Ross Report

I don't have the Ross Report (4/30/88, file
#B-4028). I need it badly. Send it quickly, and the
next cup of coffee is on me.

A template-formatted memo from a computer, aligned arrangement, multiparagraph

MEMORANDUM

TO: Samantha Evans, Vice-President, Personnel

FROM: Smedley Fahrquart, Vice-President, Accounting

DATE: 2 October 1992

RE: ROSS REPORT AND FREE COFFEE

I don't have the Ross Report (4/30/88, file #B-4028) either. I sent it to Purchasing last week, as they were concerned about some of our bidding procedures. I called them just now, and they said it would be on its way to you before noon today.

Do I still get the free coffee?

．．．．．．．．．．．．．．．
**EXERCISE D: MEMO
PLANNING SHEETS**

Discuss in class the following questions:
1. What are the advantages to listing points and then waiting a while before writing a memo?
2. What are the advantages to writing the memo immediately without planning?

Use the form on p. 55 to help organize your thoughts. A stack of these forms kept to the side of the desk allows writers to list points as they think of them during the day.

Most memos should be rewritten at least once to make them clearer, briefer, and more accurate. Blaise Pascal, the seventeenth-century French mathematician and philosopher, once apologized to a correspondent at the end of a long letter this way: "I have made this letter longer than usual, only because I have not had the time to make it shorter." He also said, "The last thing one discovers in writing a book

Memo Planning Sheet

SUBJECT _____

POINTS

1. _____

2. _____

3. _____

4. _____

is what to put first," and this is true also for preparing memos. First make the list; then decide the order in which items in the list should appear.

TRICKS TO WRITING GOOD MEMORANDA

Two tricks may help business writers compose good memos faster and easier: short introductions and repeating the content of "Re." Memos rarely need long introductions. Too many writers waste time trying to introduce the subject. Bogus introductions include such phrases as "It has come to my attention that," "Please be advised that," "As you are aware," and "You may remember that." Introductions tend to be long and rambling for one of two reasons: people begin writing before they know the subject, or they begin writing as a way to introduce the subject.

The writer will save time by defining the subject before beginning to write. Often, the subject needs no introduction; rarely does the subject require a long introduction.

The trick, if there is one, to writing good memos lies with *Re*. That is, if the first words of the text of a memo repeat the title of the memo (either verbatim or paraphrased), no distracting words occur before the subject is introduced. Because memos are short, writers do not have time or space to wander away from the subject. In addition, the important information is forced into the beginning where it belongs.

Finally, courtesy forbids referring a reader to a memo in a file. The writer, CEO or not, should attach to the memo a copy of any previous memo mentioned. This does not hold for the occasional mention of confidential memos. Here is a bad example.

Tact is after all a kind of mind-reading.

Sarah Orne Jewett
(1849–1909)

MEMORANDUM

TO: E. Lastic, Personnel

FROM: M. Phatic, CEO

DATE: 1 April 1992

RE: VACATIONS FOR SALARIED EMPLOYEES

Notice the 3½ lines of rambling prose.

As you know from our meeting of 7 March 1992 (see my 3–8 memo), during which we decided that the head office should determine whether salaried employees should be able to accumulate vacation days beyond one calendar year, my feeling was that (1) we were among only a few companies still allowing this practice, and (2) it was proving too costly to the company in both stale employees who do not take vacations and in employees who take over-long vacations (three months in one case) to be able to jump back into things quickly.

As of 1 January 1993, salaried employees must take all their vacation days within the calendar year. Vacation time begins with 1 January and ends with 30 December of *each year*.

Notice that the reader is referred to, but is not given, the file memo.

Please make this change in our policy manuals.

Here is a good example. Notice how repeating the memo's "title" shortens and guides the memo.

MEMORANDUM

TO: E. Lastic, Personnel

FROM: M. Phatic, CEO

DATE: 1 April 1992

RE: VACATIONS FOR SALARIED EMPLOYEES

Vacations for salaried employees shall no longer accumulate beyond one calendar year, as of 1 January 1993. Please make this change in our policy manuals.

As we discussed in our meeting of 7 March (my 8 March memo is attached), we are among a handful of companies still allowing the practice, and it is expensive. Employees who take no vacations grow stale, and a few take as much as three months' vacation at one time. Then they return and lose valuable time while catching up.

EXERCISE E: GOOD AND BAD MEMOS

Discuss in class some of the differences between the two examples of memos on pages 56 and 57. What makes one better than the other?

PURPOSES

Memos have dozens of uses, but four are especially important:

1. To provide a record,
2. To improve efficiency,
3. To direct, and
4. To inform.

A discussion of each follows here.

TO PROVIDE A RECORD

Although telephone calls may be logged and outlines of conversations may be written, too much room for misinterpretation remains. Written words are, or should be, a record of *exactly* what was said and done. In addition, written records tend to assign responsibility. Should someone want to know who originally had the wonderful idea that made the company millions, or who got the company into a mess, or where things began to go wrong, a file containing memos usually would provide the answer. Spoken words dissipate, but written words remain to glorify or curse their writers. Here is an example of a memo written to provide a record.

EXERCISE F: PROVIDING A RECORD

Discuss in class the following questions:

1. What does this memo provide a record of?
2. Is the memo justified?

MEMORANDUM

TO: Wanda Watt, Political Liaison

FROM: Smedley Fahrquart, Vice-President, Accounting

DATE: 28 September 1992

RE: Rep. Iambic Tetrameter

Last Thursday at 10 a.m., Rep. Tetrameter (4th Dist.) spoke with me in my office. During the conversation, he lamented our not being able to contribute to his campaign for re-election. He said, nevertheless, that he would continue to work toward a tax credit for the $750,000 scrubber we installed in the stack at this plant last May.

Sometimes information that could be conveyed orally must be recorded in writing just to verify that the information was conveyed. To say in 1994 that "I told you two years ago to buy that software" while someone else says "No, you didn't" may lead to bad feelings and bad business if there is no written record. Here is an example of a memo written for this purpose.

MEMORANDUM

TO: Seve Ballesteros
        Marina Navritalova
        Lucinano Pavarotti
        Eddie Murphy

FROM: Smedley Fahrquart

DATE: 21 November 1993

RE: REMINDER OF SOFTWARE PURCHASE OKAY

During our conversation over lunch yesterday, I mentioned that President Smith asked me to tell you that you have his okay for buying the Laffer Accounting System Software (LAS) program.

As we talked about many things, I thought you may have forgotten this important bit of information. Hope the LAS works out.

EXERCISE G: MEMOS VERSUS CONVERSATION

Discuss in class the following question: When might telephone calls or face-to-face conversations be less efficient than memos?

TO IMPROVE EFFICIENCY

Sometimes requests, directives, and instructions must be conveyed to several people. Telephone calls may be inefficient even when face-to-face conversations are impossible. Conference calls often are bothersome. Even a meeting may make conveying these things difficult because the people may not be able to convene easily or because they

Three qualities of
efficient memos

1. Clarity
2. Brevity
3. Tact

may misinterpret information. A memo conveying information to the people involved may be easier than bringing those people to the information. Moreover, if the memo is clearly written, then no misinterpretation should occur.

Three qualities create efficient memos:

1. *Clarity* promotes efficiency by assuring understanding in one reading.
2. *Brevity* promotes efficiency by requiring little time for the reading.
3. *Tact* promotes a willingness on the part of the reader to be persuaded. Although clarity and brevity create efficiency, tact is also essential. If a memo is offensive, then the qualities of clarity and brevity will be wasted; the reader will no longer be trying to understand.

Here are two examples of efficient memos.

Notice the brevity.

**Exercise H:
Efficiency in Memos**

Discuss in class the following questions:

1. What about this memo is efficient?
2. What advantage is there to listing the names of all who are invited to Jefferson Davis's house?
3. What disadvantage is there to listing those names?
4. What about the memo may be considered inefficient?
5. Sometimes memos include many names on a separate page. These are called "distribution lists." What are the advantages and disadvantages to keeping all names on the memo? To keeping names on a separate page?

MEMORANDUM

TO: Bob Lee
           Phil Sheridan
           John Gordon
           'Lyss Grant
           Tom Jackson

FROM: Jeff Davis

DATE: 22 December 1860

RE: WAR

Now that South Carolina has seceded from the Union, I think we should get together at my place Friday night (8:00 p.m., sharp) to choose up sides. See you there.

MEMORANDUM

TO: Smedley Fahrquart, Vice-President, Accounting

FROM: Samantha Evans, Vice-President, Personnel

DATE: 3 October 1992

RE: ROSS REPORT

I still don't have the Ross Report. And Purchasing says they never had it. Before I get upset with Purchasing would you save me from embarrassment by checking with your secretary once more to see whether she may have forgotten to send it? The coffee is getting cold.

Notice the clarity and the tact.

. . . .

EXERCISE I: EFFICIENCY IN MEMOS

Discuss in class the following question: Clarity, brevity, and tact are important for all memos. Why are they more important for efficiency in memos than, say, for memos in which completeness of information is most important?

TO DIRECT: MEMORANDA DOWN

Memos to subordinates should follow three directives:

1. Avoid unnecessary bossiness or criticism.
2. Be clear and accurate regarding information, direction, and requests.
3. Be examples of good writing.

Because subordinates know precisely who their superiors are, and because most resent having their superiors repeatedly reminding them, there is no need to adopt a superior tone. Directives should be made as requests; subordinates will understand that the request is a demand.

Still, writers must pay careful attention to accuracy and clarity. Subordinates should not be left to guess what they should do.

As always, superiors must set a good example. Consequently, if the writer wants subordinates to write clearly, briefly, accurately, and properly, then the writer must write that way. Here is an ineffective memo down. The bad part is in italics.

Notice that the italicized sentence is offensive to the reader.

MEMORANDUM

TO: I. Seymore

FROM: I. Younger

DATE: 17 November 1992

RE: MINOR ERROR IN MONTHLY FINANCIAL REPORT

An error was made in the monthly financial report when $5,756,023 and $373,560 were added incorrectly (lines 25–27). The sum should not be $6,682,583, but rather $6,129,583. *Because one of your people made the error, I am writing to you.*

EXERCISE J: TELLING VERSUS ASKING

Discuss in class the following question: What might be said about a society in which people are *asked* to do things as opposed to a society in which people are *told* to do things?

The memo's problem is that the tone is angry and superior; the reader is made to feel like a child being chastised for allowing his bicycle to stand out in the rain. The memo is informational, which is fine, except that the reader has no idea what to do. The reader may feel chastened but is provided no means of correcting the error. The reader may respond, of course, but reluctantly. No one wants to be chastened for the same error twice.

Here is the memo again, rewritten well. The improvements are in italics.

MEMORANDUM

TO: I. Seymore

FROM: I. Younger

DATE: 17 November 1992

RE: MINOR ERROR IN MONTHLY FINANCIAL REPORT

An error was made in the monthly financial report when $5,756,023 and $373,560 were added incorrectly (lines 25–27). The sum should not be $6,682,583, but rather $6,129,583.

These things happen occasionally, but the error must be corrected before the deadline tomorrow. Would you call the printing department and tell them I want the error corrected before the report goes out?

Notice that the revised memo, as shown by italics, (1) does not blame anyone, and (2) asks that the error be corrected.

This revised memo leaves no doubt as to who is in charge, but it does not belabor the point. Moreover, it does not slap the reader's wrists too hard. It simply states that a mistake has been made (note the passive voice), directs the reader to correct it, and tells the reader how it should be corrected.

The most important qualities of directive memos, as shown above, are clarity and tact. Clarity usually requires not only the usual care in choosing accurate words, but also great care in labeling parts and listing the order in which things should be done. The following example is a clear directive. Notice that the writer clearly labels each part and conveys the order by a numbered list. The memo concludes with an example of the new system.

Notice that the numbered list improves clarity.

MEMORANDUM

TO: All Programmers

FROM: Mayne Frayme, Director of Communications

DATE: 11 March 1992

RE: NEW POLICY ON STORING FILES ON THE ABC-6677 MAINFRAME

Policy: All programmers will use *three* numbers to identify and store computer files.

1. Project file number
2. The programmer's employee number
3. The date of contract or approval

If I were to store a file on the Bay Bridge Project today, the file would be identified as \B7562\0967\3-11-92. Using only the name of the project is causing problems because some projects go by one name in the Accounting Department and by another in Engineering. Retrieving all files on a given project, therefore, is becoming difficult. Before it becomes impossible, this change must be made. Begin today.

Although Frayme's memo is clear, and is not offensive, it could be made more tactful by making it seem less an order from on high and more the inevitable result of something employees are doing well. Here is the memo again, slightly modified. This time, Frayme uses more tact. The changes are shown in italics.

MEMORANDUM

TO: All Programmers

FROM: Mayne Frayme, Director of Communications

DATE: 11 March 1992

RE: NEW POLICY ON STORING FILES ON THE ABC-6677
       MAINFRAME

Policy: All programmers will use *three* numbers to identify and store computer files.

1. Project file number
2. The programmer's employee number
3. The date of contract or approval

If I were to store a file on the Bay Bridge Project today, the file would be identified as \B7562\0967\3-11-92.

Thanks to your efforts, the company is growing rapidly, and we now have more work than anyone can keep track of informally. Using only the name of the project is causing problems because some projects go by one name in the Accounting Department and by another in Engineering. Retrieving all files on a given project, therefore, is becoming difficult. Before it becomes impossible, this change must be made. *Please begin the new policy today.*

Notice that honest praise, as shown in italics, produces a tactful directive.

EXERCISE K: PRAISE AND TACT

Discuss in class the following questions:
1. How important is praise as an aspect of tact?
2. Must praise always be honest?

TO INFORM: MEMORANDA UP AND ACROSS

So that left hands may know what right hands are doing, memos are essential. When someone asks the boss about a subordinate's project, it is good for the boss, and even better for the subordinate, if the boss knows something about it.

Here is an apocryphal memo from the American poet T. S. Eliot, who was also on the board of an English publishing house, Faber & Faber. It demonstrates a breakdown in communication: signals were crossed, and they needed to be uncrossed quickly. If memos can correct misunderstandings between two nationalities, then they should work also in the simpler operations of business. This kind of memo belongs also to a category that could be called "Oops!"

. . . .
EXERCISE L: LEFT HAND, RIGHT HAND

Discuss in class the following questions:

1. How does this memo illustrate Churchill's remark that England and the United States are two nations divided by a common language?

2. Can you think of an occasion in business for which such a memo informing one group of the work (or mistake) of another group might be helpful?

MEMORANDUM

TO: Smedley Smythe, Chairman

FROM: Tom Eliot

DATE: 2 July 1953

RE: Meeting on 4 July

Your memo of 29 June announced a meeting on 4 July. I replied in a memo dated 30 June by asking whether England had a Fourth of July. You responded yesterday, saying "Don't be silly, Tom. Of course we have a Fourth of July." I should have said, "Does England *celebrate* the Fourth of July?" I do. So I shall not be able to attend. I shall be exploding firecrackers.

MEMORANDA UP.   Because the reader of a memo up is superior to the writer on the corporate ladder, the memo should clearly convey respect. Yet most bosses do not want subordinates to flatter them in any obvious way or to be obsequious. The following memo, for example, is too obsequious.

Notice that the memo spends more time apologizing than discussing the subject.

MEMORANDUM

TO: I. Seymore

FROM: I. Younger

DATE: 17 November 1992

RE: ERROR IN MONTHLY FINANCIAL REPORT

Please excuse me for bothering you with something that someone in your august position may think is trivial. Ordinarily, I would not presume to call myself to your attention by writing directly to you. However, because the deadline is approaching, no one but you can have the error in the monthly report corrected before that report is printed and sent out.

An error was made in the monthly financial report when $5,756,023 and $373,560 were added incorrectly (lines 25–27). The sum should not be $6,682,583, but rather $6,129,583. Perhaps you will want the error corrected before the report is sent out.

Rewritten, the memo can remain respectful without being obsequious. Note the rewritten parts in italics, below.

MEMORANDUM

TO: I. Seymore

FROM: I. Younger

DATE: 17 November 1992

RE: MINOR ERROR IN MONTHLY FINANCIAL REPORT

An error was made in the monthly financial report when $5,756,023 and $373,560 were added incorrectly (lines 25–27). The sum should not be $6,682,583, but rather $6,129,583. *Because the deadline is so close, word must come from your office to correct the error in time. If you say you want it corrected, let me know, and I'll have it done on your authority.*

EXERCISE M: DISCOURTESY: AN EYE FOR AN EYE OR TURN THE OTHER CHEEK?

Discuss in class the following question: When Chip writes "only a fool would be confused," is a respondent thus entitled to be discourteous?

The revised memo gives a nod to the reader's position but does so for a very specific reason: without a person in authority directing a change to be made, the change probably would not be made. The last sentence conveys the notion that the reader is probably busy with other things without saying "sorry to bother you"; it goes even further by offering to have the error corrected.

By remembering that the job comes first, that people in different positions have different jobs, that it is important to know those differences and just where people stand amid all those differences, the writer can avoid errors in tone.

When bosses make mistakes, they want to be told about them, but they do not like being told in a discourteous way by subordinates. When subordinates are discourteous, no one benefits. Suppose, for example, that Frayme's memo on page 65 was not a directive to subordinates, but rather one to his boss, Iva Chip. Ms. Chip specifically told people about a year ago to "call the Bay Bridge Project whatever you want to. Everyone knows what it is. And only a fool would be confused."

This is an example of a tactless memo telling her that all is not well.

Notice that the active voice connects Chip directly and tactlessly to the problem.

EXERCISE N: OFFENSIVE MEMOS

Discuss in class the following questions:

1. Where does this memo begin to offend Chip?

2. In precisely what ways might this memo offend Chip?

MEMORANDUM

TO: Iva Chip, Project Director

FROM: Mayne Frayme, Director of Communications

DATE: 11 March 1992

RE: FILE STORAGE PROBLEMS REGARDING THE ABC-6677 MAINFRAME

Last year, immediately after taking over as project director, you directed everyone to call the Bay Bridge Project by whatever name seemed reasonable. It is no longer reasonable.

We now have more work than anyone can keep track of informally. Using the name of the project is only causing problems because some projects go by one name in Accounting and by another in Engineering. Retrieving all files on a given project, therefore, is becoming a pain in the neck. It just doesn't work any more!

Here's a policy that we should send to all concerned:

All programmers will use *three* sets of numbers to identify and store computer files.

1. Project file number
2. The programmer's employee number
3. The date of contract or approval

This should correct the error.

Here is the same information written tactfully.

MEMORANDUM

TO: Iva Chip, Project Director

FROM: Mayne Frayme, Director of Communications

DATE: 11 March 1992

RE: FILE STORAGE PROBLEMS REGARDING THE ABC-6677
           MAINFRAME

Last year, immediately after taking over as project director, you cut through a
lot of red tape by directing everyone to call the Bay Bridge Project by whatever name seemed reasonable. Much time, effort, and confusion was saved,
and everyone was happy. Now, however, we have more work than anyone can
keep track of informally. Using only the name of the project is causing problems because some projects go by one name in Accounting and by another in
Engineering. Retrieving all files on a given project, therefore, is becoming difficult. In short, because the project has grown so much, what used to work no
longer does.

I suggest that something like the following policy be sent to all concerned:

All programmers will now use *three* sets of numbers to identify and store computer files.

   1. Project file number
   2. The programmer's employee number
   3. The date of contract or approval

Let me know what you think.

Notice that Chip is given credit for a good action, which only later becomes a problem.

. . . .

**EXERCISE O:
EFFICIENCY AND TACT**

Discuss in class the following questions:

1. Efficiency usually requires economical writing, whereas tact usually requires some inefficiency and, thus, more words. Why?

2. Although inefficient, tact is essential. Why?

3. We all know why we must be tactful with bosses, but why is it good to be tactful with subordinates?

A memo up, written tactfully and thoughtfully, may also benefit the writer, either directly or indirectly. Below is a memo from Saman-tha Evans to her boss. The object of the memo is to inform her boss of something important, but because she shows alertness, initiative, thoughtfulness, and tact, the memo also places her name in front of the person who has the strongest influence on her career with the company.

MEMORANDUM

TO: Norma Hartner, Vice President, Corporate Relations

FROM: Samantha Evans, Personnel

DATE: 25 November 1992

RE: Miasma Road Landfill

While running at the "Y" last evening, I overheard two men discussing legal action against us regarding the Miasma Road Landfill. I was mildly curious, so I decreased my speed to keep pace with them. They seem bent on filing a suit, but as the Legal Department assured me this morning, we have complied with all laws—local, state, and federal.

Ordinarily, two men in jogging clothes do not interest me, but in the lobby afterward, I spoke casually with them to discover who they are. J. Walker is a lawyer for the EPA, and Al Bedarn is a chemist for the Fish and Wildlife Service. Perhaps it is nothing. Probably, you already know about it. In case you did not, however, I thought you'd want to know.

Notice the many ways that Evans conveys energy and alertness to her boss.

. . . .

EXERCISE P: SELF-PROMOTION BY MEMO

Discuss in class the following questions:

1. What does the memo tell Hartner about Evans?

2. Why was checking with the Legal Department before writing the memo important?

3. Is this something one should bother writing about?

4. What would be the advantages and disadvantages of a telephone call rather than a memo?

. . . .

EXERCISE Q: CORRECTING THE BOSS IN MEMOS

Discuss in class the following question: Why do bosses, who may not mind being corrected orally and in private, dislike being corrected in print by their subordinates?

The most important thing to remember about memos up is this: although many bosses do not mind being corrected when they err, they mind very much being corrected in writing. Consequently, never correct the boss in writing.

MEMORANDA ACROSS.   Memos to corporate equals should present a tone conveying a sense of "would you do me a favor?" Memos across present problems of tone only when they are written as if they were directed to subordinates. Writers may not direct their equals in other departments to do anything; they must *ask*. Here is an example of an ineffective memo across, from the head of the printing department to the head of the accounting department.

MEMORANDUM

TO: I. Count, Accounting Department

FROM: A. Printer, Printing Department

DATE: 17 November 1992

RE: Error in Monthly Financial Report

An error was made in the monthly financial report when $5,756,023 and $373,560 were added incorrectly (lines 25–27). The sum should not be $6,682,583, but rather $6,129,583.

What's with you people?

Notice that Count may be insulted by this memo.

Here is the same opinion conveyed more effectively and more tactfully. The changes are shown in italics.

MEMORANDUM

TO: I. Count

FROM: A. Printer

DATE: 17 November 1992

RE: Possible Error in Monthly Financial Report

*Notice the tactful
uncertainty.*

*I do not know for sure, but it seems likely that between your office and mine,
an error was made in the monthly financial report when $5,756,023 and
$373,560 were added incorrectly (lines 25–27).*

Notice the tactful request.

*Would you do me a favor by checking the figures? If there is an error and you
want a correction made, I'll need to know by 9:00 a.m. tomorrow. That's my
deadline.*

ABUSES OF MEMORANDA

*People use thought only to justify
their evil-doings, and words only to
conceal their thoughts.*

Voltaire (1694–1778)

Memos are misused, even abused, when people use them to cover
their flanks excessively and overtly, when people should be talking
instead of writing, and when they should be conveying information
instead of attempting to be noticed. Too often, managers abuse memos
when they allow them to be rewritten at each rung as they move up the
corporate ladder. Finally, the most common and inefficient abuse of
memos occurs when committees try to write them.

COVERING YOUR FLANKS (CYF)

Most companies eat too much information because people keep feeding memos into the system. The system is dumb; it cannot yell "enough!" When memos are unnecessary, people should use the telephone, visit others' offices, talk to them in the hallways or at lunch. Be sure, moreover, that covering your flanks is necessary before writing a CYF memo. Here is an example of a CYF memo that is clearly unnecessary and perhaps even counterproductive.

**EXERCISE R:
PRODUCING OPPOSITE
EFFECTS**

Discuss in class the following question: Why might this memo be counterproductive—that is, why might the result be opposite the writer's intent?

MEMORANDUM

TO: Flossy Dentum, Public Relations

FROM: Alvin Plaque, Engineering

DATE: 23 August 1993

RE: RECENT ARTICLE IN GUMTOWN *ORACLE*

The recent article in the Gumtown *Oracle*, which quotes ''an unidentified source'' as saying that our company treats engineers as ''spoiled children'' was, as you have said, ''irresponsible.'' I want you to know that I was not that ''source.''

There are fewer sure signs of bad internal relations in a company than an abundance of CYF memos. There are fewer signs of good working relationships in a company than the absence of CYF memos. The lack of trust implied by many CYF memos will be detrimental in the long run to corporate health.

WRITING INSTEAD OF TALKING

When there is no reason to write, talk. When it is unnecessary to provide a record, or when people are readily available, then talk with them; do not write a memo. Here is an example of writing when talking would be better.

FIVE ABUSES OF MEMORANDA

1. *When covering your flanks is excessive and overt*
2. *When talking is better than writing*
3. *When conveying information is better than attempting to be noticed*
4. *When conveying information by rewriting memos as they move up the ladder*
5. *When memos are written by committee*

Frequent abuses of memos clog offices with piles of paper.

EXERCISE S: WRITING INSTEAD OF TALKING

Discuss in class the following question: Can you think of any specific waste—in time or money—incurred unnecessarily by the corporation because this information was written rather than spoken?

MEMORANDUM

TO: John Spaulding, Operations

FROM: John Wilson, Accounting

DATE: July 19, 1991

RE: GOLF

What say we get together at the Burning Tree for a round of golf Saturday? We could talk about your department's proposal for the new accounting system for operations on the nineteenth hole. Shall we say 8:00 a.m. tee-time? Want to see whether Al Ping and Jane Voit want to play?

When memos are simply the result of a writer's laziness, they are inefficient. Very often, much more can be accomplished by standing up and then walking to someone's office for a conversation than can be done by twenty memos.

WRITING ROT RATHER THAN INFORMATION

Even in simple memos, many people insult the reader by writing big, vague, and highfalutin words and phrases. In such instances, two things are conveyed: how many years the writer went to school and how ill-served the writer was by that schooling. Here is an example of writing rot.

Notice that this memo conveys the self-importance of the writer much better than it conveys information.

MEMORANDUM

TO: Jane Bafflegab, Corporate Accounts

FROM: Bruce Gobbledygook, VP, Research

DATE: December 10, 1991

RE: HARMONIZATION OF PATENTIZING INVENTIONS

It has come to my attention that the subcontracted corporative accounting end-users of our patentable production inventions are not being properly interfaced with this department with regard to the accounting procedures currently being processed by Corporate Accounts.

Stiflized research may be the resulting effect in this division if these sub-contracted end-users are not made accountable in dollars for the costs incurred at this end of the process.

Could you do something about it?

Business writers should remember that readers are far more impressed by clarity and brevity than they are by rot. Moreover, if writers want to influence decisions, have their ideas listened to, and rise in a company, then memos must be not only readable, but also readily understandable.

WRITING ON THE LADDER

One common misuse of memos requires special notice: editing as deciding. Memos are sometimes used as bad vehicles for deciding something. Sometimes a new staffer will propose something in a memo to the boss. The boss edits the memo by adding and deleting ideas, and then sends it on to others who add and delete ideas. When the memo finally arrives on the desk of the big boss, it bears little resemblance to the original memo, or even to some edited versions. The memo read by the big boss may have many good ideas, but the process creates two disadvantages:

1. Mere collections of ideas, recommendations, and proposals are probably unfathomable. Each successive writer fails to consult with previous writers, yet tries to preserve something of previous drafts. The result is a hodgepodge of badly expressed thoughts. By trying to convey the thoughts of many other people, writers easily lose control of their own.

2. The method is woefully inefficient. After reading the first memo, the boss should meet with those whose ideas and abilities may contribute to informed consensus and decision. Much time and work may be saved this way.

Here is a memo that might result from writing on the ladder. Notice that thoughts in this memo lack unity; that is, one idea does not always flow logically from the previous idea.

EXERCISE T: WRITING ON THE LADDER

Discuss in class the following question: Can you identify — by word choice, information, style — the parts of this memo written by different people?

Notice the lack of a single focus in this memo — caused by too many people writing it.

MEMORANDUM

TO: Mr. Big, President

FROM: Ida Fixe, Corporate Planning

DATE: April 27, 1991

RE: NEW ASSEMBLY LINE

For some time, my group has been discussing possible alterations in the assembly lines at the main plant.

Certain minor changes in purchasing may be necessary to assure that materials are properly inventoried before reaching production stages. A new assembly line would probably solve the problems we have seen for some time; a new line could eliminate bottlenecks in the old lines.

. . . .

ABUSES OF MEMORANDA   77

WRITING BY COMMITTEE

> Writing, at its best, is a lonely life. Organizations for writers palliate the writer's loneliness but I doubt if they improve his writing.

Ernest Hemingway, in his Nobel Prize acceptance speech, was talking about support groups for writers, but the statement holds for writing in another context as well. The old saying "too many cooks spoil the broth" may be applied to memos: too many writers spoil the memo. Sometimes, however, committees are charged with solving a problem and reporting on the solution by memo. When two or more write a memo, they become competitive and disagree not because words are good or bad, but because of reasons unrelated to the quality of the prose. Others avoid saying "that's rot" because egos will be damaged or because superiors do not like to be criticized.

Because too many eyes are looking at the page, each pair seeing differently, the result is foggy prose, unfocused, and undirected. Because each member has at least one pet notion that *must* be included, and because those notions often overlap, or are utterly unrelated, the result is bad.

Committees should select one person to do the writing. That person should attend the meetings, listen to comments and suggestions, and then write the memo— alone. The writing process should be repeated until there is consensus. This way, the committee's ideas are included, but the memo has a chance of having focus, clarity, and direction. Here is an example of writing by committee. Notice the shifts in emphasis, in tone, and, finally, in clarity.

. . . .
EXERCISE U: ON ABUSING MEMOS

Discuss in class the following questions:

1. How does the quotation from Voltaire on page 72 apply to the misuse of memos?

2. The art of the memo is one of brevity and clarity. What forces work against brief, clear memos?

Notice the lack of a single focus in this memo— caused by too many people writing it.

MEMORANDUM

TO: Lee Sailer, Vice President for Corporate Relations

FROM: E. Mailer, Chair, Picnic Committee

DATE: May 15, 1991

RE: ANNUAL COMPANY PICNIC

The committee has met several times to discuss the best date for the picnic and the times that would optimize the enjoyment of all our fun and games.

Some think that we shouldn't have the picnic at all. Morale is so bad, given take-over rumors, that the best date would be some time in August, after the rumors are either confirmed or refuted.

Many people are very upset by these rumors of take-over, and they are puzzled that headquarters has neither confirmed nor denied them.

Most of us believe, however, that the Saturday before the Fourth of July weekend would be the best date.

A few wanted to know if the Company would be willing to build some horseshoe courts, as many of the employees play horseshoes.

SUMMARY

1. The memo is the most common form of business writing.

2. In its titles, this part of the book uses the formal *memoranda* as the plural of *memorandum* for two reasons: it is shorter than *memorandums*, and older forms often are better in formal prose. *Memo* and *memos* are used in the text, as these are brief and commonly understood terms.

3. Good planning produces well-ordered and brief memos.

4. Good memos often are given a head start by the writer's carefully choosing titles (that which follows *Re*) and repeating them in the first line of text.

5. Although many memos are routine, writers must pay attention to the reader. They must study the reader's background, knowledge, biases, and other qualities.

6. Memos down, to subordinates, avoid a tone of "Do this, or else!"

7. Memos up, to superiors, reflect an implicit tone of request rather than of demand, suggestions rather than directives.

8. Memos across, to colleagues, make no demands that the writer would not accept, should the situation be reversed.

EXERCISES

1. *Short Memos.* Write a brief memo to your boss, the manager of the personnel department of a large company, suggesting two things: (1) that no memorandum may be longer than one page, and (2) that the company use the word "memorandums" for the plural of "memorandum."

2. *Short Memos.* Write a brief memo to your professor, a rather easy-going type, suggesting (1) that no memorandum may be longer than one page, and (2) that the word "memorandums" always be used in class for the plural of "memorandum." Be sure to include the arguments discussed in the text.

3. *Parts of memos.* Explain the importance of the first four parts of a memo. That is, why is this information listed first and not something else?

4. *The Re trick.* Using the *Re* trick, rewrite this memo for clarity, brevity, and accuracy.

MEMORANDUM

TO: J. Kaspar

FROM: K. Valenti

DATE: 21 October 1992

RE: FUEL SAMPLE BAGS

As a result of the preliminary review of the data collected during the June 1992 Moisture and Neutral Sample Study, it has been shown that the 2-mil bags currently used do lose moisture very rapidly after five days in storage. Five mil bags do not exhibit any moisture loss until after thirty days in storage.

A majority of the neutrals are called by the suppliers and analyzed at the laboratory on an average after sixteen days in storage, with 51% called between 19 and 24 days in storage. Each of the coal-handling supervisors have been contacted by phone about his change to 5-mil bags and they do not foresee any problems.

Therefore, it is recommended that the coal samples be sealed in a thicker 5-mil bag and that the coal-handling supervisors make the proper contact with the station warehouse to facilitate said changes once the quantities of 2-mil bags are depleted.

If you have any questions, please contact me.

5. *Similarities in memos going in different "directions."* What are the similarities between memos up, memos down, and memos across?

6. *Flawed Memos.* Each of the following memos is flawed: none should have been written. From the "Abuses of Memoranda" section in Chapter 3, identify *one* major flaw in each memo. Some may have more than one flaw, and some may be ambiguous (have this reason or that reason). Consequently, be prepared to support any choice.

a. TO: Jean Levi, Manager of Operations

FROM: Sam Lost, Secretary

DATE: 19 October 1991

RE: RUNNING OUT OF PETTY CASH

Just wanted you to know that I've spent $234.79 of petty cash so far this year. We'll run out soon at this rate.

b. TO: Jean Levi, Manager of Operations

FROM: Sam Yosemite, Assistant to the Manager of Operations

DATE: 17 June 1991

RE: LEFT WORK EARLY

I left work 15 minutes early yesterday. I had to close on the new house we are buying. The closing was at 5 p.m., and the drive to the bank takes 12 minutes.

c. TO: Jean Levi, Mgr., Operations

FROM: Sam Yosemite, Purchasing

DATE: 23 August 1991

RE: ORDERING WIDGITCOGS

Just a note to see how things are going and whether you will be needing any widgitcogs next month. I'm ordering them now, so be sure to let me know by tomorrow.

d. TO: Jean Levi, Manager of Operations

FROM: Sam Yosemite, Training

DATE: 5 March 1991

RE: POSSIBLE INADVISABLE MONITORING EVALUATIONINGS

This is to advise you of the potential for inadvisability that exists between the educational monitoring evaluations that we are interfacing with the traditionalized managerial supervizations.

Certain of the middle-level supervisory personnel have, or are about to have, reconsiderations of their heretofore unchallengizable authority in this area at this point in time.

7. *Revising rot.* Now that you know more about memos and about how to write clearly, rewrite the previous memo (''Possible inadvisable monitoring evaluations'') to use as few words as possible. Try also to do it entirely in one-syllable words.

8. *Writing rot.* Try rewriting this memo in plain English.

TO: Jane Bafflegab, Corporate Accounts

FROM: Bruce Gobbledygook, Vice-President, Research

DATE: 12 October 1991

RE: HARMONIZATION OF PATENTIZING INVENTIONS

It has come to my attention that the subcontracted corporative accounting end-users of our patentable production inventions are not being properly interfaced with this department with regard to the accounting procedures currently being processed by Corporate Accounts.

Stiflized research may be the resulting effect in this division if these subcontracted end-users are not made accountable in dollars for the costs incurred at this end of the process.

Could you do something about it?

9. *Memo planning sheet.* Read the article on pages 80–81. Write a memo planning sheet that includes the main points.

CASE STUDY I. BAD NEWS AND MEMO DOWN: THE RETRACTION MEMO

You are the editor of your campus newspaper. As a senior, you must spend several weeks this year off-campus interviewing for jobs. Consequently, you do not always have the tight control over editorial policy for which you are noted, a control that earned you the nickname ''Captain Bligh.''

When you return from one such trip, you receive a call from an irate Ms. Conduit, Head of Buildings and Maintenance for the university. She accuses you and your staff of utter irresponsibility in publishing an article by one A. Brasive, a new (sophomore) staff writer. Brasive, it seems, had written and, because you were not there to check the facts, published an article called ''Open Sewer on Campus.'' This article stated that, during heavy rains, the sewer system for the new student apartment buildings proves inadequate. The system clogs and raw sewage runs into a stream that flows behind the apartments and from there through the campus and into a river.

Conduit says that, while she is aware that sewage does enter the stream, the sewage comes from a private

FIRMS SEEK CURE FOR DULL MEMOS; FIND WINDY WRITERS HARD TO CURB

By Cynthia F. Mitchell, Staff Reporter of the *Wall Street Journal*

DALLAS—Where in a business memo should a piece of bad news be delivered? Right up front, says Gene Howard, a writing instructor for Communispond Inc., a company that teaches writing to businessmen.

"Where did we get the notion that we have to save the bad news for the end?" Mr. Howard asks his class of 14 middle managers, whose companies have paid $450 each for the eight-hour "Speaking on Paper" course. Give the reader your message in the first paragraph, he says.

Increasingly, companies are calling on consultants such as Mr. Howard to teach employees how to write clearly. Some send managers to one-day "tune-up" classes. Others bring in coaches for seminars lasting several days. And some provide private tutors for top executives who secretly suffer from dangling participles and suspended phrases.

Companies have come to realize that muddled memos waste time and money and can cause vital information to wind up in the trash can. Bad writing can irritate clients and lose lucrative contracts.

No Miracles

But a quick writing course won't perform miracles. "I hate to say it, but I still use the same old style," says Beth Brawner, who works in the trust department of a Tulsa bank where a writing seminar was part of her training. "I've never gotten myself motivated enough to change."

Some companies would prefer to put their money elsewhere. "We've got other priorities that are frankly higher right now," says a spokesman for American Motors Corp. "It's just not something that would pay the kind of dividends we need."

Still, most companies feel the courses are well worth it. About 34% of all organizations with 50 or more employees provide some sort of writing training, says *Training Magazine*. Most of the companies which provide writing instruction for their employees get instructors from one of two sources: Either from national or regional companies that specialize in communications consulting, or from an increasing number of English and communications professors who moonlight or who have entered the business full time.

Furthermore, companies say that employees consistently express interest in writing courses. G. D. Searle's consumer products division, for one, spent $7,000 this year to teach managers to write better. Training and sales director Leonard Swatkiewicz says he decided on the set of courses after seeing "everything from dangling participles, incomplete thoughts, backwards structure and poor spelling" in company memos. When a note riddled with misspelled words and poor grammar crossed his desk, "I stood up and said, 'My God, we've got to do something to improve this writing,'" he says.

Wipfli, Ullrich & Co., a Wassau, Wis.-based accounting firm, brought in a writing consultant last month to improve the firm's reports to clients. "You want them to be able to read it easily and understand it—not read the whole thing, then read it again, then wind up throwing it out the door because it took so long for them to read," says Ronn Kleinschmidt, a manager in charge of continuing education.

Writing instructors emphasize such basic principles as clarity and organization but use different methods to get their points across. Students in one course are sent home with an assignment to write about anything—using only one syllable words. Another consultant suggests the "sledgehammer approach." Sentence too long? Just smash it in half.

At the "Speaking on Paper" seminar, Mr. Howard exhorts his class to avoid empty phrases; substitute "prevent" for "eliminate the possibility of," he says, and use "because" instead of "in view of the fact that." He berates the class for closing memos with, "get back to me as soon as you can." "When's that?" he asks. "How? In writing? A phone call? Tablets of stone?" He suggests, "Call me Friday."

Finally, the students are told to use everything they've learned to rework the memo they wrote earlier that morning. Randy McClendon, a Southwestern Bell manager, cut 56 words from his first effort, took out dates that made his opening paragraph read like a calendar and emphasized his main points with bullets. The final memo was much more readable than the first.

On a recent morning at Amoco Corp.'s Tulsa Data Center, writing consultant Lee Johns leads 18 students in the first of five early-morning classes. She asks four participants to explain what they do when they receive a two-page memo. "If I get two paragraphs, I read all of it. If I get two pages, I read some of it. If I get a three-page letter, I lay it at the bottom of the pile," answers William Gay. "What are the implications of that?" Ms. Johns asks. Don't make memos "the great mystery novel—finally, you get to paragraph four, and there's the point."

Although many companies prefer the economy and quality of prepackaged writing courses, some consultants criticize what they call the "dog-and-pony shows" of the large training companies. "There has to be an adaptation to the needs of the client, rather than a pre-packaged pile of goods that purports to fit everybody," says Herbert W. Hildebrandt, who is a professor of business communications at the University of Michigan and a writing consultant.

Willingness to Learn

Of more general concern to businesses is whether any type of writing instruction will stick: That depends on the student's willingness to learn, the extent of the training and whether the lessons are put into practice, say the consultants.

"Honestly, I can't say that people have come up to me and said, 'Hey, this was much better and I'm much more comfortable with the whole process.'" Now, a thesaurus, dictionary and grammar book have a permanent place on his desk. And he often rewrites reports several times.

Others aren't as convinced. "There's not a single trick I'll take home and use today," says Julia Kearney, a Southwestern Bell media-relations manager who attended a Communispond seminar. Consultants warn that the training can't be done in a vacuum. "If there isn't follow-up, it can't work," says Marty Nord, a Nashville, Tenn., consultant. "You're dealing with ingrained habits."

A division manager at Chevron's Oil Field Research Co. says the company has been a "little lax" about following up on its consultant's seminars. So, he says, supervisors plan to sit down individually with employees to point out problems and review what was learned.

"Rather than practicing, polishing and using the skills we spent all this money on," says one manager, "in a crisis, we lapse back into the old, comfortable way of doing things."

apartment complex a half mile away, not from the student apartments. The university has alerted the County Board of Health, which has moved quickly to inform the owners of the offending apartment complex and to take corrective action. The university, she says, "is in no way responsible for this unfortunate, even dangerous situation."

While you don't apologize to Conduit, you do assure her that you will check into the story and, if proven wrong, you will see that a retraction appears prominently in the next issue of the paper.

After hanging up, you call the Board of Health, which confirms everything Conduit has said. Eager to appear responsible, the Board of Health even offers to send a representative to show you the problem and the reasons they believe it comes from the private complex. You accept, accompany the representative, and are faced with virtually irrefutable evidence.

In short, A. Brasive really made a mess of things.

In two hours, you must leave for three days to interview for another job. Having promised to print a retraction, and because Brasive is in class, you must write a directive telling Brasive to write a retraction.

The problem is that the newspaper has trouble finding people to write for it this time of year, as midterm examinations are approaching. You cannot afford to lose Brasive right now.

Write the directive to Brasive.

Case Study 2. Memo Down: Memo to the Lay-out Editor

Using what you know from Case Study 1 write a memo to the lay-out editor, who is responsible for which story goes where and on which page. This directive must suggest strongly that Brasive's retraction appear prominently, preferably on the front page.

Remember, however, that the lay-out editor, D. Syne, is not to be blamed for Brasive's error.

Case Study 3. Memo Down: Memo to Public Relations

Using what you know from Case Study 1, write a memorandum to the paper's PR person, Charles "Chuck" Livewell. Ask him to meet Conduit and express the paper's chagrin (look it up). Ask him also to mention that you would like to express your thanks that she came to you first with the problem.

Case Study 4. Memo Up: The Transparency Committee Memo

Your economics professor is a nice person. She is also a very good instructor. Adama Smith is challenging, demanding, and yet patient with those who do not understand things the first time they are presented. Her grading is tough, but fair. No one receives favors.

Because the students in her class fill the classroom to overflowing, several of you who must walk a half mile from previous classes to your economics class find yourselves always in the back of the room. While you have no difficulty hearing the professor, you do have difficulty seeing the transparencies. For all her good attributes, the professor writes the way a chicken scratches the ground. Her transparencies are nearly unreadable. For those who sit in the back of the room, the transparencies are completely indecipherable.

As a classroom exercise, in groups of four to six write memos to Professor Smith informing her of the problem and requesting that it be corrected. Remember to use the advice given in this chapter for avoiding writing by committee.

Challenge Exercise 1. This Book *versus* Mitchell Article: Memoranda

Much of Mitchell's article from the *Wall Street Journal* (pages 80–81) agrees with the advice given in this book. Occasionally, it differs. After reading the article and this chapter, write a memo to your instructor that provides details on the points of agreement and of disagreement.

Challenge Exercise 2. Writing by Committee

This assignment involves groups of six students. Five work together and one works alone. You and four of your classmates are assigned one of these positions: president, vice-president for marketing, director of advertising, assistant director of advertising, advertising film editor. The sixth member, working alone, may choose any of these titles.

All six work for Psycho-Ads, Inc., a $50 million a year advertising company in New York City. Your biggest account is with Howl Much, a designing company specializing in punk clothing. On Friday, you must be ready to present to Howl Much executives a $7 million television campaign for their new line of sweatshirts and jeans. On Tuesday morning, the film editor discovers some rather shocking footage in the film for three of the commercials. It seems that although nearly all of the ragged holes in the sweatshirts and jeans reveal uninteresting parts of the models' anatomies, a few reveal parts that cannot be shown on American television.

The president of Psycho-Ads is rather conservative, believing also that while short-term revenues may be great, the backlash from conservative consumer groups may diminish long-term revenues considerably;

the vice-president has pressed suggestiveness in television advertising to the limits for years. The advertising director believes that the more suggestive shots may be salvaged for magazine advertisements. The film editor does not want to see dollars taken from the film budget and given to others who handle print media.

Write a memo by committee; that is, write it as a group. Simultaneously, have one member sit alone to write the memo. Compare the two memos to see which is best.

CHALLENGE EXERCISE 3. WRITING ON THE LADDER

This assignment involves two groups of five students and follows the same scenario as Challenge Exercise 2. You and four of your classmates are assigned one of these positions: president, vice-president for marketing, director of advertising, assistant director of advertising, advertising film editor.

The assignment has three parts.

1. First, the film editor writes a memo to the assistant director of advertising regarding the problem. Second, the assistant advertising director rewrites the memo and sends it to the director. Third, the advertising director rewrites the memo and sends it to the vice-president. Fourth, the vice-president rewrites the memo and sends it to the president. The president rewrites the memo so that it might be ready should the company be required to inform Howl Much of the problem.

2. Five other students review the first and last memos and discuss the following questions.
   a. Which memo is best? Why?
   b. In part, are the memos different because the readers are different?
   c. To what degree are the memoranda different because one person wrote the first one and five were involved in writing the last?

3. The five other students then review all the memos and discuss the following questions.
   a. In which memo does the intent of the first memo disappear?
   b. Is writing memos this way always bad? Always good? Why?

COMPLEX MEMORANDA: PARTS AND SHAPES

Memorandum Forms
Multiple Readers
Writer's and Typist's Initials
Enclosure and Copy Notations
Continuing Memos on a Second
   Page
Reply Requested
Humor

MEMORANDUM REPORTS

POSTCARDS

When to Use Postcards
Postcard Format

SUMMARY

EXERCISES

Learning Objectives:

☐ Write complex memos.

☐ Understand the common format
for memorandum reports.

☐ Understand the proper use of postcards in business.

☐ Use the proper form for postcards.

4

HE WORDS ME . . .

HE WORDS ME.

WILLIAM SHAKESPEARE

(1564–1616)

 # OTHER FORMS OF MEMORANDA

Complex Memoranda: Parts and Shapes

Complex memos have the force of reports, if not quite in their formality, then at least in the importance of the material they convey. Here is a complex memo on an important matter.

MEMORANDUM

TO: S. Fahrquart, Vice-President, Sales

FROM: Dan Fino, Maintenance **DF**

DATE: 1 July 1992

RE: PROPER USE OF MAINTENANCE PERSONNEL

When maintenance delivered a modem to your house last week, in compliance with company policy, it seems that you asked that your roof be checked for leaks, as you are having problems.

Please be aware that, while no company rule was broken, had they done any work at all, company policy would have been violated.

I know you did not intend anything improper, but sometimes we all forget about company policy. This, of course, is a memo only between you and me.

DF
pdq

This memo is complex in its format and its content. The first paragraph provides some background, but also states the essential problem: Fahrquart apparently had asked company personnel to do work on a private residence. The second paragraph *tells* Fahrquart that the act, had they "done any work at all," would have violated company policy. The third paragraph tactfully tells Fahrquart never to do it again; it also provides a measure of privacy by saying that the memo is only between Fino and Fahrquart. It also tells Fahrquart something else: Fino has a copy in his files; if Fahrquart ever does it again, Fino can prove that Fahrquart had been warned. Complex memos, then, convey several pieces of information and thread their way through delicate issues.

Although memos differ from letters by not requiring an inside address, salutation, complimentary close, and other elements discussed in Chapter 5, memos sometimes do require such elements normally found in letters as reference initials, notations of enclosure, file number, and phone numbers. While many more formal memos use the signatures of the writers and the initials of readers, only memo reports require them. Special conditions and parts are given here.

MEMORANDUM FORMS

Memos are so common in business that many companies supply printed forms for them. Because most if not all offices these days have computers, however, printed memo forms are less in use. Usually, memo forms are created on a computer by the writer. In such a case, the requirements previously given still apply. Unless a company provides its own specifications or format, follow the model given in Chapter 3, pages 53–55.

MULTIPLE READERS

If the memo has two or more readers, list the names either alphabetically or in order of importance — giving the highest ranking person's name first.

Many companies add to the memo a separate page listing the names of those to whom the memo is to be sent. Such distribution lists on separate pages are cumbersome and unnecessary: cumbersome because they add a page to the memo, and unnecessary because the names should fit on the same page as the text of most routine and well-written memos. Here is one way to do it.

MEMORANDUM

TO: D. Fects _____
           B. Happy _____
           C. Moore _____
           G. Whizz _____

FROM: J. Byrd *JB*

DATE: 29 July 1992

RE: THE FAHRQUART REPORT

Here is the Fahrquart Report. When you've read it, jot your initials beside your name and send it on. Last one, please return it to my office.

Another common method involves placing the word *distribution* after the *To* and then listing the names at the end of the memo.

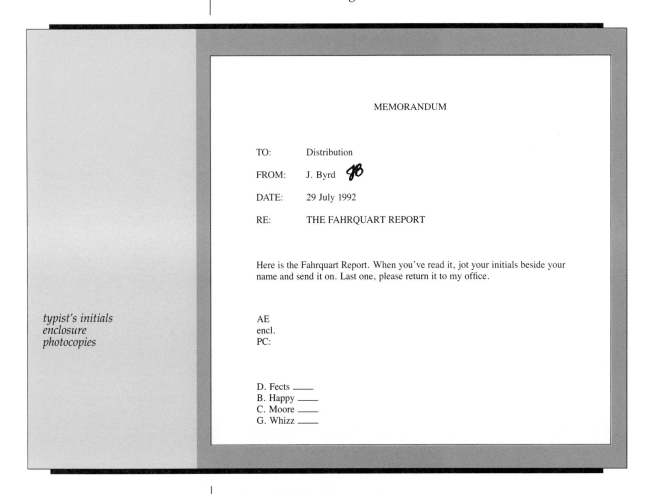

typist's initials
enclosure
photocopies

MEMORANDUM

TO: Distribution

FROM: J. Byrd

DATE: 29 July 1992

RE: THE FAHRQUART REPORT

Here is the Fahrquart Report. When you've read it, jot your initials beside your name and send it on. Last one, please return it to my office.

AE
encl.
PC:

D. Fects _____
B. Happy _____
C. Moore _____
G. Whizz _____

Either method works.

WRITER'S AND TYPIST'S INITIALS

The writer's initials appear in one of two places: typed two spaces below the last line of text and begun at the left-hand margin or handwritten beside the typed name on the *From* line.

If the typist is not the writer, the typist's initials (reference initials) appear in small letters two spaces below the last line, and the writer's initials are written beside the full name at the top.

ENCLOSURE AND COPY NOTATIONS

Enclosure notations appear one line below the reference initials. Copy notations appear one line below the enclosure notation or the reference initials when there is no enclosure notation.

CONTINUING MEMOS ON A SECOND PAGE

Rarely are memos long enough to extend beyond one page; if they do, then they are probably too long. But if a memo is longer than one page, the subsequent pages should include a heading with the writer's name, the page number, and the date. The heading can be arranged either stacked in three lines in the upper left corner or spaced evenly across the top typed line of the page. Here are examples of the two formats.

```
                         MEMORANDUM


     TO:  Smedley Fahrquart, Vice-President, Accounting

     FROM:  Samantha Evans, Vice-President, Personnel  SE

     DATE:  1 October 1992

     RE:  ADVICE ON WRITING MEMOS


     It has been said that when he was national security
     advisor to President Nixon, Henry Kissinger would
     often ask his aides to write reports.

     When an advisor gave him a report, Kissinger would
     ask that it be placed on his desk. He would not look
     at it. Next day, Kissinger would say, ''This is too
     long. Make it shorter.''

     Kissinger would say this to the advisor several
     times.
```

```
     Smedley Fahrquart
     Page 2
     1 October 1992

     When the report had been shortened to one page,
     Kissinger would read it—for the first time.

          OR

     Smedley Fahrquart          2          1 October 1992

     When the report had been shortened to one page,
     Kissinger would read it—for the first time.
```

REPLY REQUESTED

If a writer wishes the reader to reply, the memo should say so. Some advocate including *Reply Requested* between the *Date* and *Re*, but courtesy requires that the writer ask for a reply in a sentence beginning with "Please." The reader can then respond easily by noting "OK" or "No can do" on the memo. Although "please" often requires a few more words, the art of the memo is still one of brevity; consequently, the writer can be a bit more curt than is permissible in a letter.

MEMORANDUM

TO: N. Velop, Maintenance

FROM: N. Close, Hydrostatics   *nc*

DATE: 18 December 1992

RE: BAD RECEPTACLE

The outlet behind my desk keeps shorting out. Please have it fixed.

HUMOR

When everyone works for the same company, and the company is supposed to be one big happy family, informality and even humor may aid in getting things accomplished.

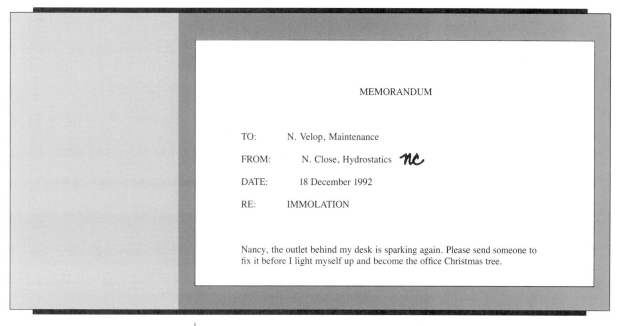

MEMORANDUM

TO: N. Velop, Maintenance

FROM: N. Close, Hydrostatics

DATE: 18 December 1992

RE: IMMOLATION

Nancy, the outlet behind my desk is sparking again. Please send someone to fix it before I light myself up and become the office Christmas tree.

There are three important caveats regarding humor.

1. Humor should be gentle, or at least not unflattering to the reader.
2. Remember that no one feels funny all the time. As humor is not a requirement in memos, one should not force it into the message. Simple clarity, accuracy, brevity, and tact will do the job well without humor.
3. Humor is most effective one-to-one. Humorous memos written *by* a group are seldom enjoyed. Humorous memos written *to* a group are seldom funny. People receiving such a memo tend to see it as far too cute and often rather precious. Avoid group humor.

MEMORANDUM REPORTS

Wit has truth in it; wisecracking is simply calisthenics with words.

Dorothy Parker (1897–1967)

Memos are the most common form of written communication in business, and memo reports are the most common form for reports. They convey more information than a standard memo but usually less than a formal report. Because memo reports are less formal than standard reports, they do not include prefatory material (title page, table of contents, abstracts) or major headings, but they do contain any necessary tables and figures. A sample memo report follows.

Notice that To From, Date, *and* Re *replace the front matter of formal reports.*

MEMORANDUM

TO: George E. Smith, CEO, PRP, Inc.

FROM: Brenda Roughneck, Comptroller *BR*

DATE: 17 November 1992

RE: DRILLING A NATURAL GAS WELL

Purpose. Petrola Reinforced Plastics, Inc., should have a natural gas well drilled on its property.

Problem. A dependency on our natural gas supplier has made Petrola vulnerable to price increases and gas shortages. Over the past five years the price of purchased gas has increased 20% a year.

Scope. After examining five drilling companies, we chose Roony and Associates, Inc. (RAI), for the project. They were chosen on the criteria of reputation, completion time, maintenance, and cost. The major points detailed in this proposal are the plan, schedule, facility requirements, personnel requirements, and cost.

Notice that minor headings remain; major headings (e.g., "Introduction") do not.

Plan. The plan involves hiring RAI to test drill for natural gas reserves under Petrola property. The test well will be drilled to 3,000 feet and, if successful, RAI will complete the well.

Schedule. RAI can begin test drilling within two weeks after receiving a signed contract. Test drilling requires about one week, and, if successful, the project would be completed in 45 days.

Facility and Personnel Requirements. No changes.

Cost. While gas exploration is risky, the potential savings are great. The risk is this: spending $43,665 for a hole in the ground. Our real risk, however, is low for the following reasons.

1. The results of an earth fracture study done by RAI at Petrola show two earth fractures. This makes Petrola's property a very good risk for drilling.
2. RAI recently completed two successful wells within 15 miles of the Petrola plant.

The cost of the project is $93,865, comprising exploration, completion, and connection costs. Details are in Table 1.

Notice that tables and figures remain.

Brenda Roughneck   2   17 November 1992

TABLE I: COST SUMMARY

	Successful Well	Unsuccessful Well
Exploration	$43,665	$43,665
Completion	43,200	—
Connection	7,000	—
Total Cost	$93,865	$43,665

Savings from this project are computed by subtracting the cost of gas production (depreciation and maintenance costs) from the cost of commercial gas. The gas well must be maintained. First-year maintenance costs are $3,000, increasing by 5% thereafter for the estimated life of the project: eight years. Commercial gas is projected to increase by 20% a year. Time to recovery is 2.5 years. Savings over five years are given in Table 2.

TABLE 2: SAVINGS OVER FIVE YEARS

Year	Cost/Year	Depreciation	Maintenance	Savings
1992	$42,688	$ 5,875	$3,000	$33,813
1993	51,226	11,750	3,150	36,326
1994	61,434	11,750	3,307	46,377
1995	73,683	11,750	3,473	58,460
1996	88,531	11,750	3,646	73,135
Net Savings				$248,111

Conclusion. Petrola should hire RAI to drill a gas well because potential benefits outweigh risks.

Notice that tables and figures remain.

Notice that the conclusion remains at the end here. Often, conclusions follow immediately after "Scope."

POSTCARDS

Postcards are hybrids. That is, they are like letters in that they include a stamp and they go outside the company. Because they are neither private nor formal, however, they are like memos.

Because they provide such a small space on which to write, postcards must avoid extraneous words and yet not appear to be cryptic, ambiguous, or, as Shakespeare would have it, equivocating.

WHEN TO USE POSTCARDS

Postcards are used primarily to acknowledge receipt of an order, an important letter, or other important material. Acknowledgments by postcard provide several benefits: they relieve the mind of the person who sent the order or letter, they keep the company's name before the customer, and they are cheaper to send than letters.

POSTCARD FORMAT

Here are an example of a postcard and format instructions.

We must speak by the card, or equivocation will undo us.

William Shakespeare
(1564–1616)

23 April 1600

Dear Mr. Shakespeare:

Thank you for submitting your manuscript of <u>Julius Caesar</u> to the Folio Press. When the editorial board has read it, a decision regarding publication will be made. When we have decided, we will let you know quickly.

Sincerely,

Samuel Daniel

Samuel Daniel

1. Standard postcards are 5½ by 3½ inches.

2. Margins are ½ inch on the left and right.

3. The top and bottom margins are ½ inch (three line spaces). The bottom margin, of course, will be larger when the text is short.

4. Given these top and bottom margins, a postcard memo/letter requires that the correspondence end by line 18.

5. The first item on a postcard is the date. It begins 4 lines below the top edge, and about half way (2¾ inches) between the side edges.

6. The second item is the salutation: "Dear Ms. So-and-so." Notice that a colon is used. The salutation begins two lines below the date at the left-hand margin. The address is omitted.

7. After leaving one space, begin the text. Use block paragraphs. Allow one space between paragraphs.

8. The closing may include a "Sincerely" and the writer's name and signature. Sometimes, in order to leave a full ½-inch margin at the bottom, the "Sincerely," the signature, and special notations must be omitted. This leaves the typed name of the writer, which begins two spaces below the last line of text and aligns with the date.

SUMMARY

1. Complex memos convey several pieces of information or thread their way through delicate issues. Length is not a criterion for relative complexity or simplicity in memos.

2. Complex memos are among the most important writing done in business.

3. Most businesses have their own style of memo form; once printed on paper, these forms now reside in computers, ready to be used on demand.

4. When several people are to receive the same memo, a distribution list is placed beside "To" or at the bottom of the memo. A complex memo also contains writer's and typist's initials and enclosure and copy notations, as necessary.

5. Humor is a constant temptation for business writers. Humor should be indulged occasionally, as long as the writer attends to three caveats: humor should be gentle, it should be flattering to the reader, and it is usually ineffective if written by a group.

6. Memo reports convey more information than simple memos but less than formal reports. They also dispense with much prefatory material common to formal reports (title page, table of contents, abstracts) and major headings. They retain tables and figures.

7. Postcards are means of business communication that resemble memos but are sent outside the company.

8. Postcards must be brief and used primarily to acknowledge the receipt of orders, important letters, and other important material.

EXERCISES

1. *Good Memos.* Write a brief, clear paragraph describing the qualities of good memos.

2. *Re.* Look up *re* in a dictionary. Why is *re* fitting as a title for memos?

3. *Titles in memos.* Write an accurate, sufficiently detailed title for the following memo.

   TO: Smedley Fahrquart, Vice-President, Accounting

   FROM: Samantha Evans, Vice-President, Personnel

   DATE: 10 January 1992

   RE:

   Here are the memoranda you asked for regarding the Fahrquart Report. I think you will find the memo of 1 September 1991 informative.

4. *Titles in memos.* Write an accurate, sufficiently detailed title for the following memo.

   TO: Niccolò Machiavelli, Chancellor

   FROM: Signore Sfrfoza, Head, Council of Ten

   DATE: 10 January 1499

   RE:

As you have now returned from your visit with Cesare Borgia, please come tell what you discovered. Say, Friday morning about ten-ish?

5. *Titles in memos.* Write an accurate, sufficiently detailed title for the following memo.

   TO: Smedley Fahrquart, Vice-President, Accounting

   FROM: Samantha Evans, Vice-President, Personnel

   DATE: 10 January 1992

   RE:

When we last spoke, you said that you would get the Fahrquart Report to me by 1-9. I know something must have come up, but could you let me know when you could get it to me?

6. *Placing information in order of importance.* Rewrite the following memo, placing the most important information first. As always, edit for brevity, clarity, courtesy, and accuracy.

   TO: Q. Upp, Printing

   FROM: A. Frump, Sales

   DATE: 3 July 1992

RE: TYPOGRAPHICAL ERRORS

It has been brought to my attention by a number of our sales personnel that the promotional literature, which they are required to give to each and every customer they see during their road trips, and which you are responsible for printing, recently has been of a very poor quality with regard to spelling, most of which seems to be due to typographical errors. My sales personnel report that customers are beginning to think that we are not exactly a first-class company. This situation is beginning to affect sales. I am sending a copy of this memo to the CEO.

7. *Placing information in order of importance.* Rewrite the following memo, placing the most important information first. As always, edit for brevity, clarity, courtesy, and accuracy.

TO: V. Neck, Sales

FROM: P. Jay, Publicity

DATE: 22 August 1992

RE: PROPER ATTIRE

As you are aware, every year in September, our publicity department begins to prepare the Annual Report for our stockholders, important customers, and others whose positions affect us. There has been some concern expressed on the part of the management and board of the company that too many of our male sales personnel, many of whose photographs we feature in our Annual Reports, probably those who are not, at the time, on the road meeting customers, do not come to their assigned appointment with our photographer properly dressed. Some need haircuts, and others wear clothing that is inappropriate for such a way that the sales personnel appear to be properly professional. Neither do string ties. White shirts, while appropriate for work, do not photograph well. Blue dress shirts are better.

  Please inform all male sales personnel that they are to be clean-shaven; have well-trimmed hair; and wear light blue dress shirts, dark blue or grey suits, and conservative ties for their session with the photographer.

8. *Placing information in order of importance by repeating title in first sentence.* Rewrite the following memo. Begin the text with the subject that follows *Re*. The objects are, of course, to get to the point immediately, to convey information briefly and clearly.

TO: Gordo Swartz, Manager, Smartmart Supermart

FROM: Delgado Mertz, Marketing

DATE: 19 September 1992

RE: Dog Food Prices at El Mercaillo

When I went to the El Mercaillo Supermarket, our biggest competitor, to check on the prices of several grocery items, something I have been doing now for several years, I noticed that they have begun to sell a fairly popular brand that we do not carry. The interesting thing is that this brand, which used to sell at a price comparable our most popular brand, is now selling at $.08 an ounce less. Perhaps we should call our supplier and make sure they know about this or we should start stocking that brand, which is called Papa Perrito's Dog Nibblies.

9. *Positioning distribution lists.* What are the advantages and disadvantages to including a distribution list at the beginning of a memo? at the end?

10. *Separate distribution lists.* Many companies attach separate distribution lists to memos. Why is this not so good an idea as placing the list on the memos themselves?

CASE STUDY 1. EDITING BAD MEMOS

Your boss is the chief of security at your college. One morning he asks you to edit the following memo to all college faculty. You have one-half hour before beginning your rounds for the day. Edit the memo in one-half hour. Although your time is limited, the revisions necessary are extensive, requiring not only corrections in formatting and grammar, but also extensive cutting. So much cutting is required, in fact, that much of this must be rewritten completely in a simpler, clearer style. Much of the problem lies in a misguided attempt to imitate legal writing to cover their flanks. Avoid the legalese while retaining the argument of the memo.

DATE: August 12, 1993

TO: All Pine State College Faculty

FROM: Remington Colt, Chief of Police & Safety Services

SUBJ: "RIGHT TO KNOW" MATERIAL SAFETY DATA SHEETS

This is to advise you that we have on file at the Department of College Police and Safety Services copies of MSDS which pertain to chemical substances found in your workplace. Also on file are a list of products and their ingredients ("PSC Hazardous Substances") by building on our campus. The MSDS are available for you, the employee, to look at and/or to get a copy, "without permission or intervention from management or a supervisor." In other words you can look through information contained on any MSDS without permission or intervention.

As our office is not open on a 24 hour basis there is always an officer on duty which can be contacted by dialing extension 6202. If there is no answer then dial extension 6543 which is our emergency number. Our officers have been instructed to assist you on getting this information you request. If by chance the officer(s) is on a emergency situation they will so inform you and upon completion of emergency contact you and make available the information you request. If you request a copy, and a copy is not available at the given time, we will within 24 hours, see that a copy is made available to you.

The requests to observe and/or gain a copy can be made either orally or by written request on a form available through our department.

Please note that we will be providing a training program, for "Right to Know" to all employees as it becomes available from Central Administration. This program will be scheduled at different times so as to be available to all employees. Additional information and schedule will be forthcoming.

If you have question please feel free to contact me. Thank you.

CASE STUDY 2. IMPROVING MEMOS

Your boss, Mr. Smedley Fahrquart, recently announced at a meeting of all staff that the quality of the memos he is receiving "would drive a saint crazy." After the meeting, Fahrquart asks you to remain. During a (mostly) pleasant conversation, Fahrquart says this to you: "You know, your memos are far and away the best I've been getting. They're clear, concise, and no-bull. I want you to write a memo to all staff outlining the qualities of a *good* memo."

While flattered by Fahrquart's praise, you fear two things:

1. Although you think you write well, and so apparently does Fahrquart, you really don't know *precisely* why you write well. And you certainly don't know why your *memos* are so much better than other people's.

2. As one of the youngest members of the staff, you fear that any advice from you on writing will anger many of your colleagues and especially many of the older people.

Although you express these concerns to Fahrquart, he is unmoved. "Just write," he says.

Fortunately, you have recently seen the Mitchell article (pages 80–81), and you think you could put together a good memo on the subject of good memos. Write such a memo.

CASE STUDY 3. PERSUASIVE MEMO

As chair of the activities committee of the Student Government Association at a large urban university, part of your job is to justify expenses. Because so many students either go home on weekends or find things to do in the city, your job has become increasingly difficult. Write a memorandum to members of your committee asking them to think about ways to attract more students to on-campus activities. Mention that if attendance does not increase soon, then the activities budget is sure to be cut drastically. A meeting to discuss members' proposals will be held on September 24, next week. You want to persuade members that well thought-out ideas will make the meeting much more productive.

CASE STUDY 4. POLICY MEMO

When you arrive at work one morning, you discover that you need a tablet of paper. When you ask the secretary for one, she says, "Someone must be hoarding those things. We're all out, but we should get more next week. I've decided to keep them in my office and make people sign for them when they want one."
Choose one of the following possibilities and write a memo appropriate to that possibility.

a. As you are the secretary's boss, you agree with the secretary. Write a memo to all subordinates telling them of the change in policy. No longer will people be allowed simply to take tablets without signing for them.

b. You are a subordinate to the secretary's boss. As you have not been hoarding tablets, you believe this new policy is a waste of time. Write a memo to the boss, Ms. Skin Flint, asking that the policy be rescinded.

c. The secretary's boss is a colleague of yours, equal in corporate rank, who happens to control office supplies. Write a memo to Flint, asking that the policy be rescinded.

Case Study 5. The Bing Pro Postcard

Your company promoted sales on a set of golf clubs by giving a very good putter to everyone who sent in a sales slip. The golf clubs, Bing Pros, were wildly popular, in part because of the promotion. Demand for the putter, then, was so great that hundreds of people will not receive their putter within the eight weeks the company asked to be allowed for shipping. Until more putters are made, none can be shipped. Write a postcard that will be sent to 837 customers who must wait for an additional but undetermined time.

Challenge Exercise 1. Uses of Memos

Students enrolled in a college or university of any size receive copies of memos at least weekly. The memos come from the dean, the director of admissions, the director of student life, dormitory presidents, club secretaries, and the like. Collect some of these, reproduce them for your class, (removing the names and organizations, of course) and evaluate them in a class discussion.

Challenge Exercise 2. Complex Memos: The Reimbursement Memo

After working for your employer for three years, you decide that to advance more rapidly you need an MBA. These days, in fact, you have noticed that most employers, not just yours, seem to promote only those who have or are working on MBAs. You enroll this semester.

Your company very generously contributes toward an MBA degree for management employees who enroll in the program at the local university offering a very fine Masters in Business Administration. Keeping an eye on ROI (return on investment), the company reimburses 100 percent of the tuition for employees who receive As, 75 percent for those who receive Bs, but nothing for any grade lower than a B.

No one has complained about this rather generous benefit, but there is one problem. Because graduate credits are $275 and each course is three credits, students must spend $825 for each course they take.

While the company has paid cheerfully, it does not pay until grades for a semester course have been received. As students must pay for all courses, and the typical student enrolls for two 3-credit courses, the outlay is $1650 a semester. Books are usually about $75 a course. Twice a year, then, students must invest $1800.

Time drags. In the fall semester, for example, students enroll (and pay) in late August. The semester ends in December. Grades are not posted until January, a week before the spring semester begins. Consequently, students are not reimbursed for more than four months.

As most students have barely begun their careers, their salaries are not high. Given the costs of raising a family and paying for a house and car, this expense burdens most students significantly. Nine employees have found the expense too great and have stopped enrolling in courses.

Write a memo to Ms. Marjorie Podolsky, Director of Corporate Education, describing the problem and asking that a significant part of the cost of the courses be paid at the time of enrollment.

Some information that may or may not be useful for making the case follows. Of some 25 employees who have enrolled in 110 courses during the past five semesters, 24 have completed all courses for which they were enrolled. Of the 110 courses taken, grades of B or better were received in 87 of the courses. Federal labor laws prohibit employers from deducting money from salaries as punishment, but educational loans from the company to employees are possible.

Challenge Exercise 3. Postcards

Last month, your student government organization announced a membership meeting for next Thursday evening at 8 p.m. Because your budget does not permit sending letters, and because many students are commuters, you are asked to write a postcard to all new students. This postcard must mention the following things: what the meeting is for, why it is important for the reader to attend, what day, what time, where. Write the postcard in the proper form. This may require using a ruler and buying a blank postcard. You could practice getting it right also by cutting paper to size.

"THAT'S A RATHER SUDDEN

PULL UP, AIN'T IT, SAMMY?"

INQUIRED MR. WELLER.

"NOT A BIT ON IT," SAID

LETTERS

SAM; "SHE'LL VISH THERE

WOS MORE, AND

THAT'S THE GREAT

ART O' LETTER

WRITIN'."

CHARLES DICKENS

(1812-1870)

THE IMPORTANCE OF LETTERS

ABUSES OF LETTERS

THE FOUR COMMON LETTER STYLES

Block Style
Modified Block Style
Semi-Block Style
Simplified Style

THE DETAILED STRUCTURE OF BUSINESS LETTERS

Margins
Heading

Opening
Body
Closing
Following Pages Headings

SUMMARY

EXERCISES

Learning Objectives:

☐ Know the differences between letters and memos.

☐ Know the advantages of letters over conversations.

☐ Know six important uses for letters.

☐ Comprehend that accuracy is essential.

☐ Write formal letters.

☐ Know the five abuses of letters.

☐ See letters as formal, intimate, and permanent.

☐ Use caution when writing letters.

☐ Use four letter styles:
Block,
Modified block,
Semi-block,
Simplified.

☐ Know and use the four parts of business letters:
Heading,
Opening,
Body,
Closing.

☐ Know the structural details of formal business letters.

SPEAK SILVER,

REPLY GOLD.

(SWAHILI PROVERB)

LETTERS:  THEIR PURPOSES AND FORMATS

THE IMPORTANCE OF LETTERS

Business letters have the same uses as memos — that is, they provide a record, improve efficiency, direct, and inform. But because they go outside the company — to customers, clients, and other companies — business letters not only convey information, but also represent the company. Because a writer is less likely to know the readers of a letter than those of a memo, letters usually are more formal than memos. Potential buyers often know the company solely by the letterhead and the text of the letter. The letterhead may look good, but should the text of the letter be sloppy and badly written, the reader may assume that the company is sloppy and badly managed. Brevity, clarity, courtesy, and accuracy are always vital to the success of anything written in business. Because problems can arise from failures in communication between companies as well as within a company, letters, like memos, are important as records of what was said and decided. Write letters with great care.

Prior to the widespread use of telephones, letters conveyed nearly as much information outside the office as did conversations. That is why Ben Franklin demanded (and got) the only nationalized service into the U.S. Constitution; a uniform, subsidized postal service was good for business. Today, letters are neither the fastest nor the cheapest means of conveying information to other companies, cities, or countries. The telephone, telex, fax and other electronic methods are faster. Yet there are times that letters are useful. Here are some reasons why, and some instances in which, letters may be more useful than telephone calls, more useful even than talking face-to-face.

No arts; no letters; no society . . . and the life of man, solitary, poor, nasty, brutish, and short.

Thomas Hobbes (1588–1679)

THE ADVANTAGE OF ACCURACY.   Because the printed word can be altered, revised, and corrected before it is finally conveyed, letters are sometimes better than telephone calls. The spoken word, once uttered, is conveyed. Once a word is uttered, it cannot be retrieved; once the telephone receiver is cradled, the conversation, unless recorded, cannot be reviewed accurately. When accuracy is essential, then, letters are a superior method of conveying information.

THE ADVANTAGE OF HANDLING COMPLEXITY.   Complex information usually must be mulled over, considered again and again, and examined in great detail. Letters or other printed methods of conveying information are superior to oral means of communication because the printed page can be re-examined, whereas conversations cannot.

THE ADVANTAGE OF FORMALITY.   In these informal days, we tend to think of formality as inevitably stiff, unfriendly, and dull. That is not so. Such negative qualities result from the writer's being stiff, unfriendly, and dull, *not* from being formal. Formality is simply an attitude of courtesy and caution. When dealing with matters of weight, and especially with someone the writer does not know, infor-

Business letters confirm and formalize arrangements that are discussed in meetings or over the telephone.

mality is more likely than formality to offend, to keep the job from being completed. Letters provide an excellent medium for conveying information formally.

Because readers of letters usually are not as well known to writers as are readers of memos, letters usually are more formal than memos, at least in arrangement. That is, they use more formal modes of address, they use contractions more sparingly, and in general they use a less familiar tone than memos.

THE ADVANTAGE OF BREVITY.   When well thought out, a few written words may say as much as an hour's conversation. When this happens, less time is spent to gain far more understanding.

WHY LETTERS ARE WRITTEN.   Business people write letters because they need to convey a little information more often than a lot of information, or to ask a few questions rather than many. Letters, like memos, are a wonderful medium for doing this. And business people know it: every working day in the United States, people write 76 million letters.

ABUSES OF LETTERS

Letters are abused in the same ways that memos are. People sometimes write letters when they are covering their flanks unnecessarily; when talking would be better; when they are conveying rot, not information; when writing on the ladder; and when writing by committee. (Information on these abuses appears in Chapter 3.) In addition, however, writers may abuse letters when they treat letters as informally and publicly as they often treat memos.

Letters, because of their long history and the uses to which they have been put—love, hate, war, and peace—convey a sense of privacy. Consequently, it is disconcerting to readers to receive letters addressed to many people. Unlike some memos, letters rarely should include the names and addresses of several people to whom the same letter is addressed. It is, as the British say, bad form.

This sense of privacy regarding letters is so much a part of Western culture that even today, when many of the old particulars of moral behavior have fallen into disuse, the notion that one simply does not read other people's mail retains its power. Consequently, letters exhibit a paradox: they are formal, yet intimate. Violating these qualities constitutes a major abuse of letter writing.

Another way of saying all this is that memos often have many readers; letters often have one. Memos therefore have the force of a newspaper: everybody reads them. Letters usually convey information from one person to another. Usually, they are meant to be private conversations in which writers often are more open than in conversation or memos, saying things they would never say if they believed others would read the letters.

Having said this, and acknowledging that no ethical person ever reads someone else's private letters, it is well, nevertheless, to remember that words in letters are permanent. Courts routinely rule that private mail be opened, which means that someday private words could be trotted out before an unforgiving world. The rule then, even for letters, is *caution*.

THE FOUR COMMON LETTER STYLES

All business letters contain four parts—heading, opening, body, closing—which usually are arranged in one of four styles—block, modified block, semi-block, and simplified. The sections that follow demonstrate each of the styles as they display the parts of the letter. A detailed discussion of the letter parts begins on page 113.

BLOCK STYLE

The block style probably is the most common form of business letters because it is straightforward and easy to follow. In a block style, all

EXERCISE A: USES AND ABUSES OF LETTERS

Discuss in class the following questions:

1. In which situations should letters be written and talking avoided?
2. In which situations should letters not be written?

lines begin at the left margin; only lists, tables, figures, long quotations, and the like are indented. Paragraphs within the body of the letter are separated by a single line space.

Here is a block-style letter written on letterhead stationery.

Heading

GLOBAL PRODUCTIONS
GLOBE THEATRE
LONDON, ENGLAND

May 4, 1660

Opening

Mr. Guy Fawkes, Sales Manager
Words Unlimited
Parliament Houses, Basement
London, England

Dear Mr. Fawkes:

Body

That certainly is a revolutionary, if not explosive idea you have. And if Ben and Kit have said it works, then I am willing to give it a try. After all, nothing ventured, nothing gained. Such a word processor could teach the torches to burn bright, even get the Romans to lend me their ears.

Still and all, it's caviar to the general, I am sure that each boy is extraordinary, but I would need a thousand of them to spruce up my poor plays. As it is, I can barely afford one boy to copy my words, and I've already got one—a lad named Webster—and he's trouble enough. Because of him, I cannot afford to get my bed out of hock, but he's a good lad, and I am enclosing a sample of his work to see if it is good enough so that you may hire him.

Annual Expenses	=	£17 and 2 shillings
Annual Income	=	£17 and 1 shilling
Result	=	Misery.

Isn't that wonderful, Mr. Fawkes?

Closing

Sincerely,

William Shakespeare

William Shakespeare

WS/jw
encl.
bc: Elizabeth, Regina

P.S. Any chance of borrowing a good worker for two weeks to see whether it works?

Here is an example of a block-style letter on non-letterhead stationery.

```
Industrial Drive
Basking Ridge, NJ 07920
7 December 1777



General George Washington,
Commander-in-Chief
Revolutionary Army
On the Delaware 93210

Dear General:

We agree that, in order to defeat the Hessians, you
and your army need boats to cross to their camp.

We have checked many many supply, sales, and rental
shops for the kind of boat you asked us to find for
you. I put four of my best people on this job. They
have worked very hard.

While we have done our best, we have been unable to
find anyone who will sell, lease, or rent any boats
to you. People naturally hesitate to rent, even sell
(because of warranties) boats that in the past have
been returned with bullet holes through them. Many,
you must agree, have not been returned at all. The
money is not very good either. There is even a say-
ing going around: "It's not worth a Continental." I
am sorry, but we cannot rent you boats.

We do have party boats available, but these are
brightly painted, stick high out of the water, and
are hard to steer. Some even have stickers reading
"I'd rather be fishin'" on them. Should, for some
odd reason, these be satisfactory, let us know.

Sincerely,

Chris Craft
Chris Craft
```

MODIFIED BLOCK STYLE

In the modified block style, the date and closing begin in the middle of the line. If the stationery contains a printed letterhead, the date is centered under the letterhead. All other lines begin at the left margin.

Here is an example of a modified block letter on letterhead stationery.

Heading

FIRST NATIONAL BANK OF AVON
STRATFORD-UPON-AVON
STRATFORD, ENGLAND

March 5, 1600

Opening

Mr. William Shakespeare
Globe Theatre
Londontowne

Dear Will:

Body

I saw your new play, *Hamlet, A Prince of Denmark* the other day, having a few hours' leisure during business in town. Banking is slow these days, so I had time to look in and see what Ol' Will was doing. I really liked the play, except, perhaps, the ghost. I mean, who believes in ghosts any more, Will?

In 1600? Still, you've come a long way from *Romeo and Juliet* and that other pretty, but youthful and lightweight stuff of your salad days. The folks back home in Stratford are pulling for you. All, that is, except the old curmudgeon, Jeremiah Fahrquart. He still has strange ideas that we shouldn't be talking about ''to be or not to be'' (that speech, by the way, is a little long for one contemplating suicide. One could grow very old just reciting it). But, heck, it's all true, and some of it is even funny. Keep up the good work.

Your wife, Anne, instructed me to tell you that things are going all right at home. Judith is turning into quite a young lady, and baby Hamnet is growing fast. She did wonder when the joiner will finish the repairs to your bed. She's made do with the second-best bed for six months now, and she says it's uncomfortable. She says you are to be home before Christmas—and bring the bed with you.

Sometimes it's embarrassing to carry her news, Will, but she also asked me when you were going to look into buying that house on the corner of Main Street? The old house, she says, is getting crowded. Anyway, Will, I know she's a bit of a nag, but she hath a way about her.

Sincerely,

Al Schwartz, Esq.

Al Schwartz, Esq.

Closing

Here is an example of the modified block style used without a letterhead.

```
                                      Industrial Drive
                                      Tonto, NJ 17654


                                      7 December 1777



          General George Washington,
          Commander-in-Chief
          Revolutionary Army
          On the Delaware 93210

          Dear General:

          We agree that, in order to defeat the Hessians, you and
          your army need boats to cross to their camp. We have
          checked many many supply, sales, and rental shops for
          the kind of boat you asked us to find for you. I put
          four good people on this job. They have worked very
          hard. While we have done our best, we have been unable
          to find anyone who will sell, lease, or rent any boats
          to you.

          People naturally hesitate to rent, even sell (because of
          warranties) boats that in the past have been returned
          with bullet holes through them. Many, you must agree,
          have not been returned at all. The money you offer is
          not very good either. There is even a saying going
          around: "It's not worth a Continental." I am sorry but
          we cannot let you have any boats.

          We do have party boats available, but these are brightly
          painted, stick high out of the water, and are hard to
          steer. Some even have stickers reading "I'd rather be
          fishin'" on them. Should, for some odd reason, these be
          satisfactory, let us know.

                                      Sincerely,

                                      Chris Craft
                                      Chris Craft
```

SEMI-BLOCK STYLE

The semi-block style is the traditional form and so is rarely used today. Each of the modern block forms developed from it, and many personal letters still use it. The first line of each paragraph is indented five spaces, and no space is added between paragraphs. More conservative than the other three, the semi-block form presents a more visually balanced page. The date and the closing begin to the right of center.

Heading

GLOBAL PRODUCTIONS
GLOBE THEATRE
LONDON, ENGLAND

March 15, 1600

Opening

Mr. Allen Schwartz, Esq.
45 Main Street
Stratford-upon-Avon

Dear Al:

Body

It was good to hear from you and to know that you like my little *Hamlet*. It's a trifle I wrote during a fortnight in February. I don't spend much time on my plays ever since Anne started the rumor that Sir Francis Bacon wrote my stuff. I think she is angry that I never write to her. Anyway, I earn more money acting than I do writing, so I'll probably give up the latter for good very soon. But then again, maybe not. Writing does pay my tab at the pubs.

It's strange that Ben Jonson says that, while I write well, I ought to edit more. Because I get paid by the word, and because Ben hasn't stood a meal for me or anyone else in a year or more, I wouldn't think he would bite the hand that pays for his sack. He may have much Latin and more Greek, but he surely never seems to have any money.

Tell Anne I'll be home for Christmas to see the children, but that I can't bring the bed with me. I can't afford to pay the joiner. So, she'll have to make do with second best. Next time you come to town, let's do lunch. We'll go to the Boar's Head, where you'll hear wondrous tales of Old Kit Marlowe. And you can tell me how the old gang at home is doing.

Closing

Sincerely,

Will Shakespeare

P.S.: There is a tide in the affairs of men, and I sometimes wish Fahrquart would get caught in the ebbing of it.

EXERCISE B: CHOOSING AN APPROPRIATE LETTER STYLE

Discuss in class the following situation: You are applying for a summer job in a bank in your hometown. Make arguments for and against using the semi-block style for your application letter.

SIMPLIFIED STYLE

In the simplified style, every line begins at the left margin, the salutation in the heading is replaced by a subject line, and the closing omits the complimentary close. The subject line can be used when the writer does not know the name of the reader or when addressing an organization employing both men and women. The simplified form is common perhaps because it is easily typed on a typewriter or word processor and because the tone can range from formal to breezy. Direct-mail sales letters frequently use this style, as shown in the example that follows.

Heading

```
EXPLOSIVE FAWKES
ROOM 1
PARLIAMENT HOUSE
LONDON


April 30, 1600
```

Opening

```
Mr. William Shakespeare
Globe Theatre
Londontowne

WANNA STEP UP PRODUCTION?

Are you the kind of playwright who just can't get
all his thoughts down on paper? Are you always
thinking of the next line while writing a line, and
then when you get to it you can't remember what you
wanted to say? If you do, then you may want to con-
sider our new WS1588 WORD PROCESSOR. What is a
WS1588 WORD PROCESSOR?
```

Body

```
It's boys. Boys from the farm, driven to the cities
by their landlords who now prefer sheep to vegeta-
bles. The same kind of English lads who whipped the
Armada only twelve years ago. And that's why we
called our word processor the 1588. Because, like
you, we're proud of our boys. And we're proud of En-
gland. WORDS UNLIMITED trains these boys to write.
They are not educated, so they have nothing to write
about, but they do know how to write. And, for a
limited time only we can offer you half a dozen for
two (that's right, TWO) shillings a month each to
write down everything you say. You never need miss
a thought again, never lose a line, never, if
you choose, actually write a word again!!! Isn't
that wonderful, MR. SHAKESPEARE? For just twelve
```

Mr. William Shakespeare   2   1-30-1600

shillings a month, you can simultaneously solve all
your writing problems, and help reduce your country's unemployment rate.

MR. JONSON and MR. MARLOWE (God rest his soul) have
said that ALL OUR CLAIMS ARE TRUE!!! MR. JONSON,
moreover, says that it has solved his problems with
writer's block. Whenever that happens, he says, he
instructs the boys to write whatever comes into
their heads. This way, MR. JONSON says HE HAS NOT
MISSED A DEADLINE IN OVER THREE YEARS!!! And he attributes all the success he is about to have in the
theatre to the WS1588 WORD PROCESSOR!!!

We think so, and we know you will agree once you've
tried the WS1588 WORD PROCESSOR on our exclusive,
money-back, six week, free-trial offer. AND if you
accept this once-in-a-lifetime offer within two
weeks, we will also offer FREE QUILLS, INK, and
PAPER!!

Isn't that wonderful, MR. SHAKESPEARE?

Guy Fawkes

GUY FAWKES, Sales Manager

P.S.: Act now, and we shall send to you, absolutely
free, a complimentary box of FAWKES'S FIREWORKS,
just chock full of noisy, exciting explosives for
your celebratory holidays!!!

Closing

....
EXERCISE C: CHOOSING THE SIMPLIFIED STYLE

Discuss in class the following situations:

1. Describe a situation in which the simplified style would be effective.
2. Describe a situation in which the simplified style would not be effective.

THE DETAILED STRUCTURE OF BUSINESS LETTERS

MARGINS

TOP MARGIN.   The top margin depends on the type of stationery being used. Because letterhead stationery has the top margin already determined, the first typed line, the date, is placed three lines below the letterhead. On blank stationery, the return address is the first part of the letter typed on the page. The top margin usually begins 1 inch (6 lines) below the top edge of the paper. If the letter is short, the top margin can be greater, or the date can be placed as much as two inches from the top of the page, to help balance the typed lines on the page.

SIDE MARGINS.   Side margins for letters are 1¼ inches on standard 8½-inch-wide paper. If the stationery is narrower (government paper, for example, is only 8 inches wide), the side margins should be set at 1 inch.

BOTTOM MARGIN.   The bottom margin must be at least 1 inch (6 lines). If a letter is so long that it needs to be continued on a second page, then the bottom margin of the first page may be as many as 2 inches (12 lines).

HEADINGS

Headings always contain two parts — the letterhead or return address and the date — and they often contain two additional parts — confidential and reference notations.

LETTERHEAD.   Although most writers use their companies' stationery (printed forms with typeset letters), some who use computers may create their own letterheads. Letterheads contain the following parts: company name; street address or post office box number; and city, state, and ZIP code. Letterheads *sometimes* contain a telephone number, fax number, or telex number. Here is an example of a letterhead in modified or semi-block style — that is, each line is centered.

FAHRQUART, INCORPORATED
1 Letterhead Avenue
Philadelphia, PA 14234
(215) 345–6789
Telex: 123456

RETURN ADDRESS.   If the letter is from an individual, then the return address should appear at the top of the page, as shown on page 115.

DATE.   Placement of the date is discussed in the "top margin" section. Always spell out the month — never write "12-5-92" — and two orders are acceptable: 5 December 1992 or December 5, 1992.

CONFIDENTIAL NOTATIONS.   When a letter is intended to be confidential, write "<u>Confidential</u>" at the left margin on the second line after the date. Be sure to underline it. Here is an example.

FAHRQUART, INCORPORATED
1 Letterhead Avenue
Philadelphia, PA 14234

13 May 1991

<u>Confidential</u>

REFERENCE NOTATIONS.   Reference notations are convenient ways for letters to refer to other documents that bear on the letters. Examples abound in letters regarding everything from bridge building to insurance claims. Suppose that a company, which subcontracted to paint a bridge that your company is building, writes regarding the number of coats of paint to be applied. Your letter may make the job easier by including a reference notation specifying the number of the contract that applies to the number of coats required. Or perhaps you are writing to someone who holds an insurance policy with your company, Everest Life and Casualty. In that letter, the insured asks whether she can buy a maternity policy after she has become pregnant. Your reply may include a reference notation specifying the policy number and the section that tells her that she cannot get after-the-act coverage.

Reference notations begin on the second line after the date or after any other notation following the date. Use "Replying to" when the letter is replying to a specific document. This avoids the wordy and old-fashioned "In re yours of the 29th instance, etc." Use "Refer to" when the letter asks the reader to see a specific document. Use "In reply to" when the letter requests the reader to respond by citing a specific document, usually the file number of that document (companies often give numbers to all correspondence).

2 Letterhead Avenue
Aardvark, Ohio 17893

13 March 1991

<u>Confidential</u>

Referring to Policy #GN32571

Mr. Smedley Fahrquart, Resource Manager
The Smedley Company
1 Industrial Drive
Tonto, NM 87654

OPENING

INSIDE ADDRESS.   Letter openings comprise the inside address and the salutation, attention, or subject line. Beginning five lines below the date or confidential notation, or two lines below a reference notation, the first line of the inside address contains the name and, if applicable, the title of the addressee. The second line contains the company name, if applicable. The third line contains the street or post office box of the addressee. Remember that streets, avenues, and so forth are spelled fully. The last line of the inside address contains the city, state, and ZIP code. If the company contains departments or divisions, add the addressee's department above the company name.

Ms. Elizabeth Bordon, Vice-President
Quality Testing Division
Sharp Axe Company
15 Wilkinson Avenue
Razoredge, PA 17453

POSTAL ABBREVIATIONS.   Formal social letters should spell out the names of states, territories, and the like. Less formal and routine business letters may use abbreviations for states but not for cities. Abbreviations of a country's name may be used for formal letters: "U.K." for United Kingdom, and so on. Remember to put "U.S.A." below the return address.

In addresses on envelopes (and consequently on letters as well), the United States Postal Service recommends that writers use the two-letter symbols for states, territories, and protectorates, shown in the second column of the list below. In the body of the correspondence, writers should either spell out or use the traditional abbreviations, as shown in the third column.

	STATE ABBREVIATIONS	
	POSTAL	TRADITIONAL
Alabama	AL	Ala.
Alaska	AK	—
Arizona	AZ	Ariz.
Arkansas	AR	Ark.
California	CA	Calif.
Colorado	CO	Colo.
Connecticut	CT	Conn.
Delaware	DE	Del.
District of Columbia	DC	D.C.
Florida	FL	Fla.
Georgia	GA	Ga.
Guam	GU	—
Hawaii	HI	—
Idaho	ID	—
Illinois	IL	Ill.
Indiana	IN	Ind.
Iowa	IA	—
Kansas	KS	Kans.
Kentucky	KY	Ky.
Louisiana	LA	La.
Maine	ME	Me.
Maryland	MD	Md.
Massachusetts	MA	Mass.
Michigan	MI	Mich.
Minnesota	MN	Minn.

	STATE ABBREVIATIONS	
	POSTAL	**TRADITIONAL**
Mississippi	MS	Miss.
Missouri	MO	Mo.
Montana	MT	Mont.
Nebraska	NE	Nebr.
Nevada	NV	Nev.
New Hampshire	NH	N.H.
New Jersey	NJ	N.J.
New Mexico	NM	N. Mex.
New York	NY	N.Y.
North Carolina	NC	N.C.
North Dakota	ND	N. Dak.
Ohio	OH	—
Oklahoma	OK	Okla.
Oregon	OR	Oreg.
Pennsylvania	PA	Pa.
Puerto Rico	PR	P.R.
Rhode Island	RI	R.I.
South Carolina	SC	S.C.
South Dakota	SD	S. Dak.
Tennessee	TN	Tenn.
Texas	TX	Tex.
Utah	UT	—
Vermont	VT	Vt.
Virgin Islands, The	VI	V.I.
Virginia	VA	Va.
Washington	WA	Wash.
West Virginia	WV	W. Va.
Wisconsin	WI	Wis.
Wyoming	WY	Wyo.

TWO OR MORE ADDRESSES.   It is common for two people to receive the same business letter. When they work for the same company, both names can be placed, one below the other, in the inside address.

    Ms. Samantha Evans
    Mr. Smedley Fahrquart
    Fahrquart Holding Company
    2 Industrial Drive
    Tonto, New Mexico 87654

SALUTATION.   The salutation, which is the formal greeting from the writer to the addressee, begins on the left margin, two spaces below the last line of the inside address. It comprises the word "Dear," followed by the addressee's name. If a particular name is unknown, write to the company using a subject line. For a more polite and formal style, write "Dear Ladies and Gentlemen" or "To Whom It May Concern." Do not write "Dear XYZ Company" or "Dear Accounting Department," because this is as personal as "Dear Occupant," although to many impersonality is less impious than being identified by gender.

While open punctuation—that is, no punctuation after the salutation and the complimentary close—is on the rise, it is always proper to place a colon after a formal salutation; commas are for informal letters to family or friends. Write "Dear Ms. Terr:."

COURTESY TITLES.   Because common titles are becoming confusing to many, here they are with their meanings and uses.

Mr.	Commonly used for all males
Mrs.	Used for married females wishing to be acknowledged as married
Miss	Used for unmarried females wishing to be acknowledged as unmarried
Ms.	Used for females who do not wish to be addressed according to their marital status
Messrs.	Used for more than one male
Mesdames	Used for more than one married female
Misses	Used for more than one unmarried female
Mss.	Used for more than one female regardless of marital status

Here are several forms of address to be used under several conditions.

1. When preferences are known.
   Dear Mr. Booper:
   Dear Mrs. Cooper:
   Dear Miss Dooper:
   Dear Ms. Fooper:

2. When preferences are unknown.
   Dear Mr. Booper:
   Dear Ms. Cooper:
   Dear Helga Dooper:

3. When the addressees are two or more men.
   Gentlemen:
   Dear Mr. Cooper and Mr. Dooper:
   Dear Messrs. Cooper and Dooper:

4. When the addressees are two or more women.
   Ladies:
   Dear Mrs. Booper and Ms. Cooper:
   Dear Mesdames Booper and Dooper:
   Dear Mss. Cooper and Fooper:

More on courtesy titles appears in the discussion of the signature, page 121.

ATTENTION LINE.   Attention lines are useful in letters when the inside address contains neither the name of the addressee nor a department of the company. When a letter is addressed more to a company or department than to an individual, an attention line sometimes replaces the standard salutation. Or if the writer does not know the name of the person who should receive the letter but does know the position held by that person, the attention line can address the job title.

The attention line usually is placed two lines below the inside address. Some company styles capitalize the entire line.

Fahrquart Holding Company
2 Industrial Drive
Tonto, NM 87654

Attention: Ms. Connie Chu

OR

Fahrquart Holding Company
2 Industrial Drive
Tonto, NM 87654

ATTENTION: ACCOUNTING DEPARTMENT

OR

Fahrquart Holding Company
2 Industrial Drive
Tonto, NM 87654

ATTENTION: DIRECTOR OF PERSONNEL

Remember that the name is not included in the inside address.

BODY

SUBJECT LINE.   Similar to the *RE* in memos, the subject line summarizes the letter and helps the reader refer to and file it quickly. Place the subject line two spaces below the salutation, either at the left margin or centered, depending on the style of the letter. The subject may be typed either in all capital letters or with an initial capital letter followed by small letters and underlined. The body of the letter follows two spaces below the subject line.

The Fahrquart Company
Personnel Department
2478 Calle Buena Vista
Basura, WY 69782

Attention: Ms. Connie Chu

Re: <u>The Fahrquart Report</u>

TEXT.   The text is the meat of the letter, and the paragraphs are distinguished either by having a line space separating them (as in the block, modified-block, and simplified styles) or by indenting the first line of each paragraph and having no extra space between them (as in the semi-block style).

Too many people end a paragraph when the mood strikes them or when the one they are writing gets too long. In business, as elsewhere, paragraphs contain information on one topic. If the topic is sufficiently large, encompassing several subtopics, then each subtopic should be given a paragraph.

CLOSING

COMPLIMENTARY CLOSE.   The complimentary close usually appears two lines below the last line of text, although it may be as many as four lines below the text to stretch out a short letter. The complimentary close is almost always followed by a comma and only the first word is capitalized: "Very truly yours." Should the complimentary close be a sentence, it would be followed by a period or some other end punctuation ("See you in San Diego." "See you in San Diego?"). These full-sentence comments usually occur only in informal letters.

The history of complimentary closings is one of increasing brevity. Centuries ago, when letters were the only means of conducting business with someone who lived far away, and when people took time to be polite even at the expense of efficiency, they commonly closed a letter as follows:

> And please be so kind as to believe me, Sir, when I say that I hold you ever in my highest regard and that I remain, as always, your most humble and obedient servant,
>
> Obadiah Fahrquart

Today, of course, this would be too much; "Sincerely" is usually sufficient, but any of these is acceptable:

Cordially,	Cordially yours,	Very cordially yours,
Sincerely,	Sincerely yours,	Very sincerely yours,
Respectfully,	Respectfully yours,	Very respectfully yours,
Yours truly,	Very truly yours,	

COMPANY SIGNATURE.   Occasionally, to emphasize that a letter reflects a company's views, the company signs the letter, not an individual. Called a company signature, it is typed in capital letters, two spaces below the complimentary close, and the first letter begins on the same column as the first letter of the complimentary close.

Sincerely,

WIDGITCOGS, INCORPORATED

SIGNATURE.   The signature must be written in ink and appear between the complimentary close and the typed name. It need not be legible, but if no typed name appears, then courtesy demands that the signature be legible.

COURTESY TITLES IN CLOSINGS.   In general, people need not sign their names using courtesy titles—*Mr., Ms., Miss, Mrs.* There are several exceptions. For example, when a person's first name could represent either sex—such as Lynn, Adrian, Sam (Samuel and Samantha)—writers may want to use a courtesy title out of respect for readers and potential respondents. A courtesy title may also be necessary if the writer goes by initials instead of a first name: J. P. Morgan, for example, is the name of an American captain of industry (man) and a once-popular American singer (woman). Women who prefer to be addressed by a particular courtesy title may specify so in the signature:

(Ms.) Jane C. Smith, (Miss) Jane C. Smith, or (Mrs.) Jane C. Smith.

TYPED NAME.   The typed name usually appears four lines below the complimentary close, although for considerations of space it can be as few as two lines or as many as six lines.

Sincerely,

Jane C. Smith

Jane C. Smith

TITLE AFTER TYPED NAME.   The writer's business title belongs on the line below the typed name. If the letterhead or return address does not indicate the writer's department, then add this information on an additional line:

Sincerely,

Smedley Fahrquart

Smedley Fahrquart
Vice-President
Specialty Widgitcog Division

If applicable, insert the academic degree or degrees on the same line as the typed name, separated from the name by a comma.

Sincerely,

Samantha Evans

Samantha Evans, Ph.D.
Director of Research

REFERENCE INITIALS.   Reference initials tell who typed the letter. Because the writer usually signs the letter, the writer's initials need not appear, but if the company style requires them, the initials of the writer appear first, followed by those of the typist. Type the writer's initials in capital letters and the typist's in capital or small letters. Separate the initials with a slash, or a colon, or a space: ABC/def, ABC:DEF, or ABC def. Reference initials appear at the left margin and two lines below the typed name and title.

Enclosures. Typed two lines below the reference initials, "Enclosures" (or "Encls.") tells the reader that information separate from the letter is enclosed in the envelope with the letter. Be sure to refer to these enclosures in the text of the letter and indicate their presence again by writing "Enclosure." Should two enclosures be included, write "Enclosures 2." Sometimes enclosures may be listed as in the example following the discussion of copies.

Mailing Instructions. When letters are not sent by first-class mail, special mailing instructions may be required. These may be such methods as registered mail, certified mail, or even private carriers like Federal Express or UPS. Such instructions are given immediately after enclosure notations.

Copies. This notation on the original letter informs readers, writers, and the company of all who received copies. It is typed one or two lines below the enclosures, at the left margin, and is followed by a colon or a space and the name of the recipient.The abbreviation "cc" means "carbon copy" or "copies." Although most are now photocopies, "cc" remains common. The use of "pc," meaning "photocopy" or "photocopies," is becoming common. The notation "bc," which means "blind copy," is sometimes used to tell the typist to send a copy to someone (e.g., "bc: Smedley Fahrquart") and include the notation on the copy for the files, but to omit the notation on the letter to the addressee. This is a way of sending copies blind — that is, without informing the addressee but of noting the additional recipient in the file copy.

typed name	A. Onassis
reference initials	AO/jo
enclosure	Enclosures:
	1. *Report on Dispersing Old Machinery* (16pp.).
	2. *Report on Buying New Machinery* (27pp.).
mailing instructions	Send by Federal Express
copies	pc: Samantha Evans

Postscript. About 350 years ago, Sir Francis Bacon complained about the common practice of using postscripts to convey essential information: "When he wrote a letter, he would put that which was most material in the post-script, as if it had been a by-matter." The problem, then, is at least three and a half centuries old.

Type the postscript two lines below the copy instructions and have it conform to the block or letter style of the letter. P.S. is an abbreviation of "post script" ("after the letter," or "Oh, by the way"), and P.P.S., used rarely, simply refers to a second and unrelated post script: "post-post script."

Do not use postscripts to convey essential information unless their appearing as afterthoughts is desirable. In justifying a request, for example, a writer may state several reasons in the text of the letter but may want to add additional motivation that is not necessarily a logical justification in a post script. Consequently, the motivation appears as an afterthought, although it really is a major justification. Remember that the last sentence read in a letter may be the most memorable sentence in the letter, as in these examples from Chris Craft's letter to George Washington.

P.S. Should "we" win this rebellion, I would hope you may look upon me as one who helped all he could.

P.P.S. I hear you are having a little trouble with your teeth; you might want to check with my brother, the barber, in Hackensack. He'll make you an excellent set, and cheap!

FOLLOWING PAGES HEADINGS

Should the sheets of a multipage letter become separated, headings would identify what letters the pages belong to and in what order they should be arranged. The heading on each successive page begins six lines from the top edge. Use only blank stationery for additional pages; never use letterhead stationery. The heading should indicate the recipient's name, the page number, and the date of the letter, and the information can be either spaced evenly across one line or stacked in three lines at the left margin. Word processors can be programmed to do this automatically. Here is an example of a following page heading in both styles.

Smedley Fahrquart   2   1-2-92

OR

Smedley Fahrquart
page 2
1-2-92

The text of the letter then continues three lines below the following page heading.

Smedley Fahrquart
page 2
1-2-92

the end of the fiscal year should show a vastly improved profitability for our manufacturing section.

Never continue to another page unless at least two lines of text remain. If only one line remains, either edit the first page for brevity so that the additonal page is not needed or—and this is the less attractive alternative—add a sufficient number of lines of text to allow for the additional page.

SUMMARY

1. Letters have the same uses as memos: they provide a record, improve efficiency, direct, and inform.

2. Unlike memos, letters go outside the company, represent the company, use a formal style, and work for the company.

3. Although oral media—telephone calls, conversations, speeches—are important, letters are more accurate, more accurately deal with complexity, and provide a formal method of conveying information.

4. Letters have several advantages over memos or oral communication: they are more accurate, more complex, more formal, and briefer.

5. Letters are abused in the same five ways as memos: writers misuse them to cover their flanks unnecessarily; to write letters when talking would be better; to write rot, not information; to write on the ladder; and to write by committee. Because letters are *private*, writers tend to be more open in letters than in such public utterances as speeches and memos.

6. Writers should be cautious about saying anything that they might not want repeated.

7. The four most common letter styles are block, modified block, semi-block, and simplified.

8. All business letters have four parts: heading, opening, body, and closing.

9. Headings always contain two parts: letterhead (or return address) and the date. There are two kinds of return addresses: typed letterhead and typed address. Two acceptable methods of writing dates are "5 December 1992" and "December 5, 1992."

10. Headings often contain two other parts: confidential notations and reference notations.

11. Openings always contain an inside address.

12. The closing may contain the following parts: complimentary close, company signature, signature, typed name, reference initials, enclosure notations, mailing instructions, copy instructions, and postscripts.

EXERCISES

1. *Letters as representatives of the company*. What does the word *representative* mean? Begin by checking a dictionary. How does it apply specifically in the statement that letters represent the company?

2. *Letters and the record*. Why are letters better legal documents than are oral contracts of memories of conversations? List three reasons and be prepared to discuss them in class.

3. *Letters and formality*. Why do letters tend to be more formal than memos? List three reasons and be prepared to discuss them in class.

4. *Uses for letters and memos*. Compare the uses of letters and memos. In what situations are they similar? In what situations are they different? Be prepared to discuss in class.

5. *Use of print for complex information*. List the reasons that complex information usually is conveyed better by print than by mouth. Be prepared to discuss in class.

6. *Use of oral exchange for complex information*. Why is complex information not always better conveyed by print than by mouth? Give an example of a situation in which conveying complex information orally is

better than conveying it by letter or memo. Be prepared to discuss in class.

7. *Abuses of letters*. The following list includes information that may be included in a private letter to the CEO of Widgitcog Industries, but not in memos. Identify which you think could be placed in memos that anyone may read and which you think should be included in the letter only.

   a. salaries of all managers

   b. lay-offs for next quarter

   c. design flaws in new engine

   d. next week's cafeteria menu

   e. rise in orders for next quarter

   f. fall in orders for next quarter

   Be prepared to discuss in class.

8. *Abuses of letters*. Remembering that letters are records, which of the items in the list for Exercise 7 do you believe should not be either in the memos or in the letters? That is, they should not appear in print at all. Be prepared to discuss in class.

9. *Parts and shapes of letters: semi-block, block, or simplified*. Using the same information as in Exercise 7,

write a letter in the Semi-Block, Block, or Simplified Style. Justify your decision by listing the advantages of your choice. That is, why do you think it is a better style for the letter you've written than the other styles. Be prepared to discuss in class.

10. *Parts and shapes of letters: naming the parts.* Write a short letter to a friend, but include *all* the parts of a formal business letter. Label those parts.

CASE STUDY 1: LETTER STYLE

Ms. Samantha Evans has just been hired as the new CEO (Chief Executive Officer) of Widgitcog Industries, Inc. You are Assistant Vice-President for Corporate and Public Relations. At lunch, during Evans's first week on the job, she mentions to you the following: "You know, I've been looking at various letters for several days, and there's something that bothers me. It seems to me that the style we use for our letters is too old-fashioned. Would you study some of the more modern forms of letter styles and recommend one for the standard to be used by this company?" After looking over numerous forms, you settle on the simplified style. Write a letter to Evans recommending the simplified style. Naturally, you must say why you think it is best, and, naturally, you should write it in the simplified style.

CASE STUDY 2: WRITING BY COMMITTEE

You are the Vice-President for Research at Fahrquart Industries, a company that makes precision widgitcogs for many industries, including excavating equipment, shipbuilding, and fast-food milkshake machines. The engineering group of one of your suppliers of bearings, Round Ball, Inc., is top-notch, filled with very bright and hard-working Ph.D.s in mechanical and electrical engineering. There is one problem, however. The letters you receive from this group seem to be written by committee. When they arrive on your desk, they are all but unreadable, not because they are ungrammatical, but rather because they are so disorganized.

Upon checking with several of these people, you realize that the letters, indeed, are written by committee. This must stop. Write a letter to Ms. Chris Stoufer, president and CEO of Round Ball, Inc., detailing the problems involved with letters by committee. See Chapter 3.

CASE STUDY 3: WRITING ON THE LADDER

Repeat the exercise for Case Study 2, but this time detail the problems involved with letters written on the ladder. See Chapter 3.

CHALLENGE EXERCISE 1: PARTS AND SHAPES OF LETTERS: MODIFIED BLOCK

While returning from a recent business trip, your boss composed a letter on note paper. Although it is a jumble, it contains sufficient information from which to make a proper letter. The next day, when the boss arrives at the office, the secretary is not there. Because the letter must go out this morning, the boss looks around, and, because it is your unlucky day, sees you. Using the modified block style, organize the following jumble into a well-written letter.

TO: Ms. (I think she's married, but I'm not sure) Una Versity. She works for Old State University, my alma mater. The address is Route 1, Master's Road, Baccalaureate, Tennessee 45637. She works for the Office of Endowments in the Lucre Building. Here we are at Fahrquart Industries, at 1111 Widgitcog Lane, in Geargrind, Michigan (29375), and there she is down there. How'm I to decide anything about endowing a chair in Gear Technology from a distance of several hundred miles? Anyway, here's what I want written.

"It was a pleasure to hear from Old State again, after so many years. You may be assured that I am, indeed, interested in endowing a chair. But we *must get together!* I want to endow the chair in a specific field, I need to know how much it will cost, whether it will be in my mother's name, and a lot of other stuff. Let me know when you can get up here to talk about this. Sincerely,

Smedley T. Fahrquart, CEO, etc."

CHALLENGE EXERCISE 2: TO WRITE OR NOT TO WRITE

An architectural company has been contracted by your firm to design a new office building. Although few problems have occurred, you get a telephone call one day from the company's chief architect, Lloyd Wright, during which he asks you about some specifications for the computer center. Those specifications are lying on your desk, and only a quick glance at them tells you that they are not as clear as they might be. Having worked closely with the architects, however, you have those specifications in your head.

The question is this: do you provide those specs over the telephone or do you tell Mr. Wright that you will send them in a letter (or telex)? The considerations involve weighing the advantages and disadvantages of each possibility. Decide which is best and write a short memo to yourself (and your instructor) justifying your decision.

MONEY AND GOODWILL: THE TWO MAIN GOALS OF LETTERS

Money
Goodwill
Preserving Money and Goodwill

PLEASANT AND ROUTINE LETTERS

Requesting and Granting Credit
Placing and Acknowledging Orders
Making and Responding Favorably
   to Inquiries
Responding Favorably to
   Complaints

UNPLEASANT LETTERS

Denying Credit
Saying No to Orders
Saying No to Inquiries
Writing Letters of Complaint
Saying No to Complaint Letters

SUMMARY

EXERCISES

Learning Objectives:

☐ Understand that all letters generate
   money or goodwill, or both.

☐ Write pleasant and routine letters,
   such as
      Letters granting credit,
      Letters ordering materials,
      Letters of inquiry, and
      Favorable responses to letters of
         complaint.

☐ Write unpleasant letters, such as
      Letters denying credit,
      Letters denying orders,
      Letters denying requests,
      Letters of complaint, and
      Letters saying no to complaints.

O AY, LETTERS—I HAD LETTERS—I AM PERSECUTED WITH LETTERS—I HATE LETTERS—NOBODY KNOWS HOW TO WRITE LETTERS; AND YET ONE HAS 'EM, ONE DOES NOT KNOW WHY—THEY SERVE TO PIN UP ONE'S HAIR.

WILLIAM CONGREAVE

(1670–1729)

LETTERS: PLEASANT AND UNPLEASANT

MONEY AND GOODWILL: THE TWO MAIN GOALS OF LETTERS

Although the benefits accrue over time, and in ways not easily documented by accountants, few tasks in business pay such high dividends as writing letters. Letters are company flags. They do not fly over corporate headquarters; rather they are mailed every day to every state in the nation and to every corner of the world. They are ambassadors charged with helping the company prosper. All letters, then, even routine letters, must be neat, grammatical, professional, clear, accurate, and courteous.

Two considerations govern all business letters: money and goodwill.

Companies thrive on two things: money and goodwill. There is no reason then to wonder why managers write letters. Letters are among a company's most important investments, for successful letters generate money and goodwill.

MONEY

It is easy to see that money is involved in some business letters. Letters of inquiry collect information that will help the company. Sales letters of all kinds persuade the recipient to buy things, so that the company may make money. Collection letters attempt to get people to pay their bills.

Even letters as routine as reservations, acknowledgments of orders, and invitations help the company make money. Letters making travel reservations make money by enabling business people to plan their time as they do business out of town. Some companies see acknowledging orders as so boring and repetitive that they use printed forms. Customers, on the other hand, may not see an order as boring; it may represent a big investment. Should a company want to be assured of repeated orders, it would do well to write good letters acknowledging those orders. Even invitations may involve money. Company money spent on conferences, banquets, and receptions produces the goodwill so important for doing business. First, however, busy clients must accept the invitation. A well-written invitation often ensures the clients' acceptance. Moreover, their attendance may produce revenues. In short, companies do not spend money for fun. They do it to make money.

GOODWILL

To some degree, at least, goodwill is part of nearly all letters, and goodwill eventually becomes money. Any letter that offends the reader lessens goodwill. No private company can survive without the goodwill of its customers or clients. Letters that are precise, accurate, grammatical, neat, respectful, and courteous do much to gain and preserve goodwill, helping the company not only to survive, but also to thrive. A good customer for twenty years is worth ten times that of a good customer for two years. A satisfied customer is a company's best advertisement and often its best investment.

....
**OPTIONS FOR WRITING
BUSINESS LETTERS**

1. Preserve both money and
   goodwill.
2. Preserve money.
3. Preserve goodwill.
4. Never relinquish both money
   and goodwill.

....
**EXERCISE A: MONEY AND
GOODWILL**

Discuss in class the following
question and situations:

1. Why is goodwill almost as
   important to companies as
   money?
2. Give two situations in which
   money is more important to
   preserve than goodwill.
3. Give two situations in which
   goodwill is more important
   to preserve than money.

....
**THREE PARTS OF PLEASANT
AND ROUTINE LETTERS**

1. *Opening.* Say yes, or provide
   the routine information that
   is the primary purpose of the
   letter.
2. *Body.* Provide details.
3. *Closing.* End briefly with a
   compliment, congratulations,
   asserting a willingness to
   serve again, or any other sincere statement that might
   please the reader and improve
   goodwill for the company.

PRESERVING MONEY AND GOODWILL

The purpose of writing business letters, then, is to gain money or
goodwill or both. The best letters preserve both money and goodwill.
Second-best letters save one or the other. Bad letters lose both. Letter
writers should keep these purposes in mind, always. And always in
this order:

1. *Preserve money* and *goodwill.* The best-written letters, even those
   containing bad news, do this.
2. *Preserve the company's money.* Always try to preserve the company's
   money; that is why the company is in business.
3. *Preserve customer goodwill.* Although other considerations are important, letter writers must always keep in mind goodwill, for it usually translates into money for the company. Although company
   policy often determines the degree to which goodwill is worth sacrificing money, the relative worth of each usually is left to the
   writer. Lose goodwill if unavoidable, but save the company money;
   lose money if unavoidable, but preserve goodwill.
4. *Never relinquish both money and goodwill.* There is no excuse for it.

PLEASANT AND ROUTINE LETTERS

In pleasant and routine letters, the method of beginning with a statement and then providing reasons for (or analysis of) it is very effective.
Pleasant letters are just that: the answer sure to please most ques-
tioners is "Yes!" And the more exclamatory (!) the yes, the more
pleased the questioner. "Here's your money," "I'd like to order the
following," and the like—good news also pleases the reader. Consequently, positive letters should convey the pleasant point first. Next,
the letter should list reasons, analysis, or details. And finally, it should
end by trying to give something else: a compliment, a hope for an
additional order, or a reaffirmation of some other kind.

Some routine letters are written so often, are so pro forma or so
mundane, that people consider them routine. Routine letters include
requesting and granting credit (personal and corporate), placing routine orders, making routine inquiries, and registering minor complaints. The greatest danger in writing routine letters is complacency.
People tend to make mistakes when they do not pay attention to form,
courtesy, accuracy, and those other qualities that make letters good.
No letters, then, are routine, for all must make the job of reading easy,
all must pay careful attention to the reader, and all must follow certain forms.

REQUESTING AND GRANTING CREDIT

Credit cards are a fact of American life. Nearly everyone has them.
Corporations operate on credit also; indeed, few could run at all
without credit. Consequently, Americans must apply for credit frequently.

PERSONAL CREDIT REQUESTS. Credit requests should ask specifically for credit and then should provide the following information.

1. Your name and your current and former addresses
2. Details about the kind of credit desired
3. Details about your recent credit history (previous or current credit—other charge accounts)
4. Employment record (recent)
5. Statement of income (approximate)
6. Former and current bank

Here is an example of a letter requesting credit. Each part is labeled.

<table>
<tr>
<td>

</td>
<td>

9604 Licorice Street
Bonbon, MI 54322

28 February 1993

Credit Department
Sugar Plum Candies
Bonbon, MI 54321

Dear Credit Department:

</td>
</tr>
<tr>
<td>

Ask for credit.

</td>
<td>

Please open a charge account for me. Normally, I would pay for candy with cash, but my family and I have an inordinate craving for Peanut Butter Meltaways, and I don't always carry sufficient cash to pay for them. I believe that $200, payable monthly, would be sufficient.

</td>
</tr>
<tr>
<td>

Give details regarding kind of credit desired.

</td>
<td>

My name is given at the end of this letter and my address at the beginning. Before moving to Bonbon, I resided at

14398 Jujyfruit Lane
Andes, FL 34794.

</td>
</tr>
<tr>
<td>

Give details regarding recent employment, residences, credit history, and approximate annual income.

List former and present banks.

</td>
<td>

Moreover, I have charge accounts with such well-known national companies as Sears, Penney's, Neiman Marcus, and Fanny Farmer.

As Vice-President for Tasting at the Himshey's Chocolates in Bonbon, my annual income is nearly $65,000.

While living in Andes, I had savings and checking accounts with

Doughnut First Federal
One Glazed Avenue
Andes, FL 34796.

My bank in Bonbon is the Turnover National Bank on Apple Street.

Sincerely,

Chuck O. Lott

Chuck O. Lott

</td>
</tr>
</table>

This example is not entirely facetious. Companies of any size use application forms. A letter such as this example, then, would be necessary only for a credit request from a very small business.

CORPORATE CREDIT REQUESTS.   Because companies change suppliers often, credit is important. When one company applies for credit with another company or borrows money, banks usually handle the details. For smaller accounts, however, companies neither go through banks nor fill out application forms. They write letters. The order in which information is given in such letters is similar to that of personal credit requests. Here is an example.

**EXERCISE B:
CORPORATE CREDIT
REQUEST**

Using the list of information important for credit requests (p. 130) and the example for personal credit requests, identify the six steps in this Button Button example. Be prepared to discuss in class.

BUTTON BUTTON
555 Stitch Street
Seam, New Jersey 12345

5 November 1993

Ms. Myser Lee
Credit Department
Buttons R Us
Hole-in-the-Wall, WY 54321

Dear Ms. Lee:

Please open an account for my company, Button Button, with a credit limit of $2,500.

The former owner, Ms. Stitch, tells me that she was always satisfied with a 30-day, same as cash arrangement. May I have a similar arrangement?

My former company, Claw Zipper, had accounts with the First Blair County National Bank, Calico Textiles, and Chintz Clothiers.

As the button business is booming, my 23 years' experience in business tells me that I will need to order many more of your fine line of buttons than ever before. Consequently, I will need a credit line large enough to handle these purchases.

Please confirm my request by mail, and let me know the approximate number of days between placing an order and receiving the merchandise.

Sincerely,

Modesty Close

Modesty Close, Owner
Button Button

GRANTING CREDIT. Extending credit is good news for everyone. Giving someone a credit card means easy spending for the cardholder and, because companies charge interest on unpaid balances, money for the company. Extending credit is really saying "we trust you" to a customer. People like to be considered trustworthy.

Letters granting credit have four parts:

1. Extend the credit.
2. Say why: because you have a good credit history and so are trustworthy.
3. Explain clearly and in detail the conditions under which credit is being extended (but avoid threats).
4. Offer to do business *now*.

Here is the body of a simple letter extending credit.

Extend credit.	Your request for an increase in the credit limit on your LISA Card has been granted. As of now the limit is $5000.
Say why.	We have been able to grant this increase because of your excellent credit history.
Explain the conditions of extending credit.	Please remember, however, that the conditions governing this increase remain the same as under your previous limit. That is, there is still an interest charge of 1.9 percent a month on any outstanding balance.
Offer to do business now.	In appreciation of your requesting a greater credit limit, we are enclosing a special offer, made only to our best customers. A special edition clock radio may be yours for only $19.95 if you charge it to your new LISA Card account.

PLACING AND ACKNOWLEDGING ORDERS

Placing Routine Orders. Orders are good news. They are such good news, in fact, that most companies provide order forms for customers. If order forms are not available, however, the customer must write a letter. Letters ordering materials or services have eight parts:

1. *A direct but courteous order.* "Please send" is more direct and clear than "We are looking for," more courteous than "We want," and more forceful than "I would like to order."
2. *What.* Name the product or service *in detail*. Include numbers given to the product or service: catalog, serial, model, part number, and

so on. When ordering parts, always include the serial and model numbers, because many models are modified periodically and parts are changed. Include size and color. If more than one thing is ordered, make a list.

3. *How many.*

4. *How much.* Unit price. Total price.

5. *Method of paying.* Standing 30-day account (this usually means paying within 30 days; no interest is charged), check, or credit card (include card name, number, and date it expires).

6. *Method of sending.* U.S. mail (1st, 2nd, 3rd, 4th class, etc.), UPS, Federal Express, passenger pigeon, slow boat.

7. *Where to be sent.*

8. *When needed.*

Here is the body of a sample ordering letter.

A direct and detailed but courteous order

What, how much, how many

```
Please send me these parts for the Todo Snow Blower,
model #L432765, serial #312578970.

    Item           Part #  Qty.  Unit Cost  Total
    Drive chain    234128   2     $13.48     $26.96
    Drive shear pin 389457  8     $ 1.20     $ 9.60
    Blower shear pin 389463 4     $ 1.20     $ 4.80
```

When needed

Where to send

```
Please send these by Federal Express, as the snow is
falling hard and fast and I need to get to work by
February 2 at the latest.

Please send them to

     S. Claus
     North Pole
     The Arctic.
```

How to send

Method of payment

```
A helicopter will be needed to ensure delivery.

Please charge my Live-It-Up account
(#89749-4774-927; exp. 5-95).
```

ACKNOWLEDGING ORDERS. Letters or even postcards acknowledging orders often are considered among the most routine of business letters. Some business people reason that promptly filled orders require no letter of acknowledgment. Others believe such letters to be, at best, mere inconveniences. Still other companies bow to what they consider a conventional formality: acknowledging orders by sending printed form postcards.

The problem is twofold. First, companies live for orders. That's how they make money: no orders, no sales, no money, no company. Second, cavalier attitudes by companies toward acknowledging orders reveal a dangerously complacent and self-centered view: the kind that eventually costs money.

It is true that orders, while important, are routine for companies. Yet orders may not be routine for the buyer. Buyers tend to re-order from companies that not only provide good service, but also convey a genuine sense of concern and gratitude for those orders. Acknowledging orders, then, may be routine, but only because it is done so often. On the other hand, acknowledging orders is far more than routine to companies that want to cultivate valued customers and capture important orders. In acknowledgments, letters are better than postcards, and separately written postcards are better than forms.

Letters acknowledging orders have five parts:

1. Acknowledge receiving the order, and specify *in detail* how the order is being filled.

2. Give details about how the order is to be sent to the customer and when it should be received.

3. When advisable, give details of method of payment.

4. Say thanks.

5. Welcome more orders.

Here is the body of a sample letter of acknowledgment.

EXERCISE C: LETTERS VERSUS POSTCARDS

Discuss in class the following questions:
1. When might it be better to write a letter? Why?
2. When might it be better to write a postcard? Why?

We received your order, dated 17 October, for a gross of AG-94 widgitcogs. Right now, the widgitcogs are being counted, boxed (one gross to a box), labeled, and addressed.

By 5:00 p.m. today, they should be crated and on their way to you in one of our own Fahrquart Industries trucks. They should be at your receiving dock by noon on Wednesday, October 21.

Payment, as always with our good customers, is 30 days/same as cash. Should you prefer some other method, please let us know by October 31.

Much as we welcome new business, it is always of our long-time customers that we are most appreciative. So, as always, thanks!

Juanita Zúñiga, our sales representative, mentions that on her last trip your production manager expressed the possibility of your making some changes in designs of your B-Class meters. Should this require modifications in the Model N-456 widgitcog, please let us know and we'll send someone there to discuss details.

MAKING AND RESPONDING FAVORABLY TO INQUIRIES

MAKING ROUTINE INQUIRIES.   Many believe that routine letters of inquiry are easy to write because they merely need to state the request first, say why the information or item is needed, and express confidence that the request will be granted. But many letters of inquiry, while routine, are not easy to write. Because people want something does not mean that they will get it. Readers often are not required to answer an inquiry; even those who must answer inquiries are not always required to do it conscientiously or even with goodwill. Companies get letters of inquiry every day: some are answered well, some poorly; some are answered quickly; some lie on a desk for a long time. Writers who make the job of answering easy for the reader are more likely to receive answers, good answers, than those who do not.

There are six parts to successful letters of inquiry:

1. *Give praise and make request*. Say something good about the reader or the company. But to convey sincerity, be specific about the praise. In order to be specific, be informed about the company. Shotgun praise does not work. Know something good — specifically good — about the company before praising it.

    Then make the request. People like to know right off what it is about. Make an accurate and precise request to yield a precise and accurate answer.

2. *State purpose*. Say why you need the information and for what. Companies are understandably wary of providing some information and want to know why the information is needed and for what it will be used.

    Demonstrate that you've done your homework. No one likes to do someone else's work. Provide details that prove a lot of work has been done already. Here is a chance to compliment the reader by showing "I have done all I can do, and because you know more than I, I come to you for help." Write letters of inquiry only after you have exhausted other ways of finding the information.

3. *Inquire*. Ask specific, clear, brief questions. Try to ask questions that may be answered in few words. *If more than one question must be asked, make a list.* A reader trying to answer questions may do so more easily and quickly when the questions have been listed and numbered. That way, no time is lost looking for questions buried in paragraphs. Questions requiring a number for an answer are best.

    Listing is most useful when the following rules are followed.

    a. Always introduce a list to connect the visuals to the text. Common introductions include "Here is a list of," "As the following list shows," "Would you please answer these four questions?" and "We want to order the four items given in this list."

b. Number the items to allow readers to refer to specific items easily.

Give praise, make request.

State purpose.

Inquire.

Make specific requests.

Give deadline.

NEW ZOOM ENTERPRISES
1 Caliente Street
Ajo, Texas 65432

1 November 1993

Mr. Frank Lee Speaking
Engineering
National Motors Corporation
123 Commerce Boulevard
Commerce, Michigan 23456

Dear Mr. Speaking:

Your article, "Casting the New Aluminum Engine," in the October issue of *Automotive Quarterly*, is the most informative account of the Aleng casting process I have read. New Zoom Enterprises is developing such an engine and hopes eventually to produce a better and cheaper aluminum engine for sale to companies such as yours. My job is to study the Aleng process and try to improve it. So far, I have read much about it, visited your plant in Michigan, and worked with aluminum-tungsten alloys.

Your article was very helpful, but I still need answers to several questions:

1. Why is a cold chamber used when a hot chamber better tempers the aluminum?
2. About how much does a die cost?
3. How many blocks may be cast before the die wears out?
4. How much does the shot weigh?
5. How many blocks may be cast an hour?

Would you please answer these questions? And would you be willing to share with me any new findings you have made since you wrote the article? Anything you give me is confidential.

My report is not due until December 1, but if you would reply by November 15, I would have time to study your information well and improve my report greatly. And, of course, I would be able to send you a copy of my findings sooner.

Sincerely,

Sierra Madre

Sierra Madre
Engineer

---

c. Keep the list short and manageable: it will make an easy reference tool.

d. List items by a principle of organization, just as you would any other writing. For example, organize lists from most important to least important, easiest to answer to hardest, and so on.

e. Items in lists should be grammatically parallel. Do not write, for example,

1) How much does the shot weigh?
2) Blocks an hour?

Write instead,

1) How much does the shot weigh?
2) How many blocks can be cast per hour?

4. *Make specific requests.* To ensure a response, especially when the reader does not have to respond, *ask* that questions be answered. *People like to be asked.* Asking in writing requires a *question mark.* Do not write, "I would appreciate any answers you could give me." Write instead, "Would you please answer these questions?"

Leave a clear opening for more information. A reader may know more than the writer knows to ask. The reader may have helpful information that will not be given unless requested.

Assure the reader of confidentiality, as necessary. Companies often refuse to give out even slightly sensitive information, unless they are assured it will not be disseminated. If you cannot assure confidentiality, then explain exactly who will receive the information. Some companies may like the free advertising.

5. *Give deadline.* Courteously set a reasonable deadline for a reply. The job of answering inquiries is not a popular one in most companies. Because the most junior employee is usually given the job, in a pile of twenty letters to be answered quickly, those containing deadlines are most likely to be answered first. (See page 136.)

6. *Say thank you.* Immediately after receiving an answer, send a brief thank you note.

Here is an example of a thank-you note.

EXERCISE D: LETTER OF INQUIRY

Letters of inquiry must be written carefully to make the job of responding easy. Discuss in class the following questions:

1. Which specific pieces of advice given in the discussion of letters of inquiry do you think are essential to all such letters?

2. Which do you see as depending on the situation?

Say thank you.

Be brief.

Dear Mr. Speaking:

The information you sent me so quickly was most helpful. Thank you. Thank you, too, for the information on your recent improvements in using hot chambers. As soon as I can digest all this information and put it with what I already had, I will send you a copy of my report.

In the meantime, I would be happy to provide any information I have that might be helpful to you.

Sincerely,

EXERCISE E: RESPONDING
FAVORABLY TO ROUTINE
INQUIRIES

Discuss in class how you might
answer the following routine
inquiry.

Dear Mom:
I know I'm supposed to mow
the lawn, take out the trash,
and feed the neighbor's cat this
evening, but I'm not sure that
they all can be done between
the time I get back from practice
at 5:00 and the time it gets dark,
around 8:30. Would you please
leave me a note telling me in
what order I should do these
dirty jobs? Moreover, Jan wants
me to come to her house tonight
to listen to a new tape she just
bought. If I get the jobs done —
or most of them — may I go?
Your obedient and loving
daughter, Jane.

RESPONDING FAVORABLY TO ROUTINE INQUIRIES.   Respond-
ing favorably to a request would appear to be easy, and it is, as long as
the writer does not become sloppy. Remember to begin with the favorable response and to answer in order each specific question.

RESPONDING FAVORABLY TO COMPLAINTS: ADJUSTMENT
LETTERS.   "To adjust" comes from Latin by way of French, *"ajuste,"*
which concerns "justice." In business, it usually means correcting an
injustice or problem. Adjustment letters, then, correct problems and
are of two kinds: those that correct problems caused by the company,
and those that correct a problem not caused by the company. In both
situations, letters are written to *adjust* the situation. That is, money is
refunded; new products are given free; or another service, within reason, is provided that will satisfy the customer.

To restore goodwill, a company should send the adjustment letter
immediately. Delay could so anger the customer that even an otherwise
full adjustment would not retain the customer's goodwill.

Letters that make adjustments as a result of a company's error
should include an apology. If the writer of the letter is uncertain as to
the legal implications — an extreme example would be apologizing for
a flaw in the design of an automobile that caused an accident and,
possibly, injury — advice should be sought from a company lawyer.

Here is an example of the body of a simple adjustment letter.

Opening

Details

Closing

EXERCISE F: SUBTLETIES
IN ADJUSTMENT LETTERS
Discuss in class the surf-
board wax letter:

1. Does the company ad-
   mit error?

2. What is gained by giv-
   ing the customer a free
   can of wax?

3. What is lost?

4. Does the word *rancid*
   seem too strong?

5. What synonym might
   be as accurate as but less
   offensive than *rancid*?

```
Here is your refund for $15.00. We are very sorry
that you were dissatisfied with Fahrquart's Natural
Surfboard Wax.

We checked the can of wax you sent us and have con-
cluded that somehow the lid, which should be air-
tight, must have been opened during shipping. By the
time you bought it, it had become rancid.

This is the first instance of an unsealed lid that
we have learned about. In addition to the check,
therefore, and because we appreciate your telling us
of the problem, we are sending you another can of
Fahrquart's Natural Surfboard Wax free. We hope it
provides you many enjoyable hours in your search for
that perfect wave!
```

UNPLEASANT LETTERS

Bad news is bad news. No one likes to receive it, and few like to give it. Bad news remains, however, a fact of life, certainly of business life. Saying no is almost always difficult. People enjoy complaining, but when they want something done as a result of their complaining, it is no longer fun, but rather hard work.

Moreover, saying no can be sad, painful, even heart wrenching. Most managers believe that saying no is the most difficult part of their jobs. Seldom are any employees so unrepentently incompetent that firing them is enjoyable. It is painful to deny people loans, raises, promotions. In a perfect world, everyone would be happy, and all would have their hearts' desires. This is not a perfect world. The best employees can do is to learn to say no properly, to provide logical reasons, to give some hope, to make people feel as good about themselves as circumstances warrant.

Ideally, employees should be straightforward. Some companies encourage employees to speak out and not to fear for their jobs, to be more willing to come right out even with the bad news *first*. General Electric is the most famous example, but so too are such other companies as Intermark, Inc., of La Jolla, California.[1] While giving the bad news first is preferable in companies run by extraordinary executives, few companies are run by executives who can handle this method of management. Consequently, we recommend the following formula for giving bad news.

While stating the point of the letter first works well for pleasant and routine correspondence, it can be disastrous for unpleasant correspondence. Conveying the bad news by saying no first, and then explaining why, does not work. No matter how sincerely or how well the facts have been marshalled, the writer will offend the reader. The reader (or listener) does not respond well to anything *after* hearing the bad news unless prepared for it. To prepare a reader, to soften the blow, to save the company's money, and to retain the reader's goodwill requires a special ordering of information, usually in four paragraphs. It is one of the few letters for which there is a formula.

Once mastered, the *no* formula works well both in print and orally. Saying no by telephone requires jotting down the main points in the proper order and then conveying them sympathetically, sincerely, and firmly. Similarly, face-to-face conversations require the speaker to keep the points in mind and in their proper order. Organizing the points saves much pain and frustration in firing people or in turning them down for big raises or promotions or transfers or projects. There is an apocryphal story about a department head who was a master of conveying bad news. His relative success was judged by others on how many hours were required for employees to come down from being told how wonderful they are and to realize that they had been fired.

Organize details.

---

[1] Larry Weber, "Peers Looking at You, Red," *Business Month*, September 1990, 16, 19.

Use proper tone.

The importance of tone in *no* letters cannot be overemphasized. Sincerity, sympathy, and professionalism must be conveyed; otherwise, much work may be undone. In *no* letters, especially, there is a specific danger to avoid: unctuousness. When the tone of conveying bad news becomes slick, when it no longer conveys genuine sympathy or regret, then no clever arrangement of words can save the day.

Here is a detailed explanation of each of the four parts of a *no* letter.

FOUR PARTS TO A *NO* LETTER

1. Agree (find a common ground).
2. Say why (explain carefully and in detail).
3. Say no (refuse politely and clearly).
4. Try to give something (encouragement if possible).

1. *Agree.* Find some common ground, an issue on which both writer and reader may agree. The common ground *must* pertain to the bad news. The easiest opening begins with "I agree." Two examples follow.

    a. The first sentence of a bad-news letter to a volunteer group that collects donations annually in the community, but which this year wants to solicit money in company offices—something specifically prohibited by company policy—might read like this:

    We agree wholeheartedly that your work is among the most important charity work done in this community.

    b. The first sentence of a bad-news letter to students who want "real world" examples of business letters for their business communication course, but which, for reasons of confidentiality, cannot be supplied, might read like this:

    We agree that "real world" examples of business letters would help immensely in your study of this most important, and often neglected, part of work in business.

    Writers should also try to find a hook to use at the end of the first paragraph, one that pertains to the *no* but does not alarm readers. Here are the two examples again. This time, notice the addition of the hooks, shown in italics:

    We agree wholeheartedly that your work is among the most important charity work done in this community, *and we will support that work to the best of our ability.*

    We agree that "real world" examples of business letters would help immensely in your study of this most important, and often neglected, part of work in business. *It is so important, in fact, that nearly all company correspondence is treated with the utmost confidentiality.*

2. *Say why.* Provide reasons or explanations for the bad news (firing, refusing to give a promotion or raise, denying money for a project). Demonstrate that the person, request, or complaint has been taken seriously.

3. *Say no.* Write *no* sympathetically but unequivocally.

4. *Try to give something.* While not required to give something in a *no* letter, the writer should try to do so: an account of the reader's or listener's good qualities, a good letter of recommendation for another job, hope for a later promotion or raise, or *part* of what they want.

EXERCISE G: *NO* LETTERS

Discuss in class the following questions:

1. Why should writers give the reasons for saying no before actually saying no?
2. Why is tone so important, especially in *no* letters?

Here is an example of a *no* letter. Because it was written in 1861 by President Abraham Lincoln, it uses language common to the time, and thus may appear a little archaic.[2] Nevertheless, although it does not begin with "we agree," it follows the general-to-specific method for *no* letters. By carefully following the argument set forth

Agree.

(Details to support the agreement)

Try to give something—in this case, hope.

Say no. (Notice that even while saying no, Lincoln gives good advice.)

Executive Mansion
Washington, December 31, 1861

Dear Sir:

Yours of the 23rd is received, and I am constrained to say it is difficult to answer so ugly a letter in good temper. I am, as you intimate, losing much of the great confidence I placed in you, not from any act or omission of yours touching the public service, up to the time you were sent to Leavenworth, but from the flood of grumbling dispatches and letters I have seen from you since.

I knew you were being ordered to Leavenworth at the time it was done; and I aver that with as tender regard for your honor and your sensibilities as I had for my own, it never occurred to me that you were being "humiliated, insulted, and disgraced"; nor have I, up to this day, heard an intimation that you have been wronged, coming from anyone but yourself. No one has blamed you for the retrograde movement from Springfield, nor for the information you gave General Cameron; and this you could readily understand, if it were not for your unwarranted assumption that the ordering you to Leavenworth must necessarily have been done as a *punishment* for some *fault*. I thought then, and think yet, that the position assigned you as responsible, and as honorable, as that assigned to Buell—I know that General McClellan expected more important results from it. My impression is that at the time you were assigned to the new Western Department, it had not been determined to re-place Gen. Sherman in Kentucky; but of this I am not certain, because the idea that a command in Kentucky was very very desirable, and one in the farther West, very undesirable, had never occurred to me.

You constantly speak of being placed in command of only 3000. Now tell me, is this not mere impatience? Have you not known all the while that you are to command four or five times that many?

I have been, and am sincerely your friend; and if, as such, I dare to make a suggestion, I would say you are adopting the best possible way to ruin yourself. "Act well your part, there all the honor lies." He who does *something* at the head of one Regiment, will eclipse him who does *nothing* at the head of a hundred.

Your friend, as ever,

A. Lincoln

---

[2]From *The Collected Works of Abraham Lincoln*, ed. Roy P. Basler (New Brunswick, N.J.: Rutgers University Press, 1953), 5:84–85.

by Lincoln, but even without understanding many of the details, the student can see clearly not only that Lincoln understood the necessity for providing reasons before the "no" and the "try to give something" at the end, but also that Lincoln knew how to lead—a quality essential to students who may want to become managers in business or leaders in other occupations. The letter was written to General David Hunter, commander of the Department of the West, early in the Civil War. Hunter, as Lincoln's letter intimates, spent much of his time complaining to Lincoln and very little time getting his job done.

DENYING CREDIT

Naturally, a few who request credit have neither a good credit rating nor any hope of achieving one. More often, however, credit is requested by people who, while well intentioned, simply are too great a risk *at the moment* to be granted credit. Young people especially have difficulty establishing a good credit rating because they have only just become old enough to establish one. Nearly all of these people will become good credit risks in short order. The difficulty, then, is to refuse them credit while not losing them as potential customers.

Refusal letters to such people will provoke positive reactions only if the reader sees the reasonableness of the refusal *and* learns what to do about it. Consequently, the *say why* portion of the letter may serve two purposes: it explains in detail (1) the reasons for the refusal and (2) how the reader can go about establishing a good rating. Page 143 contains the text of an unfavorable response to a request for credit.

SAYING NO TO ORDERS

Because orders are the lifeblood of any producer of goods, it is doubly difficult to say no: the customer is unhappy and the company is unhappy. The company may have to say no for any of four reasons.

1. *The customer cannot pay*. Should a customer order a product but have a bad credit rating, the best letter is a credit refusal letter explained in the previous section and shown on page 143.

2. *The company is out of the product*. When a company's product is so popular that manufacturing cannot keep up with demand, the company has the unpleasant job of asking the customer to wait. The company must persuade the customer that the product is worth waiting for.

3. *The company no longer makes the product*. When a company no longer makes a product, the company must persuade the customer that it makes a different product that is as good as or better than that which the customer ordered. This is the most difficult letter to write because it must refuse to fill an order while trying to sell a different product.

Agree.

Say why. (Notice the inclusion of advice about achieving a good credit rating.)

Say no. (Notice the attempt to sympathize while saying no.)

Try to give something.

EXERCISE H: CREDIT REFUSAL LETTERS

Discuss in class the following questions:

1. Do you think that Dunn's sympathy for Deed sounds genuine? If so, why? If not, why?

2. Do you think Dunn talks about himself too much in this letter?

3. Do you think that the last paragraph effectively reinforces the notion that the refusal does not mean that the lender lacks confidence in the reader?

Dear Ms. Deed:

We agree that starting out a career without being able to buy such essentials as clothing on credit can make life very difficult for a while—at least until a few paychecks come in.

Your situation reminds me very much of when I was just starting out. The best advice I received was from a banker who told me to take out a short-term loan, say two months, for a few hundred dollars. Usually, a bank will lend small amounts once you verify that you are gainfully employed. Then I applied successfully for credit.

I certainly understand how you feel, as does everyone who has been where you are now. I wish we could send you a Fahrquart Department Stores credit card, but, as you have not yet established a credit rating, we cannot.

If you take out a small loan from your bank soon, however, you no doubt will have established a credit rating very quickly. Then, when you let us know, we will happily review your application. I notice that our Fall Sales will start about the time your credit approval could come through. I'll make a note to send you a flyer.

Best wishes,

Jeremy Dunn

Jeremy Dunn,
Credit Department

---

4. *The company does not sell to individuals, but only to retail outlets.* When a company sells only to retail outlets and not directly to customers, it should supply the customer with the names, addresses, and phone numbers of the retail outlets nearest the customer. This may require such work as looking at maps, supplying price lists (if prices are uniform), and even checking with the customer's closest outlet to be sure it has the product.

Here is an example of the most difficult order refusal letter: refusing and selling at the same time.

Agree—here, a kind of congratulations for knowing to order the most popular hook for salmon.

Say why. (There's an even better hook available.)

Say no.

Try to give something—here, a discount and an order form to make ordering easy.

Dear Ms. Brookie:

We were happy to receive your order of 15 March for 13 boxes of #14 salmon hooks, model 925461. These hooks have been our most popular model for nearly 17 years. As a discriminating angler, you must know, too, that no one has made a better salmon hook in all that time, although many have tried.

Last year, however, someone did make a better hook. That someone is us. Although the best hook on the market, the 925461 did not hold its point as long as we at the Mustard Hook Company might have liked. And, as we are never satisfied with the best, we have spent a number of years looking for a salmon hook that would hold a point even longer. We found it in the model 925783.

Not wanting to make one product when we could make a better one, we stopped making 925461 last year, and have none in stock.

Because the 925783 is made from specially hardened steel, our costs are 15% greater for the 925783 than for the 925461. We are so confident that you will like the improvement represented by the 925783, however, and as you are such a good customer, we would be happy to send you 13 boxes of 100 ct. #14 salmon hooks, model 925783, at a 10% discount over the suggested retail price of $7.95 a box.

Just fill out the enclosed order form, and we'll send you these new hooks right away.

Sincerely,

Sonny Perch

Sonny Perch,
Sales

encl.

....

EXERCISE 1: REFUSING AN ORDER

Discuss in class the following questions:

1. Do you think that this example could be used as a form letter with which to answer all who order the discontinued fishing hooks?
2. Why? Why not?

SAYING NO TO INQUIRIES

Companies are in the business of pleasing customers, and a major part of pleasing customers involves answering their questions. Sometimes, however, marginal costs (as economics majors can testify) outweigh the marginal benefits. That is, it may cost the company much more to respond to a customer's request than the company can ever hope to benefit from that customer's satisfaction. The burden, then, remains on the writer of inquiry letters to make the job of responding easy.

The most common reason for denying a request is that of confidentiality. Someone studying salary rates for managers and executives may ask for such information. Understandably, the company may not want to divulge such information. Here is an example of a letter that says no to an inquiry.

Agree.

Say why. Notice the inclusion of evidence assuring support whenever possible.

Say no. Notice the blanket sentence of understanding yet saying no.

Try to give something.

Dear Professor Biddy:

We agree that salary information regarding managers and executives is important for your study of compensation rates in American industry, and we agree as well that we at Fahrquart, Inc., would benefit from knowing our competitors' pay scales, and that they would benefit from knowing ours.

As you may know, Fahrquart, Inc., has been so delighted with the enormous increase in the academic study of business that we annually give considerable sums to encourage such study even further. Occasionally, however, free academic inquiry and the demands of the so-called real world conflict. For example, when we asked our lawyers about the legality of sending to you the information you requested, we were told that, while we would like to do it, the law on such matters is clear: it is illegal.

We certainly understand your desire for such information, but we cannot risk expensive law suits in complying.

In an effort to do what we can for you, our personnel manager diligently searched our library for public information on the subject. She found a considerable amount in government publications, in Barron's, Fortune, and other magazines. We have enclosed the bibliography compiled by our staff and hope that it proves helpful. Should we be able to help you in any other way, please let us know.

Sincerely,

Clarence Darrow

Clarence Darrow,
Legal Department

WRITING LETTERS OF COMPLAINT

ROUTINE LETTERS OF COMPLAINT.   Basic complaint letters are simple because the problem should be apparent to everyone. It is important, nevertheless, to follow these guidelines:

1. Write immediately upon discovering the problem.
2. Include the solution in the first sentence.
3. Include the specific problem in the second sentence.
4. Treat the reader as a reasonable person and assume that a reasonable reply will be forthcoming.
5. Use a professional tone; never threaten, never be nasty or sarcastic.

Here is an example of a *bad* simple complaint letter.

```
Yesterday, I bought a video cassette recording of
the movie, Road Warrior at the Boy Scout Jamboree. I
thought it would be a good movie, like all other
"Road Warrior" movies I've seen.

This one was filled with unknown stars, but I
thought that that would not matter. Action is what
matters: smoke, fire, roaring engines, and stuff
like that.

Anyway, I can't get the thing to play. I put it in
my VCR and nothing happened. Other movies work in
it, but this one did not.

Please be assured that I shall never buy another
thing from your store. And if I ever do come into
your store, it will be with some of my buddies from
the Heck's Angels Motorcycle Club.
```

Here is the same situation; this time, however, the letter is well written. Each part of a simple complaint letter is labeled.

Specific request

Specific problem

Treat reader as a well-meaning, responsible person.

No nasty tone, no sarcasm

```
I would like the $19.95 I paid yesterday for the
video recording of "Road Warrior at the Boy Scout
Jamboree" refunded.

Although my VCR is fine--other movies play on
it--the movie I bought at your store does not.

I understand that any number of things can happen to
a recording, most of which you have no way of con-
trolling and no way of knowing about. This must be
one of those instances.

I enclose the recording and the receipt. Please
place the refund in my name and send it to the fol-
lowing address.

     1600 Pennsylvania Avenue, S.W.
     Washington, DC 20000
```

....

EXERCISE J: TONE IN COMPLAINT LETTERS

Discuss in class the following question: Although a writer often wants to be nasty and sarcastic in complaint letters, what is the likely effect on the reader of such a letter?

....

FOUR PARTS TO A LETTER OF COMPLAINT

1. General complaint
2. Background (why this letter)
3. Solutions (specific complaint and specific request)
4. Deadline for response

EXTRAORDINARY LETTERS OF COMPLAINT.   Extraordinary letters of complaint differ from simple complaint letters in that they are not simple. There is seldom a simple "here's the problem; fix it this way" letter. Although letters of complaint are often difficult to write well because they are composed in anger or frustration, complaint letters must be more subtle by leading the reader to a reasonable conclusion; otherwise, the bad news will not be accepted. A complaint, like revenge, should be savored as a cold dish. Consequently, good complaint letters use the general-to-specific method in four parts.

1. *General complaint.* The first paragraph should state *in general* what is wrong (broken, wrong size, etc.). Be *specific* about the product in question: provide model number, serial number, color, and other

details. If the complaint involves a service, be specific about that service. Try not to blame anyone.

2. *Background* (why this letter). The second paragraph should show that the writer is a reasonable person writing to reasonable people. Do this by recounting, calmly and coolly, the background steps taken so far. Show, in short, that the homework has been thorough, that the writer has gone through proper channels, and that writing a letter of complaint is merely the proper thing to do.

3. *Solutions* (specific complaint and specific request). Write specifically what is wrong: be detailed. Write specifically, and reasonably, what you want done about it. Mention, if true, previous business relationships; they maintain goodwill and encourage a favorable response.

4. *Deadline for response.* Set a reasonable deadline for a response. Assume that the claim will be settled quickly and to everyone's satisfaction.

Here is an example of a letter of complaint.

Dear Mr. Turtyr:

The 6.50-15 Rubberex tire that I bought on July 10 from the Standard Supply Co. (237 Broadway, Colton, NY 12040) has become cracked after only 8000 miles of use.

Because I bought the tire while on a business trip in the East, I cannot return it to the dealer from whom I purchased it. I asked your local representative, Mr. John Ostrander (5 Park Street, Galesburg, Illinois) to replace it. He has suggested that I write to you.

Because I have used your tires for the past ten years, have been pleased, have come to expect 24,000 miles from Rubberex tires, and have been considerably inconvenienced, I am certain that you will provide a new Rubberex tire at a 66 percent discount as figured on the mileage.

May I hear from you soon? My next trip begins July 31; I would feel safer riding on a new Rubberex than on my old spare.

Sincerely,

Alvin Jones

Alvin Jones

EXERCISE K: THE CONTENTS OF A COMPLAINT LETTER

Discuss in class the following request and questions:

1. Identify the four parts of a complaint letter in Jones's letter to Turtyr.

2. Does the letter contain anything *more* than those four parts? If so, what is its purpose?

SAYING NO TO COMPLAINT LETTERS

Complaints cannot always be answered favorably. Such negative responses, whether written or oral, should follow the four-part *no* letter arrangement. Here is an example of an unfavorable response to a complaint letter. Notice how carefully the letter avoids blaming Jones for an error he probably committed.

Agree.

Say why the no is coming.

Say no.

Give something.

Dear Mr. Jones:

We agree that you should expect more than 8,000 miles of service from the 6.50-15 Rubberex Tire that you wrote us about on April 10. Rubberex Tires are built to give 25,000 miles of trouble-free service under normal conditions.

Our service department has carefully examined your tire, which Mr. John Ostrander sent to us, and they find that your tire was used when seriously under-inflated; this caused the side walls to crack. To illustrate this, we are enclosing a booklet which shows a tire injured in the same way yours was injured. By following the suggestions given in the part marked in red pencil, you will have no further difficulty of this kind.

Looking at the situation from your perspective, we can understand how you feel. Our guarantee of "at least 20,000 miles for Rubberex Tires under normal conditions" still holds. But your tire, probably without your even knowing it, was abnormally strained, which no tire can withstand; it therefore does not comply with this guarantee.

Because you have been a good customer, we are willing to bear a part of your loss by offering you a new 6.50-15 Rubberex Tire at a 20 percent discount. Take this letter to your local Rubberex dealer for free installation.

Sincerely,

Wynn Turtyr

Wynn Turtyr,
Adjuster

SUMMARY

1. All business letters are written ultimately for one of two reasons: money or goodwill. Writers should try to preserve both the company's money and the customer's goodwill. Failing that, writers should always preserve either money or goodwill; writers never should lose both.

2. Pleasant letters are as one would expect. They usually include the word *yes* and end with a compliment, an order, or a reaffirmation. In such letters, the pleasant or routine information is given first and explained later. This is best because people will pay attention to the explanation after hearing the good news.

3. Letters requesting credit include the following: name, current and former addresses, details about the kind of credit desired, details about current credit history, recent employment record, approximate income, and former and current bank.

4. Letters for ordering materials or services include the following: order, title of product or service, quantity, cost, method of payment, method of shipping, return address, arrival deadline.

5. Letters acknowledging orders have five parts: acknowledging the order and specifying how it will be filled, giving details of the method of delivery and approximate date of delivery, providing details regarding method of payment, saying thank you, and welcoming more orders.

6. Letters of inquiry include honest praise (say something good), purpose (why information is needed), inquiry (ask specific questions), request (ask for specific answers), and deadline (ask for a reply by a given date).

7. Favorable responses to letters of inquiry should include a point-by-point method of answering.

8. In unpleasant and non-routine letters, the explanation for the bad news is given before the bad news. This is best because people will not pay attention to the explanation after reading the bad news.

9. The four parts to an unfavorable response (or bad-news or *no*) letter include a common ground (agree), an explanation (why), a polite refusal (no), and an attempt to give something (encouragement).

EXERCISES

1. *Money and goodwill.* Can you think of a situation in which the company's money *and* the customer's goodwill should be sacrificed? Explain on paper or discuss in class.

2. *Money and goodwill.* If you travel and the railroad fails to serve hot food during your three-day, cross-country trip, do you think you should be reimbursed for your inconvenience? How much (in percent)? Discuss in class.

3. *Money and goodwill.* Looking at the situation in Exercise 2 from the perspective of the railroad, what are some considerations that might be studied before deciding whether the traveller should be reimbursed? Discuss in class.

4. *Money and goodwill.* Assuming the railroad decides to reimburse the traveller (from Exercise 3), what considerations might determine how much should be reimbursed? Discuss in class.

5. *Credit requests.* You have just opened a new restaurant in State Village, a university town. You have been in the restaurant business for 15 years in another town, but when the major employer, East Waco, a paper mill, shut down its aging plant, the population drifted away, and the average income of those remaining fell dramatically. So, too, did your restaurant business.

   Although you have always had a good relationship with your supplier, having paid cash in the past, you cannot do so now. Your new restaurant, The Pulp Room, which serves fast foods, mostly fried, is doing very well—so well, in fact, that you need to double the amount of cooking fat you buy. Other items, such as catsup, mustard, onion salt, and premixed gravy are in such demand that they must be ordered well in advance and in greater quantities. Write a letter requesting a $5,000 credit line from your supplier: Greasy Spoon, Incorporated.

6. *Credit extension.* Here is a badly written credit extension letter. Edit the letter to make it a well-written credit extension letter. Assume that all statements made in the bad letter are true.

Dear Ms. Fahrquart:

We at LISA pride ourselves on the quality of our customers. And, although you come in at the lower end of the economic status of those customers, we are willing to grant your request for a credit card.

Unfortunately, we can allow you only a limit of $1000 as you do not qualify for our higher limit Silver Card.

We charge 1.9 percent a month on all outstanding debt, and any default, deliberate or otherwise, by the cardholder, will result in the most energetic and severe action on our part. The law even allows for jail sentences for the more stubborn offenders.

Nevertheless we hope you enjoy using your LISA Card. You have been admitted to a very select group of people. Although you probably can't afford it, we're offering a special price on a Club Ned vacation for two to Majorca for $2985 per person/double occupancy.

Our most sincere best wishes,

Alphonse La Rue,
Credit Department

7. *Orders.* Your dormitory (or fraternity or sorority) is planning an end-of-the-school-year party.

   a. A local company, Wild Times Caterers, has worked for you many times. They have always done an excellent job. Write an order requesting a detailed estimate of the cost of the things you will need.

   b. Look at several books on Brazilian culture. Write an order to International Cuisine, a company specializing in preparing foods of many countries, for those foods and accessories you think you will need for a Brazilian-style party.

8. *Letter of inquiry.* As director of corporate instruction, your job is to determine the need for, to identify participants in, and to plan Management Development Seminars for Bolling Aircraft Company. On a recent trip to Atlanta, you learned from a Ms. Scarlet Belle that her new hotel complex has just completed a hotel designed especially for corporate retreats.

   Upon returning to Denver, Bolling's headquarters, you learn that you are to plan a three- to five-day retreat for 35 managers. You have spoken with Wolford Seminars, a company specializing in communications workshops, and they have agreed to run either a three- or five-day seminar for you.

   Belle's new hotel sounds ideal, having seminar rooms, audiovisual aids, separate lunch rooms, conference calling, an auditorium, and other facilities designed for such seminars. Yet Wolford Seminars needs to confirm a date soon, as their appointment book is filling rapidly.

   Write a letter of inquiry to Belle in which you ask for more information, including fees for both a three-day and a five-day seminar, pick-up and delivery of participants at the airport, number of seminar rooms available, sample menus, and the possibility of evening tennis, squash, handball, golf, and swimming to allow participants to unwind after each day's work.

9. *Responding favorably to a letter of inquiry.* You are a junior and an economics major. One day, you receive the following note from Professor Freedman, the advisor to the Economics Club.

   Dear Fahrquart:

   Some members of the Econ. Club, especially the freshmen and several sophomores, are terribly worried about negotiating the rapids of the econ. major at this university. As a professor, my advice is suspect, naturally, and the officers of the club have asked me to recommend someone with experience to speak with them about what they see as the many little twists and turns of survival. In my experience, there has never been an econ. major here who has run those rapids more often than you and still remained afloat—so far. Would you consent to speak with them at their next meeting, at 8 p.m. on Friday, October 18? Please write and let me know before this coming Tuesday. I hope you will accept.

   Respond in writing to Professor Freedman. Say that you will do it.

10. *Credit refusal letter.* You work in the credit department of AJAX Auto Parts, the fourth largest retail autoparts franchise in the United States. You receive a credit request from a Duke Hazzard. Duke wants a no-interest credit line of $1000 for 30 days. He clearly needs it, for he has bought seven transmissions and nine clutches for a 1956 Chevrolet in the past 20 months. A credit check reveals that Duke's credit history with three other autoparts stores is less than perfect. Similar purchases over four prior years were not paid within the 30-day, same-as-cash agreement Duke had with those stores. On average, Duke required about 60 days to pay his bill.

   The problem, then, is not that Duke does not pay his bills, but that he does not pay them within

30 days. AJAX has a 30-day policy similar to the other stores, but it also has a 60-day policy that requires a 2 percent a month finance charge.

Write a letter to Duke refusing him a no-interest credit line, but offering him a 60-day, $1000 credit line at 2 percent.

11. *Unfavorable response to an inquiry*. You are the secretary of the Student Government Association of your university. One day, Ms. Ima Snoop, head of an organization called Citizens Advocating Discipline in Schools and known to some by its acronym, writes to you requesting information. Here is part of her letter.

Dear Secretary:

We are an organization vitally concerned for the future of our nation and for our young people.

In order to have facts to take to a congressional hearing on the subject of discipline in colleges and universities, we need the following information.

1. How many incidences of disorderly behavior resulted in arrests at your school between January 1, 1991 and December 30, 1992?
2. How many professors were assaulted by students during the same period?
3. How many hours a week does the average student study?

We would appreciate your answering these questions and sending them to us within 30 days.

You suspect that the answers to questions 1 and 2 are available somewhere, but, having called Campus Security, you discover that such information, while not confidential, is not given out to anyone who asks. Campus Security would not even tell you. Question 3 would require an extensive and expensive study, one that the SGA would be unable to fund even if it were interested in doing so. In short, Ms. Snoop is probably asking the wrong organization, but you have no idea what organization would be appropriate.

Write a letter to Ms. Snoop in which you decline to answer her questions.

12. *Letter of complaint*. Poverty has precluded your living in an apartment since you arrived at Old State two years ago. Consequently, you live in a dormitory and eat at a dining hall shared by seven dormitories. The manager of the cafeteria is Mr. Speece, known not entirely affectionately as Mr. Grease. Because this is the beginning of your third year, you

know that institutional food the world over is not noted for its prize-winning Beef Wellington.

Nevertheless, after two weeks of eating in the cafeteria this year, you have noted three cases of mild food poisoning, one instance of chicken so undercooked as to be raw, lima beans so hard as not to have been cooked at all, and fried eggs with no yolks.

Having complained politely to Mr. Grease, you get nowhere. His response is a curt, "Aw, you guys'd groan about the food at th' Ritz." The graduate resident in your dormitory is Mr. Grease's nephew. You know no help will come from that quarter. Write a letter to the head of food services for the entire university complaining of the food in this cafeteria. Be sure to remember to ask for specific improvements.

13. *Unfavorable response to a letter of complaint*. You are Mr. Speece, manager of a university cafeteria serving the students of seven dormitories for the past seven years. You are accustomed to hearing complaints from students about the food. Recently, however, you received a copy of a letter sent to your boss, and signed Fahrquart, in which several specific allegations were made regarding eggs with no yolks, raw lima beans, and cases of mild food poisoning. To your knowledge, none of these charges is true, except for one instance of food poisoning which caused no serious damage, other than to keep a number of students awake all night because of unusual activity in the bathrooms of five dormitories. The letter asks that Fahrquart, one who suffered from the food poisoning, be refunded 3/15 of the money charged for a 15-week semester.

Because, in general, you like students, you are concerned about the food poisoning, and have traced it to a janitor who, one Friday night, mistakenly threw a switch that turned off the refrigerators holding vegetables. Unfortunately, the night was very hot, and the beans spoiled. You were not informed until after the beans had been served. Write a response to Fahrquart saying no to the refund.

CASE STUDY I: THE CHAOS ORDER (GOOD NEWS)

Write an order to Chaos, Incorporated, in which you include the following information in the proper way:

1. Need within six weeks
2. Hand delivery
3. Thirteen 6″ x 8″ x 15″ stink bombs
4. Thirteen 7″ x 9″ x 16″ attaché cases

5. Thirteen space suits

6. One space station

7. Two sets of rations for 27 years each

8. Will pay cash upon delivery

9. Require letter assuring confidentiality

CASE STUDY 2: ACKNOWLEDGING ORDERS: McGOOCH APPLIANCE

Among your responsibilities as Shipping Department supervisor at Fahrquart Industries is that of making sure that all orders are filled promptly. A long-time customer, and your third-largest buyer, is Mr. Sam McGooch, of McGooch Appliance, a manufacturer of such small appliances as automatic potato peelers and Vetavitaveggie dicers, splicers, and cubers. McGooch insists on handling all orders himself, believing that he will get faster responses from his suppliers. He is right. Here is a short order from McGooch.

> Please send us 70,000 model W-12 widgitcogs; 50,250 model A-23s widgitcogs; and 176,000 model B-1245 widgitcogs (new design). Payment in full will be sent with our quarterly payment.
>
> Although the model W-12s and A-23s may be received anytime in the next two weeks, the 176,000 model B-1245 widgitcogs *must be here no later than November 12.*

You receive McGooch's order on November 9. Everything he asks for is in stock except that there are only 150,000 model B-1245 widgitcogs available. Having checked with manufacturing, you know that a week will be required to make the other 26,000 and another three days to get them to McGooch.

Remember that the job includes not only sending McGooch what you can, but also informing him of what you cannot. You must try to persuade him to wait ten days for the rest of the order. Write a letter acknowledging McGooch's order.

CASE STUDY 3: FAVORABLE RESPONSE TO A LETTER OF COMPLAINT: JUNIOR FAHRQUART'S SOCCER BALL (COMPANY NOT AT FAULT)

You are the newest staff member of Customer Relations for the Matex Toy Company. The company is small, having chosen to remain so in order to produce what the company and many others consider to be the best toys anywhere. The market for Matex Toys is relatively small as well, as the only line of toys MTC produces is top-of-the-line, and the toys cost between 30 and 45 percent more than other companies' deluxe toys.

MTC prides itself on producing toys that have two outstanding qualities: safety and durability. Because MTC rarely receives complaints, no employee has been assigned to respond to them. Such jobs are routinely given to the lowest (which means newest) person on the managerial staff. When your boss receives the letter shown on page 154, she hands it to you with this comment: "Give 'em what they want."

When you open the package, you find a horribly mutilated soccer ball containing what seem like thousands of tiny little puncture marks. Junior, it seems, has needle-sharp teeth. Ordinarily this would call for a *no* letter, but remember that your boss said, "Give 'em what they want." Write the adjustment letter to Ms. Fahrquart.

CASE STUDY 4: RESPONDING FAVORABLY TO A ROUTINE COMPLAINT: THE BAD BATCH (COMPANY AT FAULT)

In the pre-Christmas rush to get toys on the retail store shelves, Matex Toy Company's model X-23 soccer balls (see Case Study 3) somehow escaped Quality Control. About 70 of the balls were fitted with faulty valves, so they cannot hold air. Only 48 balls were returned before they could be sold. There is no way to learn who bought these faulty balls before they were removed from the shelves. Consequently, complaints are expected, but Ms. Fahrquart's is the first to be received. Her letter is shown on page 155. Write to Ms. Fahrquart and make the adjustment.

CASE STUDY 5: *NO* LETTER: THE NIBBLIE LETTER

Mr. Fairway Nibblie recently bought a set of golf clubs from your company, the Saint Andrews Golf Club Company. He returned his 4-iron with this note.

> You will notice that the shaft of this 4-iron is bent. Consequently, it cannot be used. As these clubs were guaranteed for one year and as I bought them only last month, would you please fix it, or send me a new one?

While examining the club, you notice black rubber marks on the heel of the club. Clearly, Mr. Nibblie bent the club on a driving range by hitting so far behind the ball as to slam the club into the rubber mat, which is usually placed on concrete. As no golf club can withstand this kind of abuse, and as the guarantee is not unconditional, but rather for defects in materials and workmanship, you cannot offer to pay for the repair or to give him a new club. Write a *no* letter to Mr. Nibblie.

9604 Williams Road
Northwest, PA 14235

28 February 1991

Customer Relations
Matex Toy Company
Toyland, MI 12345

Dear Customer Relations:

In early December of last year, we bought our 10-year-old son, Junior, a Matex soccer ball (regulation size, model X-23). Now, not three months later, the ball is broken.

We always have bought Matex toys for little Junior because they were the best, their durability pleasing us especially. We admit that Junior is a bit hard on toys, but aren't all children? Anyway, after deflating the ball for winter storage, Junior, anxious about some grades he received in school, became nervous. This nervousness became manifested in biting fits. Among the things he chewed on was his MTC soccer ball. He bit holes in it. We are returning the ball in a separate package.

Because MTC advertises that "Durability is the Name of Our Game," we would like either a new ball or a full refund. The ball cost $39.95, and a receipt is enclosed.

Sincerely,

Irene Fahrquart

Ms. Irene Fahrquart

CASE STUDY 6: LETTER OF INQUIRY: JOB COUNSELING

You have recently joined the staff of the Job Advisory and Counseling Office. This undergraduate organization was formed by your department to help place graduating seniors in industry. The office has become infamous for its lack of success. One reason is that the office is loosely coordinated. Another is that it confronts a tight job market reflecting the generally sluggish economy. In fact, the prestige of the Job Advisory and Counseling Office has fallen to the point that students regularly write nasty letters to the editor of the college paper.

Their contempt is not wholly deserved. The advice the office gives to job seekers comes largely from its extensive library of books and articles listed under the broad category of "How to Land a Job." After reading

Dear Customer Relations:

In early December of last year, we bought our 10-year-old son, Junior, a Matex soccer ball (regulation size, model X-23). The ball is broken. In fact, it never worked at all!

We always have bought Matex toys for little Junior because they were the best, their durability pleasing us especially.

The problem is that we cannot get the ball to hold air. We returned the ball to the store where we bought it, and they suggested that we write to you.

Because MTC advertises that "Durability is the Name of Our Game," we would like either a new ball or a full refund. The ball cost $39.95, and a receipt is enclosed.

Sincerely,

Irene Fahrquart

Ms. Irene Fahrquart

much from this list, you discover that the advice of several authors conflicts. Two recent articles are typical.

Writing in the *Havad Business Review*, John Sternum argues that employers are as picky about grades as graduate schools; that a record of high academic achievement is of primary importance in getting a job. Almost as important, Sternum says, is the requirement to hold office and be active in undergraduate organizations. He makes secondary such things as appearance, articula-

tion in speech and writing, and performance during job interviews. In an article appearing the same month in the *Sanford Business Review*, however, Albert Martin contradicts Sternum almost point for point. Martin's studies reveal no direct relationship between college performance and success on the job. Indeed, says Martin, success in industry may require qualities not only different from, but also opposite to those prized by colleges and universities. Employers, he believes, look for candidates who are energetic, outgoing, creative, and articulate; those who can think on their feet.

Because such contradictions are the rule, not the exception, you decide to improve the information your office gives to job seekers by getting first-hand information by surveying employers in your discipline. Generally, you want to know what criteria employers apply when choosing one candidate over another. What does the winner have that the loser does not? Because you want as much *specific* information as you can get, you realize that your questions must be written with great care. Moreover, you realize that no one need answer your inquiry, and so you must honestly and effectively move your respondents to *want* to answer.

Write a letter of inquiry in which you include a brief, easily answered, list of questions.

CASE STUDY 7: LETTER OF INQUIRY: THE DEAN'S STUDY

The dean of your college has given you one month to study the relative effectiveness of television versus live instruction for technical courses. To exclude as many variables as possible, you decide to limit the study to a single course, one taught both live and through television, and using the same syllabus and similar departmental examinations for both live and televised sections. You finally choose a basic mathematics course called Math 1 that is taken by about 500 students each semester. Enrollment is almost evenly divided between live and televised sections; each section enrolls about 25 students.

Your preliminary work discloses that the following five sources of information are available:

1. Grades for all Math 1 sections taught in the last five years are kept on file in the university's Records Office.

2. Accurate attendance records for all Math 1 sections taught in the last five years are filed in the university's Office of Student Life.

3. The opinions of former Math 1 students, written on a questionnaire, may be found in the college president's office.

4. Grades from mathematics courses for which Math 1 is requisite. Such courses are always taught live and are on file in the Records Office.

5. Podunk and Cornstalk Universities recently studied the same issue. Your one-month deadline precludes your studying *all* five sources. Choose the *two* sources that you think will yield the most reliable results. Write a letter of inquiry to these two sources requesting information.

CASE STUDY 8: COMPLAINT LETTER: THE "BLECH" LETTER

Rewrite the following letter so that it follows the arrangement and tone of a proper letter of complaint. Remember that the goal of the letter is to have a rotor that works at little or no cost to you.

Dear (!) Lace Antennae:

Who do you guys think you are? On May 11, I spent a small fortune ($79.80) for a deluxe model rotor (XI23) for a television antenna, but when I put it up, the piece of junk wouldn't turn. So, I went up the ladder again, hung over the side of my house, again, took it down, again, re-did the wiring, and climbed down the ladder. I'm not a young man. It's hard work. But I persevered: four times I checked and rechecked the connections, both on the rotor and on the TV, *carefully following the installation manual*. It still doesn't work.

When I returned to Lace Antennae, the salesman told me to check some dooflingie or other to see if that wasn't the problem. I wasn't going up there again to risk my life checking something I didn't understand. He refused to explain again. Then he told me to bring it back and he would have it checked. The problem with that is that if *you say* the problem is not in the rotor, I pay. Now how am I to know if the problem is mine or the rotor's. I have to rely on your word. And if you can make some money off me, why wouldn't you?

I'm really angry about this. Any proper business would simply replace the bad with the good. If you think I'll buy another thing from your store, you are as crazy as you are crooked.

CASE STUDY 9: COMPLAINT LETTER: LOST LUGGAGE

You went to Chicago on May 23 on a business trip. You were representing your company, Wonder Advertising, and presenting to Binky Toys a new television advertising campaign. The trip to Chicago went well until you discovered at the baggage claim that your luggage had not arrived. It was 11:30 a.m. Your presentation was to be at 2:00 p.m.

You do the obvious:

1. Register your claim with Fahrquart Airlines and Lawn Sprinkler Company.

2. Hail a taxi and go to Meiman Narcus (the fare was $12).

3. Buy clothes to wear at the presentation: suit, blouse, stockings, underclothes, shoes, makeup (totaling $336.78).

4. Keep the receipts.

5. Go to your hotel (arriving at 12:45).

6. Call Fahrquart Airlines claim desk (no luck).

7. Make your presentation (great luck!).

8. Eat dinner; go to bed; get up; fly home.

Your luggage arrives on May 25. Write a letter to the airlines requesting $348.78.

CASE STUDY 10: BOARD ROOM BIGOTRY (NO LETTER)

You are the newest staff assistant to Smedley Fahrquart, president of Consolidated Bloomers, Incorporated (CBI), a company manufacturing compact office computers. Early one morning Fahrquart's secretary hands you an envelope and tells you that he wants you to "drop everything and handle this right away." Inside the envelope you find the following letter:

Mr. Fahrquart:

I am darned annoyed!

I just went through what you people call an annual report. As I expected, it's filled with the standard piffle about "what your company is doing for you," but I'm used to that. What I am not used to is seeing photographs of women on page after page. It looks like you've finally knuckled under to Davis and the other do-gooders and sob-sisters by giving out jobs to incompetents and no-accounts just because they wiggled their ways through college.

I may just have something more to say about this situation—and about soft-headed management practices in general—at next month's stockholders' meeting.

J. C. Pants

P.S.: The only good thing about the whole report was the profit statement, and I darned well expect it to continue!

Scrawled on Pants's letter is this note from Fahrquart:

This is not the first such letter Pants has written. Subject is different each time, but the approach never varies. He's a bigot and a pest, but he owns 6200 shares of CBI, and we could use his support next month at the stockholders' meeting. That money may help us continue the good work we're doing around here! Draft a careful response for my signature.

Some points, which may or may not be useful, come to mind:

1. The law strictly prohibits discrimination in hiring. Penalties for evading or breaking the law are severe.

2. CBI has bucked a recent bear market. Its stock is now trading at $32\frac{1}{8}$, up $5\frac{1}{2}$ points since this time last year.

3. Mark S. Davis, Chairman of the Board of CBI, has a long history of supporting women's rights.

4. Many of the women recently hired have done outstanding work. A photograph of Jane C. Lewis, Sc.D., for example, appears on page 14 of the annual report. Last year she developed a way of producing memory cores that cut production costs by 30 percent. A picture of Lupe Fernández, Accounting Department, is shown on page 27 of the report. She developed a method for billing that cut postage costs by 22 percent and reduced the time from purchase to billing by half. Generally, all women managers have performed to CBI's satisfaction.

5. Just last week, CBI fired a woman, a lab technician, who allegedly sold company production secrets to a rival company. The case is now in litigation.

6. In the past five years, the CBI Annual Report has won two prestigious industrial awards: one for its straightforward reporting of company affairs, and one for excellence in style and layout.

Draft the response.

CASE STUDY 11: THE DMI LETTER (NO LETTER)

You are the newest staff member in the Office of the Treasurer of Gotham Addison, parent company of the power companies that collectively own two-thirds of the DMI Nuclear Power Installation. Two months ago, DMI narrowly averted a catastrophic nuclear accident. Since that time, the treasurer's office has been working twelve- to fifteen-hour days supplying figures on the cost of physical damage to the plant and shutdown time and figures to predict time of recovery (that is, how long will be required to make profits again).

Each time a request (really a demand) is made for information, that request is accompanied by an *if*: how much would it cost if this or that or this and that should occur. Each request thus requires an entirely new set of figures. So far, figures have been tailored for reports demanded by three state offices, ten federal regulatory agencies, and a House Congressional Special Committee in DMI. Figures remain to be included in reports for two state committees, three federal regulatory agencies, the governor's office, and the White House. New demands arrive daily, including one from the Department of Agriculture, which is responsible for monitoring the levels of radiation in cow's milk, corn, soybeans, and other crops and commodities. As you open the door to your office, the personal secretary to Ms. Jane Dawlish, the treasurer, hails you.

"Dawlish wants you to take care of this right away," he says, pulling a sheet of paper from the bottom of what appears to be a full ream he is carrying. Once in your office, you read the sheet, a letter from a well-known consumer advocate:

Dear Ms. Dawlish:

As you may know, the Consumer's Advocate Association that I head is opposed to nuclear-generated power. Although the so-called DMI accident has no doubt done more to hasten the end of nuclear power in this country than anything a group like ours could do, we do not want to judge hastily by saying that the accident resulted from sloppy management, the immoral or illegal granting of bids, or stupidity.

In order to determine causes, CAA wants to examine the accident calmly and judiciously. As part of that effort, we request that you supply us with a report detailing every aspect of the cost involved in building the DMI Installation.

This effort is being made on behalf of the American people, many thousands, perhaps hundreds of thousands, of whom had their lives threatened by the accident, and the millions who live under the shadow of other cooling towers. The American people not only have a right to know, but also you, as a *public* utility, have a responsibility to make sure that the people know what happened and why.

We would appreciate your providing us with a date when our accountants may meet with yours in a preliminary discussion regarding the kind and amount of data the public needs. This, of course, is only the first step, and any suggestions you can provide to ease the transfer of information would be helpful.

Wanda Freshwater, President
Consumer Advocates Association

Atop this letter and in Dawlish's hand the following is written:

We can't, just can't do this *now*! There's no time! No resources! We've got everybody and his uncle on our backs. We may not be able to do as she asks for months. Still, we cannot afford to have Freshwater filing a class action suit against us now. GA's President has said that the legal office is overrun by lawsuits, potential and actual.

But remember that Freshwater is no fool. She's intelligent, sophisticated, and really quite powerful.

Who knows? Ultimately, she may be good for this country. But we just cannot do it now!

Write a letter to F. for my signature saying so.

After several frantic phone calls, you discover the following information. It may or may not be useful:

1. Under the state's sunshine laws, Freshwater and her group have a right to this information if they can argue "a clear and present danger." You suspect that they would not have to argue too strenuously.

2. Until the day of the accident, DMI had the second-best safety record of the twenty-seven nuclear power installations east of the Mississippi.

3. In a referendum twelve years ago, the voters of the state favored, 73 percent to 24 percent, using nuclear energy for electricity. The results of the referendum were used widely by GA to push for rapidly completing the installation.

4. R. B. Schneidler and Co. and Scarlatti Construction, two of the contractors who built DMI, are under investigation on charges of fraud, kickbacks, and other illegalities (including sanding the concrete) while building several sections of interstate highway in a neighboring state. The job was begun fewer than seven months after they had completed their work on DMI.

5. Freshwater receives a considerable income from a trust set up by her father. That trust is administered through the Omega Fund, a Madison Avenue company once controlled by Freshwater's father. Omega sold the land now occupied by DMI to Gotham Addison.

Draft the response.

CHALLENGE EXERCISE 1: REFUSAL OF ORDERS

You are a staff member for the Ferro Carrilito Toy Train Company. Mr. Lionel Burlington wants to order a complete set—from engine to caboose—of your new, top of the line toy train, model #3745. As your company does not sell trains directly to customers, but only to dealers, you must write to Mr. Burlington refusing his order.

Some facts that may be helpful follow. The nearest dealer is Trains R Us (96 Sidecar Lane, Altoona, Pennsylvania), 25 miles from Burlington's home. Having called Trains R Us, you discover that they have sold out of their initial order. Having called inventory, you discover that orders are backlogged. In short, Mr. Burlington will not be able to buy a set from Trains R Us for about 10 weeks. Choo-Choo's, a similar dealer, does have one set, but it is in Pittsburgh, some four hours' drive from Burlington's.

Challenge Exercise 2: Saying no to Charles Darnay

Here is a letter written by an imaginative undergraduate concerning characters in Charles Dickens's novel *A Tale of Two Cities*. Darnay is in big trouble and therefore uninsurable. Identify and label the four parts of this *no* letter.

Liberté, Egalité, Fraternité, Incorporated
100 Rue Des Têtes Rollés
Paris, France 12753-0913

April 9, 1789

Mr. Charles Darnay
The Bastille
1789 Rue de la Révolution
Paris, France 12678-2134

Dear Mr. Darnay:

We agree that you would be wise to acquire considerable life insurance. As a member of the aristocracy and as the son-in-law of Dr. Manette, that prominent London physician, your business normally would be eagerly sought. And, naturally, upon the recommendation of our company's most valued customer, Mr. Sydney Carton, we would not hesitate to serve you.

Looking at the situation from your perspective, we certainly can understand how you feel. Because of the political tumult of the last few months, however, and because of your subsequent misfortune, we simply cannot issue a policy to you at this time.

Should your circumstances change, however, we would be delighted to reconsider your application.

Yours for the revolution,

Madame LaFarge

Madame LaFarge,
Interim Sales Director

PERSUASIVE LETTERS: FRIENDLY AND OTHERWISE

The Goals of Persuasion
Modern Methods of Persuasion:
    Maslow's Hierarchy of Needs
Sales Letters
Collection Letters

SOCIAL LETTERS

Letters of Congratulations
Letters of Sympathy and
    Condolence
Invitations
Reservations

INTERNATIONAL LETTERS

SUMMARY

EXERCISES

Learning Objectives:

☐ Know the goals of persuasion.

☐ Know the modern methods of persuasion: Maslow's hierarchy of needs.

☐ Write three types of sales letters:
    Solicited,
    Soft-sell,
    Unsolicited.

☐ Write all stages of collection letters.

☐ Write congratulatory letters.

☐ Write reservations.

☐ Write invitations.

☐ Write letters of sympathy.

☐ Know common rules for international letters.

7

THE REPUBLIC OF LETTERS.

HENRY FIELDING

(1707–1754)

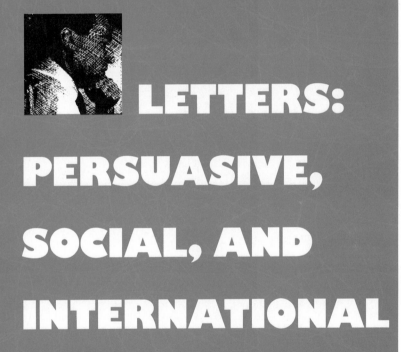

LETTERS: PERSUASIVE, SOCIAL, AND INTERNATIONAL

PERSUASIVE LETTERS: FRIENDLY AND OTHERWISE

All business letters should be persuasive. By trying to present the company or its products or services in a good light, letters persuade the reader of the company's worth, its goodwill, its competence, and its ability to provide good service, good products, and low prices. Even letters that merely convey information sell the company to the degree that they are clear, accurate, and courteous.

THE GOALS OF PERSUASION

Successful persuasion depends on knowing the goals before doing the persuading. There are five questions that, when answered precisely, define the goals.

1. *Why do I want to persuade?* We persuade people for one of two reasons: we want them to believe as we do or we want them to do something. Behind these motives lie more specific reasons, usually having to do with our own self-interest. We try to persuade people to do that which will make us money, make us look good, give us more leisure, or any of a hundred things. It is important to define *precisely* why we want to persuade in any given instance.

     A simple illustration may suffice. Your brother is being married this Saturday. This Saturday, it is also your turn to referee an intramural soccer game. Persuading a friend to be a substitute referee, so you can attend your brother's wedding, may require that you offer to substitute for your friend on more than one occasion later. This means more work for you, but attending the wedding *this Saturday* outweighs the other Saturdays by a great deal.

2. *What do I want to persuade people to do?* Precision is important here. The American Dental Association wants you to brush your teeth twice a day with a fluoridated toothpaste. Procter & Gamble, on the other hand, wants you to brush twice a day with Crest.

3. *When do I want them to do it?* When is often very important. Car dealers, for example, want you to buy a car *now*.

4. *Where do I want them to do it?* The San Francisco Chamber of Commerce wants your trade organization to hold its next convention in San Francisco. The St. Francis Hotel wants you to hold it in the St. Francis Hotel.

5. *How do I want them to do it?* Your professor wants you to write your next report on a computer. The goal is to combine a display of your knowledge of writing reports with a new skill—writing on a computer.

In addition to these five goals of persuasion and goals listed by the ancient rhetoricians (discussed in Chapter 2), writers must think about other considerations when setting out to persuade. Among these are the persuasive effects of good writing, appropriate tone, and audience analysis.

GOOD WRITING.   People are persuaded by good writing. Writing that is dull or full of rot bores readers. Writing that is ungrammatical insults readers as much as writing that is impolite or condescending.

TONE.   Tone is also important. Tone should suit both the subject and the writer's relationship with the reader. A good tone for business adapts to the demands of the information and the reader. Most often, however, routine business writing should carry a tone of efficiency, clarity, and accuracy without losing its human qualities.

Sometimes tone is more important than meaning. It can, in fact, create meaning. Notice, for example, how the difference in word choice in these two sentences creates different meanings.

1. As our *oldest* vice-president, Smedley, perhaps you know what this means.

2. As our *most experienced* vice-president, Smedley, perhaps you know what this means.

In writing, unlike speech, word choice creates most of the tone of any communication.

AUDIENCE.   When writers know their audiences, they can be more persuasive; that is, the writers know specifically what—self-interest, reason, emotion, and ethics—is likely to persuade their readers.

EXERCISE A: TONE AND MEANING

Discuss in class the following question: How many ways can you say "What do you mean by that, Smedley?"

MODERN METHODS OF PERSUASION: MASLOW'S HIERARCHY OF NEEDS

Of the many modern theories of persuasion, Abraham Maslow's hierarchy of needs remains the most prominent. Maslow said that people are persuaded by that which satisfies one or more of five fundamental needs.

MASLOW'S HIERARCHY OF NEEDS
1. *Physical:* Food, shelter, warmth
2. *Security:* Personal and financial
3. *Belonging:* Identifying with something larger or more enduring than the self: family, company, nation
4. *Esteem and status:* Self-respect and respect from others
5. *Goals:* Self-actualization—a sense of accomplishment and fulfillment

Although each of these needs belongs in classical rhetoric to the category of self-interest, Maslow went further by identifying the first two needs as *lower order*. That is, they are essential to life. The remaining three he called *higher order*. That is, once lower order needs are satisfied, we can afford to pursue higher order needs. Because there is a progression—we must accomplish the first two before we can pursue the other three—Maslow called this theory the *hierarchy of needs*.

In business, much persuasion depends on how these higher-order needs are satisfied in letters. Here is the body of a letter that appeals to all five needs.

Status

Security

Belonging
Physical well-being

Belonging and Fulfillment

. . . .

EXERCISE B: MASLOW'S HIERARCHY OF NEEDS

In a class discussion, identify the specific needs satisfied by each of the following appeals:

Lemming furnaces are warm and inexpensive.

If you are like others in your age-group, . . .

Erstwyle diamonds are known around the world for quality. . . .

To help you do the good job you want to do . . .

```
Congratulations! You have just purchased a new Whiz-
bang Blender, a state-of-the-art food processor
ready to provide you and your family with delicious
meals just brimming with health!

Your family will call again and again for all those
foods that you knew all along were good for them,
but which you could never get them to eat.

Every time you use your new Whizbang Blender, you'll
know you're giving your loved ones the very best. So
they'll be their very best all day, every day!
```

SALES LETTERS

Sales letters are persuasive with a capital *P*. They have one purpose: to sell. There are three types of sales letters: *solicited sales letters* sell things customers know or believe that they want; *soft-sell letters* sell to customers who probably will want what is being sold; and *unsolicited sales letters* are peculiar things with their own sets of rules. Soft-sell and unsolicited sales letters are extremely specialized. Unsolicited sales letters—like television commercials, the most common form of selling—reach an uncategorized audience. Thousands of tons of unsolicited sales letters, called junk mail by some, are delivered every day in the United States.

SOLICITED SALES LETTERS.   These letters are easy to write if four simple guidelines are followed.

1. Answer the reader's questions in descending order of importance to ensure that the reader gets the most important information first.

2. Create a list to make it easy for the reader to respond correctly; lists also provide a convenient method for including details.

3. Make it brief so that the reader is better disposed to order. If details make the letter long, enclose a separate list or brochure.

4. Make it easy for the reader to order. Enclose order forms, the name, address, and phone number of the nearest dealer, and so forth — these are far more effective than the standard "Just drop by your local dealer's showroom."

Here is an example of a solicited sales letter:

Answer reader's questions.

List details.

Dear Mr. Galileo:

You are right! The XL47 lens has not been approved by our company for the type of telescope you are building. We have listed below answers to your questions in the order they appeared in your letter to us.

1. Our XZ78 lens should allow you to see stars and planets better than would the XL47 lens.

2. We share your concern about the recent statement by local authorities that had Providence wanted us to see the stars better, He would have given us telescopes for eyes. We do not know what the people are saying about our XZ78 lens. They have not asked us about it.

3. Yes, if necessary, we will send one of our craftsmen to your studio to grind and fit a lens specifically for your use.

4. The cost of hiring one of our best craftsmen is 83.5 lire a day. The cost reflects a 10 percent increase from last year because higher wages were granted the Lens Grinders Guild.

5. A factory-ground XZ78 lens costs 548 lire.

Make ordering easy.

Keep letter brief.

We enclose an order form. Should you decide to order a factory-ground lens, please fill out the top half. Order a craftsman by filling out the bottom half, and please sign the release for insurance.

UNSOLICITED AND SOFT-SELL SALES LETTERS. Because selling by mail is difficult, unsolicited and soft-sell sales letters have become among the most sophisticated, finely honed methods of selling. Successful soft-sell sales letters carefully select readers and even more carefully select readers' biases. Then they hammer like the dickens on those biases.

The something-for-nothing sales pitch never goes out of style: "You have won either a BMW sedan or a Genuine Simulated Imitation Pseudo Diamond Ring! Just come to Wonderful Waterful Acres for a day, and watch a film about exciting Wonderful Waterful Acres, to claim your prize!" This kind of selling requires the expertise of advertising. Big companies spending much money on a sales campaign by mail will spend the additional money to hire professionals. Because many companies cannot afford a large professional sales staff, however, employees often write unsolicited sales letters. Consider the importance of unsolicited direct mail campaigns to many companies from this article:

> Direct mail is considered the most measurable of marketing disciplines. Marketers can determine if the false signature on a letter lifts response, for example, or whether straightening the tilt of the stamp on the envelope depresses it.

> Nearly 92 million Americans, or 51.4 percent of the country's adult population, bought goods or services by mail or phone last year [1989], up from 64.4 million Americans five years before, according to the Direct Marketing Association. Last year, 62.78 billion pieces of third-class mail—the Postal Service's category for junk—were sent, enough to grace every mailbox in the United States some 550 times.[1]

Unsolicited sales letters must follow certain rules, which differ from other sales letters only in degree. That is, while the writers must know *something* about readers for all sales letters, they must know *much more* about readers for unsolicited sales letters. Two of those rules must be followed before the letter is written: you must know all about the product and about the people to whom you are selling.

TEN THINGS YOU MUST KNOW ABOUT THE PRODUCT

1. *What it does.* Know what the product does and in descending order of importance to the reader. A wrench, for example, may be used on cars or as a nutcracker.

2. *Why it is an exceptional product.* Many companies make wrenches, but what about your wrench makes it better than other wrenches? What makes it different?

3. *Who developed the product.* Knowing the ins and outs of the product may help you sell it. These can be learned best from those who developed and made it.

---

[1]Randall Rothenberg, "Junk Mail's Top Dogs," *The New York Times Magazine* (August 5, 1990), 27, 40.

....

**EXERCISE C: SELLING AND
KNOWLEDGE OF THE
PRODUCT**

Discuss in class the following
question: Is it possible to know
too much about a product or is
it only possible to tell the reader
too much about a product?

4. *How much maintenance is required*. People want to know this.

5. *How much expertise is required for maintenance*. People want to know this, too.

6. *How much it costs*.

7. *Method of paying*. Pay in full? On time? How?

8. *How soon it can be delivered*.

9. *Safety*. Are there any safety requirements? Does the product need any, or is it so safe that it needs no safety features?

10. *Guarantees*. What assurance is given that the product will satisfy the buyer?

EIGHT THINGS YOU SHOULD KNOW ABOUT THE POTENTIAL BUYERS

1. *Income*.

2. *Marital status*. Both working?

3. *House or apartment*. Own or rent.

4. *Years of schooling*.

5. *Ages*.

6. *Occupations*.

7. *Hobbies*.

8. *Cars*. Years and makes

In addition, sophisticated methods of discovering tendencies among potential buyers include knowledge even of whether potential buyers exhibit a tendency to buy from unsolicited mail. That is, should a person ever buy one thing from unsolicited sales letters, that person will notice very soon a mailbox overflowing daily with unsolicited sales letters.

On the following page is an example of an unsolicited sales letter. It is addressed to subscribers of *National Review* (NR), a well-known national political magazine. Moreover, the magazine, now nearly forty years old, has a friendly relationship with its subscribers, as well as a particular tone of wit, charm, and informality. The letter is selling a credit card with the magazine's name on it. The magazine, as you will note, earns a small return from the credit card company each time the card is used to purchase something.

COLLECTION LETTERS

Collection letters are tricky. Because some bill collectors harassed debtors, the Fair Debt Collection Practices Act of 1978 was passed. This law prohibits harassing, abusing, or mentally distressing debtors "unreasonably." Collection letters may *not* be printed to look like letters from credit bureaus, courts, or government agencies. Postcards are prohibited: public ridicule is forbidden. Consequently, now more than ever before, companies must *persuade* people to pay their bills.

150 East 35th Street, New York, N.Y. 10016   Phone: 212-679-7330

Dear Friend of NR:

I don't know about you, but I've been thinking about summer vacation for some time now--travelling, the beach, seaside dinners, outdoor entertainment, sailing, and (of course) a new wardrobe. All perfect reasons to take advantage of the new National Review Gold Card.

Many readers have already taken advantage of this opportunity to help dear old National Review actually make some money--I'm amazed at how well it works for us (evidently you do use credit cards often!). There is no annual fee for the first year, so it's a bargain for both of us.

By the way, it is an "official" Gold Card, which I hope you'll be proud to flash at the headwaiter, or whomever: you might call it a sign of "solitarity" with NR and the values we both stand for--fun to use.

To apply, simply call toll-free 1-800-847-7378 or complete the enclosed application. As I say, it's really a good deal for both of us, and a unique way for NR to gain a financial advantage it badly needs (NR gets a very small royalty every time you use it). My thanks for your support and I hope to hear from you soon.

Faithfully,

Ed Capano

P.S.   I have the card myself, as does WFB and publisher Wick Allison, and can tell you that you won't be disappointed. National Review is prominently displayed in large black letters across the gold face of the card -- for everyone to see.

NR ng

WILLIAM F. BUCKLEY, JR. *Editor-in-Chief* · WICK ALLISON, *Publisher* · JOHN O'SULLIVAN, *Editor* · EDWARD A. CAPANO, *Associate Publisher*
RICHARD BROOKHISER, PRISCILLA L. BUCKLEY, JEFFREY HART, JOSEPH SOBRAN, *Senior Editors*
LINDA BRIDGES, *Managing Editor* · ROBERT F. SENNOTT, JR., *Advertising Director*

While there are many reasons that people do not pay bills, the most common are as follows:

1. Forgetfulness,
2. Inability to pay,
3. Irresponsibility (some companies ignore this reason, proceeding directly to reason 4), and
4. Criminality.

Remaining calm and pleasant and even solicitous is difficult when owed money, but, as the saying goes, more flies are caught with honey than with vinegar. Simple forgetfulness requires one kind of letter, inability through poverty another, irresponsibility a third, and criminality a fourth.

STAGE 1: FORGETFULNESS.   When a bill is overdue, but not long overdue, the creditor should assume that the debtor simply forgot to pay. A reminder, perhaps two or three, is called for; many companies consider two reminders sufficient. While each of these letters must be polite, each succeeding letter should be more firm than the last. At this stage, the passive voice is useful because it does not directly accuse. Letters at Stage 1 have two parts:

1. You must have forgotten to pay.
2. Please pay.

Here is an example of a *first reminder*; each part is labeled.

You must have forgotten to pay.

Please pay.

Dear Mr. Fahrquart:

December is a joyous but hectic time, and it is easy to overlook or mislay some bills that are normally paid on time. We would be pleased if the $49.79 owed us were put in the enclosed envelope and mailed.

Here is an example of a *second reminder*:

Dear Mr. Fahrquart:

Ten days ago a reminder of a bill for $49.79 was
sent to you and a request for payment was included.

We have not received payment. We would be pleased to
receive it soon.

Here is an example of a *third reminder*:

Dear Mr. Fahrquart:

A bill for $49.79 is now 45 days overdue. Would you
please send it today?

STAGE 2: INABILITY TO PAY.   After assuming forgetfulness, the creditor next must assume that, for some reason, the debtor *cannot* pay. Because the reason is unknown, the second stage becomes, effectively, a letter of inquiry: Why haven't you paid? Honey is still effective at this stage, although the letter should also include an account of the attempts to get paid. The tone of the letter should be one of concern and, as always, professionalism. The letter may express concern without appearing to be over-solicitous. After all, the customer does owe the company money. Notice also that the passive voice is used here. At this stage, the creditor does not want to accuse directly. The passive voice will be more successful than the active voice in keeping readers from becoming defensive.

There are five parts to a Stage 2 collection letter.

1. Say something nice about the reader or customer.
2. Express concern or puzzlement over the non-payment.
3. Ask specific, clear, brief questions.
4. *Ask* that the questions be answered.
5. Set a reasonable deadline for reply.
[6]. Immediately upon receiving payment, send a thank you note. It's good business.

Here is an example of a Stage 2 collection letter.

Say something good about the customer.

Express concern.

Ask questions: be brief and clear.

Ask to be paid; set a reasonable deadline.

Dear Mr. Fahrquart:

We have enjoyed your patronage for some twenty years. In all that time, you have been prompt and accurate in paying your electric bill. And we hope you have been pleased with our service in turn.

Now, we would like to help further by asking what we may do to help you. Your bill for December, now two months overdue, has not been paid, and we know there must be unusual circumstances preventing you from paying. May we help?

If, by March 15, you have let us know why you have not paid, we could help by making arrangements that would satisfy both of us. Would you please do this?

STAGE 3: IRRESPONSIBILITY. During this stage, vinegar replaces honey. Stage 3 letters contain more severe language. For example, the active voice replaces the passive so there is no mistake made about where responsibility lies. Many companies, in fact, skip this stage, moving directly to Stage 4: criminality.

There are four parts to a Stage 3 collection letter.

1. *Name the product or service and the amount of money due.* Be specific: include size, quantity, order number, and serial number. Numbers impress upon the reader that the writer has gathered all the facts and is serious about being paid.

2. *Recount the history of the overdue bill.* Begin by giving the date of purchase—for example, "You bought our Majorca pearls on September 13, 1988, and you bought them on credit." Then give the date that payment was due. List the number and dates of requests for payment. Be direct, preferably ending with a zinger: "You not only have failed to pay, but also have ignored all our attempts to find out why." This section establishes that attempts to collect have followed proper procedures.

3. *Explain what the next step will be: Pay or else!* Write something like this: "Unless we are paid by November 12, 1988, we must turn over your account to the Nasty Collection Agency and take legal action."

4. *Tell the debtor the possible results of legal action.* Make clear that the customer's failure to pay at this point will incur legal fees, court costs, and bad credit standing. Repeat the amount of payment and the deadline. Such a letter might look like this one.

Name the product and the amount due.

Recount the history of the account.

Pay or else!

Warn of legal consequences.

```
Dear Mr. Fahrquart:

In December 1991 you used 37.678 kilowatts of elec-
tricity, supplied by the Kilowatt Electric Company.
Now, three months later, you still owe $49.79 on
that account.

In January of last year, we sent you a bill for the
amount due. One month later, we received neither
money nor a reply. Successive requests on February
1, February 15, February 28, and March 15 were
greeted, apparently, with silence.

We have exhausted all methods of receiving payment
by dealing directly with you. Consequently, we shall
turn over your account to the Nasty Collection
Agency and request legal action if we are not paid
by March 30, 1992.

To avoid expensive legal fees, court costs, and a
loss of credit standing that will make it difficult
for you to do business, you must pay by March 30,
1992.
```

STAGE 4: CRIMINALITY. No more Mr. Nice Guy. This stage does not *require* a letter, but sometimes it is best to tell the debtor that the account has been given to the collection agency and that lawyers are filing suit. This is a short letter that may say no more than this:

```
Dear Mr. Fahrquart:

Because you have not paid your bill after seven
months and after six requests for payment, your ac-
count has been given to the Nasty Collection Agency,
and our lawyers have begun legal proceedings. You
shall hear from both soon.
```

SOCIAL LETTERS

An important activity for building and maintaining goodwill among business associates is writing personal or social letters. These include letters of congratulations and condolence as well as invitations and reservations.

LETTERS OF CONGRATULATIONS

Congratulations are very good news, almost as good as the news that prompted the congratulations. Notes of congratulations may range from the very informal sent by memo to the very formal written on private stationery. Generally, a hand-written note on good stationery is best.

There are many ways to congratulate people in writing. All have two things in common: they are sincere and personal. The sincerity and intimacy of the letter may be improved by something so simple as writing it longhand. Here is a list of the parts of a congratulatory letter:

1. Congratulate.
2. Give details regarding the reason for the congratulations.
3. Convey sincerity.
4. Make it as warm as circumstances allow.

Here are two examples.

February 4, 1992

Dear John,

   Congratulations on your recent award as Jaycee of the Year.

   It is a well-deserved honor, and one that brightly reflects the kind of community service all your co-workers at Shale Bank believe is important.

   Your contributions are well above and far beyond the call of duty.

   Warmest wishes,
   Samantha Evans

May 25, 1992

Dear Jan,

   Congratulations on your recent undefeated season as coach of the women's volleyball Team.

   We all knew you were a top-notch coach and a winning combination all by yourself.

   We're all pulling for you in this year's balloting for the district coach of the year.

   Warmest wishes,
   Smedley Farquart

Notice that each note begins with "Congratulations" (spelled with a *t*, not a *d*) and that each conveys sincerity and has a personal, even warm touch. Notice also that a comma follows the salutation of a personal note or letter, not the customary colon used in business correspondence.

Sometimes managers, as representatives of a company, are called on to congratulate someone they do not know well. For example, the company may be involved in a regional job-training program sponsored by the government, but the regional director of the program may live in another city. When the company hears that someone has done something outstanding, it is important to recognize it. In such a case, a warm but slightly less personal tone is called for. A letter that is too personal may convey insincerity. Properly written, such a letter also may be an opportunity for the company to reaffirm interest in the work being done. Here is an example.

....
EXERCISE E: COLONS AND
COMMAS

Discuss in class the following question: Why is a colon more formal and impersonal than a comma?

August 17, 1992

Dear Ms. Smith,

Congratulations on your recent promotion. Those at Farquart Industries who have worked in your Job Training Program know how much you deserve advancement. Although we will miss your hard work and intelligence, we will do our best to continue the good work with your successor.

   Best wishes,
   Samantha Evans

Remember, however, that congratulations are just that and should be nothing more or less. Never ask for anything in a letter of congratulations.

LETTERS OF SYMPATHY AND CONDOLENCE

When friends or business associates die, or someone in their immediate families dies, the initial response of many is to leave them to their grief, reasoning that people like to be left alone at such times. But death is universal, and knowing that others are thinking of us at such a time is a small but important comfort. Consequently, prompt, brief, hand-written, personal letters or notes conveying our sympathy (*not* empathy) is helpful, appropriate, and even necessary.

For those whom the writer does not know well, a sympathy card is usually sufficient. It should be sent promptly. For those whom the writer does know, however, letters should have three parts:

1. A brief expression of sadness and sympathy;
2. If true, a brief, personal description of how much the dead person meant to the writer;
3. A brief, affectionate closing.

Here is an example for the occasion of the death of a friend's spouse.

September 20, 1992

Dear John,

I was saddened to learn of Susan's death. I know no words of mine can lessen your grief, but I want you to know how much my family and I treasured her great warmth and quick wit over the years.

We shall all miss her very much.

Most affectionately,
Samantha Evans

INVITATIONS

Invitations usually begin with a statement of invitation ("You are invited. . . .") and include the following: who, what, where, when, why, and RSVP. The why may be obvious, but if it is not, provide some detail about the occasion that will entice the reader to accept. Finally, it is important to make responding to the invitation easy. Enclosing a stamped and addressed card or letter is helpful. So are deadlines for replying.

Of all business-related letters, invitations are perhaps the most bound by rules of propriety. Amy Vanderbilt, Emily Post, and other writers of books on etiquette provide invaluable advice for writing invitations.

Although all written invitations have a certain formality simply by virtue of their being written, some are more formal than others. The most formal are those that most of us never receive. They are engraved on expensive paper, placed in an envelope, and hand delivered by the host's employee, who usually travels in a limo. The most informal are oral: "Hey, we're having a party tonight. Wanna come?"

FORMAL INVITATIONS. In general, formal invitations are printed on card stock. Each line is centered, and unless otherwise specified by an organization all words except articles (a, an, the) and short prepositions are capitalized. The tone is formal. An example of the standard formula for formal invitations follows.

Who

Invitation

What

Where

When

RSVP

The Student Services Staff of

The Pennsylvania State University

at The Behrend College

Requests the Pleasure of Mr. Fahrquart's Company

at a Buffet Luncheon

in Room 116 of the Reed Student Union Building

on Thursday, 15 October 1991

at Noon

RSVP extension 6164

by 9 October, 1991

EXERCISE F: INVITATIONS

Discuss in class the following questions:

1. As it is notoriously difficult to get faculty to go to student events, do you think adding a "Why" here would increase faculty's participation?

2. Do you think a free lunch is sufficient motivation?

3. Should a sentence on proper attire be included?

4. Does a potential misunderstanding lurk in the phrase "The Pleasure of Mr. Fahrquart's Company"? What is it?

1. *Who.* Good manners dictate that all invitations begin with an indication of who is doing the inviting. Just as telephone conversations should begin with the callers identifying themselves, invitations should begin with the names of the hosts. An invitation primarily to one person but including a guest or spouse should include either the word "guest" (if the named person either is unmarried or the writer of the invitation does not know) or "spouse" if the named person is married.

> Ms. Samantha Evans and Guest
> Ms. Samantha Evans and Spouse
> Mr. and Mrs. Smedley Fahrquart
> Mr. Smedley Fahrquart and Guest
> Mr. Smedley Fahrquart and Spouse

Always use the full name and title of a person and the full name of an organization. Should the Student Services Staff, for example, write "The SSS of PSU/BC," many faculty would be confused.

2. *Invitation.* After announcing who is writing, an invitation should invite: "Ms. Samantha Evans invites . . ." or "The Student Services Staff . . . Requests the Pleasure of. . . ."

3. *What.* Invitations should be logically arranged. After saying who and inviting, the invitation should name the occasion. In formal invitations, be specific. Do not say only "a Party"; say, for example, "a gathering of friends in honor of Ms. Tyrone-Jones's promotion to Senior Vice-President of Fahrquart Industries."

4. *Where.* Be specific. Sometimes maps should be enclosed with the invitation.

5. *When.* Again, be specific. Include the full date and time: "December 12, 1991, at eight o'clock p.m." Unless a host plans to entertain until four a.m., the invitation should include also a time for the party to end: "eight until [not 'til] midnight." (Experience proves, however, that unless the host is especially adept at steering guests toward the door, a midnight end means an hour or two after that. Should a host desire that a party end by midnight, it is wise to write "eight until eleven.")

6. *Why.* Formal invitations should include a reason for the event. This may follow immediately the what: "In honor of Ms. Jones's Promotion."

....
EXERCISE G: INVITATIONS

Discuss in class the following question: Why should one never write "Please RSVP by . . ."?

7. *RSVP.* Traditionally, "RSVP" (or, more formally, "R.S.V.P.") is placed in capital letters at the bottom of the invitation. It is an abbreviation of the French for "Answer, if you please." So that a host can plan for food, room, drinks, and so on, good manners require that an invited guest reply. Many events are planned far ahead. For this reason, including a deadline for replying is permissible: "RSVP by December 5," "Reply by December 5" or "Please Reply by December 5," but not "Please RSVP by December 5."

INFORMAL INVITATIONS. Less formal invitations use less expensive paper and less flowery language, but they must include the same information. Often the best informal invitations list the information this way.

YOU'RE INVITED!

Who:	All Faculty
What:	Buffet Lunch
By Whom:	Student Services
Why:	Get-to-Know-Us
Where:	Rm. 116 Reed Union Bldg.
When:	Thursday, October 15
What time:	Noon
RSVP by:	Friday, October 9
How:	Call ext. 6164

RESERVATIONS

Reserving rooms, renting cars, hiring guides, and the like are best done in advance for one simple reason: it is almost always better to be expected than not to be. It is more efficient, for example, for business people to organize and plan ahead because hotels and car-rental agencies can provide faster and better service to people they expect.

For very simple reservations, telephone calls are better than letters. Most hotel chains have reservation numbers; use them. Any requirements other than the standard ones of a clean room, a warm bed, and a hot shower, however, require letters. This way, the more elaborate needs of business travelers will have a chance of being met.

Writing to reserve a room in a hotel, a conference room, or a ballroom requires the same arrangement as placing an order. Surprisingly, reserving hotel rooms seldom causes problems, but should *any* abnormal requests be made, there often are problems. Does the traveler

....

WHEN WRITTEN RESERVATIONS ARE BETTER THAN ORAL RESERVATIONS

1. When a record is desired, and
2. When the details of the reservation are complex.

need a room with a desk in it? Is the lighting good for close work? Is the occupant claustrophobic and thus requires a first-floor room with a window? There are many things to consider. Conference rooms often must include a flip chart, overhead projector, and other accessories for the conference. Ballrooms and other rooms for special occasions require even more attention to detail.

Make sure that the reservation letter contains a well thought-out and clear list of every requirement. Important also are arrival and departure times, meal times (should meals be brought into the room) and other arrangements for food: how many meals, what kind of meals (low sodium, low cholesterol, vegetarian, etc.). The details often seem endless, but a successful meeting or conference demands that the writer have all the details and that they be conveyed *clearly* to the reader. Sometimes a little tact is required, as in the following example:

> One final request: Mr. Fahrquart does not eat or drink anything white (mashed potatoes, milk, white bread, etc.). Please do not serve him anything white. We know this is unusual, and we would not bother you with it, except that he is one of our most valued clients and has been for many years. Anything you can do to make his stay more pleasant would please us greatly.

Leave nothing to chance. No matter how obvious the request, no matter how often a hotel has done something previously without being asked, ask again. Still, these things must be done pleasantly. One may write, for example,

> We have always appreciated your practice of placing a bucket of ice in each room immediately before it is occupied. It is one of those extras about which our people have often commented. We hope this service still is being offered.

As with letters of inquiry and orders, should more than one thing be necessary, make a list. Lists are easy to check, and they make the writer's job and the reader's job easy. Here is a list of items that usually are part of reservations.

1. *A direct, but courteous "reservation."* "Please reserve" is more direct than "We are looking for" and more courteous than "We want."
2. *What.* Name the services *in detail.* Include any numbers given to the services; name names of particular people or special skills required. If more than one person, skill, or thing is to be reserved, make a list.
3. *How many.*
4. *How much.* Unit price. Total price.
5. *Method of paying.* Standing 30-day account (this usually means paying within 30 days as if it were cash; no interest is charged), check, or credit card (include card name, number, and date it expires.
6. *Methods of complying.* Details of special requests.
7. *When needed.*
8. *Confirmation of everything.*

Here is an example of a simple reservation. Parts are labeled.

LERRILL MYNCH INVESTMENTS
10 Avenue of the Americas
New York, New York 01234
(212) 123-4567 TELEX: 789010

26 March 1992

Mr. James Sandman, Manager
Sandman Conference Center
1111 Concord Road
Boston, MA 12645

Dear Mr. Sandman:

Please reserve
What
How many
When

Please reserve three double rooms, thirteen single rooms, and two suites for Lerrill Mynch Investments from 3 p.m. on April 13 until 3 p.m. on April 16. There will be twenty-one people.

I understand that normal check-out time is 2:00 p.m., but because our group is following a very tight schedule, 3 p.m. check-in and check-out times are important.

Payment

Payment will be by check given at noon on April 16. We will, of course, give security in the form of a credit card on April 13.

Special requests and methods of confirmation

Would it be possible to have room service as late as 2 a.m. on April 14? Overseas guests will be hungry. We will need no other services this time.

Please confirm these reservations and the total cost, in writing, by April 1.

Sincerely,

Sacco Venzetti

Sacco Venzetti, Coordinator

When reservations are more complicated, the result may look something like the next example.

LERRILL MYNCH INVESTMENTS
10 Avenue of the Americas
New York, New York 01234
(212) 123-4567 telex: 789010

26 March 1992

Mr. James Sandman, Manager
Sandman Conference Center
1111 Concord Road
Boston, MA 12645

Dear Mr. Sandman:

Lerrill Mynch Investments is planning to hold a
sales meeting at the Sandman Conference Center beginning at 3 p.m. on April 13 and ending at noon on
April 16. Having been assured by the Assistant Manager, Lethe N. Doze, that you can accommodate us, I
have prepared the following list of requirements.
Please confirm.

    1. Languages: At least one speaker of the fol-
       lowing languages must be available to us be-
       tween 8 a.m. and 10 p.m.

          French
          German
          Russian
          Spanish
          Swedish

       These people must speak English also.
    2. Herr Guttman requires a room opening directly
       onto the swimming pool.
    3. Signore Pastore must have a room on the first
       floor.

James Sandman   2   26 March 1992

4. We would like clean white linen table cloths and napkins for <u>every</u> meal.
5. In order to assure our guests of protection, please hire two extra security guards during our stay. We will pay for this, of course.
6. I understand that your normal check-out time is 2:00 p.m., but because our group is following a very tight schedule, 3 p.m. check-in and check-out times are important.
7. We will pay in advance for these extra requirements.
8. Final payment will be by check presented at noon on April 16. Security will be given on April 13.
9. I will arrive at the Conference Center on April 12 to go over these arrangements. May I have a single room for the night of April 12?

Please confirm these reservations in writing by April 1.

Sincerely,

Sacco Venzetti

Sacco Venzetti, Coordinator

············
EXERCISE H: PARTS OF RESERVATION LETTERS

Find all eight parts of a reservation letter in this letter and label them. Discuss in class.

············
RULES FOR WRITING INTERNATIONAL BUSINESS LETTERS

1. Always sell in the buyer's language.
2. Always buy in your own language.

············
EXERCISE I: SELLERS, BUYERS, AND LANGUAGE

Discuss in class the following question: What do these two rules imply about the relationship between sellers and buyers?

INTERNATIONAL LETTERS

Opportunities for misunderstanding abound in letters sent across town. When letters are sent to people whose language and customs are different from the writers', misunderstanding is often more common than understanding. Even so, letters are the most common form of international business communication, and they serve the same purposes as letters sent across town. The differences are those of language and custom.

The most important rules for writing international business letters are these:

Always sell in the buyer's language;
Always buy in your own language.

That part of the business writer's contract concerning making the reader's job easy is especially important here. To make the reader's job easy, follow the guidelines that follow for international letters.

1. *Use only* standard *English.* English, like most languages, is filled with idioms, those little metaphorical phrases that native speakers understand but foreigners often do not. Never write, for example,

"We don't know yet if this project will fly." Most Germans who have graduated from high school understand some English, but even they may not understand the idiomatic use of "fly." If the project concerns selling the Hotel Vier Jahreszeiten in München (Munich), they might say, *"Verrückte Amerikaner! Jetzt wollen sie ein Hotel in der Luft Bauen."* ("Crazy Americans! Now they want to build a hotel in the air.") Write standard English instead: "Please give us more information. Now, we do not know whether selling the hotel will make money for us." Try not to use such contractions as "don't," "won't," "can't," "wouldn't," and "who's."

2. *Avoid abstractions.* Abstractions are words that represent things that cannot be known sensually—cannot be seen, touched, tasted, heard, or smelled. Words like "truth," "justice," "idea," "notion," and "belief," although sometimes necessary, should be avoided when they are not necessary. And some abstractions are better than others. "I think," for example, causes no difficulties for a native speaker. Foreigners, however, may wonder why they had to be told that the writer has the ability to think. "I say" may be better, but "I believe" is even better.

3. *Use simple transitions.* This one is usually easy. "First," "second," "third," and so on are the simplest and clearest transitions. They should be standard for international business conducted in English. "In other words" is better than "in short"; "but" and "except" are usually better than "however" and "although." Select the simplest and clearest transition.

4. *Use numbers and visuals.* Arabic numbers are common not only in the West, but also in the East. Use cardinal numbers (1,2,3,) almost exclusively; use ordinal numbers (first, second, third) for transitions. "Two" is not as easy for foreign readers as "2."

   Visuals—tables and figures—are always helpful. They are especially helpful to those whose English is not good. Use visuals much more often for foreign readers than for readers of English.

5. *Use common sense.* Because common sense is uncommon, this rule is included. Common sense requires that at nearly every word in a letter the writer must ask, "Will the reader understand this word, this phrase, this expression?"

6. *Write salutations and closings in the readers' language.* A little work here pays big dividends. Foreigners' most common complaint about Americans is not that they are loud and uncouth. In fact, most Europeans prefer to rent houses and apartments to Americans because, they say, Americans have more respect for others' property. The most common complaint, however, is an important one: Americans seem to *refuse* to learn even a few words of the language of the country in which they are staying. Few people expect others to be fluent in their language, but most are delighted when a few words may be exchanged. It is not only a matter of courtesy, but also of respect for the person and the country. Take time to learn the standard formal salutations and closings for business letters in the language of the reader.

Here are the standard salutations and closings of business letters in several foreign languages.

STANDARD SALUTATIONS AND CLOSINGS FOR BUSINESS LETTERS

LANGUAGE	SALUTATIONS	CLOSINGS
Chinese and Japanese	Although some books provide Western alphabetical equivalents to Oriental symbols, most business between Occidentals and Orientals is conducted *either in English or in that Oriental language*. When quizzed on the subject, a Hong Kong businessman said that salutations and closings in, say, Chinese would be seen as provincial if the text were in English. In short, write the entire letter in one language.	
French	Monsieur (man) Madame (married woman) Mademoiselle (unmarried woman) Messieurs (company)	Je vous prie de croire, [name], à l'assurance de mes sentiments les meilleurs. Je vous prie de l'agéer, [company name], l'assurance de mes sentiments distingués.
German	Sehr geehrter Herr[2] [name] (man) Sehr geehrte Frau [name] (woman) Sehr geehrte Firma (company)	Ihr Ehrgebener (man, very formal) Ihr (man, ''Yours'') Ihre Ehrgebene (woman, very formal) Ihre (woman, ''Yours'') Mit freundlichen Grüssen[3] (no gender distinction) Mit besten Grüssen
Italian	Gentilissimo Signore [name] (man; if name begins with a vowel, drop the *e*) Gentilissima Signora [name] (woman; never drop the *a*)	Distinti saluti
Spanish	Estimado Señor (man) Estimada Señora (woman)	Atentamente (''Yours faithfully'') Su seguro servidor (''Yours sincerely'') Cordialmente (''Cordially'')

Exercise J: International Letters

Discuss in class the following question: What other advice might you give to people planning to write international letters?

7. *Avoid stereotypes.* This belongs to the category of ''a little knowledge is a dangerous thing.'' National and cultural stereotypes affect writing because they are part of the baggage with which people convey tone, wording, and even information in written communication. For example, do not allow hyperbolic prose to invade writing to Italians just because we have seen on television that Italians converse by standing very close to each other, gesturing wildly, and yelling. True or not, it is silly for an American to try to imitate this behavior; do try to understand it, however. Do not allow utter misconceptions to invade writing. Moreover, Spaniards are not, as we may have been told, extraordinarily flowery in their language. Consequently, writers should not allow such a misconception to spill over into letters. The list could go on and on.

Do, however, be aware of others' cultures and customs. For instance, do remember to remove shoes before entering a home in Japan.

---

[2]As native speakers of German tend to insist on including titles, be certain to include any professional or academic titles before the name.

[3]These last two are cordial, but not excessively formal: good business-like closings.

With certain exceptions, good American manners will hold a person in good stead almost anywhere. The emphasis, however, is on *good* manners. While books on other cultures help, it is best to rely on a conservative approach to manners in another country until one learns by direct observation. International letters are not only representatives of companies, but also representatives of nations and cultures. Consequently, international letters must be written with extraordinary care.

SUMMARY

1. Writers must understand the five clear goals of persuasion:
    a. Why do I want to persuade?
    b. What do I want to persuade people to do?
    c. When do I want them to do it?
    d. Where do I want them to do it?
    e. How do I want them to do it?
2. Good writing, appropriate tone, and a sensitive understanding of the reader are important tools of persuasion.

3. Maslow's hierarchy of needs delineates several kinds of self-interest that are persuasive to the degree that they are satisfied.
4. Social letters obey certain rules peculiar to themselves but also many rules that are applicable to all letters.
5. International letters must pay careful attention to the special problems of international communications. While all people are essentially the same, vast cultural differences require that writers be especially sensitive to those differences. Often, the success of a business enterprise depends on that sensitivity.

EXERCISES

1. *Methods of persuasion.* Here is part of a letter that attempts to persuade. Analyze the letter according to Maslow's hierarchy of needs and identify the appeals the letter uses. Be prepared to discuss in class.

The most important financial decisions you will be making over the next decades will concern a home.

We at Boggy Acres Realty understand the importance of these decisions to your life and those of your family. Boggy Acres has been serving your community successfully for thirty-five years. So we know we are doing something right.

Boggy Acres is a specialty realty company, helping people find the most distinctive homes in only the most prestigious neighborhoods. Your needs and desires are our *raison d'être*.

When you next consider buying a home, we hope you will consider allowing us to serve you.

2. *Methods of persuasion.* Study the letter in Exercise 1. Can you identify any persuasive appeals that have not been discussed here? What are they? How are they different from those listed here? Be prepared to discuss in class.

3. *Methods of persuasion.* Here is another attempt at persuasion. What does it appeal to? Be prepared to discuss in class.

Buying computers from Nepal makes good business sense!

■ Nepal has American-trained specialists who know U.S. systems.
■ Software costs 40% less in Nepal than in the U.S.
■ Nepal has technical expertise, hardware capabilities, and state-of-the-art software.
■ Forty-seven of the Fortune 500 companies already use Nepalese software services.

In addition to a 40% saving on cost, when you buy from Nepal, you also get American know-how. No wonder discerning buyers are looking to Nepal for quality and savings.

4. *Solicited sales letters*. Mr. Helado, a distributor of ice cream in southwest Texas, has written to your company, which makes a very good, nationally sold ice cream similar to Häagen-Dazs. Your company has no distributor in southwest Texas because for years the area had little population. Marketing people tell you that the population now is sufficient to support a distributor. Certainly, the weather is conducive to selling ice cream. Mr. Helado has only one question: "Would you be interested in having me distribute your ice cream?" Write a letter to Helado expressing your interest in his company.

5. *Unsolicited sales letters*. Nearly everyone receives unsolicited letters every week. Save two of these letters and bring them to class. Analyze both according to the rules for writing such letters. (Your professor may want to copy these letters for distribution and discussion in class.)

6. *Unsolicited sales letters*. Compare two of the letters discussed in Exercise 5. Which does a better job of selling? Why? Discuss in class.

7. *Unsolicited sales letters*. Do some research on a product you would love to own but cannot afford. Assume that five years from now you will be married, have two children, two cars, own a home, and be able to afford the product. In five years this product may not be high on your list of things to buy. Write an unsolicited sales letter to yourself as you may be in five years. Persuade yourself to buy the product.

8. *Collection letters: Stage 1*. When the local Automobile Dealers' Association held an extravagant and expensive reception (three days long) for about fifteen executives of Detroit and Japanese car manufacturers, your company, A–Z Receptivity, was asked to handle things. And you did—to the tune of $16,350. Of that amount, you have received from the association a check for $10,000. Six weeks later, however, the promised final payment of $6,350 has not arrived. Write a Stage 1 collection letter.

9. *Collection letters: Stage 2*. Using the same information as in Exercise 8, write a Stage 2 collection letter.

10. *Collection letters: Stage 3*. Using the same information as in Exercise 8 and 9, write a Stage 3 collection letter.

11. *Collection letters: Stage 4*. Using the same information as in Exercises 8–10, write a Stage 4 collection letter.

12. *Collection letters: Group Assignment*. Dividing the class into four groups, have each group write a different stage collection letter.

13. *Congratulations*. Samantha Evans, your former roommate, has just been awarded a scholarship to study at the London School of Economics. Only 3 of 150 applicants were awarded scholarships. Evans, a finance major, was the only student of the three who is not an economics major. Write a letter of congratulations to her.

14. *Congratulations*. Ms. Rudman Hawley-Smoot, the state representative for your district in which your company, Widgitcogs, Inc., has its headquarters, has just been re-elected for another two-year term. Although she chairs the Subcommittee on Corporate Taxation of the powerful Ways and Means Committee, and will have much to say about the state's plans to correct a $3.5 billion short-fall in revenues next year, your letter cannot mention this directly. Remember that, although the letter is essentially political and good business, it should be sincere.

15. *Reservations*. You must spend two nights in Onehorse, Wyoming. Although Onehorse boasts three hotels, the Old West Inn is especially close to the offices of the Shale Oil Company, whose president you are meeting on September 9. You have tried to stay in the Old West Inn before, but either it was full or the staff had no knowledge of the reservations your secretary had made and had confirmed. This time, you decide to write for a single room for the nights of September 8 and 9. Write a letter asking for written confirmation of your reservation.

16. *Reservations*. You are entertaining an out-of-town investor who must stay at the Ritz for three days: July 9–11. Mr. Ohmigosh is a pleasant man, and a very important one. His sole peculiarity is that he likes to stay in rooms decorated in orange colors. Write a reservation for him.

17. *Invitations*. List the things you would want to know before you could decide whether to accept an invitation to a party. Does your list match those things included in formal invitations? If so, good. If not, why not? Be prepared to discuss in class.

18. *Invitations*. Your boss, who has just resigned to take a much bigger job with another company, is well liked by his staff. You are planning a farewell reception for him at your home. Because you want to do it right, the reception will be formal. Your boss has agreed to come. Write a *formal* invitation to his staff. Remember that formal invitations normally are sent to each person separately, but remember also to include spouses or guests.

19. *Invitations*. The situation is the same as in Exercise 18, but you want to keep the reception simple and informal. Write an *informal* invitation to his staff.

20. *International letters*. Choose a foreign country that interests you. Read a magazine article about the

manners and customs of that country. Write a two-page paper describing how your behavior toward someone from that country would be altered by having read that article. Precisely identify those parts of the article that seem to you to stereotype unnecessarily.

21. *International letters.* Here is a letter from a manager of sales for WorkPrefect, a computer software company, to Doctor Ernesto Jiménez-Banco, Chief of Procurement for the government of Tenibras, a stable, democratic country in South America. David O.

Save, known as "Dos," just learned that Work-Prefect has developed a Spanish-language program that controls inventory and procurement procedures. Dos wants to sell the program to Tenibras.

Because neither you nor Dos knows Spanish, the letter is in English. Even so, the errors are so egregious that they must be corrected should Work-Prefect have any hope of selling the program to Spanish-speaking countries. Correct the errors. You may want to discuss some of them in class.

WorkPrefect, Incorporated
386 Microchip Road
Silicon, California 92606
(209) 123-0987

27 March 1992

Doctor Ernesto Jiménez-Banco
Chief of Procurement
Government of Tenibras
El Hexagon
Tenibras City
Tenibras

Hola Ernie:

My company, WorkPrefect, has just developed a Spanish-language program for inventory and procurement control. Should you be interested in seeing whether such a new integrated, multi-user, package would fly in your network, I would be happy to ring you up and give you a run-through.

Jus' contact me at 1-893-555-1313 any time between 9 and 5 est. If that's not feasible, have your people contact my people and we'll tour them through our facility any time. If you're unable to break away, I'd be happy to wend my way south and we could do lunch. OK?

Sincerely,

"Dos" Save

"Dos" Save,
Sales Manager

CASE STUDY 1: COLLECTION LETTERS: THE GRUMBLY LETTER

Old Mr. Grumbly has bought his groceries from the Homogenized Food Mart for seventeen years. For the past ten years he has had his groceries delivered to his home, which is a mile from the store. He eats only gourmet foods and has several cats and dogs, as well as a beloved canary. They eat only the best food. His average weekly bill is $67.80. During four weeks in April, he bought his usual groceries but did not pay. He has not appeared in the store since April 30, although he has been seen walking his dogs near his home. It is now May 15.

Write a series of five letters, posted at two week intervals, in which you try to get Mr. Grumbly to pay. Letters one and two should be reminders from the forgetfulness stage. Letter three should reflect the inability stage. Letter four should address the irresponsibility stage.

After mailing the fourth letter, you receive the following letter from Mr. Grumbly:

Dear Homogenized:

I have not responded to any of your letters because two hours after feeding your Super Deluxe Yummy Bird Feed to my canary, Yellow Rain, on April 30, he died. If you could have seen the little fellow on the bottom of the cage, his little feet stiff and sticking up in the air, his pretty little feathers all ruffled up, and his little black eyes clouded over in death, you wouldn't pay the people who so foully poisoned him, either.

Bleck to you,

Grumbly

Respond to Grumbly's letter in a way that is both kind and firm. The firmness is demonstrated by your determination to turn over the collecting of the long-overdue bill to a collection agency and a lawyer. The kindness at this stage is unusual, but Grumbly has been a good customer for many years.

CASE STUDY 2: RESERVATIONS: THE HIGH SKY LETTER (GOOD NEWS)

High Sky, Inc., is a company that sells burials in space. For $700,000, the company will seal the deceased in a capsule, place the body in a rocket, and send it 400 miles into space, where, for all practical purposes, it orbits the earth forever. Because it must buy room on NASA's space shuttle to send bodies to space, and because NASA has recently received some bad press as a result of some bad luck (experiments have failed, rockets blown up, etc.), people who used to stand in line to buy a space burial are now hesitating. Some have even canceled their trips.

To allay the fears of potential customers, High Sky is planning a conference beginning at 9:00 a.m. on December 13 and ending at 5 p.m. on December 16 at a resort in Phoenix, near Sun City, for potential customers. Executives, even astronauts, from NASA are attending to present figures on the relative safety of space travel, to show pictures of the beauties and glories of space, its ability to preserve bodies forever, and so on. All of this is to bring more business to High Sky and to NASA.

Others have arranged the program, but you have been given the job of making reservations for the conference. Having reserved hotel rooms for NASA officials and employees of High Sky, your job is to arrange for the care and feeding of three potential customers who are not only rich and old, but also relatively infirm. Their names are Mr. Smedley Fahrquart, Sr.; Ms. Iva Smith; and Commander Mister Mister.

After many calls and much work, you discover the following things about these three people.

Fahrquart: Millionaire; 87 years young; low sodium diet; refuses to eat or drink anything white (milk, mashed potatoes, vanilla ice cream, etc.); drinks Bootles gin, straight, and lots of it; stone deaf.

Smith: Millionaire; 68 years young; always travels with 37-year-old nephew, named Chip Jones; claustrophobic, cannot use elevators; tends to pass out after three drinks; Chip seems to be well-behaved.

Mister: Millionaire; 75 years young; British Navy, retired; recovering from a broken hip, requires a walker; goes everywhere with a bulldog named Winston; demands to be wakened every day at dawn; demands a *very* dry martini every day "when the sun is over the yardarm" (noon).

Remembering that reservations are like orders, but also remembering that human beings have peculiar needs that must be satisfied, write a letter to the Thunderbird Inn in which you request the arrangements that will make Fahrquart, Smith, and Mister happy during their stays. Remember also that High Sky stands to make $300,000 dollars from each of these people should they sign up for the burial service. Here are the necessary names and addresses:

High Sky, Inc.
67 Old Santa Fe Road
Sun City, Arizona 43902

Mr. Stanley Serta
Reservation Manager
Thunderbird Inn
12586 Thunderbird Avenue
Glendale, Arizona 43835

CASE STUDY 3: INVITATIONS: SMITH

Using the information given in Case Study 2, write a letter inviting Ms. Smith to the conference.

CASE STUDY 4: INVITATIONS

Everyone knows how difficult it is to pry faculty from their ivy-tower offices, especially if they are asked to do extracurricular duty among students. Professor Maurice Cranial is such a professor, but he is also one of the most engaging and exciting lecturers on campus. In addition, he has just published a book on the history of rock music. You chair the Activities Committee of the Student Government Association (SGA), and one of your jobs is to attract interesting speakers to the monthly academic lecture series. Attendance has never been good, but it has been worse than usual since you took over as chair.

Because you want to be president of the SGA next year, the lecture series must improve attendance soon or your chances will look no better than those for the survival of the lectures. Only seven people attended the last lecture, and four of those were members of the speaker's family who came to hear an exciting two-hour slide show on the evolution of the human foot.

Professor Cranial's appearance would probably fill the auditorium. The problem is to get him to agree to speak. Write a letter inviting Cranial to speak on rock music in the auditorium on December 22, the day before the beginning of the holiday break.

CASE STUDY 5: CONDOLENCES

Samantha Evans, your former roommate, is spending a year abroad. Having corresponded with her long-time friend and colleague, Smedley Fahrquart, you learn that her pet aardvark, Antie, has died. Evans was devoted to Antie, and you think it best to write a letter of condolence to her. Write the letter.

CASE STUDY 6: INTERNATIONAL LETTERS: THE GREEK CONNECTION

Marco Panaghis, president of Avrio Water, Inc. (Tomorrow Water), a Cretan company (1 Placa El Greco, Iraklion, Crete) specializing in embalming fluid, wants to sell a new product, Agua Alto (High Water; the product is made in Mexico) to your company, High Sky (see Case Study 2). This new embalming fluid is lighter than water and lighter than other embalming fluids by 18 percent. High Sky may save an average of $6,000 on every body sent into space by using such a light embalming fluid. Your boss is interested in this product. Write a letter to Mr. Panaghis saying so. Among your concerns are these:

a. What are the normal salutations and complimentary closes in Greek?

b. Mr. Panaghis will come to the U.S. if you invite him. You want to invite him. How do you tell him that June is not a good month (eight flights occur then), but that any other time is good, and the sooner the better?

c. You need to write an itinerary for a three-day visit. Prepare it and include it in your letter to him.

CHALLENGE EXERCISE 1: GOALS OF PERSUASION

Your company is transferring you for one year from its Detroit office to its Washington, D.C., office. The question is what to do with your house. While reading a Detroit newspaper one day, you notice that an executive from California wants to rent a house for the exact period you need to rent yours. Write a letter to Mr. Caliph Dreemin persuading him to rent your house. Include and identify each of the goals of persuasion in your letter.

CHALLENGE EXERCISE 2: SOLICITED SALES LETTERS: THE CLAMPETT LETTER

High Sky (see Case Study 2) receives many requests for information. As the newest staff member, you have been assigned to answer them. When this letter arrives one morning, you decide to answer it immediately. Ordinarily, the company would send a tribe of sales people after such a large order, but Clampett clearly does not want that. After showing the letter to your boss and then to the president, Mr. Joyboy, the president says to you, "Not many people get a chance like this in a lifetime. Let's see what you can do. Pull it off, and there will be a B-I-G bonus and a B-I-G promotion in it for you. Write Clampett a letter for my signature."

During the next three days, you work out the following deal with the accountants and the designers and even, miraculously, with NASA:

1. The normal charge is $700,000 a person. The accountants have decided that a volume sale such as this one would require only $500,000 a person. Furthermore, if half were paid now, the other half could be placed in a trust. The interest would go to Mr. Clampett's trust, and the other half of the fee could be withdrawn only as one of Mr. Clampett's relatives dies. This virtually assures another generation of Mr. Clampett's relatives a substantial inheritance from the estate.

2. High Sky is a $30 million a year business. There are now no competitors, and none seems to be likely soon. Because the business deals in eternity, a 100-year agreement was signed by NASA and High Sky

```
RD #2
Back Hollow, TN 39857


17 September 1992


Dear High Sky:

I have just won $40 million in the Tennessee State Lottery.
Because my wants are small and my family large, I have de-
cided to keep $1 million, but give $1 million to each of my
19 relatives. This leaves $20 million just lying around. As
a surprise for my relatives, I am considering enrolling my-
self and all my relatives in your "Pay Now, Fly Later" pro-
gram. In order to decide, I need to know the following:

    1. How much will it cost to enroll 20 people in the
       program?
    2. Some of my relatives are very young. One is only
       six. How may I be assured that you will still be in
       business, say, 75 years from now?
    3. I want to have sent into space with me a few small
       mementos. Do you charge extra for this? Is there a
       charge by weight, or is it by item?
    4. We are a close family. Can we be assured that our
       orbits are sufficiently similar so that we may be
       said to orbit together? How closely orbited can we
       be? One mile? Ten?
    5. Many of my family and I are outdoors people, and the
       idea of being closed in is not appealing. Are there
       windows in the caskets? That is, may we be assured
       of looking out on the earth and on space? This may
       also allow future generations of our relatives to
       come up and have a look at us.

Please answer quickly, as I am 97 years young. And don't
send some city slicker to my door to pressure me into sign-
ing some papers. I've just bought some very big and very
mean dogs. Part of their training was to bite anyone holding
papers. Even the mail is delivered from a car. And don't
call, either.

Sincerely,

Jedediah Clampett
Jedediah Clampett
```

in 1980. High Sky is not a franchise; consequently, even if the business is sold, all agreements must be honored by new owners. The financial arrangement discussed in item 1 also assures a continuation of the agreement even if laws change. In short, High Sky is about as secure as the U.S. government.

3. Mementos are normally considered as extras, and the normal fee for including them on the ride is $25,000 a pound, assuming they are no larger than 6″ × 6″ × 6″. You can offer Mr. Clampett and his relatives one free memento.

4. NASA had trouble with this one. While they can place caskets in an orbit within 35 miles of each other, they cannot assure that the caskets will remain that close, and they cannot assure that the caskets can ride side-by-side in their orbits. As knowledge increases, however, NASA will work hard to place them closer to each other. NASA speculates that within 50 years they will be able to place caskets within a few feet of each other and that the orbits will be nearly identical.

5. Windows are now expensive: $75,000 for a 12″ × 12″ window. Again, however, High Sky is prepared to offer a discount of $20,000 on a window. Perhaps, as technology improves, the price will go down.

High Sky also offers a perpetual maintenance agreement for $100,000 a casket. That is, should anything go wrong (casket goes out of orbit, casket hit by small meteorite, etc.), repairs or corrections would be made free.

Write a letter for Mr. Joyboy's signature in which you follow the arrangement of a solicited sales letter, provide details of the costs, and, in short, do a good job of selling the program to Mr. Clampett.

I V

MEN MUST BE TAUGHT AS

IF YOU TAUGHT THEM NOT,

AND THINGS UNKNOWN

PROPOSED AS THINGS

FORGOT.

REPORTS

ALEXANDER

POPE

(1688–1744)

THE PURPOSE OF REPORTS

What Are Reports?
The Importance of Reports for the
   Company
The Importance of Reports for You
Formal and Informal Reports

THE REPORT WRITING PROCESS

THE PROSPECTUS

The Purpose
Anticipating Problems
The Scope and Format
The Audience

SCHEDULING TIME

RESEARCH

Gathering Primary Information
Gathering Secondary Information
Library Research

ARRANGING THE INFORMATION

Ordering the Ideas
Ordering the Data

SUMMARY

EXERCISES

Learning Objectives:

☐ Define and know the importance
   of reports—for the company and
   for you.

☐ Know the difference between formal and informal reports.

☐ Overcome the heebie-jeebies by
   understanding the process of writing a prospectus, scheduling time,
   doing research, and identifying the
   audience.

☐ Know the difference between primary and secondary research.

☐ Document and write the kinds of
   research typically employed by
   business people.

☐ Observe your behavior and that of
   others carefully.

☐ Prepare and write a brief, reliable,
   valid, and accurate questionnaire.

☐ Gather accurate and relevant data
   for reports.

☐ Work efficiently in the library.

☐ Choose a proper arrangement for a
   business report.

☐ Pay attention to the audience.

8

YOU MUST DO THE THINGS

YOU THINK YOU CANNOT

DO.

ELEANOR ROOSEVELT

(1884–1962)

REPORTS:  THE PURPOSE AND WRITING PROCESS

THE PURPOSE OF REPORTS

WHAT ARE REPORTS?

Report is a broad term used in business to describe a written or oral presentation of information. Reports may be typeset documents bound in Moroccan leather, pencil scratchings on a napkin, the president's "State of the Union" message, or a discussion over hamburgers at McDonald's. Reports, then, may be formal or informal, written or oral, long or short. They may be informational or analytical. Furthermore, they may be *ad hoc* (one-time things) or periodic (daily, monthly, quarterly, annually). Finally, while most reports are delivered *up* (to bosses, who rely on information—background, detail, and solutions or recommendations—gleaned from reports to help them make decisions), some may be delivered *down* (to subordinates) or even *across* (to colleagues on the same rung of the corporate ladder).

THE IMPORTANCE OF REPORTS FOR THE COMPANY

Reports are essential to the success of any company. Information *must* flow successfully from top to bottom, from bottom to top, and from side to side. Informal memos usually tell managers what is going on hourly or daily, but only reports can tell managers how big money was, is, or should be spent or made over time. Big and complex problems can be explained and resolved best through the report writing process. Reports provide and organize data to help managers make decisions. Effectively conveying information to those who need it builds successful companies.

THE IMPORTANCE OF REPORTS FOR YOU

In companies of any size, bosses often know their subordinates best by what and how they write. Many business and engineering students believe that they will seldom be required to write. Not so, says a study of engineers by Hewlett-Packard and reported in *Business Week*.[1] Design engineers, who write less than most other business people, spend 30 percent of an average day writing documentation; that is 2 hours and 28 minutes every day or more than 12 hours a week. Accountants, who often deal much more with the public, write even more than engineers.

EXERCISE A: MUTUAL BENEFITS OF GOOD REPORTS

Discuss in class the following question: How are good reports good for both the company and you?

---

[1]"Giving Design Engineers More Time to Design," *Business Week*, 3 February 1986, p. 63.

FORMAL AND INFORMAL REPORTS

Although most business reports look similar, their subjects are extraordinarily diverse, addressing anything from buying paper clips to changing the history of a nation. Within those boundaries, reports obey the usual rules of accuracy, clarity, and courtesy.

One way to discuss the diversity of reports is in terms of relative formality. Some reports, such as many memo reports, are informal. These reports are usually brief, use casual or conversational language, and avoid many of the formalities common in business reports. Here is an example of the simplest kind of informal report.

EXERCISE B: QUALITIES OF INFORMAL REPORTS

Discuss in class the following question: In addition to its habit of dropping the formal subject and verb ("Any chance" instead of "Is there any chance"), what about this memo report makes it informal?

```
                          MEMORANDUM


          TO:     Smedley Fahrquart, Shipping
          FROM:   Ardis Rock, Customer Service
          DATE:   December 21, 1992
          RE:     Prehensile Order


          Smed. Any chance of letting us know whether you can
          ship the Prehensile order before noon Tuesday? Pre-
          hensile needs it badly, as I can surmise from the
          three frantic phone calls they made to me between 9
          and 10 this morning. Call me ASAP.
```

In the strictest sense, anything that reports a condition, a situation, a need, a desire, or the absence of any of these can be considered a report. Some information is needed so often or is so simple that companies create forms to convey the routine information. The writer's job in these kinds of informal reports is to fill in the blanks. Trip reports and petty cash expenditures belong in this category and need no further explanation than to say that the writer should be careful to answer precisely what the questions ask. Chapter 9 addresses formal reports, and Chapter 10 addresses informal reports.

THE REPORT WRITING PROCESS

Although nearly everyone from the lowest trainee to the company's president writes reports,[2] the thought of having to write reports intimidates most people. Otherwise brave and intrepid men and women find their knees buckling, their hands shaking, and their foreheads perspiring when told "Write a report on this!"

So much time is spent writing reports and so much of success—the employee's, the boss's and the company's—depends on reports that it is time to put aside the fears and take on the process. Fortunately, overcoming the intimidation is simply a matter of being well prepared and well organized. Good writing derives from good preparation and solid organization. The steps in preparing to write a report are well defined; once done, they make the job of writing easier. These steps require as much thought as actual writing.

THE PROSPECTUS

A prospectus gathers, focuses, and defines the major components of a report. Once the prospectus is written, the writer knows four things: the purpose, possible problems, the scope and format, and the audience. These elements may change as the report progresses, but the writer always must keep each in mind.

THE PURPOSE

The purpose of the report should be stated in one sentence, but that sentence must be thought about much and rewritten often. Details about writing this sentence are given in Chapter 2. The importance of this step cannot be overemphasized. Without a clear purpose in mind and on paper, reports inevitably will go astray, thereby wasting time and money.

The purpose statement will become the first sentence of the report. Here is an example of a one-sentence purpose:

Purpose

The Jones Corporation should make and market a xenostyrene-core, steel-shaft golf club, called Fly Edition, to create maximal ball spin at impact while maintaining club feel and low cost.

THREE STEPS TO PLANNING REPORTS

1. *Write a prospectus. (Determine the purpose, any problems, and the scope and format; identify the audience and its needs.)*
2. *Schedule time.*
3. *Do the research.*

----

[2]Few company presidents write reports for their companies, but many executives volunteer to lead such community organizations as the United Way. In these capacities they often write reports. Moreover, as many people in the community read these reports, the corporate executive puts the company's prestige on the line by writing the reports well or poorly.

ANTICIPATING PROBLEMS

Make a list of problems that might impede achieving the purpose of the report. Because problems may change as the writer learns more about the subject, listing those problems keeps things on track: the writer always knows what the problems are and whether certain information is useful, thus saving time. If problems change as a result of discovering new information, then the purpose may change; again, this helps the writer keep the purpose in mind.

Here is a list of problems facing the writer of the prospectus for the Jones Corporation.

Problems

1. Two competitors already make similar clubs: Mashie Corporation makes a steel-cored, hickory club selling for $1500; and Spoon Corporation makes a graphite-cored, steel-alloy club selling for $850.
2. Xenostyrene is a relatively expensive material, as is the process of injecting it into a hollow steel shaft.
3. Research concludes that 80 percent of golfers, a huge market, will not buy a set of clubs costing more than $400.
4. Engineering is confident, but will not guarantee, that the cost of new injection procedures will allow the cost of the Fly Edition to be less than $400.
5. Our competitors doubtless soon will produce a low-cost version similar to the Fly Edition; Jones Corporation must work fast.

THE SCOPE AND FORMAT

The scope section *focuses* the report in two ways: generally, to guide the research and writing process; and specifically, to describe the organization of the report. Here is the scope section of the prospectus for the Jones Corporation's Fly Edition.

Scope

Three brands of golf clubs that impart a high ball-spin rate were analyzed before we considered manufacturing the highly dampened xenostyrene-core steel-shaft golf club, called the Fly Edition. As no other competitors seem interested in or ready for this market, their clubs were not analyzed. Criteria for analyzing the Fly Edition include performance (ball-spin rate, distance, and club feel), patent rights, and conformance to United States Golf Association (USGA) standards. A management plan showing the organizational, personnel, and facility requirements to make and market the Fly Edition is discussed in the Management section, while a detailed cost analysis appears in the Cost section.

Now that the writer knows the purpose, problems, and scope of the report, and before the writer has gathered and arranged the ideas and the data, the next step is to decide which arrangement to use for

EXERCISE C: DETERMINING SCOPE

Determining the scope of a report involves exclusion. That is, the writer must determine not only what to write about, but also what *not* to write about. To that end, choose a current political issue, define one aspect of that issue, and then list the specific points that need to be discussed and then the specific points that, while related, need not be discussed.

the report. The format that a report will follow depends on its purpose. For example, is the report a feasibility study, a progress report, a recommendation report, or a proposal? See Chapters 9 and 10 for definitions of these types of reports.

THE AUDIENCE

Although audience is covered in detail in Chapter 2, writers must remind themselves to write for a specific readership. Writers become so engrossed in the details of reports that they tend to forget whom they are gathering and organizing the information for. Throughout the planning, researching, and writing process, writers must shift from seeing information with a writer's eye to seeing it with a reader's eye and they must write the report accordingly.

SCHEDULING TIME

Depend upon it, sir, when a man knows he is to be hanged in a fortnight [two weeks], it concentrates his mind wonderfully.

Samuel Johnson (1709–1784)

One great difficulty in learning to write reports is judging how much time the whole process will require. The more reports a person writes, of course, the easier this judgment becomes. One experienced writer offers the following advice: try to decide how long the job will require if anything goes wrong. That is, the information sent for may not arrive until a week after it should, the computer may be down when it is most needed, and the dog may chew up important data. When this amount of time has been calculated, says the expert, then double it. While practical, this advice remains vague, and business writers usually do not have the luxury of setting their own due dates; they often are given a limited time in which to complete the job. Specifically, then, the writer should plan time as follows:

....
SCHEDULING TIME

1. *Always keep the due date in mind.*
2. *Know the report's degree of complexity.*
3. *Create a segment of time for completing each part of the report.*
4. *Work on the report every day.*

1. Discover when the report is due and then always keep that date in mind. The due date, as Samuel Johnson points out, is rather like the date for one's hanging: "It concentrates the mind wonderfully."

2. Identify the reasons that the project is complex, such as the degree of detail required, the level of formality required (formal reports take more time), and the number of people whose expertise will be sought (the more people queried, the more information will be available, and so the more time the writer will need for gathering and assimilating the information).

3. Allot a segment of time to perform each job. These include planning; researching, assessing, and organizing the information; creating the first draft; revising and editing the drafts; and printing and distributing the final version. (See Chapter 2.)

4. Work on at least one task of the report every day, if only for a few minutes.

Here is a schedule for a 10-page report due in two weeks.

Discuss in class the following questions:

1. Why does writing continue through editing?

2. Is it possible, or advisable, to continue writing after proofing is completed?

3. How might this schedule be revised?

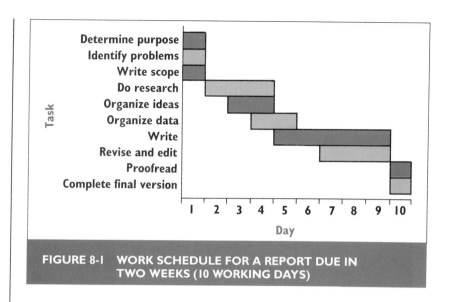

FIGURE 8-1   WORK SCHEDULE FOR A REPORT DUE IN TWO WEEKS (10 WORKING DAYS)

RESEARCH

Successful reports combine a clear, effective style and scrupulous accuracy. Accuracy derives from carefully collected and organized details, which the writer gathers through research. Research sources are of two kinds: primary and secondary. *Primary* information is from first-hand sources: interviews, questionnaires or surveys, personal observation and experience, lab reports and other experiments, original speeches, and unedited video and audio tapes. *Secondary* information is gathered from second- or third-hand sources. It comprises primary data that has passed through the filter of other people's work (such as books, articles, reports, memos, and letters) *about* the primary information—that is, anything that contains, evaluates, or analyzes primary or other secondary information. Thus, Mary Leakey's field notes about finding Zinjanthropus man in Africa are primary information; the articles about her discoveries in *National Geographic* are secondary information.

GATHERING PRIMARY INFORMATION

Among the most common methods of exploring primary sources in business are observing others, brainstorming (data gathered from one's own experiences and thoughts), constructing questionnaires (sometimes expressed as written surveys), and interviewing (direct conversation with the sources). (While interviews are major sources of information, they also are important in landing jobs; see Chapter 13.)

OBSERVATION.   Observation is both the most reliable and the least reliable method of research. Although keen eyes, photographic memories, and exact knowledge of what we are looking for produce the clearest data, few are endowed with all these gifts. Fortunately, the most important of these qualities—knowing what we are looking for—does not require the other two. For example, few of us notice how many red Chevrolets are on the road until we buy one. Then, they seem to be everywhere. In short, when we know what we are looking for, we are more likely to find it.

As a method of research, observing others requires careful note-taking. Because there is too much data to hold in our minds, keeping good notes is necessary. Another problem with abundant data is that one person seldom can gather it all. Consequently, it is important that the methods used for gathering data for a project be precisely the same for everyone. Otherwise, much work may be invalidated.

The notes below are observations of the traffic patterns of workers through some office doors. The purpose was to determine whether the doors are placed most efficiently; ultimately, the goal is to recommend whether the doors should be moved (the reception desk cannot be). The arrangement of the office is shown in the following illustration.

Notes on Traffic Patterns in Reception Area of
Fahrquart Industries, Inc.
(Monday, April 22, through Friday, April 26)

1. Number of people: 4/22: 72; 4/23: 66; 4/24: 68; 4/25: 65; 4/26: 49.
   Mean number per day: 64
2. Number of people who entered the door and proceeded straight through to the offices: 4/22: 17; 4/23: 12; 4/24: 19; 4/25: 11; 4/26: 7.
   Mean number per day: 13
   Mean percentage passing to offices: 20
   Mean percentage passing to reception: 80

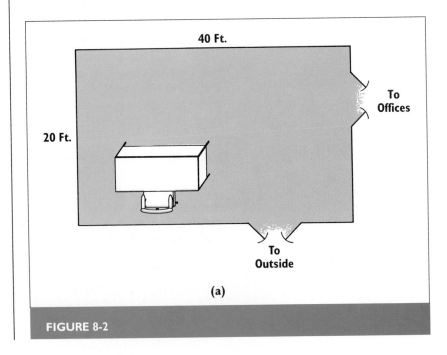

(a)

FIGURE 8-2

3. Distance traveled from door to reception desk and back to door: 30 feet
4. Distance traveled from door to offices and back to door: 30 feet.

What more is needed? Seemingly nothing, but in order to be sure, the following should be calculated:

1. How many miles/hour do people walk, on average, as they proceed from and to the door?
2. What is the cost to the company, on average, of one hour's time for these people?
3. What would it cost to replace the doors?
4. How long will the doors last?

What will this information tell us?

1. Knowing the cost of people's time and the amount of extra time people are walking as a result of the placement of the doors allows us to calculate the cost to the company of leaving the doors where they are.
2. Knowing the cost of moving the doors allows us to compare that cost with the cost of leaving the doors where they are. This allows us to determine whether moving the doors is worth it.

Let's work it out, hypothetically.

Cost of moving doors: $817.98

Average pace of walkers: 2.1 mph.

Extra distance/year: 0 miles

Average hourly cost of walkers: $45.00

Cost of not moving doors: $0.00

Benefit of not moving doors: $817.98

Results: Although the distances and the time required to go to the desk and then to the offices seem different, they are not. This seemed obvious from the start, but only by careful measurement can business objectively prove whether to do or not do something. Only given the data may one say with complete assurance that it is *not* worth making the change.

In short, careful observation is essential, but so is good data.

EXERCISE E: CAREFUL NOTE-TAKING

1. Observe the following about these notes:
   a. A careful, day-by-day counting was required.
   b. Counting included observing the direction taken by those using the door both after entering and while leaving.
   c. Careful measuring of distances was required.
   d. Notice the use of numbers throughout.
2. What might be extrapolated from these observations?

BRAINSTORMING. Gathering your own ideas may take many forms: listening to your own random thoughts; writing lists; answering journalists' questions (who, what, when, where, how, and why); puzzling through the problem from facts to connections among the facts and, finally, to solutions. Each of these methods often produces wonderful results. Do not lose the chance of finding the perfect solution to a problem by failing to consult yourself.

The most common form of this activity is called *brainstorming*. Brainstorming, which can also be done in a group, is simply tossing out ideas, connections, and solutions as they occur. Brainstorming in a group has the advantage over brainstorming alone in that ideas from others may spark ideas in you, that, in turn, generate further ideas in others. As the process continues, many surprising and insightful conclusions may be discovered.

QUESTIONNAIRES.   Questionnaires are interviews on paper, and their wording and design are as varied as their purposes. Some questionnaires seek advice about marketing methods from sales people. Others poll the public about the image of a company or one of its products. Some try to gather data for understanding the resistance of employees to seeking a second opinion on all major medical procedures. The list is endless.

The audience for whom a questionnaire is designed (or targeted) determines many attributes; length, word choice, and ease of response are only a few of the considerations involved in designing a questionnaire. A questionnaire for managers about methods of determining salary increases for managers might be long and involved because the recipients naturally are extremely interested in the subject and the result. The same questionnaire given to nonmanagers may produce bad results—low return rates, improper and incomplete responses—because the nonmanagers simply do not care about the subject.

All good questionnaires share the following attributes: they are reliable, brief, clear, objective, and valid. Moreover, all of these qualities may mean slightly different things depending on the target audience, the *sample*. Carefully selecting people to fill out the questionnaire is extremely important if the results are to be published as representing the views of an entire group. To assess the political beliefs of all Americans, for example, the audience should not be composed entirely of members of one political party.

1. *Reliability*, producing the same results no matter how many times the questionnaire is given, is only one test of a valid sample. Other tests of a sample of, say, the American people, would be that the sample represent, proportionally, income, age, gender, race, geographic location, education, and similar attributes.

2. *Brevity* is important to nearly all questionnaires because people usually respond voluntarily. Consequently, the questionnaire cannot require much time to complete.

3. *Clarity* is extraordinarily important, for everyone must understand the questions. If the respondents misunderstand words or other symbols, they will bypass the question or misinterpret it. To avoid bypassing, the writer must carefully examine word choice, so everyone will understand the question in the same way. Even the simplest question—that of filling in the respondent's job title, for example—is open to misinterpretation (sometimes intentionally):

   Question: Position?
   Answer: Usually prone.

4. *Objectivity* is crucial to good questionnaires. For example, most Americans respond to the question "Should laws be passed to prohibit the media from presenting their biased opinions as news?" by saying yes. But most Americans would also say yes to this question:

**ATTRIBUTES OF
QUESTIONNAIRES**

1. *Reliability*
2. *Brevity*
3. *Clarity*
4. *Objectivity*
5. *Validity*

"Do you think that laws should be passed to protect freedom of speech?" Questions, then, must be selected and revised with enough care to make them neutral—that is, so they do not lead the respondent.

5. Careful attention to brevity, clarity, and objectivity usually produces *validity*—the questionnaire actually measuring what it says it measures. To make the research valid, a sufficient percentage of the questionnaires must be filled out and returned. In addition to a large response, validity is measured by the quality of the questionnaire's questions. The questionnaire writer therefore must compose the questions with as few biases as possible. Fortunately, in business, many questionnaires may require only yes or no responses. This makes achieving objectivity easier, although by no means easy.

More is involved than clarity of questions. The page must be neat also. That is, few will answer a smudged, messy, misaligned, badly printed questionnaire, or one containing bad grammar or spelling or punctuation.

Here is an example of several stages in the writing of one question for a questionnaire. The respondents are members of the sales staff of a large corporation. Notice how the question becomes clearer, briefer, and more precise as it goes through three writings.

First Draft. What do you think about reducing the regional sales staffs of Fahrquart Industries?

Second Draft. Do you think the regional sales staffs of Fahrquart Industries should be reduced?

YES _____   NO _____

Final Draft. Do you think the regional sales staffs of Fahrquart Industries should be reduced?

YES _____   NO _____

If YES, by how much? Less than 5% ____, 5% ____, 10% ____, 15% ____, more than 15% ____.

Remember that questions lending themselves to numerical tabulation may be more difficult to write, but they also more readily reveal clear answers. Even so, always include a section for prose responses. Although they are difficult to tabulate, they reveal insights that one-word or numerical answers might miss. More extensive discussions on designing questionnaires may be found in any of numerous books in the library on statistical methods (very mathematical) and survey methods (less mathematical).

Page 206 shows part of a questionnaire given to police officers.

Notice the following about the questionnaire.

1. The job of completing the questionnaire is made easy by asking respondents only to circle a word or write a number. Because people are not required to fill out the questionnaire, or at least cannot be forced to do it conscientiously, the job must be made easy.

I. Job Duty

A. Are you a sworn officer of your department? (Circle the number that describes you.)
  1 yes (Continue with next question.)
  2 no (Discontinue questionnaire; return in envelope.)
B. Are you supervising other employees within your department?
  1 yes (Discontinue questionnaire; return in envelope.)
  2 no (Continue with next question.)

II. Police Activity

Following are 9 activities that police officers *may do on the job* and a scale that represents a range of time.

A. In Column A, write the number that best shows how much time you <u>actually</u> spend on the activity.

B. In Column B, write the number that best shows how much time you think you <u>should</u> spend on the activity.

C. In Column C, write the number that best shows how much time you would <u>like</u> to spend on the activity.

no time   0   1   2   3   4   5   6   7   much time

	A	B	C
1. Patrolling in cars	____	____	____
2. Patrolling on foot	____	____	____
3. Controlling traffic	____	____	____
4. Enforcing parking regulations	____	____	____
5. Investigating crime and securing evidence	____	____	____
6. Telling public about police work	____	____	____
7. Explaining crime prevention methods to citizens	____	____	____
8. Helping people in emergencies	____	____	____
9. Controlling crowds	____	____	____

2. Notice that *actually, should,* and *like* are underlined so that respondents may distinguish precisely the questions asked.

3. Notice the brevity of each of the nine questions.

4. Notice the parallel construction of each of the nine questions: "patrolling," "controlling," "enforcing," and so on.

Here are a few final *do's* and *don'ts* that affect reliability of results. *DO* include in a questionnaire of ten or more questions a few questions that restate a previous question. The answer may then be checked for validity (consistency) of response. *DO* try to give the questionnaire to several people you know before sending it out into the world. The responses from this pretest may reveal some problems you had not seen despite your best efforts. *DON'T* ask more than one question at a time. That is, make sure only one question is asked for every question mark used. See the example in Chapter 16.

Here is the cover letter that accompanies the questionnaire on police activity.

....

EXERCISE F: COVER LETTER FOR QUESTIONNAIRES

Discuss in class the following question: To what extent does this cover letter fulfill the requirements for good cover letters?

```
                    Survey of Police Work

We are interested in your views of police work and
the things that affect it. Yours is one of several
police departments around the country that has
agreed to participate in the survey. All partici-
pants within your department were randomly selected.
Your department has agreed to allow you to complete
the survey while on duty. This should take no more
than 30-40 minutes.

Of course, your participation in the survey is vol-
untary, but we hope you will take this opportunity
to express your views on policing. The information
gained from the survey will provide valuable feed-
back to your department and important data for the
study of policing.

Your individual answers will be held in strict con-
fidence. Only the staff of the Douglas Institute
will see your answers. No report will ever be made
to anyone that would allow your identification.
Findings will only be reported as statistical
summaries.

The attached survey asks for your views on police
work and things that affect it. Your answers will be
held in strict confidence. Findings will be reported
only as statistical summaries. No report will ever
be made to anyone in a way that will allow your
identification. DO NOT WRITE YOUR NAME ON THIS QUES-
TIONNAIRE.
```

One of the more intriguing innovations for business with regard to questionnaires concerns electronically designed and conveyed questionnaires. Response rates tend to be far higher than rates from printed questionnaires.

Regardless of the medium, however, questionnaires require cover letters that are written in such a way that the reader *wants to respond*. In order to have the best chance of receiving a response, the writer must include the following information.

1. *Why this questionnaire* (what are we trying to discover)? Convey also the importance of the questionnaire, both generally and specifically.

2. *How much time is required to complete the questionnaire?* Keep the time short.

3. *Will responses be confidential?*

4. *How will the information be used?* While it is not always possible to provide full disclosure on this topic, the writer should provide as much information as is permissible.

5. *Are the instructions for completing the questionnaire precise?* It is impossible to overemphasize the importance of precision here.

EXERCISE G: VALIDITY VS. TRUTH IN QUESTIONNAIRES

Discuss in class the following question: Why may information derived from questionnaires be valid but not necessarily true?

```
Most of the questions are followed by numerical
scales and instructions either to encircle a number
that describes where you stand between the two ends
of the scale or to write the number in a space pro-
vided. Unless instructed otherwise, please answer
all questions in order. Choose only one answer to
each question and circle or write your answer
clearly.

Statistical summaries of results of the survey will
be provided to your department for your information.
If you have questions or wish information about the
survey, please contact us.
```

```
John M. Magenau, Ph.D.        Raymond G. Hunt, Ph.D.
The Behrend College           School of Management
School of Business            State University of New
Pennsylvania State            York at Buffalo
University                    Buffalo, NY 14260
Erie, PA 16563
```

GATHERING SECONDARY INFORMATION

Because knowledge of the world has been doubling every few years during the past several decades, and because most of this knowledge has been recorded and stored somewhere, the odds are good that much has been written on most subjects of concern to business. The job of the writer is to find it. Most companies and college libraries now have computers to help the writer find information.

The single most common danger in gathering accurate and relevant data is not that people gather too little data, but rather that people gather too much. Many people are so afraid of sitting down to write that they prolong the data gathering until the deadline for the report looms ominously like a threatening storm cloud. For this reason, writers should set a deadline for data gathering and stick to it.

Some people, of course, wait too long to gather data, and then — again with deadline looming — they run out of time to gather sufficient data. This is not so common a problem as gathering too much data, but it is sufficiently common to warrant cautions against it.

Gathering the proper amount of data is relatively easy when the prospectus has been written carefully beforehand. Once the writer knows the purpose, the goals, and the scope of a report, the kind and amount of data are more easily discernible. Still, it is important not to gather data without some method in mind. Over the years, researchers have devised methods of data gathering, one or more of which usually satisfies the requirement of research in business.

The old way of recording research notes is to write each piece of information on an index card. Today, researchers can store such notes on computers. The trick in either method is to make sure that only one piece of information is placed on one "card"; this allows the information to be shuffled later into its proper order. Most word-processing programs include indexes. That is, each card may be labeled according to a particular category of information. When all cards have been written and labeled, the program can sort them and generate an index, thus allowing the reader to find items in any category quickly. Such a method is valuable also for the writer: simply generating the index may identify gaps in the information which may then be filled. Indexes also allow the writer to organize the information and the ideas. The researcher/writer must be sure of three things: (1) the data are accurate; (2) the data support the idea, and (3) the complete source accompanies each bit of information.

LIBRARY RESEARCH

Today, research in libraries is both easier and harder than it used to be. Not long ago, finding specific books required either travelling to distant libraries or having them sent from those libraries, usually through interlibrary loan. Today, however, computer card catalogues, microfiche, microfilm, on-line catalogues, electronic mail, data-base searching (such as on DIALOG, BRS, Microlias), government catalogues,

The traditional card catalogue at a major university

....
EXERCISE H: THE PURPOSE OF LIBRARIES

Discuss the following in class: More than 100 years ago, Thomas Carlyle said "The true university is a collection of books." What did he mean? Was it true then? Is it still true?

and other such widely available resources bring the information to the researcher. Consequently, research is more difficult because of the abundance of sources; the researcher has to choose *which* of the many sources to use. Yet research is easier because the retrieval of data is usually fast and convenient. Fortunately, libraries have begun to incorporate new methods of data retrieval, so that traditional card catalogues, various lists of periodicals, reference works, and bibliographies sit side-by-side with the many computer-search programs.

HOW TO FIND BOOKS IN A LIBRARY.   The *circulation desk* is the hub of the library. Here, librarians charge out and accept the return of books and other materials and are available to answer any questions. It is their job to help researchers locate specific books or information. When in doubt, consult a librarian.

The *card catalogue*, whether filed on cards in stacks of narrow-drawered cabinets or on computers, is a list of everything the library houses. The books in the library, all listed on the cards, are classified and stored according to a standardized system. Most large libraries, including university libraries, use the Library of Congress classification system. The system assigns each book a call number, which specifies where the book is located in the stacks. All large libraries have their cataloguing system posted on a wall by the card or computer catalogue, and many even have it posted in prominent places in the stacks.

Card catalogues cross-reference a book according to its author, its title, and its subject. Each type of card contains the same detailed information about a book, so if researchers know only the author's name, the title, or the subject, they will still be able to find the book. Each card lists the subjects that the book could be filed under.

Here is an example of an author card from a standard card catalogue, with major parts labeled; title and subject cards are similar, replacing the author at the top with the title or the subject heading.

Author	Howe, Louise Kapp.
Call number	HD6095 .H68 1977
Title *Publishing information* *Physical description*	Howe, Louise Kapp. Pink collar workers: inside the world of women's work/Louise Kapp Howe. New York: Putnam, c1977. 301 p.: ill.; 23 cm. Bibliography: p. 295–301.
Subject headings	1. Women—Employment—United States 2. Labor and laboring classes—United States. I. Title
Library of Congress number *(in right corner)*	UPCCxx 76-413002

Nearly all college and university libraries now use computerized cataloguing. The example given below is an author card from a major research university's computerized cataloguing system. Notice that this library system is spread throughout a number of campuses in different geographical areas.

Author	Daniells, Lorna M.
Title, edition	Business information sources./Lorna M. Daniells. Rev. ed. Berkeley,
Publishing information	University of California Press, c1985.
Physical description	xvi, 673 p. 24 cm. Includes index.
Subject headings *Call number* *Locations of document in* *main and branch libraries*	1. Business--Bibliography. 2. Management--Bibliography. Call #: Z7164.C81D16 1985 Reference, 1st Floor East Pattee Altoona Campus--Reference Berks Campus--Reference McKeesport Campus--Reference Delaware Campus--Reference Ogontz Campus--Reference Allentown Campus--Reference Shenango Valley Campus--Reference Mont Alto Campus--Reference Wilkes Barre Campus--Reference

Computers in use at the main branch of the New York Public Library

Many corporations also have their own libraries.

REFERENCE WORKS.   Reference works either give general information about a topic or refer the reader to other sources that can provide more detailed information. Some common types of references are listed below.

1. *Bibliographies*. Bibliographies are lists of books, articles, and periodicals (weekly, monthly, quarterly, or annual publications). Often they also include newspaper articles, and articles from specialized journals and magazines.

2. *Periodical indexes*. Periodical indexes list, usually by subject and title, the articles appearing in numerous periodicals, newspapers, and magazines. In addition to the general *Reader's Guide to Periodical Literature*, there are numerous specialized indexes such as *Business Periodicals Index, Index to U.S. Government Periodicals*, and the *New York Times Index*.

3. *Encyclopedias*. Encyclopedias are exhaustive collections of articles arranged alphabetically.
   a. *General encyclopedias*. The most comprehensive encyclopedia is the *Encyclopedia Britannica*. At the end of each entry in this encyclopedia is a general bibliography, which leads the researcher to more specialized works on the subject.
   b. *Specialized encyclopedias*. These include exhaustive and detailed articles on a specialized subject.These also contain excellent bibliographies. Among the most useful for business is *The Encyclopedia of Management*, edited by Carl Heyel.

4. *Dictionaries*. Dictionaries are essential to writers. They are tool boxes that provide not only the proper tools, but also the precise use for those tools. There are general dictionaries, such as the *Webster's Third New International Dictionary* and the *Oxford English Dictionary* (OED). There are also many specialized dictionaries that list and define words used in medicine, engineering, chemistry, economics, and the like. In fact, nearly every specialty has a dictionary.

5. *Statistical sources*. There are numerous books listing statistical sources and data. The U.S. Census Bureau has several, the most inclusive of which is the *Statistical Abstract of the United States*.

6. Books in Print. A list of all American books in print, this series organizes the books by author, by title, and by subject.

7. *U.S. Government Publications*, published monthly, lists every publication, many on business, printed by the Government Printing Office.

Here is a list of some of the most useful reference and bibliographical works for business.

1. *Business Periodicals Index* lists titles of articles from nearly 300 periodicals devoted to such business topics as accounting, economics, and finance. Other indexes useful in business include the following: *Accountant's Index, American Economic Association Index, Business Education Forum Index, Business Index, Business Publications Index and Abstracts, Catalogue of United States Government Publications, Computer Literature Index, Engineering Index, Insurance Index, Personnel Literature Index*, and *Social Science Index*.

2. *Directory of Directories* is a huge list of directories of businesses, industries, and professions.

3. *Encyclopedia of Associations* lists associations by the following categories: general subject, specific subject, name, location.

4. *Million Dollar Directory* lists more than 100,000 U.S. companies according to their net worth.

5. *Moody's Manuals* lists financial data for such specific industries as financial institutions, utilities, and multinational companies.

6. *North American Registry of Business and Industry* lists the 5,000 largest North American corporations, ranked by volume of sales and including number of employees.

7. *Standard & Poor's Register of Corporations, Directors, and Executives* lists officers, products, sales, and number of employees of nearly 40,000 major U.S., Canadian, and multinational companies.

8. *Survey of Current Business* lists data on construction, employment, finance, foreign trade, real estate, transportation, and even communication.

9. *Thomas Register of American Manufacturers and Thomas Catalog File* lists U.S. manufacturers by products and services and by name, in 16 volumes. It also includes estimated assets and a list of trademarks.

10. *The Wall Street Journal Index* lists articles on general businesses, business people, and trends.

MICROFORMS. If printed on paper, the amount of information published every day would fill several libraries. One method of dealing with the sheer volume and size of information is to use microforms, which are vastly reduced photographic copies of printed material. Although computers are gradually replacing microforms, they remain in most modern well-financed libraries as a superior method of storing and making available vast amounts of information in relatively small spaces. There are two common kinds of microforms: microfilm and microfiche.

Microfilm comprises rolls of negative-like film divided into frames. Each frame typically contains photographs of four printed pages. Microfilm is used on special machines that magnify the frames so that one may read them. Many of these machines allow the reader to print any given page onto paper. A small room of these rolls replaces many large rooms of books.

Microfiche comprises sheets of film, usually 4 x 6 inches, that contain photographs of as many as 98 pages. Microfiche is read by sliding the sheet around under the magnifier. Most librarians know how to use these machines and are happy to instruct people unsure of their use.

DATABASE RESEARCH. Many universities and businesses now use nationwide programs specifically designed for retrieving information. Huge data bases allow users to find both general and specific information in any of a number of subjects. Students and business people usually need assistance from reference librarians to narrow and hone the topic sufficiently to produce the exact information desired. Universities often charge a nominal fee, but businesses consider it part of the cost of doing business.

In *on-line database research*, the researcher's computer is connected to the source either by a satellite or other telecommunications link, or by a simple modem using existing telephone lines. Searching that database is simply a matter of pushing the proper buttons on the computer terminal.

Storing data electronically is far easier, cheaper, and faster than the old methods of printing documents and sending them to libraries where they are classified and stored. Many large corporations have their own computerized cataloguing system or have bought the services of such programs as DIALOG. These systems usually use a keyword method of organization.

Anyone planning to work in business should know something about database searches. Although the information given here is helpful, remember that knowing traditional methods of research is essential. The best way to learn to use on-line database searches is to ask a search librarian for assistance.

An example of such a search might include the following. You are researching the topic "Discrimination in the Salaries of Women Employees in the U.S.: Fact or Fiction?"

DIALOG is the largest and most common database service found in libraries; it contains nearly 200 million records. Most DIALOG databases retrieve one or more of the following kinds of information: bibliographical entries, complete texts, directories, numbers.

1. *Bibliographical entries* include the same information one normally sees on a card catalogue entry—author, title, publisher, date of publication—and many include an abstract of the document.
2. *Complete texts* are just that—the entire document. These may be printed, but usually at some cost.

STEPS TO GETTING THE MOST FROM A DATABASE SEARCH LIBRARIAN

1. *Make an appointment with the search librarian.*
2. *Take the following information to the librarian:*
   a. *One-sentence description of the topic to be searched*
   b. *Definitions of key words and phrases*
   c. *Approximately how much money you can spend on the search*
   d. *List of a few books, authors, or journals specializing in the topic*
3. *Know several terms related to the topic. The search librarian may need several of these before the terms used by the database are found.*
4. *Given this information, the search librarian should be able to narrow the search sufficiently to eliminate both extraneous information and unnecessary expenses.*

EXAMPLE OF WORKING WITH A DATABASE SEARCH LIBRARIAN

1. You call the library and ask for an appointment with Peter Rose, the search librarian.
2. You take the following information to your appointment.
   a. The one-sentence description of the topic: "Does discrimination in salaries exist for women employees in the United States?"
   b. You can think of no terms in the description that need defining.
   c. As you have $17.50 to spare from this month's income to spend on this project, you decide to tell the librarian that you have "about $15.00," but you hope it can be done for less.
   d. You know that much statistical information can be found in Moody's, in the Bureau of Census publications, and that *Fortune, Business Week, Working Woman*, and other magazines regularly publish data on income by profession and gender.
3. You have a list of several alternate key words: *female* and *woman* for *women, income* for *salary, prejudice* for *discrimination, American* and *U.S.* for *United States*, and *jobs* and *work* for *employment*.
4. The librarian cross-references the categories "women," "employment," and "income" to find 34 references. But the cost for printing it is $23.10. By limiting the years to 1988, 1989, 1990, 1991, and 1992, the librarian eliminates 10 references and reduces the cost to $16.30.

---

3. *Directories* include more than directories such as *Moody's* and *Standard and Poor's* directories of companies, product descriptions, annual sales, corporate officers, and the like. They also include dictionaries and handbooks, lists of professional associations, and other reference data.

4. *Other kinds of database systems*, in addition to DIALOG, include on-line database services that can be used with a home or office computer via a modem. These include BRS (Bibliographic Retrieval Service), COMPUSERVE, INFORMATION BANK, LEXIS (Law), NEXIS (News and Public Affairs), and THE SOURCE.

ARRANGING THE INFORMATION

ORDERING THE IDEAS

Once information has been collected, the writer must decide how to arrange the ideas presented by that information. Sometimes, it is best to arrange the ideas chronologically, sometimes spatially. Often a combination is best. Often the cause of one idea produces an effect: a second idea. The second idea produces a third, and so on. When this happens, a cause-and-effect arrangement is best. The writer must know the ideas sufficiently well to be able to plan the best ordering of them.

ORDERING THE DATA

Once ideas have been ordered, the writer may then arrange the data to support the ideas. Now that the writer knows the purpose, goals, and scope of the report and has gathered and arranged the ideas and the data, the next step is to decide which arrangement to use for the report. Is the report a feasibility study, a progress report, a description of a mechanism, or a mechanism in operation?

Once this is decided — and it may not be what was thought originally — the writer must then decide how to place the information that does not quite fit the standard format for the report. If the report is a proposal, for example, but there are two ways to solve the problem, each way having distinct advantages and disadvantages, then the proposal may have a recommendation section containing two recommendations that list the advantages and disadvantages of each. (See Chapters 9 and 10 for individual discussions of the various types of reports.)

SUMMARY

1. Reports are a means of conveying complex information objectively.

2. Reports are essential to the success of any company and may go far in aiding the success of individual employees.

3. Reports are extraordinarily diverse, encompassing the formal and informal, written and oral, long and short.

4. Overcoming intimidation of the entire process is accomplished by writing a prospectus — that is, by breaking a report into parts, and then completing each part in turn. Consequently, each task is manageable.

5. The prospectus includes identifying and writing the purpose, problem, and scope sections of a report. The report always addresses the needs and the knowledge of its audience.

6. Scheduling the time required to complete the stages of a report is vital to a business writer's success. A chart similar to the one on page 201 provides a good visual display of the writer's schedule.

7. Research is essential to most reports; the information may be divided into primary and secondary sources. Primary sources of research include direct observation, questionnaires, and interviews. Secondary sources of research — studying what others have said about a subject — requires a knowledge of resources — public or corporate libraries, traditional or electronic.

8. Knowing how to organize ideas and research data is key to writing good reports.

EXERCISES

1. *Purpose statement*. Write a one-sentence general purpose statement for a large project you must complete this semester or quarter.

2. *Problems*. Having written the general purpose for a large project, now write a list of specific problems whose resolution will lead to accomplishing that general purpose.

3. *Prospectus*. Write a prospectus for the large project.

4. *Preliminary schedule*. Having written a prospectus, now design a preliminary schedule of the time you think each of the steps of the project will require. Use the schedule on page 201 as a model.

5. *Long-range exercise*. Keep the work of Exercises 1 through 4 and try to see how closely you are able to adhere to them as the work of the project progresses.

6. *Determining purpose*. Here are two topics for business reports, each a quotation from an executive who is assigning you to write the report. Write one-sentence statements of purpose for the report that might come out of that assignment.

    a. "We've got to figure out how to reduce the percentage of faulty widgitcogs that we're sending out to our customers. I mean, it's really bad in some cases. I've just been listening to a customer complaining that fully 10 percent of the our last shipment was bad."

b. "You know, we spend $150,000 a year on that executive dining room upstairs, yet we've just asked our hourly employees to consider a pay reduction because our sales are so low. It's just not right."

7. *Observation*. Spend a few minutes each day for a week in the dining hall or in the halls between classes. Keep notes on patterns of behavior of groups and of individuals who seem to turn up most days. Record as much detail as possible. Discuss in class your findings *and* what may be made of them.

OR, if you work at least part-time, spend time each day for a week observing the traffic near your office. Keep detailed notes and try to draw some conclusions from those observations as to how that traffic could be made more efficient and whether it *should* be made more efficient (that is, does the traffic move that way for human or logistical reasons?). Remember that time-management experts are not the only people who should be able to observe keenly. Discuss findings in class.

Make sure, however, to decide ahead of time what to look for. Otherwise your observations will not be systematic.

8. *Observation*. Repeat the previous exercise, only this time do it in pairs, but do not compare notes or observations until they have been written and disseminated to the class. Notice the differences. Notice the similarities.

9. *Questionnaire cover letter*. Compare the list of requirements for writing good cover letters for questionnaires with the cover letter provided on pages 207–208. Answer in writing the following questions:

a. Does the letter fulfill all requirements?

b. Does the letter do anything more than required by the list?

c. Are there any specific places in the letter where the writing could be better (e.g., clearer, briefer)?

10. *Questionnaires*. Each of the following questions is from a questionnaire written to assess the attitudes of hourly employees (average education: high school diploma) about company health benefits. Revise each question so that it (1) is more precise, (2) is easier to answer (ideally, yes or no), or (3) will yield more information.

a. Do you think health care costs too much?

b. Should the company pay 100% of the costs involved in Osgood-Slaughter's disease?

c. How do you think the company might reduce the costs of health care without reducing benefits?

d. Do you think an in-plant pharmacological dispensary is a good idea?

e. How much is good health care worth to you?

11. *Research*. Choose a topic about which you might like to write a report. (Your instructor may give you a topic to begin thinking about for a research paper due after covering Chapters 8, 9, and 10.) Write the purpose (topic) in a single sentence. Then begin the research by compiling a list of three primary sources and ten secondary sources. The object is to determine that you can use the library effectively.

12. *Research*. Compile a bibliography of the marketing books and articles of Shelby Hunt.

13. *Library research*. Using the library, find references to Ida Tarbell from two different sources.

14. *Library research*. Using the library, find references to Jack Welsh, CEO of General Electric, from three different sources.

CHALLENGE EXERCISE 1: QUESTIONNAIRES

Compile a questionnaire in which you attempt to discover the attitudes of other students with the same major as yours or of other people who have a job similar to yours. The first job, of course, is to determine precisely what attitude you want to know about. Here are two examples of attitudes you may want to try to measure:

1. How well this institution prepares students for jobs in [insert major]?

2. How well do the policies of this institution [or company] foster students' [managers'] ability to study [work] efficiently?

This may be a group project or an individual one.

CHALLENGE EXERCISE 2: RESEARCH

Until several years ago, Blasius Industries existed in the United States as a holding company. Using library sources, find out what its name was in 1991. Be sure to document *precisely* each source you checked and where you found the answer.

THE STRUCTURE OF FORMAL REPORTS

FRONT MATTER

Letter of Transmittal
Title Page
Table of Contents
List of Illustrations
Abstract or Executive Summary

BODY

Introduction
Text
Conclusions
Recommendations

BACK MATTER

Appendices
Bibliography
Index

PROPOSALS

Introduction
Body
Conclusions
Back matter: Appendices

FEASIBILITY REPORTS

Scope
Body
Conclusions
Recommendations

RECOMMENDATION REPORTS

Introduction
Body
Conclusions
Recommendations

MIXED-PURPOSE REPORTS

ANNUAL REPORTS

SUMMARY

EXERCISES

· ·

Learning Objectives:

☐ Understand the general and specific structure of formal reports.

☐ Write good abstracts and executive summaries.

☐ Write a good proposal.

☐ Write a good feasibility report.

☐ Write a good recommendation report.

☐ Know that most reports in business are mixtures of proposals, feasibility studies, and recommendation reports.

☐ Know how to read annual reports.

☐ Write a good report.

9

NOTHING CONTRIBUTES SO

MUCH TO TRANQUILIZE THE

MIND AS A STEADY PUR-

POSE—A POINT ON WHICH

THE SOUL MAY FIX ITS IN-

TELLECTUAL EYE.

MAJOR

REPORTS

MARY

WOLLSTONECRAFT

SHELLEY (1797–1851)

....
EXERCISE A: ROT IN REPORTS

Discuss in class the following
question: Why is it better to
write "Here is . . ." than "Enclosed please find herewith
is . . ."?

THE STRUCTURE OF FORMAL REPORTS

Formal reports have three major parts: front matter, body, and back
matter. The *front matter* introduces the reader to the organization and
content of the report and typically comprises a letter of transmittal, a
title page, a table of contents, a list of illustrations, and an abstract. The
body comprises the essential details of the report, usually in three or
four sections: introduction, text, conclusions, and recommendations.
The *back matter* comprises appendices and a bibliography, if applicable.

FRONT MATTER

LETTER OF TRANSMITTAL

As the name implies, a letter of transmittal carries (transmits) a report
from the writer to the readers. If the report addresses readers within
the company, then the transmittal may take the form of a memo. If the
report addresses readers from other companies or the government,
then the transmittal will take the form of a letter. The letter of transmittal is not part of the report proper. Its job, simply and as its name
conveys, is to transmit the report to those who asked for it. Consequently, the transmittal is commonly the first page, before the title
page. The transmittal addresses the specific person or people for
whom it was written. Its tone is less formal than the report—that is, it
contains no headings—and the body comprises five parts:

1. The formula sentence "Here is the report you asked me to write" or
   "We were asked to write" should begin each letter of transmittal
   and also should include the report's title.

2. Tell the purpose of the report in a simple and straightforward manner, and justify the report to others who may read it but who did
   not ask that it be written.

3. Describe the major problem and any minor difficulties. Do not,
   however, complain.

4. Provide a broad description of the report's scope—that is, what the
   report considers and what it does not.

5. Recognize those who provided or pointed to fruitful information or
   who helped study, write, or revise the report. Sharing the credit
   displays integrity and good manners.

TITLE PAGE

The title page of formal reports usually contains four parts that are
spaced equally from each other. Center the type on each line and arrange the type as a whole just above the horizontal center of the page;
that is, make the bottom margin slightly greater than the top margin.

Here is an example of a letter of transmittal.

LETTER OF
TRANSMITTAL

1. *"Here is the report you
   asked me to write. Its title
   is. . . ."*
2. *Purpose*
3. *Problems*
4. *Scope*
5. *Here's who helped.*

Here's the report.

Purpose

Problem

Scope

Here's who helped.

GIBRALTAR INSURANCE COMPANY
P.O. Box 8471
Altoona, Pennsylvania 16650

24 March 1992

Mr. Smedley Fahrquart, CFO
Gibraltar Insurance Company

Dear Mr. Fahrquart:

Here is the report you asked me to write on 13 October 1991, entitled
"A Proposal to Buy a Software Program from Bodewell Builders, Inc."

Given a demonstrated need, this report determines whether Gibraltar
Insurance Company should buy a software program for statistical re-
trieval from Bodewell Builders, Inc., or from Multinational Business
Machinations, Inc.

Since changing computer systems, Product and Actuarial Services has
been forced to use obsolete data in order to set prices. The result could
be very expensive.

Of the several computer programs available, only Bodewell and
MBM's have everything we need. Consequently, only these two are
considered. One small difficulty—getting comparable data from these
two companies—has been overcome by the diligent work of Amanda
Jones.

Of the many people who worked hard on this project, several stand
out for their efforts and are listed here alphabetically: John Bender,
Marlene Dwyer, Jay Gadsby, Sam Secera, Brenda Smith, and Arlene
Yeats.

Sincerely,

Rebecca Sunnybrook, CPCU,
Senior Vice-President

1. *Title.* The title gives readers the essence of the report. Brief, clear,
   and accurate, it often is so important that it is written in capital
   letters.
2. *Reader's name and title.* The name and title of the person or group for
   whom the report was written appears here. Make sure to verify the
   titles and spellings.

EXERCISE B: REDUNDANCY IN REPORTS

Discuss in class the following question: A letter of transmittal involves some repetition of the abstract, purpose, problem and scope. Given that repetition usually is bad, why is it *not* bad in a letter of transmittal?

3. *Writer's name and title.* If the writer's name and title are short, then write them on one line. If either is long, then write the name on one line and the title on the next line. In either case, separate names from titles by a comma.

4. *Date.* State the due date of the report, which should also be the actual date of delivery.

Examples of title pages appear below and on pages 237 and 250.

A PROPOSAL TO BUY A SOFTWARE PROGRAM

FROM

BODEWELL BUILDERS, INC.

Prepared for
Smedley Fahrquart, Chief Executive Officer
Gibraltar Insurance Company

By
Rebecca Sunnybrook, CPCU
Senior Vice-President

14 December 1992

THE DEVELOPMENT OF A DESK-TOP REPORT

A

The writer composes and revises the report.

B

The writer explains the design needs of the report to the desk-top publishing (DTP) formatter and hands him the disk of the document.

C

The formatter retrieves the document on the desktop system.

D

He calls up the dialog box and creates the master pages.

E

He creates a master page grid and sets up the page numbers.

F

He organizes and designs the title page.

G

The formatter arranges the text into pages, highlighting and designing the report's subheads.

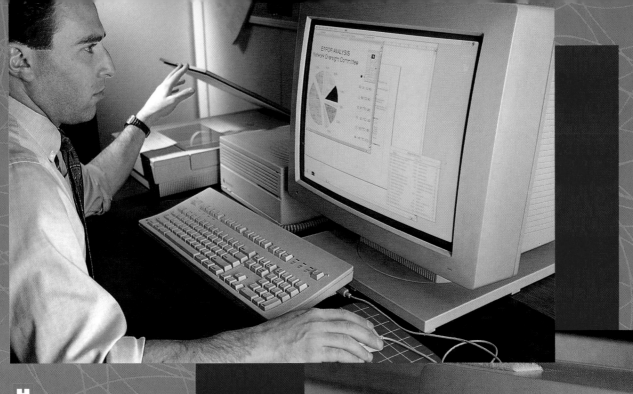

H

He inserts an illustration into a scanner and then calls up the illustration on the screen. The company is reprinting the figure (with permission) from a journal.

I

The formatter uses MockChart to add a second graphic from the writer's sketch.

J

He then places the graphics in the text, and the page make-up automatically accommodates the illustrations, moving the text as needed.

K

The formatter prints out the first proof on a laser printer and examines it to make sure all elements are arranged properly.

L

The writer proofreads the copy and discusses design revisions with the formatter.

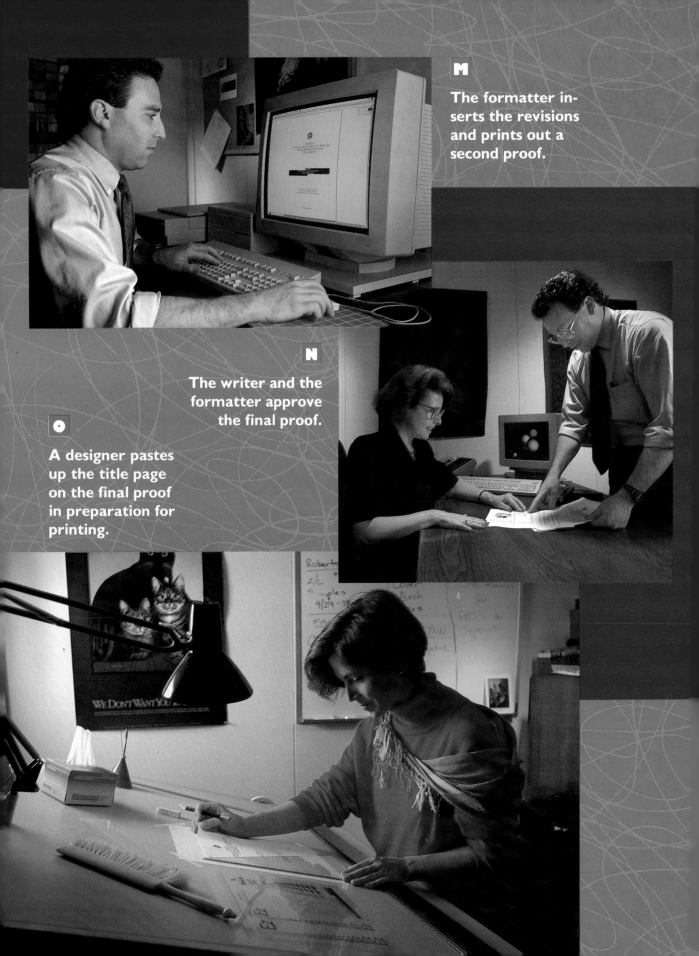

M

The formatter inserts the revisions and prints out a second proof.

N

The writer and the formatter approve the final proof.

O

A designer pastes up the title page on the final proof in preparation for printing.

P

The report is re-printed in the copy center.

Q

The writer presents the report in a management meeting.

The most common desk-top software is PageMaker® by Aldus, available in both DOS and Macintosh® versions. These two examples show the creation of a financial report and an annual report.

A popular software to create illustrations is Corel-DRAW!®, which is available in both DOS and Macintosh® versions.

Certain periodic reports, such as monthly or progress reports, are so routine that the recipients' names are omitted from title pages. Other reports may contain more than the standard four elements. Companies that require such additional elements as approval or sign-off lines, a distribution list, a file number, or a security classification will designate a specific arrangement for them on the title page.

TABLE OF CONTENTS

The table of contents lists both major and minor headings. So readers can refer easily to specific parts of a long, complex report, label the levels of the headings either by the decimal method or the Roman numeral method.

DECIMAL METHOD

1.0 First-level heading 1 1
   1.1 Second-level heading 1 2
      1.1.1 Third-level heading 1 2
      1.1.2 Third-level heading 2 3
   1.2 Second-level heading 2 3
2.0 First-level heading 2 4

ROMAN NUMERAL METHOD

I. First-level heading 1 1
   A. Second-level heading 1 2
      1. Third-level heading 1 2
      2. Third-level heading 2 3
   B. Second-level heading 2 3
II. First-level heading 2 4

Notice that the report contains at least two headings at each level. Organization is weak if any section of a report contains only one subsection. Not every section must have subsections, but if a section contains only one subsection, then the information is not organized effectively.

The table of contents for relatively short or simple reports uses only indention to indicate the level of headings. Each sublevel is indented five spaces from the level above it.

INDENTION METHOD

First-level heading 1 1
   Second-level heading 1 2
      Third-level heading 1 2
      Third-level heading 2 3
   Second-level heading 2 3
First-level heading 2 4

The front matter is paginated with lowercase Roman numerals; the body of the report, beginning with the introduction, is numbered with Arabic numerals.

EXERCISE C: OUTLINING SYSTEMS

Discuss in class the following questions: Suppose you were required to select one of the three outlining systems presented here: decimal, Roman numeral or indention. Which would you choose for a research project in economics? Which would you choose for a research project in English? Which would you choose for a research project in marketing? Are research projects in these disciplines sufficiently different to require different systems? Assuming no differences in research, which system would you choose? Why?

LIST OF ILLUSTRATIONS

Because the list of illustrations follows the table of contents, many believe it to be part of the table of contents. It is not. Should there be room, the list of illustrations may be placed on the same page as the table of contents. If not, then it appears on the next page by itself. A list of illustrations may be divided into two parts: tables and figures. Here is an example of a list of illustrations on a table of contents page.

```
                    TABLE OF CONTENTS

Abstract ...............................................iii
Introduction ............................................1
    Purpose .............................................1
    Problem .............................................1
    Scope ...............................................1
Capabilities ............................................2
    Speed ...............................................2
    Ease of Use .........................................2
    Capabilities with OPL ...............................3
Training ................................................4
Equipment ...............................................4
Cost ....................................................4
Conclusions .............................................5
Recommendations .........................................5


                  LIST OF ILLUSTRATIONS


TABLES

1. Comparing Sorting Speed...............................2
2. Comparing Training Costs.............................3
3. Five Year Cost Comparison ...........................4


FIGURES

1. Estimated Time to Recovery ..........................5
2. Comparing Training Time .............................5

                         ii
```

GLOSSARY

Reports occasionally address subjects so technical or specialized that very technical symbols or specialized words must be used. These words must be defined. Short lists can be placed following the List of Illustrations. Lengthy glossaries should be placed at the end of a report.

EXERCISE D: WHY GLOSSARIES?

Discuss in class the following questions:

1. Are glossaries the result of the writer's obligation to make the job of reading as easy as possible for the reader?

2. Using words that readers do not understand is self-defeating, but so is defining in a glossary a lot of words that readers already know. How difficult is selecting words for a glossary?

ABSTRACT OR EXECUTIVE SUMMARY

Formal reports contain either an abstract or an executive summary, which is a specialized abstract.

ABSTRACT.   An abstract is a summary that allows readers to understand at a glance the issues, processes, and conclusions of reports. Writing abstracts may be compared with distilling brandy from wine: only the essential elements are retained. Abstracts should be smooth; that is, they should retain normal English syntax. They should omit all extraneous words, ideas, and information. An abstract should not be reducible without deleting essential details. Abstracts may be longer than one paragraph, but they should never be longer than one page.

More than thirty years ago, the Institute of Electrical and Electronics Engineers published a short article on writing abstracts that remains among the best ever written to define and describe abstracts, and to help those who write them. This article is reprinted here.

The Writing of Abstracts[1]

Christian K. Arnold

The most important section of your technical report or paper is the abstract. Some people will read your report from cover to cover; others will skim many parts, reading carefully only those parts that interest them for one reason or another; some will read only the introduction, results, and conclusions; but everyone who picks it up will read the abstract. In fact, the percentage of those who read beyond the abstract is probably related directly to the skill with which the abstract is written. The first significant impression of your report is formed on the reader's mind by the abstract; and the sympathy with which it is read, if it is read at all, is often determined by this first impression. Further, the people your organization wants most to impress with your report are the very people who will probably read no more than the abstract and certainly no more than the abstract, introduction, conclusions, and recommendations. And the people you should want most to read your paper are the ones for whose free time you have the most competition.

Despite its importance, you are apt to throw your abstract together as fast as possible. Its construction is the last step of an arduous job that you would rather have avoided in the first place. It's a real relief to be rid of the thing, and almost anything will satisfy you. But a little time spent in learning the "rules" that govern the construction of good abstracts and in practicing how to apply them will pay material dividends to both you and your organization.

The abstract—or summary, foreword, or whatever you call the initial thumbnail sketch of your report or paper—has two purposes: (1) it provides the specialist in the field with enough information about the report to permit him to decide whether he could read it with

---

[1]*IEEE Transactions on Engineering Writing and Speech* EWS-4, no. 4 (December 1961): 80–82.

profit, and (2) it provides the administrator or executive with enough knowledge about what has been done in the study or project and with what results to satisfy most of his administrative needs.

It might seem that the design specifications would depend upon the purpose for which the abstract is written. To satisfy the first purpose, for instance, the abstract needs only to give an accurate indication of the subject matter and scope of the study; but, to satisfy the second, the abstract must summarize the results and conclusions and give enough background information to make the results understandable. The abstract designed for the first purpose can tolerate any technical language or symbolic shortcuts understood at large by the subject-matter group; the abstract designed for the second purpose should contain no terms not generally understood in a semi-technical community. The abstract for the first purpose is called a *descriptive abstract*; that for the second, an *informative abstract*.

The following abstract, prepared by a professional technical abstracter in the Library of Congress, clearly gives the subject-matter specialist all the help he needs to decide whether he should read the article it describes:

> Results are presented of a series of cold-room tests on a Dodge diesel engine to determine the effects on starting time of (1) fuel quantity delivered at cranking speed and (2) type of fuel-injection pump used. The tests were made at a temperature of $-10°F$ with engine and accessories chilled at $-10°F$ at least 8 hours before starting.

Regardless of however useful this abstract might be on a library card or in an index or an annotated bibliography, it does not give an executive enough information. Nor does it encourage everyone to read the article. In fact, this abstract is useless to everyone except the specialist looking for sources of information. The descriptive abstract, in other words, cannot satisfy the requirements of the information abstract.

But is the reverse also true? Let's have a look at an information abstract written for the same article:

> A series of tests was made to determine the effect on diesel-engine starting characteristics at low temperatures of (1) the amount of fuel injected and (2) the type of injection pump used. All tests were conducted in a cold room maintained at $-10°F$ on a commercial Dodge engine. The engine and all accessories were "cold-soaked" in the test chamber for at least 8 hours before each test. Best starting was obtained with 116 cu mm of fuel, 85 percent more than that required for maximum power. Very poor starting was obtained with the lean setting of 34.7 cu mm. Tests with two different pumps indicated that, for best starting characteristics, the pump must deliver fuel evenly to all cylinders even at low cranking speeds so that each cylinder contributes its maximum potential power.

This abstract is not perfect. With just a few more words, for instance, the abstracter could have clarified the data about the amount of fuel delivered; do the figures give flow rates (what is the unit of time?) or total amount of fuel injected (over how long a period?)? He could easily have defined "best" starting. He could have been more specific about at least the more satisfactory type of pump: what is the type that delivers the fuel more evenly? Clarification of these points would not have increased the length of the abstract significantly.

The important point, however, is not the deficiencies of the illustration. In fact, it is almost impossible to find a perfect, or even near perfect, abstract, quite possibly because the abstract is the most difficult part of the report to write. This difficulty stems from the severe limitation imposed on its length, its importance to the overall acceptance of the report or paper, and, with informative abstracts, the requirement for simplicity and general understandability.

The important point, rather, is that the informative abstract gives everything that is included in the descriptive one. The informative abstract, that is, satisfies not only its own purpose but also that of the descriptive abstract. Since values are obtained from the informative abstract that are not obtained from the descriptive, it is almost always worth while to take the extra time and effort necessary to produce a good informative abstract for your report or memo. Viewed from the standpoint of either the total time and effort expended on the writing job as a whole or the extra benefits that accrue to you and your organization, the additional effort is inconsequential.

It is impossible to lay down guidelines that will lead always to the construction of an effective abstract, simply because each reporting job, and consequently each abstract, is unique. However, general "rules" can be established that, if practiced conscientiously and applied intelligently, will eliminate most of the bugs from your abstracts.

1. *Your abstract must include enough specific information about the project or study to satisfy most of the administrative needs of a busy executive.* This means that the more important results, conclusions, and recommendations, together with enough additional information to make them understandable, must be included. This additional information will most certainly include an accurate statement of the problem and the limitations placed on it. It will probably include an interpretation of the results and the principal facts upon which the analysis was made, along with an indication of how they were obtained. Again, *specific* information must be given. One of the most common faults of abstracts in technical reports is that the information given is too general to be useful.

2. *Your abstract must be a self-contained unit, a complete report-in-miniature.* Sooner or later, most abstracts are separated from the parent report, and the abstract that cannot stand on its own feet independently must then either be rewritten or will fail to perform its job. And the rewriting, if it is done, will be done by someone not nearly as sympathetic with your study as you are. Even if it is not separated from the report, the abstract must be written as a complete, independent unit if it is to be of the most help possible to the executive. This rule automatically eliminates the common deadwood phrases like "this report contains . . ." or "this is a report on . . ." that clutter up many abstracts. It also eliminates all references to sections, figures, tables, or anything else contained in the report proper.

3. *Your abstract must be short.* Length in an abstract defeats every purpose for which it is written. However, no one can tell you just how short it must be. Some authorities have attempted to establish arbitrary lengths, usually in terms of a certain percentage of the report, the figure given normally falling between three and ten

percent. Such artificial guides are unrealistic. The abstract for a 30-page report must necessarily be longer, percentage wise, than the abstract for a 300-page report, since there is certain basic information that must be given regardless of the length of the report. In addition, the information given in some reports can be summarized much more briefly than can that given in other reports of the same over-all dimensions. Definite advantages, psychological as well as material, are obtained if the abstract is short enough to be printed entirely on one page. Certainly, it should be no longer than the interest span of an only mildly interested and very busy executive. About the best practical advice that can be given in a vacuum is to make your abstract as short as possible without cutting out essential information or doing violence to its accuracy. With practice, you might be surprised to learn how much information you can crowd into a few words. It helps, too, to learn to blue-pencil unessential information. It is perhaps important to document that "a meeting was held at the Bureau of Ordnance on Tuesday, October 3, 1961, at 2:30 p.m." somewhere, but such information is just excess baggage in your abstract: it helps neither the research worker looking for source material nor the administrator looking for a status or information summary. Someone is supposed to have once said, "I would have written a shorter letter if I had had more time." Take the time to make your abstracts shorter; the results are worth it. But be careful not to distort the facts in the condensing.

4. *Your abstract must be written in fluent, easy-to-read prose.* The odds are heavily against your reader's being an expert in the subject covered by your report or paper. In fact, the odds that he is an expert in your field are probably no greater than the odds that he has only a smattering of training in any technical or scientific discipline. And even if he were perfectly capable of following the most obscure, tortured technical jargon, he will appreciate your sparing him the necessity for doing it. T. O. Richard, head of the Laboratory Control Department, and R. A. Richardson, head of the Technical Data Department, both of the General Motors Corporation, have written that their experience shows the abstract cannot be made too elementary: "We never had [an abstract] . . . in which the explanations and terms were too simple." This requirement immediately eliminates the "telegraphic" writing often found in abstracts. Save footage by sound practices of economy and not by cutting out the articles and the transitional devices needed for smoothness and fluency. It also eliminates those obscure items that you defend on the basis of "that's the way it's always said."

5. *Your abstract must be consistent in tone and emphases with the report proper, but it does not need to follow the arrangement, wording, or proportion of the original.* Data, information, and ideas introduced into the abstract must also appear in the report or paper. And they must appear with the same emphases. A conclusion or recommendation that is qualified in the report proper must not turn up without the qualification in the abstract. After all, someone might read both the abstract and the report. If this reader spots an inconsistency or is confused, you've lost a reader.

6. *Your abstract should make the widest possible use of abbreviations and numerals, but it must not contain any tables or illustrations.* Because of

the space limitations imposed upon abstracts, the rules governing the use of abbreviations and numerals are relaxed for it. In fact, all figures except those standing at the beginning of sentences should be written as numerals, and all abbreviations generally accepted by such standard sources as the American Standards Association and Webster's dictionary should be used.

By now you must surely see why the abstract is the toughest part of your report to write. A good abstract is well worth the time and effort necessary to write it and is one of the most important parts of your report. And abstract writing probably contributes more to the acquisition of sound expository skills than does any other prose discipline.

There are two kinds of abstracts: informative and descriptive. In business reports the informative abstract is more common because it provides more specific information and thus is more useful. The *informative* abstract *is* the report. Here is an example of an informative abstract.

Informative Abstract

Gibraltar Insurance Company should buy a computer software program either from Bodewell Builders, Inc., or from Multinational Business Machinations, Inc. Gibraltar Insurance must retrieve data from DMS so its pricing stays adequate and its financial condition stays healthy. The software program from Bodewell Builders, called LOCUS, retrieves data from DMS; costs $120,260 over five years; sorts large record files quickly; and is compatible with One Programming Language (OPL). MBM's program, QUARK, costs $146,000 over five years; sorts large record files rather quickly; but is not compatible with OPL. Lower cost and compatibility with OPL make LOCUS a better buy.

The *descriptive* abstract tells *about* the report. Here is an example of a descriptive abstract.

Descriptive Abstract

This report discusses whether Gibraltar Insurance Company should buy a computer software program either from Bodewell Builders, Inc., or from Multinational Business Machinations, Inc. The importance of data retrieval from DMS is stressed with regard to Gibraltar's staying competitive and financially healthy. Two software packages are compared with regard to their compatibility to retrieval software and with cost. Also considered is the comparable speed of the packages.

To write a good abstract, follow these guidelines:

GUIDELINES FOR WRITING ABSTRACTS

1. Study the report. Know it well.
2. Rank the report's important ideas and information.
3. Write in one sentence the report's main idea.
4. Write in sentences the important ideas and information.
5. Rewrite so that one idea or fact leads to another.

EXERCISE E: INFORMATIVE AND DESCRIPTIVE ABSTRACTS

Do this exercise in class:

1. Write a one-sentence definition of informative abstracts.
2. Write a one-sentence definition of descriptive abstracts.
3. What are some of the similarities and differences between the two kinds of abstracts?

6. Insert sentences that include lesser ideas and information into the abstract.

7. Rewrite until the abstract sounds like normal English.

8. Make sure the abstract accurately reflects the report in tone, emphasis, and conclusions but does not contain too many of the report's phrases.

9. Rewrite using fewer words.

10. Keep rewriting until it contains nothing extraneous.

EXECUTIVE SUMMARY. *Executive summaries* are briefer, more condensed, more general, and less formal than abstracts. They give executives only the essentials of the report in a simple, visual arrangement. Beginning with the recommendations of the report, the executive summary then lists the major ideas and findings point by point, often beginning each entry with a bullet (•). The items listed need not be complete sentences, but their wording should be grammatically parallel. The following is an example of an executive summary.

EXECUTIVE SUMMARY

We recommend buying LOCUS, a program that allows us to price insurance premiums properly.

We compared two computer programs:
• LOCUS, from Bodewell Builders;
• QUARK, from Multinational Business Machinations.
We compared the two by cost:
• LOCUS: $120,260 over five years;
• QUARK: $146,000 over five years.
We compared the two by sorting speed:
• LOCUS was very fast;
• QUARK was fast, but not so fast as Locus.
We compared the two by ability to work with the programming language we now use:
• LOCUS, with minor adjustments, works well with our programming language;
• QUARK does not work at all with our programming language.
After much work, we believe unanimously that lower cost and greater compatibility make LOCUS a better buy than QUARK.

BODY

The body of a formal report commonly comprises an introduction, a text, conclusions, and recommendations.

INTRODUCTION

Introductions usually contain three parts: purpose (or definition and purpose), problem, and scope.

EXERCISE F: ABSTRACTS VERSUS EXECUTIVE SUMMARIES

Discuss in class the following questions:

1. What are the most significant differences between abstracts and executive summaries?

2. Most of those differences exist because of perceived or actual differences in the kinds of readers they attract. What are some of the differences between the readers of abstracts and the readers of executive summaries?

PURPOSE.   Business reports state their purposes immediately. Usually in one sentence, the wording is similar to the beginning of the abstract.

INTRODUCTION

Purpose

Gibraltar Insurance must determine whether to buy a software program for statistical retrieval from Bodewell Builders, Inc., or from Multinational Business Machinations, Inc.

PROBLEM.   If problems are simple, then they can be explained sufficiently by the purpose. The problem section restates the purpose but emphasizes the problem. Most problems requiring a report, however, are not so simple as that; they require more detail than merely restating the purpose.

Often, the problem section must be persuasive. Reports sometimes must persuade people that there is a problem, a serious problem, so that they will read with care and interest. Providing sufficient background and carefully chosen detail helps to persuade the reader of the importance of the problem.

Here is an example of the purpose and problem sections of a report. Notice the difference between them, especially the differences in detail.

Purpose

Gibraltar Insurance Company must determine whether to buy a computer software program for statistical retrieval from Bodewell Builders, Inc., or from Multinational Business Machinations, Inc.

Problem

Since Gibraltar Insurance Company began changing its policy issuance from DOS (disk operating system) to DMS (dual management system), Product and Actuarial Services has been unable to retrieve statistics. Without statistics, Product and Actuarial Services must set prices using obsolete data. We need valid statistics to set adequate prices. As additional lines of insurance are changed to DMS, the need for current data becomes critical. Homeowners and Private Passenger Automobile, which account for about 80%, or $400 million, of Gibraltar Insurance Company's premium income, are to be changed to DMS within the next six months.

If our prices are not adequate, especially for Homeowners and Private Passenger Automobile, then the Gibraltar Insurance Company may be jeopardized.

SCOPE.   Although comparatively short, the scope section of formal reports is vital because it focuses and organizes the report: it narrows

The formulation of a problem is often more important than its solution.

Albert Einstein (1879–1955)

the topic, describes the boundaries of the study, and filters and analyzes the information. Filtering provides an intellectual exercise in exclusion. The writer must decide which data are important and which are not, which methods of inquiry are likely to produce results and which are not. It is important to mention also those data and methods that seem to be important but that, in fact, are not. After selecting the data and methods, the writer then analyzes and arranges them so that the rest of the report will follow logically and understandably. Here is an example of the scope section of a report:

> Scope
>
> After examining seven programs, Product and Actuarial Services has narrowed the choices to two: buying a fourth generation software program called LOCUS, or buying one called QUARK. The five criteria for choosing between them are as follows: speed and ease of use; compatibility with OPL; training; equipment; and cost.

A good scope section makes a report easier to read and comprehend. Moreover, ultimately it saves the writer much time when it comes to composing the body of the report.

TEXT

The outline for the text follows the order presented in the scope section. That is, if the scope section lists criteria as "ABCD," then the text must discuss those criteria in the same order. Moreover, because the body of the report contains the details, and because those details vary in importance, headings must be selected and placed carefully. (Review the outlines on page 223.)

When typing the report, the writer should present the headings as follows.

1. *First level headings.* Capitalize every letter, underline or bold-face, and center.
2. *Second level headings.* Capitalize the first letter of each important word, underline, and place at the left margin.
3. *Third level headings.* Capitalize only the first word, do not underline, begin five spaces to the right of the left margin. Each successive subheading begins five spaces farther to the right.

Long, formal reports may add a numeral system to the headings, as shown on page 223.

CONCLUSIONS

Conclusions are statements, decisions derived from the evidence provided in the body of the report. Conclusions sections should summarize the most important findings about each criterion. Here is an example of a simple conclusion:

CONCLUSION

We conclude that LOCUS is a better buy than QUARK because the former is faster, easier to learn and use, more compatible with OPL, more compact, and less expensive.

RECOMMENDATIONS

Recommendations build on conclusions by recommending courses of action. Notice that the sample conclusion provided above simply states that LOCUS is better than QUARK and why; recommendations go one step further: "We recommend that Gibraltar Insurance buy LOCUS."

Long, complex reports may require lengthy recommendations, for there may be more than one or two things that need to be recommended, none of which has an overwhelming advantage over the others. Here is an example using LOCUS and QUARK as fairly even in their advantages and disadvantages.

RECOMMENDATIONS

Recommendation 1: Gibraltar should buy LOCUS.
Advantages: Learning LOCUS is easier than learning QUARK. LOCUS is compatible with OPL, while QUARK is not. Programs making two other programs compatible are notoriously unreliable.
Disadvantage: The initial outlay for LOCUS is $16,700 more than for QUARK.

Recommendation 2: Gibraltar should buy QUARK.
Advantage: Initially, QUARK is less expensive than LOCUS.
Disadvantages: QUARK is only slightly less easy to learn than LOCUS, but our employees should have little trouble learning QUARK. QUARK's incompatibility with OPL may be negated by the addition of a program, COMPAT, costing $39.95.

Recommendation 3: Look again.
Advantage: Given more time, perhaps a more thorough review of programs could be made.
Disadvantage: Every day that goes buy puts Gibraltar further behind in discovering proper rates for insurance.

Recommendations provide a good check for the quality of the report. A recommendation section that seems to be a mere formality — because the recommendations should be clear to all readers — probably means that the logic and evidence provided in the report make the recommendations obvious.

BACK MATTER

The back matter of a long or complex report comprises bibliography, appendices, an index, and any other ancillary material pertinent to but not properly in the report.

•••••••••••••••
EXERCISE G: DIFFERENCES BETWEEN CONCLUSIONS AND RECOMMENDATIONS

Discuss in class the following question: How may the difference between conclusions and recommendations be defined?

APPENDICES

Appendices are useful places for detailed information that supports claims made in the report proper: lengthy analyses of financial data; long letters, memos, and corroborating reports; blueprints; and computer printouts. They should not be used merely to increase the size and weight of a report. If possible, it is best to include everything in the text. Computers and photo-reducing machinery make appendices easier to create, but less necessary than they used to be. Such machinery also makes such material easier to include in the text in abbreviated forms.

BIBLIOGRAPHY

Reports that require research should contain a bibliography, which lists all sources of information used, not merely those quoted. Articles, books, journals, magazines, newspapers, bulletins, business and government reports, encyclopedias, and yearbooks are common sources. Because each discipline has its own bibliographical form, and because business has no standard form, follow the style preferred by your company or select a common form.

Generally, entries in all bibliographical forms have the same three parts: they list the author, the title, and the publishing information. The three parts of the entry are separated by periods. List the entries alphabetically by author (last name first, then a comma, then first name or initial). Capitalize the first, last, and all other words of the title except articles, conjunctions, and prepositions. Underline or italicize a book title, and put an article title in quotation marks. The publication information for a book includes the name and location of the publisher and the year of publication. The publication information for an article includes the volume number (as applicable), the full date, and the page numbers. Begin the first line of each entry at the left margin and indent all turnover lines five spaces. Here are some sample entries for a bibliography:

> Boskin, Michael. *Too Many Promises: The Uncertain Future of Social Security*. New York: Dow Jones-Irwin, 1986. [book]
>
> *Displacement of Widgitcogs, The*. U.S. Senate Committee on Aging Industries. Washington, D.C.: Government Printing Office [GPO], 1992. [government publication]
>
> Editorial. "Fahrquart's Dilemma." *The New York Times*, 30 September 1991, B-13. [newspaper article; note that the page number includes the section of the newspaper]
>
> Evans, Samantha. "The Widgitcog Factor." *Journal of Widgitcogs and Bungy Cords* 7 (February 1992): 23–47. [journal article]
>
> Fahrquart, Smedley. "Interview with Lee Youacoca." Detroit, 29 March 1991. [interview]

INDEX

A long, published report requires an index, which lists important words, names, and ideas at the very end of the report. Present the entries alphabetically and insert all page numbers on which each entry appears. Include cross-references as necessary. See the index for this book as an example.

PROPOSALS

All proposals must persuade. Whether one proposes to the school board that all sixth grades should be returned from a district's middle schools to the elementary schools or whether one is part of a team writing a proposal to compete with others for a government contract, persuasion is essential.

Proposals may be internal or external. They may propose that something change within the company (internal) or propose to do something for another company (external). Proposals may be solicited or unsolicited (self-generated). The only significant difference here is one of persuasion.When a proposal is solicited, people are persuaded already that a problem exists. An unsolicited proposal, on the other hand, is worthless should the writer fail to persuade the reader that there is a problem.

Self-generated proposals begin, as the name implies, with an employee's idea. They end, if successful, with adoption of the idea. Good self-generated proposals have catapulted their writers to the top echelons of business. After delivery, the proposal is examined by supervisors and managers, some of whom may have very little or simply very different technical knowledge.Self-generated proposals, then, must be written for readers who probably do not know as much about the subject as the writer.

Here is an outline for a formal, self-generated proposal. It is a good arrangement to begin with and can be modified to conform to the requirements of any particular proposals.

OUTLINE FOR FORMAL PROPOSALS

Title Page
Table of Contents
List of Illustrations
Abstract
Introduction
    Purpose
    Problem
    Scope
Body
    Background and Plan
    Schedule

KINDS OF PROPOSALS

Solicited *proposals are written upon others' request.* Unsolicited *proposals stem from the writer's own initiative.*

EXERCISE H: SELF-GENERATED PROPOSALS

Discuss in class the following questions: If a self-generated proposal, unlike other reports, first must persuade the reader that there is a serious problem, does the problem section of such a report require more persuasive skill than the problem sections of other kinds of reports? Why? or Why not?

> Facility requirements
> Personnel requirements
> Cost
Conclusions
Appendices

The title page, table of contents, list of illustration, and abstract are discussed in detail on pages 220–30.

INTRODUCTION

PURPOSE.   The purpose usually is a simple, one-sentence statement of the problem and solution.

PROBLEM.   This is a persuasive section. The writer must persuade superiors that a problem, a serious problem, exists.

SCOPE.   The scope briefly addresses, in order of their appearance, the major sections of the proposal. Scope is discussed in detail on pages 247–48.

BODY

BACKGROUND AND PLAN.   This section analyzes the overall method for solving the problem. It provides an overview but does not discuss the details of each phase of the report.

SCHEDULE.   Often including a flow chart, this section suggests reasonable starting and ending dates, but it acknowledges potential delays and where they are likely to occur.

FACILITY REQUIREMENTS.   Would implementing this proposal necessitate a bigger building, a different building, a change in location, or reorganized facilities? If no changes in facilities are required, this section should say so, for that is in the proposal's favor.

PERSONNEL REQUIREMENTS.   Would implementing this proposal necessitate firing, hiring, or retraining people? If no changes in personnel are required, this section should say so, for that is in the proposal's favor.

COST.   Next to the abstract, the discussion of cost is the most important section. It must be detailed, accurate, and clear, and it must explain how expenditures are to be recouped.

CONCLUSIONS

A call to action, this section re-emphasizes the proposal's main arguments. Superiors must believe there is a serious problem, must care, and must believe that this proposal offers the best method for solving the problem.

BACK MATTER: APPENDICES

Necessary documentation that cannot conveniently be placed in the text of the report is entered in appendices. (See the discussion on pages 234–35.)

Here is an example of a self-generated proposal.

A PROPOSAL FOR

ORGANIZING THE MAINTENANCE DEPARTMENT

Prepared for
John E. Pipe,
Vice-President for Operations
Widgitcogs, Inc.

by
Jeremy Frobisher

19 June 1992

TABLE OF CONTENTS

LIST OF ILLUSTRATIONS

FIGURES

TABLES

ABSTRACT

If the company combines the Facility and Building Maintenance Departments under Manufacturing, labor costs will be $1,225,000 less per year, material costs will be $500,000 less, and machine downtime will decrease.

INTRODUCTION

Purpose

This report proposes a Maintenance Department reorganization that will reduce maintenance costs and equipment downtime.

Problem

Over the past several years, maintenance cost—as a percentage of sales—has continued to rise. In 1991 maintenance costs were 4 percent of sales and are projected to increase to 5 percent in 1992. We expect to spend $26 million for maintenance this year. The rising cost of maintenance is directly reducing net income. We need to find ways to reduce the company's maintenance costs.

Scope

This report provides a comparison of the operating cost and efficiency between current and proposed restructured maintenance organizations, a plan and schedule for reorganizing maintenance, facility and personnel requirements, project costs, and resulting savings.

1

DETAILED ANALYSIS

Background

The criteria of labor cost, material cost, and machine downtime were used to compare our maintenance organization with a one-department structure. Results showed that redundancy of skills exists between the two departments and that each department separately purchases and stores material to support its work. The study indicated that maintenance responsibility for specific plant locations and equipment types is not consistent. Side-by-side machines operated by one person may be maintained by different departments. Statistics show downtime improvement ranging from 3 to 5 percent when a plant uses a central maintenance department.

Labor and material costs will be less, and machine availability will improve if all maintenance work is consolidated under one department. Charts for both organizations are shown in Figure 1. The existing structure has two departments doing maintenance work, and the proposed structure consolidates the work under manufacturing.

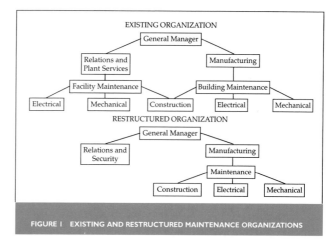

FIGURE 1   EXISTING AND RESTRUCTURED MAINTENANCE ORGANIZATIONS

2

Plan

The most important goal of maintenance is to minimize production time lost from machine breakdowns. Maintenance reorganization under Manufacturing supports the minimal downtime goal and reduces labor and material cost.

This plan requires a reduction of 35 employees to eliminate redundancy that exists because two departments do the same type of work. Table 1 shows the number of employees, by job type, that will be needed if all work is centrally logged, planned, and ranked to support production goals most effectively. Employees can be trained to select appropriate work from a job list and will require less supervision to perform well.

TABLE I EMPLOYEES REQUIRED BY JOB TYPE			
Job Type	**Existing**	**Proposed**	**Difference**
Managers	2	1	(1)
Supervisors	10	6	(4)
Planners	15	9	(6)
Electricians	120	112	(8)
Mechanics	178	168	(10)
Carpenters	15	9	(6)
Total	340	305	(35)

Material cost can be reduced significantly by constructing a central stockroom for all spare parts and construction materials. This stockroom will need only 75 percent as much floor space as the two existing stockrooms because we will not be stocking identical parts in two places.

3

Schedule

The three phases of this project are as follows: (1) combining departments and reducing employees; (2) remodeling the Building 20 office area for the new maintenance group; and (3) consolidating the stockrooms. All three phases can be completed in two months if office rearrangement and stockroom consolidation are done together. Figure 2 shows the tasks and expected timing for each phase.

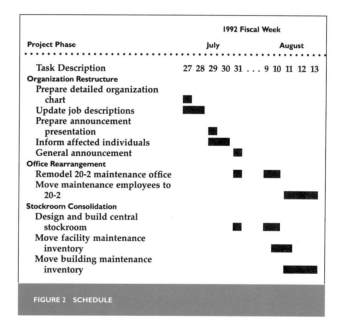

FIGURE 2   SCHEDULE

4

Facility Requirements

The existing maintenance office and stockroom in Building 20 can be remodeled so that all Maintenance Department work and inventory is dispatched from one place. This central location will support procedure changes needed for more efficient work scheduling and better inventory control. We will need to buy office partitions and shelves. This material will cost $19,250.

Personnel Requirements

Two hundred forty hours of labor are needed to remodel the office and stockroom. This is mostly construction work and can be completed by August 9 if third-shift overtime is authorized. Moving employees and inventories can be completed four days later, August 13.

Costs

Total material and labor cost for this project will be $23,479. The detail of this expense is shown in Table 2.

TABLE 2 COSTS

Description	Amount
Stockroom Consolidation	
Shelves	13,500
Labor	3,524
(300 hours @ $17.62 an hour)	
Office Rearrangement	
Partitions	5,750
Labor	705
(40 hours @ $17.62 an hour)	
Total Cost	$23,479

5

Savings

By reducing the number of employees doing maintenance work from 340 to 305, salary cost will be significantly reduced. Economy gained from consolidated purchasing and stockrooms will decrease material costs by nearly 5 percent. Table 3 compares yearly labor and material costs for the existing and proposed organizations.

TABLE 3   SAVINGS

Description	Existing Organization	Proposed Organization	Difference
Salaries and Benefits (@ $35,000 a year)	11,900,000	10,675,000	1,225,000
Materials	12,100,000	11,600,000	500,000
Total	$24,000,000	$22,275,000	$1,725,000

CONCLUSIONS

Labor costs will be $1,225,000 less; material costs will be $500,000 less; and machine availability will improve by 3 to 5 percent if all maintenance work is consolidated under Manufacturing.

A $23,749 investment can return the company $1,725,000 in savings.

FEASIBILITY REPORTS

The only constant in industry is change. Change requires ideas, and today's ideas fuel tomorrow's business success. To help choose the best ideas, companies write feasibility studies.

A *feasibility study* is a recommendation report without the recommendations. A feasibility study says "Yes, it is feasible" or "No, it is not feasible." If management is considering making a new product, buying new machinery, reorganizing a department, moving to another place, reducing the accident rate in the receiving department, then management needs to know whether such action is worth taking. Management wants to know, in the language of business, whether it is feasible. Such studies often produce surprising results, making the writer appear brilliant simply because of a report's careful and detailed examination.

Feasibility studies usually involve more than money. Here is a list of questions that feasibility reports typically answer.

- Are there people who know how to do it?
- Has machinery been made that can do it?
- Is engineering too busy trying to meet a deadline on another project to undertake this one now?
- Will the lawyers shake their heads?
- Above all, how much will it cost?

Feasibility reports are the province of everyone in business. Should city officials be considering building a new airport, for example, they would probably commission a feasibility report. Such a report would require the knowledge and work of many different people: aeronautical engineers, civil engineers, electrical engineers; experts in noise, zoning, land acquisition, city planning, traffic patterns, meteorology, environmental impact, and a host of other specialists, perhaps even specialists in terrorism.

Whereas building an airport requires the expertise of many, some feasibility reports are sufficiently limited to require only one person's knowledge. For example, a vice-president of an insurance company, who directs among other things the setting of rates for policies, may be asked to write a feasibility report about which computer program would provide the best service for retrieving information from which rates are set. Moreover, computers make it far easier than previously for one person to gather enormous quantities of data and to organize those data.

Because feasibility reports usually are read by many people, a formal, almost standard outline has evolved. Following the outline allows the concerns of all readers to be included.

STANDARD OUTLINE FOR FEASIBILITY REPORTS
Transmittal Letter
Title Page
Table of Contents

List of Illustrations
Abstract [or Executive Summary]
Introduction
    Purpose
    Problem
    Scope
        Methods
        Criteria not included (Filtering)
        Criteria (Analyzing and Ordering)
Body
    Criterion 1: Data and discussion
    Criterion 2: Data and discussion
    Criterion 3: Data and discussion
Conclusions

SCOPE

The scope section of a feasibility report requires much thought and work, for it organizes the body.

METHODS.   At their simplest, methods are merely sources: "Information about data retrieval in this report derives from Ms. Megan Byte of Multinational Business Machines and from Mr. Telemachus Modem of Bodewell Builders." Technical reports might say, "Criterion 1 was selected from the Felony Forecasting Method; Criteria 2 and 3 from the Dartboard Method of Forecasting." Specific information would be cited more fully in the body of the report.

CRITERIA NOT INCLUDED (FILTERING).   Filtering, as discussed earlier, limits the criteria of a report by eliminating certain contenders. For instance, in a report that discusses buying a new computer program for data retrieval, this section would dismiss those programs and criteria that are not being considered. The point beyond which a program becomes too expensive to be considered also may be set and mentioned here. When both sellers offer the same important service at the same cost, mentioning or not mentioning it requires judgment. A site license, for example, is permission given to the buyer to copy the software program without cost. An insurance company may buy one software program and pay a permission fee to copy it however many times are required. Should two sellers offer a similar site license for a similar price, the writer would need to decide whether the service is sufficiently important to be mentioned.

CRITERIA FOR ANALYSIS.   Once the limits of cost and time have been determined, programs falling within those limits should be listed. But the programs themselves are not the criteria. The criteria that will form the sections of the body of the report concern what those programs will do and how they will do it. Speed, within certain limits, is a criterion. Cost, within certain limits, is a criterion. But there are costs other than those of just buying the program. What are the costs of the maintenance agreements? Reliability involves cost: how often do the various programs fail? Other criteria include operating speed (how fast do the programs compute?), storage, and the ability of the program to work with other programs in other departments of the company. The writer must also consider the cost of learning the program (training time).

For example, the criteria section of a report on selecting an outside restaurant to cater the college dining hall (something nearly everyone would applaud) might include a ranked list of criteria such as the one provided below.

CRITERIA FOR DINING HALL FRANCHISE SELECTION

Criterion 1. *Price:* Average meal of meat (8 oz.), fresh green veggie (8 oz.), potato (average size A1), milk (8 oz.) or soft drink (12 oz.).

Criterion 2. *Service:* Survey each of three restaurants for 3 hours to discover average time from ordering to delivering.

Criterion 3. *Quality:* Student survey (345 people) of perceived quality of meals: excellent = 5; good = 4; satisfactory = 3; bad = 2.

ORDERING (LIST OF MAIN SECTIONS).   After selecting the criteria, the writer must select a logical order in which to discuss them. Often, they are ranked; that is, they are listed from most important to least important, or vice-versa. For example, cost is most important and normally would be placed first. Perhaps, however, as various tables explain costs, and those tables appear in the cost section (which appears last), cost could be listed last. Here the programs would be compared not only regarding the cost of purchase, but also of maintenance. A second criterion may be capability; that is, what will the programs do? How fast are they? How easy are they to use? How compatible are they with other systems being used by the company? A third criterion may be training. A fourth criterion may concern the equipment required to use the program.

BODY

Now that the criteria have been selected and ordered, the writer creates an outline for the body of the report in which each criterion forms a section. There is no need, however, to list and discuss those criteria satisfied by all systems under consideration. These should be mentioned in a paragraph at the beginning of this section. Here the writer would mention, for example, that all the sellers of programs being considered will provide free updates of the programs whenever they are written. The first criterion listed in the scope section becomes the first criterion examined in detail in the body. Here is the outline.

OUTLINE FOR BODY OF FEASIBILITY REPORT
Criterion 1: Capability
    Speed
        Program A
        Program B

Ease of Use
  Program A
  Program B
Compatibility with Other Software
  Program A
  Program B
Criterion 2: Training
  Program A
  Program B
Criterion 3: Equipment
  Program A
  Program B
Criterion 4: Cost
  Program A
  Program B

A more concrete example may be derived from the "Criteria for Dining Hall Franchise Selection" provided previously. Here is a list of data regarding those criteria from which a writer may derive further explanation and justification.

CRITERIA DATA FOR DINING HALL FRANCHISE SELECTION
Criterion 1: Price
  MacGrease: $2.75
  MacFry: $2.45
  MacBurg: $2.25

Criterion 2: Service
  MacGrease: 3:24 minutes
  MacFry: 2:22 minutes
  MacBurg: 3:45 minutes

Criterion 3: Quality
  MacGrease: 4.5 approval rating
  MacFry: 3.4 approval rating
  MacBurg: 4.0 approval rating

CONCLUSIONS

The writer now draws conclusions from the information provided in the body. This section does not recommend; it simply discusses the relative advantages, disadvantages, and importance of each program.

RECOMMENDATIONS

A strict feasibility study contains no recommendations. In practice, however, many bosses ask for feasibility studies but require recommendations from the writer. Recommendations are drawn from conclusions. Each recommendation should be one sentence. Should more than one recommendation be made, each would be numbered.

Here is an example of a feasibility report about buying a new software system. It includes the most common parts of most formal reports.

EXERCISE I: CRITERIA FOR DINING HALL FRANCHISE

Discuss in class the following question: What other criteria can you think of that might be important to those responsible for selecting one of the outside restaurants for providing dining hall service?

EXERCISE J: CONCLUSIONS AND RECOMMENDATIONS IN FEASIBILITY REPORTS

Some feasibility reports place conclusions before recommendations, while others place recommendations before conclusions. Discuss in class the following questions:

1. When is it better to conclude before recommending?

2. When is it better to recommend before concluding?

THE FEASIBILITY OF BUYING A SOFTWARE PROGRAM

FROM

BODEWELL BUILDERS, INC.

Prepared for
Smedley Fahrquart, Chief Executive Officer
Gibraltar Insurance Company

By
Rebecca Sunnybrook, CPCU
Senior Vice-President

14 December 1992

TABLE OF CONTENTS

LIST OF ILLUSTRATIONS

TABLES

ABSTRACT

This report determines whether GIS should buy a computer software program called LOCUS or one called QUARK.

To maintain adequate prices and financial health, Gibraltar Insurance must retrieve data from DMS using the best possible software program.

The software program from Bodewell Builders, called LOCUS, costs $120,260 over five years, sorts large record files very quickly, and is compatible with One Programming Language (OPL).

MBM's program, called QUARK, costs $146,000 over five years, sorts large record files rather quickly, but is not compatible with OPL.

Lower cost and compatibility with OPL make LOCUS a better buy.

iii

INTRODUCTION

Purpose

This report determines whether GIS should buy a computer software program from Bodewell Builders, Inc., called LOCUS, for statistical retrieval, or one called QUARK.

Problem

Since Gibraltar Insurance Company began changing its issuing of policy from DOS (Disk Operating System) to DMS (Dual Management System), Product and Actuarial Services has been unable to retrieve statistics. Without statistics, Product and Actuarial Services must set prices using obsolete data.

We need valid statistics to set adequate prices. As additional lines of insurance are changed to DMS, the need for current data becomes critical. Homeowners and Private Passenger Automobile, which account for about 80 percent, or $400 million, of Gibraltar Insurance Company's premium income, are to be changed to DMS within the next six months.

If our prices are not adequate, especially for Homeowners and Private Passenger Automobile, then the Gibraltar Insurance Company may be jeopardized.

Scope

After studying seven programs, Product and Actuarial Services has narrowed the choices to two: buying a fourth-generation program called LOCUS or buying one called QUARK. No others satisfy the criteria.

After discussions with A. Schmidt, Vice-President for Corporate Communications, we have narrowed the criteria for choosing to three: capabilities (speed and compatibility with OPL), ease of use (training), and cost.

1

CAPABILITIES

Analysts in the Actuarial Department tested both software programs for three weeks. Testing allowed the analysts to perform ordinary jobs common to each system in order to judge performance.

Speed

Because the six-month and year-end record files are large, sorting speed is important. LOCUS and QUARK can select and sort much data; when a sorting test with two record files of different sizes was performed on both systems, LOCUS was faster than QUARK. The results are in Table 1.

TABLE I COMPARISON OF SORTING SPEED			
Number of Records Read	Quark CPU Time	Locus CPU Time	Percentage Difference
20,000	137 sec.	103 sec.	24.8%
211,149	1478 sec.	1085 sec.	26.6%

Locus CPU Time
$(100 \times$ Quark CPU time $-$ Locus CPU time)/Quark CPU time

Compatibility with OPL

Most of Actuarial's rate-making programs are written in OPL. Software systems not compatible with OPL require about 250 hours of work before they become compatible. An option that interfaces with OPL may be bought with QUARK. LOCUS has no OPL interfacing problem.

2

EASE OF USE

Both systems are designed for non-programmers. The analysts found the two systems easy to learn and use. Because these analysts may understand programming better than others in the Actuarial Department, other employees also used these systems. Although most found both systems easy to use, they preferred LOCUS to QUARK.

Training

The Actuarial Department has 17 employees who would need to learn the program. Both companies will provide training at our home office. A comparison of training costs appears in Table 2.

LOCUS includes in the license fee five days of on-site training for one person. Bodewell Builders also will train as many as 15 at our office for $900 a day, plus $40 a day for each additional person.

QUARK includes in the license fee five days of on-site training for one person. MBM also will train as many as 20 at our office for $1,000 a day.

TABLE 2 FIVE DAYS' TRAINING FOR 17 EMPLOYEES	
Locus	**Quark**
15 for 5 days @ $900/day = $4500	17 for 5 days @ 1,000/day
1 for 5 days @ $ 40/day = $ 200	
1 for 2 days @ $ 40/day = $ 80	
1 for 3 days = $0000	
$4780	= $5000

3

Equipment

LOCUS requires no additional equipment. QUARK requires eight new keyboards to replace Actuarial's OPL keyboards. Each new keyboard costs $150.

COST

Both systems require a one-time license fee and a yearly maintenance fee.

LOCUS would cost $85,900 initially and $8,590 in each following year. QUARK would cost $69,200 initially and $19,200 in each following year.

The costs of each system over five years are compared in Table 3.

TABLE 3 COSTS COMPARED OVER FIVE YEARS		
Year	Locus	Quark
First	$ 85,900	$ 69,200
Second	94,490	88,400
Third	103,080	107,600
Fourth	111,670	126,800
Fifth	120,260	146,000
TOTAL	$515,400	$538,000

Although QUARK initially is cheaper, in the third year its costs exceeds that of LOCUS by $4,520. Over five years QUARK's cost exceeds LOCUS's by $22,600.

4

Notice that while the conclusions clearly favor LOCUS, the writer does not *formally recommend it.*

CONCLUSIONS

1. LOCUS sorts record files faster than QUARK.
2. LOCUS is easier to use than QUARK.
3. Training costs for LOCUS are slightly less than for QUARK.
4. LOCUS requires no additional equipment; QUARK requires eight keyboards costing a total of $1,200.
5. LOCUS costs $25,740 less than QUARK after five years.

5

RECOMMENDATION REPORTS

Recommendation reports differ from feasibility reports in· that they recommend. Feasibility reports do not need to recommend any action; they usually determine only whether a course of action is feasible. In practice, there is little difference between feasibility and recommendation reports, for even if a writer recommends several possible solutions to a problem, the boss may want to know the writer's preference.

Recommendation reports differ from proposals in that recommendation reports may recommend more than one action, while proposals tend to say "Let's do this."

Recommendation reports often provide several solutions to a problem. Although the writer clearly prefers one solution, all solutions must have advantages that outweigh disadvantages. Otherwise, there is no point to providing them. A writer may say, for example, that should the company desire speed more than range of performance, Machine A should be bought. Should range of performance be preferred, then Machine B should be bought, and so on. Advice given freely is usually worth what one has paid for it. The advice given in recommendation reports, however, is hard won. Each solution must be thought out carefully, presented logically and clearly, listing advantages and disadvantages.

Here is an outline for a recommendation report. When written in and for the company, such reports seldom contain letters of transmittal. Abstracts and other front matter may or may not be included depending on the requirements of the company or the boss or on the complexity of the subject:

One gives nothing so freely as advice.

Duc de la Rochefoucauld
(1613–1680)

OUTLINE FOR RECOMMENDATION REPORT
Introduction
    Purpose
    Problem
    Scope (Methods and Criteria)
Body: Presenting and Interpreting Information
    Criterion 1
        Definition
        Discussion
        Interpretation
    Criterion 2
        Definition
        Discussion
        Interpretation
    Criterion 3 (etc.)
Conclusions
Recommendations
    Recommendation 1
        Advantages
        Disadvantages

Recommendation 2
  Advantages
  Disadvantages
Recommendation 3
  Advantages
  Disadvantages

INTRODUCTION

The introduction of a recommendation report follows the arrangement standard for formal reports. Should the report be informal, a memorandum form is used. Usually the only differences are of arrangement: the formal report comprises a title page, headings, and subheadings; the memorandum report includes "to," "from," and so on and includes fewer headings and subheadings. The arrangement, purpose, problem, and scope, however, must be discussed.

PURPOSE. One sentence is usually sufficient: "This report recommends. . . ." Such a sentence, when well stated, leads the reader to the question "What is the problem?" The answer is provided in the next section.

PROBLEM. Defining the problem is crucial. Defining it precisely is essential. Readers who do not understand the problem will not understand the recommendations, no matter how carefully explained. The problem, then, often requires more than one sentence of definition and explanation.

Two concerns dominate the definition of a problem in business: money and time. Business is vitally concerned with time and money. Reader support may be enlisted when the report focuses clearly on these common interests.

SCOPE (METHODS AND CRITERIA). Most scope sections simply delineate the criteria. In recommendation reports, as well as feasibility reports, however, the methods for finding information sometimes must also be listed.

Major sources for methods come from research literature, databases, survey, observations, interviews, and just plain hard work. The discussion of criteria lists the standards by which a problem is examined. These could be anything from cost, speed, and accuracy to truth, beauty, and goodness. Those criteria not included, but which others may believe ought to be included, must be mentioned also. For example, "'The Finger-Counting Forecasting Method,' formerly used in similar reports is not included here because recent studies show it to be unreliable." Another might be this: "Although 'justice' and 'the American way' usually accompany 'truth,' 'beauty,' and 'goodness' as criteria for examining the public writings of Thomas Jefferson, we believe that 'justice' and 'the American way' are subsumed in 'truth' and 'goodness,' and that to treat them separately is to muddy the waters."

BODY

Each criterion must be named, listed, and discussed separately under its own heading in the body of the report. Each is listed in the order in which it was listed in the scope section. Normally, definition, discussion, and interpretation require only a single paragraph. Sometimes, however, clarity is improved by separating one or more of these. Separating definition, discussion, and interpretation occurs most often in complex reports. Here, also, tables and figures are placed to provide details. Remember not to rely on the reader to interpret data. The writer must tell the reader what the data mean.

CONCLUSIONS

Following the body of the report, in which criteria are listed and information is discussed and interpreted in detail, the writer must draw general conclusions. Normally, one conclusion is required for each criterion.

RECOMMENDATIONS

By now, the reader should be well prepared to understand the recommendations. In fact, each recommendation should be little more than a well-worded expression of what the reader already understands.

Each recommendation should be one sentence, underlined, numbered, and in a separate paragraph. Two paragraphs should follow each recommendation. The first should list the advantages, and the second the disadvantages of that recommendation. If the disadvantages of any recommendation outweigh the advantages, the recommendation is a bad one and must be deleted.

MIXED-PURPOSE REPORTS

Reports infrequently come ready-made. That is, the pure report, one that is only a recommendation report or only a feasibility report or only a monthly report, seldom comes along. More often, reports are mixtures requiring some of this and some of that, a bit from this kind of report and a lot from that kind.

ANNUAL REPORTS

Annual reports are periodic reports written by public relations departments. They are often elaborate and expensive, costing American corporations more than $2 billion a year.[2] In fact, the worse the company's

EXERCISE K:
RECOMMENDATIONS

Discuss in class the following questions:
1. Why is it important to write a recommendation using only one sentence?
2. Why is it important to underline each recommendation sentence?

---

[2]Meg Cox, "Snap, Crackle, Give: How the Kellogg Foundation Decides Who Receives Its Generosity," *The Wall Street Journal*, 5 May 1988, 20R-21R.

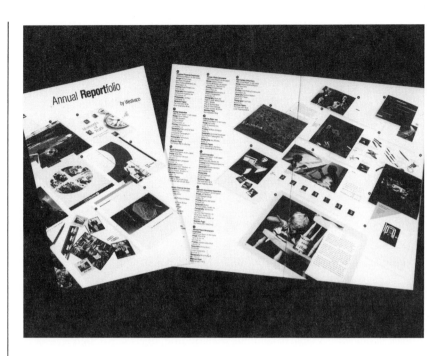

Example of a company's annual report.

financial performance, the more glossy and expensive such reports may be.

The Securities and Exchange Commission (SEC) requires all companies issuing public stock to publish annual reports. Annual reports present the state of the company: how much money it made (or why it did not make money, but did better than the year before), what new projects it undertook, what projects it completed, and the like. The Chief Executive Officer's (CEO's) letter usually opens the annual report and paints the company prettily. Major problems and developments are discussed (and sometimes dismissed) here.

Annual reports written for small companies are often one-page letters from CEOs to other employees and shareholders. Those written for large corporations are usually expensive booklets printed on glossy paper and include color photographs, elaborate charts, and interviews with executives and other important people. In general, annual reports are not read casually. They often are subject to intense scrutiny by people other than shareholders: financial analysts, lawyers, and board members. All have special interests; all want to see special things.

All annual reports should have financial statements that are easily understood by stockholders and employees. Knowledgeable readers usually turn first to the *independent auditor's report* and then look in the text for such waffling qualifying phrases as "except for those" and "this is, of course, subject to." In these statements often appear the company's problems. Of course, all good reports use accounting methods that cast the company in an attractive light, but those methods should be clear to readers not especially knowledgeable about accounting.

SUMMARY

1. Formal reports contain three major sections: front matter, body, and back matter.

2. Front matter includes letter of transmittal, title page, table of contents, list of illustrations, and an abstract or executive summary.

3. The body contains the introduction (purpose, problem, scope), the text, conclusions, and recommendations.

4. Back matter contains the bibliography, appendices, and — in very long reports — an index.

5. Kinds of major reports include proposals (solicited and unsolicited), feasibility reports, recommendation reports, mixed-purpose reports that contain elements of other kinds of major reports, and annual reports.

6. Feasibility reports address the feasibility of doing or not doing something. They determine whether something can or cannot be done, not necessarily whether doing it or not is a good idea.

EXERCISES

1. *Table of contents.* A table of contents is an outline. Beginning with one of the following lists, fill in an appropriate word from one list after the appropriate decimal outline form (admittedly incomplete, as 1.0 has no complementary 2.0).
   List a: University, College, Department, Macro Economics, Triangular Trade
   List b: Chair of the Board, CEO, V-P for Finance, Head of Accounting, Actuary
   List c: Universe, Galaxy, Solar System, Earth, Western Hemisphere

   1.0
      1.1
         1.1.1
            1.1.1.1
               1.1.1.1.1

2. *Writing abstracts.* Return to the preface for this book. Write a 75-word abstract of it following the advice given in this chapter.

3. *Glossary.* Suppose that you are going to write a report about your field of study. Compile an alphabetized glossary of ten terms that would be required by anyone *not* in your field of study but who might want to read your report. Define those terms briefly, clearly, and simply.

4. *Proposals.* Write the introduction (purpose, problem, scope) to a self-generated proposal.

5. *Proposals.* Write a self-generated proposal. Your idea for the proposal may come from any campus- or work-related problem. Unfortunately, these are not difficult to find. Everyone, at one time or another, perceives a problem *and* a solution. That is, each of us has complained that "the parking problem here is terrible," "the food on this campus (or in this plant) is not fit for insects," and "the organization here is unnecessarily complicated." Next we say, "If only they would just. . . ." Well, here is your chance to solve, formally, one of the problems to which you perceive a solution.

6. *Feasibility reports.* Choose three topics from a campus wish list ("I wish the university would . . .") as potential subjects for a feasibility report. After class discussion of these topics, choose one to write for a grade.

7. *Feasibility reports.* Write a feasibility report on one of the following subjects.
   a. Charging all full-time students exactly half-price for season football tickets.
   b. Increasing tuition so that each entering full-time student receives, without additional charge, a microcomputer.
   c. Leasing the commuter cafeteria (or company lunch room) to a fast-food chain in exchange for reduced prices.

8. *Recommendation reports.*
   a. Using the same topic chosen for the self-generated proposal (Exercise 5), write a recommendation report that presents at least *three* possible solutions as recommendations.
   b. Choose a problem to which you think you have the solution, and then write a recommendation report that presents at least *two*

solutions as recommendations. Remember that *both* solutions must be good.

9. *Recommendation report*. Obtain information about two brand-name 19-inch portable color television sets. Compare these sets — two key comparisons might be warranty and price — and then write a recommendation report about which one should be bought for Fahrquart's Beauty Salon.

CASE STUDY I: REVISING PROPOSALS

Your boss says to you, "I just read this report by Campe. It's good, but it could be a lot better. Most of the difficulty lies in its being too long. Could you make it shorter? Also, there are one or two minor problems in organization. Would you fix them?" You, of course, say "Sure!" Revise the report and submit it to your professor, indicating in the margins every change.

A PROPOSAL TO START A TRAINING PROGRAM

FOR

NEW PROGRAMMERS AND COLLEGE INTERNS

Prepared for
Top Cat, Applications Programming Manager
Ultimate Corporation

By
Shirley Campe
Senior Programmer
14 May 1992

TABLE OF CONTENTS

LIST OF ILLUSTRATIONS

TABLES

ii

ABSTRACT

Poor programming techniques with LOBOC, Datumget, LEC, CALCU-
LATOR, Writer, QED, and disregard for department standards cost us
$29,400. We spent 600 hours in fifteen months solving problems caused
by these errors. A thorough, uniform training program for the two new
programmers should start in June. It would cost $960, take four days,
save 370 hours and $11,840, and be taught by programmers.

iii

INTRODUCTION

Problem

Before 1984 the Programming Department had little employee turnover. Since then the turnover has left us with few experienced people. Thus, new programmers and interns are given more difficult beginning assignments than in the past. Because we have a cap on the number of employees, we have also been hiring interns and replacing them every six months when they return to college. The interns and new programmers have little time to learn our systems and become productive employees.

In the past several months the Programming Department has had five new employees. We trained none of these formally, and we cannot guarantee that the training they did receive was thorough and uniform. During those months Systems and Programming spent much non-chargeable time solving many problems. We would have avoided many of these problems if programmers used proper programming techniques. These errors cost the Information Systems Group $29,400.

Moreover, the time spent on the problems could have been spent on new systems and systems improvements. This time is chargeable, saving Information Systems money and producing money-saving systems for the corporation. Thus, the corporation loses and the cost of these errors mushrooms.

Purpose

I propose we start a formal programming training program for all new programmers and college interns beginning in June 1987.

Scope

This report does not detail the employees involved with problem solving or the specific people to do the training. It includes a study of the problems encountered, a training curriculum and schedule, personnel requirements, and program costs.

1

PROBLEM DETAILS

Problem Costs

Programmers' time is charged to other budget centers at $30 an hour and analysts' time is charged at $35 an hour. Table 1 shows 600 hours costing $29,400 were spent solving problems. These hours are not chargeable. Had this time been spent on planned projects, the Information Systems Group would have charged that $29,400 to other budget centers.

Causes

Table 2 shows which subjects cause the most trouble. From most to least troublesome, they are LOBOC, Datumget, LEC, CALCULATOR, Writer, QED, and Department Excellent. Table 2 also shows that 370 hours and $11,840 would not have been lost if programmers had known more about these subjects. Writer, CALCULATOR, and QED are OMNISYS processors learned on the job. Our LOBOC and Datumget programming, along with Department Excellent, are specific to Ultimate. Previous work experience and education cannot replace on-the-job training in our department.

Results

Information Systems has a reputation for data integrity, system access, and speedy turnaround time. Poor programming techniques causing job reruns, incorrect data, and system delays jeopardize this. We can measure how this problem-solving time delays other projects, but we canot measure the loss of our credibility to the rest of the corporation.

2

TABLE 1   TIME-SOLVING PROBLEMS

Month	Systems Hours	Systems Cost	Programming Hours	Programming Cost
January	30	$ 900	20	$ 700
February	20	600	15	525
March	25	750	15	525
April	15	450	20	700
May	25	750	35	1225
June	20	600	30	1025
July	10	300	15	525
August	15	450	15	525
September	20	600	15	525
October	10	300	10	350
November	25	750	20	700
December	20	600	25	1175
January	15	450	20	700
February	20	600	15	525
March	10	300	20	700
TOTAL HOURS	280		320	
TOTAL DOLLARS		$8400		$21,000

TABLE 2   PROBLEM CAUSES

Cause	Hours In Use	Percent of Time Down	Avoidable Hours*
Writer	667	6.0	40
LOBOC	240	37.5	90
LEC	533	15.0	80
QED	583	6.0	35
CALCULATOR	150	13.3	20
Datumget	479	16.7	80
Dept. Excellent	625	4.0	25
TOTAL AVOIDABLE HOURS			370

*This number is based on a study from previous years.

3

SOLUTION DETAILS

Table 2 shows the subjects the errors were found in. The training program curriculum will emphasize the subjects which cause the most problems and give us the most benefits. For example, the most time and
money will be saved if LOBOC techniques are improved, and the least
time and money will be saved if knowledge of CALCULATOR is increased. However, the program will include all topics.

Writer

Although Writer is not the worst offender, it should be the first topic
taught. Programmers need it to work on anything else. Writers are similar from one system to another. Only the core commands will be taught:
insert, change, delete, ditto, and print. The remaining commands are
easily learned from the manual.

LOBOC

All programmers have used LOBOC before they are hired, but many
need a refresher course. Typical errors caused by the misuse of loops,
indices, subscripts, and internal sorts will be included. The program will
also include program skeleton use and compiling procedures.

4

Datumget

All programmers have learned database theory, but many have not programmed on a MODASYL database. Subtopics will be schemas, subschemas, DML, currency, standard error handling, multi-thread, single-thread, and restoring the database.

LEC

LEC is slightly less useful than Datumget, has the third highest number of hours in use (533), and yet shares with Datumget the second highest number of avoidable hours (Table 2). On the other hand, it provides a quicker retrieval than does QED.

QED

QED does not cause as many problems as the other topics, but it logically follows Datumget and is needed for program testing. Included will be ad hoc queries, report writer, single-thread, multi-thread, building records and files, and updating the database.

Department Excellent

All department standards in the DAPEM (Data Processing Excellence Manual) pertaining to programmers will be discussed. However, a separate session will not be necessary. These standards will be included with their corresponding subjects.

CALCULATOR

Most new employees go through a formal CALCULATOR training. We, however, do not schedule our new employees for this. We rely on peers to do the training. The proposed training program includes time for the CALCULATOR instructor to teach the new programmers this processor.

TABLE 3	TRAINING PROGRAM TOPICS AND SCHEDULE		
Topic	Day	Hours	Cost
Writer	1	1	$ 30
LOBOC	1, 2	10	300
LEC	2	2	60
Datumget	2, 3	9	270
QED	3, 4	8	240
CALCULATOR	4	2	60
TOTAL HOURS		32	
TOTAL COST			$960

PERSONNEL

All instructors will come from the Programming Departments (Applications and Software). One exception may be the CALCULATOR instructor. Systems Analyst Ted Kline now teaches CALCULATOR and could teach this session.

FACILITIES AND MATERIALS

Room 222 will be reserved for the first week in June. It has one terminal and chalkboard. The operations manager will have another terminal moved in.

The documentation clerk has ordered manuals for the new employees. She will check with OMNISYS to ensure their timely delivery.

6

COSTS

The program's cost—$960—includes only instructors' time. OMNISYS does not charge for the manuals, and Room 222 is already charged to the Information Systems Group. This charge is not passed to Programming.

CONCLUSION

If we initiate this formal training program, $10,880 ($11,840 − $960) would be saved. We could easily conduct this program at a low cost compared to the benefits reaped. And doing so would cause little disruption to programmers' schedules.

I recommend we begin the program for the two new programmers starting in June.

CHALLENGE EXERCISE 1: WRITING ABSTRACTS

Write a 50-word *informative* abstract of the article on abstracts on pages 225–29.

CHALLENGE EXERCISE 2: FEASIBILITY REPORT

Using the following criteria, write a feasibility report to determine whether return on investment or time saved can justify the purchase of a new fax machine for Fahrquart's Real Estate. If a fax is feasible, recommend one of them. Note that it now becomes a recommendation report.

	FAX 1	FAX 2
Initial Cost	835.00	965.00
Installation	65.00	55.00
Est. Service Costs/yr.	90.00	30.00
Paper Costs (special)	$5.00/100	$1.00/100
Projected Use (pgs./yr.)	600	600
Transmittal Cost/pg.	.35	.15
Estimated down time/yr.	3 days	1 day

Expected new business from fax equals two sales/yr. Average commission per sale: $3,000.

Learning Objectives:

☐ Write informal reports.

☐ Write progress or periodic reports.

☐ Write justification reports.

☐ Write letter reports.

☐ Write minutes of meetings.

WRITING IS THE ACT OF

SAYING *I,* OF IMPOSING

ONESELF UPON OTHER PEO-

PLE, OF SAYING *LISTEN TO*

ME, SEE IT MY WAY, CHANGE

YOUR MIND.

JOAN DIDION

(1934–)

MINOR

REPORTS

THE STRUCTURE OF INFORMAL REPORTS

The reasonable man adapts himself to the world; the unreasonable one persists in trying to adapt the world to himself. Therefore all progress depends on the unreasonable man.

George Bernard Shaw
(1856–1950)

Informal reports are usually brief, use casual and conversational language, and avoid many of the formalities common in business reports.

Because of their casual presentation, informal reports seldom require the front and back matter common to formal reports. The best informal reports, then, contain only essential parts—essential to the reader and the subject matter. Exactly what parts of the structure of the body of formal reports are used or discarded by informal reports depends on the demands of the material, the aim of the readers, and the degree of informality.

Some information is needed so often or is so simple that companies create abbreviated informal reports called forms. The writer's job is to fill in the blanks. Trip reports and petty cash expenditures belong in this category and need no further explanation than to say that the writer should be careful to answer precisely what the questions ask.

PROGRESS OR PERIODIC REPORTS

All progress is based upon a universal desire on the part of every organism to live beyond its income.

Samuel Butler (1835–1902)

Progress or periodic reports tell about the status of a project—that is, about work completed, being completed, and yet to be completed on a project during a given period. Such reports may be written weekly, monthly, quarterly, or periodically at any other time determined by the needs of the company. Annual Reports are a formal form of periodic report (see Chapter 9, page 260). Some companies make a disnction between progress reports and periodic reports. They use the term "progress reports" to describe projects that have clear beginnings and endings and the term "periodic reports" to describe projects that have no foreseeable end. A bridge project, because it has a definite end, requires progress reports; reports on quality control, because striving for perfection never ends, are periodic reports. This text will use the term "progress report" to mean both progress and periodic reports.

Progress reports either are internal (written to be read by company employees) or external (written for someone outside the company: usually someone who has hired the company). Progress on projects is reported periodically to every corporate level from first-line managers to boards of directors. The form these reports take and the amount of information included depend on the company, the project, the manager, and the level of management. Most, however, find some way to include the following:

1. The name, goal, and schedule of the project.

2. A statement about whether the project is on, behind, or ahead of schedule and why.

3. A statement about whether the project is on, over, or under budget and why.

4. Recommendations.

If the reports occur regularly and are written for company employees, a memorandum form often is adopted; if the report goes outside the company, a letter form is more commonly used. Usually, letter forms are short and routine. Unlike formal reports, explanations are extremely brief. People want facts, and they want to know why. Progress reports in many companies have been reduced to one line. More often, they are a paragraph or two. Occasionally, they fill out one page, but rarely should progress reports occupy more than one page. Although there are at least as many types of progress reports as there are companies using them, two types predominate: one-line and one-page.

ONE-LINE PROGRESS REPORTS

Managers often oversee dozens of projects at one time, so it becomes impractical for them to read one-page progress reports routinely. Consequently, they often keep abreast of the projects they manage by requiring weekly progress reports that do little more than provide one line of information, usually in tabular form. Notice in the example below that everything is reduced to numbers, but that time and money remain the most important information. By comparing the percentage of the money allocated for the project, the amount spent, the time allotted for the project, and the percentage of time used to date, managers easily may determine problems. For example, in this illustration, only one project (Z5093) has a big discrepancy between the percentage of the budget spent (67) and the percentage of time used (15). Consequently, a checkmark placed next to that project would indicate that the manager wants to know additional information about it.

MEMORANDUM

TO: Genghis Khan

FROM: Kublai Khan

DATE: April 1, 2180

RE: Status of Projects

Here is the table indicating the status of my projects for March. Please place a checkmark next to any project about which you wish further information.

Project No.	Dollars Budgeted	% Spent	Hours Budgeted	% Spent
A123	1,000,000	50	100	50
R8409	4,567,231	25	200	24
D8402	500,000	95	500	90
C89034	15,503,000	15	550	18
Qv840983	3,098,000	45	250	42
W9832-2	1,000,000	78	50	75
Z5093	79,000	67	15	10

Although this example contains only seven entries, many managers receive reports like this one that contain more than a hundred one-line progress reports.

ONE-PAGE PROGRESS REPORTS

Another form of progress report explains in depth the status of a single project. Contained on one page, the report usually gives a project overview; describes the activity on the project for the period in question, the status of the project's schedule, and the status of expenses; and provides a list of recommendations. The report should explain any deviations from the projected budget, schedule, or result. Here is an example of a one-page progress report.

MEMORANDUM

TO: Genghis Khan, CEO

FROM: Kublai Khan KK

DATE: March 1, 2180

RE: Zeal/Profit Projects

1. Project overview. Studies dramatically showed us that as zeal among our soldiers (hordes) fell, so did profits. Two subsequent reports have shown that insurance may be the answer: given insurance for themselves and their families, the hordes should perform much better and profits should rise.

2. Description of the project for the period. A test group of 1,000 marauders was insured and then sent to pillage a village. A control group (uninsured) was sent to pillage a similar village. After 20 repetitions, we compiled results that show zeal in the insured group to be 27% higher than in the uninsured group.

3. Time.
          _____ Project is behind schedule. Why?
          _____ Project is ahead of schedule. Why?
          ____X_____ Project is on schedule. Why?

4. Money.
          _____ Project is over budget. Why?
          _____ Project is under budget. Why?
          ____X_____ Project is on budget. Why?

5. Recommendations.
    a. Run the test once to increase its reliability.
    b. Compare increase in zeal with increase in profits.
    c. Compare price of insurance and increase in profits to determine whether insurance is cost effective.

A more elaborate report, which would still be only one page long, might contain both words and visuals. The more elaborate form would be sent to executives, who want to see progress at a glance (the visual) and, if they have concerns, answers to their questions (words). Here is an example.

MEMORANDUM

TO: Smedley Fahrquart, Director of Research

FROM: *GB* Gothic Buttress, Engineer

DATE: April 1, 1992

PROJECT TITLE: R3445; The Galesburg Bridge Wind Problem

1. <u>Project overview</u>. A $10 million project to alleviate the problem of extraordinary winds threatening any standard design for the Galesburg Bridge project.
2. <u>Description of project for this period</u>. A preliminary design for stabilizers for the Galesburg Bridge has been completed.
3. <u>Graph of total project with this period sectioned</u>.

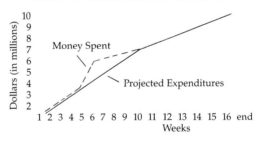

4. <u>Explanations and Recommendations</u>.
   a. The clear over-expenditure in week 6 derived from the discovery of an unforeseen flaw in the design.
   b. The flaw has been corrected.
   c. Because the flaw occurred in the calculations for metal fatigue, allocations for week 11 will not be spent, and we should be able to recoup the over-expenditure from week 6.

JUSTIFICATION REPORTS

Justification reports are typical of short, informal reports. People daily must justify to someone why money was spent, why it was spent for one project and not another, and why certain procedures should change or not change. Justification reports are arranged in one of two ways.

ARRANGEMENT 1: CONCLUSIONS FIRST

Should the boss mainly want to know why, or simply want a report for the files, the report would be arranged so the conclusions appear first and the justification afterward. No one is contesting what was done, but a written record is needed. This is commonly the case when an employee is asked to write it up and put it in the file. Here is a report written this way.

MEMORANDUM

TO: Ghengis Khan, Chief Executive Officer

FROM: Kublai Khan, Executive Vice-President KK

DATE: 1 December 2179

RE: BUYING INSURANCE FOR MARAUDING HORDES

Conclusions

Our study shows that buying insurance for our marauding hordes would not only stop the fall in annual profits, but also produce for The Pillage Company a net increase of 6,153,147 yen annually.

Justification

We suspect that the zeal for which our hordes are justly famous has slackened of late. Many employees have complained that when soldiers are maimed or lost and no longer of service to this company, they and their families are often left to fend for themselves. Nearly half die, and more than a third merely subsist. More importantly, since complaints began four years ago, our profits have fallen by 19.5 percent to a low this year of 400,785,370 yen. Insurance for the hordes may solve the problem.

Costs

Revenue lost annually from lack of zeal	78,153,147 yen
Cost of insurance for 342,834 soldiers	−72,000,000 yen
Annual savings	6,153,147 yen

ARRANGEMENT 2: JUSTIFICATION FIRST

Occasionally, writers are not *asked* for a report but come up with brilliant ideas on their own. A new element thus complicates the issue: persuasion. Brilliant ideas often come in a flash; presenting them in such a way as to persuade others of their brilliance, unfortunately, does not. Ghengis Khan, for example, is not likely to be persuaded easily of the benefits of insurance for his marauding hordes, even by his son, Kublai.

MEMORANDUM

TO: Ghengis Khan, Chief Executive Officer

FROM: Kublai Khan, Executive Vice-President   KK

DATE: 1 December 2179

RE: BUYING INSURANCE FOR MARAUDING HORDES

Justification

We suspect that the zeal for which our hordes are justly famous is sliding because they have no insurance. The cause may be that on those occasions when soldiers are maimed or lost and no longer of service to this company, they and their families are often left to fend for themselves. Nearly half die, and more than a third merely subsist. More importantly, since complaints began four years ago, our profits have fallen by 19.5% to a low this year of 400,785,370 yen.

Conclusions

Our study shows that buying insurance for our marauding hordes would not only stop the fall in annual profits, but also produce for The Pillage Company a net increase of 6,153,147 yen. This, of course, assumes no increase in zeal. Should zeal increase, profits would rise.

Costs

Lost annual revenue:	78,153,147 yen
Cost of insurance for 342,834 soldiers:	72,000,000 yen
Annual savings:	6,153,147 yen

....
Three Parts to Persuasive Justification Memos

1. *Painting a bleak picture*
2. *Painting a pleasant picture*
3. *Proving the pleasant picture*

Occasionally, an employee must justify expenses. The boss wants to know why money was spent, and the report will be scrutinized before it is filed. Kublai does not have to worry about being scourged, but perhaps the frown of Ghengis, even on his son, would not bode well for Kublai's career. After all, Ghengis has many sons. The persuasive justification memorandum contains three parts:

1. *Painting a bleak picture.* The Pillage Company wants to make money. When profits fall, describe how the picture is bleak.

2. *Painting a pleasant picture.* The Pillage Company wants to make money, not lose it. When the fall in profits may be stopped, describe how the picture is pleasant.

3. *Proving the pleasant picture.* Proof must be presented by using numbers and words persuasively.

Letter Reports

Although most informal reports circulate within a company, some are sent outside. Usually sent to a customer or supplier with whom a company has a long-standing and comfortable relationship, letter reports are an effective vehicle for expressing goodwill and a businesslike tone. Small tables and figures occasionally may be added.

A letter report might be written like the example below. Notice the changes in form: Kublai now works for a consulting firm hired by Ghengis to study the problem of falling profits. This is his preliminary report. Notice that authorization, purpose, and problem are contained in the first paragraph; in long, formal reports they have their own headings. Notice the increase in detail.

WARRIORS INSURANCE OF PEKING
1 Ghengis Avenue

1 December 2179

Ghengis Khan, Emperor of China and Manchuria
Encamped near Han, Chungking Province

Dear Emperor Khan:

In October 2179 you asked us to study your company, Marauding Hordes, Inc., and to recommend a way to stop the recent fall in corporate profits. We believe that insurance for the hordes is the answer. The falling profits of Marauding Hordes, Inc., have corresponded to a fall in the zeal for which your hordes are justly famous. When zeal slackens on one side, resistance tightens on the other side: more of your people are lost, the cost of materials (horses, swords, food for long sieges) is greater, and profits are lower. Details are shown in Table 1.

TABLE 1   THE ZEAL-PROFIT RELATIONSHIP

Zeal	No. Marauders Lost	Cost of Materials	Profits
99%	20,567	117,679,843	515,000,000
89%	23,955	134,753,895	498,000,000
73%	26,374	153,390,782	478,000,000
53%	30,782	191,930,278	451,000,000

Extensive and covert interviews were conducted by our people to determine just why zeal has fallen off of late. Many marauders noted that when they were young and without responsibilities, no one cared for much but the joy of battle and the subsequent pillaging. Those who were lost or maimed had taken their chances with everyone else, and such was considered to be simply one of the risks involved with the gains. As time passed, however, most of these marauders married, had families, and thus gained responsibilities. On those occasions when soldiers are maimed or lost and are no longer of service to this company, they and their families are often left to fend for themselves. Nearly half die, and more than a third merely subsist. More importantly, since complaints began four years ago, your profits have fallen to a low this year of 451,000,000 yen.

Emperor Khan   2   1 December 2179

Although our work is not complete, we have decided to pursue two possible solutions. One is to point out to the hordes that zeal has fallen by 45 percent in four years, and that losses have risen by nearly 6,000 annually. Perhaps, by explaining this to the hordes, zeal will improve. Experience has shown, however, that this is usually only a short-term solution, and thus no solution at all. Perhaps the better approach is to buy insurance for the hordes. Because the hordes would no longer need to worry about their families' welfare should a man be lost or maimed, they would no longer need to withhold zeal. The only drawback to insurance is cost. So far, we have been able to find insurance that only would stop the fall in profits and provide a small increase. It does not, unfortunately, bring profits back to their levels of four years ago. On the other hand, spending less for materials during sieges, and increasing zeal, would indeed bring profits back to their former levels. This is still being studied.

Buying insurance for The Pillage Company would increase profits 6,000,000 yen. See Table 2. This, of course, assumes no increase in zeal. Should zeal increase, profits would rise.

TABLE 2   SAVINGS

Lost Annual Revenue	64,000,000 yen
Cost of Insurance for 342,834 Soldiers	− 58,000,000 yen
Annual savings	6,000,000 yen

Sincerely,

Kublai Khan
Consultant

CUREÉ MEDICAL CENTER
101 State Street
Alexandria, Pennsylvania 16624

27 October 1993

Dr. Alphonse Jones, Director of Purchasing
Clinical Pathology Center
5572 Northview Drive
Huntingdon, PA 16635

Dear Dr. Jones:

Our discussions during the past 18 months regarding our joint purchase of a Boulter
X-PLUS MYKR or the DEMIPATH 2000 to perform routine complete blood counts
(CBCs) and differentials at your Central Laboratory have produced considerable excitement and even more study here at the Medical Center. Finally, however, we have
concluded that the sooner you buy X-PLUS MYKR, the better for all of us.

Our relationship with you has been long and mutually beneficial. Given the number of
patients we send you and the high quality of your work, we believe that we can save
$79,502.06 annually in labor, material, and service contract costs. This breaks down to
a savings for you of 46 percent (or $36,570.95) and for us of 54 percent (or
$42,931.00).

Consequently, should it meet with the approval of your board, Cureé Medical Center is
prepared to pay 54 percent of the cost of the machine, if Clinical Pathology is willing to
pay 46 percent.

Not only could we reduce or eliminate certain labor costs and the rising cost of materials, but also dramatically reduce the turnaround time for performing CBCs and
differentials.

As you may remember, we had some discussion regarding whether, should we buy
anything, the X-PLUS MYKR or the DEMIPATH 2000 would be an excellent machine
for our purposes.

These two pages provide yet another example. This time, the situation is contemporary.

MINUTES

There are several problems with meetings. The most serious is that
they must occur at all, next that one must attend them, and finally that
someone must act as secretary. The secretary records the minutes of
the meeting. The anguish of writing minutes may be diminished by
remembering that minutes are fairly standardized; that is, over the

Dr. Jones   2   27 October 1993

Here is a breakdown of the differences between the machines.

Annual Time-Savings for Performing 300 CBCs per Day
X-PLUS MYKR versus DEMIPATH 2000

	X-PLUS MYKR	DEMIPATH 2000
Start-up	5 minutes	20 minutes
Sampling & Review time	1 hr./45 min.	5 hrs.
Hours consumed (312 days/year)	2756	452
Hours saved (312 days/year)	2756 − 452 = 2304 hrs./year	

In addition our study shows that the X-PLUS MYKR uses $12,374.20/day in materials to run 300 CBCs; the SEMIPATH uses $15,687.70. Savings, then, is $3313.50/day.

Moreover, annual contract fees for the SEMIPATH would cost $19,248, while X-PLUS MYKR contract fees would be $1,798; the X-PLUS MYKR thus would save us $17,450 annually in contract fees.

Overall, savings would be as follows:

Salaries:	2304 hrs. × $15.48/hr	$35,665.92
Materials:	312 days	$1,033,812.00
Contracts		$ 17,450.00
Total savings		$1,086,927.92

We found these figures convincing, to say the least. Do you think we should ask our respective boards to discuss and, I hope, recommend buying the X-PLUS MYKR? Do you think we should get together to discuss purchase/lease alternatives, as well as Return on Investment?

Sincerely,

Smedley Fahrquart,
Chief Financial Officer

years a loose formula has been created for writing minutes. Minutes usually contain the following:

TYPICAL CONTENTS FOR MINUTES OF A MEETING

1. *Name of the group.*
2. *Kind of meeting* (regular, ad hoc, etc.).
3. *Date, place, and opening time.*
4. *Topic.* Some meetings have several topics; some have none. Try to describe several topics under one topic heading. If a meeting has no identifiable topic, then it is an ineffective meeting.

Name of group; kind of meeting; date, place, and time

HUMANITIES & SOCIAL SCIENCES DIVISION MEETING, 8-20-1991, Theatre, 3:30 p.m., Elections, Changes to English Major

Attendees

Present: J. Banker, S. Buckwald, J. Davis, S. de Hart, C. Dubbs, J. Fernandez, R. Fiordo, D. Frankforter, M. Ichiyama, Z. Irwin, B. Lane, A. Loss, T. McCracken, G. Morris, M. Podolsky, M. Simmons, R. Sweeting, G. Vanneman, C. Wolford, B. Zaranek

Approval of minutes

Minutes of previous meeting were approved.

Old business

OLD BUSINESS

Petty cash reimbursements are limited to $20.00; anything more requires a purchase order.

Please remember that making coffee is not part of the job for the secretaries, so try to cooperate with them.

We have no budget yet. J. Burke thinks we will have about the same amount as last year.

R. Mester was congratulated for controlling scheduling problems and class section sizes.

Z. Irwin gave a report on the Flower Committee. Traditionally, Assistant Professors give a donation of $10.00, Associate Professors $15.00, and Professors $20.00. Any donation will be appreciated.

A. Loss reported that the Search Committee for Division Head was formed over the summer. The ad will be placed in the Chronicle shortly.

5. *Attendees.* Record the names of those presiding at the meeting. Record the names of stand-ins for officers, and note that they are standing in. If roll is called, note it, and also note how many are present.

6. *Approval (or not) of the previous meeting's minutes.* Show whether the minutes were approved, approved as read, approved as amended, or not approved. See *Roberts' Rules of Order*.

7. *Old business.* The secretary need only listen to and record motions of old business items and their disposition. That is, record *exactly* a given motion (and who made and seconded it); then record whether the motion carried, failed to carry, was tabled, amended, or sneered at. Beyond motions and amendments, the secretary needs to pay attention to little except *actions*.

8. *New Business.* The same rules apply here as for old business; the difference is that the secretary must be more alert during new

New business

Roll-call vote

Time adjourned

Signature of secretary

NEW BUSINESS

B. Zaranek was elected to replace D. Zimmerman on
the Program and Policy Committee.

G. Vanneman was elected to replace S. Buckwald on
the Recruitment Committee.

Three minor changes in the English major were approved by the Program and Policy Committee last
spring. They are as follows: ELISH 494-6 credits,
changed to 3 to 8 credits with a 494 R designation;
eliminate ELISH 210 and 211; substitute with Engl 3
and Engl 2.

M. Simmons amended the motion to read, "Change 8
credits to a maximum of 6 credits." J. Davis seconded the amendment. The amendment carried. The
original motion with amendment, seconded by M. Simmons, carried.

The discussion then moved to the topic of the research money. The basic question was should the
money be distributed for use by faculty giving a paper or otherwise taking part in a conference only,
or should it also be distributed for use in research
in other ways, such as attending conferences but not
taking an active part, subvention for books, etc.

A motion was moved and seconded that money should be
used for legitimate scholarly purposes and distributed as in the past. The motion carried but discussion showed there was confusion as to what had been
voted on. It was decided that another meeting should
be held to continue the discussion. Faculty should
come to the meeting with motions prepared.

The meeting was adjourned at 5:15 p.m.

Submitted by Ms. Carol Theuret

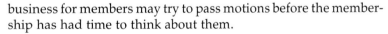

business for members may try to pass motions before the membership has had time to think about them.

9. *Roll-call votes.* Sometimes the vote of each member is recorded.

10. *Time adjourned.* Record the time of adjournment and the time and
place of the next meeting. Many assume that the membership
must vote on adjournment. Not so. Usually, the chair says "Because there is no further business, this meeting is adjourned."

11. *Signature of secretary or recorder.* Notice in the following example
that the "Respectfully submitted," once a standard and still very
common form of closing, is no longer preferred.

Minutes tend to include more passive voice than normal discourse
because the action is usually more important than the actor. Minutes,
however, should not be written exclusively in the passive voice.

SUMMARY

1. Informal reports are brief and use casual language and few formalities. A given report is called by a particular name—periodic, justification, proposal—because it is *predominantly* that kind of report, not because it does not have elements of other reports in it.

2. Progress or periodic reports are status reports that confine themselves to specific periods (weekly, monthly, annually, or periodically) in the life of a project (progress) or a continuing concern (periodic) of the company.

3. Justification reports justify an action or lack of action. These usually are limited to specific and limited actions.

4. Letter reports are like memoranda reports except that they go outside the company. Because they are letters, letter reports usually are more formal than memo reports, and often contain tables and figures.

5. Minutes provide a record of meetings. They tend to be organized formally and follow the meeting's agenda. They are signed and dated.

EXERCISES

1. *Memo and letter reports.* List the primary differences between memo and letter reports. Be prepared to discuss them in class.

2. *Forms: Petty-cash reimbursement.* Here is a common request for petty-cash reimbursement form used in business. Why is it superior even to an informal report required from each person each time this information is needed?

PETTY CASH VOUCHER   DATE

PAY TO

AMOUNT	AMOUNT (Written)
$	

EXPLANATION
(Give full details for accounting purposes of nature and purpose of this payment and attach supporting documents. Receipts are required for all expenses of $25.00 or more.)

COMPANY	ACCOUNT	CENTER	TITLE CODE - AUTHOR - EMPLOYEE NUMBER	MATERIAL CODE	$ AMOUNT
				TOTAL	

REQUESTED BY (Print)	(Signature)
APPROVED BY (Print)	(Signature)

Received Payment

3. *Forms: Trip reports.* Here is a common trip report used in business. Why is it superior even to an informal report required from each person each time this information is needed?

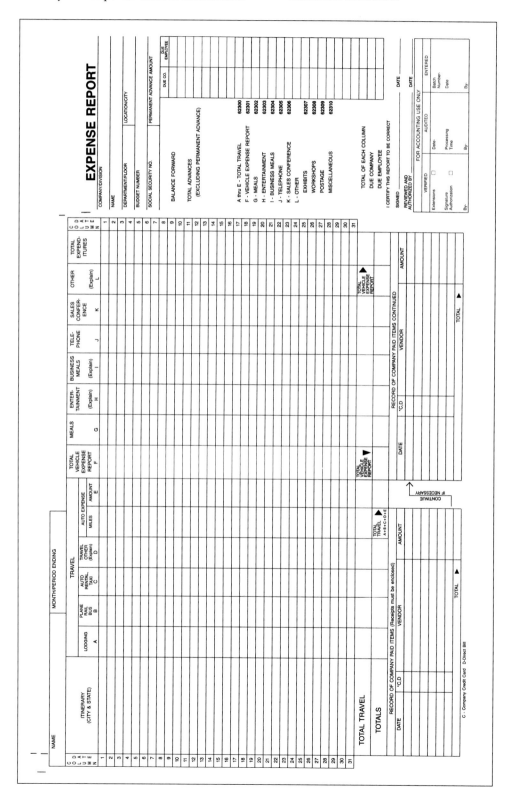

4. *Letter reports.* Here is a *formal* report. Rewrite it as a *letter* report to Ms. Josephina Bungy. Bungy is very picky about spelling, grammar, and organization. She becomes particularly upset when presented with irrelevant information. Neither does she like to see in appendices those figures that should be included in the text of the report. Consequently, in addition to reorganizing the report as a letter report, remember to correct the many errors as well.

A PROPOSAL TO BUY SOFTWARE FROM

MART SOFTWARE, INC.

OR TO CONTINUE USING

ORCHESTRA SOFTWARE, MOTUS, INC.

Prepared for
Josephina Bungy, Comptroller
Ocean Bank

By Juan Fernández

12 October 1992

TABLE OF CONTENTS

LIST OF ILLUSTRATIONS

Tables

ABSTRACT

The report determines whether the Finance Department of Ocean Bank should buy a software program from Mart Software, Inc., or continue to use Orchestra Software from Motus, Inc.

The Finance Department needs the bankwide economics of scale that are developing in other departments.

Mart costs $2,500. Mart allows the user to create spreadsheets faster than Orchestra and provides more diverse accounting applications.

The Finance Department is the only department not using Mart.

Economies of scale and spreadsheet versatility make Mart a smarter buy.

iii

INTRODUCTION

Purpose

This report determines whether the Finance Department of Ocean Bank should buy a software program from Mart Software, Inc., or continue to use Orchestra software from Motus, Inc.

Problem

The Finance department has been using Orchestra for three years. During that time, Ocean's Information Center has been recommending Mart software to all other departments in the bank.

Other departments, such as investments, Commercial Lending, and Trust, have developed economies of scale while using Mart. These departments have reduced their long-term average data-processing costs while income has increased substantially. Departments using Mart have greater specialization of resources, more efficient use of equipment, and a more successful match between department growth and software use.

Mart is superior to Orchestra in many practical ways. Unless the finance department buys and uses Marts now, current spreadsheet problems will become worse.

Scope

Methods. Ocean's Information Center has given the finance department an introductory Mart diskette. The diskette has given two Orchestra users a chance to compare packages and to decide which package would suit the finance department's needs best. They tested the time need to learn Mart and the practicality of both software packages.

Criteria. Mart is a leader in accounting software, and it is used in 34 percent of the Fortune 500 companies, including Ocean's holding company, Mar Financial. Criteria include companywide consistency, cost, practicality, and training time.

COST

Cost-indifference and break-even points can be computed, as well as a variety of other cost-volume-profit analyses, without a lengthy analysis.

Mart will cost $2,500, a one-time cost that includes all installation costs and unlimited use of the Mart. Table 1 breaks down the initial installation cost and provides a yearly comparison to the cost of Orchestra.

1

TABLE 1   TOTAL 1992 COSTS

	Mart	Orchestra
Installation Cost	2,500	n/a
Fixed Costs		
Annual Depreciation	500	435
Maintenance Contract	0	100
Insurance and Misc.	0	350
Total	3,000	885

The $2,115 price differential is small when opportunity cost—the value of the alternative not chosen—is considered. If the Finance Department stays with Orchestra, it will lose all the software experience gained by the other departments. In this case, opportunity cost is experience.

Data processing consistency must be considered also. Mar Financial stresses consistency and practicality. If the Finance Department marches to the beat of a different drummer, Finance will be violating a major corporate objective.

TRAINING TIME

Training time refers to the time required to train the accounting staff to use Mart efficiently. Table 2 shows the time needed for four users to get to know Mart well.

TABLE 2   TRAINING TIME

Name	Hours Needed for Training
Mandy	23
Sandy	26
Andy	34
Randy	26
Total	109

The 109 hours is yet another example of opportunity cost. Finance lost 24 percent of its hours while four accountants learned Mart. Considering future time savings, 24 hours is trivial.

2

VERSATILITY

While Mart and Orchestra share many qualities, there are some important differences.

Mart allows the user to create spreadsheets faster by prompting the user at every stage of spreadsheet development. If the accountant wants to know, for example, whether enough memory remains on the computer, a quick check of the bottom of the computer terminal will provide the answer. In short, command list keys are always displayed, so that the user will spend little time searching for answers to problems.

While Mart allows the practiced user to eliminate many time-consuming routine steps, Orchestra requires the user to perform seven routine commands simply to boot the software. Mart not only creates spreadsheets in half the time of Orchestra, but it is far more versatile.

Graphics

The greatest advantage to the Mart user is the ease and versatility of creating graphics. Orchestra has *no* capability of making graphs.

CONCLUSION

Ocean Bank's Finance department should buy the Mart software package. Although a few full-time hours are lost while accountants learn Mart, Mart is so much faster, more versatile, and more compatible with other departments that, ultimately, it is not only better but cheaper than Orchestra.

3

CASE STUDY 1: FIRST PROGRESS REPORT: MY CHECKBOOK BELONGS TO DADDY AND MOMMY

You are a student at Old State. Your name is Leslie Fahrquart. Last year you overspent (to put it mildly). During the summer you had one of those heart-to-heart talks with your parents in which they asked you if you might have somehow got the notion that the Fahrquarts were closely related to the Rockefellers. You naturally expressed surprise.

After many protestations on your part and accusations on theirs, you and your parents agreed to the following on July 19.

1. Smedley and Irma Fahrquart agree to do the following:
   a. Pay for one twenty-minute phone call home each month.
   b. Pay for your automobile insurance, license, and registration.
   c. Pay for three round-trip airplane tickets a year at super-saver rates as follows:
      1) to Old State in September/to home in May,
      2) home and back at midyear break,
      3) Old State/Fort Lauderdale at Easter.
   d. Pay tuition, fees, and books for the academic year.
   e. Pay room and board in the dormitory.
   f. Pay $100 a month in spending money for "laundry."

2. Leslie Fahrquart agrees to do the following:
   a. Give to Smedley and Irma Fahrquart half of monthly paycheck from summer job.
   b. Mow the grass weekly during the summer.
   c. Reduce expenses for the car at school from $60/month to $40/month.
   d. Reduce fraternity/sorority assessments (beyond normal fees) from $80/month to $0/month.
   e. Never again to have a bill sent home from the Varsity Grill for entertainment, from Sharper's Clothier for high-top sneakers or Guici pumps, from Honey's Pet Shop for an alligator, or from any other store.
   f. Submit in writing to Smedley and Irma Fahrquart a progress report regarding the achievement or lack of achievement of these conditions at the end of each semester.

It is now December 18. Final examinations are written, and you are faced with writing your progress report. You have tried. You really have. But there were unusual expenses this semester.

1. Otello, your beloved alligator, grew very quickly. When the bill for raw meat exceeded $15 a week, you had to get rid of him. Fortunately, you had to pay the zoo only $70 to take him. Prior to the day the zoo received him, you had paid out $255.

2. The potted palm thrown through a window at the fraternity/sorority resulted in the only extra assessment for the semester: $55. But this was small compared with the $418 assessment last year for cleaning the rugs after that unfortunate but minor episode with the incontinent armadillo.

3. The clerk you were dating dumped you in September: "too tired," was the reason stated. Because the clerk lives across town, you saved $25 a month (four months) on automobile expenses.

4. Your parents have balked at paying $28 for the "Erotic Arts Magazine" to which you subscribed.

Write the first progress report to your parents, using the guidelines provided on pages 276–77.

CASE STUDY 2: SECOND PROGRESS REPORT

It is now early May. Write the second progress report to your parents. The following points, showing much improvement, may be helpful:

1. No new pets.
2. New friend, but lives on campus. Car expenses increase only $10/month (January to May).
3. Barred for three months from attending fraternity/sorority activities (for "conduct unbecoming," etc.). A bummer, but savings result of $40/month for three months.

This is the second report. It requires an introduction, a body, and a conclusion.

CHALLENGE EXERCISE: THE HARVEY CORPORATION TAKEOVER

The Harvey Corporation, with sales of about $180 million, 1,600 people, and headquartered in Chicago, is a recent acquisition of the Pulpy Paper Company. It is a diversified company which manufactures paper, envelopes, business forms, packaging materials, and stamped metal products. It distributes paper, graphic arts, and office supplies.

A steering committee to coordinate and assist the transition of Harvey into an operating division of Pulpy has been established. You are a member of the steering committee responsible for coordinating personnel matters during the transition. Mr. Randolph Reeves, Vice-President of Pulpy, is responsible for acquisitions and their integration into your company. He is aso the chair of the Harvey Steering Committee. Here is a first progress report to Reeves regarding this takeover.

MEMORANDUM

TO: R. A. Reeves

FROM: D. A. Loss

DATE: 10 December 1992

RE: Harvey Integration: Personnel Progress Report No. 1

My visit to the Harvey Corporation on Friday, November 6, 1992, was primarily to review their concerns about providing a severance policy for salaried personnel. This visit is the first of many over the next few months to coordinate the integration of their personnel systems with ours and any restructuring that is completed.

I discussed the severance policy concerns with Walk and Corp. They had reviewed our policy, which you had sent to Jay Walk, and both agreed it was appropriate to apply it to Harvey salaried personnel. I recommended they follow our practice when computing pro rata pay of granting not less than one week of severance pay. Walk is concerned about losing the following employees.

DIRECT REPORTS (second level)
J. Walk   —Vice-President, Law
W. Eigh   —Vice-President, Manufacturing
J. Clamp   —President, Bankon Division
R. Enogh   —Director, Human Resources
T. Bucks   —Vice-President, Finance

DIVISION MANAGERS
A. Hemm   —Armmate
O. Mye   —Harvey Paper Sales
E. Gregious   —Harvey Business Forms
Z. Bart   —Ramcot
H. Eyejay   —Maplegrove
K. Ellem   —Sword Paper Company
N. Opey   —Chicago, Bankon
P. Quare   —Emeryville, Bankon
S. Teeyou   —Glendale, Bankon

THIRD LEVEL   —Headquarters
A. Lago   —Internal Audit Manager
C. Garr   —Treasurer
B. Begun   —Controller
F. Stop   —Director of Data Processing
J. Kay   —Director of Manufacturing Systems

R.A. Reeves   2   10 December 1992

FOURTH LEVEL —Headquarters
Y. Degrin   —Assistant Treasurer
N. Mitty   —Manager of Support Services
E. Normity   —Assistant Controller
J. Fernàndez   —Assistant Controller

FIFTH LEVEL   —Headquarters
M. Molient   —Benefits Administrator

We discussed possible enrichments to this severance policy for
the above-named individuals.

1. Provide each individual with a letter from Baumann with the
   following provisions:
   a. Severance pay would be not less than 16 weeks.
   b. No relocation more than 25 miles.
   c. The agreement is to be kept confidential.
2. In addition to number 1, an enrichment would be added for <u>only</u>
   those five direct reports. It would be a "golden handcuff"
   bonus payment of 12 weeks base pay if the individual remained
   at Harvey until January 1, 1993. The total cost for this enrichment is $100,270.

We also discussed calculating the bonus awards for September
through December of 1992 and making the payment in March of 1993.
This short-term handcuff may require a revision of the bonus plan
language. The 1993 bonus would be based on the full year, January
through December, and paid in 1994. This change would also co-
incide with the change in fiscal reporting to a calendar year.

Randy Corp spent time orienting me to their personnel systems. He
is sending me compensation and benefits material and I will summarize it in the next report.

I recommend they adopt our severance policy as soon as possible
for all exempt and nonexempt salaried personnel and nonbargaining
personnel. I also recommend they enrich the severance policy for
the four levels of personnel previously listed but not the fifth
level. By including the fifth level, we would be discriminating
against others in that reporting level.

I am in favor of the handcuff bonus for the top five people, especially when you consider the centralized approach of Harvey and
the dependency of the divisions on the headquarters for systems
support. I also favor the bonus cutoff and payment in 1993.

SF 2218GB.Mem

Attachment

Write a progress report for the next month. Mention that half of all employees listed above have been given notices so that their employment ends on February 1. Each has been given one month's severance pay. You must indicate which employees have been fired and which have been retained, and how long those remaining will be retained. Rewrite it in no more than one page, but be sure to retain the important information.

V

ONE OF THE TOUGHEST

HURDLES YOU'LL EVER

OVERCOME IS LANDING

YOUR FIRST JOB.

THE JOB

LEE IACOCCA (1924–   )

HUNT

ORGANIZING TIME

SELF-SEARCHING

JOB SEARCHING

School Placement Service
Contacts
Job-Hunting Bibliography
Reading Want Ads

SUMMARY

EXERCISES

Learning Objectives:

☐ Organize your time for job
hunting.

☐ Search yourself and identify your
personal and professional
strengths and weaknesses.

☐ Find places and people to help you
search for the right job: placement
services, contacts, bibliographies,
and want ads.

▲
CHECKLIST

TO GO BEYOND IS AS

WRONG AS TO FALL SHORT.

CONFUCIUS

(551–479 B.C.)

PLANNING THE JOB HUNT

ORGANIZING TIME

Finding a job is a job, but, fortunately, like most difficult activities, job hunting is more likely to succeed when it is well planned. Planning seizes the task by the throat before the task seizes you. When planned from scratch, the job hunt requires several activities. The best method probably is to take a page from business practice by constructing a job-hunting schedule. Here is one such schedule.

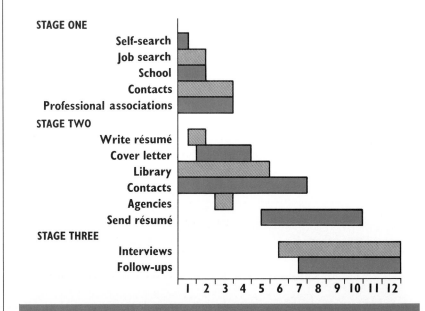

THE PROCESS OF JOB HUNTING

Good planning requires job hunters to do a lot of honest self-searching and job searching. Self-searching involves deciding on your strengths and weaknesses, as well as your likes and dislikes. Job searching involves evaluating the job market, studying companies you like, and discovering which companies are hiring.

If this sounds like the advice your high-school counselor gave you, that is probably because it *is* the same advice. The important difference between now and then is not in the advice, but rather in the person receiving it: you are a different person now, your circumstances are different, and the world appears to be a far more competitive place than it seemed a few years ago. Now it's for real, and now you are probably ready to listen carefully.

SELF-SEARCHING

A cold, rational eye is required of anyone who sets out to list personal strengths and weaknesses. It is all too easy to fool ourselves into thinking that what others think are our strengths and weaknesses really are our strengths and weaknesses. Although honest comments from others are important, helping us to shape and reshape ourselves, the most interested party is also the most knowledgeable: we ourselves. The only requirement is that we be honest about ourselves.

Many books avoid telling us that we need to look squarely at our dislikes and weaknesses, as well as at our likes and strengths. This is probably a mistake, for it is not enough to find a job by relying solely on our likes and strengths. Many jobs, while exercising the best in us, may also contain elements that bring out the worst in us. Consequently, the qualities that make us suited for a particular job may, indeed, be outweighed by qualities that make us unsuited. Moreover, we can learn much about our strengths by studying our weaknesses, for often each is the flipside of a given quality. Honesty, for example, usually is considered to be a strength. Being too bluntly honest, the other side of honesty, may be considered a weakness.

Analyze yourself by constructing a self-assessment sheet in the following way:

EXERCISE A: SELF-SEARCHING

Discuss in class the following question: Why is it important to know ourselves — our weaknesses and strengths — before embarking on a job search?

1. Begin by making a list of the strengths that each of your parents possesses. Then cross out those that you think you do not have (but save them, as you may add their opposites — antonyms — later to your weakness list).

2. By contrasting yourself with your parents, add strengths to the list that you possess but that you have not noticed in your parents.

3. Once the strengths list is complete, make a weakness list. Write the antonyms to each of your strengths. (You may wish to consult a dictionary or a thesaurus, one that includes antonyms.)

4. Next, cross off from the weakness list the items that do not apply to you.

5. Follow the same procedure for the likes and dislikes lists.

6. Construct a self-searching chart that includes strengths, weaknesses, likes, dislikes, and similar categories for education, work, fun, and geography. Rank the items on each list from most significant to least, and include the reasons why. It is in the "why" that you discover most about yourself, and thus what kind of job you will be able to do best and make you happiest. Such a list might look something like the one on the next page.

JOB SEARCHING

The job search is expressed in part by Lee Iacocca, famous Chairman of the Board of Chrysler Corporation: "First, do your homework. Get informed about the job and the company."[1] Many mistakenly glide through their senior year of college believing that freedom from study is just around the next final exam. "After this year," they say to themselves, "I can go out, get a job, and enjoy the fruits of these terrible

---

[1]Quoted in *Careers* 3 (October 1985): 6.

EXERCISE B: SELF-
ASSESSMENT

Discuss in class the fol-
lowing questions:

1. What elements of
   the Self-Assessment
   Form tell individuals
   the most about
   themselves?

2. What elements of the
   Self-Assessment Form
   tell individuals the
   least about themselves?

SELF-ASSESSMENT FORM

Parents   **Me**
Strengths: Strengths:
Weaknesses: Weaknesses:
Likes: Likes:
Dislikes: Dislikes:

Education
What I liked most about courses in my major and why:
What I liked least about courses in my major and why:

My best <u>specific</u> accomplishments in my course work:
My worst <u>specific</u> accomplishments in my course work:

Courses outside my major that I liked best and why:
Courses outside my major that I liked least and why:

Work
Jobs I liked best and why:
Jobs I liked least and why:

Jobs in which I accomplished most and why:
Jobs in which I accomplished least and why:

Fun
What I like most to do in my free time and why:
What I like least to do in my free time and why:

Geography
A ranking of the geographical areas I most prefer, considering such
factors as urban-suburban-rural, cold-hot, dry-humid, and so on:

Other
I prefer working
　　☐　alone.
　　☐　as part of a team.
　　☐　sometimes alone and sometimes as part of a team.
I like being a
　　☐　big fish in a little pond.
　　☐　little fish in a big pond.

years of reading and studying." Sad to say, this is not true. A college
diploma is a piece of paper with Latin phrases all over it saying only
"This person knows how to learn." Those who want a good job must
study not only the potential jobs and companies but also how to get a
job. Study the companies' performances in the market. Study their
annual reports and other publications. Talk with people who know
about the companies. Keep a detailed list of their performances and
practices.

Job fairs and career counseling are two resources that students should take advantage of.

SCHOOL PLACEMENT SERVICE

Having done a lot of self-searching, you are well prepared to benefit from a bonafide objective view of your qualifications: career counseling. Counselors are trained to analyze your likes, dislikes, strengths, weaknesses, and qualifications and to recommend the types of jobs that match your skills and talents. In addition, the placement service may direct you to a substantial library of information on jobs and job hunting. Even corporations, interested as never before in finding good people, have begun to supply brochures and video tapes outlining the kinds of people they seek.

Usually for a nominal charge, the placement service will keep on file your dossier — which includes your transcript, résumé, reference letters, and the like. An additional value of this service only appears later, when you are terribly pressed for time: many of your inquiries may result in a company's requesting that you send your dossier. All you need to do is call or write the placement service to have the dossier copied and sent to that company.

Nearly all university placement services, as well as consortia of smaller colleges, organize job fairs to bring employers to prospective employees (students) for gathering information and interviewing. Ask about such a service and how to become involved.

CONTACTS

Contacts are people. Three kinds are especially useful: friends, professors, and acquaintances in business. Too often this category is woefully overlooked by people just entering the job market. Perhaps this fact will persuade you of its importance: 70 percent of all job openings are not advertised.

FRIENDS. Too many job hunters overlook friends and their friends' contacts. Friends probably will not provide you with an inside track for a job that they have their eyes on, but often they know of jobs in which they are neither interested nor qualified, but for which you may be. Do not wait for them to tell you about the jobs; ask them how their interviews have gone, what kinds of jobs they are applying for, and so on. Often they will give you information valuable for your job search.

Moreover, should you be a member of a service or social organization, such as a sorority or fraternity, other members — especially those graduates already working in the area you are studying — can be very helpful. Job-search advice from these extracurricular sources is invaluable.

PROFESSORS. Professors are not always so isolated from the real world as many students believe. Many consult for companies, others study job markets, and many have friends in business. Professors, then, are good sources for information on jobs. Ask them about their consulting, their research, and their lives in business. You may be surprised by the wealth of information they can provide to help your job search.

PROFESSIONAL ASSOCIATIONS. Every academic discipline enjoys an association of its practitioners. Although most have student memberships for a relatively small fee, even those who do not belong may receive information regarding jobs from the association. As a graduate, or proto-graduate, you should belong. A nearly complete list of professional associations may be found in either of the following books: *Career Guide to Professional Associations: A Directory of Organizations by Occupational Field* or *National Trade and Professional Associations of the United States and Canada*.

BUSINESS ACQUAINTANCES. Those who have held part-time or summer jobs, or who have been fortunate enough to have worked as interns for a company, know people in business. Should those jobs have been at all related to the kind you are looking for, these people may be of great help. Either the company you or a friend worked for may be looking for permanent employees with your qualifications, or the people you know in that company may know people in other companies who are looking for people like you. Check it out.

Job hunting, therefore, should begin long before your senior year and should be a continual activity. People for whom you worked part-time or during the summer should be cultivated in the sense that you should do your best work for them; try to be liked and remembered by them. When you are actively job hunting, you may find these people eager to help you.

Here is a short list of questions you might ask acquaintances in business:

QUESTIONS FOR BUSINESS ACQUAINTANCES

1. What did you do during your job search?
2. What attracted you to your job?

3. What do you like best about your job?

4. What do you like least about your job?

5. What kinds of qualifications do you think make people suited to work for your company?

6. How are chances for advancement with your company?

7. How does one usually become employed by your company?

8. What are the long-range prospects for your industry?

9. What are the long-range prospects for your company?

10. What are the long-range prospects for people with your kind of job?

············

EXERCISE C: QUESTIONS FOR BUSINESS ACQUAINTANCES

Discuss in class the following question: Can you think of any other questions that you might ask business acquaintances?

There are, of course, many more questions that might be asked, and even some of these might be more diplomatically phrased. The point, however, is that before discussing employment opportunities, you should convert your list of likes and dislikes, strengths and weaknesses, into carefully phrased questions that neither embarrass nor offend. These questions also should be phrased so that, if honestly answered, they will provide you with significant answers. No one can provide you with a list that, if memorized, would be perfect for you. You are the only person who knows precisely what you want, what you would do well and poorly. Consequently, only you are qualified to construct proper questions. As always, however, this requires both perspiration and thought.

JOB-HUNTING BIBLIOGRAPHY

Libraries are wonderfully useful for the job hunter. Those serious about finding the right job will use the library fully; moreover, they will have a leg up on those who do not. Here, for example, is a bibliography of books and periodicals commonly held by libraries. The sole purpose of these books is to help you prepare for and engage in the job hunt.

Aima, Hillsdale College. *Job Search: The College Graduate's Guide to Securing a Job.* Dubuque, IA: Kendall-Hunt, 1986.

Allen, Jeffrey G. *How to Turn an Interview into a Job.* New York: Simon & Schuster, Fireside Books, 1985.

Bolles, Richard N. *What Color Is Your Parachute?* Berkeley, CA: Ten Speed Press, annual.

Camden, Thomas M. *The Job Hunter's Final Exam.* Chicago: Surrey Books, 1990.

Eyler, David R. *Resumes That Mean Business.* New York: Random House, 1990.

Half, Robert. *How to Get a Better Job in This Crazy World.* New York: Crown, 1990.

Hochheiser, Robert M. *Throw Away Your Resume.* Hauppauge, NY: Barron's, 1990.

Korda, Michael. *Power! How to Get It, How to Use It*. New York: Ballantine Books, 1987.

Maltz, Maxwell. *Pyscho-Cybernetics*. New York: Pocket Books, 1989.

Meyer, John E. *How to Get the Job You Want: A Guide to Resumes, Interviews, and Job-Hunting Strategies*. Englewood Cliffs, NJ: Prentice-Hall, 1990.

Molloy, John T. *Dress for Success*. New York: Warner Books, 1984.

_____ . *The Woman's Dress for Success Book*. New York: Warner Books, 1984.

Reed, Jean. *Resumes That Get Jobs*. New York: Arco, 1990.

Ringer, Robert J. *Looking Out for Number One*. New York: Fawcett Crest Books, 1985.

Smith, Michael H. *The Resume Writer's Handbook*. New York: Barnes & Noble Books, 1980.

Thompson, Charlotte E. *Single Solutions: An Essential Guide for the Single Career Woman*. Boston: Brandon Publishing, 1990.

Waitley, Denis E. *The Psychology of Winning*. Chicago: Nightingale-Conant, 1988.

Zunin, Leonard, with Natalie Zunin. *Contact: The First Four Minutes*. New York: Ballantine Books, 1988.

Make sure also to check such references and indices as *Standard & Poor's Index* and *Moody's*, which almost every library holds. They are indispensable for everyone looking for the right company. So, too, are such additional sources as the bibliographies of periodicals and newspapers (*Reader's Guide to Periodical Literature* is good) for recent articles on specific companies. Look under the entry for the company's name, but also such entries as the company's major product and the name of the CEO. Pay special attention to articles in the *Wall Street Journal* and trade journals. See also the bibliography in Chapter 8.

Another invaluable source is *Dun's Employment Opportunities Directory: The Career Guide*. *Dun's* annually lists employers alphabetically, geographically, and by industrial classification. Moreover, it provides tips on conducting a job search, statistical analyses of national employment trends, an overview of each employer and career opportunities, and names of people in each company who provide employment information. Finally, it lists each major employer and each discipline it employs.

The *Thomas Register of American Manufacturers and Thomas Catalog File* lists U.S. manufacturers by name and product in 16 volumes. Using standard corporate terminology, *Thomas Register* serves as a glossary of terms for many industries. Consequently, those interested in using professional terminology in their cover letters and résumés would benefit from scanning this book.

Once you have determined several companies to be promising, the next step is to secure copies of the annual reports. Most business libraries in colleges and universities keep current annual reports of major businesses on file. Should your library not keep annual reports, you might have good luck by writing to the company or by finding someone who holds stock in the company and would probably save copies of the annual reports.

READING WANT ADS

Everyone has seen want ads in the newspaper, but no one ever teaches people how to read them, and that is not surprising, as there is only one way to read them: skeptically. That is, read want ads not only from the perspective of "does this job fit my qualifications and desires," but also from the perspective of the potential employer: "How should this ad be written so that I'm likely to get the applicants I want?" The healthy skeptical mind may read want ads well simply by removing all hyperbole. Here is an ad that might appear in a New York City newspaper.

Minor agency
New company?
Vague

COPYWRITER

Northern N.J. advertising agency looking for medical Copywriters in growing, creative agency. Health care agency exp a must. Cardio-vascular product exp a +. Gd bnfts. Sal commens w/exp. Send resume to: T2030 Box XYZ at this newspaper.

• • • • • • • • • • • • • •

EXERCISE D: VAGUENESS IN ADS

Discuss in class the following questions:

1. You doubtless have noticed that much of the copywriter ad is vague. Why might this be purposeful?
2. What are the advantages to the company to be vague?
3. What are the disadvantages?

A critical reading of this ad reveals the following. "Northern N.J." means that the agency is not in Manhattan and, consequently, may not be a major agency. The hyperbolic "growing, creative" probably means the company is reasonably new and, if it were not growing, would probably be in trouble. "Creative" is a term that appears everywhere in the advertising business. Would any advertising agency write of itself that it was *un*-creative? Next, what about "health care experience" and "cardio-vascular accounts"? Just what are "cardio-vascular accounts"? They probably have something to do with the fitness industry that includes everything from running shoes to multi-vitamins. A couch potato, lacking interest in this sort of thing, probably should not apply for this job. "Sal commens w/exp" (salary commensurate with experience) tells very little. The ad and explanation provide only a very small example of conventional want ads and how to interpret them.

As if interpreting conventional ads were not sufficiently difficult, new kinds of want ads are appearing as a result of the widespread use of computer bulletin boards. Here is an add for a software programmer that might appear in a computer conferencing network.

```
      FILE: A TIP R OLD STATE UM/ZA CONTROVERSIAL
                   MONITOR SYSTEM

Path: pasdf!qwerty2!state!oldivy!rutabega!goodl!mush
From: mushemupl.CCCP (Mad Dog Smith)
Newsgroups: Jobs
Subject: NEED SW DEVELOPERS, OURS ABDUCTED BY
WALLSTREET...
Keywords: Muc, TOP, Doors, Graphics, Suply, Pre-
Script, employment, Job
Message-ID: <mushemupl.CCCP>
Date: 14 Nov 92 07:24:12 GMT
Distribution: all
Lines: 30

SW DEVELOPERS ABDUCTED BY WALLSTREET!

        It had to happen.... World Class engineers who
        are redefining the DUix universe at MUSix Soft-
        ware, a well-funded start-up, have been ab-
        ducted by Wallstreetgoons. We developed Mirror,
        the counter-revolutionary desktop publisher. We
        need more world class engineers with brains and
        vision. Of special interest are creative devel-
        opers with expertise in Muc, TOP, mirrors and
        graphics. We want to meet KEY CONTRIBUTORS with
        experience in SUply, Prescript, MUCH, BIgTalk,
        Z.09, Olds, and multimedia systems development.
        We offer an unparalleled working environ-
        ment.... all the right stuff! What do you
        really know about breaking technical barriers
        if you don't know about MUSix? If you're very
        good, we're very interested. Find out more
        about us. Ask for our exclusive agent Mad Dog
        Smith at (619) 555-4321 PST, Fax (619)
        444-1234.
```

EXERCISE E: CONSIDERING THE PERSPECTIVE OF EMPLOYERS WHO WRITE WANT ADS

After gathering in small groups in class retrieve a Reader Profile from Chapter 2. Discuss what attributes the employer wants in people who respond to this ad. Fill in the profile, and then compare your group's profile with those of other groups.

Notice that this is not conventional in any sense. Consider, then, the perspective of the potential employer. One way to handle an interpretation of a want ad such as this one is to use a Reader Profile (see Chapter 2) to determine from the employer's perspective the kind of applicant MUSix is looking for. Completing the profile will allow the various signals put out by the ad to be interpreted and then understood.

Reading job advertisements requires job seekers to be skeptical and resourceful. Placing the right kind of ad in the right place enables companies to attract the applicants they want. Consequently, job seekers should look for job advertisements in the trade journals in their disciplines. Many of these journals will be found in college libraries.

SUMMARY

1. Although it can be done in less time, the job hunt, properly done, requires about a year.

2. Planning comprises three steps: planning time, searching the self, and searching for the right job.

3. Planning time is best done by constructing a chart that plots the time and length of the job hunt's various activities.

4. Self-searching is best done by looking hard at ourselves (our likes and dislikes; strengths and weaknesses) and at our geographical, social, and psychological preferences. This, too, may require a self-assessment chart.

5. Job searching can be done by seeking and studying information from people (placement service, friends, business acquaintances, and professional associations) and from the wealth of job information stored in libraries.

6. Reading want ads is important for finding jobs, but the job hunter must read them skeptically.

7. Electronic bulletin boards are important sources for jobs that involve the computer industry.

EXERCISES

1. *Job-hunting schedule.* Construct a job-hunting schedule. Your schedule may differ from the example on page 302 because you have less time, your résumé has been written, you have been to the placement service, or because of any number of reasons. Justify in writing each of the categories with regard to duration (the time you give yourself to do it) and placement (just *when* during the search you plan to do it).

2. *Self-assessment chart.* Construct a self-assessment chart. Be tough on yourself.

3. *Discovering the placement office.* Go to the placement office and ask about its services, list those services, and decide which may help you. Decide how and when you plan to use those services.

4. *Asking the right questions of those who know.* Plan a list of questions (refer to the list on page 306) that you want to ask a professor whose subject interests you as a career. Interview that professor. Take notes. Report on the answers in writing to the professor from whom you are taking this course.

5. *Reading the literature.* Read one book from the bibliography on page 307–308.

6. *Analyzing want ads.* Choose from a newspaper a want ad that solicits applications from people holding qualifications you have, will have, or would like to have. Write a short analysis of the ad, discussing buzz words with special meanings and any qualifications not listed that may prove important. That is, look at the ad from the employer's perspective.

Learning Objectives:

☐ Know the purpose of résumés.

☐ Write three kinds of résumés: standard, active, and functional.

☐ Write a cover letter.

☐ Write follow-up letters.

ALL EXPERIENCE IS AN

ARCH, TO BUILD UPON.

HENRY BROOKS ADAMS

(1838–1918)

WRITING RÉSUMÉS, COVER LETTERS, AND FOLLOW-UP LETTERS

Style in Résumés and Cover Letters

....

Exercise A: Analysis of a Quotation

Discuss in class the following question: What has Adams's statement—"All experience is an arch, to build upon"—to do with résumés?

Style for résumés and even cover letters encompasses two major concerns: wording and shape. The proper shape of résumés will be discussed later in this chapter; words will be addressed here.

Wording in résumés should be *tight*, *bright*, and *active*. *Tight* wording means precisely what it means in abstracts: no extraneous words. Do not write, for example, "I was mainly responsible, with, of course, three other people, for reducing the cost of shipping widgitcogs by approximately 16%, more or less, by combining the invoice and docking departments." Instead, write, "Part of team that reduced shipping costs by 16%." *Bright* means up-beat, assertive but not aggressive, positive not negative, and interesting rather than dull. Dull, vague, wordy passages such as "During my four years in the marketing department, I was able to progress from one rather low-level position to the next highest and so on, until finally, last year, I was made one of the assistant managers of the marketing department" bore the reader. Instead, write, "Promoted five times in four years, rising from copywriter to assistant manager of marketing." *Active* means active verbs. Do not use such abstract, inactive verbs as "was able to progress" or "was made." Notice how those phrases in the boring and ineffective sentence quoted above become effective in the revised example.

Here is a list of relatively active verbs commonly used in good résumés:

Active Verbs

act	act as	attain	authorize	award
balance	change	climb	control	create
decrease	design	develop	direct	establish
evaluate	execute	expand	gain	generate
increase	inform	initiate	install	launch
maintain	manage	monitor	operate	organize
oversee	plan	produce	promote	purchase
represent	resolve	revise	rise	secure
select	set up	study	supervise	test
train	update	upgrade	win	work

Adjectives, used selectively, can also enliven a résumé. Here is a short list of expressive adjectives common in persuasive résumés:

Expressive Adjectives

strong	extensive	efficient	important	motivated
high	low	proficient	responsible	eager

....

Exercise B: Active Verbs and Expressive Adjectives

Discuss in class the following question: Why are active verbs and expressive adjectives so desirable in résumés and cover letters?

Professional jargon is similarly important in résumés and cover letters. Just as a carpenter does not shave wood with a "woodshaver," but rather with a "plane," so accountants do not speak of "making" money and "losing" money, but rather of "profit" and "loss." Money owed is usually a debit. Learn the terminology of your profession and use it, but use it judiciously. Do not burden résumés and cover letters with excessive jargon.

SUBSTANCE IN RÉSUMÉS AND COVER LETTERS

Before writing a résumé, study what qualities companies want in employees and then how you can acquire (and convey in the résumé) those qualities. Although each company wants specific qualities in its employees, and you should know the company well enough to know what those qualities are, you should know also (and convey in the résumé) the general attributes most companies want in their employees.

Here are examples from résumés and cover letters. Notice that those from résumés are not written as sentences because résumés should not be written in sentences.

QUALITIES THAT COMPANIES DESIRE IN EMPLOYEES

1. *The ability to work well with others, to be a team player*

   Appointed chair of two group projects charged with streamlining the offices of the Student Government Association.

2. *The ability to grow, to adapt to change, to find new ways of thinking*

   Appointed as the only student member of Faculty Search Committee for a new head of the Department of Management. Received written commendation from committee chair for my ability to appreciate faculty, as well as student, concerns.

3. *The ability to make money for the company*

   My major is plastics engineering, the revenues from which, according to the *Wall Street Journal*, are expected to grow tenfold in the next decade.

   While working part-time as a short-order cook at Harry's Mash House, I discovered a way of ordering and serving meals that decreased time from ordering to serving by 29 percent. On an average day, this method increased gross revenues by $137, or 9 percent.

4. *Discipline*

   As a member of the cross-country team that took second place in our conference, I learned the hard way about the trials and benefits of self-discipline.

   Although the project eventually required my running the data through the program 27 times in three days, I persevered until it worked. My efforts produced substantial savings for the community blood bank.

5. *The ability, even desire, to take risks*

> Although our used book cooperative paid off—saving students an average of $7.00 for each book and making us $3.50 for each book—my idea was not without risks. For example, I had to authorize an outlay for a computer and accounting program that amounted to 78% of our sorority's working capital for the year. It was a risky decision, but it paid off.

6. *High standards for oneself and for others*

> Although my project received an *A*, I was not satisfied. Because two sets of data did not seem to support my hypothesis, I continued working until I discovered my error and corrected it so that my hypothesis was supported completely.

> Although everyone wanted to quit by the end of the day, we were not satisfied. Fortunately, we discovered the problem after another two hours.

RÉSUMÉS

For about two decades after World War II almost any cleanly written résumé produced interviews. Beginning in the late 1960s, however, getting a job became at least a full time job because great numbers of young people began to take college degrees. Today, more people are looking for jobs requiring college degrees than ever before, jobs that seem to be outnumbered by the people seeking them, and competition is fierce. This seems grim, but competition is a rule of life, not an exception.

It is also true, however, that people with the best grades, the most tasteful clothes, and the most pleasing personalities do not always get the best jobs. Because more people are qualified for good jobs than there are good jobs, it is important to prepare very carefully.

After you study many companies and are ready to create a résumé, do not rely on professional résumé writers to write it. Even for $100 to $500, these people simply do not have the stake in a job that you do. After all, a job is worth much more than $500. Find the latest editions of *What Color Is Your Parachute?* (R. N. Bolles, Berkeley, CA: Ten Speed Press) and *The Résumé Writer's Handbook* (M. H. Smith, New York: Harper) and follow their advice.

A résumé is a sanitary autobiography. It comprises facts only, and presents to employers a bright, brief summary of your life. The best résumé conveys those qualities you possess that companies desire. The purpose of your résumé is to get you an interview. To be sure that your résumé helps you get an interview, remember that it must be perfect and selective.

RÉSUMÉS AND PERFECTION.   Résumés must be as letter perfect as anything else you ever write. One engineering executive, for example, hires by the dozen. He instructs his secretary to make two piles of

Job hunters attend a résumé-writing workshop.

résumés: one in which *everything* is perfect, another in which everything is not. If sufficient candidates for interviews are found among the pile of perfect résumés, then the imperfect pile is never perused. Why? The executive reasons that should engineers, who must be attentive to detail, not care enough about something so important to them as a résumé, they would not attend to detail when working for someone else. What is true for engineers, moreover, is just as true for accountants, lawyers, secretaries, loan officers, and janitors. Perfection of this kind means a résumé that contains no misspelled words, no smudges, no bad grammar, no bad anything.

SELECTIVITY.   Many job seekers succumb to the temptation to put everything in the résumé, but employers initially glance at résumés, on the average, for only 45 seconds. Consequently, explanations, detailed job descriptions, unusual educational experiences, and the like should be written about in the cover letter, *not* in the résumé.

LENGTH.   Some say that the ideal length for a résumé is one and a half pages. For recent graduates, one page is ideal; in fact, 68 percent of chief personnel officers of Fortune 500 companies prefer one-page résumés.[1] In either case, never extend a résumé to just a few lines beyond the first page.

---

[1]Nelda Spinks and Barron Wells, "Letters of Application and Resumes: A Comparison of Corporate Views," *The Bulletin* (September 1987): 9–16.

PAPER. Formerly white, the standard color for résumés is now off-white. The quality of that paper should be the best you can find, and it should be heavy: 20 lb. An off-white—egg-shell or ivory—makes a résumé easier to read and thus, should a reader have hundreds to look at, will be a gift to the reader because the eyes will not be strained so much as they would be by reading black on white. A résumé for a job in advertising, communications, or something similar may use a more flamboyant color. But it is best, usually, to be conservative. The print should be black—always.

USE OF SPACE. Always design a résumé so there are no large empty spaces in it. A résumé should always look full, but not crowded. Students who have little experience, and whose résumés consequently have little to make them full, should space the words so that white spaces are fairly evenly distributed. Moreover, to make the résumé look squared off, make sure that the four corners are occupied by something.

THE STANDARD RÉSUMÉ

The following arrangement for a résumé is standard today in the sense that its form is the most common. The standard résumé usually comprises the following parts:

PARTS OF A STANDARD
RÉSUMÉ

1. *Heading*
2. *Objective*
3. *Experience*
4. *Education*
5. *Honors*
6. *Activities and memberships*
7. *Languages/travel*
8. *Personal data*
9. *References*

1. *Heading.* Include your full legal name, address, and telephone number. Laws against discrimination have removed the requirement to include height, weight, age, gender, marital status, and so on. Do not include a photo.

2. *Objective.* Including a sentence on career objectives is common. Many think, however, that it is a waste of time and space because at best it means nothing and at worst it can prejudice employers. If the career objective is to be president of GM, others will see the applicant as unrealistic; if the desire is to be head janitor, others will dismiss the applicant as unambitious. A realistic and particular career objective, "management trainee leading to position as buyer," may cut off the job hunter from other areas later seen as desirable. Certainly, most companies do not want to hire college graduates willing to do *anything*, but perhaps particular long-range goals are best reported in the cover letter or orally in an interview.

   A career objective *should be included* under the following circumstances: if you have the inside track on a particular job, and you know precisely the qualifications required, then a career objective may reflect those qualifications; in some areas, such as advertising and public relations, applicants are routinely expected to list career objectives.

3. *Experience.* List experience in reverse chronological order. In particular, provide the job title, company name, employment dates, and a *brief* listing of duties most pertinent to the job for which you are

applying. Include also military service and volunteer work pertinent to the job. Be honest but selective: do not, for example, advertise that year spent in the army's stockade at Fort Dix.

4. *Education.* Place education before experience in a résumé whenever you have more education than experience. Experience appears first whenever you have either more of it or it is more important than the education section. Under education, list your degree, your major, the date awarded, school (if small and not nationally known, provide the address). Mention also a few *pertinent* courses that employers may think important but have not considered. Do not list courses that all students in your major may have been expected to take. Marketing majors, for example, should not list Marketing 101. If grades are well above normal, list the average here, and give it its own line.

5. *Honors.* Awards should be listed on separate lines but in the same category. Awards such as dean's list, outstanding student legislator, IBM salesperson of the year, and so on, are good. So are military commendations, community service awards, and the like. This is not a time to be modest, but neither is it a time to lie.

   Still, be selective. Be careful about including high school awards. Certain exceptional honors, such as scholarships, may be included, but remember that employers assume that college students and graduates have high-school diplomas. It may be best to assume that life begins the day after graduating from high school.

6. *Activities and memberships.* List only a few and only those taxing physical and mental abilities. Most employers do not look at hobbies. On the other hand, syndicated columnists Steve Strasse and Tom Bateman, who write *Working It Out*, have this to say:

   > To what extent does including personal interests . . . help you get an interview?
   >
   > Once employers have narrowed down the list of candidates to those who possess the technical skills and experience a job requires, they are likely to turn their attention to a very different question: What kind of person am I considering for an interview? Listing your personal interests can begin to answer this question.
   >
   > Personal interests serve as perfect examples. Listing that you have earned master points in bridge or were an Eagle Scout, or that you are active in the Big Brother or Big Sister program may help to make a very positive impression. The general rule: If your personal interests can help you secure an interview, then list them.[2]

Bateman and Strauss give good advice; unfortunately, the problem is that job hunters seldom know whether a particular interest will help secure an interview. Whether to list social activities on a résumé often depends on the kind of job being sought. On one end of the job spectrum lie advertising and sales, both of which *require*

---

[2]*Erie Daily Times*, 28 May 1987.

employees to be interested in other people; on the other end is engineering, which often does not require so much social interaction. You should try to discover where on the spectrum your professional and personal interests lie and respond accordingly. Consequently, if you list interests, do so wisely.

The final decision about whether or not to include information about personal interests may be determined by limitations of space. You may wish to pad a skimpy résumé a little by adding your significant interests. Conversely, you may benefit by deleting your interests from an over-stuffed résumé.

7. *Languages and travel.* Today, more than ever, knowing a foreign language helps in business. Travel is broadening; it makes the traveler less provincial. A well-traveled candidate who knows a foreign language will almost always get the job over an otherwise equally qualified candidate.

8. *References.* Two sets of instructions are given here because requirements regarding references differ for newly graduated or about-to-graduate job hunters and those who have been around a while.

a. *College students.* Give at least three references, having first received permission to use their names. Provide name, job title, business address, and business phone. Strive for three kinds of references: one who knows your work; one who knows your educational background, preferably in your major; and one character reference.

Many experts suggest that applicants write "References available on request" or "References available from XYZ placement bureau." They may be right. But consider the following before deciding whether to include names, addresses, and phone numbers of references. Employers usually make two phone calls *after* they are interested. If they are in a hurry, they want to make the calls *now*, not after another exchange of letters. This can determine who gets the job. About 40 percent of one hundred companies surveyed still check references in some instances.

If you are looking at a specific job and company, the best course may be to ask whether they require references.

b. *"Old timers."* Write "References available on request" or omit the category altogether. Litigation and other governmental activities have eliminated, or nearly eliminated, references from the résumés of job hunters. Write or call a previous employer and the response will be in two parts: "You'll have to contact our personnel department" and, from the personnel department, "Yes. Mr. Smedley Fahrquart worked for Widgitcog International from June 1, 1982, to December 25, 1991. . . . I'm sorry. We cannot give you any other information." That is about it.

Here is an example of a standard résumé:

```
                    SAMANTHA FAHRQUART
                        7896 Wimp Way
                    Peoria, Illinois 42091

    (317) 555-1212 [home]          (317) 555-1234 [office]

    EDUCATION
        Bachelor of Science in Management
        J. L. Furguson University and Truckers' Academy,
        Perkins, Kansas. June 1992

    EXPERIENCE
        Demonstrator. Willie Walker Toy Company, Peoria, IL.
        Demonstrated and sold Willie Walker toys house-
        to-house. 1991-present

        Retail Sales. Wimpburgers, Inc.; Peoria, IL.
        Sold hamburgers and other fast foods. 1990-1991

        Meatgrinder. Fahrquart Groceries; Peoria, IL.
        Ground 14 kinds of meat. 1988-1990

    ACTIVITIES
        YWCA, member of board
        Athletic Advocates of Peoria, vice-president
        Mugwump Spelunkers Association, outings organizer
        Water Ski Waxers of Illinois

    REFERENCES
    Mr. Smedley Fahrquart          Mr. Harry Shirt,
    (unrelated)                    Manager
    Vice-president                 Wimpburgers, Inc.
    Willie Walker Toy Co.          321 Grease Drive
    123 Milton-Bradley St.         Peoria, IL 42989
    Peoria, IL 42995               (317) 555-4567
    (317) 555-8901

    Ms. Becky Thatcher,            Parson Brown,
    President                      Minister
    Mugwump Spelunkers             Easy-Marriage Chapel
    15 Huck Avenue                 Newbird Lane
    Hannibal, MO 45678             Snowman, ME 12345
    (314) 555-9083                 (207) 555-9280
```

THE ACTIVE RÉSUMÉ

Active résumés are relatively new, but they are catching on fast. In a few years, they may be standard. The essential difference between standard and active résumés is that standard résumés list the duties accruing to a job, while active résumés list those things accomplished in a job.

Notice the following differences between standard and active résumés, most of which involve brevity and efficiency:

1. *Dates are reduced to years only.* The only exception may be the month of graduation. Some employers want to hire people immediately after graduation.

2. *The number of numbers is increased.* People are impressed by numbers. Numbers sometimes provide a sense of precision, security, and truth where none exists.

3. *Claiming partial credit for a group's success is acceptable.* In the active résumé that follows, Fahrquart implies that her work at Wimpburgers helped increase sales. This is fine. On the other hand, an assembly-line worker for GM should not claim credit for increased sales of automobiles.

4. *Irrelevant activities are not included.*

5. Again, *list accomplishments*, not merely job history. It is also true that employers do not always expect to find much work history in the résumés of newly graduated people. One specialist, for example, says

> The standard chronological résumé stressing "work history" is no longer required or expected of college graduates.[3]

Yet what is required or expected may be one thing; what impresses may be something else. Should a young college graduate have worked hard, then that is looked upon favorably. Should you have held a job or two pertaining to the subject of your studies, and, consequently, your career, that, too, could make the difference in whether you are hired.

6. Again, *be economical*. No one appreciates long-winded writing. Think of a résumé as a one-page list summarizing your life: tight, controlled, no-nonsense. Do *not* write, for example, "I managed to complete all my requirements for my bachelor's degree in accounting in the very short time of only three years." *Avoid sentences; they take up too much space, and do little else.* Write instead: "Completed requirements for B.S. degree in three years."

   In the active résumé shown on page 323, those parts conveying accomplishments are printed boldly as examples; such highlighting is *not* done in actual résumés. Some parts are lettered and are discussed under corresponding letters on page 327.

   a. To have completed the customary four years of study in three is a considerable accomplishment and should be noted here. It shows that the applicant is a motivated worker.

   b. This is an extraordinary action. It conveys accomplishment, something that merely giving the job title does not do. More-

[3]Suzanne Stinson, career counselor, Princeton.

SAMANTHA FAHRQUART
7896 Wimp Way
Peoria, Illinois 42091

317/555-1212 (home)   317/555-1234 (office)

EDUCATION
Bachelor of Science in Management; J. L. Furguson University and Beautician Academy, Perkins, Kansas
June 1990
Completed all requirements for B.S. in three years. [a]

EXPERIENCE
Demonstrator. Willie Walker Toy Co.; Peoria, IL. 1991–Present
Gross sales were 23% above the average for all part-time demonstrators. [b]

Retail Sales Clerk. Wimpburgers, Inc.; Peoria, IL. 1990–1991
Profits increased 17% during this time. [c]

Meatgrinder. Fahrquart Groceries; Peoria, IL. 1988–1990
Named "meat-grinder of the month" seven times.

ACTIVITIES
Mugwump Spelunkers Association: **organizer for three outings a year**.
YWCA: member of board [d]
Vice-president: Athletic Supporters of Peoria, 1991.

REFERENCES
Ms. A. Milquetoast,   Mr. Harry Shirt, Manager
Chair of Board   Wimpburgers, Inc.
YWCA   321 Grease Drive
Peoria, IL 42876   Peoria, IL 42989
(317) 555-9722   (317) 555-4567

Ms. Becky Thatcher,   Parson Brown,
President   Minister
Mugwump Spelunkers   Easy-Marriage Chapel
15 Huck Avenue   Newbird Lane
Hannibal, MO 45678   Snowman, ME 12345
(314) 555-9083   (207) 555-8402

over, because it is listed immediately after the fact of graduating in three years, having held a part-time job, and having done it well, this notation will not be missed by employers.

Note, however, that not all experience must include accomplishments. On the following page is an example from a résumé in which one of four jobs listed (highlighted in boldface type for illustrative purposes only) does *not* include accomplishments.

EXPERIENCE
Public Health Program Representative. Fulsom County Department of Health; Fulsom, AL
Coordinated program on communicable diseases. Established program on AIDS. 1988–Present.

Environmental Protection Specialist. Fulsom County Department of Health; Fulsom, AL
Certified as Sewage Enforcement Officer and Environmental Health Sanitation. 1983–1988.

Human Services Aide. Fulsom County Board of Assistance (Alabama Department of Public Welfare); Fulsom, AL. 1982–1983.
Increased county's participation in treatment program (EPSDT) by 22%.

Substitute teacher. Fulsom County, AL 1979–1981.

c. This seems to be a case of taking credit for others' accomplishments. It may be also that market forces, new products, or any of many things other than one's appearance on the scene caused this increase. Do not worry. It is customary in résumés (and elsewhere) to take partial credit for a company-wide accomplishment, whatever the reason for that accomplishment.

d. Notice that the active résumé reverses the order of these items as listed in the standard résumé. The reason is that the board of the YWCA is probably more important than the vice-president of a spelunker's club, at least to a nonspelunker.

THE FUNCTIONAL RÉSUMÉ

Functional résumés serve those well who have more experience than education or who have a great many activities (clubs, fraternities, sororities, service organizations) for which they did much work. They also work well for students who need more information to fill out the page of a résumé. Notice that the major difference between an active résumé and a functional résumé is that active résumés list employers, job titles, and accomplishments together; functional résumés, conversely, separate employers from job titles and list job *functions* rather than specific accomplishments. Here is Fahrquart's functional résumé.

SAMANTHA FAHRQUART
7896 Wimp Way
Peoria, Illinois 42091

(317) 567-1212 [home]   (317) 555-1234 [office]

EDUCATION
  Bachelor of Science in Management; J. L. Furguson
  University and Beautician Academy, Perkins, Kansas.
  June 1988

EXPERIENCE
  DEMONSTRATOR
    Aggressive door-to-door demonstration and sales.
    Recommended several new sales techniques to sales
    manager. Made sales at a level 23% above the av-
    erage for all part-time demonstrators.

  RETAIL SALES CLERK
    Worked part-time during busiest periods of days
    and seasons. Profits increased 17% during this
    time.

  MEATGRINDER
    Learned in five days to grind all meats to speci-
    fications. Named ''meat-grinder of the month''
    seven times.

EMPLOYERS
  Willie Walker Toy Co.   1990—Present
  Peoria, IL.

  Wimpburgers, Inc.   1989—1990
  Peoria, IL.

  Fahrquart Groceries   1987—1989
  Peoria, IL.

ACTIVITIES
  Organizer for three annual outings of Mugwump
  Spelunkers Association.

  Active board member for local YWCA.

  Active officer—vice-president—for Athletic Supporters of Peoria.

REFERENCES
  Available on request

Cover Letters

The Importance of Cover Letters

Many people believe that a résumé is sufficient for job applications, a cover letter thus being redundant and superfluous. A recent survey of chief personnel officers of *Fortune* 500 companies, however, reveals that about 80 percent prefer cover letters to accompany résumés.[4]

Although the following is written for those beginning a career, the old and experienced may also be edified.

1. Understand the purposes of cover letters:
   a. To highlight noteworthy parts of the résumé;
   b. To make the writer more human than a résumé can;
   c. To demonstrate good writing, which demonstrates good thinking;
   d. To get you an interview;
   e. To bring the résumé to life by rounding out and more fully explaining special parts of the résumé;
2. Use a lively style, active voice, vivid verbs, economical prose. Do not ramble; do not waffle.
3. Do not lie.
4. Do not write *anything* negative about yourself.
5. Let the facts speak for themselves. That is, do not usurp the job of the reader, which is to determine who is worthy of an interview, by writing "I feel qualified for," "My résumé shows that I can do a good job," or "As you can see, I am a hard worker."
6. Show that you have studied the company well enough to contribute some specific—and positive—comments about the company.
7. Do not write a "me" letter. That is, do not write, for example, "Your job is great for me because. . . ." Rather, remember that you must sell yourself to the employer, and the employer wants to know what you can do for the company, not what the company can do for you. Consequently, write something like this: "Here are the skills I can bring to your business."

The Parts of a Cover Letter

A cover letter has four parts: opening, description of education, description of experience, and a request for an interview.

Opening: Getting Their Attention.   There are four ways to open a cover letter.

---

[4]From Nelda Spinks and Barron Wells, "Letters of Application and Resumes: A Comparison of Corporate Views," *The Bulletin* (September 1987): 9–16.

1. *Standard.* "I am applying for the job of accountant recently advertised in the *New York Times*." This does not pique interest, but at least it is simple, direct, and accurate. Do *not* write "I *would like to* apply" because "would like to apply" is not applying.

2. *Name.* In many cases, it is not only what you know, but also who you know that counts. That is, simply being qualified for a job often is not sufficient for getting the job. Should you know a respected person in the company, and should you receive permission to use that person's name, then use it. Getting permission is sometimes done by calling the person, asking if that person thinks you should apply, and upon receiving a yes, opening the cover letter with this: "*Jane Smith*, Vice-President for Purchasing at your company, *suggests that I apply for the job of accountant recently advertised*." Notice that the name is the first thing to appear in the letter. Do *not* bury the name by writing "It has been suggested by your vice-president for purchasing, *Jane Smith*, that I apply." The purpose of the opening is to get the attention of employers. Seeing first the name of someone they know and respect will do it.

3. *Assertive.* Writers can be assertive without being aggressive, and it is important to know the difference. It is also important to assert *facts* and not opinions. The assertive opening, therefore, must dazzle with facts, but not be aggressive — that is, *not* cause the reader to mumble "What a jerk!" Such openings require much thought, much work, and much rewriting. Here are two examples.

   > I have a 3.6 average from a good university, have won two service awards, was president of the accounting honor society, and would like very much to work for Fahrquart Industries.

   > I'm hungry. I'm so hungry that during the last four years I worked 20 hours a week as Assistant Manager of a local Alby's Restaurant, belonged to three service organizations, and maintained a 3.2 average in my major: Hotel and Food Administration. Now I am applying for a job with Hilton Hotels.

   Notice that each of these grabs the reader's attention and then presents impressive facts. Each is energetic and up-beat, but not weird.

4. *Outrageous.* Outrageous openings are to be avoided by almost everyone. They seldom amuse and often produce snickers among those who review applications. Such applicants often are described as strange or weird. Nevertheless, should you have sufficient experience to be desirable, outrageousness may get you a job.

DISCUSSION OF EXPERIENCE. If you have more experience than education, then put experience first. You may mention facts given in the résumé, but do not repeat them word-for-word. Do not give opinions; give facts. That is, do not say "My experience makes me qualified for a job as. . . ." It is the job of the person doing the hiring to decide that.

DISCUSSION OF EDUCATION. If you have more education than experience, then put education first. Again, do not give opinions; give

facts. Explain research projects in which you helped a professor. Discuss courses not in your major but which may provide additional knowledge sought by the employer. Discuss anything important in your education not mentioned in the résumé.

ASKING FOR THE INTERVIEW. Most applicants fail to ask for an interview. Nearly all say something like this: "I am available for an interview any time after graduation day: May 29." Not good enough. There is a subtle but important difference between saying one is available and saying "May I please have an interview?" *Always ask for an interview!* Getting an interview is, after all, the purpose of a cover letter and résumé. Remember to place a question mark at the end of the sentence that asks for the interview.

Then discuss your availability for the interview and include a deadline for a reply. It is important to use a pleasant tone. An excellent example, supplied to us by a professor and consultant in California, is this: "With the tax season so near, I know that you are very busy. So, if I don't hear from you, I'll wait until February 15 to follow up on arranging a date for an interview."

FOLLOW-UP LETTERS

It is both courteous and helpful to send a *brief* thank-you note a day or two after the interview. Such a letter needs to say only "thanks for the interview," add some little touch about the interviewer, and remind the interviewer of your continued interest in the job. The most important effect of a thank-you note is this: the name of the writer is once more placed in front of the person deciding, from among all those interviewed, who gets the job. Be sure to chat during the interview with the interviewers. Discover something personal about them: Do they like to fish? Are they going to Palm Springs for a holiday soon? A follow-up letter that includes thanks, a semipersonal comment, and reminder of interest in the job, might read something like this:

EXERCISE D: RÉSUMÉS AND RULES

Discuss in class the following questions: In résumés, all rules, at one time or another, may be violated. Why? Why not?

Thanks

Some small, semipersonal things picked up and remembered

Reminder of interest in job

Dear Mrs. Borgia:

Thank you for the interview last Tuesday regarding a job with Borgia Pharmaceuticals.

You were very kind to ask about Professor Alexander, under whom we both studied as students. He asks to be remembered to you, one of his most "enterprising" students.

I hope your holiday in Brazil went well and that you found the exotic flowers you were looking for.

Please remember me as one sincerely interested in a job with your company, and I hope to hear from you soon.

Esperanza Curare

SUMMARY

1. Because competition is great for most good jobs in business, résumés are very important. The purpose of a résumé is to get the subject an interview.

2. A résumé is a list comprising facts that are arranged to make the subject look fully qualified.

3. Résumés must be perfect; that is, *they must be free of errors of any kind*—grammar, spelling, misalignments, even smudges.

4. Undergraduates, seeking their first full-time job, should write a standard résumé; those who have held full-time managerial or professional jobs should write an active résumé.

5. Cover letters (sometimes called application letters) are written to provide more detailed information, to demonstrate good writing, and to secure an interview.

6. Follow-up letters to interviewers serve two purposes: to show courtesy and to put the subject's name once more before the prospective employer. Follow-up letters should be brief, courteous, and say something personal (within the bounds of propriety) about the interviewer.

EXERCISES

1. *Standard résumé.* Write your own résumé in the *standard* format.

2. *Cover letters for standard résumés.* Write a cover letter to accompany the standard résumé.

3. *Active résumés.* Write your résumé in an *active* format.

4. *Cover letters for active résumés.* Write a cover letter to accompany the active résumé.

5. *Differences between standard and active résumés.* List in detail the differences between the standard and active résumés written in Exercises 1 and 3.

6. *Cover letter openings.* Rewrite the first paragraph of the cover letter using one of the openings you did *not* use the first time: standard, name, or assertive.

7. *Cover letter openings.* Rewrite yet again the first paragraph of the cover letter using the opening you did *not* use the first or second time: standard, name, or assertive.

8. *Follow-up letters.* Write a follow-up letter to Mr. Smedley Fahrquart, who interviewed you for a job as an accountant (or economist, management-trainee, systems analyst, or whatever your major is) with Widgitcog Industries. During the interview, you discovered that both you and Mr. Fahrquart shared a hobby: wind surfing. In fact, Mr. Fahrquart mentioned that he was beginning a two-week vacation the day after your interview. He planned to wind-surf at a beach resort in Southern Portugal near Cabo de São Vicente.

9. *Cover letters.* Here are four qualities that employers look for in job applicants:

Team player	Ability to grow
Adapts to change	Ability to make the company money

Using no more than three sentences for each quality, write what you might say in a cover letter that would capture the attention of the reader regarding these qualities. Remember to be honest—with yourself and the reader—as you probably will have to live up to your answers in an interview.

CASE STUDY: EXECUTIVE RÉSUMÉS

On page 330 is a *Harvard Business Review* example of an exemplary executive résumé. First, notice the simplicity of it and try to emulate that simplicity on your own résumé. Second, try to make it even better. (Hint: Remove "Résumé of" in the heading.)

CHALLENGE EXERCISE I: THE RÉSUMÉ OF ODYSSEUS

On page 331 is the résumé of Odysseus (Ulysses to the Romans), Homer's resourceful, cunning warrior who conceived the idea for the Trojan horse, spent ten years getting home from that long war, and who had many life-threatening adventures with gods, goddesses,

```
                        RESUME OF GARY WILSON

        OBJECTIVE
          To create value for shareholders

        SKILLS
          Innovative financing
          Strategic planning

        WORK EXPERIENCE
          1985 to present: The Walt Disney Company
          Executive vice president, chief financial officer,
          and a director
          Responsibilities include financial management, and
          worldwide real estate development

          1974 to 1985: Marriott Corporation
          Executive vice president and chief financial offi-
          cer, promoted from vice president and treasurer
          Responsibilities included financial management,
          strategic planning, hotel and corporate develop-
          ment, and management of Marriott's Inflight Serv-
          ices Division

          1964 to 1974: Trans-Philippines Investment
          Corporation
          Executive vice president and a director
          Responsibilities included financial management and
          commodity trading

        EDUCATION
          Masters of Business Administration, 1963
          Wharton School of Business of the University of
            Pennsylvania

          Bachelor of Science, 1962
          Duke University, accounting major

        OTHER EXPERIENCE
          Board of Visitors of the Fuqua School of Business
          at Duke University

          Past chairman of IREFAC, the financial advisory
          board of the American Hotel & Motel Association
```

semimortals, and mortals along the way. Were he to apply for an executive's job with a Fortune 500 company, his résumé might look as this one does. Identify and mark the active parts of Odysseus's résumé.

CHALLENGE EXERCISE 2: FOLLOW-UP LETTERS

Unable to take a final exam on December 11 because of an important job interview, you go to Professor Fahrquart to ask him whether he would agree to give you a make-up final. The interview is informal, but, although he is polite, you do manage to discover that not only must Professor Fahrquart compose an entirely new examination, but also he must postpone a trip to a professional conference to give the exam to you on December 12. In the end, he agrees. Write a follow-up letter to this interview.

```
                              ODYSSEUS
                           7896 Hero Drive
                           Rugged, Ithaca
                         (messenger; no phone)

        EDUCATION
        855 B.C.        Ph.D. War and Defense
                        Athena's Mercurial Mercenary Academy
                        College Island, Greece
                        Summa Cum Laude

        EXPERIENCE
        850 B.C.—       King. Ithaca.
        Present.           Rule 3968 subjects.
                           Settle, on average, 672 disputes a year

        805             Warrior. Self-employed. Rugged, Ithaca.
                           Thwarted take-over attempt by numerous
                           suitors.

        805             Free-lance, Self-employed Actor. Rugged,
                        Ithaca.
                           Perfected the character of a beggar,
                           convincing numerous relatives,
                           acquaintances, and enemies.

        807—806         Underworld Pioneer. Hades.
                           First mortal to visit Hades and return
                           alive.

        808—807         Warrior. Self-employed. Land of Cyclops.
                           Outwitted the giant Polyphemous and
                           saved numerous men in my employ.

        825—815         War Hero. Veteran of Trojan War. Ten
                        tours.
                           Conceived, developed, and produced the
                           Trojan Horse Project, which won the war.

        ACTIVITIES
                        President, Artemis's Archery Club
                        Member, Nine Muse Thespian Society
                        President, Hermes Halcyon Travel Club
                        Past president, Giant-Slayers
                        International
                        Exercise Director, Calypso's Island

        HONORS AND AWARDS
                        Archer of the Year Award, 804
                        Traveler of the Decade Award, 804
                        Consort of the Decade Award, Goddess
                        Society, 807
                        Contractor of the Era Award (for Trojan
                        Horse Design)
        REFERENCES
                        Pallas Athena          Redhaired Menelaus
                        Goddess of Wisdom      King
                        321 Mount Olympus      Royal Palace
                        Call by sacrifice      Sparta, Lacedaemon
                                               Messenger
```

INTERVIEWS

The Etiquette of Interviews
The Parts of Interviews
Job Interviews
Preparing for Job Interviews
The Tasks of Job Interviewers
Performance Appraisal Interviews

ACCEPTING JOB OFFERS

REJECTING JOB OFFERS

RESIGNING FROM JOBS

RECOMMENDING OTHERS FOR JOBS

SUMMARY

EXERCISES

Learning Objectives:

☐ Know the importance of good manners in interviews.

☐ Know the various types and parts of interviews.

☐ Know how to conduct persuasive interviews.

☐ Know the most common questions asked by job interviewers.

☐ Know some uncommon questions asked by job interviewers.

☐ Know twenty characteristics interviewers like to see in job applicants.

☐ Write acceptance letters.

☐ Write rejection letters.

☐ Write letters of resignation.

☐ Write letters of recommendation.

13

To know that you do not know is the best. To pretend to know when you do not know is a disease.

LAO-TZU

(C. 604–531 B.C.)

JOB

DECISIONS

INTERVIEWS

Although people in business make decisions every day, some of those decisions are more important than others. Some are especially important and often irrevocable: preparing for interviews, accepting and rejecting job offers, resigning from jobs, and recommending others for jobs are perhaps the most important professional decisions anyone ever makes. The first of these decisions requires a thorough knowledge of interviews.

Much research ink has been spilled over the relative importance of the interviewee's ability to write (e.g., résumés) and to communicate orally (e.g., interviews). Each skill is extremely important, but excellent writers are given the nod over excellent speakers when the job requires better writing than speaking; the reverse is true when the job requires better speaking than writing.[1] In short, it is best to be good at both writing *and* speaking.

In a sense, any situation in which two or more people communicate orally and visually may be called an interview.[2] Consequently, when people get together to buy or sell, to instruct or be instructed, to inform or learn, to help or hinder, an interview is occurring. For business, however, it is most practical to define *interview* as any conversation in which at least one person wants something more than the time of day.

Interviews can be informational, persuasive, or a combination of both. *Informational interviews* are so common that we seldom think of them as interviews. When we ask directions of someone on the street, we are interviewing. We give information: "Would you please tell me where I can find East Third Street?" And they give information: "Surely. Just turn right at the second stop light on this street and you will be on East Third." When we give the symptoms of our illness to a physician, we are giving information. When the physician tells us what we have and how to cure it, the physician is giving us information. When we stand at the counter of a fast-food restaurant, we give information: "I would like a MacWhopper, please." The cashier gives us information: "That will be $2.25, please."

To one degree or another, informational interviews require people to listen carefully and to speak clearly. Otherwise, customers could get catsup and onions when they really wanted mustard and pickles. Similarly, it is vital that a patient be sure to take two pills six times daily as opposed to six pills twice daily; the difference could be that the former cures and the latter kills.

---

[1]Steven Michael Ralston, "An Exploratory Test of Contingency Approach to Recruitment Interview Decisions," *The Journal of Business Communications* 26 (Fall 1989): 347–60.

[2]Telephone interviews usually are preliminary interviews from which prospective employers prepare a short list of those people who will be invited to a face-to-face interview. Many times, sales interviews are conducted over the telephone. Questionnaires, too, are executed in this way.

Sometimes called sales interviews, *persuasive interviews* are crucial to business. The best persuasive interviews have two winners: the seller wins by selling, and the buyer wins because the product or service is the best for the price. All participants in such interviews must be ready to ask important questions, to accept limitations, and to provide relevant information.

THE ETIQUETTE OF INTERVIEWS

Manners not only reflect the way civilized people should behave but also increase everyone's chances of winning in the long run. In persuasive interviews the persuader should observe the following good manners.

GOOD MANNERS AND PERSUASION

1. Use solid detail as a method of persuasion. People who know the facts and provide them usually can persuade others to their point of view.
2. Never become ill-tempered, at least not outwardly.
3. Remain cool, calm, and collected.
4. Never whine about losing; never crow about winning (not publicly, at least).

THE PARTS OF INTERVIEWS

Interviews may be loosely or tightly structured, open-ended or moving toward a specific and predetermined goal, informal or formal. Nearly all interviews, whatever the kind, have similar parts.

INTRODUCTION.   Nearly all interviews, for example, begin with introductions — sometimes formal, sometimes so informal that participants, who already know each other, simply say "Hi." A typical introduction in an interview between interviewer A, interviewer B, and interviewee Samantha Evans might occur as she enters the room.

> Interviewers stand.
>
> Interviewer A: "Good Morning, Ms. Evans. I'm A. May I introduce B? Ms. Evans, this is B. (To B) Ms. Evans is looking us over for a job in our actuarial department.
>
> Evans: "How do you do, Ms. B? I'm very pleased to meet you."
>
> Interviewer B: "Delighted. Shall we begin?"
>
> Evans: "Certainly."
>
> Interviewer A: "Shall we sit down?"

BODY.   The body of an interview comprises the substance — the information, the persuasion, or the argument. Specifically how these proceed depends on the people themselves, the environment, even on

---

EXERCISE A: INTERVIEW INTRODUCTIONS

Discuss in class the following questions:

1. Why does Interviewer A say "Ms. Evans is looking *us* over," rather than "We are interviewing Ms. Evans for a job"?
2. Is this an example of good manners? Why? Why not?

the complexity of the information. The body of a formally structured interview may include a predetermined list of questions. The most common example of this kind of structure is that of interviewing heads of state (or others who must be extremely careful of what they say). Some formal interviews may be relatively unstructured. That is, while the questions are formal, they are not predetermined; while a formal sense of decorum is apparent, no one has decided beforehand which questions may be asked and which may not.

A body of a typical job interview comprises many questions. Some of the most common appear in ''Common Questions in Job interviews,'' found on page 337.

CONCLUSION.   Very formal and highly structured interviews may conclude according to a set plan written years ago; interviews with royalty, for example, sometimes end according to very precise, and very old, protocol. Less structured interviews end formally or informally, depending on how well the interview progressed. It is usually best, however, to err on the side of formality in concluding interviews with people you have never met before.

A typical interview usually concludes when one of the interviewers says something like this:

Interviewer A: ''That was an intriguing way to put it, Ms. Evans. And it completes all the questions I have. Ms. B, do you have anything more to add?

Interviewer B: ''I don't, but perhaps Ms. Evans does. Ms. Evans, do you have any other questions for us? We'd be happy to answer.

Evans: No, I don't think so. You've been very thorough and forthright. I've really enjoyed our talk.

Interviewer B: Thank you. We have, too. May I walk out with you?

JOB INTERVIEWS

Except proposals of marriage and other momentous personal conversations, the most important one-on-one conversation people ever have is a job interview. The résumé and cover letter have proven successful, allowed the applicant to enter the stream. Now the job hunter must negotiate the rapids of interviews before being told ''We would like you to work for us.''

The job interview is not so much an examination as it is a process of learning. During the interview, the applicant tries to learn whether the job would be suitable, challenging, and rewarding. The interviewer tries to learn whether the applicant offers the combination of skills and attributes that the company needs and wants. Each side is using the interview to learn more about the other. The job of both sides is to provide honest answers and to ask those questions that will allow each to make an informed decision. Curiously, the amount of talking appropriate to each side is not equal. Stewart and Cash recommend

....
EXERCISE B: INTERVIEW CONCLUSIONS

Discuss in class the following questions:

1. Why does Interviewer B say ''May I walk out with you?'' rather than something like ''You'll be hearing from us soon''?

2. Is this an example of good manners? Why? Why not?

that the interviewee do about 70 percent of the talking and the interviewer only about 30 percent.[3]

PREPARING FOR JOB INTERVIEWS

The job of the résumé and cover letter is to get an interview; the job of the interview usually is to get the job. Most of the questions an interviewer asks will be these or variations of these questions listed below; and most of the work for the interviewee involves preparing thoughtful answers to them.

COMMON QUESTIONS IN JOB INTERVIEWS

1. Goals
   a. Why do you want this job?
   b. Where do you want to be in five (ten, twenty) years?
   c. What do you want from a job?
   d. What is your definition of professional success?

2. Education
   a. Why did you choose this major?
   b. Why did you choose this school?
   c. How did you finance your education?
   d. What was best about college?
   e. What was worst about college?
   f. What single most important thing did you learn in college?

3. Experience
   a. What did you like most (least) about your last job?
   b. Why do (did) you want to leave the job you have (had)?
   c. This job requires _____ and _____. What experiences have you had in _____?
   d. What important things did you learn from your last job?

4. Describe Yourself
   a. What are your strong points?
   b. What are your weak points?
   c. How have you changed during the last _____ years?
   d. How well do you work with others?
   e. How well do you work alone?
   f. Why should we hire you?
   g. Are you willing to relocate?

EXERCISE C: INTERVIEW QUESTIONS

Discuss in class the following: Several, perhaps many, people in your class have undergone job interviews. What questions do you remember being asked that are not on the list of common questions?

---

[3]C. J. Stewart and W. B. Cash, Jr., *Interviewing: Principles and Practices*, 3rd ed. (Dubuque, Iowa: Brown, 1984), 4.

5. Knowledge
    a. What do you know about this company?
    b. What do you know about this job?
    c. What do you think qualifies you for *this* job?
    d. What do you think is the most difficult part of this job?

6. Inquiry: Do you have questions for me?

Many employers now ask more difficult questions, such as "Suppose two of your subordinates are not on speaking terms, yet they must communicate often. As their boss, what would you do?" Although it is difficult to prepare for such questions, at least you should not be caught off guard completely when they are asked.

Preparing for a job interview requires a great deal of attention to detail, much of which must be practiced. That is, a job applicant cannot decide one hour before an interview to be knowledgeable about current affairs. Such knowledge is one of the characteristics that interviewers observe in the people they interview. Here is a list of other characteristics that reflect well on a job candidate.

COMMON CHARACTERISTICS DESIRABLE IN JOB CANDIDATES

1. Clean and neat application form
2. Well-groomed; stylish but traditional clothing
3. Assertive, but not aggressive; confident, but not overbearing
4. Enthusiastic, but not nervous
5. Interested in money, but not *overly* interested
6. High college-grade ranking
7. Well mannered and tactful
8. Responsible; not an excuse maker
9. Pleasantly humorous
10. Interested in many things
11. Active in the community
12. Not critical of former employers
13. Formal without being stuffy
14. Sure about goals, but not inflexible
15. Well spoken
16. Knowledgeable of specialty and willing to learn more
17. Knowledgeable about the prospective company
18. Curious and inquisitive about company and job

THE TASKS OF JOB INTERVIEWERS

Interviewers may have as many as five discrete tasks. They must define the job, seek applicants, interview applicants, offer the job, and make the first days pleasant for the new employee. Some companies divide these five tasks among several people. For example, in large companies, the manager seeking to fill a position may do the interviewing and may work with the new employee, while various people in the Personnel or Human Resources Department handle other tasks.

DEFINE THE JOB.   In small companies, interviewers also may be engineers, accountants, or almost anything else. That is, people in small companies must be more versatile than those in large companies. Versatility is often the reason people choose to work for small companies. Known also as practitioners or field interviewers, these people have the advantage of being able to define the job because they work every day with those who do that work.

Still, *all* interviewers, whether trained for interviewing or not, must be able to put into words *precisely* the abilities desired in a prospective employee. Large companies hire people whose sole job is interviewing. While these recruiters usually are very good at interviewing, they often have the disadvantage of not knowing the job as well as they should. For this reason, many companies may have the recruiter do an initial interview to screen applicants and then send the strongest applicants to do a second, more exhaustive, interview with the manager or supervisor who has the job opening.

Whatever the definition of the job, interviewers must be very clear on its meaning, specifically the responsibilities of the job. This, of course, means knowing many things not in an advertisement, such as typical hours, where the employee will work (office, city, region of the country, etc.), normal attire, number of people in the department, and so on.

SEEK APPLICANTS.   Normally, there are three ways to let potential applicants know that your company has a job opening. The first way is *word of mouth*. Because new college graduates are not in the grapevine, however, this method is reserved for older, more experienced applicants. The second way is through *advertisements*. Because they are expensive, ads must be placed in newspapers that people with the training the company wants will see. Sometimes efficient advertising means placing advertisements in trade journals catering to that specialization. The third way is to go to *job fairs* at universities. Sometimes a group of small colleges in the same area will combine to hold job fairs.

INTERVIEW APPLICANTS.   While each interview is different, all interviews have certain characteristics that allow interviewers to discover whether the applicant is the best person for the job. Here is a list that should help interviewers do a good job.

CHECKLIST FOR INTERVIEWERS
1. Be assertive, not aggressive.
2. Let interviewees talk to reveal whether they know as much as the résumés suggest.
3. Prepare and follow a list of questions for *each* interviewee.

4. As questions tend to beget questions, be ready to ask questions *not* on the list; be ready also to answer questions from the interviewee.

5. Answer interviewee's questions objectively. Try to use facts, not opinions.

6. Use questions to guide interviewee back to the topic at hand.

7. Don't take extensive notes during the interview. (Tape recording is a bad idea: it lulls interviewers and unnerves interviewees.) Notes should comprise one- or two-word entries that may be expanded just *after* the interview.

8. Remember (and use frequently) the interviewee's name.

9. Avoid too many questions allowing a yes or no answer; these use time and do not always reveal much information.

Almost every interviewer these days is nervous about unconsciously violating laws regarding hiring. In general, the law is this: illegal questions include those asked for the purpose of discriminating against an applicant's race, religion, color, gender, national origin, marital status, or age. The key is "for the purpose of discriminating." An employer hiring people to drive automobiles may legitimately ask for proof of age. Moreover, the U.S. Supreme Court has ruled that the important point is that of "business necessity."[4] To make it clearer, here is a list of questions that *may* be asked and those that *may not* be asked.

LEGAL AND ILLEGAL INTERVIEW QUESTIONS

Legal

1. Asking for legal proof of age to support working with vehicles or alcohol

2. Asking whether the applicant is an American Citizen

3. Asking what foreign languages the applicant speaks

4. Asking the applicant about work experience

5. Asking for names of family or relatives who work for the company

6. Asking whether the applicant will abide by rules of dress, grooming, etc. set by company

7. Asking the applicant whether reliable transportation to work is available

8. Asking the applicant about military service

9. Asking the applicant for names of references

Illegal

1. Asking whether the applicant has ever worked under another name

2. Asking for the applicant's, parents', other relatives' birthplace

---

[4]H. A. Medley, *Sweaty Palms: The Neglected Art of Being Interviewed* (Belmont Cal.: Wadsworth, 1978), 164.

Both interviews and interviewees need to know which questions are legal and which are illegal.

3. Asking the applicant to state or give proof of age when age has no bearing on the job
4. Asking the applicant's religious affiliation
5. Asking for the applicant's police record or type of military discharge
6. Asking the applicant to supply the names of relatives other than immediate relatives
7. Asking the applicant to supply the names of minor dependents
8. Asking for the applicant's marital (or sexual) status, height or weight, maiden name, or mother's maiden name
9. Asking for names of the applicant's social affiliations (clubs, lodges, etc.)
10. Asking for a photograph
11. Asking for the type of transportation applicant will take to work
12. Asking whether applicant owns or rents a residence

OFFER THE JOB. Although some candidates are so impressive that interviewers are tempted to offer the job immediately after the interview, this is seldom good practice. Job offers are made later, after everyone involved agrees, and although informal offers are sometimes made over the telephone, the formal offer should always be in writing.

MAKE THE FIRST DAYS PLEASANT. The permanent perception an employee has of a company is often influenced greatly by the first

EXERCISE D: THE
INTERVIEWER'S TASKS

Discuss in class the following
question: Why is it important
for job hunters to know something about the tasks of
interviewers?

days on the job. Consequently, during those first days the new employee should be welcomed and introduced to colleagues, bosses, procedures, and methods of all kinds.

Ideally, the person assigned to making a new employee's first days
pleasant should be the interviewer, who is, after all, the single link a
new employee has to a company. If the interviewer cannot do so, then
the interviewer should introduce the new employee to the person who
will be making the new employee's first day pleasant.

PERFORMANCE APPRAISAL INTERVIEWS

Supervisors periodically meet with employees individually to appraise
their performance. These appraisals usually occur annually, although
some jobs and companies require more or less frequent appraisals.
Such appraisals have two parts: How well has the employee performed in the past, and what goals will the employee strive for in the
future? That is, the supervisor says, here's how you did last year, and
here's what we want you to accomplish next year.

The best approach for employees undergoing performance appraisal is to assume goodwill on the part of the supervisor. Defensiveness is not productive. Employees should have documentation of their
accomplishments readily available and should be prepared to present
it at the appropriate time.

Supervisors, on the other hand, need little help when the appraisal is a very good one. If the appraisal is not very good, then the
supervisor should be tactful and specific in discussing what the employee has not achieved and what the employee reasonably might
achieve in the months to come. Like bad-news letters (pages 140–142),
appraisals of bad performance should begin by finding something
good to say about the employee's work, then should lay out the documentation of the bad performance, present unambiguously the bad
appraisal rating, and finally offer specific goals and hope for better
appraisals in the future.

ACCEPTING JOB OFFERS

ACCEPTANCE LETTERS
SHOULD CONTAIN THE
FOLLOWING:

1. A clear acceptance of the job
2. A clear naming of the job
   accepted
3. A repetition of the salary
   accepted
4. Mention of benefits (vacations, insurance, etc.)
5. Date, time, and place of reporting to work
6. Eagerness to begin

Accepting a job offer often is exciting: new job, new place, more
money, new life. In the excitement, however, it is easy to overlook
important details. Acceptance letters should be written within a week
of the offer. If this cannot be done, a letter should be sent (or phone call
made) asking for more time. Acceptance letters should begin by saying "I accept!" Specifics should follow that restate those conditions in
the formal offer, such as precisely how much money, what kind of
benefits (insurance, medical, vacation), and when and where to report
on the first day of work. Detailing such information provides employee and employer with a clear legal record of what's what. Although the tone of the acceptance letter should be up-beat, it should
not be bubbly.

Here are two examples of an acceptance letter:

Dear Ms. Faust:

I am happy to accept your offer of $_____ per month as Research Chemist for the Margo Drug Company. The benefits package that arrived with your offer is also attractive.

Be assured that I shall arrive at the Margo plant in Inferno, Arizona, on June 1 at 9:00 a.m. sharp, ready to begin work.

Sincerely,

Marie Curie

Dear Mr. Swartz:

I happily accept your offer of the job with Ritestuff Magazine as Staff Photographer. The salary of $34,000 per year, as well as the benefits--three weeks paid vacation, full dental and medical coverage, use of the magazine's photographic equipment and studios--mentioned in your letter of April 27, is also acceptable. Having an office and dark room of my own is also a pleasure for which I thank you.

Although photography is demanding and difficult, I am sure you will find me a diligent employee. I am eager to meet you again when I begin work at 8 a.m. on June 22 at the Chicago office, 111 Gale Avenue, Room 439.

Sincerely,

Albert Kaupth

REJECTING JOB OFFERS

Rejecting a job offer is a grand luxury, but a rejection should not be written from the mountain top of self-congratulations. Remember that the world is very small, and that even the thousands of American companies compose a much smaller world. A rejection letter should not say anything that would insult or anger the company offering the job. The same person who rejects a job offer may be required later to buy from or sell to that company, and companies have employees endowed with prodigious memories.

Rejection letters are variations of *no* letters and should be written in a similar way (see Chapter 6).

PARTS OF A JOB REJECTION LETTER

1. *Say thank you.* Mention something about the generosity of the offer, the opportunities the job affords, or such other benefits as these. Make them feel good.

2. *Explain circumstances.* Do not say "I got a better offer" in a way that casts a bad light on the company making the offer.

3. *Say no.*

4. *Give something* (optional).

5. *Never say anything disparaging* about the company or one of its employees.

Say thank you.

Explain circumstances.

Say no.

Give something.

Dear General Achilles:

Thank you for your most generous offer to be your armor-polisher. I am both pleased and honored to have been asked by such an illustrious warrior. The salary is excellent, and such fringe-benefits as a holiday in Asia Minor are very hard to pass up.

Three days before your offer arrived, however, my father signed papers with a General Odysseus from Ithaca, making me his personal carpenter. General Odysseus seemed particularly impressed that my specialty is carving horses. In fact, he offered my father nearly twice the going rate for carpenters.

Although armor-polishing is an exciting job, and working for you would be even more exciting, I must decline your offer.

I shall be meeting the rest of the fellows at the Bay of Aulis next month. Should time permit and Odysseus agree, I would be happy to do any special jobs you might like done.

Sincerely,

Socrates Hoplite

On the previous page is an example of a rejection letter, with the parts labeled. The final item on the list above that letter is achieved by the writer saying nothing disparaging about Achilles.

RESIGNING FROM JOBS

While letters of resignation are formulaic, they are perhaps the only permanent record an employee leaves behind. Such letters usually require tact, clarity, and some warmth. Disraeli once remarked, ''Never complain, never explain.'' Although *some* explanation is often required, an employee should look on Disraeli's advice as a guideline for resignation, whether from a job or a club, and, in general, of life.

A letter of resignation contains four general parts:

1. *Resign.* Be brief: do *not* say ''This is to notify you that as of . . .''; rather, say ''I am resigning as of [such-and-such a day].'' Be sure that the date mentioned is the last day you plan to work for the company. Try to give at least two weeks' notice.

2. *Say why.* Be careful. Say nothing that reflects badly upon the company or its employees.

3. *Assure support.* Assure the employer of your willingness to train a replacement, to complete a given project, and so on, before the last day. If you cannot give such assurance, then allow the last day of work to be soon enough that the company can proceed with business.

4. *Say something nice.* Writing that your working for the company was enjoyable, or any other related comment, is optional but advisable.

....
EXERCISE E: GOOD OR BAD ADVICE?

Discuss in class the following question: Although Disraeli's ''Never complain, never explain'' is good advice, does it follow that ''the squeaky wheel gets the oil'' (complainers get treated well) is an adage that provides bad advice?

Resign.
Say why.

Assure support.

Say something nice.

```
Dear Ms. Evans:

I am resigning as Accounting Supervisor as of 5 No-
vember 1992, having accepted a job as Chief Finan-
cial Officer with another company.

Please be assured of my continued support until I
leave. I would be happy to help my replacement in
any way deemed advisable.

I do not leave without regrets. My five years with
Fahrquart Industries have been challenging and pro-
ductive. I have made many friends, and I leave with
genuine hope for the continued success of this fine
company.

Sincerely,

Pat Ross
```

Although most resignation letters should follow these rules, exceptions abound. Occasionally, it may be advisable to provide an extensive explanation in writing. Occasionally, when nothing you may say would help, it is best to write a one-sentence resignation: "I am resigning as of 5 November 1992." Usually, however, something like the following example on page 345 should be written.

RECOMMENDING OTHERS FOR JOBS

The general rule for writing letters of recommendation is to be honest, yet to do one's best for the candidate. Damning with faint praise is better than no praise at all. In short, write the truth, but write it in such a way as to avoid saying bad things.

Robert J. Thornton, Professor of Economics at Lehigh University, wrote in a February 1987 issue of *The Chronicle of Higher Education* the following humorous, but not entirely impractical, advice about letters of recommendation. The case here is, of course, overstated, and Thornton's amusing examples are not to be relied on too heavily, but understand that writers must be *very* careful about what they say in letters of recommendation.

"I Can't Recommend the Candidate Too Highly": An Ambiguous Lexicon for Job Recommendations

Letters of recommendation are becoming increasingly unreliable as a means of evaluating candidates under consideration for academic [and corporate] employment. The chief reason is that the contents are no longer strictly confidential. In all but the rarest of cases a letter is apt to be favorable, even when the writer knows the candidate is mediocre or unqualified. This is so because the writer fears the candidate may later exercise the legal right to read the letter, and perhaps even sue if the contents are not to his liking and are insufficiently substantiated.

While abolishing the practice of requiring letters of recommendation may at first seem like a good idea, there is really no better way to get reliable information about a candidate's qualifications than to ask the people who have had close contact with him or her. What is needed is a means by which the letter writer can convey unfavorable information in a way that the candidate cannot perceive it or prove it as such.

To this end I have designed a Lexicon of Inconspicuously Ambiguous Recommendations, or LIAR. Here are a few samples:

- To describe a candidate who is woefully inept: "I most enthusiastically recommend this candidate with no qualifications whatsoever."
- To describe a candidate who is not particularly industrious: "In my opinion you will be very fortunate to get this person to work for you."
- To describe a candidate who is not worth further consideration: "I would urge you to waste no time in making this candidate an offer of employment."

- To describe a candidate with lackluster credentials: "I cannot say enough good things about this candidate or recommend him too highly."
- To describe an ex-employee who had difficulty getting along: "I am pleased to say this candidate is a former colleague of mine."
- To describe a candidate who is so bad that the position would be better left unfilled: "I can assure you that no person would be better for this job."

Because nothing is safe any longer from litigation, letters of recommendation should be placed on the list of endangered species. Confidential letters of recommendation have been ordered opened in court so often that few people are willing these days to write them, or at least to write them fully honestly. Should a prospective employer call a company, the company will refer the employer to the Personnel Department. The Personnel Department will say, "Yes. [So-and-so] worked here from 1 June 1984 to 13 September 1989." And that is all that most companies will say.

Sometimes a letter of recommendation must be written. Such letters obey three rules: they are true, they are pertinent, and they are immune to litigation.

Truth is especially important. This does not mean that the letter must parade all the ugly facts about the candidate. Often, what is *not* said is as important as what is said. If the letter of recommendation is positive, then nothing bad about the candidate should be in it. Truth is also important because it is such a small world. Suppose Smedley Fahrquart is applying for a job with a company to which he once sent a glowing letter about a person who, hired on the strength of his recommendation, turned out to be a disaster at that company from the first day of employment. Can Smedley expect to get the job?

Pertinence is similarly important. Should a candidate be applying for a job in central Kansas, it is irrelevant to mention that the candidate was a first-class sailor in her youth. The writer must understand something about the job for which the candidate is applying and provide information that applies to that job.

Here is a list of qualities that readers of recommendation letters need to know. If the writer knows nothing about certain qualities, then the letter should say so.

NINE QUALITIES TO BE CONSIDERED IN RECOMMENDATIONS

1. Intelligence
2. Ability to work hard
3. Creativity
4. Organization
5. Ability to work alone
6. Ability to work with others
7. Ability to complete the job
8. Ability to communicate
9. Qualities of dress, speech, and deportment

....
THREE RULES FOR LETTERS OF RECOMMENDATION

1. They must be *true*.
2. They must be *pertinent*.
3. They must be *immune* to litigation.

EXERCISE F:
RECOMMENDATIONS AND
LITIGATION

Discuss in class the following question: The text says that nothing is immune from litigation, and then it says that letters of recommendation must be immune to litigation. What gives? That is, is the text overstating the case to make its point, and what it really means is that letters of recommendation must be as carefully crafted to avoid litigation as possible?

Immunity from litigation is important and should be watched carefully, for almost nothing is immune from prosecution. Remember also that, win or lose, litigation remains expensive, if only in time. If a writer can recommend another without reservation, then there is no problem. The writer simply uses the good news method: recommend the applicant, and then say why. If the candidate cannot be recommended unreservedly, then the writer must be very careful. Truth, of course, is the best defense. But an even better defense is truth that the writer can *prove* to be true. Records, copies of memoranda, and the like will go far in proving the truth.

A letter of recommendation should follow an order similar to this:

OUTLINE FOR A LETTER OF RECOMMENDATION

1. Recommend.
2. Describe the candidate's relationship with the writer.
3. Discuss the candidate's qualifications for the job: professional qualifications first, personal qualifications second.
4. Recommend again.

Here is an example of a letter of recommendation written by a person who perhaps has reservations about a student applying to a graduate school of business.

Dear Ms. Dunbar:

Mr. Charles Hiller has asked me to write a letter of recommendation for admission to your MBA program. Mr. Hiller and I worked in the same department for two years. During that time, he seemed to me to get along well with people and to do his job satisfactorily. At least, I never heard any complaints about the way he did his job.

In my judgment, Mr. Hiller should be able to complete the MBA program successfully.

Sincerely,

Stephen Miller

Here is an example of a positive letter recommending a student for admittance to a graduate school of business.

Dear Ms. Dunbar:

I am delighted to support Mr. Charles Hiller's application for admission to the doctoral program in the School of Business at Three Rivers University. As a member of the graduate faculty at Old State, I think I have some notion regarding those qualities that most benefit the institution and the student. In my judgment, Mr. Hiller has all of these: maturity, desire, intelligence, energy, and--important anywhere, but especially in business--personability and presentability.

I have known Mr. Hiller for two years in two situations. First, as an instructor in the School of Business, Hiller demonstrated his ability not only to grasp material, but also to convey it well to students. His evaluations from students are among the highest given to instructors. He is very well liked by faculty, and his extensive experience in business makes him the target of many questions from new and established faculty. I also have found him to be intellectually curious--a quality I think essential for anyone who aspires to university research and teaching. Second, I have had the pleasure of sharing some consulting work with Mr. Hiller. His role has been varied, but most often he has been sought by local industries in Erie and environs for his expertise in marketing. He has displayed at those times an invariable ability to see the problem, suggest solutions, and simultaneously to take charge of meetings with some senior executives when his advice was being sought. In short, I am impressed by his business sense, intelligence, leadership ability, and his thoroughness.

One concern doubtless in the minds of your admissions committee is that of time and logistics regarding Mr. Hiller. That is, how could he live in Old State and survive not only the rigors of the doctoral program but also the debilitating efforts of virtually commuting to Three Rivers? For most people, I admit that I would feel bound to present this as a caveat. For Mr. Hiller, however, I see few problems. He is a man of almost limitless energy. I have seen him in long meetings just warming to the task when all others have begun to flag. This is not to say that Mr. Hiller is hyperactive or, as many of us have experienced in others, a nervous trotter-out of trivia. On the contrary, he knows what is important and what is not, and he is a finisher. I also know that many who return to graduate programs many years after completing a B.S. or M.B.A. never complete requirements for the Ph.D. In my judgment, the committee may feel secure that, should they admit Mr. Hiller, he would finish.

To these inner qualities may be added his pleasant personality and appearance. In all senses, then, Mr. Hiller is the kind of man who would benefit immensely from the fine program at Three Rivers. And I believe that the university would benefit from Mr. Hiller's presence both immediately and ultimately.

Sincerely,

Robin Watt

EXERCISE G: ASSESSING RECOMMENDATIONS

Discuss in class the following question: Given that this example is far from perfect, discuss its good and bad qualities. How could it be made better?

Asking for a letter of recommendation requires tact and good sense. Ask people you trust and who can write a strong, positive letter. College students should supply their references with documentation (usually a résumé and G.P.A. are sufficient) and with stamped, addressed envelopes. Remember that the letter is written as a favor, that it requires a great deal of work, and that the writer therefore should not incur any costs other than time.

SUMMARY

1. Broadly defined, an *interview* is any situation in which two or more people communicate.

2. *Business interviews* may be defined as any conversation in which at least one person wants something more than the time of day.

3. Good business interviews require good manners.

4. Although there are many kinds of interviews, all interviews—like reports—contain an introduction, body, and conclusion.

5. *Informational interviews* occur daily and include everything from asking directions to providing a physician with a list of the symptoms of your illness.

6. *Persuasive interviews* might include selling widgitcogs, campaigning for election, or convincing a professor that the dog really *did* eat your assignment. In business, these interviews are crucial, and the best ones conclude with everyone's having won.

7. *Job interviews* include those in which one is applying for a job, but also those involving performance appraisals and exit interviews. These must combine the informational and the persuasive interviews. Moreover, the interviewer and interviewee have equally difficult jobs.

8. The job of the interviewer involves (1) defining the job, (2) seeking applicants, (3) interviewing applicants, (4) offering the job, and (5) making the new employee's first days pleasant.

9. Accepting jobs is fun, but it also requires careful writing that includes clearly accepting; clearly naming the job; repeating the offered salary; mentioning benefits; mentioning the date, time, and place for reporting to work; stating enthusiastically an eagerness to begin.

10. Follow-up letters must be sent quickly after the interview: be brief, say thanks, restate your interest in the job, and try to say something pleasantly personal.

11. Rejecting job offers uses the *no* letter format, and must reflect the company positively by saying thanks, saying something good about the company, explaining the circumstances forcing the rejection, saying no clearly, but *never* saying anything bad about the company.

12. Letters of resignation include four parts: resign, say why, assure support, and say something nice about the company.

13. Letters of recommendation must be written carefully, with full attention paid to legality, honesty, and fairness.

14. When asking another to write a recommendation, do everything possible to make the job easy: supply envelopes, stamps, addresses, and pertinent information.

EXERCISES

1. *Dressing for job interviews.* Whenever interviews are to be discussed in class, come to class dressed for an interview. When the discussion describes proper dress, compare your clothing with that considered to be appropriate.

2. *Group exercise: Buyers (employers) and sellers (job hunters).* Divide the class into two groups: employers and job hunters. Group 1 should include three people. These should be the most experienced members of the class—usually older stu-

dents—who have held full-time jobs before. The rest of the class falls into the job-hunting group (Group 2). Group 1 should write six ''Employee Wanted'' newspaper advertisements and post them on the board. Members of Group 2 then decide which they will apply for. Over a period of time to be decided by the professor, Group 1 should interview each member of Group 2. Discuss each interview in class.

3. *Writing other people's résumés.* Using your observations of the interviews performed as part of Exercise 2, write a résumé for the person you think did the best job of being interviewed. This requires, of course, that you pay careful attention to the interviews.

4. *Recommendation letters.* Having observed the interviews performed as part of Exercise 2, write a letter of recommendation to a prospective employer (details should be forthcoming from Group 1 during the interview) for the person you think did the best job of being interviewed. This requires, of course, that you pay careful attention to the interviews.

5. *Resignations.* We have all had jobs we did not like. Recalling the good and the bad things about your worst job, write a letter to the boss resigning from that job.

6. *The Interviewer's tasks.* What are the five tasks of an interviewer? List them. Why is each important? Explain in writing.

7. *Learning from the interviewer.* What can an interviewee learn from knowing the five tasks of an interviewer?

8. *Practicing the answers to interviewers' questions.* Discuss in class the common questions of job interviewers. Why do they ask these questions? What kind of answers might they be seeking?

9. *What interviewers like in interviewees.* Discuss in class each of the qualities interviewers like to see in job hunters. Identify why interviewers like each of these qualities.

10. *The job interview as informative and persuasive.* Explain in writing in what ways a job interview combines the qualities of the other types of informational and persuasive interviews.

CASE STUDY 1: ACCEPTING THE JOB

Ms. Samantha Evans of Widgitcog Industries has offered you a job as an accountant. It pays $27,500. The benefits are good. She asks you begin work in Phoenix, Arizona (59th Ave. and Thunderbird Road), at 9 a.m. on

7 July 1990. Evans was one of several interviewers who met with you. You did not think the interview went well because you did not like Evans. It seemed clear that she did not like you, either. At one point during the interview, she grudgingly gave in to the other interviewers' compliments about your academic achievements by saying that you ''looked pretty good for graduating from a football factory.'' Although you have some doubts about whether you could work for Evans, write a letter to her accepting the job.

CASE STUDY 2: REJECTING THE JOB

Following the same conditions as in Case Study 1, write a letter to Evans rejecting the job.

CASE STUDY 3: GOOD RECOMMENDATIONS: THE BALONEY LETTER

Lebanon Baloney, the daughter of an old family friend, has asked you to write a letter of recommendation. Baloney is twenty-one and will graduate with high honors from Harvard next month. She has a degree in Finance and wants to work in investment banking, eventually planning to direct the trust funds of wealthy people. She presents an engaging and professional demeanor. She is well spoken, highly thought of, intelligent and hard working. During the past two summers, she has worked for you in your accounting business, always doing what was asked and sometimes more. Write a letter of recommendation for Ms. Baloney.

CASE STUDY 4: BAD RECOMMENDATIONS: THE DRAWER LETTER

File Drawer, the son of an old family friend, has asked you to write a letter of recommendation. Drawer is twenty-seven and will graduate with a 2.0 average from Southwest Eastern Northern College of Calligraphy next month. He has a degree in Scuba Diving and wants to work in investment banking, eventually planning to direct the trust funds of wealthy people. His idea of dressing for work is to wear a pair of Hawaiian cut-offs and a ragged tee-shirt—that is, when he cares to go to work. Although he says very little, he nevertheless has trouble keeping his lower jaw sufficiently tight against his upper jaw so that the back of his mouth is not visible. During the past two summers, he has worked for you in your accounting business, emptying waste baskets. He was employed to empty baskets every other Thursday. He came to work four times in two summers. Once he emptied fourteen incomplete tax returns into the incinerator. Write a letter of recommendation for Drawer.

CASE STUDY 5: RECOMMENDING THE PROF.

Write a letter to Oxford University, recommending your favorite professor for a professorship there. You are qualified, of course, to speak only about the professor's teaching and out-of-class involvement with students.

CASE STUDY 6: HELPING THE NICE PERSON WHO AGREED TO WRITE A RECOMMENDATION FOR YOU

Pretend that you are your favorite professor, and that professor has agreed to write a letter of recommendation about you to a company for which you would like to work. This assignment is not so easy as it looks. Make a list of your strengths and your weaknesses. Remember to be honest and to emphasize the strong points.

CASE STUDY 7: RECOMMENDATION: THE SLEAZE LETTER

Write a letter of recommendation for A. Sleaze. Sleaze has applied for a job as chief of security at Chase Manhattan Bank. Two years ago, when he worked for your company as chief of security, he was fired for alleged embezzlement. To avoid panic, no charges were filed. You were the person responsible for discovering the loss of money, and the probability that Sleaze took it is great.

CHALLENGE EXERCISE 1: RESIGNATION: THE SWIMRITE LETTER

You have worked in sales for Swimrite, Inc., for three years. The base pay is good, but your territory is northern Canada. Although your best customers have been in Thunder Bay, you have believed for a long time that northern Canada is not the best place in the world for selling swimming pools. In addition, your boss, John Weismuller the sales manager, has been chiding you for

six months for not selling more pools. He never tires of citing Harley Working's record of seventeen pools in one month. He dismisses as trivial the fact that Working sold these pools in Miami during its worst heat wave in thirty years. It's clear that he does not like you, and almost equally clear that you do not like him. Remembering that a letter of resignation must be cool and professional, write a letter of resignation to the president of Swimrite, Neva Working.

CHALLENGE EXERCISE 2: LETTER OF RESIGNATION

For seven years you have worked in the Quality Control Division of Fahrquart Industries as a laboratory technician, while completing your engineering degree at night. Fahrquart Industries paid half of your tuition. Upon taking your degree, you applied for an engineering job with Fahrquart, but none has been open for a year now. Last week, you accepted a job as engineer with another company. Write a letter of resignation to your boss, Mary K. Kreps, Director of Quality Control.

CHALLENGE EXERCISE 3: LETTER OF RESIGNATION

You have been a technical writer in the Printing Department of the Bord Corporation for three years. The department prepares, prints, and disseminates everything from in-house newsletters to technical manuals accompanying Bord's products. You liked your job until four months ago, when a Mr. Prolixity was hired as the new head of the Printing Department. He disparages your work constantly, making such remarks as "This is too terse," "That's not long enough," and "This doesn't flow smoothly. Make it longer." Prolixity comes from a modern school of communications, and you think his approach is flat-out wrong. You have applied, interviewed, and been hired for a similar job with another company. Write a letter of resignation to Prolixity.

V I

LEARNING IS NOT AT-

TAINED BY CHANCE; IT

MUST BE SOUGHT WITH

ARDOR AND ATTENDED TO

WITH DILIGENCE.

ABIGAIL ADAMS

(1744–1818)

OTHER

MODES

OF

COMMUNICATION

LISTENING

Impediments to Listening
Rules for Good Listening

SPEAKING

OVERCOMING JITTERS

THE KINDS OF SPEECHES

Impromptu
Extemporaneous
Written
Recited
Combination

PREPARING A SPEECH

Choose a Subject.
Choose a Clear Purpose.
Choose a Persona.
Analyze the Audience.
Study the Subject.

Organize the Speech.
Write the Body.
Write the Introduction and
Conclusion.
Decide on Examples and Illustrations.
Study the Room and Decide on the
Equipment.
Create Visual Aids.
Insert Some Humor.
Practice on Tape.
Anticipate Questions.

ORAL REPORTS

The Differences between Public
Speaking and Oral Reports
Outlining Oral Reports

DICTATION

SUMMARY

EXERCISES

Learning Objectives:

☐ Know the impediments to listening
well.

☐ Know the rules of good listening.

☐ Know the kinds of speeches: impromptu, extemporaneous, written, recited, and a combination.

☐ Know the step-by-step methods for
preparing a speech, from choosing
a subject to anticipating questions.

☐ Understand the differences between public speeches and oral
business reports.

☐ Know ways to prepare an oral
report.

☐ Understand the guidelines for
good dictation.

14

SPEAK SILVER, REPLY GOLD.

SWAHILI PROVERB

TALKING AND ELOQUENCE

ARE NOT THE SAME: TO

LISTENING

SPEAK, AND TO

AND

SPEAK WELL, ARE

TWO THINGS. A

SPEAKING

FOOL MAY TALK, BUT A WISE

MAN SPEAKS.

BEN JONSON

(1573–1637)

LISTENING

People in business spend 80 percent of their time communicating. Of that time, 30 percent is used for speaking, but 45 percent of the time is spent listening.[1] Moreover, research demonstrates that those who listen well not only communicate with others well, but also tend to rise higher in corporations.[2]

IMPEDIMENTS TO LISTENING

While impediments to listening in business are numerous, most involve fundamental facts about people. Knowing those facts helps both speakers and listeners to understand and overcome the impediments to listening. Here is a list of the most important obstacles to listening.

1. *Long speeches impede retention.* The percentage of the information in a speech that listeners retain, especially detail, decreases as the length of the speech increases. Listeners should try to identify and retain the main points that occur throughout the speech.

2. *When buried in the middle, important points are forgotten easily.* As in written communications, the beginning and the end of a speech are the most important parts because people tend to remember them. Listeners tend to forget the middle. Consequently, speakers should place the most important information at the beginning and the end of a speech. And listeners should get the main points from the beginning, and pick up at the end what they may have missed in the middle. In a typical 30-minute speech, for example, attention begins high, but then slides to a low at about 15 to 25 minutes, and then rises again at the end.

3. *Audiences distort information.* Distorting information is a common error in listening. Because people by nature are always looking for ways to make life easier, we tend to distort information in the following ways.

    a. Because it is easier to see the world as black or white, right or wrong, correct or incorrect, we tend to simplify information. Good speeches usually reflect the world as it is, and, consequently, they address many gray areas. We tend to disregard these complexities in favor of an oversimplified view.

    b. Because it is easier to have our prejudices confirmed than denied, to hear confirmation of our preconceptions, we tend to distort information so that it agrees with what we believe.

    c. Because it is easier to agree with authority than to make up our own minds, we tend to accept the statements of experts

---

[1]George R. Bell, "Listen and You Shall Hear," *Association Management*, March 1984.
[2]See Beverly Devenport Sypher, et al., "Listening, Communication Abilities, and Success at Work," *The Journal of Business Communication* 26 (Fall 1989): 293–303.

Listeners should try to identify and retain the main points of a speech.

rather than to think hard about the information and make up our own minds about the degree to which we agree and disagree with authority.

d. Because we believe we understand the views of people who have spoken to us often, we tend not to listen, but rather rely on what we already believe the speaker believes.

4. *Because attention spans are short, listeners tend to let their minds wander.* They may be distracted by any of the following preoccupations.

   a. Preoccupation with the shape of the cloud outside the window — daydreaming.

   b. Preoccupation with the ways in which we are being perceived by others in the audience or by the speaker.

   c. Preoccupation with the process. We tend to pay attention to and be concerned with the mechanics of the situation. We lose track of what is being said in the attempt to make sure things continue to be said.

   d. Preoccupation with the speaker rather than the speech. We tend either to become involved in the emotions of the speaker or to become detached by watching the speaker's gestures, clothing, or physical characteristics. In either case, the information becomes a dull rumble in the back of our minds.

5. *The time of day affects the quality of listening.* People listen best in the morning, and the quality of their listening goes into a long slide as the day progresses.

6. *When people believe that the speaker is saying things irrelevant or contradictory to their interests, they tune out.* While it is good for us as listeners to be skeptical, automatically assuming that the speaker is

saying things that we disagree with is not good. Just because we disagree with statement A does not mean that we will disagree with statement B. Try to hear each discrete statement afresh; that is, take each statement separately, and agree or disagree with it on its own merits. Moreover, listeners should try to see things from the speaker's perspective before trying to see them from their own.

7. *Poor hearing is a severe impediment.* Listeners who sometimes miss what is said should sit close to and in line with the speaker.

8. *Listening solely for facts impedes understanding.* Unless listeners understand the major generalizations, the facts may be useless.

RULES FOR GOOD LISTENING

Good listening is active: good listeners are alert, attentive, and involved in the speech. Listening well is not like watching television. Speakers react to their audiences so much that a good audience may make the speech better than it might otherwise have been, whereas the television show will proceed in the same way — becoming no better or worse — regardless of whether ten or ten million people are watching and listening. Much can be learned by listening carefully. Here is a list of the most important qualities of good listening.

THE QUALITIES OF A GOOD LISTENER

1. Above all, pay attention.

2. Reinforce the speaker by laughing at funny jokes, smiling at unfunny jokes, looking solemn when the speech is serious, and appearing seriously attentive when complex ideas are being presented.

3. During a question-answer period, formulate one or two questions that clarify or exemplify the information given in the speech.

4. Avoid automatically countering with objections based on your own biases. Such give-and-take is important at times, but do not go into a speech looking for a fight.

5. Because we think faster than anyone can speak, we should use lag time to review what we have heard, and then apply it to what we are hearing.

6. Pay attention to more than words: intonation, pauses, speed of delivery. Often these give clues to emphasis.

7. Remember that speeches are organized so that abstract ideas are followed by concrete examples, facts, or statistics. Keep the abstraction in mind as the speaker is giving the examples.

SPEAKING

Using language orally has been the most common method of conveying information and persuading others since the day millennia ago that the first human being spoke and another understood. Today, people give speeches for any of four reasons.

WHY WE WANT TO SPEAK IN PUBLIC

1. *People pay us for our opinions.* Whether we are paid directly for the speech or indirectly for doing our job, money is a big reason for giving a speech.

2. *We want recognition.* Fame, even in small doses called recognition, provides us with much satisfaction.

3. *We want to persuade.* Public speaking provides the most rapid method of persuading the most people that our ideas are good ideas, or that our company's products and services are good products and services.

4. *We want to make things happen.* While persuasion is a forceful reason for speaking, it is even better that, once persuaded, people will *act* as a result. When our speaking causes others to act and follow our ideas, we often receive money and recognition.

OVERCOMING JITTERS

Although everyone, albeit secretly, wants to speak in public, speaking is perhaps the only activity that gives people the jitters more than writing does. In fact, more than twice as many people fear public speaking than fear death.[3] Demosthenes, the greatest orator of ancient Greece, was so frightened by and ashamed of his mumbling, halting speech that he practiced with his mouth full of pebbles. When he could speak clearly with such a full mouth, he felt ready to speak without pebbles. One of the greatest speakers of this century, Winston Churchill, had great difficulty speaking. As his biographer William Manchester relates, Churchill overcame a weak voice by practicing every syllable over and over again, every stress, every rise and fall of his voice. Indeed, Churchill also prepared by practicing responses to comments he thought might come from others. In short, few people become good speakers because of a natural gift. Like good writing, good speaking is infinitely perfectible and derives from hard work; speaking, like writing, is a skill. And skills are learned. Indeed, we may paraphrase Thomas Mann's remark on writers by saying that an effective speaker is one for whom speaking is more difficult than it is for most people.

Overcoming the jitters of speaking derives solely from preparation. No one with a normal voice and sufficient preparation should be frightened of speaking, for the speaker who controls the words, the tone, and the delivery usually controls the audience.

Nearly everyone is nervous before speaking to a group. Actually, nervousness is beneficial. It is analogous to being psyched up before competing in a sport. Athletes know, for example, that intense concentration is a requirement of performing well. And getting the adrenalin flowing helps concentration. Nervousness stimulates adrenalin. People

. . . .
EXERCISE A: OVERCOMING JITTERS

Many people have developed methods for overcoming the jitters caused by public speaking. Discuss some of these methods in class and decide what may or may not work for everyone.

---

[3]That is, 18.7% fear death, but 40.6% fear public speaking. David Wallechinsky and Irving Wallace, *The Book of Lists* (New York: Morrow, 1977).

in show business tell us that they worry only when they are not nervous. So do not worry about being nervous before speaking.

The trick, however, is to *control* nervousness, to turn it to one's advantage. Nervousness is unproductive only when it leads to mumbling, halting, rambling speech. Such impediments may be eliminated by one thing only: thorough preparation. A well-prepared and slightly nervous speaker is the best speaker.

THE KINDS OF SPEECHES

The first question the wise speaker always asks before agreeing to speak is "What kind of speech?" Here is a list of the kinds of speeches business people are likely to encounter.

IMPROMPTU

Surprise! There you were sitting in a meeting, minding your own business, thinking about whatever. From somewhere comes a voice saying, "Smedley, this is your area. Why not give us a few words on the subject?" Impromptu speeches should be plain and simple. Usually, they call for your *opinion*, not for some detailed, well-digested, and highly organized speech. When you are asked to give an opinion, think for a moment and gather your thoughts into one sentence that summarizes the opinion. You can support this statement by reasons or facts, or a little of both. Then sit down.

EXTEMPORANEOUS

Although *extempore* means "without preparation," in speech it means "without writing it out." An extemporaneous speech is a prepared speech; it is not written out word for word. Given from an outline, an extemporaneous speech may contain as little as three main points or as much as the main points plus illustrative anecdotes, facts, opinions, an introduction, and a conclusion. If the extemporaneous speech is long, then the speaker may use notes to keep the speech organized.

WRITTEN

A speaker delivers a written speech by reading from a prepared manuscript. A written speech can be dull, especially when the speaker never deviates, never looks up from the page. Although information, especially when it is difficult, complex, and perhaps arcane, requires some reading, speakers should know the material sufficiently well that they may look at the audience and talk extemporaneously on the subject. Such stepping away from a manuscript must be planned carefully, for the advantage of written speeches is that they protect the speaker from being misquoted or from saying indelicate things. Moreover, pressures of time sometimes are so severe (as with televised speeches) that practicing the speech from printed copy may keep its length within a few seconds of the time allowed.

Recited

Except for short speeches in very formal situations, recited or memorized speeches are boring and dangerous. Although everyone advises against memorizing speeches, some novice speakers are so frightened of forgetting that they do it anyway. The most likely kind of speech to fail is that which is recited. Do not succumb to the temptation to memorize. We have all been embarrassed by and for the speaker who recites for two or three minutes and then forgets the rest of the speech. Either there is dead silence for a few looong minutes before the speaker remembers or there is dead silence and the red-faced speaker must sit down.

Combination

Some of the best speeches combine the types mentioned here. Parts are extemporaneous, parts are memorized, and parts are written. A seasoned speaker still must prepare carefully for each speech, but such speakers also know when to deviate from that preparation.

Preparing a Speech

Here is a list of requirements for preparing a speech. Some changes in the order may be necessary depending on the kind of speech, the kind of audience, and other limitations.

How to Prepare a Speech
1. Choose a subject.
2. Choose a clear purpose.
3. Choose a persona.
4. Analyze the audience.
5. Study the subject.
6. Organize the speech.
7. Write the body.
8. Write the introduction and conclusion.
9. Decide on examples and illustrations.
10. Study the room and decide on the equipment.
11. Create visual aids.
12. Insert some humor.
13. Practice on tape.
14. Anticipate questions.

CHOOSE A SUBJECT

There are three criteria for choosing a subject. The audience must be able to understand it and be interested in it, the speaker must know or be able to discover a lot about it, and it must be encompassable by the limits of a speech. Given that a well-prepared speech will create interest and enable understanding, and that a speaker can usually discover sufficient information on nearly any subject, the most important question in choosing a subject is "Can it be discussed adequately in the time allowed?"

The process of limiting a topic is extremely important (see Chapter 2), for a speaker must give an audience the sense that the subject has been discussed fully, or at least certain parts of it have been examined thoroughly. For example, if a speaker has twenty minutes to inform an audience of anglers about fishing, clearly the topic must be limited. One cannot in twenty minutes discuss adequately all forms of fishing: salt water, fresh water, surf fishing, stream fishing, lake fishing, and many others. Consequently, the speaker must limit the topic to, say, stream fishing. Once again, the topic is too large. There are big streams and little streams; there are streams that empty into oceans or lakes or other streams. There are mountain streams and lowland streams, cold water and warm water, white water and still water. Streams in Colorado contain different fish than streams in Pennsylvania. Yet again, then, the topic is limited to, say, fishing in streams feeding Lake Erie in Pennsylvania. After studying the topic, the speaker discovers that those streams contain coho salmon, chinook salmon, brown trout, rainbow trout called steelheads, and even palomino trout. At different times of year these streams have more of one kind of fish than another. The topic may be encompassable, finally, with this topic: "Fishing for Steelhead Trout in Pennsylvania's Lake Erie Feeder Streams."

After much research and organization, this topic may be broadened slightly to include salmon or narrowed even more to fit the twenty-minute limit by discussing only fishing with dry and wet flies, rather than also with live bait and artificial spinning lures.

CHOOSE A CLEAR PURPOSE

The main purpose of a speech usually falls into one of two categories: persuasion or information (see Chapter 2). The speech is primarily persuasive if the purpose is to persuade anglers to go to Lake Erie to fish for steelhead trout. The speech is primarily informative if the purpose is to provide information regarding any the following: how the fish got there, when they are in the streams, or how they may be caught.

A promotional speech by someone from the Pennsylvania Tourist Bureau would include both purposes, but primarily it would discuss those things that would persuade people to come to Pennsylvania's part of Lake Erie to fish. Consequently, such a speech would emphasize ease of travel, how clean the lake is compared to twenty years ago, costs associated with fishing there, and the likelihood of catching many fish.

An informational speech by an outdoor writer or promoter would discuss both purposes, but primarily the speech would emphasize methods of catching steelhead. The promotional speaker should remember, however, that helpful information may result in successful fishing trips, thus bringing many people back to Pennsylvania streams and bringing in more dollars for the commonwealth.

CHOOSE A PERSONA

One of the most enduring and pervasive questions lurking in the back of the brains of every member of an audience is the question ''Who is this person?'' Yet the question is not one to which audiences want a thorough answer. Audiences are not interested in the great complexities, contradictions, fears, and hopes of the speaker; they are interested in a simple answer that will allow them to understand where the speaker is coming from. There are three essential personas, or roles, a speaker may adopt in order to satisfy an audience: authority, colleague, and beginner.

AUTHORITY.   The persona of authority falls into two categories: the leader and the expert. The leader is one whose position reserves the right to decide but is concerned that the goals of the organization be achieved. The stance is one that says ''here are the problems and here are some possible solutions. Let's talk about them. I need your knowledge and experience to help me make the best decision for us all.''

The persona of the expert is based on knowledge and experience. The audience recognizes this person as knowing much more about the topic than anyone else the members are likely to hear. Although ''I don't know'' is the best response when a speaker does not know the answer to a question posed by the audience, not knowing enough will destroy the speaker's rapport with an audience.

COLLEAGUE.   This persona conveys to an audience the sense that ''we're all in the same boat, and although I've thought a lot about this topic, you probably have also.'' This persona is much more approachable than the authority. Speakers using this stance seem warmer than those using authority, but the result is that the speaker should be prepared for much audience response and interaction.

BEGINNER.   The persona of the beginner makes up for a lack of knowledge with excitement. Having recently discovered the topic, the speaker using this persona awakens or reawakens excitement in the audience. Although a speaker may sometimes adopt more than one of these personas during a speech, one persona must dominate. Otherwise, the audience may be confused, or at least may be left wondering ''Who is this person?''

This speaker exemplifies a persona of authority.

ANALYZE THE AUDIENCE

The audience for a speech can be analyzed in the same way that multiple readers are analyzed. That is, the reader profile provided in Chapter 2 (page 31) may be lifted whole from that chapter and considered as an audience profile. One major difference may lie in the attention the speaker pays to possible differences in opinion. Because of the immediacy of audience responses, a speaker must prepare well to answer those responses. Responding in writing allows the writer to spend time thinking of answers before responding. Responding orally allows little time for pondering. Preparing to answer questions from the audience requires speakers to think carefully about the kinds of questions they are likely to get *before* they get them. Consequently, audience analysis is vital to successful speaking.

To be successful, comments made during a speech benefit from a thorough analysis of the audience. An audience comprising two groups — say, commercial anglers interested in raising the legal limit of fish allowed to be taken in the lake and lowering the limit in the streams; and recreational anglers interested in the opposite — might require a careful tiptoeing around an issue if it is not part of the *primary* purpose of the speech. Raising controversial side issues is sure to defeat the speaker's primary purpose. Part or all of the audience will be unsympathetic to the entire speech if angered only by some part of it. Again, a careful analysis of the audience is vital.

Another difference between the nature of readers and audiences lies in the nature of the situation. That is, readers tend to come to a document individually, whereas members of an audience share the fact of their being in the room. They may be there as part of a conference on a given theme, or they may be part of a service organization at a monthly or annual meeting. Knowing these things allows the speaker to analyze the audience even better than a writer can analyze the readers. One would never give a speech about killing, cleaning, and eating trout to a conference entitled "Global Hunger in the Twenty-First Century: A Vegetarian Response." Clearly, speakers need to analyze many details about an audience, but they also must not forget to analyze the big picture.

WHAT AUDIENCES LIKE.   In addition to discovering the things that audiences do not like, speakers should also consider the things that audiences do like. Audiences respond favorably to the following qualities in speakers.

QUALITIES AUDIENCES LIKE IN SPEAKERS

1. *Knowledge.* Good speakers project a sense of knowing whereof they speak. Allusions to experience and study far beyond that given explicitly in the speech give audiences a sense of security, a sense that they are hearing things from someone who really knows.

2. *Sincerity.* Worthless without logic and knowledge, sincerity is a worthwhile addition to logic and knowledge. In short, a speaker must believe.

3. *Vitality.* Energetic, dynamic, enthusiastic speakers convey energy, dynamism, and enthusiasm to their audiences. And audiences respond, so that the room is charged with excitement.

4. *Confidence.* Audiences respond well to speakers whose demeanor conveys a sense of competence, of knowing where they have been, are, and are going. That is, the vitality conveyed must be controlled and focused. The audience must believe that it is in good hands. Confidence and vitality combine to produce the ideal audience, a curious paradox: one that is relaxed, but intensely interested.

5. *Clarity of purpose.* Audiences like to know from the beginning just what the point of all this is, and they like to be reminded frequently throughout the speech.

6. *Clarity of organization.* Audiences may be kept from straying into boredom or daydreams by knowing exactly where they are in the life of the speech. That is, they are pleased when they know that "now we're hearing the purpose; now we're hearing an example; now the speaker is making another point; now the speaker is going to summarize." Good speakers make it so easy for audiences to know where they are that audiences need not think about it; they just know.

7. *Pertinence.* Audiences generally, and listeners individually, are made comfortable, even flattered, by language they understand, examples they have experienced, subjects in which they are interested, information that is practical, and a length that does not tax

EXERCISE B: AUDIENCE ANALYSIS

Discuss in class those qualities of speakers that audiences do *not* like. List them and then place them into categories.

their capacity for paying attention. One would never speak about the glories of fifty-foot sail boats to an audience whose average individual income is $30,000 annually.

8. *Memorability*. We have all heard speakers who sounded good, but when we thought about the speech afterward, or discussed it with others, we could not remember much. Instantly, we revise our opinion of the speech. Memorable speeches have several vivid, concrete statements, each of which is memorable, as well as one big idea that is virtually unforgettable.

9. *Inspirational*. Not unlike good sermons, good public speeches inspire audiences to *act*, to rise to the occasion, to dig down into themselves to do better jobs, to be better people. Sometimes, of course, the speech attempts to persuade people *not* to act. Often this is the more difficult job.

10. *Humor*. No speech should be soooo serious as to be humorless. Of course, humor must be appropriate to the subject and must not overwhelm the point of the speech. But should the subject of the speech admit of *no* humor, the subject is probably inappropriate for a speech.

STUDY THE SUBJECT

Few things demonstrate the truth of the old saying "still waters run deep" so well as a speaker's knowledge of the subject does. Speakers should never deliberately show off their knowledge by providing arcane information that no one really needs, but when challenged, the speaker should always be ready to trot out that knowledge. Another way of saying it is that for everything said in a speech the speaker should know ten or twenty things.

Such knowledge comes only from study. Rarely, if ever, does a person pick up enough knowledge over the years to negate the necessity for studying a subject before speaking about it to a knowledgeable audience. When writing, the speaker should keep notes not only of generalities but also of specifics. These provide a store of information to draw from when sitting down to write the speech.

ORGANIZE THE SPEECH

Organizing a speech involves a number of steps. Although the order may vary, beginning speakers should determine the purpose, identify the major points, outline the speech, fill in the gaps, and write the introduction and conclusion.

DETERMINE THE PURPOSE. After studying and compiling information, a speaker must begin to organize the speech. What is the *purpose* of the speech? Is it primarily to inform or to persuade? Although the speech may inform *and* persuade, the speaker must choose one as the *primary* purpose.

IDENTIFY THE MAJOR POINTS.   The more knowledge a person has, the more difficult it is to winnow that knowledge into a few important points. The tendency is to choose too many points. We have all been bored to tears by speeches entitled, "The Eighty-Eight Keys to Effective Selling." Although more palatable, even "The Eight Keys to Effective Selling" is a bit much. To be effective, a speech must be capable of being absorbed almost whole by the minds of the audience. Although speeches are often recorded on videotape, few people actually review them after the fact. Members of an audience can remember three points; they cannot remember twenty-three. Sometimes, of course, two points are sufficient; sometimes four points are needed. The number of points made is partly determined by the subject and partly by the length of the speech. Remember, however, that audiences do not have long attention spans. In general, then, choose three major points about the subject.

CHOOSE THE METHOD OF DEVELOPMENT.   There are a number of patterns that can be used to organize the speech.

1. *Temporal*. The temporal—having to do with time—may be *chronological*, in which the speaker relates a narrative of events in the order they occur. A report that conveys a manager's review of office organization in four offices around the country or region may be given chronologically. The speaker begins with the office examined on Monday, then the one on Tuesday, and so on. A variation on this is to begin with the present and work backward.

   Another temporal method is *cause and effect* (or chain of events). Using this method, the speaker relates the series or chain of events that led to a particular situation, problem, or solution. This method is best used when it is important for people to understand just how a situation or problem arose, and when understanding that series provides a key to the solution.

2. *Categorical*. The categorical method is familiar to everyone who has taken high school biology. Using this method, the speaker simply divides the subject into categories in the same way that, say, a biologist separates all living things into two categories: flora and fauna. Political philosophies may be categorized as conservative and liberal. Government is more complicated and may include democracy, oligarchy, monarchy, and so on.

3. *Priorital*. The priorital method assumes a hierarchy of importance. That is, should the topic be rescue from fires, the speaker may address such priorities as saving people first, then animals, then things. The priorital method can produce marvelously interesting (and controversial) speeches, but it usually requires a great deal of research in preparation.

4. *Spatial*. The spatial method is best used for organizing speeches or parts of speeches that describe something physical. That is, should an image be described from the top down to the bottom, left to right, right to left, inside to outside?

5. *Topical*. The topical (or newspaper) method organizes speeches in the same way that news stories are written. That is, the speaker must answer who, what, when, where, why, and how. This organization is very efficient and is often used to great effect in oral reports.

WRITE THE BODY

The body of a speech contains the guts, the information, the data that either inform or persuade, or both. The first job is to choose the major points. These points should be arranged so that the discussion follows naturally from one point to the next. The most common method for informative speeches is chronological. The first major point of a speech on how to fish for steelhead trout may begin, for example, by discussing what to do *before* fishing. That is, what equipment is best, what stream conditions (high or low water, deep or shallow water) are best, what type of bait given certain conditions, and so on. The second major point may be what to do *during* fishing. Should the sun be at one's back or in one's face, fish upstream or down, tight line or slack, how to land the fish, and so on. The final point might discuss what to do once the fish is landed. Such things might be discussed as how to clean them, keep them, and even cook them, although the last of these doubtless would provide subjects for many speeches.

Each of these major points must be organized. Typically, major points are presented in three parts: illustrations or examples, facts, reviews and transitions. Outlined, the body of a typical speech may look like this:

OUTLINE OF THE BODY OF A SPEECH

I. Point 1
    a. Illustrations
    b. Facts and Opinions
    c. Review and Transition

II. Point 2
    a. Illustrations
    b. Facts and Opinions
    c. Review and Transition

III. Point 3
    a. Illustrations
    b. Facts and Opinions
    c. Review and Transition

ILLUSTRATIONS. Often the best illustration is a story. Sometimes a speaker can gain the interest of an audience by telling a story that captures the audience's imagination or that the audience can identify with. For instance, the first major point, preparation, might begin this way:

I well remember the first time I went fishing for steelhead. Although I had fun, it was not because I had fun that I remember it. I remember it because of the disasters. I took along my little twelve-inch net, only to find that the average fish was twenty-four inches long. I used four-pound test line only to find that the average fish weighed seven pounds and fought so hard that, had the line not broken every time, my rod might have been torn from my hands. I took only small, inland-stream size sinkers, so that in fast water, the fly sped well above the fish I was trying to catch. And I failed to bring along felt-bottomed shoes, so that I spent most of the day practicing ballet from rock to rock, and I fell several times. The average steelhead, once hooked, will force you downstream about 125 yards. An exciting time, yes. A fun time, certainly, but only if you are prepared for these monsters from the deep.

FACTS AND OPINIONS.   Facts come in many forms. The most impressive facts involve numbers. While studying the subject, the speaker should gather as many facts and statistics as can reasonably be found — many more than will be used in the speech. Regarding steelhead trout, for example, the speaker could learn the following: between March of 1987 and February of 1988, the anglers on the Lake Erie tributary streams in Pennsylvania caught one steelhead, on average, for every two hours that they fished.[4] In contrast, the typical angler required eight hours of trying before catching a coho salmon. The average steelhead trout entering the streams is about twenty-three inches long, although the state record exceeds thirty-six inches. Given that the average inland trout caught is less than half the length of the average steelhead caught, such statistics should excite many anglers. The Pennsylvania shoreline of Lake Erie is 42 miles long, and into the lake run about a dozen fishable streams. In a typical year, about 500,000 steelhead fingerlings are released into the streams where they imprint. That is, they remember that stream and return to it two to four years later to spawn.

How much of this information will be used is determined later, as the speech is written. Nevertheless, there are two reasons that it is better to have too much information from which to draw than not enough. First, the speaker may pursue a line of thought that requires information originally not thought useful. Second, the speaker will remember much of the information not used in the speech, ready to be retrieved by questions from the audience.

REVIEWS AND TRANSITIONS.   Should any major point require support that occupies more than five minutes, it is usually best to summarize at the end of each major point, recapping the information. It also is best to wait until the body has been written before thinking about how to insert transitions, how to move smoothly from one point to another. The example used here initially had a chronological order:

---

[4]Information supplied by Robert Lorantas of the Pennsylvania Fish Comission, Fairview Fish Cultural Station, Fairview, Pennsylvania.

before, during, and after fishing. A good transition from ''before'' to ''during'' might be something as short as an introductory clause: ''After we've gathered all this paraphernalia, the time has come to have some real fun.'' While the order is selected initially *before* writing, only *after* the writing does the speaker decide finally on the proper order. Often speeches take an unforeseen direction during the writing, one that makes the best order of presentation different from that initially thought workable. The key here is to think about the order again after the writing.

WRITE THE INTRODUCTION AND CONCLUSION

Because the introduction and conclusion are rhetorically closer to each other than to the body, they should be composed at about the same time. Some writers and speakers prefer to write the conclusion before composing the introduction. Whether written first or last, introductions and conclusions should be brief.

INTRODUCTION.   Openings should get to the point as soon as circumstances and culture allow. Rather than flounder about for an interesting, attention-getting opening, the speaker should look to the body or the conclusion for a way to open the speech. In this instance, the humor implicit in the term ''steelhead'' may be used:

> Imagine with me for a moment a late-February morning on a stream two hundred yards from the shores of Lake Erie. The temperature is seventeen degrees, the wind is thirty miles an hour and whipping off the lake. The edges of the stream flowing into the lake are ridged with ice. On this ice stands an angler, the line in the water and the pole shaking almost as much as the angler.
>
> It's cold, it's miserable, and any sane person would never, it seems, refer to such a situation as exciting. Sane people, then, have never spent a day fishing for steelhead trout. Such people, some of them otherwise thoroughly admirable, respond to anglers' tales of steelhead fishing by asking whether the term ''steelhead'' refers to the trout or to the angler. One must, they say, have a head of solid steel to be out in such weather voluntarily.
>
> What is it that causes men and women, loving fathers and mothers, upstanding citizens who avoid football games if it drizzles, hunting if the wind is high, and exercising during heat waves, to endure such misery and call it fun? . . . Steelhead trout.

There is almost always something in the body or conclusion that may be developed for the introduction. Notice also that the last two words of the introduction are the subject of the speech.

At times, getting the audience's attention is a more immediate problem than can be solved by an opening that eventually provides a sense of completion. This problem occurs most often with bored or hostile audiences, those that the speaker senses want first to be entertained. Here are three common attention-getting openings for problem situations.

1. *Silence.* Five or six seconds of silence, while the speaker surveys the audience, can be an effective attention-getter. This device can create anticipation and interest in an audience.

2. *State a problem the audience has.* If the audience is homogeneous, and the subject of the speech is to solve a problem common to most members of the audience, simply stating a specific case illustrating that problem will get the audience's attention.

3. *Say something cryptic, puzzling, or intriguing.* It should not frighten or anger the audience, but it should puzzle them. This gains their attention. Be sure, however, to enlighten them before the end of the speech, and be sure the puzzle is related directly to the subject of the speech. Often this method works well in connecting the introduction and conclusion.

4. *Thanks.* In all public speeches, as in oral business reports (see pages 379–81), speakers should thank the person who introduces them. The thank-you may be brief, prosaic, or humorous, but it must be there, if only because courtesy, good manners, and tradition require it. Public speeches often require a thank-you that involves thanking the introducer in a personal but appropriate way, or thanking certain members of the audience for the opportunity to speak. In oral reports, a thank-you may be just that, with the first words being nothing more complicated than "Thank you" or "Thank you, Ms. Fahrquart."

CONCLUSION.   Once the body has been written, or at least a first draft of it, the conclusion can be composed. The conclusion summarizes the main message, the single most important thing one wants the audience to remember, to talk about afterwards, even to change their lives in some small way. The speech on fishing for steelhead trout might close this way:

> These trout are big, fast, and usually fighting mad to get off your hook. They are ghosts, disappearing from before your eyes, hiding in clear water, doing more to avoid the net than any other freshwater fish you are likely to encounter. After a full day on the streams, your back will ache, your arms will be tired, your legs will be rubbery, your eyes will be bloodshot, and your body will be nearly frozen. And yet, you will no longer wonder why you did this to yourself, no longer wonder whether "steelhead" refers to the fish or the angler. You will have had one of the most satisfying, intensely engrossing times of your life. All these statistics and stories will be replaced by your own stories and facts that may lead others to the conclusion you will have reached: The steelhead trout creates the most exciting stream fishing in America.

The necessity for brief closings derives from the power of brevity. If you want people to remember what you say, do not say too much. Lincoln's Gettysburg Address, perhaps the most famous speech ever by an American, has fewer than 300 words.

Choosing similar topics for introductions and conclusions gives the audience a sense of completion, a sense that the speech has come full circle, but that now they know much more than they knew at the beginning. Audiences want to be entertained, to be sure, but they also like to be informed and persuaded. Conclusions that return to the beginning remind audiences of what they have learned, and wrap the speech and the audience's new knowledge into a nice, tight package. The topic is then unwrapped by the speaker, displayed to the audience in an organized and entertaining way, and then is wrapped again, folded neatly, tied in a pretty bow, and presented to them. And everyone likes the giver of gifts.

DECIDE ON EXAMPLES AND ILLUSTRATIONS

Having studied the subject and gathered a wealth of data, examples, and illustrations, the speaker must decide which of these is best suited to the speech. That is, which illustrative stories, which examples, which data best support the major points of the speech. Many humorous or riveting stories, many telling statistics and illustrations may grab the audience, but if they have nothing to do with the major points of the speech, then they do not serve the speaker or the audience well. Often a speaker may abbreviate an example or illustration by culling those parts not germane to the speech and yet retain the parts that support the major points.

STUDY THE ROOM AND DECIDE ON THE EQUIPMENT

Much of the success of a speech depends on the room in which the speech is given. No room is perfect, no room is completely unsuitable, but every room will pose one problem or another. Speakers should know the room as ballet dancers know the dance floor, as hunters know the terrain, as the Boston Red Sox know Fenway Park. If they do not, they will not do the best job they might have done.

THE ROOM.   The old slapstick routine of the speaker tripping on the steps leading to the podium derives from real experience. Speakers have tripped over steps, microphone cords, chair legs, and ridges in the wood flooring. They have bumped their heads on ceilings, walls, and screens. Their elbows have slipped from podiums and caused them to fall to the floor. Their chairs have tipped over backward, taking them along and exposing the audience to the hole in the sole of a shoe. More subtle traps include bad acoustics, noisy air conditioners, and squeaky chairs. By checking for such things, a speaker may avoid problems by asking members of an audience to avoid certain areas of the room, even certain seats. Knowledge of the acoustics will enable the speaker to know how loudly to speak. *A speaker should always spend some time in the room with the sole purpose of discovering the traps and ways to avoid them.*

THE EQUIPMENT.   Few rooms these days lack all the equipment available to speakers. Slide and overhead projectors, flip charts, chalkboards, and the like all allow the well-prepared speaker to do a better job. Speakers need to know what kind of equipment will be available so that they can plan effectively. Moreover, they must know how to use that equipment.

1. *Slides.*

    a. Advantages. Slides can project a clarity and detail beyond that of any other commonly used equipment. They project photographs, complicated graphs, and colorful charts very well. Because detail is fine and colors are vivid, slides rivet the attention of the audience. Everyone has heard people say upon leaving a presentation, "Wasn't that wonderful? The slides were magnificent!" No mention is made of the speech, but it must have been wonderful because the slides were wonderful.

    b. Disadvantages. To present slides well, a speaker must turn off the lights. Doing so not only encourages napping, but also prevents note taking. Should the audience need to take notes, slides may not be acceptable regardless of their advantages.

    c. Traps. Among the traps are these: the slides may be out of order in the carousel, the focusing device may be broken, the remote control (which allows the speaker to stand or sit some distance from the machine itself yet advance to the next slide or return to a previous one) may not work. Be sure to have a spare bulb on hand and know how to change it. Be sure everyone in the room can see the slides.

2. *Overhead projectors.*

    a. Advantages. Overhead projectors are nearly as clear as slides, but they have the additional advantage of being able to project images created on the spot.

    b. Disadvantages. Again, the room must be dark, unless the projector and screen are very good. Using overhead projectors requires speakers to stand by them, and, while writing, to turn their faces from the audience. Speakers should learn to arrange themselves so that only the head must be raised in order to see the audience, not so that the body needs to be turned also.

    c. Traps. Make sure that the marking pen actually marks the transparency well. Often, felt-tipped pens are water-based and the ink beads on the transparency, leaving illegible drops of color on the acetate. Again, be sure to have a spare bulb and know how to change it. Be sure everyone in the room can see the transparency.

3. *Flip charts.*

a. Advantages. Flip charts are excellent for audiences that need to take notes, for the lights need not be turned off. Moreover, what is written on them remains; that is, should a speaker need to return to a particular sheet of paper, the information is still there. In the interest of economy, many people erase transparencies.

b. Disadvantages. Flip charts are not so vivid as slides and transparencies. Flipping the page is a nuisance: it becomes noisy and distracting. Although it is difficult to face an audience while writing, practice makes it easy to write while half-turned toward an audience. This method allows the speaker to turn the head toward the audience without having to turn the body also.

c. Traps. Some flip chart stands can fall over at the slightest touch. Consequently, it is best for a speaker to test the flip-chart stand for stability.

4. *Microphones.* There are several kinds of microphones. All are used to amplify the voice, but some do it better than others, and some allow more freedom of movement than others.

a. Stationary microphone. These are of two kinds: the genuinely stationary and the supposedly stationary. The first kind is old and heavy. Its advantages are that it usually works, and because it is heavy it is both stationary and imperturbable. Its disadvantages are that its size limits the speaker's movement and may even hide the speaker's head. The supposedly stationary microphone is new and light. Its lightness allows it to be moved more easily, giving the speaker more freedom of movement. Its newness means that it is more temperamental, working well sometimes, not at all sometimes, and working sometimes most of the time. Sometimes the cord is heavier than the microphone, which can result in the microphone being dragged off the podium by the cord.

b. Lavaliere with cord. Lavalieres are small microphones that often clip to an article of clothing near the speaker's mouth. The cord extends from the microphone to an amplifier. Advantages of the lavaliere are that it frees the speaker's hands and allows considerable freedom of movement around the stage. Disadvantages are that the cord can get tangled, and the speaker can trip on the cord, pulling the microphone off the clothing; or the speaker can forget about the cord and walk beyond its reach.

c. Lavaliere without cord. These marvels of technology are wonderful when they work well. The most common problem concerns the placement of the lavaliere on clothing. Sometimes it becomes covered by a bit of cloth; when this happens, either no one can hear or the movement of the microphone against cloth creates weird and often unpleasant scratching noises. Make sure the clip is strong and that the space between the speaker's mouth and the microphone is filled only with air.

5. *Handouts*. Although not part of the room initially, when handouts are brought to the room, they become part of the equipment.

    a. Advantages. As members of the audience receive a set of handouts, they become a relatively intimate part of the audience-speaker relationship. Handouts are a kind of small gift from the speaker to the audience, and are appreciated as such. Moreover, each member may look at a given handout when it is convenient for the member, not necessarily for the speaker or for other members.

    b. Disadvantages. The individual convenience of handouts, however, is both advantageous and disadvantageous, for handouts also may distract audiences from the speech. Members of an audience also cannot see the speaker while looking at a sheet of paper.

    c. Traps. Make sure, when you refer to "Handout #1," that the information to which you are referring is indeed on "Handout #1." Few things distract and confuse audiences more than mislabeled handouts. As with all written material, make sure that the handouts display accurate spelling, perfect punctuation, and neatness. A polished speech may be ruined by sloppy handouts.

6. *Posterboards*. Posterboards are precisely the same sheets of colored cardboard that you used in grade school to show how flowers bloom in the spring. They work well for adults, too.

    a. Advantages. Vivid colors can be seen from great distances, and color-coding items on the board can help show differences and similarities. Moreover, they can be prepared in advance of the speech.

    b. Disadvantages. Posterboards are relatively small (usually about two feet by three feet) and cannot be used effectively to illustrate a great deal of information. Posterboards are most effective with simple information.

7. *Magnetized Boards*. These are about the same size as posterboards, but they are magnetic. Accompanying the board are smaller pieces, also magnetic, but of the opposite pole so they stick to the board.

    a. Advantages. Magnetized boards have the same advantages as posterboards, primarily that they can be prepared in advance. In addition, each piece of information can be presented as it is discussed, the smaller pieces added as the speech proceeds. Moreover, the highlights of the speech become plainly visible to all, reinforcing the main ideas and giving comfort to the audience. Finally, and importantly, the speaker also can write on these boards.

EXERCISE C: VISUAL AIDS

As veterans of the classroom, college students have nearly unequaled exposure to visual aids. Discuss particular glories and miserable failings that you have seen or heard.

A flip chart is a good visual aid for listeners who need to take notes.

b. Disadvantages. Magnetized boards attract gadgetry. In spite of their many advantages, magnetized boards often cause otherwise sensible people to create a picture that is much more complicated than the information that picture is supposed to simplify. In short, do not overdo it.

CREATE VISUAL AIDS

Visuals (graphs, charts, other figures, and tables) are extremely powerful — so powerful, in fact, that they sometimes distract the audience from the words of the speech. To keep the audience attentive to the point at hand, a visual must illustrate *only* the given point. Extraneous data are the worst enemies of good visuals. Keep visuals simple and keep them on the subject. Decide, of course, which method of presenting each visual works best for the kind of speech, and for the limitations and advantages of the room and audience. In addition to the types of equipment mentioned on pages 373–75, see the section on visuals in Chapter 16.

INSERT SOME HUMOR

Humor depends as much on its manner of presentation as it does on the words presented. Humor somewhere in a speech is almost always helpful, but inappropriate humor is almost always disastrous. Humor must be appropriate to the audience, to the subject, and to the place in the speech.

MANNER OF PRESENTATION. Study stand-up comics. Try to learn a bit about timing and intonation. Remember also that humor that attacks others is most difficult to achieve, and can be inappropriate; humor that attacks oneself is most easy to achieve, and has the advantage of being received better.

Do not say, for example, *"I once saw a man, much like you, Sir (pointing),* fishing in a boat at night. After forty minutes of *his* companion's catching fish and *his* not catching anything, *he* checked his line only to discover that he had cast his line into the bottom of the boat itself. What a fool! Always check your line every few minutes." Say, rather, *"I once sat in a boat,* fishing at night. After forty minutes of *my* companion's catching fish and *my* not catching anything, *I* checked my line only to discover that I had cast *my* line into the bottom of the boat itself. What a fool! Always check your line every few minutes."

APPROPRIATENESS. What you think is funny is not necessarily what others think is funny. Make sure that you know the audience sufficiently well before inserting a joke or humorous story into the speech. An otherwise excellent speech may be ruined by humor considered inappropriate by an audience, or even by certain members of an audience.

PLACEMENT. Do not place all the humor in one place in a speech. Use it to reinforce a point or as comic relief, or both. That is, when a long train of depressing, dull, or otherwise serious information begins to overload the audience, they will begin to become bored. Appropriately placed humor may regain their attention. Remember that audience attention begins high, slides fast, and climbs in anticipation of the end. Humor may help keep the audience's attention from sliding too far.

THE VALUE OF HUMOR. Many people believe that humor has no place in business, that people should be all business. They are wrong. Robert Half, International, a large recruiting company, commissioned a study of executives in one hundred of the largest 1,000 companies in the United States regarding the place of humor in business. Of them, 84 percent believe that employees with a sense of humor do a better job than humorless employees.[5]

PRACTICE ON TAPE

Good speeches are made in a small room, the speaker being alone with a tape recorder. Flaws in organization, intonation, emphasis, and clarity first become apparent here. Because speeches may *look* well organized on paper, but may fail utterly when spoken, speeches must be practiced orally. Finding out that the speech needs to be reorganized in the middle of delivering it to an audience is an unsettling experience

---

[5]Margaret M. Bedrosian, *Speak Like a Pro* (New York: John Wiley & Sons, 1987), 161.

for speaker and audience alike. Moreover, by then, the damage is done. Practicing a speech is the equivalent of editing a report, and is a good time to listen to certain qualities of your own voice, specifically tone, intensity, enunciation, and pronunciation.

TONE. Good posture not only improves appearance, but it also improves the tone of voice. By relaxing the voice and speaking from the diaphragm, speakers may lower and enrich their voices, both desirable effects. By lowering the normal pitch of the voice (but not so low that it sounds affected), speakers increase the range of their voices, enabling them to express a greater range of emotion than would be possible otherwise. Remember also that a voice should be sufficiently loud to be heard by all, but should not be so loud that it damages the eardrums of the audience.

ENUNCIATION. Many people tend not to enunciate the syllables of words. "Government," for example, often is pronounced "guvment." Slurring syllables is so pronounced and so common that many people never realize that they do not enunciate or articulate their words. Fortunately, speakers can correct easily and simply the tendency to elide syllables by paying attention to the words they speak and doing their best to enunciate syllables more clearly. The real trick is to practice enunciation until syllables are articulated without speaking more slowly than normal.

Just as it is important to enunciate the syllables, it is equally important to pronounce words separately. People speak many phrases quickly without significant loss of meaning, but most strings of words benefit the speaker and the listener when they are spoken as separate words.

PRONUNCIATION. Enunciating words in a pleasant and varied tone is a great step toward good speaking, but it goes for naught should the words be pronounced incorrectly. Speakers should consult a dictionary for any words they are not sure how to pronounce. This may require looking at the pronunciation key that most dictionaries provide at the bottom of every page. It also is a good idea to practice the speech before a few people who can identify which words are pronounced incorrectly.

Although a speaker can do little about some things, there are many things a speaker must do. Here is a list of common concerns and common methods of dealing with them.

SPEECH-MAKING CHECKLIST
Before making a speech, answer each of these questions.
1. How loudly must I speak in order to be heard by everyone?
2. Will *everyone* be able to hear no matter the seat?
3. Will *everyone* be able to see me and the visuals?
4. Will *everyone* be comfortable for the duration of the speech?
5. Do I know enough about the microphone to use it effortlessly?
6. Are all visual aids clear and simple?

......

EXERCISE D: ENUNCIATION

Practice the following words out of class and then in class. Try first to enunciate each syllable, and then to enunciate each syllable without speaking more slowly.

continent	remember
proposition	measure
hallow	freedom
altogether	dedicated
unfinished	consecrate
remaining	detract
liberty	devotion
created	resolve
power	government

......

EXERCISE E: ENUNCIATION

Practice the following, the first paragraph of Lincoln's Gettysburg Address, until a listener can hear each word separately.

Fourscore and seven years ago our fathers brought forth on this continent, a new nation, conceived in Liberty, and dedicated to the proposition that all men are created equal.

......

EXERCISE F: PRONUNCIATION

Here are a few words commonly mispronounced. Consult a dictionary, and correctly pronounce each word ten times.

comptroller	Uranus
filet	fillet
data	accidentally
cretin	motel
valet	liquidity
err	hotel

7. Am I dressed appropriately and well groomed?
8. Do I know the kind of audience that will be there?

By now it should be clear that speaking is different from reading and writing. Reading and writing are intimate. Something happens between a page and the eye, and it all occurs in the space of a few inches. Speaking is different. Speaking is affected by the size of a room, the number of chairs and their arrangement, the lighting, and the voice and words of the speaker. Moreover, to all this must be added unforeseeable vagaries of the world: jack hammers pounding away outside the room, broken heating systems, dingy walls, chewing gum on chairs, people with hacking coughs, and late arrivals, to name only a few.

ANTICIPATE QUESTIONS

The more experience speakers have, the better able they are to anticipate the questions that come from audiences. Speakers who have presented the same subject a number of times, also have heard almost all the questions before and have developed answers for most of them. Even here, however, they may find a question coming from a direction not anticipated. New discoveries and recent events conspire to provide new angles on the subject, and speakers should be prepared to respond to them.

Beginning speakers need to spend much time anticipating questions. Perhaps the best ways are these: (1) know the subject extremely well and think much about it; (2) give the speech to a friend or several friends, asking them to formulate questions. These allow the speaker to revise the speech in anticipation of the questions.

ORAL REPORTS

Oral reports are among the most important means in business of conveying information. The ability to present oral reports well is also among the most important attributes of successful managers. Good oral reports earn the presenter the admiration of subordinates, the respect of colleagues, and promotions from superiors. This ability is so important, in fact, that an employee cannot hope to rise far in a company without it.

THE DIFFERENCES BETWEEN PUBLIC SPEAKING AND ORAL REPORTS

Although good public speakers tend to give good oral reports as well, it is not only because they have practiced qualities common to all good speaking. It is also because they know the differences between public speeches and oral reports. Here are those differences.

DIFFERENCES BETWEEN PUBLIC SPEECHES AND ORAL REPORTS

1. Most oral reports are internal — that is, given within the walls of the company. Because both the audience and the speaker are employees, the audience knows the speaker and the subject better than public audiences may know the speaker and the subject.

2. Although persuasion is often as important in oral reports as in public speeches, the appeals in oral reports are confined to facts and reason; emotional appeals carry little weight.

3. Oral reports are more often interrupted by questions than are public speeches. This complicates the attempt to keep to a strict schedule and organization.

4. Oral reports are typically informative, brief, and have both captive and interested audiences.

OUTLINING ORAL REPORTS

Because oral reports are no-nonsense presentations, they tend to follow a no-nonsense outline similar to those of written reports. Two significant differences between written and oral reports are that the speaker first thanks the person who performed the brief introduction and that tables and figures normally appearing in a report are transferred to one or more of the visual methods (transparency, slides, and so on) for speeches discussed previously. Here is a typical outline.

OUTLINE FOR ORAL REPORTS

I. Introduction
    Purpose
    Problem
    Scope

II. Body
    Main Point 1
        Factual Support
    Main Point 2
        Factual Support
    Main Point 3
        Factual Support

III. Conclusion
    Summary
    Recommendations

INTRODUCTION.   An oral report contains no jokes, no stories, no warming up other than perhaps a brief overview of the purpose of the report and a reminder of the problems faced by the company regarding the subject of the speech. The scope section becomes merely a statement of the organization of the body of the report. For example, a speaker might end the introduction by saying the following:

As many of you may know, having been part of the discussions, the company has been forced to consider a smoking policy for all employees for three reasons: recent state and local legislation, discoveries of enormous health costs associated with smoking, and complaints from employees regarding smoking. The purpose of this report is to provide information regarding the *kind* of policy the company will promulgate and enforce.

A brief statement like this one introduces the subject and outlines the body of the report in one sentence, requiring about twenty seconds to utter. Moreover, the statement cuts off any discussion regarding *whether* such a policy should be introduced. That, it is clear, has been decided already. Speakers should always anticipate potential polarizations. Even a speech about smoking policy provokes much strong feeling on both sides among a few people, and much rational argument to be gathered from both sides. This talk, however, is to discuss the *kind* of policy, *not* whether there will be one; consequently, the introduction does well to snip off this side branch before it has a chance to grow.

BODY.   The body of the report may then begin, without further introduction, with the first main point: recent state and local legislation. Facts, preferably numbers, provide most of the support. The speaker might say, for example,

> A survey by the Bureau of National Affairs discovered that of the 662 companies responding to the survey, 59 percent either had or were considering smoking policies. Of these, 28 percent established smoking policies because of state laws or local ordinances.[6] Of this 28 percent (185 companies), 41 percent (76 companies) complied with the minimal requirements of the laws banning smoking in open offices and shared work spaces, and 56 percent (104) permit smoking in private offices. Only two percent (4) banned smoking within all company property.

The second main point would discuss the policy from the perspective of health costs: lost time related to smoking and direct medical benefit costs. Most likely, visuals would provide this information. The third main point would discuss the policy from the perspective of complaints by non-smoking employees: turnover, lawsuits, lowered productivity.

CONCLUSION.   A good closing to an oral report involves perhaps two parts: The first part is a summary of the discussion in the body, the second part concerns recommendations. If the body presents facts, the closing draws conclusions and makes recommendations derived from those facts.

---

[6]Bureau of National Affairs, "Where's the Smoke?" (Washington, D.C.: GPO, 1986), 7.

DICTATION

Dictation seems to be a simple matter, but it is more common than oral presentations, and more commonly done badly than oral reports. Were it not for intelligent secretaries, many dictated letters and memoranda would be incomprehensible. Fortunately, many secretaries are more literate than those around them. The following list presents guidelines for dictating correspondence to secretaries.

RULES FOR DICTATION

1. *Outline.* List and rank the points to be made.

2. *Instruct.* List special requirements: double spacing, number of photocopies, letterhead.

3. *Enunciate.* Each word must be spoken clearly. Be precise with numbers. Do not chew on clothing, handkerchiefs, golf tees, or rubber ducks while speaking.

4. *Spell* difficult words (fluorescent), unusual names ("Taliaferro" is pronounced "Talliver") or unusual spellings of names ("Smyth," "Sean," or the occasional American spelling of "Sean": "Shawn"), and others easily misunderstood for other words (e.g., "allude," "elude").

5. *Avoid sounds used to fill the mouth* when the mind is empty: "well," "um," "ah," and "ya'know." You know?

6. *Prepare typists* for capital letters, parentheses, underlines, and initial quotation marks by mentioning these things before the word is spoken. Indicate end quotation marks and end parentheses immediately. "Oh, by the way, the last sentence should be underlined" is a sure way to have your paychecks disappear, your coffee cold, and your memoranda sent next door by way of Murmansk.

7. *Announce a new paragraph* before it is begun.

8. *Say "period"* at the end of declarative sentences, "question mark" following interrogative sentences, "colon" and "semicolon" whenever fitting.

9. *Proofread transcriptions.* Correspondence is the responsibility of the person whose signature appears there. Do not blame secretaries for illiteracies. No one else will.

10. *Do not cough, mumble, or gargle* in front of a recorder; do not take coffee breaks, play with your putter, or otherwise create long pauses on a recording tape. Doing so tries the patience of secretaries and wastes their time.

EXERCISE G: DICTATION

Play a tape recording of a dictated letter in class. Each student should write the good and bad qualities of the dictation. Discuss those qualities.

SUMMARY

1. Impediments to listening include long speeches, important points not emphasized, the many ways audiences distort information, short attention spans, the time of day, irrelevant or unwelcome information, poor hearing, and listening solely for facts.

2. Of the many rules of good listening, two are especially important: pay attention, and listen actively.

3. Overcoming the fear of speaking in public is best done by preparing well and remembering that a few butterflies are not only normal, but also beneficial to good speaking.

4. We speak in public because we want recognition or money, we want to persuade, and we want to make things happen.

5. There are several kinds of public speeches: impromptu, extemporaneous, written, and recited. Most speeches are combinations of these kinds.

6. Preparing to speak involves choosing a subject; defining a purpose; selecting a persona; analyzing the audience; studying the subject; organizing the speech; writing the body, conclusion, and—usually *last*—the introduction; studying the room and equipment, deciding on examples and creating visual aids; inserting humor; anticipating questions; and practicing, practicing, practicing.

7. Planning a speech must include choosing a method of development: temporal, categorical, priorital, spatial, or topical.

8. The following order for writing the parts of speeches is common: (1) detailed body, (2) conclusion, and (3) introduction.

9. Planning the delivery of a speech includes preparing attention-getting devices and pertinent examples, illustrations, visuals, and humor.

10. Oral reports differ from public speeches because they are internal to the company. Therefore, they are no-nonsense speeches that go immediately to the point and proceed without fanfare to the conclusion. And yet, also because they are internal, oral reports are less formal than public speeches.

11. Good dictation requires speakers to place themselves in the position of the typist. If a manager wants good, clear letters, then good, clear speaking is necessary.

EXERCISES

Many of the following exercises ask you to evaluate speakers and speeches from a variety of perspectives. The following chart may be used to evaluate a speaker or speech from any or all perspectives. The evaluation form is arranged to provide for a five-point rating scale (5 is excellent, 4 is good, 3 is average, 2 is poor, and 1 is very poor).

NAME _____

DATE _____

TOPIC _____

		5	4	3	2	1
Organization	Introduction					
	Body					
	Conclusion					

		5	4	3	2	1
Content	Research					
	Details					
	Materials					
Delivery	Posture					
	Voice					
	Eye contact					
	Timing					
	Totals					

COMMENTS

1. *The jitters.* List the causes of your jitters from public speaking. List the solutions to most of those jitters. Be prepared to discuss the problem in class.

2. *Paying attention.* Attend a speech. During part of that speech, list all the distracting inanimate objects in the room: air conditioners, lights, colors, shapes, and so on. Later, describe in good prose why each of these was distracting (3–4 paragraphs); or be prepared to discuss the problem in class.

3. *Observing the speaker.* Attend a speech. During part of that speech, list all the distracting actions of the speaker: gestures, noises, hems and haws, "you knows," and movements. Later, describe in good prose why each of these was distracting (3–4 paragraphs); or be prepared to discuss the problem in class.

4. *Following the organization of a speech.* Attend a speech. During part of that speech, list all the main points of that speech. Afterward, try to reconstruct the outline of the speech. If a classmate attended also, then compare lists. You may find they are different. Discuss why that is so.

5. *Impromptu speech.* Give a two-minute impromptu speech on one of the following subjects.

    When I graduate I want to . . .

    The thing I like best about this school is . . .

    The thing I dislike most about this school is . . .

    When I retire, I want to . . .

6. *Extemporaneous speech.* After five minutes of preparation, give a two-minute extemporaneous speech on one of the following subjects.

    When I graduate, I plan to . . .

    The best professor I ever had was good because . . .

    Ice cream

    Peanut butter

7. *Writing a speech.* Write a one-minute speech on any of the subjects provided in Exercises 5 and 6. Try to write so it will sound good when delivered orally.

8. *Analyzing an audience.* Attend a speech. Using the Reader Profile on page 31, analyze the audience. Do not be afraid to generalize, but be prepared to support your claims with more than feeling; and be prepared to discuss the problem in class.

9. *Analyzing one member of an audience.* Attend a speech. Using the Reader Profile on page 31, analyze *one* member of the audience. Do not be afraid to generalize, but be prepared to support your claims with more than feeling; and be prepared to discuss the problem in class.

10. *The big speech.* Prepare a full-blown, all-out, ten-minute speech on a subject about which you know much, or must know much by the end of the semester or quarter.

11. *Practicing.* In front of a friend, practice the speech you wrote for Exercise 10. Discuss the good and bad points and how the bad points might be eliminated or improved.

12. *Examining the speech.* Examine your ten-minute speech for places in which you might be able to use visual and oral aids effectively. Integrate those aids and practice again.

13. *Dictation.* Dictate your one-minute written speech into a tape recorder. Have a classmate listen to the tape and type what you said. Read the dictation, and then play the tape, listing all the good and not-so-good points. Then repeat the process, only this time you type for your classmate.

CASE STUDY: FIVE-MINUTE SPEECH

You are a newly hired (right out of college) member of the staff of Fahrquart Industries, Inc. Smedley Fahrquart, CEO, has asked you to represent the company as the after-dinner speaker at the local Rotary Club. The subject he suggests for your speech is "Undergraduate Preparation for the World of Work." You've got a week to prepare, but fortunately, Fahrquart tells you, "For goodness sake, don't talk for more than five minutes. And make it lively. Those people get sleepy and bored after dinner." Write the speech and deliver it in class.

CHALLENGE EXERCISE 1: THE ETHICS OF GOOD LISTENING

Knowing that speakers are manipulated—encouraged or discouraged—by our listening methods, what distinguishes ethical manipulation from unethical? Is there such a thing as ethical manipulation? If so, provide examples; if not, how should we listen? Be prepared to discuss this exercise in class, and be prepared to argue your side of the issue of ethical manipulation, yes or no.

CHALLENGE EXERCISE 2: A BIG SPEECH

Prepare and give in class a fifteen-minute speech.

CHALLENGE EXERCISE 3: ORAL REPORTS

Choose one of the reports that you wrote for Chapter 9 or 10. Convert that written report into an oral report of, say, 10 minutes.

CHALLENGE EXERCISE 4: FIVE-MINUTE SPEECH

Choose a hot campus issue and prepare a *lively* five-minute public speech.

CHALLENGE EXERCISE 5: IMPROMPTU SPEECH

In class, write on a piece of paper the topic of a business-related issue, encompassable by a three-minute speech.

Then fold your paper and place it in a box. Each student then draws a topic from the box and gives a three-minute impromptu speech.

CHALLENGE EXERCISE 6: EXTEMPORANEOUS SPEECH

Each student gives a five-minute speech on a topic selected by the instructor.

CHAPTER OUTLINE

▼

Learning Objectives:

☐ Know the importance of nonverbal
communication.

☐ Use nonverbal communication, including body language, grooming,
and dress.

☐ Work with small groups to solve
problems.

☐ Choose the best group organization for solving problems.

☐ Know the different roles of group
leaders and members.

☐ Know the technology of international communications.

☐ Recognize the need for understanding and patience in intercultural communications.

▲

CHECKLIST

[PEOPLE SHOULD] NOT
BE JUDGED BY THE COLOR
OF THEIR SKIN BUT BY
THE CONTENT OF THEIR
CHARACTER.

MARTIN LUTHER
KING, JR.
(1929–1968)

THE INNER AND OUTER WORLDS OF COMMUNICATION

THE BEST PART OF HUMAN
LANGUAGE . . . IS DERIVED
FROM REFLECTION ON THE
ACTS OF THE MIND ITSELF.

SAMUEL TAYLOR
COLERIDGE
(1772–1834)

Talking without Words

Because nearly everyone has eyes as well as ears, communication occurs without words. In fact, Americans are so bombarded with pictures—billboards, neon signs, television—that we depend more heavily on them than perhaps any other people. Some researchers suggest that we receive more than half our information from nonverbal forms of communication.[1] One suggests that only 7 percent comes from words, while 93 percent comes from other sources.[2]

People think almost exclusively in words, but communication involves other activities also. Perhaps nonverbal communication is the predominant way in which people convey how they *feel*. And, since feelings are an integral part of how we think and behave, a study of nonverbal communication is important for business.

Nonverbal communication is important also for speakers and listeners. Speakers who consciously use nonverbal methods of communication help their audiences learn and understand better. Listeners who closely observe the speaker may learn more than they would by listening only to the speaker's words.

The difference between verbal and nonverbal communications is one of *precision*. Words can be precise; many gestures, kinds of dress, and other forms of nonverbal communication cannot always, or even most often, be so precise. Nonverbal communications are easily misinterpreted. Consequently, speakers and audiences must not rely solely on nonverbal communications. It is possible that someone who smiles is angry, not pleased. A speaker who holds hands up with palms toward the audience may not be warding off comments, but actually inviting them. Shaking the head does not always mean that one is saying no. Nonverbal communications are very subtle, and one can seldom take a single clue and generalize an entire attitude from it. Still, that very subtlety demands that speakers and audiences attend to nonverbal communications carefully.

Body Language

American businesses and corporations will generally reward, through increased salary and promotions, those professionals who project effectively. A well-polished image gives you a genuine competitive edge and stamps you as someone on the way up.

Susan Bixler,
The Professional Image

Body language includes everything we do with our bodies, other than actually speaking, to convey information. Facial expressions, postures, and body movements convey feelings, and they serve either to reinforce words or to contradict them.

Gestures. The most obvious nonverbal communication is in the form of *symbolic gestures*. During World War II, for example, Winston Churchill used his index and middle fingers to form a V. This sign

---

[1] Randall Harrison, *Beyond Words: An Introduction to Nonverbal Communication* (Englewood Cliffs, N.J.: Prentice-Hall, 1974).

[2] Albert Mehrabian, "Commmunication without Words," *Psychology Today* (September 1968), 53–55.

People convey how they *feel* through nonverbal communication.

became famous among the allies, standing for "Victory." Churchill used the sign when appearing before crowds and cameras. Millions of people saw it, identified with it, and repeated it. Napoleon's formal pose included placing part of his hand inside his jacket. Now everyone who wants to mock a formal pose does the same. The Nazi salute is a gesture, and people who want to mock ruthless totalitarianism sometimes use it.

Other gestures include the referee who draws the edge of a flattened hand across the back of the calf to indicate a clipping penalty in a football game or the traffic officer who holds an arm out, palm facing drivers, to indicate "Stop!" When a television program director whirls a hand in a circle it tells the person before the camera to hurry or to finish quickly; the sponsor wants a commercial. Similarly, looking at a watch repeatedly indicates impatience, and placing the hands palms down indicates "slow down" or "calm down."

The old saying "She wears her heart on her sleeve," meaning that her every emotion is visible, is really inaccurate. Most of us wear our hearts on our faces. These emotional gestures are sometimes difficult to control, and sometimes we are not even aware that our emotional reactions are so transparent. The most obvious of these is the red face that comes from embarrassment. Others include shifting the eyes when not telling the truth, smiling when pleased, and frowning when displeased.

When we turn our heads away and place our arms and hands in front of us, we are expressing fear or are warding off danger. They are reactions that our primordial ancestors used and that we still use. Few of them are controllable. When we meet someone on the street, but we have no time to speak, we tend to smile or raise our eyebrows in recognition of the other person.

Does the man's body language convey agreement or disagreement with what the speaker is saying?

THE HEAD.   The head, of course, is the most expressive part of the body. Everyone is familiar with nodding to mean "yes" or "I agree" or "Tell me more; I understand," and with shaking to mean "No" or "I think you're wrong" or "I don't want to hear any more." There is much more. Holding the head high and looking down at someone conveys just what we always thought it did: a sense of superiority. Similarly, holding the head down, looking up at someone, conveys the opposite: submission.

Eyes that look directly at another's register attention. People who do this may agree or disagree with us; the only thing certain is that they are paying attention. Raised eyebrows often indicate surprise or interest. Pursed lips may suggest anything from thoughtfulness to disagreement. And, of course, the entire face expresses many moods. Closed eyes indicate sleepiness, boredom, or an attempt to close out what the other person is saying. Rarely does it mean concentration on the words being spoken. Staring at the ceiling indicates boredom.

The wise speaker or listener is constantly looking at people's expressions, trying to determine what they mean. Most people have idiosyncratic expressions, peculiar only to them, that tell us much about what they are thinking and feeling.

THE BODY.   The body that leans toward us is either interested in us or being aggressive toward us. Conversely, the body leaning away is uninterested or passive or just trying to get away from us or what we are saying.

Posture, or how we hold our bodies while sitting or standing, often telegraphs our thoughts or emotions. Our mothers were correct

As distances shrink, members of other cultures may begin to look Western, but they still retain their own ways of thinking and acting. Bridging these differences is the challenge of international communication.

No man is an island, entire of itself; every man is a piece of the continent, a part of the main.
John Donne (1572-1631)

INTERNATIONAL COMMUNICATION

No man or woman, no company, and no country — metaphorically — is an island. The recent technological revolution in communications, the merging of European economies, and the lifting or easing of trade barriers among other nations have all but erased the geographical and tempo-ral barriers that have defined international business for centuries. They have changed for-ever the way that people conduct business internationally.

The one barrier that re-mains, however, is cul-ture. Conducting international business successfully will depend less on our training in technology and more on our ability to understand cultural similarities and differences. This is as true today as it was for Donne's time: understanding those unlike ourselves is the foundation of international communication.

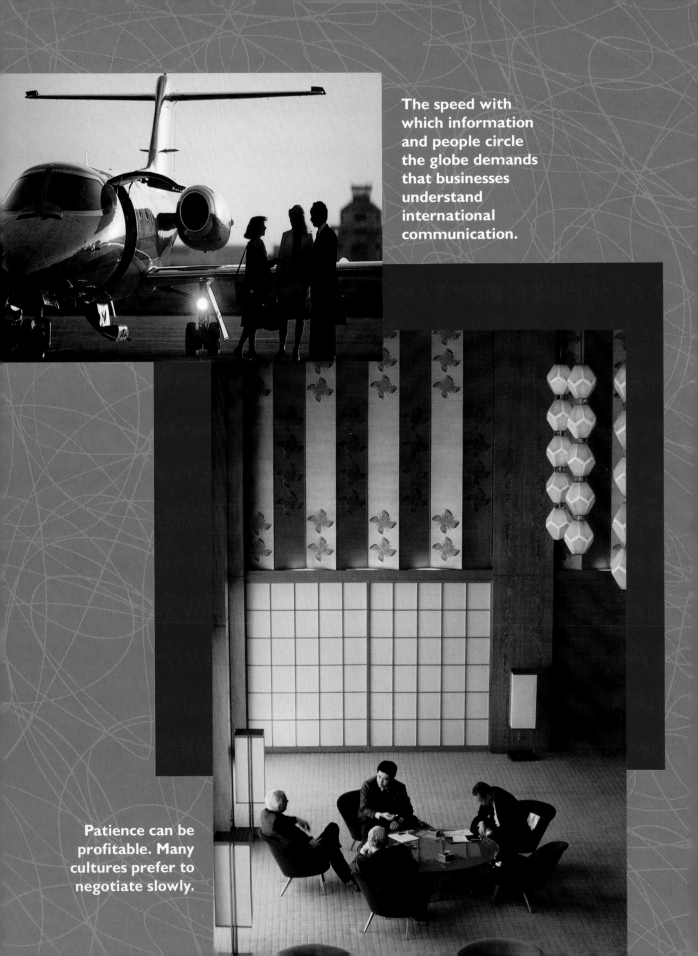

The speed with which information and people circle the globe demands that businesses understand international communication.

Patience can be profitable. Many cultures prefer to negotiate slowly.

Clear communication with nonnative speakers of English requires listening carefully, speaking slowly, simplifying words and sentences, and using numbers and visuals.

Similar interests create the foundation for agreement among people of all cultures.

FAX machines have revolutionized international business, sending documents inexpensively and almost instantaneously across continents and across the world.

To decode body language, we must pay attention to each other's gestures, expressions, and posture, while remembering that interpretation of these nonspoken messages differs from one culture to another.

The sociology of international communication is as complex as the nations, races, religions, and ethnic groups that form the world.

Computer-to-computer transfer of data and documents can be conveyed electronically to anywhere in the world.

when they told us to stand or sit straight. An erect, almost ramrod-straight back conveys confidence and competence to others. The way we hold and move our shoulders is similarly expressive. Hunched shoulders indicate uncertainty, and squared shoulders convey certainty.

Arms are extremely expressive. When folded across the chest, arms display defensiveness. Held high over the head, arms convey either surrender or jubilation. Hands placed behind the head, elbows forward, while the person is sitting, convey superiority. A person whose elbow is on a table and whose chin is resting in the palm of the hand is often expressing boredom.

Crossed legs pointed away from another person is a defensive posture. Uncrossed legs, body leaning toward another person, indicate openness, sometimes intimacy. Crossed ankles sometimes display a mild fear. Moving a foot while the legs are crossed often indicates boredom. Standing pigeon-toed, head down, Huckleberry Finn fashion, conveys shyness or submissiveness.

Finally, body language provides clues to the thoughts and emotions of others and of ourselves. While we should not rely solely — or even primarily — on body language, knowing something about the way people use their bodies consciously and unconsciously to convey thoughts and emotions is helpful to people in business. Such knowledge is most helpful to those who want to control their own body language.

GROOMING AND DRESS

EXERCISE A: WHAT IS "APPROPRIATE" DRESS?

Discuss in class the appropriate dress for the following situations:

1. An ordinary day at the office
2. A business golf date
3. Dinner with a client at a good restaurant

Dressing properly for white-collar work requires some effort. Just as our body language should not distract from our speech, so our dress should not draw attention away from what we are saying or doing. Manner of dress should reinforce, even improve, an image of composure. How we look provides others with their first impression of us, and first impressions, as we know, are extremely important. People who are properly dressed and groomed are accepted and listened to more readily.

To learn how to dress for business, observe carefully the successful business people you know, and read such books as *Dress for Success* and *Dress for Excellence*.[3] One common fallacy is that business people need large and expensive wardrobes. Clothing can be well pressed, appropriate, and good looking without being expensive. Should you belong to a college business club, you would do well to invite a respected clothier in town to come to a club meeting (or even to class) and discuss some of the tricks to dressing appropriately, well, and inexpensively.

While it is important to pay close attention to dress (corporations, like all tribes, have their own styles of dress), the temptation also exists

---

[3]John T. Molloy, *Dress for Success* (New York: Warner Books, 1984); Lois Fenton and Edward Olvott, *Dress for Excellence: The Executive Guide to Looking Like a Leader* (New York: Rawson Associates, 1986).

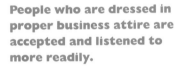

People who are dressed in proper business attire are accepted and listened to more readily.

to become obsessed with clothing—especially after we begin, for the first time in our lives, to make money. Remember that although everyone *notices* the grooming and dress, do not succumb to the temptation to *talk about* grooming and dress in business situations. Grooming and dress, while very important, are not supposed to be very important. Those who talk about these things too much are seen as silly and as people who cannot distinguish between form (grooming and dress) and substance (the individual's abilities).

Unused to dressing up, many students are uncomfortable when they do. Because they are uncomfortable, everyone else is uncomfortable also, including interviewers and audiences. Students can overcome this discomfort by dressing up every day for about a week before the interview or the speech. For students who do not have extensive wardrobes or extensive bank accounts to pay for cleaning bills, such activity is impractical. It is not impractical, however, to dress occasionally for a date, a party, religious services, or even class. The point is to dress often enough to get used to it, so as not to be tugging constantly at a collar or a skirt during a speech.

COMMUNICATING IN SMALL GROUPS[4]

In business, "small group" has a particular definition: five to seven people working toward a common goal. Fewer than five people seldom have sufficient information to proceed effectively, and more than seven people tend to lose the individuality required for decisive action.

---

[4]Further information may be found in numerous books about speaking in business. One good example is Kenneth B. Mayer, *Well Spoken: Oral Communication Skills for Business* (San Diego: Harcourt Brace Jovanovich, 1989).

THE ADVANTAGES OF SMALL GROUPS

PROBLEM SOLVING.   Small group discussions can be excellent ways to bring together people who know about or are affected by a problem. By having several people address and analyze a problem, that problem can be resolved to everyone's satisfaction, or at least with everyone's concurrence. Often, a side benefit occurs: people with differing points of view come face to face to present their perspectives and to reconcile them. Often people may change their minds or at least understand and appreciate other perspectives when those views are aired in a small group.

EFFICIENCY.   Small groups may be gathered to receive information that otherwise must be delivered in writing. If everyone concerned can hear a report at the same time, they can gather, exchange, and modify information at one meeting. Moreover, they can work out disagreements more quickly in a meeting than if each person responded to a report in writing. Finally, small groups often provide an efficient means around the inevitable bureaucracy that forms in organizations.

TRAINING.   Rather than introducing each person to a new procedure or directive individually, introducing these to people in small groups provides more efficient use of time, and an opportunity for these people to learn from each other.

THE DISADVANTAGES OF SMALL GROUPS

Small groups in the guise of committees get much bad press, as illustrated by the saying "a camel is a horse designed by a committee." Too often the criticism is deserved, for small groups often are badly led. To avoid some of the disadvantages of small groups, people should be aware of the disadvantages.

COST.   If five people earning an average of $40,000 a year meet weekly for two hours, the annual cost to the company would be $10,000. Consequently, the benefits — the value of the advice received and information provided — should be worth $10,000 a year before calling that small group together every week. The committee chair might do better to ask whether meeting once every two weeks ($5,000) or even every four weeks ($2,500) might not be more cost effective.

Other considerations include travel time and expense, three- and four-hour meetings, as well as typing and distributing the agenda or reports. In fact, the real cost of small-group meetings is best determined by doubling the direct labor costs.[5] For example, the annual direct labor costs of the hypothetical small-group meeting given in the previous paragraph is $10,000, but the true cost is closer to $20,000.

PRESSURES: TIME AND HIERARCHY.   Although small groups work well only if they are efficient, other pressures may undo an otherwise productive effort. When members agree to end the meeting only so they can get back to work, the agreement may not provide the best solutions. Moreover, subordinates may feel pressured to agree with a boss's proposal. Sometimes, subordinates mistakenly believe that bosses want such responses. The job of persuading small groups that this is not the case belongs to the boss. Finally, small groups inevitably conform to an unspoken social rule: the majority is more important (and "more right") than the minority. That is, majorities tend to pressure individuals to conform, and part of that conformity results in individuals acceding to the majority, even if the individuals believe that the majority is wrong. To avoid this problem, members must listen as objectively to the opinions of individuals as they do to those of the majority.

Hidden Agendas. Too often, one or two people within a small group want a particular decision from the group before the group ever gets together. When these people are prepared to sacrifice the best decision for the decision they want for their own reasons, the group process breaks down. Individuals must examine their motives and realize that their decisions are not always the only right ones.

The Kinds of Small Groups

Staff Meetings. The most common kind of small group, the staff meeting usually is a regular meeting of a boss and several subordinates. The tasks here are to inform, to plan, and to solve. Members are given information they need to know; they plan activities, and they solve problems. Sometimes the consensus becomes the decision (consultative meetings); sometimes the boss gathers information and opinions from members and then makes the decision alone (advisory meetings).

Committees. There are two types of committees: standing and ad hoc. Standing committees meet regularly and have a general charge. They may be charged with planning policy, carrying out policy, or assessing policy. Such committees are most effective when staffed with people who have different points of view and different kinds of knowledge. Ad hoc committees are one-time groups appointed to address a specific question, problem, or situation. A paper company may create an ad hoc committee to assess the effects on their industry of a new environmental law. Another company may create an ad hoc committee to determine the kind of computer system that will be best for the company for the next ten years.

Training groups. These groups are rather like college classes. One person (or several people, each with a particular expertise) in-

---

[5]Kenneth B. Mayer, *Well Spoken: Oral Communication Skills for Business* (San Diego: Harcourt Brace Jovanovich, 1989), 184.

A one-to-one training
session.

structs, and the rest learn. Such situations are not solely lectures from
the instructor. Questions from the group are encouraged, and because
many group members have a great deal of experience, contributions of
their knowledge are encouraged as well.

CONFERENCES.   Often companies decide to make big changes. To
decide what to do, they hold conferences. That is, they announce a big
theme, say, "Fahrquart Industries in the Twenty-First Century," and
then small groups form around this theme, each group addressing a
more specific question: "Office Design for the Year 2000," "Just-in-
Time Manufacturing: How Soon Can We Have It?" Because conferences can be expensive, they must be extraordinarily well planned,
and the planning often is given over to a conference director and a
small group that forms an ad hoc committee.

THE METHODS OF WORKING IN SMALL GROUPS

Although there are as many ways of working well in small groups as
there are small groups, it is best in the beginning to choose a specific
method that seems to fit the group or the job best. As members of a
group become accustomed to working together, the method will modify to take advantage of the peculiar strengths of that group.

DEMOCRATIC METHOD.   As its name implies, the democratic
method stresses the individual and minimizes hierarchies. This method

allows individuals of whatever rank or status in the organization to have their views aired. The steps are these.

1. *State the problem*. The leader carefully delineates the problem, being careful not to imply any particular direction for finding solutions.
2. *List the ideas*. Each member compiles a list of ideas addressing the problem.
3. *Record the ideas*. Members individually read aloud from their lists and the leader records them on paper, a chalkboard, transparency, or some other medium.
4. *Vote*. Members vote for each idea, on a scale of 5 (best) to 1 (worst). Scores are summed and posted.
5. *Discuss*. Members talk about each item, fully airing its advantages and disadvantages.
6. *Revise*. After the discussion, members revise, delete, or add to the ideas.
7. *Final Vote*. Members vote again, and the ideas with the highest number of votes win.

BRAINSTORMING METHOD. At its best, this method produces free-wheeling discussions that the uninitiated might think are merely noisy. Brainstorming can be extremely effective when ideas come by free association — that is, without careful thinking. Still, there are steps to follow.

1. *Define the problem*. The leader first defines the problem. The leader's only other role is to try to keep the ideas from going too far from the problem at hand.
2. *Brainstorm*. Beginning with the first idea, others think out loud by speaking their ideas.
3. *Record the Ideas*. The leader records these ideas on a chalkboard. Because ideas come so often and so quickly, the person acting as leader may change several times during the session. People wear out.
4. *Discuss the Ideas*. Only after everyone runs out of ideas, or the time runs out, does the group begin to discuss the details of the ideas presented.

ROUND-TABLE METHOD. The round-table method may be used with any other method. It makes the procedure seem more democratic; that is, bosses and subordinates are not placed in superior or subordinate positions in the room, but rather everyone is in an equal position.

ROLE-PLAYING METHOD. Especially effective for training and retraining employees, role playing essentially is an extemporaneous drama in which actors are given roles to play. To learn better methods for interviewing prospective employees, for example, personnel managers might be given the job of interviewing a ''prospective employee,'' while other members of the group watch, listen, and com-

············
EXERCISE B: BRAINSTORMING

Discuss in class the following questions:
1. What are the four steps to the brainstorming method?
2. What are the advantages and disadvantages of brainstorming?

············
EXERCISE C: ROUND-TABLE METHOD

Discuss in class the following questions:
1. Would a round table or a rectangular table be better for creating a sense of equality among members? Why?
2. What are the advantages and disadvantages to using a round table for a meeting of internationals?

ment on particulars. Sometimes, these dramas are taped and replayed for the members. Role playing is most often used to teach people new ways of doing such subtle things as leading, selling, deciding, planning, and giving and receiving criticism.

THE ROLE OF THE LEADER

The essential role of the leader is to guide and motivate the members of the group. Two common methods of guiding occur in setting the agenda and keeping the discussion moving toward a goal. Motivation may be stimulated by the leader's careful attention to and encouragement of everyone's comments. Although personality, company policy, pressures of time, and the mix in the group influence the efficiency of a leader, a number of common practices, if followed carefully, usually can ensure a productive meeting.

STATE THE GOALS CLEARLY.   When people know the goal at the outset, they are more likely to reach it. Should the leader be unable to define the goals, then perhaps there is no good reason to meet. Sometimes, in democratic sessions, the leader may provide a tentative agenda, asking the members to discuss and complete it. A related objective is motivation: the leader must explain to members the benefits of their achieving a good solution.

MANAGE THE TIME.   Because small groups are expensive, and because people have other things to do, wasting time is inexcusable. The job of the leader is to use every minute effectively by preparing well, beginning and ending on time (for instance, do not wait for latecomers), and keeping the agenda moving. When a specific problem has been solved or exhausted, move on immediately to the next problem. Should speakers be allotted specific times, make sure those times include beginning *and* ending times. And stick to them.

GUIDE THE DISCUSSION.   Whenever a member begins to get off the topic at hand, the leader must interject politely to bring the discussion back to the topic. For example, "That certainly is a problem, and it's one we must attend to. Right now, however, we've got to return to the problem of quality control." To get the full benefit of everyone's thoughts and experiences, leaders must occasionally prod the silent members to speak. For example, "That's interesting. Joan, you've worked in quality control. What do you think about Jane's idea?"

REFEREE.   A good leader is a good referee, not only as arbiter, but also as peacemaker. The leader must constantly be attentive to ways of reconciling differing opinions, ideas, even personalities. Some theories suggest that stating things generally — that is, not attacking people or their ideas — helps productivity. General Electric, under Jack Welch, however, has been managed extremely well with a straight-talk style of management. In either case, leaders should take care to head off any gratuitous unpleasantness.

Another job of the leader-as-referee is to summarize the ideas of several people into one idea. If done well, this often unites a group and can advance the agenda of the group. Finally, the leader's job is to summarize the entire discussion at the end of the meeting.

ASK QUESTIONS.   Questions have the effect of forcing people to think and to respond. Well-focused questions are therefore excellent rhetorical devices for initiating and moving ideas and people toward a goal. Several types of questions can help a leader control, direct, and advance a meeting.

....
EXERCISE D: DIRECT AND INDIRECT QUESTIONS

Asking questions is an important activity both for leaders and members of small groups. Discuss in class the following questions:

1. In what circumstances do direct questions (How many widgitcogs should we buy, Smedley?) work well?

2. When might indirect questions (Smedley knows about widgitcogs; perhaps he could help us out here) be more effective?

1. *Group questions.* These are general questions, usually including the overall problem at hand. When this question is asked — and there should be only one, and usually at the beginning of a meeting — a long pause often occurs while members consider it. Allow sufficient time for that consideration and for members to formulate their answers. A leader might say, for example, "Well, you can see the problems on the agenda. What are some of your ideas regarding the first one?"

2. *Directed questions.* These questions are directed to a specific person. Consequently, it is best to use that person's name as the first word. The leader can involve shy and reticent people by directing questions to them, and such questions can elicit information from people known or suspected to have specific information. Directed questions can be intimidating because they put people on the spot; when overused, they can create an atmosphere of interrogation. While appropriate in classrooms, such questions should be used sparingly in business meetings.

3. *Combination questions.* These combine the general and directed questions by asking the same question of several people. "John, what do you think about using a computer billing system?" "Joan, have you anything to add to John's ideas?" "Jean, what do you think about it?" Such questions have a way of forcing people to think about the question at hand.

4. *Throw-back questions.* Members of the group may throw a question back to the questioner — whether the leader or another member. "I'm not quite sure, Samantha. What do you think?" is also a way, however, *not* to answer the question.

5. *Hypothetical questions.* These are questions that begin with "What if" or "Suppose that." Such questions, well hypothesized, can set an entire group thinking along lines suggested by the questions. Often they stimulate extremely creative responses — some good, some not so good.

6. *Questions of personal experience.* These questions work best when the questioner knows well the person to whom the question is directed: "Joan, you worked in billing for a month or two when you first started here. What do you think?"

REACH HONEST CONCLUSIONS.   To avoid the problems of small groups — agreement for the sake of ending a meeting, clock watching, boredom—a leader should stick closely to the timetable and the agenda. In addition, the leader may deliberately attempt to thwart a too-easy agreement by including members whose views are bound to differ, encourage them to disagree, and solicit different perspectives. Moreover, it is a good idea to provide some time toward the end of the meeting for a re-evaluation of consensus. That is, when the group seems to agree, introduce the possibility that there may be a better way, thus inviting alternate perspectives.

DO SOMETHING.   Should a leader gain a reputation for soliciting advice or consensus or ideas from a group but then *not* act on them, the leader would soon have difficulty getting people to take meetings seriously. Moreover, the leader should be sure to inform members of the actions resulting from the meeting. The leader should never underestimate the importance of satisfaction people get from seeing their efforts bear fruit.

THE ROLE OF THE MEMBER

As international competition has forced American companies to become leaner, including eliminating entire levels of middle management, the middle manager, a typical member of small groups, must be more efficient, more alert, and more able to contribute visibly to the company. Still, although companies spend millions each year on leadership seminars, few companies spend sufficiently on teaching managers to be better participants. Moreover, reluctant, ill-prepared, or ill-trained group members may thwart the best leadership. Here are some guidelines for group members.

SHOW UP.   "Eighty percent of success is showing up," says actor Woody Allen. A member of a small group not only should show up regularly, but also should show up on time. Every minute that a participant is late is lost company time and must be multiplied by the number of members of the group, as well as by the time lost in recapitulating and restarting the meeting. No one appreciates no-shows and late-comers.

SPEAK UP.   While showing up is crucial, it is also important to speak up. Having taken the trouble to go to the meeting, a member might as well have some good come of it by contributing to it. Do not forget, however, that economy in oral expression is as great a virtue as economy of written expression. In short, participate but keep it brief.

STICK TO THE SUBJECT.   One of the most common problems in small groups is the seeming inability to stay on the subject. While keeping the discussion relevant to the issue is an important job of the group leader, it is also a responsibility of members.

Each member of a small group must be efficient, alert, and make a contribution.

BE TACTFUL. Although facts speak for themselves, it usually is not necessary to offend people by attacking them personally, and certainly not by showing contempt for their ideas. Groups work best when each member is treated as a colleague worthy of respect and courtesy.

BALANCE INDIVIDUALISM AND COLLECTIVISM. While respecting and eliciting individual ideas, always remember that the goal is to reach conclusions and solutions. Never obstruct for the sake of obstructing, and never place personal agendas before the agenda of the group. In short, be neither a nay-sayer nor a yea-sayer; but forced to choose, help the group achieve consensus.

LISTEN, RESTATE, QUESTION. People learn by listening, avoid misunderstanding by restating others' arguments, and advance the agenda through questions. These common-sense rules are the meat and potatoes of small-group discussions. When everyone follows them, the group almost always works; when no one follows them, the group seldom works.

LOSE GRACEFULLY. Almost everyone wins gracefully; too few people, however, lose gracefully. Because we all lose more often than we win, learning to lose gracefully is essential. Moreover, it marks us as mature, dignified, and intelligent—intelligent because winners often see graceful losers as having seen the error of their ways. Finally, losing gracefully is a moral virtue, and needs no acclaim from the group to make it a virtue.

INTERNATIONAL COMMUNICATIONS

Considering the great challenge of working in small, homogeneous groups, imagine the difficulties of dealing with groups of other nationalities and cultures. Even so, successful international communications is the key to America's business future. International communications involves an understanding of technology and culture.

THE TECHNOLOGY OF INTERNATIONAL COMMUNICATIONS

Technology has virtually eliminated time and distance as impediments to business communication. This technology includes such systems as Telex, satellite link-up, and other electronic systems that allow nearly instantaneous communications between and among most places in the world.

TELEX (TWX) is an inexpensive method of sending information over great distances. Using telephone lines, TELEX reproduces written communications quickly.

Satellites have revolutionized international communications. CNN, for example, put the Persian Gulf War live in homes worldwide by means of satellites. This technology is available to business as well, although the expense limits it to the biggest companies.

Other systems include computer-to-computer transfer of data, reports, indeed, any information that can be conveyed electronically. In short, the instantaneous transfer of information from any point on the globe to any other point is theoretically practical. As business students, you should get to know the various technologies of communications, their immense possibilities, and the speed with which information can move from point A to point B. You should realize also, however, that the very ease of conveying information makes any communication part of a competitive system. When ten pieces of information are sent to Timbuktu, all ten are read carefully; when ten thousand are so conveyed, only those that are well-written or otherwise presented or perceived as important will be read carefully.

THE CULTURE OF INTERNATIONAL COMMUNICATIONS

The sociology of international communications is extraordinarily complex, as complex as the different cultures associated with the various nations, races, and ethnic and religious groups that make up the world. A culture is a set of beliefs that governs the thoughts and actions of a group of people. This set of assumptions involves religion, morality, and even, ultimately, the characteristics of the land. For example, Arab cultures tend to place enormous value on water because the culture developed in the desert areas of the Middle East. That is why the Moors of Spain (descendants of North African Moslems) believed that the city of Granada was situated directly below heaven: it had water in abundance. The Alhambra, the fortress and palace of the Moorish kings of Granada, displays fountains, pools, baths, and small aqueducts everywhere, for by doing so, the kingdom displayed its greatest wealth. Conversely, a culture developed in a rain forest might not see a fountain as an example of great beauty or a grand display of wealth. People tend to value those things that are scarce.

This example is only one of hundreds of thousands that could be considered by anyone trying to learn about a culture. It is impossible for anyone ever to know even the rudiments of getting along in every culture. There simply are too many cultures, too many rudiments. Students may learn, of course, quite a bit about several cultures, but this takes much time, and much travel. Few students, still young, have been exposed to a sufficient number of cultures for a sufficient length of time to know many of them well. A survey of culture as it applies to international communication, then, may only expect realistically to present to students some of the common features of cultures, so they may know at least what to look for, and perhaps what to learn should their work send them to another country or to another culture within this country.

UNDERSTANDING. The first criterion for understanding a culture is to be open to it. The Japanese eat raw fish, and the Spanish eat salads from a common bowl. Travelers need to recognize that, although their customs are different, the Japanese and Spanish are very civilized people. Essentially, understanding, by its very nature, stems from the belief that one way of doing things is not always the only way; that is, it is possible for other ways to be better for other people. This is not so difficult for most Westerners to accept as some have suggested. Western culture has a long intellectual history of openness to differing ideas and ways. The English language, for example, although hardly representative of all Western culture, not only is the repository of a heritage, but readily includes words and phrases from other languages. The United States itself comprises the widest variety of cultures, races, and ethnic groups in the world.

Both understanding and patience contribute to another necessity for intercultural communications: accepting ambiguity. Americans are especially famous (or infamous) for talking straight. That is, Americans tend to be direct in their negotiations, and can become frustrated, even angered, by those whom they perceive to be evasive. Ambiguity—not getting a clear answer—is the stock in trade of many cultures; ambiguity serves them well in their business dealings also.

Patience and understanding are involved also in the necessity for Americans to withhold judgment about people of other cultures with whom they do business. That is, do not judge too quickly. Americans tend to believe that by having said yes to everything proposed, the Japanese have agreed to our requests. Such a belief may prove fatal to negotiations because the Japanese often say yes in the sense of "Yes, I understand," not "Yes, I agree." Consequently, do not judge or assume that what appears to be the case is the case. Wait and withhold judgment until time has revealed more of the facts.

Because people have similar needs, fears, and hopes, those dealing in international business should try to find ways to emphasize this sameness. Such commonality may occur also on more particular levels. Moslems and Christians, for example, have much in common in their religious heritages. The religious ancestry of both groups includes Abraham, Christ, and many others. Christians and Moslems are all, as the Moslems say, "People of the Book." This common ground may be found on many levels, in many areas, and in many cultures. The wise and prudent person will find it.

PATIENCE.   Patience takes many forms. In intercultural communications, patience is especially helpful and often profitable. People from many cultures are less hurried than Americans. The Japanese, for example, usually are content to wait us out until we will agree to virtually anything just to make the deal. Many Arab, Mediterranean, and African peoples spend what we consider to be great amounts of time before settling down to discuss business. Still, it is less important to learn the details of each of these cultures than it is to learn patience. Consequently, when selling, one should seldom be the first to bring up the subject of business. When buying, one should try to gauge the seller's interest in getting down to business and wait for a decent interval.

OVERSIMPLIFICATION.   Books about other cultures are extremely helpful and, if they are good ones, extremely enjoyable as well. Yet, be careful. Too many books and too many people tell us that people from other cultures *always* believe this or *always* do that. There is a tendency, for example, for Americans and northern Europeans to think that people in Central and South America *always* take siestas in the middle of the day. While this may be true for some people some of the time, it is not true for all people all of the time. In summer, when the heat is greatest in mid-day, people tend to stop working during that time, and then work later in the day. In many large cities in Hispanic countries, however, because of air conditioning and the need to compete with other nations, businesses keep the same hours as American and northern European nations.

We are told constantly about the differing notions of time indigenous to various cultures. The Japanese and Germans consider it rude to be anything other than exactly on time for a meeting. The Spanish consider it acceptable, even obligatory, to be late, sometimes even very late. Generally, this is true. Specifically, there are always exceptions. The lesson is that Americans should be try to be on time, but should not be frustrated by those whose cultures have a different notion of tardiness.

BODY LANGUAGE.   Americans nod to say yes; rural Greeks shake their heads to say yes. The Japanese move their right hands to suggest no; some Italians raise their chins to suggest no. Americans consider it polite to look another person in the eye; Japanese consider it impolite. But again, it is easy to oversimplify. One textbook says, "North Americans stand about five feet apart when conducting a business conversation."[6] Which North Americans? Bostonians, Los Angelenos, Mexicans from Tijuana or those from Yucatan? Such oversimplification in interpreting body language can cause problems. Still, it is true that citizens of the United States, who have been there for several generations, tend to stand farther apart than do people from almost all other cultures.

The best cure for oversimplification is to fight one's own cultural tendencies in areas that have no moral value. For example, while talking with Italians, French, Spaniards, Indians, or anyone from a culture in which people tend to speak nose-to-nose, fight the natural tendency to back away. This way, it does not matter with whom one is talking. Allowing the other person to set the conversational distance eliminates the problem.

LANGUAGE.   When conversing with a person for whom English is a second language, remember that there is a vast difference between knowing a language well and knowing it intimately. The following list provides a number of hints about being understood by others (see also Chapter 7).

SPEAKING AND WRITING ENGLISH TO NON-NATIVE SPEAKERS OF ENGLISH

1. *Use short sentences.* By confining one idea to one sentence, we allow the listener time to understand.
2. *Use short, common, accurate words.*
3. *Speak slowly.* Many people must translate mentally the words of one language into another before they understand.
4. *Avoid slang.* This is essential, but it is important to remember that many words and phrases normally used by native speakers are not immediately recognized as slang by those speakers. We must weigh our words carefully, thinking about their effect on the listener or reader. "No sweat," for example, is common to us, but could be incomprehensible, even vulgar, to non-native speakers and readers.
5. *Simplify, even oversimplify, the structure of conversations.* "First, second, third, last" often seem simplistic to native speakers, but they help a non-native speaker immensely.
6. *Use numbers and visuals liberally.* Arabic numerals are understood worldwide, and pictures seldom need translation. Using these things often greatly eases the job of understanding.

---

[6]Courtland L. Bovée and John V. Thill, *Business Communication Today*, 2nd ed. (New York: Random House, 1989), p. 391.

SUMMARY

1. Nonverbal communication (body language) is important because it can direct audiences toward our words. When it contradicts our words, however, nonverbal communication can distract and confuse audiences.

2. Grooming and dress are further examples of nonverbal communication. Because they create the first impression that others have of us, grooming and dress must be attended to carefully.

3. Small-group communication is especially important because so many decisions come out of it. The disadvantages are largely those that create inefficiency, such as time wasting, unnecessary disagreement, and lazy agreement. The advantage of small groups is that — well run — they solve problems with the collective wisdom and creativity of several people.

4. Four kinds of small groups common to business are staffs, committees, training groups, and conference groups.

5. Several methods have been developed for running small groups efficiently: democratic, brainstorming, round-table, and role-playing.

6. Both leaders and members have particular responsibilities. Leaders should state the goals of the group, manage its time, guide discussions, referee disputes, ask questions, articulate honest conclusions, and act on the information gathered and conclusions reached. Members should be sure to show up on time, participate in discussions, stick to the subject, try to be tactful but not obsequious, win graciously, and lose gracefully.

7. The technology of international communications is improving so rapidly that we must be open to learning about those improvements daily. It is theoretically possible for two people to communicate nearly instantaneously from almost any points on, beneath, or above the earth.

8. The cultural problems of international communications remain as they always have been: difficult. Doing business internationally requires a special sensitivity to the differences and similarities among the many peoples of the earth.

9. When speaking with someone not fluent in English, use short sentences; short, common, accurate words; speak slowly and avoid slang; use short, simple structures for conversations; and use numbers and visuals liberally.

EXERCISES

1. *Using body language to project an image in print*. Examine a magazine advertisement containing a person or people. Write a 250-word analysis of how body language is use to sell the advertised product.

2. *Using body language to project an image in print*. Clip a magazine advertisement containing a person or people. Mount the ad on a piece of paper with arrows drawn to postures and positions that suggest a body message. Label these messages.

3. *Using body language to project an image in print*. Construct a photo montage of parts of many advertisements in which you select *one* mode of body language. Write a short explanatory paragraph telling what kind of body language is being illustrated and how it is used to sell products.

4. *Using body language to project an image in television and film*. Discuss in small groups in class how television and films use body language. Mention some films, television shows, directors, and actors that are particularly effective in using body language. Each group will then present these findings to the class. Be sure to demonstrate just *why* your group believes they are effective.

5. *Observing a speaker's body language*. Attend a speech. List on paper examples of the speaker's body language. After the speech, add to each example in your list whether it was used effectively. Support your claims with details. If classmates attended the same speech, compare lists.

6. *Observing an expert in body language*. Most colleges

employ a mime at least once a year to entertain students. Attend such a performance and watch the mime closely, for no other performers are so attentive to body language. Write a one-page report of what techniques the mime used and how effective they were.

7. *Having others observe your body language.* Give a two-minute speech before the class, and elicit comments on your body language. Your classmates need not be experts in speech to know, given careful attention, which of your movements during the speech were effective and which were distracting or even annoying.

8. *Grooming and dress.* Clip five advertising photographs of business men and women from such business magazines as *Fortune, Business Week*, and *Forbes*. In groups, discuss their dress and how appropriate dress is for working in a corporation. Each group then presents its findings to the class.

9. *Grooming and dress.* Discuss in class how one should dress for an interview with Chase Manhattan Bank in New York City in March. Discuss whether a similar interview in March in Atlanta would require different dress.

10. *Grooming and dress.* Compare your attire for an interview with Chase Manhattan Bank in March with that you might choose as proper dress for an interview with the National Park Service.

11. *Small groups.* The best exercise for small groups is practice. Divide the class into groups of five to seven people; choose a topic of common concern (grading policies, library hours, campus safety, final exam policies, requirements for a major); choose a group leader; choose the type of small-group practice to be followed; come to an agreement of possible solutions to the chosen concern.

12. *Leading small groups.* Brainstorm in class about the problems of leading a small group. Those in the class with experience can take turns as leader. Those with good ideas may be able to provide examples — real and hypothetical — illustrating solutions to those problems. Be sure to follow the brainstorming method.

13. *Small groups: Democratic method.* List on the board several controversial campus issues. Choose one of these to resolve in groups of five to seven people. Use the steps of the democratic method to reach consensus in each group. Once consensus is achieved, then discuss with the entire class your group's conclusions and your successes and failures in attempting to achieve agreement.

14. *Managing time: Phil, Oprah, and Geraldo.* Managing time is difficult for leaders of small groups. Hosts of television talk shows are masterly in their ability to bring discussions to a seemingly natural close by the deadline.

In small groups and in class, role-play different talk shows and decide which of your hosts is best at managing time. The shows may be live or may be videotaped in advance of class. Be sure to provide specific examples, and be sure to be specific about how the time is well managed.

15. *Small groups and side issues: Phil, Oprah, and Geraldo.* One of the major problems of small groups is to remain focused on the problem. Too often, side issues arise that take the group off into relatively unimportant areas, thus wasting time. For example, small-group discussions abound these days on television, especially if the studio audience is not considered. Watch one of these shows, and note how many times the announced topic is shunted aside for another issue. Note also whether the group leader, the host, is able (or even tries) to bring the discussion back to the subject.

CASE STUDY: SMALL GROUPS AND INTERNATIONAL COMMUNICATION

Discuss in class the following problem in the technology and culture of international communications. Assume that your class is the top management in New York of an international corporation with offices in fifty foreign cities, including Hong Kong and Tokyo. In order to keep records of employees' salaries, health records, and the like, the head office in New York needs to have all employee records on computer files. Your job is to discuss ways to have those records sent from each office to New York. One problem is that you cannot ask the records to be sorted alphabetically by name, because Chinese does not have an alphabet in the sense that English has an alphabet. Moreover, many languages are written from top to bottom, not left to right as in English. Records from Tel Aviv will arrive in Hebrew, which is written right to left. Your job is to *try* to find some ways that your subordinates may pursue a solution.

CHALLENGE EXERCISE: SMALL GROUPS AND INTERNATIONAL COMMUNICATION

Discuss in class the following problem in the technology and culture of international communications. Assume that your class is the top management in New York of an international corporation with offices in fifty foreign cities. In order to keep records of employees' salaries, health records, and records of their children also, the head office in New York needs to have on computer files information on these people. Your job is to discuss ways to have those records sent from each office to New York. Among the problems is that different cultures assign different kinds of names to people. The offices in Caracas, Venezuela, and in Barcelona, Spain, send names such as "Fernández-Jiménez, Juan." "Fernández" is not a middle name, but part of the last name. In Hispanic cultures, the names of both father and mother become the last name. Juan's father's name is "Fernández-García"; his mother's last name is "Jiménez-Mendoza." In other cultures, last names may include those of one's father, grandfather, and great-grandfather. In still other cultures, the last name always appears first.

You need to find a way to sort names in such a way that each person's records, and those of the children, may be organized in some helpful way that will not do violence to the various cultures to which these people belong. Having the proper order of their names garbled would undoubtedly cause employees to think less of their employer, and of their importance within the company. Your job is to *try* to find some ways that your subordinates may pursue a solution.

AUTOMATION IN THE OFFICE

Word and Data Processing
The Advantages and Disadvantages
  of Longhand, Typing, and Word
  Processing
Electronic Mail Systems
Teleconferences
Integrated Office Systems

VISUALS

Tables
Figures

SUMMARY

EXERCISES

**4
0
8**

Learning Objectives:

☐ Be familiar with the importance of
technological innovations in business offices.

☐ Know the kinds of automation
used in business offices.

☐ Use visuals effectively in business
communications.

▲
CHECKLIST

PICTURES FOR THE PAGE

ATONE.

ALEXANDER POPE

(1688–1744)

THE MEDIUM IS

THE MESSAGE.

MARSHALL

McLUHAN

(1911–1980)

THE AUTOMATED OFFICE

AUTOMATION IN THE OFFICE

Automation, a system or method of performing or controlling processes by means of self-operating machinery, has transformed the business office so much that it would be hardly recognizable to some visitor from a hundred years ago, when telephones and primitive manual typewriters had only just appeared on the scene. An office, however, is still defined as any place occupied by managers, other professionals, secretaries, or clerks and in which the primary job is that of handling information. Together, automation and offices provide so many changes that any student contemplating a career in business must have a good idea of the many extraordinary technological innovations that are revolutionizing the way people think about business offices.

For example, computers have gone far toward eliminating time and distance — two great enemies of communications — as problems for business offices. Whereas telephones have been used for years to send audible messages long distances, computers are relatively new means of sending and receiving information visually almost anywhere in the world.

Automation produces enormous savings to companies. A few years ago, for example, researchers reported that those companies using only one electronic device — voice mail — saved between $540 and $2,328 a year *for every user*.[1] A large company, then, employing 5,000 managers, would save between $2.7 million and $11.6 million every year, solely by changing to a more efficient system of communication. Multiply those figures by the number of managers working in the United States, and the savings would be billions of dollars.

The office of the 1990s is filled not only with many machines whose speed, intelligence, and usefulness increase almost every day. These machines include telephones, computer systems, copiers, printers, plotters, and facsimile machines. These machines enable people to be more productive by being more efficient and allow entire offices to work as well-integrated units that can produce, assimilate, store, and convey information rapidly and reliably.

About one-third of all American workers are office workers, but two-thirds of all wages and benefits are paid to office workers. Because even non-office workers do some paper work, about 60 percent of all working hours is given to managing information, while 40 percent goes into actual production. Consequently, any technology that increases the efficiency of managing information increases the efficiency of at least 60 percent of all work in business. Machinery that improves productivity, therefore, is essential to business, given that salaries, benefits, and overhead account for more than 90 percent of the operating budgets of offices.[2]

---

[1]Gail Siragusa, "Voice Mail Takes Off," *Administrative Management* 47 (April 1986), 44.

[2]Paul Strassmann, *Information Payoff: The Transformation of Work in the Electronic Age* (New York: Free Press, 1985), 43.

**Word and data processing
are essential in modern
offices.**

WORD AND DATA PROCESSING

Data processing was the original use for computers, and it remains one
of their main functions. Data processing often means number processing, for the computer is an excellent, even indispensable tool for making sense of great collections of numbers. Databases, however, may
comprise any information that can be organized by categories, because
the matchless accuracy and speed of computers is mathematical, enabling computers to perform all kinds of complicated, time-consuming
calculations. Because business offices must collect, sort, store, and
make sense of many numbers for the purposes of everything from
sales projections to inventory control to employees' performance records, data processing is an essential job of computers in modern offices. Computers not only make the jobs easier, but also, in many
cases, make the jobs possible.

   Word processing is to words what data processing is to numbers.
Word processing is an unfortunate but accurate phrase for creating,
manipulating, storing, and moving words with the speed of electricity.
Combined with other electronic methods such as Electronic Mail, Local Area Networks (LAN), and even Global Networks, word and data
processing can increase the amount and improve the quality of information created, conveyed, and received across the room and across
the world.

   Students who do not know how to use word and data-processing
should learn. Word and data processing are easy to learn. Ten hours of
diligent study and practice should be enough for most students to
learn to use a word-processor sufficiently well to produce papers and
reports. Such students will then see typewriters as antiquated and
long-hand as prehistoric.

Learning data processing may take more or less time than learning word processing, depending on the level of sophistication of the kind of data processing a student is attempting to learn. Of course, there are a few disadvantages to both processes, but the advantages outweigh them greatly.

THE ADVANTAGES AND DISADVANTAGES OF LONGHAND, TYPING, AND WORD PROCESSING

Longhand has a personality to it; no two hands write the same. Consequently, messages written in longhand are more intimate and more warm than those that are typed. Furthermore, longhand is not tied to a location so much as are typing and word processing. That is, given a pencil—or even a charred stick—a person can write virtually anywhere on anything. Although there are portable typewriters and laptop computers, they normally may not be carried to dinner at a restaurant; pencils may be. Yet, longhand is not only terribly slow, but correcting it is laborious, tedious, and sloppy.

Although Thomas Jefferson once invented a machine that would write another copy of a letter as he was writing the first, it was impractical, and the idea never caught on. Consequently, there is usually only one copy of a handwritten document: the original. Businesses usually need multiple copies of written documents for their records to prove that such-and-such was indeed sent, complied with, received, and so forth.

Typing is less personal but much faster than longhand; most trained people can type between 60 and 100 words a minute, faster than most people can write longhand. Moreover, by using carbon paper, typists can make several copies of a document. Because copies are on paper, and must be stored in filing cabinets, offices can be overwhelmed by file copies. Further, although more easy to correct than longhand, typing errors are still not easily corrected. Most people slap a white, fast-drying paste over an error and then retype the passage.

Word processing is at least as fast as typing, but its real advantages lie in editing and storage. Everyone has experienced the agony of discovering, after typing an entire page, an error at the beginning of the page. Consequently, many of us gauge the seriousness of the error and decide whether it is worth correcting—that is, worth retyping the page. Word processing allows writers to correct errors in seconds. Because correcting is easy, two things result: more correcting gets done; and, because more correcting gets done, the final product is better.

Storage is also easy. One small two-megabyte disk—3½ inches square and ¹⁄₁₆ inch thick—can store several hundred pages. Finding any given page is easy and fast.

Computer software has been developed to improve, or at least make easier, a number of perennial problems people have with writing. This software often includes spell checkers and writing analyzers. *Spell checkers* are programs run after a writer has finished a piece. By pressing a few buttons, the writer can ask the computer to make sure all words are spelled correctly. This is a fast and painless way to simplify proofreading. The problem with spell checkers, however, is that no means has been developed for deciding whether the word used is the correct word. For example, for the sentence "And so the trapped minors were lead to safety from the mine," spell checkers will not correct "lead" to "led" nor "minors" to "miners" because, although they are not the correct words in the context, they are correctly spelled words nevertheless. So, while spell checkers find errors such as "*recieve*," they do not eliminate the problem of proofreading.

Writing analyzers have come a long way in a few short years. They are capable, for example, of distinguishing in most instances between active and passive voice. Usually, the computer will tell the writer that "63% of your sentences are in passive voice." That is good to know because, almost always, that is too high a percentage of sentences in passive voice. The writer still must know the difference between active and passive voice and how to change from one to the other. Such programs will also point out the percentage of long words in a piece of writing. While long words are fine when needed, business writing must display simplicity whenever possible. Some programs even include a list of clichés that, when they appear in a piece of writing, are identified as no-no's for the writer.

Although computers are immensely helpful to writers, writing is so complex that people are in little danger of having computers write for them. Imagine, for example, what a writing analyzer would say about a sentence that is eight-pages long. Yet such a sentence was written by one of the greatest American writers: William Faulkner in a short novel called *The Bear*.

ELECTRONIC MAIL SYSTEMS

WRITTEN SYSTEMS. *Electronic mail*, often called "E-Mail," is common, and may be as simple as a telephone-line connection between two computers or as complex as connections between hundreds of computers dispersed on several continents. Such systems replace paper correspondence by sending messages via computers. Sent over telephone lines, the message is placed (or "parked") in the electronic mailbox of one or more other computers and opened when the user goes to that mailbox. Only when a printed copy is needed will the mail be placed on paper. In fact, not long from today, the United States Postal Service will be reduced to carrying only holiday presents and junk mail, for all business mail and most personal correspondence may be sent electronically.

FAX systems (for *fac*simile) use telephone lines to send the image of a printed copy from point A to point B. That is, a FAX machine attached to a telephone scans a sheet of paper, converts it to electrical signals, and transmits those signals over telephones lines to another FAX machine, which reconverts the signals to words or visuals and prints them on another sheet of paper.

Computer-assisted design is a visual system that is replacing mechanical drafting and is saving businesses millions of hours and dollars.

ORAL SYSTEMS. *Voice mail*, which uses telephones, is the corporate equivalent of an answering machine. In business, it works like this: Person A calls person B, who is not in the office. A recorder stores the message on B's machine and replays the message when B returns. The answering machine may be specific to person B or it could serve many employees. Person B may retrieve only the relevant calls by providing a code number to the big answering machine. Further, a voice mail system can transfer calls automatically to another telephone (call forwarding) and can be programmed to override all calls except those from specific telephone numbers.

Conference calls allow many people to talk on the telephone together. Often, this method eliminates the cost of and time required for gathering many people in the same room. Sales managers in Florida, Arizona, Washington, and Maine, for instance, can make collective decisions during conference calls, and no one needs to leave the office.

VISUAL SYSTEMS. *Computer-assisted design*, known as CAD, not only creates pictorial versions of mathematical constructions, but also can be sent to other computer terminals. FAX systems may transmit pictures as well as words. In fact, almost any system that can send words can send pictures. An example of the potential for mail systems is *Videotex*, or television shopping. Items for sale are displayed on a television screen; to buy an item, the viewer uses the computer to send relevant information over telephone lines to the company selling the item. The importance for this to business is not only in retail markets, but also in its applicability to home offices. That is, many jobs eventually may be performed at home, and the traditional office may simply be a place where information is gathered and disseminated. The savings in travel time, not to mention gasoline and its attendant problems, could be revolutionary.

ELECTRONIC QUESTIONNAIRES. One prime example of the kind of office innovation brought about by technological improvements is the electronic questionnaire used by General Electric's Joseph Podolsky in the early months of 1990. Knowing that written questionnaires produce a relatively small return, yet wanting and needing information from employees about various information provided to employees by the company, Podolsky decided to try a voluntary phone-in survey concerning a presentation made to employees by someone from corporate headquarters.

The telephone and a tape recording were programmed to ask questions and to record answers. The survey used 100 randomly distributed cards asking the recipients to respond by calling a number. A 20 percent return on written questionnaires is good. The responses exceeded 50 percent of those surveyed. Incredibly, many of the 100 people asked to respond then gave the card to other people, so that a total of 175 people responded. Here are the instructions and the results of the survey.

COULD YOU HELP ME FOR ABOUT TWO MINUTES?

We've put together a phone-in survey to find out how well we're getting business information to you. Please help us by testing it.

From any touch-tone phone, call x5555 (875-5555 from outside the plant). When "Jane" answers (she's the system voice), push 1111. Then you'll hear a few questions, which you can answer by pressing the appropriate numbers on your phone.

Be straightforward with your answers. The system can't tell who's calling.

Please call anytime this week, *before noon on Friday, February 20*.

I really appreciate your help. If this works well, we'll use it often.

PHONE SURVEY #1: WEEK OF FEBRUARY 16–20, 1990

Starting on the afternoon of Friday, February 13, we handed out about 100 cards randomly throughout the plant, to hourly people as well as exempts. This drew a total of 175 responses. Here are the questions and the responses:

1. First, about the information presented. Was it too detailed, not detailed enough, or just about right?

Too detailed	20	11.4%
Not detailed enough	27	15.4%
Just about right	126	72.0%

2. From what you heard, do you expect Transportation Systems business in 1990 to be better than 1989, worse than 1989, or about the same?

Better than 1989	16	9.3%
Worse than 1989	53	30.8%
About the same	99	57.6%

3. How about the format of the meeting? Was it okay, or would you prefer a smaller, less formal meeting?

Okay	78	45.3%
Smaller, less formal	89	51.7%

4. Mr. Y_____ talked about an ombudsperson. Do you know what one is?

Don't know	30	17.4%
Grows flowers	6	3.5%
Finds answers	135	78.5%

5. Would you participate in this kind of survey again, and encourage others to do it, too?

Yes	159	93%
No	12	7%

NOTE: This is a tabulation of valid entries only. When invalid numbers were pressed, they were disregarded. This accounts for deviations from 100% on some questions.

TELECONFERENCES

One method common in business today combines, potentially at least, voice, pictures, and writing: the teleconference. The teleconference, like a conference call, adds television pictures. Consequently, people may be seen as well as heard, and visuals (charts, graphs, and so forth) may be seen by all. Teleconferences are more expensive than conference calls, but often they provide satisfactory compensations, not the least of which is that they are 75 percent less expensive than actual person-to-person conferences.[3] The most important compensation, however, is that people pay attention more. A television screen commands attention; as a result, participants are better prepared, more alert, and more active during teleconferences than during conference calls.

INTEGRATED OFFICE SYSTEMS

INTEROFFICE.　Computers can be connected in almost any way people want them to be connected. Two examples here, one at either end of a broad spectrum, will suffice to demonstrate this ability.

Local Area Networks (LANs) connect computers and other communication equipment in a limited geographical area: office, building, complex of buildings. Such networks may connect several computer terminals to a computer large enough to allow people to work on all terminals simultaneously. In addition, each terminal may be able to send and receive information from other terminals. The possibilities are endless. Several computers may be connected in numerous ways.

Wide Area Networks (WANs) take the notion of LAN and extend it to computers that, potentially, could be anywhere in the world. The WAN is a simple idea that remains an ideal in most instances because it is difficult to achieve practically. Although aggressively pursued by many multinational corporations, and by such organizations as the

EXERCISE A: OFFICE SYSTEM JARGON

Here is a list of several terms commonly used to describe kinds and parts of LANs. In class, try to define them. Someone in class may know what they mean; if not, perhaps someone who does could be invited to explain these terms.

star network	ring network
bus network	loops

---

[3]Marvin Kornbluh, "The Electronic Office: How It Will Change the Way We Work," in *Career Tomorrow: The Outlook for Work in A Changing World* (Bethesda, Md.: World Future Society, 1983), 63.

Soon, Wide Area Networks (WANs) will allow companies to do business efficiently almost anywhere.

consultative committee on International Telephony and Telegraphy, there are many problems. In Taiwan, for example, the country's Postal Telephone and Telegraph (PTT) authority has rules and regulations that make it extremely difficult for a foreign company to set up data links with offices outside the country. The trade magazine *Computerworld* reports that when a Mexican company built a microwave station, the Mexican government took it over, magnanimously allowing the company to use "half the station free."[4] Any company wanting to install a network in, say, three countries may do so technologically, but must comply with the laws of three different countries. Solving such problems has proven difficult, sometimes impossible, in the past. For example, in order to protect their own computer industries, many countries require that all computers and associated peripherals be bought from an indigenous manufacturer. The problem is that these machines may not be compatible with those of other countries or of the machinery used by the multinational company. Fortunately, many countries are beginning to realize that such regulations may impede their own economic development and are beginning to change their laws.[5] For more on the technology of international communications, see Chapter 15.

---

[4]Avery Jenkins, "Networks in a Strange Land," *Computerworld*, 9 September 1987, 25–27, 30.

[5]See John Highbarger, "Diplomatic Ties: Managing a Global Network," *Computerworld*, 9 September 1987, 45–46.

INTRAOFFICE. Integrating the machinery in an office is essential to getting the fullest use from that machinery. For example, one computer may be connected to printers, copiers, telephones, micrographic machinery (microfiche and microforms), FAX machinery, and optical scanners that read a page or photograph into a computer, where it may be stored and used. Moreover, many of these machines may be connected with each other as well.

Software programs can process words, analyze data, and create graphics. For example, desk-top publishing software, combined with a laser printer, can produce a typeset document (memo, letter, report, manual, book) that includes words, tables, and figures. A mail merge program can then send that document to a thousand people. One file contains the document, and another contains the names and addresses of those thousand people. When the two are combined, one name and address are printed automatically on one copy of the document.

Databases simply are stored information. They are different from books in that they are organized so that one may find specific information very easily and quickly. For instance, a company that has just patented a new glue for bonding rubber to metal may want to send an information sheet to all manufacturers of products that bond rubber to metal, but only to those states whose laws allow the use of this particular kind of highly volatile glue. A database containing a list of 4,000 manufacturers in the United States could sort those 4,000 companies 1) by the states in which the glue is legal, and 2) by the companies manufacturing products that bond rubber to metal. Should there be one hundred of these manufacturers, the company has saved printing, paper, clerical work, and postal costs for 3,900 mailings. The computer can produce a list in minutes, whereas the people performing such a job would have required hours, if not days.

VIUAL

"What is the use of a book,"
thought Alice, "without pictures?"
Lewis Carroll (1832–1898)

Because numbers are concrete symbols, people use numbers to illustrate and to persuade. People like numbers because numbers are precise, take the place of many words, and, properly presented, do not lie. The problem is that understanding lists of numbers is not always easy; sometimes lists confuse; they need to be interpreted. Consequently, numbers in lists can violate the writer's contract with the reader, for the writer must make the job of reading easy. To make reading and understanding easier, writers use illustrations, which in business are commonly called visuals. In writing, a visual is anything that is not a word, but which helps to convey information. Notice, for example, that the dollar signs ($) in the title of this section make the word *VISUALS* as much a figure as a word.

There are many types of visuals: graphs, charts, lists, and photographs. Business reports usually divide the visuals into two categories: *tables* arrange words and numbers into rows and columns; *figures* use linear illustrations such as charts, graphs, maps, drawings, and sometimes photographs.

Anything *not* part of the text—that is, the writing—is a visual. Visuals are very powerful, arresting the eye, demanding attention, and getting it. Use visuals only to convey information that words cannot convey as well. Reserve the emphasis granted to visuals to those things deserving emphasis.

RULES FOR VISUALS

1. *Place visuals conveniently and logically for the reader.* Logic and convenience dictate that visuals occur on the same page as the first important textual reference to it. Move heaven and earth before placing a visual on a different page. Those reports printed on two sides of a sheet may include the reference on one side and the visual on the facing page. The point is to avoid the reader's having to turn pages to find a visual.

2. *Connect all visuals to the text.* That is, the writer must refer to a visual in the text. The reader has no reason to confront a visual not mentioned in the text.

3. *Keep visuals simple.* Avoid using so many words that the visual becomes cluttered.

4. In complex visuals, *label the parts.* Place the explanations in a Key at the bottom of the visual.

5. *Cite the source of reprinted visuals.* Place the complete citation at the bottom of the visual.[6]

6. *Place long or complicated visuals in an appendix.*

TABLES

Add to golden numbers, golden numbers.

Thomas Dekker (1572–1632)

Tables are groups of words or numbers that are arranged vertically and horizontally to enable readers to compare the elements displayed. Tables are better than words for conveying many specifics at a glance. Tables are more accurate than most figures, for they usually present numbers rather than representations of numbers. Because tables place numbers in rows and columns, comparisons of those numbers are easy. Here are several guidelines for using tables.

GUIDELINES FOR TABLES

1. *Give each table a title and a number.* A report containing only one table, however, does not need to be numbered.

2. *Arrange the table effectively.* Study the information before choosing a form for a table. Merely arranging numbers in columns and rows does not guarantee the reader's understanding. Contracts often specify the form of tables.

3. *Make sure the column headings accurately describe the columns.*

---

[6]If the report or publication is to be sold, then the writer *must* seek permission from the source to reprint the table or figure.

4. *Express units of less than one as decimals*, unless fractions are standard (e.g., parts of inches).

5. *Use standard symbols for column headings*. This saves space. Arcane symbols must be accompanied by an explanatory key.

6. *Exhaust all possibilities before continuing a table on another page*. The title, table number, and the word "continued" must occur at the top of a table continued on a second page. Column headings must be repeated also.

The most common parts of tables appear in the following list, although not all tables will contain all parts.

- *Table Title*. Accurate, precise, and short, the title is capitalized, centered, and placed at the top.

- *Stub*. The stub lists the names of things being compared in the table. It is the first left-hand column.

- *Column headings*. These are placed inside the boxhead and directly above the column of data to which they apply.

- *Ruler lines*. Ruler lines separate rows and sometimes columns in the body of the table.

- *Body*. The body contains the guts of the table: the numbers. Note that the numbers are aligned on the decimal point.

- *Notes*. Notes are placed near the bottom of the table to explain those things requiring many words. Footnote numbers are not used, but rather such symbols as asterisks (*), daggers (†), bullets (•), and the like.

Here is an example of a table.

	TABLE I AVERAGE PERCENTAGE OF SUNSHINE FOR NINE CITIES					
Table number and title						
Column head	City	Average	Jan.	Apr.	July	Oct.
Rule	Phoenix	86	78	88	85	88
	Tucson	86	81	91	79	89
	Boston	60	53	56	65	61
	Chicago	57	43	53	69	61
Stub	Los Angeles	73	71	69	82	73
	Miami	66	68	*	69	59
	New York	59	51	59	65	61
	St. Louis	58	51	56	71	62
	Portland, Or.	47	24	*	68	39
Table source	Source: U.S. Department of the Interior.					
Table note	*Data unavailable.					

FIGURES

Figures are photographs, drawings, pie charts, line graphs, bar graphs, maps, flow charts, schematic diagrams, pictographs, and other forms of illustration that convey information in reports without relying primarily on words. Here are several guidelines for using figures.

GUIDELINES FOR FIGURES

1. *Give each figure a number and a title.*
2. *Label parts of figures clearly and consistently.* Make sure that the letter or number given to a part of a figure is the same as that given to the explanation.
3. *Make figures self-sufficient.* That is, although figures must be referred to in the text, each figure must be well labeled and explained: should it fall from a report, and be picked up and read, the figure would be understood without the text.

In routine business reports, the three most common figures are *pie charts, bar charts*, and *line graphs*. Each of these is useful, and each has advantages and disadvantages.

PIE CHARTS.   Pie charts or circle charts, like pies, have wedges that show the relationship of parts to the whole. The best way to learn about pie charts is to make one. Because it fluctuates so much, the cost of gasoline provides an interesting example. Suppose the price of a gallon of gasoline is $1.39, and you want to discover how that price is derived.

BREAKDOWN OF THE COST OF ONE GALLON OF GASOLINE

.74	Producing crude
.22	Refining, storing, transporting
.06	Refining profits
.04	Federal tax
.14	State, local taxes
.19	Service stations
$1.39	Total

To present the data visually, follow this procedure:

1. Add each part to produce a whole: $1.39 a gallon.
2. Divide each part by $1.39 to produce the percent of the whole.

Producing crude:	.74 ÷ $1.39 = .532 =	53.2%
Refining, storing, transporting:	.22 ÷ $1.39 = .158 =	15.8%
Refining profits:	.06 ÷ $1.39 = .043 =	4.3%
Federal tax:	.04 ÷ $1.39 = .029 =	2.9%
State, local taxes:	.14 ÷ $1.39 = .101 =	10.1%
Service station:	.19 ÷ $1.39 = .137 =	13.7%

PLOTTING A PIE CHART

1. *Add each part to find a whole.*
2. *Find the percent of the whole for each part.*
3. *Multiply each percentage by 360°.*
4. *Draw a circle sufficiently large to represent each part clearly.*
5. *Using a protractor, mark off the degrees belonging to each part. Mark them along the arc.*
6. *Label each part.*

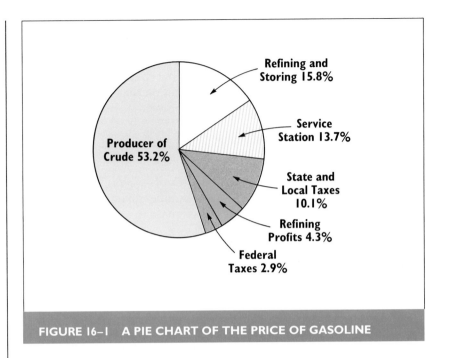

FIGURE 16–1   A PIE CHART OF THE PRICE OF GASOLINE

3. Multiply each percentage by 360° to produce the following degrees for each part of the whole.

Producing crude:	.532 × 360° =	191.5°
Refining, storing, transporting:	.158 × 360° =	56.9°
Refining profits:	.043 × 360° =	15.5°
Federal tax:	.029 × 360° =	10.4°
State, local taxes:	.101 × 360° =	36.4°
Service station:	.137 × 360° =	49.3°

4. Draw a circle large enough to depict six parts.

5. Beginning at 0°, mark in order 191.5° (this requires marking first 180°, then moving the protractor and marking another 11.5°), 56.9° more, 15.5° more, 10.4° more, and 36.4° more. That should leave 49.3° unmarked, which completes the whole. If not, recalculate and re-mark, for something went wrong.

6. Each wedge may be sufficiently large to allow a label to be placed inside. If not, or if the labels are lengthy, place the labels outside the pie and draw arrows to the wedges. Figure 16-1 is the result.

BAR CHARTS.   Bar charts compare items over time or compare the sizes of related items. Bar charts have vertical and horizontal axes that direct the plotting of the bars. The decision to place bars on the horizontal axis or on the vertical axis is guided by limitations of space and concern for aesthetics.

Magazines and newspapers commonly use simple bar charts. Figure 16–2 is an example of a bar chart oriented horizontally.

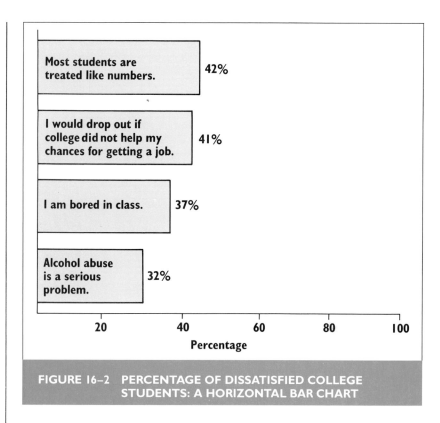

FIGURE 16–2   PERCENTAGE OF DISSATISFIED COLLEGE
STUDENTS: A HORIZONTAL BAR CHART

Suppose a bar chart were required comparing 1969 prices to 1979 prices for several goods: bread, margarine, hamburger, and gasoline. A *segmented bar chart* would be the most effective method to display this information (see Figure 16–3, which is oriented horizontally).

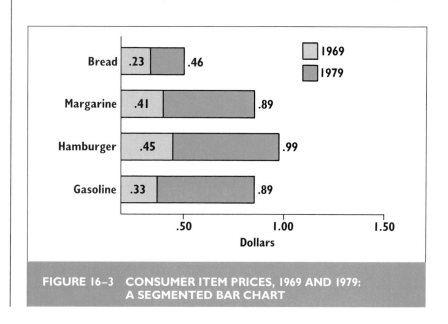

FIGURE 16–3   CONSUMER ITEM PRICES, 1969 AND 1979:
A SEGMENTED BAR CHART

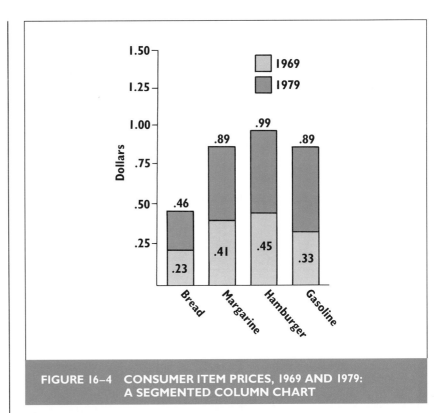

FIGURE 16–4   CONSUMER ITEM PRICES, 1969 AND 1979: A SEGMENTED COLUMN CHART

Column charts, which use vertical bars, tend to make differences look more dramatic than they are. Figure 16–4 is the bar chart from Figure 16–3 oriented vertically.

Line Graphs.   Line graphs make much more accurate comparisons than bar charts, and line graphs can compare many variables. To make a line graph, follow these steps.

How to Make a Line Chart

1. Draw a grid with horizontal and vertical lines.
2. Choose one variable to be represented by the horizontal axis, usually the independent variable.
3. Choose one variable to be represented by the vertical axis, usually the dependent variable.
4. Choose a system of numbering for the lines on the grid.
5. Plot the points.
6. Connect the points with straight lines.
7. Properly label the chart and each variable and constant.

Suppose a graph were needed for comparing the prices of coffee between 1969 and 1979. The independent variable would be the year (for the year changes independently of the price of coffee). The depen-

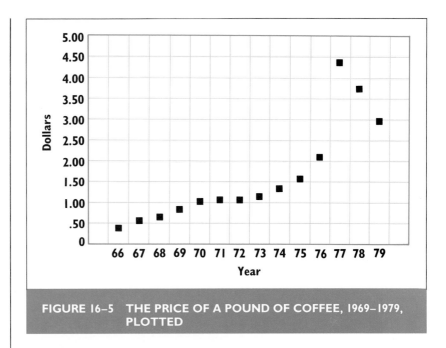

FIGURE 16–5 THE PRICE OF A POUND OF COFFEE, 1969–1979, PLOTTED

dent variable would be the price of coffee (for the price changes and seems to be dependent on the year). Figure 16–5 shows how the line graph should be set up and plots the coffee prices.

Figure 16-6 then joins the plotted points to display the trend of coffee prices.

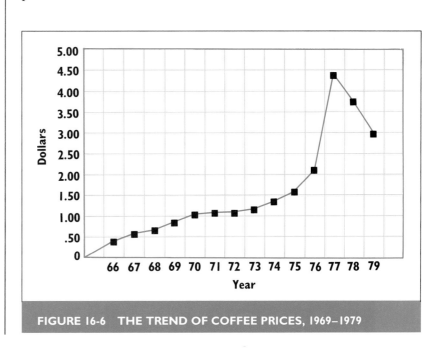

FIGURE 16-6 THE TREND OF COFFEE PRICES, 1969–1979

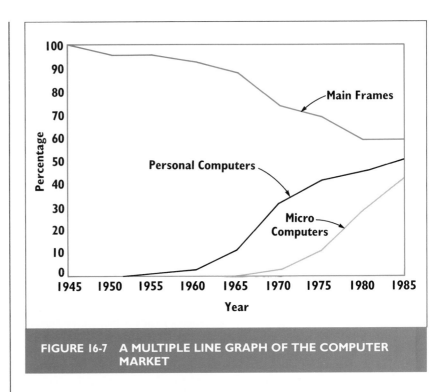

FIGURE 16-7   A MULTIPLE LINE GRAPH OF THE COMPUTER
MARKET

Commonly used, *multiple line graphs* compare different items over
time, as shown in Figure 16-7.

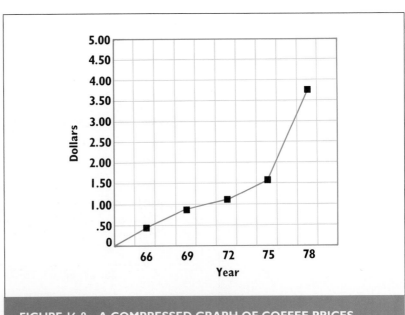

FIGURE 16-8   A COMPRESSED GRAPH OF COFFEE PRICES,
1969–1979.

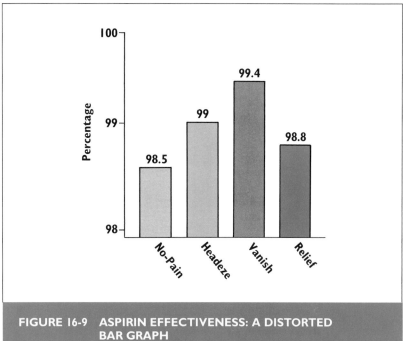

FIGURE 16-9   ASPIRIN EFFECTIVENESS: A DISTORTED BAR GRAPH

GRAPHIC DISTORTIONS OF INFORMATION.   Charts and graphs can distort information easily. The rise in the price of coffee was indeed precipitous between 1969 and 1979, but the rise may be made even more dramatic by compressing the graph. This is done by narrowing the graph, representing, say every three years, rather than every year.

Figure 16-8 shows *horizontal* compression, but a graph can distort through *vertical* compression also. The bar chart in Figure 16-9 illustrates vertical distortion by displaying only a 2 percent difference between the highest and lowest points on the vertical axis. As plotted, the effectiveness of the four aspirin brands seems significant until the reader discovers that the difference between the most and least effective brands is only 9/10 of a percentage point.

FLOW CHARTS.   A flow chart diagrams the stages of a process, depicting each stage in its proper place as the process flows from one stage to the next. A flow chart, for example, may depict the structure of a company, as in Figure 16-10 on the next page.

Or it may depict, for example, transportation costs, as in Figure 16-11.

MAPS.   Most of us think of highway or street maps when we think of maps, but a quick check of the atlases in any library shows us that maps can chart many different things, many of which are important

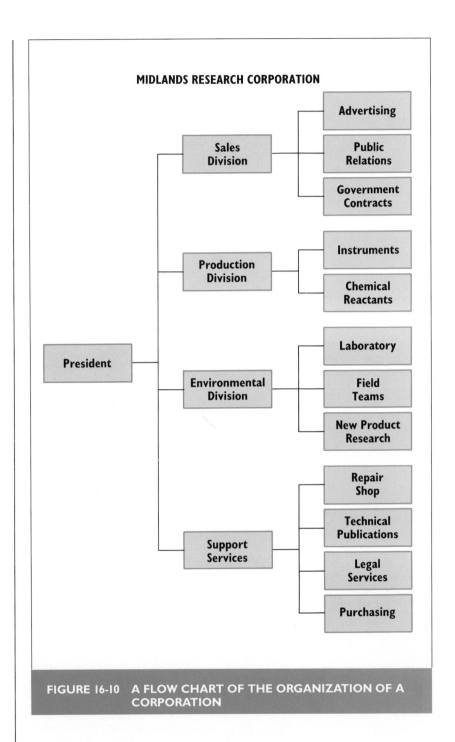

MIDLANDS RESEARCH CORPORATION

FIGURE 16-10   A FLOW CHART OF THE ORGANIZATION OF A CORPORATION

for business. Maps can show transportation costs for various geographical areas; manufacturing density for such heavy industries as steel, autos, and plastics; the mix of manufacturing and service; the population of workers having particular skills in any given geographical area. Figure 16-12 depicts the power plants in Greater Los Angeles.

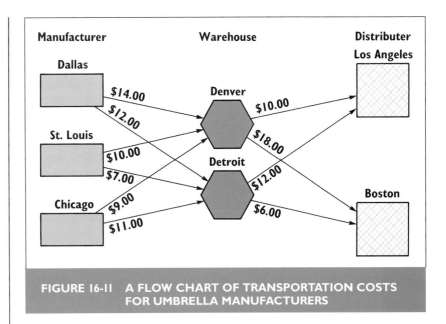

FIGURE 16-11   A FLOW CHART OF TRANSPORTATION COSTS FOR UMBRELLA MANUFACTURERS

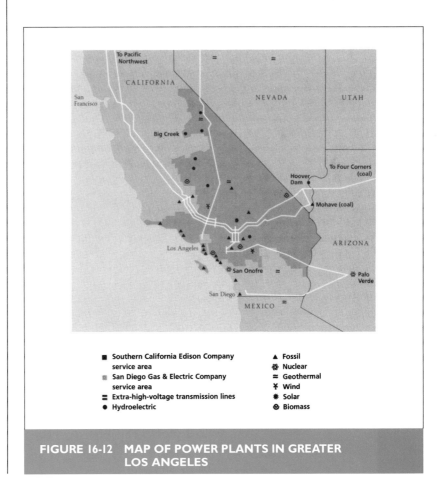

FIGURE 16-12   MAP OF POWER PLANTS IN GREATER LOS ANGELES

Here is a list of do's and don'ts for creating maps.

DO'S AND DON'TS OF USING MAPS IN BUSINESS

Maps are figures. Label them so and follow the rules for figures: see page 419, 421. For example, maps, like all figures, should be clear and simple. Shading will create easy differentiation.

Maps should contain only the necessary information. Nothing is more distracting and confusing than a map containing 500 points, only 10 of which are needed for doing the job.

Maps should contain a scale — inches or feet to miles or hundreds of miles.

Maps should identify boundaries clearly.

Maps should indicate north.

PHOTOGRAPHS.   Photographs often are worth a thousand words — as long as the picture is good, clear, simple, and above all, relevant. Here is a list of do's and don'ts for using photographs. See the color inserts for examples of photographs and their captions.

DO'S AND DON'TS OF USING PHOTOGRAPHS IN BUSINESS

Photographs are figures; label them so. In fact, photographs must follow all the rules for figures.

Photographs for business should strive for clarity. Unless the photo is to be used for advertising, it should be relevant before being beautiful.

Mount photographs on white paper, with wide margins. Remember that computer scanners now may reproduce a photograph as a file and then insert it into almost any document.

If no scanner is available, *attach photographs with glue or tape*, not with clips or staples.

Do not write on a photograph; use overlays.

Do not fold, spindle, or otherwise mar a photograph.

DRAWINGS.   Drawings are as important as, if not more important than, photographs. This is especially true since computers have begun to draw intricate and complicated pictures with a precision and speed unknown only ten years ago. While mechanical drafting is an important skill, if only for historical perspective and for use when the electricity goes off, most technical drawing is now done by computers using such programs as CAD (computer-assisted design). CADs may be so intricate that they have qualities both of graphs and of photographs. To use them properly, a writer should remember that drawings are figures, and that they are extremely useful. See the color examples of CADs in the "High-Tech Office" color insert, after page 438.

SUMMARY

1. The automated office saves time and money by improving efficiency and by increasing the speed of communications, production, and billing.

2. The automated office comprises word and data processing, electronic mail systems, integrated office systems, and other sophisticated voice and visual communications systems.

3. Getting the most from visuals requires that the writer use them effectively by employing logical arrangements: simple designs, labels, and citations.

4. Visuals should be placed precisely in the text where they are discussed or near that which they illustrate.

5. The two kinds of visuals are tables and figures. Tables are groups of words or numbers that are arranged vertically and horizontally to enable readers to compare the elements displayed. Figures are graphs, charts, maps, photographs, and a host of other visuals that are not tables.

6. Computer-assisted design (CAD) is spreading quickly throughout industry, and is already the best and easiest method of creating most visuals.

EXERCISES

1. *Advantages of instantaneous communications.* List the advantages to business of eliminating virtually all problems of time and distance with regard to communications. Discuss in class.

2. *Disadvantages of electronic communications.* List the disadvantages to business of eliminating virtually all face-to-face meetings. Discuss in class.

3. *Understanding the jargon of the automated office.* Define the following terms as they apply to the automated office. Your paper should list each term, provide a one-sentence definition, and include also a short paragraph explaining the function of each item in the automated office.

CAD	voice mail	database
FAX	word processing	software
LAN	E-mail	WAN

4. *Problems with local networks.* Although Wide Area Networks have glaring problems, local networks have less glamorous ones. Local problems are serious and perhaps even cause a greater number of problems for a larger number of people. Discuss some of these and seek solutions.

5. *Defining "connected to the text."* What does the rule mean that says "all visuals must be connected to the text"? How does the rule make the reader's job easier?

6. *Bar graphs.* Study the table on page 432 and construct a bar graph from it.

7. *Line graphs.* Study the table on page 432 and make a line graph from it.

8. *Pie charts.* Study the table on page 432 and make a pie chart from it.

9. *Comparing charts.* Which of the figures in Exercises 6–8 does the best job of displaying the information graphically?

10. *Figures and tables.* Give three examples of situations in which tables are more effective than figures. Write these examples on paper and prepare to discuss them in class.

11. *Figures and tables.* Give three examples of situations in which figures are more effective than tables. Write these examples on paper and prepare to discuss them in class.

12. *Figures and tables.* Give three examples of situations in which photographs are more effective than tables or graphs. Write these examples on paper and prepare to discuss them in class.

13. *CAD versus the drafting table.* Discuss in class the advantages of computer-assisted drawings over mechanically drafted ones.

14. *CAD versus the drafting table.* Discuss in class the advantages of mechanically drafted drawings over computer-assisted drawings.

15. *Small groups.* Choose one of the foregoing exercises and do it as a small-group exercise in class.

FACULTY SALARIES (1988–89)   (in thousands of dollars)

Professor		Associate		Assistant	
U. of Virginia	64.1	U. of Michigan	47.5	U. of Michigan	39.3
U. of Michigan	62.9	U. of Virginia	44.1	U. of Maryland	36.5
U. of Texas	61.9	Ohio State	43.5	U. of Illinois	36.2
Ohio State	61.1	U. of Maryland	42.7	U. of Virginia	36.0
U. of Maryland	60.3	Penn State	42.2	U. of Texas	35.9
Purdue U.	59.7	U. of Iowa	41.4	Ohio State	35.8
Penn State	57.9	Purdue U.	41.2	U. of Colorado	35.7
U. of Illinois	57.7	U. of Texas	40.8	U. of Iowa	35.3
U. of N. Carolina	57.5	U. of Illinois	40.7	Penn State	34.5
U. of Iowa	55.0	Iowa State	40.1	Iowa State	34.4

Source: Association of American Universities

CASE STUDY: THE ELECTRONIC OFFICE

One day you receive the following from your boss, Smedley Fahrquart, CEO of Widgitcog Industries, and the instructions to perform the task A.S.A.P. Here is the memorandum: ''I have been asked by the business school of State University to present to a meeting of business majors a lecture entitled, 'The Business Office in the Year 2000.' Would you please write for me a one-page speech (without intro or closing) simply detailing the kinds of electronic components likely to be in most business offices by the end of this decade?'' Write the one-page speech.

CHALLENGE EXERCISE 1: INTERPRETING DATA

Here are some numbers and other data. Make an intelligible table from them.
- 1989: sales amounts for January by personnel. Fahrquart: $657,000; Harcart: $792,000; Marbart: $865,079; Gephart: $800,000.
- 1990: sales amounts for January by personnel. Fahrquart: $483,000; Harcart: $392,000; Marbart: $804,345; Gephart: $900,000.
- 1991: sales amounts for January by personnel. Fahrquart: $657,000; Harcart: $712,000; Marbart: $632,567; Gephart: $750,500.
- 1992: sales amounts for January by personnel. Fahrquart: $657,000; Harcart: $452,000; Marbart: $568,090; Gephart: $995,000.

CHALLENGE EXERCISE 2: PROBLEMS WITH WIDE AREA NETWORKS

Some of the problems of Wide Area Networks may be illustrated by the following in-class exercise. Half the class is France, and gets red 3x5 cards; the other half is Italy, and gets white cards. On these cards, we pretend, are messages. Only two Italians understand French, and only two of the French understand Italian. All messages between these countries must go through these two people for translating.

This is a problem in language, but the same is true for electronic ''borders.'' The French system will accept only red cards; consequently, each white card sent to France must be copied onto a red card before it can proceed. Europe in 1992 will eliminate the red card/white card problem, theoretically. There are other red card/white card problems, however; for example, there are legal problems between borders, even currency problems between borders. It will take time to work these problems out, but each gives headaches to the technology of Wide Area Networks.

Your job, as a class, is to discuss possible solutions to these and other similar problems that reduce the effectiveness of Wide Area Networks.

CHALLENGE EXERCISE 3: COMPUTER-ASSISTED DESIGN

Should you know word processing and want to learn data processing, use the data from the chart to construct a number of different kinds of visuals from a CAD or similar computer program.

1989 sales amounts for January by personnel
    Fahrquart: $657,000;
    Harcart: $792,000;
    Marbart: $865,079;
    Gephart: $800,000.
1990 sales amounts for January by personnel
    Fahrquart: $483,000;
    Harcart: $392,000;
    Marbart: $804,345;
    Gephart: $900,000.

1991 sales amounts for January by personnel
    Fahrquart: $657,000;
    Harcart: $712,000;
    Marbart: $632,567;
    Gephart: $750,500.
1992 sales amounts for January by personnel
    Fahrquart: $657,000;
    Harcart: $452,000;
    Marbart: $568,090;
    Gephart: $995,000.

Be sure to read the color section "The High-Tech Office" following page 438.

APPENDIX OUTLINE

▼

AND NOW I SEE WITH EYE

SERENE,

THE VERY PULSE OF THE

MACHINE;

A BEING BREATHING

THOUGHTFUL

BREATH,

A TRAVELLER BE-

TWEEN LIFE AND DEATH.

WILLIAM WORDSWORTH

(1770–1850)

TECHNICAL WRITING

435

Accounting, economics, management science, operations management, statistics, human resource management, as well as the entire range of social sciences, are only a few of the many disciplines that follow scientific methods. Anyone majoring in any of these subjects must become acquainted with several methods used in technical writing to organize and define products, procedures, and manuals.

Many reports, especially those including much technical information, require more than a simple, single-sentence statement of purpose. Technical reports often require definitions of unusual terms or terms likely to be unfamiliar to the reader. Such definitions have two parts: a formal sentence definition and an expanded or amplified definition.

Formal Sentence Definition

Formal sentence definitions are not a recent invention. Aristotle, for example, defined terms by separating them from everything else in the universe. His *formal sentence definition* method, which is still used today, divides the term into three parts. First, the term is given a *name*; then it is placed in a *class*; and finally it is *differentiated* from everything else in its class. When a term has been isolated from everything else in the universe, said Aristotle, that term has been defined. A formal sentence definition, then, has three parts: name, class, and differentia. It may be written as a formula:

Name   = Class + Differentia
Resistance = a force + opposes motion.

Thus, we have

Resistance [name] is a force [class] that opposes motion [differentia].

A computer [name] is an electronic machine [class] that performs calculations and other jobs by using a system of relays [differentia].

A contract [name] is a binding agreement [class] between people or parties [differentia].

Although the formula for writing formal sentence definitions saves much time and anguish, it does not solve all problems for the writer. Writers remain responsible for choosing proper and accurate names, classes, and differentiae.

Names

In business writing, the writer must define any word in the sentence definition that the reader does not know. Because writers often know certain arcane words very well, they often assume that readers know them also. Or, because some words have several meanings, writers must place a limiting phrase at the beginning of the formal sentence definition to restrict the word's meaning to only one thing: "As it is used here, a tree is a drawing shaped rather like a real tree that shows the relationships among all departments of the company."

CLASSES

The Aristotelian notion of definition isolates a term from everything else. Because there are so many things in the universe, it is helpful first to place the term in a class of things, thereby isolating it from most things in the universe. The problem for writers, then, is one of choosing a proper class in which to place the term. If the class is too big, then the term becomes lost in the class.

Here is a formal sentence definition in which the class is too big: A Widgitcog can opener is a thing for opening cans. Clearly, "thing" is a useless class for this can opener; there are simply too many terms in the universe for "thing" to be helpful to the reader. The following example further limits the class: A Widgitcog can opener is *an electric machine* for opening cans.

DIFFERENTIA

Differentiae isolate terms from their classes. Here writers must take care to do just that. One common problem is the circular definition. The second example above has such a problem, for the name of the object describes what it does. It is clear to everyone that a can opener opens cans; so merely writing that can openers open cans is not especially helpful, even if it is unavoidable. As there are can openers that only punch holes in cans, "opening" in the differentia is therefore insufficient, and the silliness of saying that can openers open cans may be diminished by adding this: "for removing lids from cans." Then, finally, the word "metal" is included, as there are now plastic cans on which can openers are useless. The result, after all this toying with names, classes, and differentiae, is this:

> A Widgitcog can opener is an electric machine for *removing lids* from *metal* cans.

AMPLIFIED DEFINITION

Because of unavoidable ambiguity or unfamiliar terms within the definition, even well-written formal sentence definitions often prove inadequate as clear explanations for readers. Consequently, such defini-

---

EXERCISE A: AMPLIFIED DEFINITIONS

Classify the dominant rhetorical modes used in the following amplified definition. Be ready to support your classification.

What is Small Business?[1]

One of the snags in trying to develop a usable definition of small business is simple relativity. For instance, it's clear that Amtrak, the top-ranked passenger railway, with $436 million in 1980 sales, isn't a small operation. But relative to Conrail's 1982 revenues of $3.6 billion, it's *small*. We all know that a one-woman dog-walking service is small business, but what about the local kennel with employees and revenues of $750,000? The answer is, of course, that neither Amtrak nor Conrail is a small business.

Perhaps the best definition is the one used by Congress in the Small Business Act of 1953, when it said that a small business is one that's independently owned and operated and doesn't dominate in its field of operation.

tions must be *amplified* or expanded so that readers might thoroughly understand the meaning of a term. Amplification usually is achieved through particular ways of writing that help clarify terms. These ways of writing are called *rhetorical modes*. Three rhetorical modes—analysis, comparison, and example—are especially helpful to technical writers.

ANALYSIS. Analysis means to divide something into its parts. Things may be defined by being analyzed. Here is example: "The 'Doppler Effect' results from two things: the speed at which sound travels and the speed at which the source travels. If the source is travelling in the same direction as the sound, the sound waves compress, raising the pitch. If the source is moving away from the sound, the sound waves are farther apart, lowering the pitch."

COMPARISON. A (the unknown) is like B (the known). When done well, comparison is perhaps the most useful method for defining things. Here is a good example from the *U.S. Steel Supervisor's Handbook*: "The Standard Cost System is a control for comparing what we actually spend (the strokes we took) with what we should have spent (par)." The Standard Cost System is like the scoring system for golf.

EXAMPLE. Examples are simple stories used to help define or explain. The best are very simple, so the writer can be sure that the reader understands the example. Here is a simple example of "resistance": "If children run through rooms with the doors open, they encounter little resistance. If one of the doors is closed, resistance occurs."

EXERCISE B: AMPLIFIED DEFINITIONS

1. Choose a process, term, or phenomenon peculiar to your major subject or to a special interest. Write an amplified definition.
2. Write an amplified definition of one of these terms.
   mountain
   accounting
   life
   freezing
   amortization
   love
   selling
   radar
   truth

DESCRIPTION OF A MECHANISM

For some reason business and technical writing have come to be considered discrete kinds of writing. They are not. Like most things, they are different only in their extremes. No one would confuse annual reports and the writing of specifications, but nearly all work-related writing, whether attempted by executives or engineers, obeys the same requirements. Reports commonly thought to be technical often follow arrangements similar to those of business reports. While it is true that microbiologists seldom write annual reports and personnel managers seldom write specifications, both write memos, résumés, letters, progress reports, feasibility studies, and many other forms of reports. In fact, most kinds of writing in business are done by most people regardless of their specialties.

Many formal business reports, for example, use an expanded version of the very simple arrangement of the technical writer's

A The paper office

B The electronic office

THE HIGH-TECH OFFICE

Until the 1970s, most businesses relied on calculators and manual computations to generate data and on typewriters to produce correspondence, and they stored their files on paper.

The challenges of the space program, however, produced the microchip in 197X, enabling the computer industry to develop the affordable desktop computer in the late 1970s. The advent of personal computers and the rapid technological advances since then have enabled office workers to streamline their work and in many cases to double their output. Computers enable businesses to manipulate enormous amounts of data easily and swiftly; to create three-dimensional designs of immense complexity; to make mathematical projections in minutes that had previously taken days or weeks; to communicate electronically across the office and, via satellites, across the world; to revise documents heavily without retyping them; and to store an entire filing cabinet of information on a single 3½-inch disk.

The types of computers used today range from huge mainframes, which can process more than 1000 million instructions per second (mips), and theoretically can accommodate an infinite number of terminals; to minicomputers, which can process as many as 75 mips; to desktop (personal) and portable (laptop) computers, which can process as many as 25 mips.

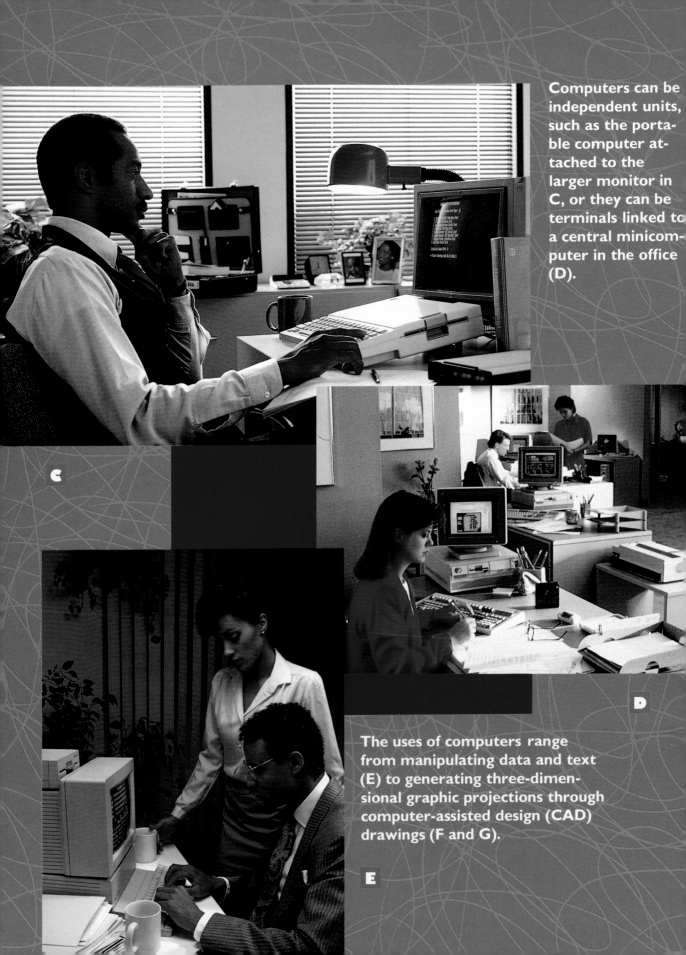

Computers can be independent units, such as the portable computer attached to the larger monitor in C, or they can be terminals linked to a central minicomputer in the office (D).

C

D

The uses of computers range from manipulating data and text (E) to generating three-dimensional graphic projections through computer-assisted design (CAD) drawings (F and G).

E

G

F

Communication technology links business people with their offices and their customers. Locally, cellular telephones use radio waves beamed from local transmitters (H).
To communicate beyond the range of local transmitters, companies relay the radio waves via satellites (I).

H

I

J

Portable, or laptop, computers and cellular telephones enable business people in the 1990s to work almost anywhere, anytime.

VOICE - 64Kbps = $\bar{o}_a$
DATA - 16Kbps = D

WORKSTATION 5

K

Current technology combines computers with televisions, telephones, and printers. A conference call can connect people in three different countries so they can not only speak to each other but also see each other, manipulate the same text and graphics, and print out that material via facsimile machine.

description of a mechanism. Technical writers who write good descriptions of mechanisms can write good business reports. Those who normally write business reports may improve those reports by learning to write simple technical reports. Versatility in business is important, and the less one tries to separate technical writing from business writing, the more one will do well. Although all writing must pay attention to the reader, business writing is nothing more than technical writing that must attend to people more than technical writing typically does. Descriptions of mechanisms provide an opportunity for writers to write the unadorned truth: no embellishments, no ambiguity, just the facts clearly stated. The description of a mechanism is, in fact, the prototype for all reports. Moreover, a mechanism is any system of definable parts, whether they compose a machine or an organization. Although each mechanism may require a special tailoring of the outline, the standard outline for a description of a mechanism follows.

OUTLINE FOR DESCRIPTION OF A MECHANISM
Title

I. Introduction
  A. Definition and purpose
  B. General appearance
  C. List of main parts
II. Detailed description
  A. Part one
    1. Definition and purpose
    2. Appearance
      a. Size
      b. Shape
      c. Material
      d. Location
      e. Attachment
  B. Part two
    1. Definition and purpose
    2. Appearance
      a. Size
      b. Shape
      c. Material
      d. Location
      e. Attachment
  C. Part three [etc.]
III. Summary

TITLE

Titles should be short but detailed. A title, for example, should read "Description of a Seven-Inch Model 240 Widgitcog," not "Description of a Widgitcog." Descriptions of widgitcogs must describe a specific widgitcog, not a general one, because widgitcogs come in many sizes and shapes. So do windows, door handles, office computers, books, trees, cars, electric can openers, and the absence of any of these things.

To describe a mechanism properly, a writer should be able to look at it while writing a description.

Here are some titles that are too general.

Description of a Hair Drier

Description of a Word-Processing Center

Description of a Felt Tip Pen

Here are the same titles made specific:

Description of a Prostyle 2000 Hair Drier

Description of the Fahrquart Company's Word-Processing Center

Description of a Blue Ink Ritewrite Model 3 Felt Tip Pen

Unlike formal reports, a description of a mechanism does not have a title page, although the report's title and the writer's name, job title, department, and company name are centered. Center the title two inches from the top of the first page, and place the writer's name one inch below the title. Immediately below, place the writer's title, and below that the department and the company name, each with its own line. Last comes the date.

INTRODUCTION

The introduction follows the title information, beginning about one-third of the way from the top of the page, but at least one inch below the date. The introduction orients the reader by defining the mechanism, describing the way it looks as a whole, and by listing its main parts. After reading the introduction, the reader should have sufficient information not to be confused by the description that follows.

DEFINITION AND PURPOSE.   The *definition* tells what the mechanism is, and the *purpose* tells what the mechanism does. The purpose—here, in detailed descriptions of the main parts, and in summary—is the only concession made to process; that is, the definition and purpose section is the only introductory section that says anything about what the mechanism does.

GENERAL APPEARANCE.   The section on appearance should say how big, how wide, and how tall the mechanism is. Sometimes a simple figure is helpful here. Sometimes a comparison works best, as long as the reader can be expected to know well what the mechanism is being compared with. Because nearly everyone knows what a jeep looks like, a writer might say "a dune buggy looks like a stripped-down jeep with big tires."

LIST OF MAIN PARTS.   The one-sentence list of the main parts is formulaic: "A Model 16 Widgitcog has four main parts: 1, 2, 3, 4." Before composing the sentence, however, the writer must decide the order in which to list the parts: the section on description takes each of those parts in the order they appear here. Moreover, because mechanisms are logical (those that work, anyway), their main parts must be listed logically, or at least according to a logical method. The writer can list them from outside to inside, inside to outside, left to right, right to left, top to bottom. The writer should not order the main parts by what each does, however. A description of how the mechanism works belongs in the detailed description section.

A description of the operation of a mechanism is called a "Description of a Mechanism in Process." It is important to separate what the mechanism is as a thing existing in space from the mechanism's process, which exists in time.

DETAILED DESCRIPTION

The detailed description of each part in its turn usually requires only one paragraph. The topic sentence for each paragraph should begin with a formal sentence definition. Next comes a short statement of purpose. The rest of the paragraph describes the part's appearance, usually in the same order as in the other paragraphs: size, shape, material, location, and how it attaches to the other parts. Sometimes figures help; sometimes comparison works better.

SUMMARY

This short section describes briefly just how the parts of the mechanism work together. Should the mechanism be simple and sufficiently described in the purpose section in the introduction, this section would be omitted. Here is an example of a description of a mechanism.

DESCRIPTION OF AN AUGEAN FLOWSPLITTER
SHUTOFF VALVE

Smedley Fahrquart
Sophomore, FSU
30 April 1992

INTRODUCTION

Definition and Purpose

The Augean Flowsplitter Shutoff Valve is a green,
plastic, 2.4 cm connector that screws into two
threaded hoses and a threaded water faucet. The
flowsplitter shutoff valve splits one flow of water
into two. It also increases or decreases the flow
in one or both hoses. Gardeners and others use the
valve to direct water from one water source to two
different places simultaneously.

Overall Description

Looking like a thick Y, the valve is 11.4 cm long,
8.9 cm across the top of the Y, and 2.4 cm wide at
the base of the Y. Each of these three ends is
threaded: the base has standard female threads; the
branches of the Y have standard male threads. Each
branch of the Y houses a switch that controls flow.

Main Parts

The main parts of the Augean Flowsplitter Valve are
the flow splitting assembly, internal flow restrictors, switches, and locking screws.

DETAILED DESCRIPTION

Flowsplitter Assembly

Housing the internal parts is the plastic flowsplitter assembly that, as the name implies, splits the
flow of the water from the faucet. The Y-shaped assembly comprises two branches (or arms), each 4.2 cm
long, and 2.4 cm in diameter, and a trunk (or base)
2.1 cm long. A small, flat plastic triangle, .3 cm
thick, sits in the Y's apex. A small hole, drilled
in the middle of the triangle, is used only to hang
the valve on a nail on a wall during storage. A 1.4
cm × 3.1 cm hexagonal nut is attached to the end of

the base. The nut includes female threads and a rubber washer. Immediately below the threads on each
branch is a small hole.

Internal Flow Restrictors

The internal flow restrictors control the flow of
water in each branch of the valve. Housed in the
middle of each branch, the plastic restrictors are
spheres 2.1 cm in diameter. Each sphere has two opposed holes, 1.0 cm across, allowing water to pass.
A small notched cylinder, .6 cm across and .3 cm
high, centered atop each sphere, attaches to the
flow switch.

Flow Switches

Each of two plastic flow switches, 2.5 cm long and
shaped like electric light switch toggles, turns a
flow restrictor, thereby altering the amount of water passing through the holes in the flow restrictors. At the rounded end of each switch is a notched
hole.

Locking Screws

A locking screw, 1.8 cm long and .3 cm in diameter,
connects each flow switch to an internal flow restrictor. The locking screw passes through the
notched hole of a flow switch, the hole below the
threads in each branch of the Y, and attaches to the
small notched cylinder of a flow restrictor.

SUMMARY

As water flows from a faucet through an open flowsplitter, half flows through one branch of the Y and
half through the other. If one flow switch is turned
slightly, the restrictor turns also, making the restrictor's hole smaller and allowing less water to
pass. Turned to off, that restrictor stops all water
flow through that branch of the Y. If the other restrictor is turned to off, then no water passes.
Each restrictor may be adjusted to allow the water
to be distributed between the branches as needed.

MANUALS

Companies sell more than machinery and services. They also sell instructions about how to assemble, use, maintain, and repair that machinery and how to use and maintain those services. Manuals may be very simple: "Your new Handy-Dandy bottle opener is very easy to use. While gripping the handle, just place the loop over the bottle cap, with the near end under the cap, and pry up." Or manuals may be very complex: "To get a precise fingerprint of any wine, it is very important to perform the 237 tests presented here precisely in the order they are presented. The first 79 tests require a gas spectrometer, the operation of which must be understood first."

Simple manuals, the kind that come with simple tools bought in grocery and hardware stores (carrot peelers, hand pipe-cutters, and the like), are read by everyone from Ph.D.'s in English to those whose first language is not English. To make sure that nearly everyone who buys a Handy-Dandy peeler will be able to use it properly, the language of these manuals is usually pitched near a seventh-grade level. (See the fog index in Chapter 1.)

Complex manuals, usually written for business clients or industrial customers and read only by engineers, accountants, or computer analysts, are pitched much higher, on an eleventh- or twelfth-grade level. Most of the difference derives from vocabulary and complexity of sentence structure. Some machinery is so complex that it must be accompanied by separate manuals for assembly, operation, maintenance, and the like.

In-between manuals Most manuals are written for business and industry. But the audience, while not so difficult to reach as a general one, is nevertheless diverse. A gas spectrometer, for example, a machine that analyzes and measures the complex chemical components of liquids, may be assembled by an engineer, operated by a chemist, maintained by a technician, and repaired at the factory. Consequently, the manual must be clear and precise, written for an intelligent but general audience. The intelligent lay audience is one that can figure many things, but it must be told what technical words mean and how technical processes work.

KINDS OF MANUALS

The four most common kinds of manuals are assembly, operation (use), maintenance, and repair manuals. In large companies, manuals are written by people hired to do nothing else. In middle-sized and small companies, anyone with a little knowledge may be asked to write, or at least to oversee the writing of, the manuals. Because the most common kind of manual is an operation manual, that kind will be discussed here.

OPERATION MANUAL

Here is a detailed description of the parts of an operation manual.

OUTLINE FOR OPERATION MANUAL

Title page

Table of Contents

List of Illustrations

Glossary

Introduction

    General Description

    Theory of Operation

Detailed Description

    Training Session

    Maintenance

    Trouble-Shooting

Index (long manuals only)

Appendices (long manuals only)

TITLE PAGE.   The title page of an operation manual is like that of other formal reports (see Chapter 9). The title must be complete, detailed, and accurate.

TABLE OF CONTENTS.   The full table of contents of an operation manual, containing many subsections, is more detailed than other types of manuals because people may refer to an operations manual dozens of times. After the first few times, they may want to see only a particular section. The table of contents must make that section easy to find. The decimal system is used so that people may refer others to a particular section without having to cite the name of the heading. The decimal method, in short, is used to make the reader's job easier. See the examples on pages 449–57.

LIST OF ILLUSTRATIONS.   A list of illustrations for an operation manual is almost always required. Operation manuals must be written simply, and visuals, usually figures, greatly aid the reader in understanding a machine and its operation. Because visuals appear frequently in manuals, a list that gives the title and page number of each is included after the table of contents. (See page 449.)

GLOSSARY.   A glossary of terms is often useful because almost every machine has parts with abstruse names, because many operations have strange titles, and because the reader cannot be expected to follow the manual without knowing the meaning of those names. Moreover, because any of these names may occur often throughout a manual, a single definition in the text is insufficient. Although readers may learn the meaning of a term on page 4, they probably will have forgotten it by the time they see the term again on page 25. For these reasons, and because defining a word each time it appears takes up space, a glossary of terms helps the reader greatly.

INTRODUCTION.   In addition to the standard introductory material—type of manual, detailed name of the machine (model numbers, etc.) and manufacturer—the introduction to an operation manual also includes the following:

- What the reader needs to know before attempting to operate the machine. If the machine requires no special knowledge or training, then this sentence may be omitted.

- Where the reader may find additional information, related manuals, and the like.

- A section on how to use the manual because operation manuals have no scope section.

Such sections mention the glossary, advise readers to learn the description sections before attempting the training session, and so on.

GENERAL DESCRIPTION.   This section describes the machine and its operation. It contains a formal sentence definition, an amplified definition, and a list of the main components. A figure depicting the entire machine placed here is helpful. Each of the main components should be labeled with a name and a letter or number. The component labeled "1" or "A" should be the first discussed in the detailed description. That labeled "2" or "B" should be second, and so on.

THEORY (OR PRINCIPLE) OF OPERATION.   The theory of operation section is where readers and operators go when all else fails. The operators need to know why the machine works and what principles make it work. Clearly written theories of operation inform readers sufficiently so that by understanding a problem they might solve it.

The theories and principles by which a machine works must be written simply and concretely:

DO'S AND DON'TS FOR WRITING THE PRINCIPLE (OR THEORY) OF OPERATION SECTION

- Do explain each principle and theory in relation to the machine.

- Do use visuals, but don't use *complicated* visuals and arcane symbols.

- Do give each theory and principle a separate paragraph.

- Do begin each paragraph with a formal sentence definition. Amplify the definition only so far as the reader requires for understanding.

DETAILED DESCRIPTION.   The detailed description follows the arrangement set forth in the introduction. Each main part of the machine is described, as well as each process dealing with it. Again, a formal sentence definition and an amplified definition are required if the main part is sufficiently complex to warrant such definition. Do not define simple things: a toggle switch, for example, or a simple control knob. Simply mentioning which way to flip the switch or turn the knob for on and off is adequate.

There is one major difference between a manual and a description of a mechanism: the reader of a description of a mechanism is looking at one thing, the description; the reader of an operation manual is looking at two things, the manual and the machine. Labels given to each part, and included in the text as well as the figure, allow the reader to move from the page to the machine again and again without becoming lost.

The detailed description of a main part may divide the main part into smaller parts. When this is advisable, do it. Remember that each paragraph in a manual has a decimal number included in the heading. Remember to create a further indention and add another decimal each time a part is divided into smaller parts.

TRAINING SESSION.   The training session is a step-by-step explanation that leads the reader through the operation. Give directions as if they were orders, using the second person imperative: "Do this. Then do that."

MAINTENANCE.   The maintenance section of an operation manual is sometimes called "routine maintenance" to distinguish it from "trouble-shooting," which is, of course, maintenance that is not routine. The maintenance section, like the training session, is written as a series of directions ("Do this. Do that."). Figures are helpful here also. Consider the order of those directions carefully.

TROUBLE-SHOOTING.   The best trouble-shooting sections divide the page into two parts: trouble and solution. See page 457 for an example of a trouble-shooting section.

APPENDICES.   Sometimes such related material as other manuals, manufacturer's specifications, blueprints, and the like are too long to include in a manual but may help readers. These should be included, each as a separate appendix. Should a manual contain more than one appendix, entitle the section Appendices. Capitalize and center "appendix" as the main heading.

INDEX.   The index alphabetically lists all important ideas, names, principles, and theories in a manual. It includes page numbers and cross-references for related items. The index is the last section to contain regular pagination. See the index of this book for an example. Capitalize and center "Index" as the main heading.

Some computer writing programs create an index by flagging words, phrases, and ideas. They then do wonderful things, such as sort the flagged items, place them in alphabetical order, note page numbers, and even display cross-references.

Creating an index by hand is best done with index cards. Note each item and its page number on a separate card. Then place the cards in alphabetical order. Check the pile for cross-references and write each down. Then type the index from the pile of cards.

OPERATION MANUAL FOR THE
WIDGITCOG ELECTRIC FUZZ REMOVER

Prepared for
Samantha Evans,
President and CEO,
Fahrquart Industries

By
Smedley Fahrquart,
Technical Writer

22 June 1992

TABLE OF CONTENTS

LIST OF ILLUSTRATIONS

<u>Figures</u>

1.0 INTRODUCTION

After repeated washing and wearing, clothing's fabric fibers often get tangled, forming little balls of fuzz. These balls become visible and very unattractive. The Widgitcog Electric Fuzz Remover removes fabric fuzz from all kinds of fabrics from woolens to wash-and-wear synthetics.

2.0 GENERAL DESCRIPTION

The Widgitcog Electric Fuzz Remover is a hand-held, battery-operated machine used to remove fuzz balls from clothing. Coming in pink or blue, weighing 6.5 ounces, and using a Size C battery, the fuzz remover has five main parts: battery cover, motor case, fuzz-catching case, fuzz-removal dish, and rotating unit (see Figure 1).

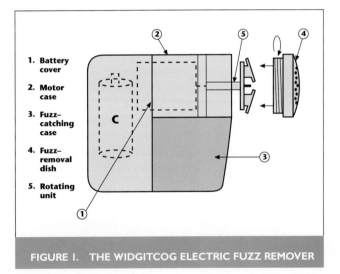

1. Battery cover
2. Motor case
3. Fuzz-catching case
4. Fuzz-removal dish
5. Rotating unit

FIGURE I.   THE WIDGITCOG ELECTRIC FUZZ REMOVER

3.0 THEORY OF OPERATION

A direct-current motor, powered by a 1.5 volt battery, drives the fuzz remover. Current passes through the motor by means of two electrical terminals, one at each end of the battery (see Figure 2). When current is supplied, the motor rotates an axle that fits into the rotating unit.

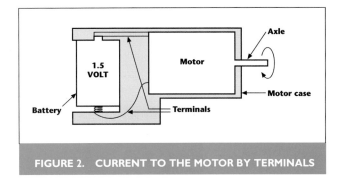

FIGURE 2.   CURRENT TO THE MOTOR BY TERMINALS

4.0 DETAILED DESCRIPTION

4.1 Parts in Operation

4.1.1. The Battery Cover

The battery cover protects the battery by snapping onto the motor case. The cover must be removed gently from the motor case before the battery can be inserted (see Figure 3).

4.1.2. The Motor Case

L-shaped, the motor case houses all the other parts.

The battery is inserted by placing it between the two arms of the motor case. The battery's positive end must touch the positive arm, and the negative end of the battery must touch the negative arm of the motor case (see Figure 3).

2

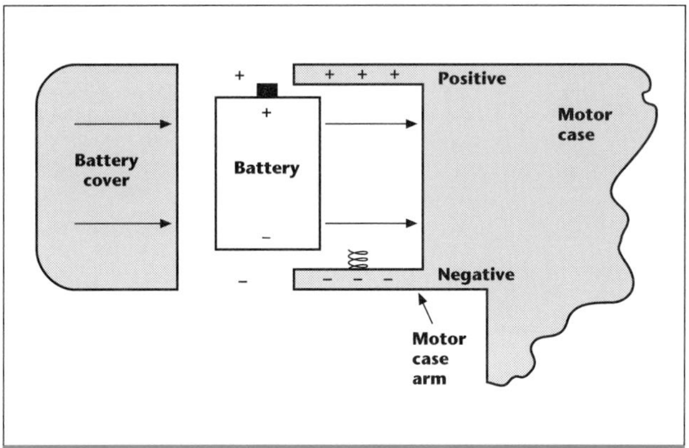

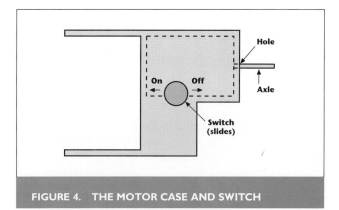

FIGURE 3. INSERTING THE BATTERY

The direct-current motor also is housed by the motor case. Here, too, are attached the axle and the on/off switch (see Figure 4).

FIGURE 4. THE MOTOR CASE AND SWITCH

4.1.3. The Fuzz-Catching Case

Attached beneath the rotating unit on the motor case, the fuzz-catching case catches the fuzz. When full, the case may be removed by pulling it from the motor case gently.

3

4.1.4. The Fuzz-Removal Dish

The smooth, chrome, mushroom-shaped fuzz-removal dish actually collects the fuzz by moving across the fabric. On top of the mushroom are many holes through which the fuzz travels from the fabric to the catching case. The dish screws into the motor case at a point directly over the rotating unit (see Figure 5).

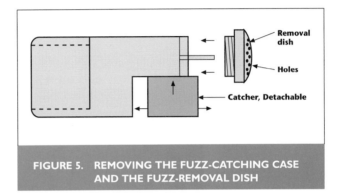

FIGURE 5.   REMOVING THE FUZZ-CATCHING CASE AND THE FUZZ-REMOVAL DISH

4.1.5. The Rotating Unit

The rotating unit fits between the motor's axle and the fuzz removal dish (see Figure 6).

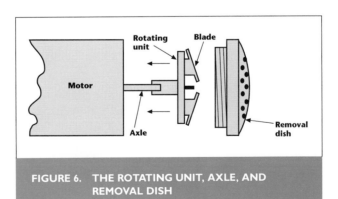

FIGURE 6.   THE ROTATING UNIT, AXLE, AND REMOVAL DISH

4

The rotating unit is a light, flat, plastic disc that holds three metal blades. The blades are angled in the disc so that, when power is supplied and the unit rotates, they create a vacuum in the removal dish (see Figure 7).

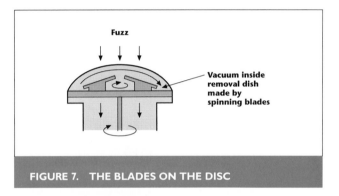

FIGURE 7. THE BLADES ON THE DISC

Fuzz is pulled through the holes of the dish and cut by the whirring blades. The vacuum causes the fuzz to be pulled down and into the fuzz catching case (see Figure 8).

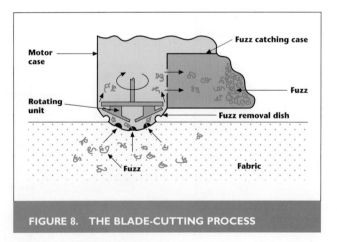

FIGURE 8. THE BLADE-CUTTING PROCESS

5

5.0 TRAINING SESSION

5.1 Warnings

Improper use may cause the blades to cut the fabric of clothing. Also, unscrewing the fuzz-removal dish while machine is operating is dangerous because the cutting blades will be exposed and turning fast.

5.2 Operating the Fuzz Remover (see Figure 9)

Place the fabric on a hard, smooth surface. Check to see that the Fuzz Remover's parts are tight. Turn on the Fuzz Remover. Gently lay the removal dish flat against the fabric. Slowly and gently rotate the dish across the fabric. Periodically check the catching case. When the catching case is full, turn off the Fuzz Remover. Remove the catching case from the Fuzz Remover. Then remove the fuzz from the catching case. Replace the catching case, and begin again.

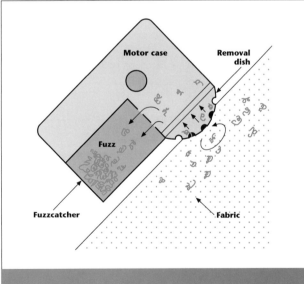

FIGURE 9. OPERATING THE FUZZ REMOVER

6

6.0 MAINTENANCE

Like all knives, the blades of the Fuzz Remover eventually become dull and must be sharpened. To sharpen the blades of the Fuzz Remover with an emery board, unscrew the fuzz removal dish. Pull the rotating unit from the motor axle. Holding the dish in one hand and the emery board in the other, pass the emery board lightly over the edge of the blades (see Figure 10). After each pass, look to see whether the blades are sharper. Once the blades are sharp, reassemble the unit.

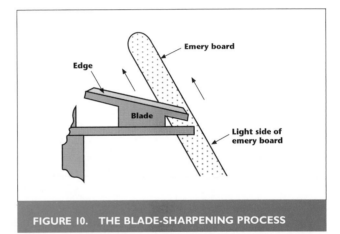

FIGURE 10.　THE BLADE-SHARPENING PROCESS

7

7.0 TROUBLE-SHOOTING

Problem	Cause and Solution
7.1. Remover will not remove fuzz.	1.a. The catching case is full; empty it.
	1.b. The blades are wrapped with fuzz. Remove fuzz with tweezers.
	1.c. The Fuzz Remover is being moved too quickly across the fabric; move more slowly.
	1.d. The blades are dull; sharpen the blades.
7.2. Remover will not run.	2.a. Battery is weak or dead; replace it.
	2.b. Battery is incorrectly inserted; see Figure 3.
	2.c. Electrical circuit is broken; take the Fuzz Remover to a small-appliance repair shop.

APPENDIX OUTLINE

▼

You write with ease to

show your breeding,

But easy writing's curst

hard reading.

EDITING

R. B. Sheridan

(1751–1816)

I am the Roman

Emperor, and am above

grammar.

Emperor Sigismund

(1361–1437)

Grammar, which knows

how to control even

kings.

Molière (1622–1673)

WHY EDIT?

The quality of writing is determined largely by carefully, even painstakingly, changing the first draft into a finished draft that is concise, organized, and clear. This process is called *editing*. The busy manager who believes that time is too precious to waste on editing should consider the example of John Kenneth Galbraith, the famous economist, businessman, author, and statesman, who says that after much experience, he usually can produce passable prose after only four drafts.

Consider the differences between these two sentences, the second being an edited version of the first.

> UNEDITED: Accidents that are fatal head-on collisions often occur in a manner that is severe enough to result in the death of the occupants of the vehicles involved.

> EDITED: Head-on collisions can be fatal.

The unedited sentence has 27 words; the edited sentence has 5 words. If an unedited report this badly written contained 100 pages, then an edited report might have fewer than 20. No one in business would choose to read 100 pages should the same information be contained in 20 pages. Moreover, it takes about six seconds to read and seven seconds to understand the unedited sentence and about one second to read and understand the edited version. An edited report, then, can be read in about 20 to 25 percent of the time required to read the unedited report. Although careful editing adds about 25 percent to the time required to write a report, the overall savings in time is considerable if more than one person must read the report.

Admittedly, this is an extreme example. Yet, should a well-edited report cut the number of original words in half — a common occurrence — a well-written report costs very little more to write than a badly written one. When one adds monetary value to clear, concise, accurate reports; to the reader's ability to understand, not misunderstand; to do what is expected as a result, not what is unexpected; to coordinate activities properly, not create a hopeless tangle of schedules; to produce the first time what everyone believes ought to be produced, not produce it after five or six tries, the savings could be in the millions of dollars.

The job of editing is made easier by knowing what to look for. There is more to do than reduce the number of words. When many sentences are reduced to plain English, it becomes apparent that they state the obvious and probably should never have been written. Telling people what they already know wastes time. Misspellings and bad grammar often escape several copy-editing jobs. In spite of much work, the writer has not clarified some points well. Some deadwood and redundancy are nearly invisible, the obvious not obvious. Polishing is the writer's last chance to produce clean and shining prose.

COPY EDITING

Because no one wants to retype a memo or report to correct each error as it occurs in each draft, writers make marks on pages to insert and delete, change and rearrange words. Over the years writers have agreed on a set of symbols for editing copy. *Copy* means anything written for publication that needs editing before it is sufficiently good to be printed. Learning these symbols saves much time for the typist or typesetter and makes writing better.

THE KINDS OF COPY

Writers edit so much that over the centuries names have been given to those drafts that occur from the first draft to the final product.

FOUL COPY.   The initial writing, which usually contains only a rough outline and a few words identifying each heading in the outline, is called a *foul* copy. This is a good name, for it describes well the quality of the writing and the ideas therein.

FAIR COPY.   The copy that is almost ready to send to the printer (or typist) is called a *fair* copy. This copy usually contains numerous but minor changes written in the margins and in the text. Between the foul copy and the fair copy, there are usually many other copies that are fairly foul or foully fair depending on their proximities to the foul or fair copies. These have no specific names, although they are usually called *drafts*.

FINAL COPY.   This copy is sent out into the world. Even more frightening is that this copy is sent to the boss. The work that occurs between the foul copy and the first full draft is usually organizational, consisting of re-arranging the order in which information is presented, of filling in detail. After producing a full draft, however, copy editing occurs. Business and technical writers copy edit. They seldom proofread.

Most have heard of proofreading, but that is what is done to the final draft when it returns from the typist or typesetter. The most common kind of editing is copy editing.

THE ADVANTAGES OF COPY EDITING

Much writing and rewriting is required in this text, but learning a set of simple copy editing symbols before beginning to write and rewrite will make the job much easier. Moreover, although perfect copy is preferable, it is possible, given the professor's permission (or the secretary's), that final copies submitted for a grade (or for posting) occasionally may contain a few copy editing symbols without sacrificing that grade.

THE SYMBOLS OF COPY EDITING

DELETING LETTERS, WORDS, AND PHRASES. To delete a letter, strike through it and mark the space created by the deletion to be closed up:

judgement

To delete a word or phrase, cross it out:

She liked the green ~~color~~ on the cover of the report.

Furthermore, ~~in addition,~~ that company is nearly bankrupt.

Notice that the comma after "addition" must also be deleted.

INSERTING LETTERS, WORDS, PHRASES, AND SPACES. To insert anything, put a caret (∧) under the appropriate place and print the item to be inserted in the space above the line. (This is why manuscripts are double-spaced—to make room for such markings.) If little space exists between the characters where the new item needs to be inserted, draw a line between the characters:

misspelling

Smedley is *not very* good at his job.

To insert a space, use the symbol for "number":

Smedley Fahrquart

DELETING AND INSERTING SIMULTANEOUSLY. To replace letters or words, strike through the incorrect elements, place a carat beneath the line to indicate the insertion, and print the correct letters or words in the space above the line:

knowledgeable

What are the *boundaries* ~~parameters~~ of this discussion?

This method, *moreover* ~~in other words,~~ saves retyping a page.

REVERSING LETTERS, WORDS, AND PHRASES. To reverse the order of letters, words, or phrases, put a transposition mark (∽) around the elements to be switched:

This is the correct spelling of "recieve."

He wanted to carefully search all the files.

CREATING A NEW PARAGRAPH. To break up a paragraph into two or more paragraphs, insert a line break symbol (⌠) and a paragraph symbol (⌗):

. . . The second stage ends with cleaning the spark plugs. The third stage begins with putting them back. . . .

**EXERCISE A:
DELETING LETTERS**

Delete letters from the following misspelled words:

occassional

passtime

cemmetary

exhillarate

parallell

sallary

**EXERCISE B:
DELETING WORDS**

Delete the redundant words in the following sentences:

1. A round circle would be most efficient.
2. It is essential and extremely important to avoid redundancies.
3. Smedley is living off memories of the past.

**EXERCISE C:
INSERTING A LETTER**

Correct the spelling of these words by inserting the appropriate letter:

accomodate

aparatus

commitee

paralel

EXERCISE D: INSERTING WORDS AND PHRASES

Insert the bracketed words and phrases where indicated in the following sentences. Be careful also to insert the appropriate punctuation.

1. The project director may be nasty, or she may be accommodating. [particularly]

2. There are several ways   to play Trivial Pursuit. [, however,]

3. There are several ways to play Trivial Pursuit [, however]

4. It is probable   that Smedley will wear a lamp shade at the office Christmas party again this year. [, but not certain,]

EXERCISE E. DELETING AND INSERTING SIMULTANEOUSLY

Delete the words in italic and insert the words and phrases in the brackets. Be sure to note any other changes required by the deletions and insertions.

1. These reports, *as well as* their appendices, are well done. [and]

2. The Treasurer wants all sales personnel to submit their travel expenses to the Treasurer's Office on a regular basis. [regularly]

3. I shall be ready momentarily. [in a moment]

CHANGING A CAPITAL LETTER TO A LOWER-CASE LETTER.

To change a capital letter to lowercase, draw a slash mark through it:

the President

CAPITALIZING A LETTER.

To capitalize a lowercase letter, draw three short lines beneath it:

president Lincoln

SPELLING OUT AN ABBREVIATED WORD.

Sometimes writers abbreviate in early drafts. To make sure abbreviations are spelled out in the final copy, circle the abbreviation:

As an undergraduate, Smedley Fahrquart was the social director of the Student Gov. Asso.

I GOOFED; IGNORE THESE COPY-EDITING MARKS.

Sometimes editors err in their editing. That is, they make changes and discover later that the original was fine. To undo the editing, circle it and write "stet." This is an abbreviation for the Latin for "let it stand."

I KNOW THIS LOOKS ODD, BUT IT IS CORRECT.

Occasionally, English has peculiar or variant spellings of words. When a word looks misspelled but is not, circle it and write "ok" above it:

Yesterday I called Windinthewillows Smith.

CENTERING WORDS.

When a word or phrase needs to be centered on a line, such as in a title or a main head, enclose it in reverse brackets:

]Hamlet[

MOVING WORDS TO THE RIGHT OR LEFT.

To create or remove indentions or to adjust alignment, draw single brackets indicating the direction that the words need to go: an open bracket (⊏) for moving to the left and a close bracket for moving to the right (⊐). To specify how many spaces the words should be moved, write the number and the space symbol and circle them:

Maine
New Hampshire
⊏ Vermont
Massachusetts
Rhode Island
Connecticut

 I wish to persuade women to endeavor to acquire strength, both of mind and body, and to convince them that the soft phrases, susceptibility of heart, delicacy of sentiment, and refinement of taste, are almost synonymous with epithets of weakness, and that those beings who are only the objects of pity and that kind of love, which has been termed its sister, will soon become objects of contempt.[1]

GRAMMAR

Grammar comprises the rules and conventions that help clarify the meanings of words.

PARTS OF SENTENCES: DEFINITIONS AND EXPLANATIONS

DEFINITIONS.

Adjective   A word that modifies a noun or pronoun: short, tall, rich, green, hard-working, warm.

Adverb   A word that modifies a verb, adjective, or other adverb, and occasionally other parts of speech. Most words ending in -*ly* are adverbs—quickly, correctly, hardly, considerately—but so, too, are such intensifiers as "too" and "very."

Article   Indefinite articles are "a" and "an." The definite article is "the."

Conjunction   A word that links words, phrases, or clauses: and, but, or, nor, for, so, yet, and many more.

Expletive   The use of "there" or "it" to begin a passive construction: "There is . . ." or "It is . . ."

Gerund   Verbals used as nouns, ending in -*ing*. Gerunds may be subjects: "*Seeing* (gerund) well is helpful." Or, they may be objects, even objects of prepositions: "She is tired of *working* (object of the preposition, 'of') hard."

Infinitive   The fundamental form of a verb, usually preceded by *to*: "to run," "to think," "to sit."

Interjection   A word outside normal construction, used to express strong feelings or to gain attention: "Oh," "Gee," "Goodness."

Noun   A person, place, thing, or idea: Jane, home, book, truth.

Participle   A participle in its true form is a verbal used as an adjective: "I've had a trying day." Usually, it ends in -*ing*. Often, they take objects: "The judge *trying* [part.] the *case* [object] . . ."

Preposition   A word that indicates position and introduces a phrase: at, on, onto, in, into, up, down, to, from, about, with, of, across, for, by, among, between.

Pronoun   A word used in place of a noun. Personal pronouns (person speaking or writing and person spoken or written to) include the

---

[1]Mary Wollstonecraft, *A Vindication of the Rights of Women* (New York: Norton, 1975). Originally published in 1792.

following: I, me, mine, we, us, ours, you. Demonstrative pronouns (pointing out) include the following: he, she, it, him, her, his, hers, its, they, them, theirs. Interrogative and relative pronouns (uncertain identity) include the following: who, whom, whose, which, what. Other pronouns include the following: one, someone, somebody, anybody, nobody, none, both, all, each, either, neither, whether.

Verb   A word or group of words describing the state or the action of a noun: go, get, receive, catch, play.

EXPLANATIONS.

Case   Every noun and pronoun in a sentence serves one of three functions, or cases: *subjective*, actors (I, we, they); *objective*, receivers of action (me, us, them); *possessive*, possessors of a thing or quality (my, ours, his, hers, its, yours, theirs).

Clause   A group of words containing a subject and a verb. Some are complete thoughts (independent clauses): "He went home to be with his family." Some are incomplete thoughts (dependent clauses): "When he went home."

Comparatives   Comparatives are the second of three adjectival or adverbial comparisons: good, *better*, best; bad, *worse*, worst; tall, *taller*, tallest.

Double negatives   A statement that contains two negatives, thereby having a positive meaning (the two negatives cancel each other to create a positive meaning). Thus, *"I do not have nothing"* means *"I have something."*

Person and number   Person identifies who the subject is: *"I"* and *"we"* are first person; *"you"* is second person; and *"he," "she," "it," "one,"* and *"they"* are third person. Number indicates whether the subject is singular or plural: *"I," "he," "she," "one,"* and *"it"* are singular; *"we"* and *"they"* are plural; and *"you"* can be either singular or plural. The form of the verb must always agree with the person and number of the subject. Using the present tense of the verb *be*, the following table demonstrates how person and number relate:

Person	Number	
	Singular	**Plural**
First	I am	we are
Second	you are	you are
Third	he, she, it, one is	they are

Phrase   Any group of grammatically related words that is not a clause is a *phrase*.

Tense   Verbs exist in time—past, present, future, among others—and each distinction in time is called a *tense*.

EXERCISE F: PERSON AND NUMBER

Give the person and number of the following statements:

1. I know
2. she considers
3. we ate
4. you left
5. they are
6. it ran
7. one owes
8. he arrives

....
COMMON GRAMMATICAL PROBLEMS

1. *Subject/verb agreement*
2. *Noun/pronoun agreement*
3. *Dangling modifiers*
4. *Misplaced modifiers*
5. *Spelling errors*
6. *Subjective and objective forms*
7. *"Is when" constructions*
8. *Parallel constructions*
9. *Changing tenses*
10. *Subjunctive mood*
11. *Who/whom*
12. *Predicate nominative*

....
EXERCISE G: SUBJECT/VERB AGREEMENT AND PREPOSITIONAL PHRASES

Make the verbs and subjects of the following sentences agree:

1. Each of the books (is, are) boring.
2. A majority of Democrats (is, are) considered conservative.
3. The purpose of the meetings (is, are) unclear.

....
EXERCISE H: SUBJECT AND VERB AGREEMENT WITH *AS WELL AS*

Choose the proper verb in the following sentences to make their subjects and verb agree:

1. Smedley, as well as his sister, (was, were) hired on April Fool's Day.
2. Smedley and his sister (was, were) hired on April Fool's Day.

GRAMMATICAL PROBLEMS COMMON TO BUSINESS PROSE

Although writers make too many errors to count them all, twelve grammatical errors commonly appear in such business prose as memos, letters, and reports.

SUBJECT/VERB AGREEMENT.   In grammar, subjects and verbs must have the same person and number; that is, they must agree in person and number. Singular subjects agree with singular verbs; plural subjects agree with plural verbs. A number of conditions cause problems. They are discussed here.

1. *Separation of subject and verb.* Agreement is easy when subject and verb are close; no one, for example, errs in writing "Trees are pretty." Nearly everyone occasionally errs, however, when subject and verb are separated by, say, a prepositional phrase, especially when the object of the preposition differs in number (singular or plural) from the subject of the sentence: *Which* of the boys *is* going?" Some people may write "Which of the boys are going?" because "boys" is so close to "is." But the subject is "which." "Which" is singular, and the verb must also be singular: "is." This is a natural error, one to which even the best writers succumb at times. Good writers, however, correct the error when they edit.

2. *Separation of the subject from the verb by* as well as. Some people mistake "as well as" for "and," and in a sense they are the same, but it does not make a subject plural or compound. Here is a sentence containing a compound subject: "That *manager and* this *mechanic are* hard workers." When the sentence replaces "and" with "as well as," it looks like this: "That *manager,* as well as this mechanic, *is* a hard worker." "As well as" emphasizes one of two subjects: "Newspapers, as well as magazines, convey more information than television." But when emphasis is unnecessary, write "Newspapers and magazines convey more information than television." If "and" can replace "as well as," and emphasis is unnecessary, use "and."

3. *Verb choice with "neither . . . nor."* The verb following "neither . . . nor" (or "either . . . or") is singular or plural depending upon whether the noun closest to it is singular or plural: "Neither the president nor her *advisors* are coming." Compare "Neither her advisors nor the *president* is coming."

4. *Indefinite pronouns as subjects.* Indefinite pronouns are the following: each, every, one, either, neither, any, none, everyone, anyone, everybody. Indefinite pronouns take singular verbs.

   Each of the reports *is* due next week.

   None of the managers *is* here today.

   Neither project *is* ready.

   Everybody knows the condition of the department.

EXERCISE I: SUBJECT AND VERB AGREEMENT WITH NEITHER . . . NOR

Choose the verb that properly agrees with the subject of the following sentences:

1. Neither Smedley nor his sister (celebrate, celebrates) April Fool's Day.
2. Neither Smedley nor his brothers (celebrate, celebrates) April Fool's Day.

EXERCISE J: SUBJECT AND VERB AGREEMENT WITH INDEFINITE PRONOUNS

Correct the errors in agreement in the following sentences:

1. Everyone among us know that Smedley may be in trouble.
2. Neither of them need to answer to Smedley.

EXERCISE K: COLLECTIVE NOUNS AND SUBJECT-VERB AGREEMENT

Choose the correct verb to make the following sentences' subjects and verbs agree:

1. Smedley, the president's office called and (want, wants) you to get over there right away.
2. The jury (was, were) deliberating when news of the defendant's escape arrived.

Any of the secretaries *is* able to do the job.

Either of the plants *is* able to produce the part.

Collective nouns take a singular verb: "The staff *is* well paid."

NOUN/PRONOUN AGREEMENT.   Make sure the pronoun agrees in number with the noun. Do not write, for instance, "If a *person* wants to succeed in business, *they* had better be prepared to work hard." Who are "*they*"? Write "If a *person* wants to succeed in business, *he* [or *she*] should work hard." Or make the noun and pronoun plural: "If *people* want to succeed in business, *they* should work hard."

DANGLING MODIFIERS.   A phrase or clause "dangles" from the beginning of a sentence if it does not clearly modify the subject of the sentence. Do not write, for example, "Unless well cooked, people should not eat pork." A well-cooked person could not eat anything. Write, instead, "Unless it is well cooked, people should not eat pork."

MISPLACED MODIFIERS.   Dangling modifiers are only the most obvious of misplaced modifiers, for all modifiers must be placed so they clearly identify the word, phrase, or clause they modify. This is usually done by placing the modifier as close as possible to the part modified. In the sentence "He sang a song at the convention that was lewd," the modifier ("that was lewd") should modify the noun "song." Because it immediately follows "convention," however, it modifies "convention." The convention, indeed, may have been lewd, but that is not what the writer is trying to say. To read correctly, the modifier must be moved close to the word it modifies: "He sang a song that was lewd at the convention." Better yet, revise and shorten the sentence: "He sang a lewd song at the convention."

SPELLING ERRORS.   Bad spelling not only ruins the writer's authority regarding spelling, but also ruins the writer's authority on any subject. It usually does not matter how memos, letters, and reports become spelled correctly—proofreading carefully, asking others to check them, or using the computer spell-checker—it matters only that words be spelled correctly.

SUBJECTIVE AND OBJECTIVE FORMS: "I" IS SUBJECTIVE, "ME" IS OBJECTIVE.   When choosing one of these for the object of a sentence or a preposition, select "me." When choosing one of these as the subject of a sentence or clause, select "I." Never write "While others were deciding the fate of the proposal, *her* and *me* were playing golf." Write "While others were deciding the fate of the proposal, *she* and *I* were playing golf." Never write "They wrote to *he* and *I*." Write "They wrote to *him* and *me*."

"IS WHEN" CONSTRUCTIONS.   Whenever we write "is when" or "was when," we often confuse space and time: "One example of Caesar's respect for his soldiers was when he slept outside in a storm

Rewrite the following sentences
in two ways to correct the dangling modifiers:

1. When a baby, my mother
   used to drive race cars.
2. After taking in a constant
   flow of beer for two days, the
   engineer should note that
   the vats are nearly full.

The following sentences contain
dangling and misplaced modifiers. Rewrite the sentences,
placing the modifiers correctly:

1. While walking through the
   shop, the manager's hard hat
   disappeared. [Note that the
   hard hat, not the manager, is
   walking through the shop.]
2. Those who work quickly develop anxieties. [This misplaced modifier is called
   a squinting modifier; that is,
   it seems to modify both
   "work" and "develop."]

with his men because the tent had room for only one person." The best
way to correct an "is when" or "was when" problem is to change to an
active verb: "An example of Caesar's respect for his soldiers *occurred*
during a storm. Caesar slept outside with his men because the tent had
room for only one person."

PARALLEL CONSTRUCTIONS.   Place equivalent ideas in equivalent grammatical constructions to create strong, dynamic, and grammatical sentences. Here is a sentence that is not parallel: "To put it
simply, Sulla knows only two methods of communication: *dictate* and
bribery." Because "dictate" is a verb and "bribery" is a noun, the phrase
is not parallel. Here is the rewritten sentence: "To put it simply, Sulla
knows only two methods of communication: *dictation* and *bribery*."
Do not write "He is prompt, has good manners, efficient, and hard-
working." Each item in the series must agree separately with "is"; otherwise, the sentence is not parallel. Write instead, "He is prompt, well-
mannered, efficient, and hard-working."

CHANGING TENSES.   Time should remain consistent in a sentence.
Do not write "When General Lucius Cornelius Sulla *needed* resources,
he simply *takes* whatever he wants." Although the reader can, after a
second or two, decipher the meaning, the reader should not be required to do it. Meaning should be clear; time should be consistent.
Rewrite the sentence: "When General Lucius Cornelius Sulla *needed*
resources, he simply *took* whatever he wanted."

SUBJUNCTIVE MOOD.   Because business people often suggest,
recommend, doubt, regret, and the like, some knowledge of the subjunctive is necessary. "If" requires the subjunctive. Do not write "If
there *was* time, I could show you the shop floor." Write "If there *were*
time, I could show you the shop floor." Do not write "I suggest that
billing time *is* decreased." Write "I suggest that billing time *be* decreased."

WHO/WHOM.   Use "who" for the subject of a sentence or clause;
use "whom" for the direct or indirect object of a clause: "*Who* did it?"
"*Whom* are you calling?" "You gave it to *whom*?" But "You said to give
it to *whoever* asked for it." Here "whoever" is not the object of the
preposition "to" but the subject of the clause "whoever asked for it."

Some suggest that the use of "whom" is dying. It is not dead yet,
and far too many people still know how it should be used for a writer
to risk misusing it. Also, write "people who," not "people which."

PREDICATE NOMINATIVE.   A *predicate nominative* is a noun that
follows the verb and complements the subject: "The children are *monsters*." Writers and speakers sometimes confuse predicate nominatives
with objects when answering a question such as "Who is there?" The
correct response is "It is I," not "It is me," because "me" is an object,
not a subject.

EXERCISE N: "IS WHEN" CONSTRUCTIONS

Rewrite the following sentences, correcting the "is when" constructions:

1. Pompey's ability to organize is impressive. Just one example of this ability is when he and his troops were opposed by three enemies: Carina, Cloelius, Brutus.
2. A fine example of Caesar's ability to organize is when his troops came under attack by the Helvatti.
3. One other way Pompey motivated his men is when they thought they had come across a land of treasure and did not want to leave. He made them dig until they begged him to move on.

THE FIVE USES OF APOSTROPHES

1. *To form possessives: "Smedley's memo"*
2. *To form contractions: "You'll," "won't"*
3. *To indicate a single quotation mark: "She said 'Hello'"*
4. *To indicate deletion of centuries in dates: "class of '94"*
5. *To indicate feet: "11'"*

PUNCTUATION

Speech clarifies meaning by using inflections and pauses, whereas writing clarifies meaning by using punctuation. The following is a discussion of punctuation marks commonly used in business.

APOSTROPHE (')

APOSTROPHES FORM POSSESSIVES. A word is *possessive* if it owns the word it describes. In "Jane's report," for example, "Jane" is possessive because Jane owns the report. Compare "the report of Jane." Most singular nouns require an apostrophe and an *s* to demonstrate ownership: "the company's policy" and "the employee's benefits." The apostrophe and *s* are a shortened form of "the policy of the company" and "the benefits of the employee."

> Dan's encyclopedia
>
> the report's appendices
>
> golf's vagaries

Some writers have difficulty with singular nouns ending in *s*. If a singular noun ending with an *s* does not end in an *s* sound, add an apostrophe and an *s*:

> Arkansas's Sam Walton
>
> Francois's directive
>
> Des Moines's grain elevators

If a singular noun ends with a pronounced *s*, add an apostrophe and an *s* to show possession. The additional *s* will create another pronounced syllable.

> Jones's department
>
> the process's failure
>
> Harris's promotion

Possessives of plural nouns that end in *s* require only the apostrophe:

> the companies' goals
>
> the shareholders' gain
>
> the bonds' dividends
>
> the Joneses' house
>
> the bosses' meeting

Possessives of plural nouns that do not end with an *s* require an apostrophe and an *s*.

> the women's room
>
> the men's room

the children's homework

the criteria's relevancy

the data's importance

APOSTROPHES FOR CONTRACTIONS. A *contraction* is a shortened word or a combination of two words into a single word. The contraction is indicated by an apostrophe. Contractions should be used rarely in formal prose, but because much business prose is informal, the use of apostrophes for contractions is included here.

o'clock   (of the clock)

can't   (cannot)

could've   (could have, *not* could of)

should've   (should have, *not* should of)

APOSTROPHE AS A SINGLE QUOTATION MARK. When a quotation contains a quotation itself, indicate the internal quotation by single quotation marks, which on typewriters and keyboards are usually the apostrophe:

Ms. Fahrquart remarked in her speech, "The president said to me, 'This is an exciting time for our company; we must take advantage of it and do our best.'"

APOSTROPHES TO INDICATE DELETION OF CENTURIES IN DATES. Informal business prose may use apostrophes to abbreviate certain dates: "the crashes of '29 and '87," "the class of '95." Formal prose rarely abbreviates dates.

APOSTROPHES INDICATE FEET BESIDE A NUMBER. The apostrophe is often used as an abbreviated form of the word *feet*: "The cantilever, at its highest, is about 75' from the floor." Used regularly in technical prose, this abbreviation should not be used in formal business prose.

ASTERISK (*)

The asterisk in informal writing often replaces a footnote number. Place the asterisk in the text immediately following the word or phrase requiring the footnote and again at the bottom of the page, where the footnote begins as follows:

And so, as Professor Spooner* once said to a student he kicked out of college, "You have deliberately tasted two worms and you can leave Oxford by the next town drain."

_____

*Oxford don, famous for "Spoonerisms."

•••••••••••••
EXERCISE O: APOSTROPHE

The first word in some of the following phrases is possessive. Place an apostrophe appropriately.

1. the news department
2. Quality Controls belief
3. the earnings statement
4. the business meeting
5. the sales strategy
6. Joans appointment
7. the auditors investigation
8. Assets inventory
9. the analysis report
10. Products sales

Discuss in class those phrases that could be possessive or not.

BRACKETS [ ]

Brackets indicate either an insertion that is not part of a quotation or a parenthetical note within an item already in parentheses:

> The president said, "The annual meeting for 1987 shall be held in Albany [his mother's hometown] and for 1988 in Albuquerque [his sister's home]."

> When he arrived in Brussels, Smedley was awed ("It ain't Altoona [his hometown]!").

CAPITAL LETTERS

Writers should memorize such common uses of capital letters as those listed below:

Proper names: Smedley Fahrquart (person's name), Katmandu (city), Chrysler Motor Corporation (company), Church of the Latter-Day Saints (church), Hawley-Smoot Act (titles of treaties and laws), Tylenol (brand names), Sierra Nevada (mountains and mountain ranges), Tuesday (days), Pluto (planets), Fifth Avenue (names of streets, avenues, ways, lanes, and cul-de-sacs), February (months), Labor Day (holidays)

The first word of a complimentary close: Sincerely, Yours truly

Regions (but not directions): the East (*but* east of Singapore, she's heading west), the Southwest (*but* San Diego is southwest of here)

Adjectives describing nationality: Polynesian, French, American Indian

Salutations: Dear Smedley

I (always)

Figure and table numbers: Figure 3, Table 6, Section 4 (*but* page 153)

Deities, sacred books: Allah, God, the Koran, the Bible

Titles when combined with names: Chairman Iacocca, Mayor Fahrquart (*but* the chairman, the mayor)

Languages: English, German, Spanish

Titles of books, but prepositions and conjunctions in titles are seldom capitalized, except when they are the first word: *Of Mice and Men*. Articles (a, an, the) are not capitalized except when they are so by custom or are the first word of title: *The Grapes of Wrath*.

COLON (:)

Colons announce lists, quotations, and directives. In formal prose, colons must follow an independent clause. Do not write "Present at the meeting were: Scarlet, Ashley, and Butler," because "Present at the meeting were" is not an independent clause. Write "Present at the

---

EXERCISE P: COLONS

EXERCISE P: COLONS

Place colons in or remove them from the following (you may rewrite):

1. The manual contained three badly labeled sections introduction, body, and conclusion.
2. The manual contained badly labeled sections on the introduction, body, and conclusion.
3. There are five parts to the fishing rod butt, seat, handle, guides, and rod.
4. The five parts of a fishing rod are: butt, seat, handle, guides, and rod.
5. Here he comes, folks: Give him a hand.

meeting were Scarlet, Ashley, and Butler" or "The following were present: Scarlet, Ashley, and Butler." Use colons in informal prose after one word to introduce a list. Write informally "Options: sell it, lease it, or use it." Or write formally "The company has three options: sell it, lease it, or use it."

Colons also follow the salutation of all formal letters,

Dear Ms. Fahrquart:

Dear Ladies and Gentlemen:

Capitalize the first letter following a colon only if the capital begins a complete sentence or if the word should be capitalized itself (such as if it is a proper noun).

COMMA

Commas separate one part of a sentence from another and show the relationship between the parts. They help make a sentence clear: "To Jane, Smith is among her most agreeable subordinates." (Compare: "To Jane Smith is. . . .") In general, commas serve seven functions:

1. They set off introductory dependent clauses.
2. They set off nonrestrictive elements.
3. They set off interruptions, such as asides, editorial elements, and direct address.
4. They set off appositives, such as titles, dates, and addresses.
5. They separate items in a series.
6. They join related adjectives.
7. They set off independent clauses.

One comma should *never* separate the subject from the verb.

INTRODUCTORY DEPENDENT CLAUSES. When a *dependent clause*—that is, a clause that contains a subject and a verb but cannot stand alone as a complete thought—introduces a sentence, insert a comma after it to set it apart from the main or independent clause.

> *Before we go to the gym*, we must call to reserve a court.
>
> *As the president has said many times*, communication among the departments must improve dramatically.

If the dependent clause follows the independent clause, do not set it apart by a comma:

> We must call to reserve a court *before we go to the gym*.
>
> Smedley went home *because he was not feeling well*.

RESTRICTIVE AND NONRESTRICTIVE ELEMENTS. Restrictive phrases and clauses limit, or restrict, the nouns they modify; nonrestrictive phrases and clauses do not. Restrictive phrases and clauses

---

EXERCISE Q: COMMAS IN NONRESTRICTIVE PHRASES

Place commas in the appropriate places in the following sentences (rewrite as necessary):

1. The manual which contained three badly labeled sections was discarded by the CEO.
2. The manual that contained badly labeled sections was discarded.
3. The John Jones who is head of finance is leaving. [In a big company there may be many John Joneses.]
4. John Jones who is head of finance is leaving. [Note the absence of *The* here.]

are essential to the meaning of a sentence; nonrestrictive phrases and clauses are not. Restrictive phrases and clauses are not set off by commas; nonrestrictive phrases and clauses are set off by commas. Restrictive clauses often begin with *that*; nonrestrictive clauses often begin with *which*.

To determine whether an element is restrictive or nonrestrictive, simply try to delete the element from the sentence. Restrictive clauses and phrases cannot be removed from a sentence without greatly changing the meaning of the sentence. "Widgitcogs that pass our strictest quality control tests cost more than other cogs" contains a restrictive clause. Remove it and the sentence reads "Widgitcogs . . . cost more than other cogs." The original sentence limits the number of widgitcogs that cost more than other cogs; the second does not. Removing the clause alters the meaning. "Widgitcogs, which pass our strictest quality control tests, cost more than other cogs" contains a nonrestrictive clause. Here the meaning is clear: all widgitcogs cost more than other cogs.

Sometimes restrictive clauses can be distinguished from nonrestrictive clauses only by the commas. The difference in meaning is nevertheless clear. "People who are prejudiced cannot be educated" means that some people are prejudiced and uneducable. "People, who are prejudiced, cannot be educated" means that all people are prejudiced and uneducable. The lowly comma is important here. Similarly, "I like accountants who do not fudge figures" conveys one meaning. "I like accountants, who do not fudge figures" conveys another meaning, that no accountant fudges figures. Again, the only difference is a comma.

INTERRUPTIONS. Interruptions break the flow of a sentence. They may take the form of asides, editorial comments, or direct address. And they may appear at the beginning, in the middle, or at the end of a sentence. When a word or phrase interrupts, commas are required:

Clearly, we must solve the problem.

Could we not give, *say*, ten thousand for the retraining?

Cheryl Arbuckle completed the audit on time, *in spite of Fahrquart's interference*.

Asides, like those in drama, are thoughts added to sentences for emphasis or as afterthoughts. They give a slightly different tone to the main part of the sentence:

There are two days, *I think*, remaining before the deadline.

Reply to this memo, *please*, before Friday.

Did she tell us, *really*, to have the figures completed by 5 o'clock?

Editorial elements provide ways for the writer to make editorial, or author's, comments. The most common of these is the transitional word or phrase:

We must do it now. We must, *nevertheless*, do it carefully.

. . . .
EXERCISE R: COMMAS AND EDITORIAL ELEMENTS

Place commas in the appropriate places in the following sentences (rewrite as necessary):

1. It is of course a difficult decision.
2. The decision is however not to be made by any of us.
3. They are sure aren't they that the shipment is here?

. . . .

Other transitional words and phrases include "however," "otherwise," "although," "next," "too" (when meaning "also"), "therefore," and "thus." Some editorial elements appear as afterthoughts: "They are sure that the shipment will arrive, aren't they?"

APPOSITIVES. *Appositives* are nouns or noun phrases that follow and describe another noun. Titles, dates, or addresses, appositives are commonly set apart by commas.

> Jack Potter, *the marshall of Yellow Sky*, surveyed the dusty street.
>
> Boston, *Massachusetts*, is more than 350 years old.
>
> March 15, *1993*, will be a special Ides of March. [*but no commas in* 15 March 1993 *or* March 1993]
>
> Samantha Evans, *Ph.D.*, is a cornerstone of the corporation.

For labels following personal names, add a comma before "Jr." (unless otherwise specified by the individual), but do not add a comma before Roman numerals. For labels following names of organizations ("Inc.," "Ltd."), add a comma unless otherwise specified.

> Douglas Fairbanks, *Jr.* [*but* "William F. Buckley *Jr.*" if he prefers to omit the comma]
>
> Smedley Fahrquart *III*
>
> Fahrquart Industries, *Inc.*

When a full address is written out in the text, separate all of the elements except the state and zip code by commas:

> Please contact me at 111 Hardscrabble Road, Erie, PA 16523, by January 15.

COMMAS IN A SERIES. Commas separate items in a series of three or more. If "and" is used to join the items, no comma is used. If the series uses only one "and," or none at all, then commas separate all items.

> Good writing requires hard work and good thinking and much time.
>
> Good writing requires hard work, good thinking, and much time.

COMMAS AND ADJECTIVES. When two or more adjectives modify one noun, separate the adjectives by commas.

> Carol gave an interesting, intelligent speech to the Rotary Club. ["Interesting" and "intelligent" modify "speech."]
>
> Jim is a hard-working, sympathetic manager. ["Hard-working" and "sympathetic" modify "manager."]

SETTING OFF INDEPENDENT CLAUSES. Commas alone cannot join two independent clauses. Joining two independent clauses with a comma, but without a coordinating conjunction, is called a *comma*

. . . .

EXERCISE S: APPOSITIVES

Place commas in the appropriate places in the following sentences (rewrite as necessary):

1. The manual "The Care and Feeding of Widgitcogs" has three badly labeled sections.

2. The woman a CPA was distressed to discover that her bill for the lunch was incorrectly summed.

3. The CPA Ms. Numba Cruncher was distressed to discover that her bill for lunch was incorrectly summed.

4. Both of us Joan and I were rewarded with a bonus.

5. Smedley Fahrquart head accountant was angry.

splice. "We are going to the gym, we must reserve a court first." To correct the comma splice, insert a *coordinating conjunction* ("and," "but," "or," "nor," "for," "so," or "yet") after the comma:

> First, an inventory must be done, *and* then we must decide how to organize it.

> We are going to the gym, *but* we must reserve a court first.

> Either we modernize this plant, *or* we shut it down.

> Neither can we afford to modernize this plant, *nor* can we afford to shut it down.

COMMAS BETWEEN SUBJECTS AND VERBS.   While two commas may set off a word or group of words that occurs between the subject and verb of a sentence, one comma may never occur between a subject and a verb. Here is an example of a sentence ruined by a single comma that separates the subject from the verb: "Writing [subject] a report for my meticulous boss, is [verb] hard work." To make the sentence grammatical, remove the comma: "Writing a report for my meticulous boss is hard work."

DASHES

More emphatic than commas, dashes mark abrupt changes in a sentence's continuity. They are commonly used also to set off phrases and clauses that have commas in them.

> When Japanese companies sold their stockpiles—dumped them, really—the American steel industry was hit hard.

If the phrase or clause appears at the end of the sentence, do not type the second, or closing, dash—unlike parentheses. The period is sufficient to close the thought, as demonstrated in the preceding sentence.

To type a dash, use two hyphens with no space on either side of them: ". . . stockpiles--dumped . . ."

ELLIPSIS

Ellipsis indicates the deletion of a word or words in a quotation. Writers use ellipsis to quote concisely, to omit any extraneous words not pertinent to their arguments. But writers must make sure to use ellipsis ethically; they must *never* use it to alter the meaning of the quotation.

If the omission appears in the middle of a sentence, type three equally spaced ellipsis points. If the omission begins or ends at a comma, place the three ellipsis points before or after the comma, as appropriate, to keep the sentence sense. If the omission concludes a sentence, type four ellipsis points, with the first point serving as the period for the sentence.

ORIGINAL: Johnson Creek, where it flows into the North Fork of the Boise River, was about three times as wide as a boy is tall when I discovered it. It is a fast creek, cutting its path through granite mountains as it descends from lakes high in Idaho's Sawtooth Wilderness. There are log jams there that have made a great array of holes, pools, backwaters, and riffles, all hiding trout.

SHORTENED: Johnson Creek, where it flows into the North Fork of the Boise River, was about three times as wide as a boy is tall when I discovered it. . . . Log jams there . . . have made a great array of holes, pools, . . . and riffles, all hiding trout.   —Jack Trueblood, ''For a Love of Fishing''

EXCLAMATION POINT (!)

Exclamation points express surprise or disbelief: ''No! You don't say! It can't be true!'' In formal writing, use exclamation points rarely. As with periods, type two spaces after an exclamation point.

If an exclamation is within a quoted sentence, place the exclamation point inside the final quotation marks:

She said, ''I don't want to have to tell you again!''

If the sentence is exclamatory, but the quoted part is not, place the exclamation point outside of the final quotation marks:

Smedley actually had the nerve to say ''Have a nice day''!

PARENTHESES (   )

Parentheses serve two functions: they enclose information supplementary to a sentence, and they enclose numbers or letters used for enumeration.

Parentheses, like commas and dashes, set off nonessential information in a sentence. They are more emphatic than commas but less emphatic than dashes. They also commonly enclose text citations in research reports.

Smedley was opposed (violently) to their plans for reorganization. [Compare: Smedley was opposed — violently — to their plans for reorganization.]

Smedley referred to Lee Youacoca's book, *Corporate Organization* (2nd ed., 1991), for guidance.

For guidance, Smedley referred to Lee Youacoca's book, *Corporate Organization* (2nd ed., 1991).

Notice that the punctuation follows, not precedes, the parentheses.

When a list is run in the text, put parentheses around the numbers or letters.

Here are our choices: (1) buy it, (2) sell it, or (3) lease it.

When a list is in outline form, use parentheses for enumeration as shown in the example below:

I. The universe
  A. The galaxy
    1. The solar system
      a. The Earth
        1) The Western Hemisphere
          a) South America
            (1) Equador
              (a) Quito

PERIOD (.)

Use a period after a statement and after an indirect question.

> She filled out the form quickly. [statement]

> It was then that I asked who was going to write the report. [indirect question]

Use a period for common abbreviations: a.m., p.m., Jr., Ms., U.S., etc. If a sentence ends with an abbreviation, the period of the abbreviation also serves as the period to close the sentence.

> His appointment at 7 a.m. tomorrow is with the president.

> He has an appointment with the president tomorrow at 7 a.m.

QUOTATION MARKS (" ")

Enclose direct quotations in quotation marks. Do not enclose indirect quotations in quotation marks.

> Samantha asked, "Will we recoup our investment?" [direct quotation]

> Samantha asked whether we would recoup our investment. [indirect quotation]

QUOTATION MARKS WITH OTHER PUNCTUATION. Place periods and commas before the final quotation mark, and place colons and semicolons after the final quotation mark.

> Hamlet said, "To be, or not to be."

> "To be," Hamlet said, "or not to be."

> Samantha said emphatically, "We will recoup our investment in two years"; she did not persuade the board, however.

> Samantha said emphatically, "We will recoup our investment in two years": The board was not persuaded.

QUOTATION MARKS FOR EMPHASIS OR SLANG. Do not use quotation marks for emphasis (for example, "Smedley said we were 'not' to do it"). Use underlining or italics instead: "Smedley said we were *not* to do it."

Rarely use quotation marks to set off slang. Formal prose should not use slang; informal prose need not call attention to slang. Do not write "Our president's speech was 'awesome.'" Write formally "Our president's speech was awe-inspiring." Write informally "Our president's speech was awesome."

QUOTATION MARKS FOR TITLES. Book, magazine, journal, and newspaper titles are underlined. Article and report titles are placed in quotation marks when others refer to them:

> On August 14, Smedley submitted "The Fahrquart Report," which is attached as an appendix to this report.

Chapter titles and section titles of long, formal reports are placed in quotation marks when others refer to them. Do not, however, place such standard terms as Preface in quotation marks.

> Chapter Four of the plan for the next century, "Standardizing Widgit-cogs," is an outstanding example of gobbledygook.

QUOTATION MARKS WITHIN QUOTATION MARKS. When a quotation appears within another quotation, identify the internal quote by single quotation marks:

> "It is unfortunate," said Jane, "that Smedley felt called upon to mention 'The Fahrquart Report' in that context."

SEMICOLONS (;)

Semicolons join independent clauses of equal importance. Notice this example from Winston Churchill's speech in June 1940 regarding a likely invasion from Nazi Germany. The first five independent clauses are joined by (actually separated by) commas. The last independent clause is joined to the others by a semicolon. Churchill included a semicolon here to make the final clause equal to the other clauses combined.

> We shall defend our island, whatever the cost may be, we shall fight on the landing grounds, we shall fight in the fields and in the streets, we shall fight in the hills; we shall never surrender.

UNDERLINING OR ITALICS

Underlines in typewritten material produce italics in printed material.

Underline foreign expressions unless they are common in English. Underline, for example, the foreign phrase in the following sentence: "You are going to stay to hear the speaker, es verdad?" On the other hand, because the French phrase "laissez-faire" is commonly used in English, do not underline it: "Smedley is a believer in laissez-faire economics."

Underline the titles of books, reports, magazines, newspapers, paintings, operas, etc. When referring to a company of the same name as its newspaper or magazine, do not underline the name. That is, "The latest issue of <u>Forbes</u> has an article about takeover stocks," but "Smedley just wrote to Forbes regarding their interest in buying our company."

Follow the style of the discipline or the company regarding continuous or separate underlining.

VIRGULES (/)

Virgules, or slashes, have several uses and a common misuse.

1. Virgules indicate certain omissions. Many people have two offices and, consequently, two telephones. Sometimes, although people have an office phone, they are so often elsewhere—say, on the shop floor—that the telephone there must be listed also. Virgules are thus often used to list two telephone numbers with the same exchange: 898-6324/6010.

2. Virgules separate numerators from denominators in fractions: 2/3 (two-thirds or 2 of 3 parts).

3. Virgules indicate certain omissions. The most common of these are "ft/sec" (feet per second), "m/h" (miles per hour), and "c/o" (in care of).

4. *Do not* use virgules in formal prose to create ungrammatical expressions. Here are some examples.

he/she	Write "he or she."
s/he	Very ugly
either/or	Write "either this or that"; "either/or" is a specialized term used in philosophy.
and/or	Write "this or that, or both"; "and/or" is a specialized term used in philosophy. "Either/or" and "and/or" are commonly used as a kind of shorthand, but only in the most informal prose.

The purpose of this glossary is fourfold:

1. To introduce the common errors in words, phrases, and grammar used in business communication, to point out the problems with them, and to suggest better choices.

2. To help create a habit of mind, so that scrutiny of the language becomes second nature, thus improving the quality of writing, expressing, and thinking.

3. To suggest that *formally correct* usage often is the best — clear, accurate, and economical — usage.

4. This glossary does *not* want to suggest that the *formally correct* is *always* the best. On the contrary, the glory of English is its flexibility. By knowing the *formally correct*, however, readers and writers are better able to use informal English well, and to manipulate the language so that logic need not be sacrificed to the casual. To the eloquent quotation by John Stuart Mill should be added this one by Ralph Waldo Emerson: "A foolish consistency is the hobgoblin of little minds."

TO QUESTION ALL THINGS; NEVER TO

TURN AWAY FROM ANY DIFFICULTY;

TO ACCEPT NO DOCTRINE EITHER

OURSELVES OR FROM OTH-

ERS WITHOUT A RIGID SCRU-

TINY BY NEGA-

TIVE CRITICISM;

LETTING NO FAL-

LACY, OR INCOHERENCE, OR

CONFUSION

OF THOUGHT, STEP BY UNPER-

CEIVED; ABOVE ALL, TO INSIST ON

HAVING THE MEANING OF A WORD

CLEARLY UNDERSTOOD BEFORE

USING IT, AND THE MEANING OF A

PROPOSITION BEFORE ASSENTING

TO IT.

JOHN STUART MILL (1806–1873)

A GLOSSARY FOR COMMUNICATORS

481

A

ABILITY/CAPACITY

- "Ability" concerns the power to do something, such as read this book; "ability" involves the potential to move outside oneself.

- "Capacity" concerns the power to contain or absorb something, such as learn what is in this book; "capacity" concerns bringing something inside oneself.

- Clearly, these are different terms. Most people have a greater *capacity* for watching others work than they have an *ability* to work themselves. One may have the capacity for understanding a problem, but not have the ability—because of time or resources—to do anything about it.

-ABILITY

- The suffix "-ability" is so insidiously attractive that even those who profess to study and know the language often succumb to it. The most common example is "readability," which is, logically, the substantive form of "read-able." The problem with "readability" is not with grammar, but rather with the specializations that create long and ugly phrases from short and pleasant ones.

- "Readability" becomes "readability scale," or "readability quotient," which is a measure of how easy or difficult something is to read. The uninitiated and intelligent should write "easy to read" or "difficult to read."

- "Mobility" is acceptable because it has been long in use, but in America mobility is acceptable only so long as it is upward. "Moveability," on the other hand, is unacceptable. See **profitability**.

ABOVE

- While "above" has become acceptable in most writing as a way of referring to something previously mentioned, it is often vague. Good writing in general and business writing in particular should be so clear that "above" is almost always unnecessary.

- Avoid writing "The above tables show fiscal 1992's gains" if "Tables 9 and 10 show fiscal 1992's gains" is clearer. Should all else fail, the following are useful: "The goods previously mentioned arrived damaged," and "The tables on pages 11, 12, and 14 show fiscal 1992's gains."

- Never write "The above goods arrived damaged"; those goods are "listed" in the text. The goods themselves are not there. After all, one does not write "The below items in the within letter to the without people are listed in the above statements."

- These words on "above" hold similarly for "below." See **items**.

ABSOLUTELY

- "Absolutely" means "completely, and without qualification." As few things in this world are so unqualifiably true as to admit of no qualification, "absolutely" should be used sparingly, if at all, in business prose.

■ Do not use "absolutely" to mean "certainly," "yes," "very," or simply for emphasis. Avoid writing "She is absolutely correct." Write "She is correct."

ACCEPT/EXCEPT

■ "Accept" means "receive." "Except means "exclude."

■ Do not confuse the meanings, especially as they are nearly opposite.

ACCESS

■ Until recently, "access" was used mainly as a noun meaning "the action or power of getting near to" or gaining the use of something. Now it is among the more common and vague verbs in the language, meaning "to penetrate," "to get at," "to have on one's side" (civil servants like to "access the private sector"). "To read a computer file," "to consult," and "to use" are each more precise and therefore more proper than "to access."

■ Do not use "access" as a verb. Avoid writing "We have to access that computer file." Write "We have to see (or use or read) that computer file." One would never say, for example, "Let me access the refrigerator and I'll let you input this great new brand of Brie I've found."

ACCORDING TO

■ Acceptable, but often wordy.

■ Seldom write "According to these reports. . . ." Write "These reports show (prove, suggest) [that]. . . ."

■ Avoid writing "According to Ms. James. . . ." Write "Ms. James says (thinks, believes). . . ."

ACCOUNTABILITY/RESPONSIBILITY

■ "Accountable" means "answerable." Those who are accountable are not only responsible for their actions, but also must be able to provide reasons for their actions, or pay penalties or gather rewards.

■ "Responsible" means that one is judged by certain actions regardless of whether one can provide reasons for them.

■ Avoid writing "accountability" when "responsibility" is meant. See **responsible**.

ACCOUNT FOR

■ Often misused to mean "consists of," "account for" means to "make amends," "provide satisfactory reasons," or "to be the cause or source of."

■ Avoid writing "Most of our products are accounted for by widgitcogs." Write "Most of our products consist of widgitcogs." Write "The sale of widgitcogs may account for most of this year's profits."

ACQUIESCE

- To give in quietly. One acquiesces *in*; one does not acquiesce *to*. Avoid writing "They have decided to acquiesce to our demands for more equity." Write "They have decided to *acquiesce in* our demands for more equity."

ACQUAINT WITH

- A stuffy and often wordy expression.
- As "acquainted with" is linguistically anaerobic, do not write "I *acquainted her with* aerobic dancing." Write "I *told her about* aerobic dancing." See **familiarize**.

ACRONYMS

- To save time and space, acronyms are created from parts of other words. They save time only if readers understand them. Avoid writing "Project managers are asked to report to the BO at 9 a.m. Monday" unless they know that "BO" is the acronym for "Boss's Office."
- Some acronyms have become accepted as words; "scuba," for example, is the acronym for Self-Contained Underwater Breathing Apparatus.
- Some acronyms have become clichés: "TLC."
- Words that have been *initialized*—post meridiem, p.m.; and Anno Domini, A.D., and the like—differ from acronyms in that a period follows each letter of an *initialism*.
- Uncommon acronyms are often a mark of their user's insecurity: "I mean, come on, Smedley. Give the APV a little TLC, and MIS will give you a lot of ROI. OK?"

ACTION

- Often found in wordy constructions. Avoid writing "The company must take action." Write "The company must act."
- Although "act" is usually better than "action," both often are vague. Avoid writing "The company must act" when that act should be known specifically. Write "The company must act" when the act should not be known to others or, as is more common, the writer does not know what must be done.

ACTIVATE

- Avoid, except in chemistry.
- "Begin" is better than "activate" because "begin" is shorter and simpler, and because one begins (motivates, spurs) human actions; one does not "activate" them.
- Use "start" for machinery: "Start the engine." Use "begin" to avoid ugly prose. Avoid writing "Activate the activities."

- That which spurs human action usually "stimulates"; it does not "activate": "Poverty after graduation from college usually stimulates [not activates] a desire for a good job." This holds also for "activation." See **up**.

ACTUAL/ACTUALLY

- Avoid "actual" and "actually," especially with "fact." As "fact" itself is nearly always unnecessary, to append "actual" is to compound the silliness.

- Avoid writing "Although we believed it to be true, in actual fact, it was false." Write "Although we believed it to be true, it was false."

- Avoid writing "Actually, I am not sure" in formal prose. Write "I am not sure" or "I am uncertain."

- Common in speech, "actually" is usually a silly and unnecessary word in writing.

ADDRESS

- Not a synonym for "speech." An "address" is a particularly formal speech, usually for an important occasion or by an important person. Consequently, you and I speak; Henry Kissinger addresses.

ADEQUATE

- Means "to measure up," "be equal." "Her qualifications are *adequate enough* for the job" is redundant. Write "Her qualifications are adequate for the job."

- Similarly, "more adequate" and "less adequate" are absurd because, just as nothing may be "more equal," so nothing may be "more [or less] adequate." Write "adequate."

ADJECTIVE   See Appendix II, page 464.

AD VALOREM

- Latin for "To the value of" (money, goods, property).

- Usually, a tax on the value of something: commonly called "value-added tax."

- At Joe's Discount Jewelers, say, "The value-added tax on these diamonds makes them expensive." At Tiffany's, say, "These diamonds are taxed *ad valorem*, and thus they are more desirable."

ADVERB   See Appendix II, page 464.

ADVERSE/AVERSE

- "Averse" connotes repugnance, stronger than "disinclined."

- "Adverse" means acting against, physically resisting.

- "Adverse" requires physical action; "averse" does not.

- One may be averse without becoming adverse. Write "I am averse to changing the production schedule now, during the peak season, but the president wants to do it. So, what can I do?" Write "I am so adverse to changing the production schedule now, during the peak season, that I wrote a memo to the president."

ADVICE/ADVISE

- "Advice" is a noun: "She gave me good advice."
- "Advise" is a verb: "She advises me on fiscal responsibility."

ADVISE

- A common business word uncommonly pretentious when used to indicate anything other than advice, "advise" once meant to give formal notice, usually of a transaction. This construction is obsolete: "Please be advised that on 1 July 1986, we intend to. . . ." Write "On 1 July 1986, we intend to. . . ."
- Do not "advise" unless giving advice; do "tell." Even "inform" is sometimes better than "advise." Avoid writing "Let me advise you as to the outcome of the meeting." Write "Let me tell you about the outcome of the meeting."

AFFECT/EFFECT

- "Affect" means "to influence" or "to adopt a pose."
- "Effect" means "the result" or "to bring about."
- "The fire that gutted ABC Corporation's plant will affect the company's merger with DEF Corporation" means something different from "The fire that gutted ABC Corporation's plant will effect the company's merger with DEF Corporation."
- In psychology and education, "affect" relates to feelings. The "affective domain," then, would refer to the domain of feelings.

AFFIRMATIVE

- "Yes."
- "Affirmative" is commonly used in the military to avoid confusing "yes" and "no" because of the noise of battle and the static of field telephones. Business does not normally need to say "affirmative" (four syllables) because "yes" (one syllable) is understandable. Avoid writing "She answered in the affirmative." Write "She said yes."

AFFLICT/INFLICT

- Afflict *with*. Inflict *on* or *upon*. One is never "inflicted with" anything, even in-laws. Avoid writing "Poor Smedley is being inflicted with his in-laws for three weeks." Write "Smedley's in-laws inflicted themselves on him for three weeks." Write "Smedley was afflicted with severe depression when he heard that his in-laws were arriving for a long visit."

AGENDA

- Originally the plural of "agendum," "agenda" now requires the singular: "The agenda is. . . ." The plural is "agendas." Some words, such as "data," have not succumbed to this change. See **data/datum**.

AGGRAVATE/IRRITATE

- "Aggravate" originally meant "to burden"; now it means "to worsen by adding to or intensifying." Write "Our fiscal problems were aggravated by inflation."

- While among the lesser meanings are those of "provoke" and "embitter," "aggravate" does not mean simply "to make angry," "to annoy," or "to irritate." Consequently, it is best to avoid writing "I am aggravated" in formal prose. Write "I am annoyed" or "I am angered." "Irritate" means "to excite anger, impatience, or other kinds of displeasure." See **angry/mad**.

ALL

- Often used for emphasis — "*All* of them are going!" — "all" is wordy when not used for emphasis. Write "They are going."

- "All of" is often unnecessary; even when "all" is desired, "of" may be omitted. Avoid writing "All of the board members were entertained lavishly." Write "All board members were entertained lavishly" only when emphasis is desired for the "all." Otherwise, write "The board members were entertained lavishly."

ALL AROUND

- Acceptable in informal prose, "all around," means "including everything in a given circle," "comprehensive" or, when describing a person, "versatile." Consequently, "all around" is rather too vague to be used often in business. In formal prose, use "comprehensive" and "versatile."

- Avoid writing "She is an *all-around* manager." Write "She is a *versatile* manager." Avoid writing "Management trainees enroll in an *all-around* course of study." Write "Management trainees enroll in a *comprehensive* course of study." Informally, however, one may "buy Cokes all around."

ALL RIGHT/ALRIGHT

- "All right" is two words and means "all is correct."

- "All right" does not mean "acceptable." Avoid writing "The meeting went all right." Write "The meeting went fairly well."

- "Alright" is an obsolete word meaning "just" or "exactly." Perhaps it should remain so. Avoid "alright."

ALLUDE/REFER

- "Allude" concerns indirect references: "He alluded to management's methods during the 1950's."

- "Refer" concerns direct references: "She referred to this memorandum."

A LOT

- Never "alot." Always "a lot." Always. Remember that "allot" means "to portion out" and has nothing to do with "a lot."

ALSO

- "Also" means "additionally"; it is not a synonym for "and."

- Avoid using "also" to begin a sentence or other clause. An exception is the "*not only . . . , but also . . .*" construction. Write "Not only did they default on the loan, but also they negotiated for a loan from another bank."

- Place "also" carefully. Try to place it next to the word it is intended to modify. Avoid writing "Also, we are expected to be prompt." Write "We are expected also to be prompt."

ALTERNATE/ALTERNATIVE

- Often incorrectly used to mean "different," "alternative" is a noun meaning one of two possibilities or choices.

- Although "alternative" occasionally includes more than two possibilities or choices, it is best to be precise in business by distinguishing between two and more than two.

- As an adjective, "alternate" means "done or changed by turns": "She and I go to class on *alternate* days." "Alternate" usually *precedes* the noun, as in "alternate days" or even "alternate alternatives."

ALTHOUGH/THOUGH

- "Although" is usually more appropriate in formal prose than "though" because "though" — while a very old word meaning "in spite of that," "nevertheless," "yet" — is now considered colloquial. Avoid writing "Though he went to the meeting, he learned nothing." Write "Although he went to the meeting, he learned nothing."

- Avoid writing "She behaved *as though* she expected to be promoted any day." Write "She behaved *as if* she expected to be promoted any day."

- Many people use it informally, *though*.

AMERICA

- It is best sometimes to write "United States" when writing to others whose nations compose North and South America, all of which is properly "America." Occasionally, Canadians politely or silently object to citizens of the United States referring to themselves as "Americans" while others are "Canadians," "Mexicans," "Brazilians," and so on. To people of these nationalities, write "I am from the United States," not "I am an American." To express a geographical kinship with Canadians and others of the Western Hemisphere, write "We are Americans."

- To most Europeans and Asians, write "I am an American." They seldom distinguish or are offended.

AMONG/BETWEEN

- Although rarely confusing today, the distinction between "between" and "among" did not become clear until recently. In general, use "between" for two; for more than two, use "among."

- Writing formal prose, serious students of English will choose "between" when more than two share something *equally*, and "among" when the sharing is not equal. Write "The discussion among those at the meeting became incomprehensible." Write "Discussions between GM, Ford, and AMC concerning import quotas were planned secretly" if each spoke with the other equally.

AMOUNT/NUMBER

- Use amount for the uncountable: "amount of wealth."

- Use number for things countable: "number of dollars." Always use number for living things: "number of fish," "number of people."

AMPLE ENOUGH

- Redundant. Write "ample." See **adequate**.

ANATIONAL

- Formerly called "multinational," an "anational" company is spread across the world and may be richer than some countries. "Anational" companies have little or no allegiance to any country.

- The prefix "a-" indicates a separation. As "*a*moral" differs from "*im*moral" in that "amoral" means morality is treated as irrelevant, so "anational" means that nationalism is irrelevant.

AND

- "And" may begin a sentence if that sentence equals in importance the sentence immediately before it. And such sentences should be uncommon. Write "The Dorchester Hotel was bought in May for $100 million. And it was sold in September for $125 million."

AND/OR

- "And/or" is often used because it sounds exact. It is not. Avoid writing "Policy meetings must be held in Albany and/or New York." Write "Policy meetings must be held at Albany or New York, or both."

ANGRY/MAD

- "Angry" means "wrathful." "Mad" means "insane."

- Avoid writing "I am mad at Smedley." Write "I am angry with Smedley," but write, humorously, "I am mad at the insane asylum."

ANTICIPATE/EXPECT

- "Anticipate" implies preparing for expected or even unlikely occurrences.

- "Expect" does not. One may expect something to occur without preparing to do anything about it; that is, an event may be expected but not anticipated. Write "Although he expected the take-over bid, he had not anticipated it. Consequently, he lost control of the company." Conversely, it is possible that an event may be anticipated but not expected. For example, nuclear arsenals are created to *anticipate* a war that is not necessarily *expected*.

- "Anticipation" also implies a mental accommodation not implied by "expect." When one "anticipates" an exciting Super Bowl, "anticipation" connotes excitement. When one "expects" an exciting Super Bowl, one simply expects it.

ANXIOUS/EAGER

- Because only one of the lesser meanings of "anxious" involves eagerness, it is best in business to distinguish the two words.

- "Anxious" means "worried"; "eager" means "impatient with a keen desire." Avoid writing "She is anxious to begin her new job." Write "She is eager to begin her new job."

APOSTROPHES

- Learn t' use 'em properly. See Appendix II, pages 469–470.

APPENDIX

- One "appendix," two "appendices" or, more informally, "appendixes."

APPOSITIVES   See Appendix II, page 474.

APPRECIATE

- Because "appreciate" is overused and because the most important meaning of "appreciate" in business is "to increase the value of" (opposite of "depreciate"), one seldom should write "appreciate" to convey its most common meaning — "I understand the worth of."

- Write "Your opinions are thought-provoking" (or "important" or "considered carefully" or whatever else is true and precise). See **value**.

APPROACH

- The noun "approach" is used too often to mean "method" or "tactics."

- Use "method" or "tactics" if only because "method" and "tactics" are shorter and clearer than "approach."
- Avoid writing "Smedley's approach to solving this problem should be. . . ." Write "Smedley's method for solving this problem should be. . . ." Write "Smedley's tactics should be. . . ." Write "Smedley's solution to the problem should be. . . ."

APPROPRIATE

- Adjectivally, "appropriate" is often written better as "fitting"; "fitting" is shorter by two syllables.

APPROXIMATELY

- "Approximately" implies more accuracy than "about," but when such precision of measurement is not important, write "about"; "about" is shorter by three syllables and eight letters.

ARBITRATE/MEDIATE

- One who arbitrates (an "arbiter") decides. One who mediates (a "mediator") may only persuade.
- The term "binding arbitration," much used in business, is redundant in that a decision "arbitrated" is binding or it is not, strictly, "arbitration."
- "Arbiter" is a general term used when one cannot put a name to the arbiter.
- "Arbitrator" is a specific term used when the person named to settle a dispute is identifiable.

AREA

- Although defined as any extent conceived by the mind, "area" is often vague and consequently not so fitting as some more precise term.
- The phrase, "in the area of," is especially wordy. Avoid writing "She is an expert in the area of industrial psychology." Write "She is an expert in industrial psychology." See **field of**.

AROUND

- "Around" means "surrounding." "Around" as "approximately" or "about" is colloquial and should not be used in formal prose.
- Avoid writing "We have hired around 100 people this quarter." Write "We have hired about 100 people this quarter."

ARRIVE AT CONCLUSIONS

- Wordy. Do not "arrive at conclusions." Write "conclude."
- More wordy is "arrive at the point at which." Avoid writing "We have arrived at the point at which. . . ." Write "We may now. . . ."

ARS LONGA, VITA BREVIS

- Latin for "Art is long, life is short." One cannot live long enough to learn the business.

ARTICLE   See Appendix II, page 464.

ASAP   See **as soon as possible**.

AS . . . AS/SO . . . AS

- Most problems with "as . . . as/so . . . as" are solved by the following explanations. "As happy as" expresses equality. "Not so happy as" expresses inequality, usually negatives. Do not use "as . . . as" to express inequalities.

AS FAR AS

- Refers to distance; otherwise, "as far as" is a wordy and vague way to express "to a certain extent."
- Write "She flew as far as Pretoria." Avoid writing "As far as our finances are concerned, we are on solid ground, but morale is slipping." Write "Our finances are sound, but morale is slipping."

ASIDES   See Appendix II, page 473.

AS IF

- Requires the subjunctive. Avoid writing "He walks as if he was late for work." Write "He walks as if he were late for work."

ASPECT

- A good word, "aspect" is overused to mean "part" or "facet." Avoid writing "This aspect of the merger" too often. Write "This part of the merger."
- "Aspect" is an astrological term; use when guiding the company by horoscope.
- "Aspect" also refers to the exposure of a building or plot of ground; use when planning the view from a veranda.

AS PER   See **per**.

ASSETS

- Originally, money or property that may be used to pay debts. Now, anything owned that has value, from buildings ("fixed assets") to good will and patents ("intangible assets").
- Originally, "assets" had no singular because "assets" was always plural. ["Data" is another word used only in the plural.] Now, "asset" is common, but usually is used to describe "attributes." Avoid

writing "Intelligence is not Smedley's greatest asset." Write "Intelligence is not Smedley's greatest attribute."

- Avoid writing "assets" except to mean money or property; otherwise, write "intangible assets" or a more specific term.

ASSIST

- A good word, "assist" is overused in business. Sometimes it assists in creating wordy expressions, such as this one. "Help" is often better because it is shorter. People needing "assistance" may never get it; the word is so long.
- Seldom "assist to do." Regularly "assist in doing." Regularly "help to do" or "help do."
- Avoid writing "She was hired to assist in the promotion of our new line of products." Write "She was hired to assist in promoting our new line of products." Write "She was hired to help promote our new line of products."

ASSOCIATE/IDENTIFY

- Never confuse the verbs "associate" and "identify." See **identify**.

AS SOON AS POSSIBLE   Acronym: ASAP.

- Although one cannot do anything sooner than possible, the phrase, "as soon as possible," proves the exception to the rule of never saying or writing the obvious. Merely writing "soon" is indefinite. "Now" is different from "as soon as possible." Consequently, "as soon as possible" may be used as there seems to be nothing better. When "as soon as possible" is not necessary, try "soon" or "now" or "quickly."
- In memos and informal prose, write "ASAP."

ASSURE/ENSURE/INSURE

- "Assure that"; "assure of"; "ensure of"; "ensure against."
- As most good writers prefer "assure" to "insure," use "insure" only with reference to insurance.
- Each of these words has caused legal problems. Do not use in manuals, instructions, or any other writing that has the legal force of a guarantee, without company lawyers' approval.

ASTERISK (*)   See Appendix II, page 470.

AS THOUGH   See **although/though**.

AS TO

- Omit.
- Avoid writing "As to our replying to the charge, I do not think we should." Write "I do not think we should reply to the charge."

AS WELL AS   See Appendix II, page 466.

AS YOU KNOW

- If they know, why tell them? To be both polite and accurate, write "As you may know." See **obviously**; **needless to say**.

AT ALL TIMES

- Write "Always."

AT THAT POINT IN TIME

- A phrase made popular by witnesses during the televised "Watergate" hearings; use after being caught breaking and entering. Otherwise, write "then."
- Avoid writing "At that point in time, I was in Reggio, Italy." Write "Then, I was in Reggio, Italy." Write "I was in Reggio, Italy, then."

AT THIS POINT IN TIME

- "Now." Write "now."
- Use "now" also for "at this juncture."

AUGMENT/SUPPLEMENT

- "Augment" means to increase something.
- "Supplement" means to add to something.
- An augmentation is absorbed by that which is augmented. A supplement adds to, but remains separate from, that which is supplemented. One augments a salary by getting a raise. One supplements a salary by moonlighting.

AVERSE/ADVERSE   See **adverse/averse**.

AWARE

- A word much overused, especially as a noun, "awareness."
- Avoid writing "We must be in a state of awareness" not only because the phrase is wordy, but because it is redundant: "awareness" means "a state of consciousness." Write "We must be ready."
- "Do you know that . . . ?" is better than "Are you aware of . . . ?" See **oblivious/unconscious**.

AXIS

- In business, this term usually refers to one of two planes on a two-dimensional graph: the horizontal "axis" or the vertical "axis."
- One axis; two axes.

B

BAD/BADLY

- Commonly misused. Never write "I feel badly." Write "I feel bad." Write "The report is written badly."

- "State of being" verbs—"am," "is," "were," "are," and "feel" (in an overall emotional sense)—often separate subjects and modifiers. Consequently, the modifiers do not describe the verb, but rather the subject. "Badly," then, is the wrong word in this example, because what is described as "I." Adverbs ("badly") do not modify nouns ("I"). Adjectives ("bad") modify nouns ("I").

BALANCE

- Properly used, "balance" refers to a sum still outstanding on a debt. Consequently, whenever "balance" is used metaphorically ("The balance of the report will be completed next quarter"), be sure that it cannot be confused with debt. If confusion is possible, write "The remainder of the report will be completed next quarter."

- Even accountants should use "remainder" in those rare moments when they are not writing about other people's debts. "Balance of payments" and "checking account balance" are fine, but notice that the latter refers to money owed by the bank to you.

BASED ON

- While not incorrect when used to refer to a foundation—logical, firm, or otherwise—"based on" is much overused, and is often the occasion for grammatical infelicities. For example, do not write "Based on these data, I believe we should not renew our contracts with that company." What is "based?" Write "I conclude from this data that we should not renew our contract."

- Even "Our conclusions are based on these data" may be written more economically as "Our conclusions derive from these data." See **basis**.

BASIC

- A basic, but much overused word.

- Here are several basic combinations that may be avoided, basically by deleting "basic."

basic appreciation	basic information
basic basics	basic machinery
basic facts	basic problems
basic fundamentals	basic terms.

- When conveying the notion of something indispensable, try "fundamental" or "essential."

- As a computer term, BASIC is an acronym for Beginner's All-purpose Symbolic Instruction Code, a computer language relatively easy to learn.

BASIS

- One basis; two bases.

- Often used in such wordy expressions as "on a regular basis." Write "regularly." Do not use this construction: "on a _____ basis." Avoid writing "Our research must be run on a more efficient basis." Write "Our research department must be run more efficiently." See **based on**.

BECAUSE

- Sometimes misused for "that," especially in "is because."

- Avoid writing "The reason you are being hired is because we need your experience." Write "The reason you are being hired is *that* we need your experience." Write "We are hiring you for your experience."

- "Because" is usually much better than "due to" and "since." See **due to**; **since**; **being**.

BEFORE/PRIOR TO

- The distinction between "before" and "prior to" is seldom useful in business. Use "before."

BEGIN/COMMENCE/START

- Use "begin"; "commence" is stuffy. For example, "begin" a meeting; do not "commence" it. Because "start" derives from the same root as "startle," use "start" only when motion is required.

- Avoid writing "In this section we start to develop procedures for representing each vector in a vector space as a linear combination." Write "In this section we begin to develop. . . ." See **up**.

BEING

- As commonly used, "being" usually betrays an immature style and is often awkward and wordy.

- Avoid writing "As regards your being promoted, Smedley. . . ." Write "Regarding your promotion, Smedley. . . ." Avoid writing "Being an avid golfer, I try to play every weekend." Write "An avid golfer, I try to play every weekend."

- "Being as" and "being that" are substandard phrases. Use "because."

BELOW   See **above**.

BETTER THAN

- "Better than" implies quality but often is used incorrectly to mean quantity. Clarity and precision are improved by replacing "better than" with "more than" when quantity is meant.

- Avoid writing "The building cost better than nine million dollars." Write "The building cost more than nine million dollars." Yet, "She writes better than he" refers to quality and is correct.

BETWEEN/AMONG   See **among/between**.

BI-/SEMI-

- "Bi-" means "two"; "semi-" means "half."
- Regarding time, "bi-" means occurring once every two periods; "semi-" means occurring twice every period. A semi-annual meeting, then, occurs four times as often as a biennial meeting. See **biannual/biennial**.

BIANNUAL/BIENNIAL

- "Biennial" means every two years.
- "Biannual" means twice a year; so does "semi-annual." Because "bi-annual" is easily confused with "biennial," use "semi-annual" to mean every half-year. Remember, however, that "semi-annual" connotes "every six months" (say, January and July), while "bian-nual" does not. That is, biannual reports may occur at any time during a year so long as they occur only twice.

BLANKET WORDS

- "Blanket words" are imprecise. Their popularity in business and government is explained by the ease with which they may be used without thinking. Examples are "activity," "contact," "communication," "facility," "process."
- While occasionally useful, blanket words usually are used when the writer has nothing specific to say. See **rot**.

BLOC/BLOCK

- A "bloc" is a political alliance: "communist bloc nations."
- "Block" is a verb meaning to forestall and a prefix for "head."

BOARD

- Because business people spend much time getting on and off airplanes, they would be well served to learn that one "boards" an airplane. One does not "onplane." See **disembark/deplane**.

BOTTLENECK

- A good word used properly in business to refer to a place receiving input faster than it can produce output.
- A vivid noun that should not be overused. When emphasis is not required, use a less emphatic word, such as "congestion," "jam," or "obstruction."

BOTTOM LINE

- "Bottom line" correctly refers to the bottom line in a column of figures. Loose and vague when used to mean "in the end," "finally," or "when you get right down to it."

- Avoid writing "The bottom line is that we must." Write "In the end we must" or "We must finally."

BOYCOTT/EMBARGO

- Boycotts involve people and businesses. Boycotts end all relations between the parties.

- Embargoes involve nations. Embargoes may be laid by governments on particular branches of commerce. Embargoes do not necessarily end all relations between nations or between a nation and a branch of commerce.

BRACKETS ([ ])   See Appendix II, page 471.

BUT

- "But" may begin a sentence if that sentence is equally opposed to the sentence immediately before it. But, used often, such sentences may lose effect.

C

CAN/MAY

- Can means "possible" or "to have the ability to."

- "May" means "permissible," or rather, "lacking prohibitive conditions." "May" implies possibility only in a sense of uncertainty: "I may be in my office Saturday morning; but, then again, I may not be."

- Children can be taught this lesson in grammar at the dinner table. When they say "Can we be excused?" parents should respond with "Yes." When the children attempt to leave, they should be told, "No, you may not be excused." When the children express surprise, they should be told that while they can be excused, they have not been excused. Only after receiving a "yes" to "May we be excused?" may they leave the table. That is, it may be *possible* to leave a table, but that does not necessarily make it *permissible*. Subordinates can learn the same lesson during meetings that extend beyond 5 o'clock.

CANNOT

- One word, unless one wants to emphasize the "not." Because shorter, "I cannot" usually is better than "I am unable to."

- "I may not" is better than "I am unable to" when one could but is not permitted to do something. See **can/may**.

CAPABILITY

- "Capability" is a condition of ability. A computer, for example, may have a "capability" of 75 MIPS (millions of instructions per second), but may not use it always. The problem is not so much with meaning as with wordiness.

- Avoid writing "This computer has the capability of performing 75 MIPS." Write "This computer can perform 75 MIPS."

- The notion of capability often may be omitted, as in "The computer performs 75 MIPS." See **ability/capacity**.

CAPITAL/CAPITOL

- "Capitol" refers to buildings in which a government performs, tries to perform, or pretends to perform: the capitol building.

- "Capital" refers to all other meanings: money, goods, death penalties, tops of columns, upper-case letters, and a city serving as the seat of government. "Seat of government" is as unfortunate a phrase as it is accurate.

CAPITALIZATION   See Appendix II, page 471.

CARGO

- One cargo; two cargoes.

CARPE DIEM

- Latin for "Seize the day." Grasp the opportunity. Live for the moment. Go for it.

CAR POOL

- Two words.

CASE

- A blanket word meaning "instance," "example," "state," or "position," "case" is too often used in place of a more precise word and often creates wordy constructions. Avoid writing "There are many cases of projects running behind schedule." Write "Many projects are running behind schedule."

- The three important grammatical cases are subjective, objective, and possessive. See Appendix II, page 465.

CAVEAT EMPTOR

- Latin for "Let the buyer beware."

CENTER AROUND

- By definition, a "center" is "around" nothing. Center *in* or *on*.

- Avoid writing "The project's problems center around an inventory control." Write "The project's problems center on inventory control."

CENTER/MIDDLE

- The center is a geometrical position. Write "The center of a circle."
- Occasionally, "center" may be used metaphorically. Write "the center of activity."
- "Middle" should be used more often than "center." Thousands of offices, for example, may be in the middle of town, but only one may be in the center. Write "the middle of town."

CEO

- Chief Executive Officer.

CHAIR/CHAIRMAN/CHAIRWOMAN

- Write "chair" to refer to the position.
- Write "chair" when the gender of the chair holder is unknown or pointedly to be ignored.
- "Chairman" and "chairwoman" remain acceptable in many companies. "Chairperson" is lengthy.

CHARACTER

- Wordy when used to mean "kind" or "type."
- Avoid writing "The XYZ Analogue Computer is different in character." Write "The XYZ Analogue Computer is a different type."

CIRCUMSTANCES

- Means "that which surrounds materially, morally, or logically."
- "Circumstances surrounding" is redundant. Write "The circumstances are."
- "Under the circumstances" is incorrect. Write "Considering the circumstances, . . ." Write "In the circumstances, . . ." See **center around**.

CITE/SIGHT/SITE

- "Cite" refers to a source: "Smedley frequently *cites* Alexander Haig's speeches as new sources for rot."
- "Site" is a specific location: "This is the *site* of the new plant."
- "Sight": surely this word is not a problem.

CLAUSE   See Appendix II, page 465.

CLICHÉ

- Clever phrases, the cleverness of which is destroyed by overuse. "Thoughts that snore in words that smoke" (Ambrose Bierce).
- Avoid writing "a tried and true method"; write "proven." Avoid writing "she wasn't born yesterday"; write "experienced," or "not naive." Avoid writing "He let the cat out of the bag"; write "revealed."

- Avoid writing "We have a cash-flow problem" when "broke" is meant, unless writing to a creditor.
- A reputation for wit may be gained by cleverly altering clichés. A director of highways may alter the cliché, "Leave no stone unturned," to "Leave no turn unstoned." Bird haters may "leave no tern unstoned." Often deplored by stodgy grammarians and rhetoricians, lively and accurate idioms are excellent for business prose and are not to be confused with clichés. They give energy, humor, and force to language. "Quaking like a leaf" is a cliché, but "nervous as a fly in a frog pond" is a good American expression.

CLIENT/CUSTOMER

- A "client" is one who employs the services of professional or business people. Lawyers and businesses offering services have clients.
- Customers buy products; clients buy professional services.

CO-

- Beware of this prefix. Journalists are beginning to use it to describe anything done by two people. George Hackett, for example, errs grievously by writing that Deborah Allen, the song writer, "cowrote most of the songs on the LP with her husband" (*Newsweek*, 28 Jan. 1985). "Allen and her husband wrote most of the songs on the LP" is more literate.

COGNIZANT

- From the Latin "to know," "cognizant," meaning "knowing," is a bit pompous.
- Avoid writing "We are cognizant of your needs." Write "We know that you have needs" or "We know about your needs."

COLLECTIVE NOUNS   See Appendix II, page 467.

COLONS (:)   See Appendix II, pages 471–472.

COMMAS (,)   See Appendix II, pages 472–473.

COMMON/MUTUAL

- "Mutual" means shared between two entities.
- "Common" means shared among (or "between" if shared equally) more than two entities.
- "A mutual friendship" is redundant; "We two have a mutual friend" is not. "Mutual interest" is written better as "shared interest."

COMMON SENSE

- Two words as a noun: "She has common sense." One word, hyphenated, as an adjective: "a common-sense directive."

COMMUNICATE

- Use "tell," "write," "speak with" when brevity and precision are required.

COMMUNICATE TO/COMMUNICATE WITH

- One cannot communicate "to" anything because communication is either mutual or common or it is not communication. Communication never occurs on one-way streets. The traffic of information must flow at least two ways. One may *convey* information from point A *to* point B, but one may communicate only if information flows from A to B *and* from B to A.
- One may "communicate *with*" (although it is better to "talk" or "discuss"). One may "convey *to*." One may "tell," "discuss," and even "say."
- Avoid writing *"Communicate* our decision *to* him." Write "Tell him our decision" or *"Convey* our decision *to* him."

COMMUNITY

- A useful word when used alone. When modified by adjectives, "community" is over-used and often unnecessary.
- Avoid "banking community," "intelligence community," "welfare community," "corporate community," "educational community." Write "banking" or "bankers," "intelligence" or "intelligence services," "welfare," "corporations," and "education" or "educators." See **sector**.

COMPARE/CONTRAST

- "Compare" means to point out similarities and differences, or simply to point out similarities.
- "Contrast" means to weigh those differences.
- Consequently, use "contrast" to make differences stand out so they can be weighed; use "compare" to note similarities or only to note differences, not to weigh them. One usually "compares to." One usually "contrasts with." Write "We want to compare her work to his"; write "We want to contrast her work with his."

COMPATIBLE

- An action, idea, or person able to exist harmoniously with another act, idea, or person is "compatible." "Compatible" does not mean "acceptable" or "convenient."

COMPENSATION

- When compensation means money, write "pay." When "remuneration" or "recompense" means money, write "pay."

- Use "honorarium" instead of "pay" when money is given in exchange for a speech. Use "compensation" when remuneration does not mean money necessarily: "The compensation which the borrower pays to the lender" (Adam Smith, *Wealth of Nations*).

COMPLEMENT/COMPLIMENT

- "Complement" means "to complete," "to go well together."
- "Compliment" means to praise with the truth (as opposed to "flattery" or "sycophancy").
- The difference between "flattery" and "compliment" lies in the intent, "flattery" being insincere and "compliment" being sincere. A tie may (or may not) complement a suit; a string of pearls may (or may not) complement a dress. One may compliment someone on his tie or her pearls; or, in some places, the reverse of these.

COMPOSE/COMPRISE

- "Compose" in business means "to put together parts to make a whole"—that is, "to consist of." Parts compose the whole: "Five divisions compose the company's organization"; "The organization is composed of divisions."
- "Comprise" works from the other end; the whole comprises the parts: "The company's organization comprises five divisions."
- For those uncomfortable with "compose," substitute "contain," "embrace," and "make up."

CONJUNCTION   See Appendix II, page 464.

CONNECT

- Some forms of "connect" are wordy and useless; "connected with" and "in connection with" are often redundant. Avoid writing "A is connected with B." Write "A and B are connected."
- Avoid writing "She is connected with plant operations." Write "She works for plant operations."

CONNOTE/DENOTE

- "Denote" indicates specific meaning; "connote" includes those meanings, often subtle, suggested by a word or action other than denotative or "dictionary" meaning.
- "Adequate" *denotes* "satisfactory," "having given satisfaction." That it *connotes* something else is evident from the disappearance from many companies of those people who receive only "adequate" job ratings. "Adequate" has come to *connote* "barely squeaking by."

-CONSCIOUS

- As a suffix used to create new words, "-conscious" is much overused.

- Avoid writing "security-conscious," "production-conscious," or any other "-conscious." Write "concerned about security," "concerned about production." Always be word-conscious.

CONSENSUS OF OPINION

- Usually redundant. While there may be a consensus of forces or functions, business nearly always uses "consensus" for "unanimous opinion." As consensus therefore requires opinion, write only "consensus."
- Avoid writing "The consensus of opinion among the project's directors is. . . ." Write "The project's directors agree. . . ." Write "The consensus among the project's directors is. . . ."

CONSULT

- "Consult" is a verb meaning "to ask for someone's advice or opinions." In such cases, one usually "consults with." Too often, "consult" is used in business prose to describe any conversation.

CONSUMER

- A consumer is not "one who uses," but rather "one who destroys by consuming," or in a commercial sense, "one who uses up" a product.
- "Buyer" is a better word and more accurate.

CONTACT

- Often vague when used as a verb: "I contacted him." "Call" her, "phone" him, "reach" her, "meet" with him, but do not "contact" her.
- As a noun ("She is my contact in their firm"), "contact" is used by all but the discerning. The discerning write "I know her" or "I am to call her." See **touching base; blanket words**.

CONTINUAL/CONTINUOUS

- "Continual" means "frequent."
- "Continuous" means "uninterrupted."
- For example, "All our pumps—Teuton III, Teuton IV, and the Triton I—are made to run contin*ual*ly" means the pumps may turn on and off thousands of times. That is, they are built for frequent but not contin*uous* use. On the other hand, "All our pumps—Teuton III, Teuton IV, and the Triton I—are made to run contin*uous*ly" means the pumps may run 24 hours a day, 7 days a week, until they wear out or break down.

CONTRACTIONS

- In formal prose, don't use 'em.
- *Say* "I don't know what I'd do, Smedley," but *write* "I do not know what I would do, Smedley." See Appendix II, page 470.

CONTRAST/COMPARE   See **compare/contrast**.

CONVENIENCE

- "At your earliest convenience" is absurdly polite, ridiculously wordy. Write "soon." See **as soon as possible**.
- "For your convenience" is a blanket euphemism for many distasteful possibilities. Locks on hotel room doors are not provided for safety but for "convenience." Cheap, skinny tires, good for only fifty miles have replaced good, solid spare tires not, say automobile makers, because cheap tires save Detroit money, but "for your convenience": they provide more trunk space. This euphemism and others often say the opposite of their meanings. Use euphemisms cautiously.

CONVINCE/PERSUADE

- "Persuade" often is followed by an infinitive: "persuade to."
- "Convince" never is followed by an infinitive: "convince that."
- "Convince of" and "persuade of" are correct.
- "Convince" connotes the satisfaction of all doubts and reservations. "Persuade" connotes the use of argument to gain assent. "I am persuaded to believe that something is true or false," but "I am convinced that something is true or false."

COPY

- As a verb, "copy" is often incorrectly used, as in "Copy the staff on this memo." Write "Send copies of this memo to the staff," because the staff presumably is human. To "copy the staff" would be to "act as the staff acts." Paper, on the other hand, may be copied. Write "Copy this memo and send it to the staff."

CORODY

- A maintenance allowance dispensed as charity. A corporation may give computers to a college or other nonprofit organization, and that is charity. Should the corporation give money to maintain those computers, that is charity called a "corody."

CORPORATISM

- The organization of a society into industrial and professional corporations that influence politics and people.

COST/PRICE

- "Cost" refers to that required to do or to produce something: time, money, work, things.
- "Price" refers to the money to be paid for something. Write of the *cost* of producing a product, and of the *price* for which it sells.

COULD OF

■ An illiteracy, "could of" sounds like "could've," which means "could have." Similarly, "would of" sounds like "would've" which means "would have"; "should of" sounds like "should've" which means "should have."

COUNCIL/COUNSEL

■ A "council" is an advisory or deliberative group. "To counsel" is to advise.

CREDIBLE/CREDITABLE

■ Credible means "believable." Creditable means "worthy of praise or respect."

CREDIT

■ As a noun, "trust," "belief," or "something creditable." As a verb, "to trust," "to believe."

CRISIS

■ One "crisis," two "crises." Hyperbolic and much overused. Do not use, except to describe emergencies.

CRITERION/CRITERIA

■ One "criterion," two "criteria." "Criterion" refers to a standard of judgment.

CRITICAL

■ Too often used incorrectly to mean "we have a problem."
■ A medical term, "critical" means "hanging between life and death."
■ In business, "critical" should be used to indicate "at a turning point between success and failure." Because "critical" implies "turning point," and because "turning point" defines "juncture," the phrase "at this critical juncture" is redundant.

CURRENTLY

■ Popularly used to mean "now," "currently" is overused and often unnecessary. "Currently" correctly refers to that which is in common use at a given time.
■ Avoid writing "We are currently reviewing the 'Cost' section of your report." Write "We are reviewing the 'Cost' section of your report."

CUSTOMER/CLIENT   See **client/customer**.

D

DANGLING MODIFIER   See Appendix II, page 467.

DASHES ($-$)   See Appendix II, page 475.

DATA/DATUM

- "Datum" is singular but rarely used. "Data" is plural and commonly used to mean facts or numbers that compose information.
- Never write "The data *is*." Always write "The data *are*."

DATE

- Used in wordy expressions. "On [or At] an early date" indicates "soon," unless one plans to attend a matinee. "On [or At] a later date" indicates "later," unless one plans to attend an all-night film festival.
- "Exact date" is redundant; dates are exact.

DECISION MAKING

- Almost always, "deciding" is a better word.
- Avoid writing "We are engaged in decision making." Write "We are trying to decide."
- A "decision-making process" is vague because such a process could involve anything from gathering mountains of information to simply tossing a coin.

DECREASE OVER

- "Decrease over" or "decrease under" should be used carefully or not at all.
- Avoid writing "There was a five percent decrease over the profits of last year." Write "This year's profits were five percent less than last year's."

DEFINITELY

- "Definitely" is definitely one of the most overused emphatic words in the language. Any word too often used for emphasis definitely loses its power to emphasize. Such words, used repeatedly or not, are usually unnecessary.
- Should emphasis definitely be required, the following would at least create variety: assuredly, certainly, clearly, decidedly, indeed, no, yes.

DEGENERATE/DETERIORATE

- "Deteriorate" means "to make or become worse." "Degenerate" means "to make or become worse morally."

- Everything deteriorates; only people may also degenerate, because only people have a moral sense.

DELETE/OMIT

- "Delete" means to remove. "Omit" means not to insert or include.
- Consequently, one "deletes" something in a preliminary report. One "omits" by not inserting something into a report. Write "I think we should delete from the memo those nasty remarks about Smedley" if they are already there. Write "I think we should omit from the memo those nasty remarks about Smedley" if they have not been included yet.

DEMONSTRATE

- Write "show" more often than "demonstrate." "Demonstrate" means "to make evident or display by reasoning."

DENOTE/CONNOTE   See **connote/denote**.

DENY/REFUTE

- "Deny" means merely to assert the falsity of an accusation.
- "Refute" means to prove an accusation false.
- People may deny things interminably, and they usually do. Many of these people have trouble refuting things. See **rebut/refute**.

DEPLETE/REDUCE

- A thing "reduced" is merely lessened.
- A thing "depleted" is exhausted or otherwise harmfully reduced.

DEVELOPMENT

- Often creates wordy expressions.
- Avoid writing "in the development of." Write "in developing" or "while developing."

DIALOGUE

- A "dialogue" refers to two or more people talking. "Duologue" means two people talking, but is rarely used. Although "dialogue" is acceptable for describing a conversation, "discussion" or "conversation" usually is more conventional. See **meaningful dialogue**.

DIFFERENT THAN/DIFFERENT FROM

- Although many say that "different than" is acceptable when followed by a clause, rarely write "different than" in formal prose. Write "different from."
- Avoid writing "It is different than I remember it." Write "It is different from my memory of it."

DIFFER FROM/DIFFER WITH

- One thing may "differ from" another thing. In an argument, one person may "differ with" another.
- Write "A 16-bit computer *differs from* an 8-bit computer in several ways." Write "Smedley *differs with* Samantha on almost every issue."

DILEMMA

- "Dilemma" denotes a difficulty of choosing between two possibilities. If more than two present themselves, then the situation is not, strictly, a "dilemma," but rather a real pickle.

DIMINISH/MINIMIZE

- "To diminish" means "to lessen."
- "To minimize" means "to make least," or "to reduce as much as possible."
- Do not use "minimize" when merely "lessen" is meant.

DISCONTINUE

- "To discontinue" means "to stop." One who writes "discontinue" clearly went to school; one who writes "stop" clearly conveys meaning in three fewer syllables.

DISCREET/DISCRETE

- "Discreet" means "prudent." "Discrete" means "separate" or "distinct."
- One may use "discreet methods" and "discrete methods," but the second means using more than one method to achieve an end, while the first implies cautious, careful, and prudent methods that either avoid hurting feelings or avoid letting others know that one is doing it at all.
- A good device for remembering the difference is this one: In "discre*t*e," the *t* separates the *e*'s.

DISEMBARK/DEPLANE

- Airline personnel say "When deplaning, please be sure to take with you any belongings that you may have brought on board."
- Airplanes are ships, and the correct terminology should be that associated with ships. One "disembarks." One does not "deplane" or "offboard."

DISINFORMATION

- Lies.

DISINTERESTED/UNINTERESTED

- "Disinterested" means "unbiased," "impartial." "Uninterested" means "not interested."

DIVIDED BY/DIVIDED INTO

- Never confuse the two. Nearly always, they yield different results. Ten divided *by* two equals five: $\frac{5}{}$. Ten divided *into* two equals .20: $\frac{.20}{10\,\overline{)2.00}}$. $2\,\overline{)10}$

DONE

- Avoid writing "Smedley is done," unless he is being served up as a meal. "Done" in this context means "to be finished cooking": "The roast is done." Write "Smedley has finished."

DOUBLE NEGATIVES   See Appendix II, page 465.

DOWN

- A term often used to describe a computer that is not working. "Sorry, the computer is down."

DRACONIAN

- Harsh. From an ancient Athenian law-giver, Draco, whose laws were severe.

DRASTIC

- "Drastic" does not mean "extreme." "Drastic" means "vigorous," even "violent."
- Do not write "drastically reduced prices." Write, instead, "drastic actions."

DUE TO

- Correctly used with "is," "was," "were," "will be": "His absence was due to illness." Otherwise, use "because of" or "owing to," or "on account of": "He failed because of illness." See **because**.
- Notice that "was [or is] due to" usually follows a noun: "Her *promotion was due to* hard work." Notice that "because of" usually follows a verb: "She *was promoted because of* hard work."

DURING

- Often used in wordy expressions. Avoid writing "during the course of the. . . ." Avoid writing "during the time that. . . ." Write "while."

E

EACH/EITHER/NEITHER   See Appendix II, pages 466–467.

EACH AND EVERY

- Redundant.

EACH OTHER/ONE ANOTHER

■ No rule governs here, but precision may improve should "each other" be used for two and "one another" for more than two.

EAGER/ANXIOUS   See **anxious/eager**.

ECONOMIC/ECONOMICAL

■ As an adjective, "economic" concerns the economy.

■ As an adjective, "economical" concerns the prudent use of money or other resources.

EDITORIAL ELEMENTS   See Appendix II, pages 462–464.

EFFECT/AFFECT   See **affect/effect**.

EFFECTIVE

■ Avoid writing "Effective 1 June 1993 and running through 30 September 1993, the work day will begin at 7:30 a.m. and end at 3:30 p.m." Write "From 1 June 1993 through 30 September 1993, the work day will begin at 7:30 a.m. and end at 3:30 p.m."

EFFICIENT

■ "Efficient" means "effective," especially "effective without waste." Always praised and often overrated, "efficient" is sometimes used to mean "practical," although the practical is not always efficient. When practicality is desired, rather than "efficient," write "practical."

EFFORT

■ "Effort" refers to especially strenuous labor, and, as such, is related to "work." But "work" may be "effortless"; consequently, when "effort" has the same meaning as "work," write "work."

E.G.

■ *exampli gratia*; Latin for "For the sake of example." Not to be confused with "i.e.," *id est*, meaning "that is."

■ Write informally "She has had a long career in creative financing; e.g., she has owned nine companies in seven years—one at a time."

■ Do not use "e.g." in formal prose. Write "for example." See **i.e.**

EITHER/EACH/NEITHER   See Appendix II, pages 473–474.

EITHER/OR

■ Used in sentences, "either/or" is a special construction for logic. Do not use in business prose.

■ Avoid writing "It's an either/or situation." Write "We must either do this or do that."

EITHER . . . OR

- The form of the verb in this construction is determined by the subject nearest the verb.
- Write "Either Joan or *they are* attending the meeting." Although this sentence—"Either they or *Joan is* attending the meeting"—is correct, it is awkward and should be avoided.
- This holds also for "neither . . . nor."

ELLIPSIS (. . .)   See Appendix II, pages 475–476.

EMBARGO/BOYCOTT   See **boycott/embargo**.

ENCLOSED

- Avoid writing "Enclosed herewith is." Write "Here is," "Enclosed is," or "I have enclosed."

ENCROACH

- To trespass or intrude on one's rights, property, or privileges, or, as some say, "space."

ENDEAVOR

- As a noun, it means "a strenuous attempt."
- As a verb, "endeavor" should not replace "try" or "attempt" unless one wants to convey the involvement of great effort.
- As a noun, "endeavor" should not replace "job" or "project" unless one wants to convey the involvement of great effort.
- Try "try." Try "job."

ENHANCE

- Overused. Write "improve" more often than "enhance."

ENHANCEMENT

- Stuffy, overused word meaning "the act of making greater," and usually referring to attractiveness, desirability, or value.
- The common phrase, "enhancement value," is redundant.
- When "improvement" is meant, write "improvement."

ENORMITY

- "Enormity" means "monstrously wicked crime" against morality, ethics, or society.
- "Enormity" does not mean "big."

ENSURE   See **assure/ensure/insure**.

ENTHUSE

- Avoid "enthuse." Avoid writing "I am enthused." Write "I am excited" or "I am enthusiastic."

ENVIRONMENT

- "Environment" concerns more than simply "climate"; it concerns the "big picture," the world. Linking "business" and "environment," as in "The trouble with today's business environment," cheapens both. Write "The trouble with business is. . . ."

EQUAL

- "Equal" has no comparative. One cannot be "more equal" or "less equal" except, says George Orwell, in certain political systems.

ERR

- To err is to make a mistake; to lie is to say a deliberate falsehood.

-ESE

- A suffix indicating jargon or other language difficult to understand: computerese, educationese, legalese.
- Do not create "-ese" words.

ESSENTIAL

- Anything so important as to be "essential" cannot be done without. "Important essentials," then, is redundant. "High priority important essentials" is doubly redundant. Even "very essential," "most essential," and "totally essential" should cause one to cast a cold eye on the writer.

ET AL./ETC.

- Abbreviation for the Latin "et alii," meaning "and other people." Normally, "et al." is used in bibliographical citations after a principal author to indicate multiple authorship: Nixon, Richard, et al. *The Watergate Scandal.* Do not use "et al." to mean "and other things."
- "*Et cetera*" means "and other things," not "and other people." Do not use "etc." in formal writing, nor in a sentence with "such as," "in addition," "for example," or "and."
- Informal writing may include "etc.," as in the following: "Bow hunters must carry with them camouflage clothing and paint, scent maskers, a bow, arrows, a quiver, a rope, a knife, etc."

EUPHEMISM

- Nice expression replacing a unpleasant one. While some civilize the world a little—"Would you like to get together sometime?"—most are silly ("He went to that big brokerage house in the sky" for "He died"), or deliberately obfuscating ("rapid oxidation" for "fire," or "revenue enhancement" for "tax increase"). Business uses too many euphemisms: "It is unfortunately not within the purview of this company to grant you a refund" for "no."

■ Job titles are subject to euphemisms. People who collect garbage are "sanitary engineers," elevator operators are "vertical transportation corps employees," junk yard workers are "surplus property disposal agents," and mail clerks are "correspondence review employees." The problem is that in attempting to ameliorate what people do, name givers must provide abstractions. The result is that the job no longer sounds demeaning, but neither does the name any longer describe the job. See **facilitate** and **facilitator**.

EVENT

■ Because an uncountable number of events occurs each second in this world, one should be cautious about labeling any occurrence as an "event," especially in formal or business prose.

■ Avoid "Smedley's promotion party was a real event." Write "Smedley's promotion party was memorable." See **in the event that**.

EVERYBODY/EVERYONE   See Appendix II, page 466.

EX-/FORMER

■ "Ex-," used with a title, refers to an immediate predecessor.

■ "Former," used with a title, refers to those who came before the "ex-."

■ Last year's student body president, for example, is "Ex-President Fahrquart." The student body presidents from all previous years are "former presidents." Similarly, one may have only one "ex-spouse," even if one has been married several times. Those spouses previous to the immediate past one are called "former spouses."

EXCEPT/ACCEPT   See **accept/except**.

EXCITING/FASCINATING

■ Seen daily in advertisements and television commercials, "exciting" denotes motion, "fascinating" immobility. The connotations of "exciting" include strong emotions, either pleasurable or painful. The connotations of "fascinating" include the pleasurable ones of "irresistible" and "charming."

■ Do not use "excited," "exciting," "fascinated," or "fascinating" whenever "pleased," "pleasing," "admirable," "excellent," or "good" is better. An "exciting new mouthwash" is rarely "new" and never "exciting."

EXCLAMATION POINT (!)   Hey! See Appendix II, page 476.

- Rarely use exclamation points in formal prose!
- Use sparingly in informal business prose to indicate surprise or indignation: "His hotel bill for two nights was $1750!"

EXIST/SUBSIST

- "Exist" means "to have being." "Subsist" means "to support life."
- Avoid writing "I don't know how she exists on such a diet." Write "I don't know how she subsists on such a diet."

EXPATIATE/EXPOUND

- "Expatiate" means "to explain at great length." "Expound" means merely "to explain."

EXPECT/ANTICIPATE   See **anticipate/expect**.

EXPEDIENT/EXPEDITIOUS

- "Expedient" means "advantageous." "Expeditious" means "completed quickly."

EXPEDITE

- "To do quickly." Much overused.
- Avoid writing "Please expedite your decision." Write "Please decide soon."

EXPLETIVE   See Appendix II, page 464.

EXPOUND/EXPATIATE   See **expatiate/expound**.

EXTEND

- To "extend" one's sympathies or congratulations is weak. Better to "offer" or "send" sympathies and congratulations. Better yet, "sympathize" and "congratulate."

F

FACET

- A "facet" is a smooth, flat surface, usually of a cut gemstone. A cut diamond, then, has many facets. Use "facet" sparingly to refer to a portion or side of a many-sided, finished argument, problem, or piece of work.
- Write "There are many facets to the president's white paper." Write "There are many sides to Smedley's argument."

FACILITATE

- "To make easier," "to smooth the path," "to ease." A good word overused. People cannot be "facilitated," only activities.
- Avoid writing "New employees must be facilitated." Write "We must facilitate the adjustment of new employees." Write "We must ease [or make easier] the adjustment of new employees."

FACILITATOR

- Commonly used in psychology and education, "facilitator" is overused and vague.

FACILITY

- A euphemism for a public toilet, "facility" is also vague in its other meanings. Be specific.
- Avoid writing "Our locomotive facility in Erie. . . ." Write "Our locomotive plant in Erie. . . ." See **euphemism**.

FACT

- Facts are facts, as they say, and need to be stated, not introduced.
- Avoid writing "The fact is that we are overstocked." Write "We are overstocked." Avoid writing "accurate facts," as facts are accurate by definition. See **true fact**.

FACTA NON VERBA

- Latin for "deeds, not words." Do not tell me about it. Just do it!

FACTOR

- Often wordy and vague.
- Avoid writing "The most important factor in our success has been hard work."
- Write "Hard work contributed most to our success."

FAMILIARIZE

- "To become familiarized with" is a common and uncommonly wordy business phrase. Write "learn about," "learn," or "get to know."
- "To familiarize with" is similarly bad. Write "tell," "explain," or "teach."
- Avoid writing "She familiarized herself with FORTRAN." Write "She taught herself FORTRAN." "He is familiar with," on the other hand, while wordy and a trifle vague, is acceptable. See **acquaint with**.

FARTHER/FURTHER

- "Farther" refers to distance: "How much farther is the nearest town?"
- "Further" refers to "more" — that is, to the temporal or to degree: "How much further must this report be studied?"

FAULT

- In most formal prose, it is better to "blame" someone than to "fault" them.

FEASIBLE

- "Feasible" means "able to be done."
- Although the dictionary gives subordinate meanings — "easily done" and "probable" — business would be better off with these; otherwise an important distinction between possibility and probability may produce mixed signals, and thus confusion. Something is "feasible," then, simply because it may be done. Building the pyramids and the Panama Canal was feasible, but not easily done, or even probable.

FEATURE

- Use "feature" to describe the structure, form, or appearance of a person or thing. Write "One feature of this computer is a full-size keyboard."
- Do not use "feature" to describe what a thing will do. Avoid writing "One feature of this computer is that it is twice as fast as an IBM PC."

FEEDBACK

- Except when discussing machinery, "response" is a better word than "feedback" because "response" has been used with regard to humans for centuries while "feedback" usually has been associated with electronic or mechanical information.
- Avoid writing "The feedback from Smedley is favorable." Write "The response from Smedley is favorable."

FEEL

- Weak and vague, and therefore bad business prose, when used in place of "think," "believe," "say."
- Avoid writing "She feels that we should reorganize the department." Write "She believes that we should reorganize the department."

FEMALE/MALE

- Avoid "female" and "male" except as legal or scientific terms; use "woman" and "man."

- Women should not be called "girls"; men should not be called "boys." Women should be called "ladies" only in situations in which men are called "gentlemen," and vice-versa. See **gender**.

FEWER/LESS

- While the meanings of these words overlap, they are beginning to be distinguished as follows.
- Write "fewer" for things countable: "fewer dollars," "fewer grains of sugar," and "fewer people." Write "less" for the uncountable: "less money," "less sugar," "less humanity."
- Time is different. Write "The meeting took less than three hours" if the amount of time is indeterminate, that is, if it did not end on an hour. Writing "The meeting took fewer than three hours" is unnecessary and vague and probably incorrect. For the same reasons, it is best to say "less than twenty minutes." Similarly, money may be different. Write "It costs less than twenty dollars" when the amount, like the time, is indeterminate.

FIELD OF

- Usually wordy. Avoid using "field of" in formal prose except literally, as in "A field of corn."
- Avoid writing "The field of electrical engineering"; write "electrical engineering." Avoid writing "the field of genetic research"; write "genetic research." See **area**.

FINAL DESTINATION

- This common phrase of flight attendants is uncommonly frightening to many business people and should be avoided.
- Common phrase of morticians who did not know the dead person and refuse to speculate upon a "final destination." Write "destination."

FINALIZE

- An ugly word meaning "to finish" or "to complete."
- Avoid writing "Let's finalize the agenda." Write "Let's complete the agenda."

FINAL OUTCOME

- Redundant. "Outcome" is sufficient, but even "outcome" is seldom needed.
- "Outcome" is so often misused by so many that one often reads of some outcomes being only "temporarily final."
- Avoid writing "The final outcome of the meeting was that nothing was decided." Write "We decided nothing at the meeting." See **outcome**.

FIRM

- Correctly used when referring to a partnership, or to a company owned by two or more people, but not incorporated.
- Incorrectly used to refer to companies owned by one person or by many stockholders.

FIRSTLY, SECONDLY, THIRDLY

- Because "first," "second," and "third" are adverbs without "-ly," write "first," "second," "third."

FISCAL

- Formerly used only to describe public revenue, "fiscal" is now used only when describing or discussing large amounts of money.
- Corporations may have "fiscal problems." You and I and Pete's Restaurant, sadly, may have "money problems."

FLOUNDER/FOUNDER

- "Flounder" means to flop about like the beached fish of that name. "Founder" means to bog down or sink. Consequently, "flounder" conveys the idea of struggling with difficulty, and "founder" conveys the notion of being ruined. A corporation usually "flounders" before it "founders" or receives a federal loan.

FORCEFUL/FORCIBLE

- Although their meanings overlap, "forceful" generally describes persuasive power: "Her arguments were forceful."
- "Forcible" generally describes physical power: "She was forcibly removed from the boardroom."

FORECAST

- "Forecast" differs from "predict" in that prediction connotes prophesy or intuition, while forecasting connotes research and thought. Given the accuracy of their "forecasts," economists and meteorologists would be more accurate should they use "predictions."
- The past tense is "forecast," not "forecasted."

FORMAT

- A noun. Originally printers' jargon for the size, shape, and general arrangement of a book or other printed matter, "format" has become acceptable as a verb *only* in computer jargon. Otherwise, it remains an unacceptable verb in formal business prose.
- A computer disk may be "formatted," but do not write "The report needs to be formatted better." Write "The report needs to be designed [or arranged] better."

FORMER/LATTER

- Stuffy and sometimes confusing. "Former" and "latter" make work for the reader unless it's clear to whom or what "former" and "latter" refer. Either repeat the specific words or be sure the reader immediately recognizes the references.

FORTUNA FAVET FORTIBUS

- Latin for "fortune favors strength."

FOR YOUR INFORMATION

- "FYI," quickly penned on memos, is efficient and helpful. "FYI" is used most often when one sends copies of something to someone else and does not want to bother writing anything much about it. "FYI" is clear only when what is sent is clear, and when the purpose for sending it is also clear. Spelled out in a sentence of a memo or letter, "for your information" is unnecessary unless the reader does not know the meaning of "FYI."

FRACTION/PORTION

- A "fraction" describes a piece or portion broken off and separated from a whole. A "portion" is any part of a whole. In informal prose, "fraction" also connotes a small portion.
- In formal prose, do not write "These are only a fraction of the errors the engineers made regarding the architect's design." Write "These are only a portion of the errors the engineers made regarding the architect's design."

FRIENDLY

- "Friendly" often has strange connotations in business. The phrase, "friendly take-over," for example, is an oxymoron. There is no such thing as a friendly take-over. Some take-overs are merely less hostile than some others.
- The easier a computer program is to use, the more "friendly."
- "User-friendly" is a marketing claim that could bring trouble to a computer company. One cannot prove "friendliness" because one cannot control the intelligence of the "user."

FULFILLMENT

- Often used to mean the completion of a job, "fulfillment" has many other meanings and should not be used often.
- Avoid writing "What is the fulfillment date?" Write "What is the completion date?"

FUNCTION

- Meaning "to perform one's duty," "function" is often vague and wordy. Try "work," "act," or "do."

- Avoid writing "Management functions to help." Write "Management helps." Avoid writing "The machine functions to sort our mail." Write "The machine sorts our mail."

- "Function" is often written in bureaucratese as the object of many nouns turned adjectives: "research and development functions," "needs assessment function," "procurement function," "function function." In such instances, "function" is never needed.

- Oddly and connotatively biological, "function" is often disheartening when applied to one's work. I am happy, or at least not upset, to be told that my heart "functions" well. I am distressed to be told that in my work I merely "function."

FUNCTIONAL

- "Functional" means "workable" and "doing its part." An adjective, "functional" is much overused and often useless ("nonfunctional").

- Avoid writing "functional illiterate" unless one needs to convey that the illiterate "functions" in spite of illiteracy; usually, "illiterate" is sufficient. This holds also for "functional planning"; write "planning."

FUNDS

- Used incorrectly and indiscriminately to mean money under any circumstances, "funds" means money available, not merely money. "Funds are available" is redundant.

- Avoid writing "Are there funds available for this project?" Write "Are there funds for this project?" Write "Do we have money for this project?"

FUTURE

- Normally concerned with the knowable, business people are oddly given to citing the unknowable. "We must be sure to examine our present and future needs" would be more profitably and economically written as "We must be sure to examine our needs." "Although I am leaving Star Industries, it has my best wishes for its future endeavors." Delete "future" because it is futile to wish luck (good or bad) in past endeavors. Better yet, delete everything after "wishes."

- A common but redundant construction is this: "We look forward to working with the Fahrquart company in the future." How else can one "look forward" except to the future?

- "In the near future" is more economically written as "soon."

- "The foreseeable future" is a common absurdity since it is futile to speak of the "unforeseeable future."

G

GENDER

- "Gender" is sometimes a euphemism for "sex," but "gender" has only one meaning: sexual identity; "sex," having become descriptive of an action, has many.
- In business prose, to indicate the gender of anyone, write "gender."

GENERALLY ALWAYS

- Contradictory. "Generally" means "usually"; something that happens generally does not happen always.
- Write either "generally" or "always," depending on which is meant.

GERUND   See Appendix II, page 464.

GLANCE/GLIMPSE

- One "glances." One catches a "glimpse."

GOAL/OBJECTIVE

- "Objective" has three syllables; "goal" has one. "Objective" has nine letters; "goal" has four. Why waste two syllables and five letters? Write "goal."

GOOD/WELL

- "Good" is an adjective.
- "Well" is an adverb (except when it refers to health: "I feel well").
- "She is a good analyst," but "she analyzes well." Do not use sports announcers or professional athletes as arbiters of correct English. They may play "good," run "good," hit "good," talk "good," even be paid "good," but they should also speak well.

GOT

- Often redundant with "have." "Have got" and "had got" are often used in wordy constructions.
- Avoid writing "I've got the report." Write "I have the report."
- Often a bad substitute for "must." Avoid writing "She's got to work harder." Write "She must work harder."
- As a noun, "got" is executive jargon for one who has "made it": one is a "got." A "polygot" is a "got" who wants more; and "antigot" is usually a revolutionary "nogot" who wants to take away the system that made gots gots. "Got" is short, but has little else to recommend it.

GOTTEN

- Originally proper, "gotten" has become colloquial except in the cliché "ill-gotten gains."

- Avoid writing "gotten." Write "got." Even better is "have." See **got**.

GRATIFIED/GRATEFUL

- Often misused for "grateful," "gratified" means "to be pleased or satisfied." One may be gratified by a fine meal, a good wine, or a substantial bonus.
- "Grateful" means "thankful" or "feeling gratitude." One may be grateful for a straight drive on a narrow fairway or gratified by it, or both.
- One is gratified *by* an experience; one is grateful *for* an experience.

GRESHAM'S LAW

- Bad money tends to drive out good money. See **Vanneman's corollary to Gresham's law**.

GROSS PROFIT

- The profit before expenses are subtracted. See **profit margin**.

H

HANDS-ON EXPERIENCE

- Unnecessary and wordy. Write "long experience," or even "experience." All "experience," except vicarious experience, is "hands on," at least metaphorically.
- Hands off "hands on."

HEREINABOVE/HEREINAFTER

- Used by business people in the mistaken belief that imitating lawyers is to imitate the most precise language. In most such instances the imitation is of incoherence.
- "Hereinabove" is usually used to mean "here is" or "this means."
- "Hereinafter" is usually used to mean "the following means."

HESITANT

- As "hesitant" implies a faltering, usually in speech, do not write "She was hesitant about asking him" to mean "she had doubts." Write "She was doubtful about asking him." "She hesitates to ask him" means that, after hesitating, she will ask him.

HESITATE

- "Please do not hesitate" is wordy.
- Avoid writing "Please do not hesitate to call if you have any problems with the order." Write "Please call if you have problems with the order."

HIGHLY

- Highly overused, "highly" is often attached unnecessarily to such words as "complex." There is no need to use "highly complex" unless examples of the "lowly complex" exist with which the "highly complex" could be confused. Similarly, "highly technical," "highly unlikely," and "highly improbable" are silly phrases.

HIM/HIS

- About the only common error made in the use of "him" and "his" lies in sentences such as these: "Smedley opposed *him* attending the meeting." What Smedley opposes is not "him," but rather "attending the meeting." Consequently, the form should be "his" because it is possessive "Smedley opposed *his* attending the meeting."
- Avoid writing "Smedley was delighted by *him* giving the speech." Write "Smedley was delighted by *his* giving his speech."
- This holds also for "me" and "my."

HOBSON'S CHOICE

- "Where to elect there is but one,/'Tis Hobson's choice, — take that or none" (Thomas Ward, 1577–1639). That is, no choice. To hire one of Hobson's horses, one had to take the horse nearest the stable door. A famous example is Henry Ford's statement: "People can have any color Ford they want, so long as it's black."

HOME/HOUSE

- A home cannot be bought or sold.

HOMO HOMINI LUPUS

- Latin for "man is a wolf to other men."

HOPEFULLY

- Ninety-nine times in a hundred, "hopefully" is used incorrectly. "Hopefully, I will be finished tomorrow" is meaningless. Write "I hope to finish tomorrow."
- One may "speculate hopefully."

HUMAN RESOURCES ADMINISTRATION

- Euphemism for "personnel work."

HYPERBOLE

- Exaggeration. Business prose should avoid hyperbole.

I

IDENTICAL

■ Most things said to be "identical" are really "similar," for very few are truly "identical."

IDENTIFY

■ Almost a blanket word in business, "identify" becomes vague when its many meanings become confused. "Identify" may be psychological jargon in that one may "identify with." One may "identify" (define) problems. Instead of "identifying problems," try "defining," "discovering," "finding," or even "labeling" problems.

I.E.

■ *Id est*, Latin for "that is." Not to be confused with "e.g., for example."

■ Used to explain further: "The executive vice-president was incapacitated; i.e., he had influenza."

■ Do not use in formal prose. Use "that is." "The executive vice-president was incapacitated; that is, he had influenza." See **e.g.**

IF

■ Good word underused. "In the event that," which means "if," is overused.

IF AND WHEN

■ Redundant. Write "if or when," not "if and when." Avoid writing "If and when she calls you, . . ." because the uncertainty is not conveyed by "if and when." Write "If or when she calls you, . . ."

IF . . . THEN

■ In the most formal prose, "if" may be half and "then" the other half of a construction of "supposing." That is, "*If* this happens, *then* that happens." Using "if . . . then" keeps the logic tight and makes understanding more rapid. In short, "if . . . then" helps reduce fuzzy thinking. Use it.

IF/WHETHER

■ "If" may introduce one possibility. "Whether" introduces two or more. See **whether or not**.

IGNORANT

■ "Ignorant" does not mean "ill-mannered," "stupid," or "foul-mouthed."

- "Ignorant" means simply "ill-informed" or "unaware." An "ignorant" person, then, may be intelligent and proper, but simply lack specific knowledge.

I/ME   See Appendix II, page 467, Subjective and Objective Forms.

IMPACT

- When used as a verb, "impact" means "to press closely together"; unfortunately, it often is used incorrectly as a verb to mean "influence" or "affect." Seldom write "impacted on." Write "influenced" or "affected."

IMPLEMENT

- As a noun, "implement" is often imprecise. Name the "implement." Farmers, for example, pick corn with a corn picker, not with a "farm implement."
- As a verb, "implement" is often stuffy and vague. Try "carry out" or "do."
- "Implement" is occasionally used to mean "complete": Avoid writing "The job must be implemented by next Friday. We shall not otherwise have implemented our obligations." Write "The job must be completed by next Friday. Otherwise, we shall not have completed our obligations."

IMPLEMENTATION PHASE

- Common bureaucratese, the phrase "implementation phase" is beginning to appear in business.
- Avoid writing "We have now entered the implementation phrase." Write "We are doing it now." Write "We have begun."

IMPLY/INFER

- "Imply" means "to suggest," even "to insinuate." One may "imply" that Smedley is competent by telling others of his hard work.
- "Infer" means "to conclude." One may "infer" that Smedley is competent by learning of his hard work.

IN CAMERA

- Latin for "in a room." Refers to a secret or closed meeting.

INCIDENT

- "Incident" has many meanings, but as commonly used ("Did you hear about the incident between Smedley and the health spa?"), it is a vague word useful only when one wants to be vague.

INDICATE

- An eight letter word, "indicate" often means "show," a four letter word. Use "show" more often than "indicate."
- "Indicated" is often misused to mean "advisable." Avoid writing "One can infer from the report that a better method of taking inventory is indicated." Write "One can infer from the report that a better method of taking inventory is advisable."
- Business writing is addicted to "indicate." Break the habit by not using "indicate" for a few weeks. There are dozens of replacements, most of which are more precise. Here are several: assert, declare, imply, mean, say, show, suggest.

INDICT/INDITE

- One "indicts" a person for wrongdoing.
- In business, use "indite" to mean "to put formally in writing."

INFINITIVE

- A grammatical term for the form of a verb expressing being or action without reference to a subject or tense. Usually, infinitives comprise "to" followed by a singular form: "to be," "to run," "to think." See **split infinitive**. Also see Appendix II, page 464.

INFLICT/AFFLICT   See **afflict/inflict**.

INFORM

- Avoid writing "This is to inform you that on 1 July 1995 we intend to. . ." The clause is obsolete and wordy. Write "On 1 July 1995 we intend to. . ." See **advise**.

INFORMATION

- A simple, useful noun, often absurd when used as an adjective. Avoid writing "information dissemination" or "information transfer." Write "Tell them."
- "Information package" is vague. Be specific: write "book," "brochure," "report."

-ING

- Participles, many of which end in "-ing," are often champions of economical writing. Use them.
- Avoid writing "She is engaged in making a survey of the plant managers' attitudes." Write "She is surveying the plant managers' attitudes."
- "-Ing" words may be used as nouns called "gerunds." As such, they sometimes must be modified by possessive forms of nouns and pronouns: "Smedley's forgetting to post the proposal cost us the contract."

IN/INTO

- "In" refers to position. "Into" means movement toward "in."
- "She is into aerobics" is meaningless; aerobics is not something into which one can go. To be "into" something is slang.

INOPERATIVE

- A legal term meaning "without practical force," "inoperative" is too often used as a way of saying "we were wrong" or "we lied." "Inoperative" was made famous by President Nixon's press secretary: "Previous statements about this matter are inoperative."
- "Inoperative" also means "does not work." Write "does not work."

IN ORDER THAT

- "So that" is shorter and usually followed by "I [we, she, he, they, it] may" or "might." Sometimes followed by "shall" or "should." Never followed by "can," "could," "will," "would." Try "so that."
- Avoid writing "In order that she could persuade him to buy Widgitcogs, Inc., she rented a limousine." Write "So that she might persuade him to buy Widgitcogs, Inc., she rented a limousine."

INPUT

- A verb and a noun, "input" is probably the most common example of computerese: "Input the input, Smedley."
- As a verb, "input" is vague because it has come to mean so many kinds of contributions. When one "inputs" information, for example, the information may be oral, written, or photographic; it may be a request, a demand, a suggestion, a hope, a belief, a thought, a hunch, an example, an analogy, or other disparate things.
- Avoid writing "Give us your input on this, Smedley." Write "Give us your ideas [notions, thoughts, and so on] about this, Smedley." "Please input the data" means "Please type in the data."

INSERVICE

- An especially ugly verb in business, and originally used in education to describe what teachers do in school on those days when students need not attend, "inservice" has made some inroads into business to describe training seminars for employees. Avoid "inservice" because it is vague; use the term that best describes *specifically* the activity undertaken.

INSIDE OF

- Wordy. "Inside" is sufficient.

INSOLUBLE/UNSOLVABLE

- "Insoluble" means incapable of being dissolved.

- "Unsolvable" means incapable of being solved.
- As something may be "solved" without being "dissolved," there is a difference. An "insoluble" problem just won't disappear; an "unsolvable problem" will remain a problem, but may be shunted away somewhere out of sight.

INSTANCES

- "In many instances" is wordy. Write "often" or "frequently."

INSURE   See **assure/ensure/insure**.

INTEGRATE

- "Integrate" means to form a whole out of parts. Often "coordinate" is better.
- Writing "All departments must integrate their marketing efforts" would require moving separate marketing sections into one marketing section. Because most companies have only one marketing section, "integrate" is misused. Writing "All departments must coordinate their marketing efforts" allows separate marketing sections to remain separate.

-INTENSIVE

- A suffix much overused in business writing, usually by people too lazy to find the proper word. "-Intensive" is often appended to "labor," "capital," and "computer" to create "labor-intensive," "capital-intensive," and "computer-intensive" to describe the predominant work or requirement of a given industry. Do not overuse.

INTERFACE

- As a noun, "interface" refers to a translator allowing two or more parts of a computer system to work together.
- "Interface" is an ugly verb.
- Avoid writing "To speed production, we must interface quality control and engineering design." Write "To speed production, quality control and engineering design must work together." Write "To speed production, we must coordinate quality control and engineering design."

INTER/INTRA

- "Inter" means "between" or "among." "Intra" means "within."
- Do not use such constructions as "inter-departmental interfaces interrupting the internal intra-workings of . . ." They tend to be interminable. For example, "Intercollegiate" sports refers to contests between or among colleges. "Intra-mural" (or "intracollegiate") sports refers to contests within a college.

INTERJECTION   See Appendix II, page 464.

IN TERMS OF

- Wordy and almost always useless; omit.
- Avoid writing "We must think about this in terms of public relations." Write "We must consider public relations."
- "In terms of" may be replaced by prepositions such as "at," "by," "for," "from," "in," or "to."
- Avoid writing "We must look at this in terms of the average person." Write "We must look at this as average people do."

INTERRUPTIONS   See Appendix II, pages 473–474.

IN THE EVENT THAT

- Write "if." See **if**.

IN THE NEAR FUTURE   See **future**.

INVESTIGATE

- everyone "investigates"; no one "studies" because "to investigate" makes one sound important, especially to oneself. Write "study"; it is shorter and probably more accurate.

IRREGARDLESS

- No such word.
- "Regard" means "looking at," "having esteem for." "Regardless" means "lacking that esteem." "Irregardless" means "lacking a lack of esteem," which, theoretically, means "having esteem," or "regard."
- Write "regardless," which, in business, most often means "in spite of": "We shall go ahead regardless of the consequences."

IRRITATE/AGGRAVATE   See **aggravate/irritate**.

"IS WHEN" CONSTRUCTIONS   See Appendix II, pages 467–468.

ITEMS

- A vague substitute for the precise term required. Be precise.
- Avoid writing "These items arrived damaged" when "These computer components arrived damaged" more accurately describes what was dropped from the loading dock.

IT GOES WITHOUT SAYING   See **needless to say; obviously**.

-ITIS

- A medical suffix indicating inflammation of an organ, "-itis" is often misused to mean an exaggerated liking of or concern with. Desiring profits to the exclusion of safety is not "profititis." Profits are not organic and cannot become inflamed.

- Coining words is dangerous even if one knows the meanings of the parts of those words. If one does not know their meanings, the result is often disastrous.

IT IS I   See Appendix II, page 468.

ITS/IT'S

- "It's" is a contraction for "it is." Always.
- "Its" is a possessive pronoun meaning "belonging to it." No possessive pronoun requires an apostrophe, except "one," as in "one's book."
- Confusing these words is one of the most common and unnecessary errors in business writing. It's also one of the most annoying to professors and bosses, betraying, as it does, great carelessness on the writer's part. The only way to get it right is to proofread carefully. One method we like is to replace every "its" and "it's" with "it is." If the sentence makes sense, then "it's" is correct; if the sentence sounds ridiculous, then, "its" is correct. For example, "Smedley's office was ready to have *it's* furniture replaced" is shown to be incorrect by replacing "it's" with "it is": "Smedley's office was ready to have *it is* furniture replaced."

-IZE

- There are plenty of "-ize" words already: summarize, apologize, scandalize, brutalize, canonize, cauterize, sympathize, disorganize, and philosophize. Recently created "-ize" words are everywhere advertised, recognized, merchandised, and overprized. One must criticize the exercise to publicize a lack of vocabulary and an aestheticized, sensitized ear for the language.

J

JUNCTURE   See **at this point in time**.

K

K

- In finance, "K" represents "kilo," or "1000."
- In computerese, "K" stands for "1024"; "8K" is "8192."
- In most of Europe, "kilo" is a measure of weight of about 2.2 pounds.
- In chemistry, "K" represents "potassium."

KIND

- "Kind" is singular (in both senses). Write "This kind of accident is. . . ."

- "Kinds" is plural. Write "These [or those] kinds of accidents are. . . ." See **kind of**.

KINDLY REQUESTED

- Usually inane. Avoid writing "You are kindly requested to attend the open house on Friday"; kindness is here attributed to the person requesting, not as intended, to the reader. Write "Please come to the open house on Friday."

KIND OF

- except literally ("A cow is a kind of bovine."), "kind of" is colloquial.
- Avoid writing "The meeting was kind of tiresome"; write "rather" or "somewhat." Write "The meeting was rather tiresome."

L

LAST

- Avoid writing "the four last sections of the report." A report can have only one "last section." Write "the last four sections of the report."

LATTER/FORMER   See **former/latter**.

LAY/LIE

- The difference between lay-laid-laid and lie-lay-lain is not difficult to remember. The two verbs share only one word, "lay," and they are used for different tenses.
- "Lay-laid-laid" are forms of the verb meaning "to place."
- "Lay" is the present tense of "to place": "Please lay the squash ball on the counter." "I laid the squash ball on the counter." "I have laid the squash ball there many times."
- "Lie-lay-lain" are forms of the verb meaning "to recline." "I lie down for ten minutes every day at noon." "I lay down yesterday at noon." "I have lain down every day at noon for years."
- "Lay" requires an object: "lie" does not.

LEAVE/LET

- "Leave" means "to go away from": "Leave me!"
- "Let" means "to allow": "Let him alone!"
- "Leave me be!" is colloquial and ungrammatical.

Le Chatelier's principle

- When altered, a stable system attempts to restore its original condition.

LESS/FEWER   See **fewer/less**.

LESS THAN/UNDER

■ Although "under" may mean "less than," never write formally, "The finance department estimates the cost to be under the cost first projected." Write "The finance department estimates the cost to be less than the cost first projected." "Under" is less precise than "less than."

■ The same imprecision occurs when "over" is used instead of "more than."

LET/LEAVE   See **leave/let**.

LEVEL

■ A useful word for builders and surveyors and for those dealing in concerns of society, morality, or thought, "level" is sometimes unnecessary when used in such constructions as "noise level," "crowd level" (what is "crowd level?"), and the ubiquitous "socio-economic level."

■ A "level" must describe a position such that falling below or rising above it would produce a different "level." People tend to use "level" without supplying readers with specific gradations. If gradations are not provided, would not "high socio-economic level" be more clear written as "rich"?

■ Avoid writing "The noise was at an acceptable level." "The noise was acceptable" conveys as much in three fewer words.

LEVERAGE

■ Originally confined to psychics, "leverage" has come to mean "power," but it is a weak noun for conveying such strong qualities.

■ Avoid writing "Because we have 25 percent of the market, we have the leverage to set standard sizes for bottles." Write "Because we have 25 percent of the market, we have the power to set standard sizes for bottles."

■ Rarely use "leverage" as a verb; try "pry" or "force." As an adjective "leverage" is used frequently in financial and management circles: "leveraged buy-out" (LBO).

LIE/LAY   See **lay/lie**.

LIFESTYLE

■ No one whose life has any style uses this word. One should speak rather of one's "way of life." The word is so pervasive, however, that BMW dealers no longer sell BMW's: they sell "lifestyle concepts."

LIKE

- Not to be used for "as." "Like" is used for nouns and pronouns, "as" for verbs and verbals. Advertising agencies often use substandard grammar ("Winston tastes good, like a cigarette should").
- "Like" takes the objective case (me, him, her, them): "Like him, I am nervous about the Bay-to-Breakers race tomorrow." "As" takes the subjective case (I, he, she, they): "I believe as she does about the advisability of leasing the store front."
- "Like" expresses similarity.
- "As" expresses equality. See **such . . . as**.

LITERALLY

- Often redundant or illogical.
- Redundant: "He was literally in tears over the Annual Report." Either he was or he was not "in tears."
- Illogical: "Although literally dead on her feet, she managed to walk from the airplane." Zombies and vampires can do this; mortals cannot. People in business are mortal.

LOAN

- Traditionally, a noun. One grants or receives a loan. One lends something.
- Avoid writing "The bank has agreed to loan us money." Write "The bank has agreed to lend us money." "Lend" things; do not "loan" them.

LOCATE

- Often used unnecessarily in place of "find," "locate" also means "place." One can "locate a nice little weekend chalet at Sun Valley" only by building one. One can "find a lovely old farmhouse in the Berkshires."
- "Locate" often may be omitted. Avoid writing "The master cylinder is located under the hood on the driver's side of the car." Write "The master cylinder is under the hood in front of the driver's seat."
- This holds true also for "situated": a master cylinder need not be "situated" under the hood, but simply be under the hood.

LUNCHEON

- A "luncheon" is a formal lunch.

M

MAD/ANGRY   See **angry/mad**.

MAINTAIN

- One "maintains" machinery. One never "services" machinery. See **serve/service**; **claim**.

MAJORITY

- More than half, and usually applied to countable things: "She received a majority of the votes." When numbers are not involved, "most" would seem to be a better word: it is shorter than "majority."

- Avoid writing "He remained for a majority of the meeting." Write "He remained for most of the meeting." Even when numbers are involved, "most" is often more economical than "a majority of." Write "Most of [not "The majority of"] our employees are not using the lunch room."

MAKE

- Often unnecessary, "make" sometimes creates wordy expressions. A given occurrence, for example, may not so much "make history," as it "is historic."

Do not	make a profit	Do	profit
	make an announcement		announce
	make a decision		decide
	make an effort		try
	make a bid		bid

- "Made" and "making" are similarly unnecessary and contribute to wordiness.

MALE/FEMALE   See **female/male**.

MANNER

- Often unnecessary and wordy.

- Avoid writing "The negotiations were handled in an unsatisfactory manner." Write "The negotiations were poorly [badly, unsatisfactorily] handled."

MANY/MUCH

- Use "much" with things uncountable: "much wealth."
- Use "many" with things countable: "many dollars."

MASTERFUL/MASTERLY

- "Masterful" is said of people and refers to domineering or imperious qualities. Good leaders often are "masterful."

- "Masterly" is said of actions and refers to the great skill with which people perform those actions.

- Write "She is masterful." Write "Her handling of the grievances was masterly." One could be referred to as "masterly" only when one's actions are so.

MATRIX

- Although it has broad biological and medical meanings, "matrix" in business means "a rectangular array of data, usually a table." Do not use "matrix" in any other ways.
- Avoid writing "The Employee Benefits Division provides a matrix of services"; services are not an array of data, rectangular or otherwise. Write "The Employee Benefits Division provides many services."

MATTER

- Avoid writing "The main problem was a matter of cost." Write "Cost was the main problem." Except in "Does this matter?" and "What's the matter?" and "The matter is closed," or as a name for one of the two parts of the universe (void and matter), "matter" is a matter of wordiness only.

MAY/CAN   See **can/may**.

MAYBE

- Although a good word, in formal prose, write "perhaps."
- Do not confuse "maybe" with "may be." "May be" cannot substitute for "perhaps," but "maybe" can.
- Avoid writing "Maybe we should fire Smedley." Write "Perhaps we should fire Smedley." Avoid writing "It *maybe* that we should fire Smedley." Write "It *may be* that we should fire Smedley."

MEA CULPA

- Latin for "my sin." My error. I goofed.

MEANINGFUL DIALOGUE

- Business should assume that all its discussions are "meaningful." Avoid writing "We had a meaningful dialogue about the shortfall in the sale of Adidas running shoes." Write "We had a good discussion about the shortfall in the sale of Adidas running shoes."
- Meaningful dialogues are for weekends at Big Sur, *not* for business.

MEDIATE/ARBITRATE   See **arbitrate/mediate**.

MEDIUM/MEDIA

- One medium; two media.
- A medium is one mode of expression. In business, it usually means a "news medium." The "media" are commonly television, radio, and newspapers.
- Avoid writing "Representatives of the television media are coming tomorrow" for television is *one* medium. A "happy medium" is a seer whose predictions have come about.

MEGA-

- A prefix meaning "one million," but hollywood hyperbole for "big": "mega-blockbuster movie."
- A mega-vague and mega-ugly word.

ME/MY

- "Me" is objective and is used as a direct object of sentences or an object of a preposition.
- "My" is possessive and concerns ownership.
- The most common error regarding "me/my" is called a "fused participle." In "Is there a problem with [me/my] arriving late?" the object of the preposition "with" is "arriving," a participle acting as a noun, not "me." "Arriving" must be modified by the possessive "my." Write "Is there a problem with my arriving late?" Write "Is there a problem with the report's arriving late?"
- This holds for "he/his," "she/her," and "they/their."

MENS SANA IN CORPORE SANO

- Latin for "a sound mind in a sound body" (Juvenal (60–c. 130).

MESSAGE

- A good word, "message" should not be used for "letter," "phone call," or "instruction." The falsely tough phrase, "send a message" is puerile, as in this example: "Some expressed concern that the arrests would send a message that friends of the chancellor are held to a different standard." "Convey an idea [or notion]" is usually more accurate: "Some voiced concern that the incident would convey the idea that friends of the chancellor are held to a different standard."

METICULOUS

- Often misused to mean "good at detail," "meticulous" means "overly concerned for detail." "Too meticulous," then, is redundant. Referring to someone as meticulous, even in business, is not complimentary.

MIDDLE/CENTER   See **center/middle**.

MIGHT OF   See **should of**.

MISPLACED MODIFIERS   See Appendix II, page 467.

MITIGATE

- To cause to be less hostile or harsh. Some use "mitigate" to mean "to lessen" or "to reduce," but the word may be used only when referring to hostility or harshness. Consequently, while one may "mitigate ill will," one may not "mitigate good will."

- "Mitigating circumstances," then, are those that reduce hostility or harshness, not, as commonly thought, to justify an action.

MONEY IS NO OBJECT

- Do not use this phrase: money *is* an object. See **object**.

MONOPOLY

- One may have a monopoly *of*, not a monopoly *in* or monopoly *on*.

MORE THAN/OVER   See **less than/under**.

MUCH

- A much underused word, "much" will often replace such wordy phrases as "a great deal."
- Avoid writing "He derived a great deal of pleasure from seeing you." Write "He derived much pleasure from seeing you." Avoid writing "These reports require a whole lot of time and work to complete." Write "The reports require much time and work to complete."

MUCH/MANY   See **many/much**.

MURPHY'S LAW

- If it can go wrong, it wil. Note example in previous sentence! See **Vanneman's Corollary to Murphy's law**.

MUTUAL/COMMON   See **common/mutual**.

MYSELF

- Often incorrectly used for "me," and sometimes for "I."
- Avoid writing "Smedley and myself will present the report." Write "Smedley and I will present the report."
- "Myself" is redundant when used with "I." Avoid writing, in formal prose, "I myself will present the report." Write "I will present the report."
- Informal prose may correctly write "I myself will present the report," but solely for emphasizing *who* will do it.

N

NATURE

- Often used in wordy constructions. Avoid writing "nature" except when used to mean the universal force, or that part of a person or thing partaking of that force. Avoid writing "The welding process was of an unsatisfactory nature." Write "The welding process was unsatisfactory" or "The welding was bad."

NEAR/NEARLY

- "Near" is a preposition: "Smedley lives near the office."
- "Nearly" is an adverb: "Phoebe lives nearly five miles from the office."
- Seldom write "nowhere near": "Phoebe lives nowhere near the office." Write "Phoebe lives far from the office."

NEEDLESS TO SAY

- If something does not need to be said, then do not say it. Avoid writing "Needless to say, production must not be delayed." Write "Clearly, production must not be delayed." See **obviously**.

NEGATIONS

- Generally, the work required to comprehend negative statements is greater than that required to comprehend positive ones meaning almost the same things.
- Avoid writing "It is impossible for Phoebe to fail." Write "Phoebe will succeed." Avoid writing "not a few"; write "many." Avoid writing "Samantha cannot fail to do the job"; write "Samantha must [or "will"] do the job."

NEGLIGENCE

- A good word to use in performance appraisals, especially when firing someone. "Negligence" is a failure to do what a reasonable person should do in given situations. Because lawyers make much money debating "reasonable," one should have good cause to use "negligence."

NEGOTIABLE

- Anything transferable. Most things are therefore negotiable.

NEITHER/EACH/EITHER   See Appendix II, page 466.

NEITHER . . . NOR   See **either . . . or**; see in Appendix II, page 466.

NETWORK

- As a noun, "network" describes a group of lines regularly crossing one another.
- As a verb, it is jargon meaning "to make or use a network." "Coordinate" is usually a better verb than "network."

NICE

- "Nice," like "interesting," is too often used when one is asked to judge something about which nothing pleasant may be said. "Nice" is coming to having a meaning opposite the colloquial one of "agreeable" and "pleasant": "a nice visit to the dentist."

■ The original meaning — "fine," "precise," — still holds: "The departments of the manufacturing division fit together nicely."

NO

■ One "no," two "noes."

NON-

■ Avoid writing "nonproductive," "nonhuman," "noncaring," "nonfrequent." Write "unproductive, "inhuman," "uncaring," "infrequent." There are, however, a few acceptable words beginning with "non-": "nonflammable," "nonsense," "nonrestrictive."

NONE

■ "Not one" or "no one," "none" requires a singular verb.
■ Avoid writing "None of the reports are completed." Write "None of the reports is completed." Write "None of the vice-presidents is here."

NOR/OR

■ Use "nor" after "neither";
■ use "or" after "either."
■ When "or" or "nor" joins two subjects, the verb agrees with the nearest subject. Write "Neither she nor her colleagues were there."
■ If both subjects are singular, use the singular: "Neither he nor she is attending the meeting."

NOT ONLY . . . BUT ALSO   See **also**.

NOUN   See Appendix II, page 464.

NOUN-PRONOUN AGREEMENT   See Appendix II, page 467.

NUMBER

■ *"The* number" takes the singular. *"The* number of reports *is* increasing."
■ *"A* number" (in the sense of "many") takes the plural: "A number of reports *are* missing from the files." See Appendix II, page 465.

NUMBER/AMOUNT   See **amount/number**.

NUMERALS

■ In business writing, use Arabic numerals almost as commonly as in technical writing. The conventions for numerals in formal prose rule rather more strongly in business writing than in technical writing. Both business and technical writing, however, should obey the following conventions.

- When several numbers are used, clarity may require combining numerals and words. Avoid writing "The company may buy 11 or 12 747s." Write "The company may buy eleven or twelve 747s."
- Spell out numbers smaller than 11.
- Never begin a sentence with a numeral. Avoid writing "76 kazoos led a big parade." Write "Seventy-six kazoos led a big parade." Obeying this rule may require recasting a sentence. "Forty-four thousand eight hundred dollars were spent last week for shop maintenance," for example, is unwieldy. It should be recast so that the number does not appear first, as in "Shop maintenance cost $44,800 last week" or "Last week, . . ."

O

OBJECT

- Often ridiculous, as in "money is no object": money is an object. "Time is no object" is also ridiculous; everyone knows that time is not an object.
- Write "Money is no obstacle" or "Time is no obstacle." Write "Money [or time] is not our primary concern."

OBJECTIVE/GOAL   See **goal/objective**.

OBJECTIVELY

- Seldom write or say "objectively speaking" or "looking at this objectively." Because objectivity should be assumed in business, do not announce it.

OBLIVIOUS/UNCONSCIOUS

- "Oblivious" means "unaware," "unmindful," or, sometimes, "forgetful."
- "Unconscious" means "out cold."
- Avoid writing "He was unconscious of their maneuvers." Write "He was oblivious to their maneuvers." Write "He was unaware of their maneuvers."

OBSERVANCE/OBSERVATION

- "Observance" refers to compliance with custom or law. One "observes" religious holidays and speed limits.
- "Observation" refers to what the eye sees. It also means "remark."
- Avoid writing "She made the observation that. . . ." Write "She observed that . . ." Or she remarked that. . . ." See **make**.

OBSTACLE   See **object**.

OBVIOUSLY

- Do not use. If something is obvious, then why write it? Avoid writing "Obviously, we must do something." Write "Clearly, we must do something."
- Many, however, belabor the obvious. See **needless to say**.

OCCAM'S RAZOR

- So named for William of Occam, who divided problems into their simplest parts, and thus gained fame for his ability to reason and analyze. Given two competing systems, he reasoned, one should choose the simpler. A simple system has fewer parts to break. In short, *simplify*.

ODD

- Commonly used, "odd" means "abnormal." In business, however, writing "The report contains 400-odd pages" creates ambiguity. Are there no *even* pages? Are all 400 pages abnormal in some way? Write "The report contains more than 400 pages."

OF WHICH/WHOSE   See **whose/of which**.

OMIT/DELETE   See **delete/omit**.

ON/ONTO

- "On" implies position. Write "She saw Smedley lying *on* the floor."
- "Onto" implies movement toward a position. Write "She saw Smedley falling *onto* the floor."

ONE ANOTHER/EACH OTHER   See **each other/one another**.

ONGOING

- Business rot for "continuing" or "active." Usually redundant.
- Avoid writing "It is an ongoing program" because a program is not a program if it is not ongoing. Write "The program continues." Avoid writing "Our ongoing projects are working well." Write "Our projects are working well."

ON LINE

- Computerese: "The machine must be on line by April."
- English: "The machine must be working by April."

ORAL/VERBAL

- "Oral" means "by mouth." "Verbal" means "by word."

- Although these distinctions have blurred, business would be served better if, instead of "verbal agreements," people said "oral agreements."

ORIENTATE

- The correct verb is "orient," not "orientate."
- "Orient" is nearly always superior. A follower of Islam "orientates" himself toward Mecca at times; that is, he places himself so that he may bow toward Mecca, toward the East, toward the "Orient."
- Everyone else should be "oriented," pointed in the "true" direction.
- New employees, Islamic or otherwise, often face "Orientation Meetings." A noun ("Orientation") should not modify a noun ("Meetings"), but even so, during such a meeting, one is "oriented," not "orientated."

OUTCOME

- Often redundant, as in the following sentence: "The outcome of these meetings may create bad blood between the board and management." Write "These meetings may produce bad blood between the board and management." See **final outcome**.

OUTPUT

- The computer's product.
- Computerese (verb): "Smedley is going to output the committee's conclusions." As a verb, "output" is not only ugly, but also vague. "We output the data" could mean "We printed the data" or "We ran the program." These are very different acts and should not be confused. English (noun): "The output from Smedley's committee has been enormous."

OUTSIDE OF

- Redundant. "Outside" is sufficient.

OVER   See **less than/under**.

OVERALL

- Write "general" or "generally."

P

PARAMETER

- A quality that remains constant in the particular, but varies when applied to other cases, as in "The desire to make money is a parameter of the free-enterprise system."

- Business people have taken the noun to mean "boundary," or "perimeter." Do not use "parameter" to mean "boundary." Write "boundary."

PARENTHESES ( )   See Appendix II, pages 476–477.

PARTICIPLE   See Appendix II, page 464.

PARTS OF SPEECH   See Appendix II, pages 464.

PARTY

- A legal term, "party" should be avoided in business prose. Write "person" or "people" or "company," not "party."

- "Party" is acceptable when it means "group": "Her party met us on the nineteenth hole." But writing "The party of the first part's party met the party of the second part's party at the company's party" is as silly as it is confusing.

PEOPLE/PERSONS

- Write "people" far more often than "persons."

PEOPLE-PLUCKER

- An employee of a company paid to steal executives from one company for another company. A corporate phrase beginning to replace "head-hunter." It is one of those cute alliterations common in business. Unlike many, this one has the virtue of being accurate.

PER

- Omit "As per. "As per your request of 29 May" is perhaps the most common letter and memorandum opening and among the most wordy. Write "As you requested on 29 May."

- Some Latin uses for "per," which means "through," "on account of," or "by means of," are useful: "per diem" (a day), "per annum" (a year), and the like. Sometimes, however, changing the Latin to English works better. There are times that this sentence—"The company allows sales personnel a per diem allowance of $85 and per annum automobile allowance of $20,000."—would read more clearly to many people if it were written this way: "The company allows sales personnel a daily allowance of $85 and a yearly automotive allowance of $20,000."

PER CAPITA

- "Per capita" is an adjective, meaning regarding a head count: "per capita gain."

PERCENT/PERCENTAGE

- "Percent" applies to a specific amount ("45 percent"); "percentage" needs a descriptive adjective ("greater percentage").

- Write "The greatest percentage of one's income is spent on housing." Avoid writing "The greatest percentage of one's happiness (or unhappiness) is created by one's marriage." Write "The greatest portion of one's happiness (or unhappiness) is created by one's marriage."

- Remember that "percentage" and "percent" take the singular: "The greatest percentage of one's income *is* spent on housing"; "Of the 25 percent that *survives*, half will be stunted."

- "There is no percentage in it" is either obvious or meaningless.

- Avoid using "%" in formal prose.

PERIODS   See Appendix II, page 477.

PERSONAL/PERSONALLY

- Used orally for emphasis, "personal" and "personally" are unnecessary in writing. "I" means "personally." Run when someone begins a sentence with "personally." It is a harbinger of bad news: "Personally, I liked your presentation. The president, on the other hand, . . ." Write "I liked your presentation."

- Do not "extend personal sympathy," feel sorry for someone's "personal loss," have a "personal" physician or accountant or checkbook. Rather, be sympathetic, be saddened by someone's loss, have a physician, an accountant, and a checkbook.

- Because we have such a good word as "privacy," we should use it; we should not use its wordy equivalent: "personal life."

PERSON AND NUMBER   See Appendix II, page 465.

PERSONNEL

- Sometimes "staff" is better because it is more restrictive; when "employees" is meant, use "employees." Occasionally misspelled as or confused with "personal."

PERSPECTIVE   See **point of view**.

PERSUADE/CONVINCE   See **convince/persuade**.

PERUSE

- Does not mean "to read cursorily," "to glance at," "to skim." "Peruse" means "to read carefully."

PHENOMENON/PHENOMENA

- One "phenomenon," two "phenomena."

- Avoid writing "This phenomena is interesting." Write "This *phenomenon is* interesting." Write "These *phenomena are* interesting."

PHILOSOPHY

- Do not use in business writing. A "plan," no matter how good, or an "idea," no matter how brilliant, has come, erroneously, to be called a "philosophy."

- Philosophy is the love of wisdom; as a discipline in the humanities, philosophy is the pursuit or study of wisdom, which makes the following common phrase ridiculous: "Her philosophy of business is . . . ." Write "She believes business is . . ."

PICKET

- In strikes or protests, a "picket" is one person, and "to picket" is to stand as a picket fence.

PLAN ON

- Avoid writing "plan on doing." Write "plan to do."

PLEASE BE ADVISED   See **advise**.

POINT OF VIEW

- "Viewpoint" is better because it is shorter.

- "Perspective" is better because it is more precise.

POSITION

- The common business phrases "We are in a position to" and "We are not in a position to" are pompous and wordy, and one might be excused for thinking that those positions could be compromising ones. For "we are in a position to" write "we can." For "we are not in a position to" write "we cannot."

POSSIBLE

- Seldom required. "If it is possible" is ridiculous in "if it is possible, let me have" because if it is not possible, they cannot "let me have." Phrases like these abound: "if at all possible," "when possible," "as soon as possible."

- "Can" has the same effect. "When you can" is unnecessary because until one can, one cannot! The attempt here is to be polite while expressing urgency without asking the impossible. Because it is futile to ask the impossible, write something like "May I please have X very soon?" See **as soon as possible**.

POSTERIOR TO

- "After" or "behind" are better.

PRACTICAL/PRACTICABLE

- "Practical" means "workable, useful."
- "Practicable" means "that which may be workable, useful, but which has not yet been tried."

PRACTICALLY

- Because it is often ambiguous, "practically" is not appropriate for business prose when used to mean "almost." "The construction is practically completed" means that the construction is not complete. Write "almost" or "nearly"; each is shorter.

PRECIPITATE/PRECIPITOUS

- "Precipitate," as an adjective, means "ill-considered, rash, frenzied."
- "Precipitious" means "steep," as in "a precipitious decline" or "a precipitous rise."

PREDICT/PROGNOSTICATE

- Physicians are paid to sound learned; they prognosticate.
- Business people are paid to be clear; they predict.
- Consequently, business people should write "prediction," not "prognosis."

PREFACE

- Preface "with": "Complex figures need to be prefaced with explanatory remarks"; "Let me preface my remarks with these comments."

PREFER

- "I prefer to" is much shorter and more fitting than "I would like to." Moreover, "I would like to" suggests wishfulness; "I prefer to" suggests simple preference.

PREPLANNING

- All planning is "pre" doing; at least, one would hope so. "Preplanning" is therefore redundant and useless. Write "planning."

PREPOSITION   See Appendix II, page 464.

PREREQUISITE

- Often unnecessary. Avoid writing "Knowing a subject is a prerequisite for writing about that subject." Write "Knowing a subject is necessary for writing about that subject."

- Normally, "prerequisite" is a noun, not an adjective. The proper adjective is "requisite," as in "requisite number"; usually, "required number" is plainer and clearer.

PRESENTLY

- Two meanings: "now" or "for the time being," and "soon." "Now": "Ms. Fahrquart is presently executive vice-president." "Soon": "She will be arriving presently."
- Because misunderstanding is costly to business, use "now" or "soon" instead of "presently."

PREVENTATIVE/PREVENTIVE

- "Preventative," as commonly used, is a noun. Exercise is a "preventative" against heart disease.
- "Preventive" is an adjective. Exercise is a "preventive" measure against heart disease.

PRICE/COST   See **cost/price**.

PRINCIPAL/PRINCIPLE

- "Principal" means "first," "foremost," or "chief," or "that which earns interest at the bank."
- "Principle" means "a rule of law, doctrine, assumption, conduct."
- Write "The principal principle of my high school principal was that one should live by the principal's principal principles."
- "In principle" means "theoretically." "On principle" means "governed by morality or ethics."

PRIORITIZE

- Common but wordy. "To rank" is better. See **rank order**; **-ize**.

PRIOR TO/BEFORE   See **before/prior to**.

PROACTIVE

- Governmentese for "preplanning." Because "preplanning" is redundant, use "planning." See **preplanning**.

PROBLEMATIC

- Difficult to decide; hard to solve. Often incorrectly used to mean "debatable."

PROCESS

- As a verb, "process" means to do whatever is normally done to a new employee, a file, a report, an idea, an application, a delivery, a steer, a broken toe (hospitals "process" illnesses and other maladies).

- "Process" is often vague. "Orient" a new employee, "file" a file or report, "consider" an idea or application, "handle" a delivery, "butcher" a steer, "fix" or "mend" or "set" a broken toe.

PROCESSING

- "Processing" is overused, vague, and commonly heard in computer rooms.

- Avoid writing "data processing center." Write "data center" or "computer room."

PROCUREMENT

- A long word meaning "buying" or "getting."

PROFITABILITY

- Avoid writing "What's its profitability?" Write "Is it profitable?" Avoid writing "What's its profitability potential?" Write "Is it potentially profitable?" Write "Do you think we could make some money from it?" See **position**.

PROFIT MARGIN

- Profit expressed in percentage.

- Avoid writing "The profit margin is four dollars on every sale." Write "The profit margin is 34 percent." Write "The profit is four dollars on every sale." This holds true also for "gross profit."

- "Profit margin" does not consider operating expenses and retail overhead, but does include the cost of production.

PROGNOSTICATE/PREDICT   See **predict/prognosticate**.

PRONOUN   See Appendix II, page 464.

PROTOTYPE

- "Prototype" means an original, the first of its kind, a model, but often is misused for "predecessor." A machine may have many "predecessors," but it has only one "prototype."

PURCHASE

- "Buy."

PURCHASING AGENT

- "Buyer." See **vendor**.

PURSUANT

- Legalese for "regarding," or "following."

Q

QUALITY

- "Quality" does not denote excellence. To speak or write of a "quality program" means nothing: the quality could be good, bad, or irrelevant.
- Too many write of "high quality" or "top quality" programs. Write "excellent programs."

QUANTITY/NUMBER

- Use "quantity" for things uncountable: "a quantity of sparkling water."
- Use "number" for things countable: "a number of bottles of sparkling water." See **amount/number**.

QUID PRO QUO

- Latin for "this for that," which assumes "this" and "that" are of equal value, connotes the same as the longer but more mundane "You scratch my back and I'll scratch yours." "Quid pro quo" is so common that one may use it without fear of showing off.

QUITE A FEW

- Write "many."

QUOTATION

- "Quote" is most commonly a verb, not a noun.
- "Quotation" is a noun.
- In formal prose, do not write "Is that a quote?" Write "Is that a quotation?" You may quote us on that.

QUOTATION MARKS (" . . . ")

- Avoid placing words in quotation marks solely to emphasize those words or to indicate trendy phrases. Arrange the sentence to show emphasis. See Appendix II, page 477–478.

QUOTE   See **quotation**.

R

RAISE/RISE

- Things "rise" on their own, or seemingly on their own (bread, prices, the Dow Jones); things "raised" require the help of others (corn, pigs, and cattle are "raised" by farmers, girders by construction workers, stakes by card players).

- Children, however, are "reared."

RANK ORDER

- Commonly used and regularly redundant. "Rank," in the phrase "rank order," implies a relative standing of importance. Otherwise, "rank order" must refer to a particularly odoriferous group of Elks or Moose or Rainbow Girls. Avoid writing "We must rank order our priorities." Write "We must order our priorities." To "order priorities" simply means to organize them, not necessarily to place them in positions of relative importance.

- To indicate a desire to place priorities in positions of relative importance, write "We must rank our priorities." See **prioritize**.

RARE/SCARCE

- Things rare are always hard to find: honesty, compassion, a good cigar, candles when the electricity is off.

- Things scarce are temporarily hard to find: gasoline in 1976, Trivial Pursuit in 1980, calm airline passengers in 1985.

RE

- Latin for "concerning the matter." Used in memo headings.

REACTION

- Commonly misused in business prose for "opinion."

- Avoid writing "What is your reaction to this, Smedley?" Write "What is your opinion of this, Smedley?" Even better is "What do you think, Smedley?"

REALIZE

- Often creates wordy phrases, as in "We stand to realize much profit from this venture." Write "We could profit greatly from this venture."

REASON

- Avoid the redundant "The reasons *why* he did it are obscure." Write "The reasons *that* he did it are obscure." Similarly, avoid writing the redundant "The reason is *because* . . . ." Write "The reason is *that* . . . ."

REBUT/REFUTE

- "Rebut" means to answer in contradiction or denial. "Refute" means to prove something to be in error. An important distinction. See **deny/refute**.

RECEIPT

- "To be in receipt of" and "to acknowledge receipt of" are long-winded. Avoid writing "We are in receipt of your order of 16 March."

Avoid writing "This is to acknowledge receipt of your order of 16 March 1992." Write "We received your order of 16 March 1992."

RECIPIENT

- Often found in annual reports and company news letters, "recipient" is usually wordy.
- Avoid writing "Director Sally Jones was the recipient of the Engineer of the Year Award at the society's annual banquet last week." Write "Director Sally Jones received the Engineer of the Year Award at the society's annual banquet last week." Avoid writing "The recipient of much applause" or "the recipient of congratulations." Write "was applauded" and "was congratulated."

RECYCLE

- "Recycle" means to rejuvenate something to make it usable again, said of aluminum cans and newspapers. Unfortunately, it is also said of jobs that are elminated and, by extension, of the people who held those jobs. In this context, "recycle" is a dehumanizing, even foul, term.

RED HERRING

- Something that distracts from the real issue.
- In securities law, a red-bordered prospectus not yet approved by the Securities Exchange Commission or a similar state agency, is called a "red herring." See **stalking horse**.

REDUNDANCY

- "Redundancy" concerns repeating, repetition, writing or saying something twice or thrice, as in this sentence. "Redundancy" is a linguistic disease, often fatal.
- Several redundancies are common in business: "circular in shape" ("circular" is a shape), "green in color" ("green" is a color), "past memories" (what else?), "basic essentials" (all essentials are basic). See **tautology**.

REDUCE/DEPLETE   See **deplete/reduce**.

REFER/ALLUDE   See **allude/refer**.

REFERENCE

- A perfectly good noun, "reference" has some uses as a verb among those who study and work with computers. Normal business prose, however, should never use "reference" as a verb.
- The correct verb is "to refer," not "to reference."
- Avoid writing "We must reference page 16 of the attached report." Write "We must refer to page 16 of the attached report."

REFUTE/DENY   See **deny/refute**.

REGARD

■ Never write "in regards to." Write "in regard to." Even better is "regarding" because less wordy.

REGRETFUL/REGRETTABLE

■ People may be "regretful" (meaning "full of regret") when they have done something wrong or have been caught doing something wrong.
■ That which happened may be "regrettable."
■ Avoid writing "It was a regretful incident." Write "It was a regrettable incident." Write "She felt regretful for having lost the contract."

RELATE

■ Avoid writing the colloquial "I can relate to what you are saying." Write "I understand what you are saying."

REMUNERATION   See **compensation**.

REPERCUSSIONS

■ A long word much overused, "repercussions" does not mean "negative effects." Causes produce "repercussions"; more simply, causes produce "effects."
■ Do not often write "If we do this, we invite several repercussions." More often write "If we do this, we invite several effects" (or consequences or results).

REPLACE/SUBSTITUTE

■ Replace *with*. Substitute *for*. But the past tense of "replace" uses "by," not "with." Write "replaced by" and "substituted for."

RESOURCE PERSON

■ Usually, a specialist asked to help one out of trouble. Write "specialist."

RESPECT

■ Never write "with respect to," except when referring to a person. Write "regarding."
■ In conversation, especially when rebutting an argument, "respect" may be used this way: "With respect to Smedley, I do not think his idea for increasing the speed of the assembly line will work." See **regard**.

RESPECTFULLY/RESPECTIVE/RESPECTIVELY

■ "Respectfully" means "full of respect."

■ "Respective" refers to two or more things taken separately, but usually for comparison: "Let's look at Smedley and Joan's respective sales records."

■ "Respectively" means "in the order given": "Jim, Sally, and Irv work for IBM, AT&T, and Honest John's Used Cars, respectively." Be precise, "First, second, and third prizes went to Jane, Al, and Barbara, respectively" is correct.

RESPECTFULLY YOURS   See **sincerely**.

RESPONSIBLE

■ Only people can be responsible for events. Animals, plants, stones, and events may *cause* events, but they cannot be *responsible* for them. Mrs. O'Leary's cow was *not responsible* for the great Chicago fire. Mrs. O'Leary's cow may have *caused* the great Chicago fire.

■ Avoid writing "The oil embargo of 1973 was responsible for the high inflation rates of the 1970s." Write "The oil embargo of 1973 caused the high inflation rates of the 1970s."

RESPONSIBILITY/ACCOUNTABILITY   See **accountability/responsibility**.

RESTRICTIVE AND NONRESTRICTIVE ELEMENTS   See Appendix II, page 472–473.

REVENUE

■ Money, or goods convertible to money, received for other goods or services.

RISE/RAISE   See **raise/rise**.

ROT

■ The bane of English.

■ Avoid writing "Normative evaluational techniques are necessitated by the requirement to distinguish qualitative differences" when "Testing requires tests" has the same meaning. Rot is often useful in winning government grants and contracts. Not even government will pay to discover that "testing requires tests"; call tests "normative evaluational techniques" and the money will roll in.

■ Remember that writing rot is work without production. Work without production will destroy individuals, companies, nations. The company run by the CEO who recently remarked that "We must efficiencyize interdialogues during our intenseful natural interfacings" is in big trouble.

S

SALIENT

- "Salient" means "that which stands out from the rest." Consequently, a "salient point" is probably an important, or even the most important point.

SAME

- A good word except when used in place of "it" or "them."
- Avoid writing "We received the machine and shall return same after testing." Write "We received the machine(s) and shall return it (them) after testing."

SAY'S LAW

- Supply creates demand.

SCAN

- Misused to mean a quick examination, "scan" means "to scrutinize," "to examine closely."
- Avoid writing "Employers spend an average of 15 seconds scanning a résumé." Write "Employers spend an average of 15 seconds glancing at a résumé." See **peruse**.

SCARCE/RARE   See **rare/scarce**.

SECTOR

- In geometry, a figure bounded by two radii and part of the arc of a circle. Sometimes a military term identifying a location. Too often a bureaucratic term identifying (or rather failing to identify) anything.
- Avoid writing "the public sector," "the corporate sector," "the banking sector," or most other "sectors." Write "the public," "corporations," "banks," or "banking."

SEE YOUR WAY TO

- Avoid writing "I should appreciate it if you would see your way to help us." "See your way clear to" is equally bad writing. Write "Please help us."

-SELF

- The "-self" words include "himself," "herself," "myself," "yourself," and "themselves."
- "-Self" words have two purposes: (1) *emphasis*, "I'll do it *myself!*"; (2) *reflection*, "She drove *herself* to the hospital."
- Beware of overusing the "-self" words. Remember that removing them from the two examples may not change the meaning of either sentence substantially.

SEMI-/BI-   See **bi-/semi-**.

SEMICOLON (;)   See Appendix II, page 478.

SERVE/SERVICE

- Write "serve" for people and companies, "maintain" for machinery. As a verb, "service" can have a barnyard connotation and should be avoided.

SERVE TO

- Often part of nonsensical phrases such as "These facts serve to give an idea" (meaning "these facts suggest"), "serve to" is wordy even when it makes some sense. Avoid writing "These charts serve to illustrate the following." Write "These charts illustrate the following."

SHAPE

- Often redundant.
- Avoid writing "The flip chart is rectangular in shape." Write "The flip chart is rectangular."

SHORT SUPPLY

- Wordy. Avoid writing "Widgitcogs are in short supply." Write "Widgitcogs are scarce."

SHOULD OF

- "Should of" is an illiteracy that comes from "should've," which comes from "should have." See **could of**; **would of**; **might of**.

SHRINKAGE

- Euphemism for theft by employees. Theft by employees or by anyone else should be called "theft" or "stealing." "Shrinkage" is useful for soothing customers who must pay more for a product because of it, but among employees and employers, "shrinkage" is a silly word.

SHUTTLE BACK AND FORTH

- Redundant. "Shuttle" is sufficient.

"SIMPLIFY. SIMPLIFY. SIMPLIFY."

- Henry David Thoreau (1817–1862) *Walden*. A maxim for writing, business, and life in general.

SINCE

- "Since" properly refers to that period after something occurred. Use "since" in place of "because" sparingly.

- Avoid writing often "Since I had to see her about the project, I took along the report." Write more often "Because I had to see her about the project, I took along the report." See **because**.

SINCERELY

- Perhaps the best closing for a business letter, "sincerely" is short and, one hopes, accurate.
- "Very truly yours" is long;
- "Cordially," which means "from the heart," is a bit overdone; usually, only hate mail and love letters are "from the heart."
- "Best wishes" is fine for Christmas cards and other informal notes.
- "Respectfully" smacks of sycophancy or clever petulance.

SITE/CITE/SIGHT   See **cite/sight/site**.

SITUATED

- Omit. "The plant is situated in rolling farm country ten minutes from Baltimore" is better without "situated." See **locate**.

SIZE

- Often redundant. Avoid writing "The microchip is small in size." What else can it be? Small in color? Write "The microchip is small."
- Sometimes sentences only seem to be useful. Given the meaning of "micro," a "microchip" must be small. "Small" becomes redundant.

SKILLS

- Much overused, especially when preceded by certain adjectives—for example, "people-," "teaching-," "organizational-." Try "abilities, "methods," "talents."

SO . . . AS/AS . . . AS   See **as . . . as/so . . . as**.

SOMEWHAT

- Illogical when used with absolutes and superlatives.
- Avoid writing "somewhat essential." Something is essential or not. Avoid writing "somewhat unique," "somewhat factual." Write "essential," "unique," factual."

SOONER

- A strange invention, "sooner" means "more soon than soon," but what does that mean?
- "Sooner" is also used colloquially to mean "rather." For formal writing, avoid "I would sooner see *Rigoletto* than *My Fair Lady*"; write instead "I would rather see *Rigoletto* than *My Fair Lady*.

SORT OF

- Colloquial; use "rather" or "somewhat." See **kind of**.

SPEAKING

- Never write "Confidentially speaking, I can say that . . ." Never write "Speaking for myself, I believe that . . ." When one writes, one is writing, not speaking. Write "Between you and me, I believe that . . ." Write "I believe that . . ."

SPELLING

- Good spelling reveals an attentive, careful mind. See also Appendix II, page 467.

SPIN-OFF

- In business and manufacturing, "spin-off" refers to the benefit to one industry of discoveries in another. The NASA space program, for example, had produced many spin-offs in private industries, including plastics, computers, and weather prediction.

SPLIT INFINITIVE

- In general, try not to split infinitives; that is, do not place words, usually adverbs, between the "to" and the verb: "to completely rely." Instead, move the qualifiers either to precede or to follow the infinitive: "to rely completely." See Appendix II, page 464.

SPOUSE

- Because "spouse" may include either married men or women, use "spouse."

STALKING-HORSE

- That which conceals the real purpose. A horse behind which an Indian hunter hid while approaching a buffalo or other animal.

STAND

- "The company should not stand for this" is bad business writing. Do not use "stand" to mean "withstand." Write "tolerate" or "endure" or "withstand."
- "The company stands to gain from this" is bad business writing because "stands to" is imprecise, meaning "may" or "will." Write "The company may [or will] gain from this." See **realize**.

STATE

- Overused and wordy.
- Avoid writing "He was in a state of euphoria." Write "He was euphoric." Moreover, one seldom needs to write "the state of Texas,"

except when the state of Texas is in a state of euphoria. Write "Texas." Exceptions include "state of Washington" and "state of New York" when confusion between states and cities may result.

STATEMENT, MAKING A

- Only people state, objects do not make statements.

STATIONARY/STATIONERY

- "Stationary" means "fixed to one place." "Stationery" refers to writing paper.

STATISTICS

- As a branch of mathematics, "statistics is." As numbers, "statistics are."
- A "statistic" does not mean just any "number" or "fact." Properly defined, a statistic is a descriptive measure computed from and describing a sample. For example, the statement "Smedley is 49 years old" is a fact. The statement "President Smedley Fahrquart has a 29 percent approval rating taken from a sample population of 1,000 from the general population of 250 million" is a statistic. Consequently, "number," "fact," and "statistic" are discrete terms and are not to be used interchangeably.
- The adjective is "statistical."

STRATEGIC PLANNING   See **strategy**.

STRATEGIZE

- The acceptable noun "strategy" is incorrectly used as a verb, "to strategize." Write "to plan." See **-ize**.

STRATEGY

- Whenever managers use the word "strategy," they almost always mean "tactics" or a "plan." Properly used, "strategy" involves the coordinated plans of the military, economic, and political forces of a nation or group of nations, or by diminution, the overall perspective of a commander-in-chief, or the political leader of a nation. For example, the plan for conducting a war may be called a "strategy"; but the plan for conducting a battle in that war may be called "tactics."
- "Strategic planning," then, is almost always redundant and almost always hyperbolic.

STRUCTURE

- A strong noun, a weak verb. Avoid writing "We must structure the project well." Write "We must organize the project well."

SUBJECT-VERB AGREEMENT   See Appendix II, pages 466–467.

SUBSTITUTE/REPLACE   See **replace/substitute**.

SUCH . . . AS

- An efficient construction rare in business prose. Use it. "We are such stuff as dreams are made on."

SUPPLEMENT/AUGMENT   See **augment/supplement**.

SUPPLY   See **short supply**.

SURE/SURELY

- "Sure" is an adjective meaning certain: "I am sure." "Surely" is an adverb.
- Do not respond to "May I borrow your 8-iron?" with "Sure." Say "Surely" or "Buy your own."

SURROUNDING CIRCUMSTANCES

- Redundant. "Circumstance" means "surrounding."
- Avoid writing "the circumstances surrounding the meeting." Write "the circumstances of the meeting."

SUSPICION

- Often creates wordy constructions. Avoid writing "I have a suspicion that." Write "I suspect that."

SYNOPSIS/SYNOPSES

- One "synopsis," two "synopses."

T

TACTICS

- Taken from military jaron, "tactics" are plans made during or immediately before a battle and while facing the enemy. A "tactic" is a piece of tactics, but the word must be used carefully and rarely to mean one part of a tactical plan.
- A adjective is "tactical." See **strategy**.

TARGET

- As a noun, "target" is usually followed by "area," creating "target area." In government and increasingly in business, there are "target communities," "target consumers," "target products," and "target services" at which government and business are "shooting."

- As a verb, "target" is illogical. "To target" is used to mean "to aim at," "shoot at," but logically should mean "to set up as a target." Avoid writing "to target" or "targeting."

TASK

- "To task" is uncommonly vague and wordy. Avoid writing "We should task Quality Control with this job." Write "Quality Control should do this job."

TASK FORCE

- "Task force" is a military term. "Committee" is a civilian term. Write "committee" unless planning to invade another country.
- "Task force" is not a verb.

TECHNICAL WRITING

- A form of business writing that attends almost solely to technical matters. Precise technical writing cannot be misunderstood.

TERMINATE

- A word for "kill" used by gangsters and spies. Corporate word for "fire."
- Most would rather be "fired" than "terminated."
- Business has nearly stricken "fired" from English except when used to describe a rifle recently "fired" or clay placed in a kiln. Use fire.

TERMINUS

- One "terminus," two "termini."

TERMS   See **in terms of**.

TERRA INCOGNITA

- Latin for "an unknown region." Write "When we decided to make microchips, we entered terra incognita."

THANKING YOU IN ADVANCE

- Do not thank anyone in advance. As presumptuous as it is common, thanking others in advance presumes they are going to do what has been asked. By asking, one assumes that those asked are not required to do it.

THAT/WHICH

- Write "The merger that is referred to here sets an important precedent." Write "The merger, which sets an important precedent, is referred to here."

- "Which" hunts are usually productive. Burn many. If a comma cannot be placed before "which," perhaps "that" sounds better. See Appendix II, pages 472–473.

THEIR/THEY'RE

- "Their" is possessive: "their equipment."
- "They're" is a contraction for "they are."

THERE ARE/THERE IS

- A passive construction, sometimes necessary but overused. Adequate: "There is much dead wood in the company" (passive). Better: "The company has much dead wood" (active). See Appendix II, page 464.

THEY

- Before writing "they," make sure the reader knows who "they" are. Be sure also that "they" refers to more than one.

THINKING

- An admirable pastime, "thinking" expresses illiteracy in the following common sentence: "What's your thinking on this, Smedley?" Write "What do you think, Smedley?"

THIS

- Before using "this," make sure the reader knows what "this" refers to.
- Be sure that "this" refers to one, "these" or "they" to more than one. See **they**.

THOUGH

- Write "although" more often than "though" in formal writing. Avoid writing "as though"; write "as if." See **although/though**.

THRUST

- Commonly misused in business, as a noun, "thrust" ought to be reserved for discussions of jet propulsion. The "thrust" of an argument refers to its power and not, as many believe, to its main point or direction.

THUS

- A good word much overused. When overused, "thus" conveys stuffiness and pomposity to writing, as well as uncertainty of transition and of logical procedure.

TIME FRAME

- A common but illogical phrase meaning a length of time. Represented spatially, time is linear; a frame is rectangular, oval, or some other closed shape. Consequently, time "frames" are impossible.
- Write "length of time" or "duration."

TIME HORIZON

- Rot for "as far as we can see." Since one cannot see farther than one can see, neither time horizon nor "as far as we can see" is useful.
- Omit.

-TION

- A much overused suffix which robs language of variety and life.
- Avoid writing "Administration authorization of perforation evaluations requires signaturization." Write "Before testing for perforations, get the boss's signature."

TOTALLY

- A totally useless word employed for emphasis where none is needed. Seldom use it.

Avoid writing	Write
"totally alive"	"alive"
"totally controlled"	"controlled"

Avoid writing	Write
"totally involved"	"involved"
"totally finished"	"finished"
"totally dead"	"dead"

TOUCHING BASE

- A baseball metaphor; in business, do not "touch base." Do "call," "write," "stop by." "Touching all the bases" is impossible except in baseball. See **contact**.

TRADEMARKS

- The use of apostrophes with trademarks is frowned on by those who own the trademarks. Apparently they believe it sullies their name when used possessively. If one works for, sells to, or writes to such a company, one should not use a trademark possessively.
- Avoid writing "I am sure GE's representative meant well when he said . . ." Write "I am sure General Electric's representative meant well when he said . . ." Avoid writing "IBM's record during the last forty years is impressive." Write "International Business Machine's record during the last forty years is impressive."

TRANSPIRE

- Means "to become known by degrees," not, as many believe, "to occur." In business, as in politics, what occurs and what transpires are usually different.

TRENCHANT

- Effective and articulate. Usually said of remarks.

TRIGGER

- A much-abused verb. It connotes force, speed, and power, but it should not replace all words denoting causation. Try "cause," "induce," "start," "begin," or "produce."

TRUE FACT

- Redundant. A fact is true by definition. See **fact**.

TRY AND

- Avoid writing "try and." Write "try to."
- "Try and find it" is really two requests or demands: "try" is one, "find" is the other. "Try to find" is more brief, precise, and polite than "try and find."

TYPE

- Avoid using "type" except when referring to a method of printing letters. Use a more precise term.

U

UNCONSCIOUS/OBLIVIOUS   See **oblivious/unconscious**.

UNDERLINING   See Appendix II, pages 478–479.

UNDER THE CIRCUMSTANCES   See **circumstances**.

UNINTERESTED/DISINTERESTED   See **disinterested/uninterested**.

UNIQUE

- "Unequalled," "one of a kind in quality." Too often wrongly used to mean "different" only.
- "Unique" is difficult to modify. For example, "The new production system is totally [very, completely, entirely] unique" is silly and redundant.

UNITED STATES See **America**.

UNIVERSALLY ACCEPTED

- Write "generally accepted." Who is to know that something is accepted by the universe? Write "generally rejected" for the same reason. "Commonly accepted" and "commonly rejected" are also acceptable.

UNSOLVABLE/INSOLUBLE See **insoluble/unsolvable**.

UP

- Often colloquial, substandard, and redundant.
- Avoid writing "start up the machine," "run up the bill," "head up the committee." Write "start the machine," "increase the bill," "chair the committee." See **tautology**.

USAGE

- Except when referring to English usage, do not use "usage." When an acceptable three-letter word, "use," has the same meaning as a five-letter word, be brief. Always.

UTILIZATION

- Means "use." When an acceptable three-letter word has the same meaning as an eleven-letter word, be brief. Always. "Utilization" is almost never preferable to "use."

UTILIZE

- Means "use." When an acceptable three-letter word has the same meaning as a seven-letter word, be economical. Always.

V

VALUE

- A favorite verb of administrators and managers ("I value your opinion, Smedley, but . . ."), "value" is insipid and condescending. Write "You have good ideas, Smedley, but . . ."

VANNEMAN'S COROLLARY TO GRESHAM'S LAW

- Bad words tend to drive out good words. See **Gresham's Law**.

VANNEMAN'S COROLLARY TO MURPHY'S LAW

- If it can be misunderstood, it will be. See **Murphy's Law**.

VENDEE

- Some companies call buyers "vendees." An unnecessary word, slightly uglier than "vendor." Write "buyer."

VENDOR

- Some companies call sales people "vendors." A vendor used to be the fellow who sold hot dogs at the ball game or roasted chestnuts on the street.
- Write "sales people" or "sellers." See **purchasing agent**.

VERB   See Appendix II, page 465.

VERBAL/ORAL   See **oral/verbal**.

VERY

- Very overused. Use very sparingly by very carefully deleting "very" from prose very often.

VERY TRULY YOURS   See **sincerely**.

VIA

- Latin for "by way of," via indicates a direction, not a method of transportation.
- Avoid writing "We went to Los Angeles via airplane." Write "We went to Los Angeles by airplane." Write "We went to Los Angeles via San Francisco."

VS.

- In formal writing, spell it out: "versus."
- In informal writing use the abbreviation: "vs."

VIABLE

- Means "capable of living on its own outside the womb." Grossly misused to mean "feasible," "workable." A research group seldom produces "viable alternatives." If it produces sufficient numbers of good products, that group may separate from its department and become a "viable department"; that is, it may become capable of existing on its own outside the womb of the parent department.
- "Nonviable" is also a nonviable word choice. See **alternate/ alternative**.

VIEWPOINT   See **point of view**.

VIRGULE (/)   See Appendix II, page 479.

VISIT

- Never "visit with." "Visit" is sufficient.

VOICE

- Avoid writing "He voiced the opinion that . . ." Write "He said that . . ." Avoid writing "She voiced an objection to . . ." Write "She objected to . . ."

W

WAIT

- One waits *on* tables. One waits *for* people.
- Avoid writing "We waited on him for an hour." Write "We waited *for* him an hour."

WE

- Acceptable, even preferable, when speaking or writing in the name of the company, the corporate "we" is short and clear.

WELL/GOOD   See **good/well**.

WHEN AND IF   See **if and when**.

WHETHER OR NOT

- Seldom write "whether or not." "Whether" is sufficient.
- But write "Whether he wanted to sign the merger or return it unsigned we never knew." See **if/whether**.

WHILE

- "While" describes a period of time. "While" does not mean "and" or "although."
- Avoid writing "While Smedley is good with numbers, he sometimes has difficulty with people." Write "Although Smedley is good with numbers, he sometimes has difficulty with people." Avoid writing "Smedley is good with numbers, while Albert is good with people." Write "Smedley is good with numbers, and [or "whereas"] Albert is good with people." Write "While Smedley studied the company's data, Albert studied the company's management."

WHO/WHOM   See Appendix II, page 468.

WHOLE

- Often unnecessary.
- Avoid writing "She wanted to do the whole job." Write "She wanted to do the job."

WHOSE/OF WHICH

- Use "whose" for people: "The people whose jobs were lost have found new ones."
- Use "of which" for things: "The machinery, many parts of which are substandard, was returned."

-WISE

- Once reserved for "clockwise" and "otherwise," "-wise" now threatens to append itself to every noun in the language.
- "-Wise" is generally used by the inarticulate in search of the inexpressible, jargonwise: "Profitwise, economywise, and reinvestmentwise, we may be wise to prioritize our buying, portfoliowise." See **-ize**.

WITH

- Often used imprecisely. "With the shipment arriving, we worked feverishly." Are we working hard because the shipment arrived or in expectation of its arrival?
- Use "with" to mean "accompanying."
- Often used in a prepositional phrase in place of an adverb. Avoid writing "We must approach this problem with caution." Write "We must approach this problem cautiously."

WOLFORD'S LAW

- The more complex the idea, the simpler the language should be.

WORKSTATION

- A place with a computer and peripherals or with a computer that is connected to peripherals elsewhere. One person may complete a job there without having to move elsewhere.
- Phrases such as "learner/scholar workstation," "programmer/manager workstation" are silly. A workstation is a workstation and needs no fancy adjectives. Many times, "workstation" is unnecessary. Write "work place" or "desk" or "office."

WOULD OF

- An illiteracy, "would of" means, "would've," which means "would have." See **could of**; **should of**.

Y

"YOU" APPROACH

- The darling of "communications experts," the "you" approach is becoming standard. Yet, in spite of what those experts have told us, or perhaps because of it, "you" has lost its force in establishing automatic "communication links" between writer and unknown readers. "You" should be used when writer and reader know each other. Otherwise, use it judiciously and sparingly.

- The "you" that is understood (not written, but grammatically there) is permissible, even preferable, in instructions; for example, directions for assembling a machine, technical manuals, writing handbooks.

YOU KNOW

- Seldom written with purpose, "you know" is a common phrase uttered by Americans. "You know" is used when thought lags behind speech and indicates that one is merely flapping one's gums. You know what I mean?

Z

ZZZ

- Represents the sound of someone snoring or sleeping — something we hope this glossary has not caused you to do.

ILLUSTRATION CREDITS

Page 6: © Ursula Markus/Photo Researchers, Inc.; page 74: © Stan Fellerman/TSW, Inc.; page 105: © Steve Niedorf/The Image Bank; page 210: © 1990, Virginia Blaisdell/Stock, Boston Inc.; page 212 (right): © Barbara Alper/Stock, Boston Inc.; page 212 (left): © 1987, Rafael Macia/Photo Researchers, Inc.; page 261: © Wetvaco Corporation; page 287: © John Waterman/TSW, Inc.; page 305 (left, top): © Ellis Herwig/Stock, Boston Inc.; page 305 (left, bottom): © 1988, Martha Everson/The Picture Group; page 305 (right): © 1985, Stuart Rosner/Stock, Boston Inc.; page 317: © Richard Sobol/Stock, Boston Inc.; page 341: © Dick Luria/Photo Researchers, Inc.; page 357: © Four By Five, Inc.; page 364: © Four By Five, Inc.; page 376: © 1990, Rafael Macia/Photo Researchers, Inc.; page 389: © 1990, Dale Higgins Photography; page 390: © Superstock; page 392 (left): © 1990, Lionel Delevigne/Stock, Boston Inc.; page 392 (right): © Superstock; page 395: © Four By Five, Inc.; page 400: © Superstock; page 411: © Spenser Grant/Photo Researchers, Inc.; page 414: © T. Tracey/FPG, Inc.; page 417: © Peter Yates/The Picture Group. *The High-Tech Office:* (A) © 1985, David Frazier/The Stock Market; (B) © International Business Machines, Inc.; (C) © 1989, Arthur Tilley/FPG, Inc.; (D) © International Business Machines, Inc.; (E) © 1987, Michael A. Keller/FPG, Inc.; (F) © 1991, Issam Karkoutli/Urban Dynamics; (G) © 1991, Issam Karkoutli/Urban Dynamics; (H) © 1990, L.O.L., Inc./FPG, Inc.; (I) © 1989, Charles Krebs/The Stock Market; (J) © 1989, Ronnie Kaufman/The Stock Market; (K) © 1989, Wayne Eastep/The Stock Market; *International Communication:* (A) © Four By Five, Inc.; (B) © 1989, Michael Hart/FPG, Inc.; (C) © FPG, Inc.; (D) © 1990, Jon Feingersh/The Stock Market; (E) © 1989, James Marshall/The Stock Market; (F) © Jon Feingersh/The Stock Market; (G) © 1985, Harvey Lloyd/The Stock Market; (H) © Ray Ellis/Photo Researchers, Inc.; (I) © 1991, Dale Higgins Photography; *The Development of a Desk-Top Report:* All photos (A through Q) are by Dale Higgins Photography, copyright 1991. Computer images R and S are from the Aldus Corporation and T from the Corel Corporation.

INDEX

A 2
B 3
C 4
D 5
E 6
F 7
G 8
H 9
I 0
J 1